THE NEW SPORT MANAGEMENT READER

THE NEW SPORT MANAGEMENT READER

John Nauright and Steven Pope, Editors

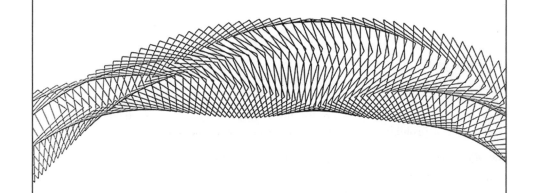

FiT

Fitness Information Technology
a Division of the International Center
for Performance Excellence
West Virginia University
262 Coliseum, WVU-PASS
PO Box 6116
Morgantown, WV 26506-6116

Copyright © 2009

Library of Congress Card Catalog Number: 2009934546

ISBN: 978-1-935412-01-4

Cover Design: Bellerophon Productions
Production Editor: Val Gittings
Indexer: Val Gittings
Typesetter: Bellerophon Productions
Printed by Data Reproductions Corporation

10 9 8 7 6 5 4 3 2 1

Fitness Information Technology
A Division of the International Center for Performance Excellence
West Virginia University
262 Coliseum, WVU-PASS
PO Box 6116
Morgantown, WV 26506-6116
800.477.4348 (toll free)
304.293.6888 (phone)
304.293.6658 (fax)
Email: fitcustomerservice@mail.wvu.edu
Website: www.fitinfotech.com

To the memory of Sam Reith (1971–2007) and Mick Green (1957–2009).

They left us far too early . . .

CONTENTS

PART III • EMERGENT THEMES: DEVELOPMENT, HUMAN RIGHTS, MEDIA CULTURE, AND SPORTS TOURISM

Sport, Events, and Tourism

Democracy, Human Rights, and Development in Sport Management

FOREWORD

The management of sport is a developing and rapidly growing area. With professional athletes receiving multi-million dollar contracts and governments spending large amounts of taxpayer money on sport-related issues, it becomes more important that we understand the management of sport and the various disciplines that make up this area of study. Every credible university in the world now offers a minimum of one course related to the management of sport. There are at least three English-language journals that publish articles related to this field. Each of the major associations holds conferences at which issues related to sport management are presented and discussed, and they produce a journal that is circulated worldwide and read by academics and practitioners. The North American Society for sport management produces the *Journal of Sport Management*, the European Association of Sport Management produces the *European Sport Management Quarterly* and the Sport Management Association of Australia and New Zealand publishes the *Sport Management Review*. Journals, both those that are sport related and those that deal with management in general, have much to say for this discipline. Early research in our field was conducted through questionnaire studies of the leadership qualities of NCAA athletic directors and coaches or studies that attempted to determine why fans attended a particular game. More recent and refined studies have utilized the concepts and theories from the business disciplines to examine sport and the organizations that deliver it. However, both types of studies see sport as a pure and neutral activity, but sport, like other phenomena we find in social life, is subject to the inequalities of race, gender, economics, and politics.

Each of the chapters in this book rejects the purity and neutrality of sport; as such they add to our understanding of sport and the organizations that deliver it. Their ideas come from the original critical theorists, the Frankfort school (Horkheimer, Marcuse, Adorno, etc.). The ideas of these critical theorists have most frequently been embraced by sociologists. Indeed most of the chapters of this book are written by people who identify themselves as sport sociologists. Those scholars who study sport management have traditionally not used the ideas of the critical theorists. Scholars who identify with the management of sport are in the minority in this book. However, sport management has not kept pace with developments in the general management field where scholars have used the ideas of the critical theorists to inform their work (see, for example, the writing of people like Acker, Alvesson, Burrell, Calas, Clegg, Willmott, etc.). While globalization and feminism are the two topics where the ideas of critical theory are most often found, the ideas can, as the chapters in this book have shown, be applied to a variety of topics. Ideas from critical theory force us to rethink our conceptualizations of sport and other organizational phenomena and their relationship to social life. Critical theory challenges our epistemology and requires us to use different methods. While it is laudable to use the concepts of critical theory, the data for the majority of chapters in this book come from North America or Western Europe. If we are to fully understand the management of sport we need to expand the geographic areas that are included in our studies. With Africans dominating middle and long distance running, African and South American footballers (soccer to North Americans), Scandinavian ice hockey players, Serbian tennis players, New Zealand rugby players, Australian swimmers and cricketers, and Chinese divers all increasingly starring on the world stage, it is more important that we understand the role of sport in the culture of these countries and how sport is delivered. The two largest sporting events in the world, the Olympic games and the FIFA World Cup, one that was staged in China and the other to be staged in South Africa, bring focus to the global reach of sporting events. If we use the ideas of critical theory and expand the geographic scope of our research we will be able to improve an expanding and rapidly growing area of study.

—Trevor Slack
University of Alberta

ACKNOWLEDGMENTS

Appreciation is expressed to Caleb Chamberlayne for his administrative assistance in the production of this book.

Appreciation is also expressed for permission granted to print previously published articles, as noted below:

Chapter 1, Rupture: Promoting Critical and Innovative Approaches to the Study of Sport Management. Reprinted by permission from *Journal of Sport Management*, 2005, (19)4, 355–366. © Human Kinetics, Inc.

Chapter 2, Hockey Capital: Approaches to the Study of the Sports Industry. Reprinted by permission from *Business and Economic History On-Line*, 2006. © Business History Conference.

Chapter 3, Feminist and Gender Research in Sport and Leisure Management: Understanding the Social-Cultural Nexus of Gender-Power Relations. Reprinted by permission from *Journal of Sport Management*, 2005, (19)4, 422–441. © Human Kinetics, Inc.

Chapter 4, Addressing Epistemological Racism in Sport Management Research. Reprinted by permission from *Journal of Sport Management*, 2005, (19)4, 464–479. © Human Kinetics, Inc.

Chapter 5, Urban Regimes and Sport in North American Cities: Seeking Status Through Franchises, Events and Facilities. Reprinted by permission from *International Journal of Sport Management and Marketing*, 2008, 3(3), 221–241. © Inderscience Publishers.

Chapter 6, Sport and the Repudiation of the Global. Reprinted by permission from *International Review of Sociology of Sport*, 2003, 38(3), 281–294. © International Sociology of Sport Association and Sage Publications.

Chapter 7: The Four Domains of Sport Marketing: A Conceptual Framework. Reprinted by permission from *Sport Marketing Quarterly*, 2008, 7(2), 90–109. © West Virginia University.

Chapter 8, Sporting Sign Wars: Advertising and the Contested Terrain of Sporting Events and Venues. Reprinted by permission from *International Journal of Sport Management and Marketing*, 2005, 1(1–2), 17–36. © Inderscience Publishers.

Chapter 9, Expressing Fenway: Managing and Marketing Heritage within the Global Sports Marketplace. Reprinted by permission from *International Journal of Sport Management and Marketing*, 2005, 1(1–2), 37–55. © Inderscience Publishers.

Chapter 10, From Beckham to Ronaldo: Assessing the Nature of Football Player Brands. Reprinted by permission from *Journal of Sponsorship*, 2008, 1(4), 307–317. © Henry Stewart Publications.

Chapter 11, Dangerous Liaisons: How Can Sports Brands Capitalize on the Hip Hop Movement Barbara Manivet and Andre Richelieu. Reprinted by permission from *International Journal of Sport Management and Marketing*, 2008, 3(1–2), 140–161. © Inderscience Publishers.

Chapter 12, Supporters, Followers, Fans and Flaneurs. Reprinted by permission from *Journal of Sport and Social Issues*, 2002, 26(1), 25–46. © Sage Publications.

Chapter 13: A Model Used to Explain Support in Spanish Football. Originally published as a Munich Personal RePEc Archive (MPRA) paper, 2007. © Angel Barajas.

Chapter 14, El Rey de Los Deportes: Bodies, Business, and Identity in Mexican Baseball. Paper presented to the Conference on Globalization and Sport in Historical Context University of California, San Diego, March 2005.

Chapter 15, Us and Them: Australian Professional Sport and Resistance to North American Ownership and Marketing Models. Reprinted by permission from *Sport Marketing Quarterly*, 1997, 6(1), 33–39. © Fitness Information Technology.

Chapter 16, Mechanisms of International Influence on Domestic Elite Sport Policy. Reprinted by permission from *International Journal of Sport Policy*, 2009, (1)1, 51–69. © Taylor & Francis Group.

Chapter 17: Policy Transfer, Lesson Drawing and Perspectives on Elite Sport Development Systems. Reprinted by permission from *International Journal of Sport Management and Marketing*, 2007, 2(4), 426–441. © Inderscience Publishers.

Chapter 18: Change and Grassroots Movement: Reconceptualising Women's Hockey Governance in Canada. Reprinted by permission from *International Journal of Sport Management and Marketing*, 2007, 2(4), 344–361. © Inderscience Publishers.

Chapter 19, Sport, Human Rights, and Industrial Relations. Reprinted by permission from *Australian Journal of Human Rights*, 2000, 6(2) 129–159. © Australian Human Rights Centre.

Chapter 20: Sport and the Transnationalizing Media Corporation. Reprinted, by permission from *Media Economics*, 2003, 16(4), 235–251. © Taylor & Francis Group.

Chapter 21: Recovering (from) Janet Jackson's Breast: Ethics and the Nexus of Media, Sports, and Management. Reprinted, by permission from *Journal of Sport Management*, 2005, (18)4, 315–334. © Human Kinetics, Inc.

Chapter 22, Corporate Training: Identity Construction, Preparation for the Sydney Olympic Gamesand Relationships between Canadian Media, Swimmers and Sponsors. Reprinted by permission from *Olympika: The International Journal of Olympic Studies*, 2001, 10, 1–32. © International Centre for Olympic Studies.

Chapter 23, The Juxtaposition of Sport and Communication: Defining the Field of Sport Communication. Reprinted by permission from *International Journal of Sport Management and Marketing*, 2007, 2(3), 193–207. © Inderscience Publishers.

Chapter 24, The Influence of Policy Makers' Perceptions on Sport-Tourism Policy Development. Reprinted by permission from *Tourism Review International*, 2006, 10(4), 227–240. © Cognizant Communication Corporation.

Chapter 25, Modern Sport and Olympic Games: The Problematic Complexities Raised by the Dynamics of Globalization. Reprinted, by permission from *Olympika, The International Journal of Olympic Studies*, 2008, 17, 1–40. © International Centre for Olympic Studies.

Chapter 26, Assessing the Impact of Sports Mega-events in Transition Economies: EURO2012 in Poland and Ukraine. Reprinted by permission from *International Journal of Sport Management and Marketing*, 2007, 2(5–6), 496–509. © Inderscience Publishers.

Chapter 27, Can New Orleans Play Its Way Past Katrina? The Role of Professional Sports in the Redevelopment of New Orleans. Reprinted by permission from *International Journal of Sport Management and Marketing*, 2(5–6), 2007, 541–554. © Inderscience Publishers.

Chapter 28, A New Social Movement: Sport for Development and Peace. Reprinted by permission from *Sport in Society*, 2008, 11(4), 370–380. © Taylor & Francis Group.

Chapter 29, Reaching the "Hard to Reach": Engagement, Relationship Building and Social Control in Sport-based Social Inclusion Work. Reprinted by permission from *International Journal of Sport Management and Marketing*, 2007, 2(1–2), 27–40. © Inderscience Publishers.

Chapter 30, Women and Children First? Child Abuse and Child Protection in Sport. Reprinted by permission from *Sport in Society*, 2004, 7(3), 322–337. © Taylor & Francis Group.

INTRODUCTION

"What are we [in sport management] helping to promote and exactly
why are we doing it? I fear that we are simply going along with the seemingly inevitable tide. In the process, we have become pawns to the prevailing sport establishment by riding the wrong horse."[1]

—Earle Zeigler

Prologue

Sport management is a relatively young field as academic areas of study go.
Most programs can trace their origins only to the 1990s, though a few, which
emerged under the rubric of "athletic administration," go back as far as the
1970s. The history of professional societies in the field demonstrates that it is,
indeed, new as a recognized subject area. The North American Society for
Sport Management (NASSM) was founded in 1985 and organized its first
conference a year later. The European Association for Sport Management
(EASM) was established in 1993, while the Sport Management Association of
Australia and New Zealand (SMAANZ) emerged in 1995. Together these
three associations form the International Sport Management Alliance. In 2002,
the more narrowly focused Sport Marketing Association (SMA) appeared.[2]
Research on the business aspects of sport is not limited to these associations
and their journals, however. A vibrant scholarship has emerged that examines
the many facets of the sports industry internationally within sport history and
sport sociology in particular and that informs and contextualizes research
within "sport management."[3]

One of the central arguments underpinning this particular volume is that
although sport management students are increasingly taught a wider range of
sports-related areas in the course of their studies, the core focus of the academic field of sport management has evolved to the point whereby the prag-
matic, technical-training aspects of professional preparation have been privileged while simultaneously, critical, interdisciplinary thinking has become
marginalized. As John Amis and Michael Silk argue in this book's first chapter, "what currently holds the center in sport management research is a somewhat narrow definition of the field that, in many ways, blinkers sport management scholars in their ability and potential to provide a critical examination of
the operations and machinations of sport-related industries and institutions."
Moreover, as Amis and Silk argue, "too often research in sport management

has been presented as neutral and value free, with little regard for the histori-cal, social, political, and cultural context in which the work takes place."[4] We find this problematical for the long-term development of sport management. *The New Sport Management Reader* was conceived and developed as a clarion call for a more critical, reflexive approach to sport management education and practice. As such, we do not anticipate this book will be universally greeted with consensus and without disagreements. We expect and encourage discus-sion of opposing ideas. It is only through vigorous debate that any field of en-quiry can be moved forward. This book has been designed to spark debate, discussion, and reflection and hopefully to better inform research questions and professional practice in the future.

Broadening Horizons

One of the key challenges on the horizon for U.S. scholars is to better contex-tualize (and conceptually de-center) the vast research on intercollegiate sport. To date, there has been and continues to be an inordinate amount of attention devoted to developing theoretical frameworks based upon the idiosyncratic and cultural anomaly that is big-time (and essentially professionalized in all but name) college sport. To be sure, this is not a new critique or mandate for the field. As early as 1995, Trevor Slack reported that, in his analysis of the *Journal of Sport Management*, 65 percent of research was devoted to American physical education and intercollegiate athletics. In her 2001 Zeigler address, Brenda Pitts lamented how little had changed in terms of this topical preoccu-pation. "When one reads the totality of our literature," according to Pitts, "one gets the distinct impression that sport management is nothing more than the study of managing college athletics and some professional sports . . . Sport management textbooks reveal the same heavy focus," which leads to the per-ception "that sport management is just a new and contemporary buzzword for athletic administration." Pitts argued that sport management scholars had "a responsibility to expand the scope of our research and add the other areas of the sport industry."[5] As American-born (and trained) academics who have taught sport studies abroad, we (the editors) were forced to come to grips with the utter, cultural disconnect of the NCAA-based environment outside the United States.[6] Thus, despite the voluminous literature on "amateur" intercol-legiate (American) athletics that has occupied such a dominant portion of the sport management research agenda to date, it remains marginally relevant to scholars, students, and practitioners working outside of the United States.

Fortunately, there is a current (and hopefully a burgeoning) effort to glob-ally contextualize sport management cultures. The key concept underpinning this effort is the word "culture," which connotes the core assumptions and val-ues held by individuals in particular communities and societies.[7] A cultural studies perspective of the field would, for example, take into consideration the ways in which management decisions are undertaken by people who are mak-ing choices based upon their values and beliefs within specific human environ-ments. Vassil Girginov affirms the need to "transcend the Western scientific rationality, which is no longer sufficient to explain the whole multiplicity of ontologies that organize human experience and to urge sport management students to pay attention to the cultural meaning of management by generating local knowledge and solutions to sport problems." Such a global awareness of the "cultural meaning of management" would enable sport managers to better understand both "the cultural diversity of their own work force and in developing appropriate cross-cultural skills needed for running international events, marketing campaigns, sponsorship deals and joint ventures."[8] Girgoniv highlights the following issues for scrutiny: theoretical perspectives on culture and sport management; culture of sport organizations; managing diversity in sport organizations; the politics of multiculturalism in sport; culture and organizational performance; culture and participation in sport; culture and interpersonal communications in sport; sport marketing and sponsorship across cultures; and teaching sport management in a multicultural environment and across national borders.

We concur with Girgoniv that such issues should, at least partially, delineate the future research agenda for the field of sport management. Sports leagues are unique entities in capitalist economies as, unlike other areas of business, sports leagues need to cooperate in order to succeed. Yet, there is not one accepted model of business practice in the organization of professional sports internationally. This makes sport different and not easily tied down by principles taught only in schools of business. For example, the North American practice is to have single leagues that exist as private entities shared by the owners of professional teams. In much of the rest of the world, professional sports operates on a promotion-relegation system whereby teams can move up or down between leagues depending on their performance. If a team finishes last in the National Football League (NFL), there is no threat of dropping to a lower league. In fact, the team is rewarded with the first draft pick for the following season. In 2009, the powerful English soccer club Newcastle United performed poorly and was relegated to the league below the Premier League. This demotion will cost the club millions of £s (pounds sterling) in lost television revenue, further jeopardizing its ability to compete with the top clubs. In Australia, teams have traditionally been publicly owned, as Nauright and Phillips attest in this book, which has resulted in fan-led campaigns to save beleaguered teams threatened with mergers or relocations. Attempts to create North American models of sport ownership there failed largely because they were anathema to Aussie sporting practices. In the Nordic countries and other parts of Europe, the multi-sport club format is common, which caters to mass participation and elite sport within a single entity. These examples point to the need to understand the social and cultural role of sport in any given society, which is as important as understanding the sport marketplace in and of itself. This book, then, is an attempt to broaden the terrain in sport management once and for all to view sport first and foremost as a social technology—to borrow from sport historian Mark Dyreson, one that is enmeshed in society and not viewed simply as a commodity to "sell."

We believe, as do the authors whose work is represented in this volume, that sport plays too powerful a role in societies around the world to be analyzed within a narrow, culturally insular lens. Again, we reference Amis and Silk's call to understand sport management in its wider political, economic, and ideological context and be concerned with exposing patterns of inequality and intervening in local communities. Researchers who place sport management within the material contexts of everyday life and multiracial, economic, and political democracy can, as Ian Henry maintains, effectively address the imperatives of consumption; the dynamics of the marketplace; commercial space; the sweeping reach of neoliberal ideology, power, and influence; the production of knowledges and identities; nation-states; globalization; freedom; and community.[9]

Trends in Sport Studies

What is the state of sport management? To what extent can those working in the Americas, the United Kingdom, Europe, Australasia, and elsewhere agree on central methodological, theoretical, pedagogical, and professional issues? What constitutes the field of sport management and what should aspiring sport managers and sport business researchers know? NASSM defines the essential common body of knowledge in sport management as being cross-disciplinary. This knowledge "relates to management, leadership, and organization in sport; behavioral dimensions in sport; ethics in sport management; sport marketing; communication in sport; sport finance; sport economics; sport business in the social context; legal aspects of sport; sport governance; and sport management professional preparation."[10] Although the existing NASSM guidelines usefully delineate key topical areas, there has been only limited debate on the present state or future trajectory of the field. As scholars who participate and circulate in other sport studies circles, we (the editors) have been surprised by the modest level of intra-disciplinary self-scrutiny within sport management. Despite NASSM's self-professed interdisciplinary orientation, its 2008 conference theme was "Good Sport Makes Good Business"—which caused us (the editors) to reflect critically upon Zeigler's provocative question and lamentation at the beginning of this essay. Zeigler's comment arises from a critical philosophical position on the nature of sport itself. There is a sense that sport management scholars have followed what he characterizes as "uncritical popular wisdom that sport is good thing for society to encourage and more sport is even better." To date, with some notable exceptions there has been little explicit, reflexive engagement with such concerns emanating from a founding father of the field.[11]

Such a scenario is different from that of the "sister" fields of sport history and sport sociology. Although several scholars lamented the lack of reflexivity and the limited use of theory during the 1990s,[12] there has been a fledgling body of literature dealing with wider developments on theory, methodology, and epistemology during the past decade.[13] Sport history emerged as a recognized academic area of study in the mid-1970s at precisely the time when historical scholarship shifted dramatically from a political-diplomatic-history of ideas orientation to one focused upon social history. The "new" social history derived from two European intellectual trends: a social scientific approach linked to the French *Annales* school and the British Marxist tradition. Complementing these two schools was the important influence of anthropologists and sociologists, particularly Max Weber, Clifford Geertz, Norbert Elias, and Michel Foucault, whose work expanded historians' understanding of such concepts as society, community, modernization, culture, and power. During the 1980s sport historians transformed their infant field beyond recognition.[14] The cutting edge of the field currently finds itself within a third wave of development and moving toward a paradigmatic shift.[15]

Sport sociologists have been more aggressive in terms of aligning their disciplinary identity within the "parent" disciplines of sociology and cultural studies in terms of breaking out of their institutional place (within physical education and kinesiology departments) to engage with broader social theory and sociological research. During the 1980s, several sociologists brought a more critical theoretical approach into the mainstream of sport studies that inspired scholars to analyze sport as a medium of class, gender, racial domination, and resistance.[16] During the 1990s, sport sociologists within North America pondered whether, as Peter Donnelly and Alan Ingham articulated the matter in 1997, "sociology of sport is an apt description for what we are now doing . . . [or whether] social studies of physical culture may best describe the cultural formation that once was the sociology of sport."[17] The field remains contentious and dynamic in terms of discussions of methodology and theory.[18]

Sport psychology is a third and final, instructive example of a sport studies discipline undergoing a fundamental reassessment led by a small, but growing, group of researchers influenced by the field of cultural studies and the "cultural turn" (a permutation of the postmodernist critique of the production of knowledge that has swept through the social sciences since the 1970s). The mainstream knowledge base within sport psychology has and continues to be underpinned by positivistic theoretical assumptions as applied to research with white male athletes. Building upon the interdisciplinary field of cultural studies as well as the pioneering work of feminist, critical race, and queer scholars of sport, an emergent challenge predicated on the notion of "cultural praxis" (a methodological approach linking theory to practice) has emerged, according to Tatiana Ryba and Handel Wright, as a way of opening up sport psychological research to issues of transnational identities, competing notions, and sites of belonging and contested cultures that are enmeshed with power and ethics and that constitute the pressing actuality of our complex, globalized world.[19] The issues brought about by the "cultural turn" relate to epistemological, analytical, and moral concerns that challenge conventional theories of representation of older paradigms underpinning sport psychology. In particular, sport psychologists have insisted (and continue to insist) upon the reputedly neutral, value-free, "scientific" foundations of their research and, thus, have been slow to embrace discursive-based understandings of "culture." The emergent critique within sport psychology focuses upon language and culture as fundamental to peoples' embodied experiences in the social world by highlighting the fact that the human psyche is cultural and politically constructed and not merely a matter of neurological processes and cognition of the individual subject. As such, this burgeoning critique of epistemological and methodological assumptions within the field focuses upon interdisciplinarity (as well as anti-disciplinarity and post-disciplinarity); cutting-edge theorizing; an explicitly political approach (concerned with issues of power, difference, and social justice); praxis-driven (not a purely academic endeavor but rather one that attempts to address real, contemporary socio-cultural issues); contextual (the fact that such an inquiry is rooted in specific geographical and historical conjectures); and self-reflexive (an approach that realizes the potential incongruity and transient nature of the knowledge it produces). The cultural studies vanguard, the "cultural turn" within the humanities and social sciences has prompted the scholars to re-examine the assumptions that underlie sport psychological research and practice so as to address the urgency of socio-cultural difference in theory, practice, and research in their field.[20]

In short, the fields of sport history, sport sociology, and sport psychology have undergone various paradigm shifts and all three are currently engaged with the implications of "cultural turn" for research agendas in their respective fields. What is the state of such disciplinary re-evaluation within sport management? Zeigler notes how the literature on poststructural and postmodern discourses within sociology, as well as within various other areas such as gender studies, cultural geography, social policy, leisure, and tourism, have been virtually ignored within sport management,[21] there has been a fledgling critique of the field of sport management in recent years by scholars who, like their colleagues in other areas within sport studies, have lamented the lack of theoretical reflexivity, interdisciplinarity, and cross-cultural acuity within the mainstream.[22] Reflective of this emerging self-scrutiny, Wendy Frisby argues that sport management research must be conducted from multiple paradigms. As a former editor of the flagship journal, *Journal of Sport Management*, she reflected that "very few manuscripts crossed my desk that operated from a critical stance" (on sport and its broader contextualization) and speculated that this neglect is related to the positivistic orientation within the field. Without a critical perspective and method for evaluating marketing, accounting, human resource management, and the like, practitioners and students alike miss the sheer messiness, the ambiguity, and the politicized and fragmented nature of sport management. When students are trained primarily in the technical functions of organizational planning, organizing, and controlling events and processes — without appropriate attention to the prevailing cultural, historical, economic, and political contexts characterized by asymmetrical power relations — they are ill-equipped to think outside the textbook box. Frisby recommends a wider use of critical social science inquiry that "goes beyond surface illusions to uncover the real structures of the material world in order to help people change conditions and build a better world for themselves."[23]

Similar sentiments are echoed by the contributors to the first section of this book—all of whom share a commitment to critical, interdisciplinary theory and methodology for better understanding sport management practices. Such contributions to the emergent critique of the field are intent on interrogating the dominant explanatory frameworks currently deployed within sport management and, as such, envision "a messier, challenging environment in which competing ontological, epistemological, and political positions exist alongside one another," which promises to "expand our intellectual horizons and offer the additional theoretical and practical insights that our rapidly developing field requires."[24]

This Book

The chapters that comprise this collection are divided into sections that can be further subdivided as needed for instructional purposes. We have attempted to provide a representative selection of core areas of focus within sport management research globally. Not all of the work in what we call a new approach to sport management is represented here. Yet, we believe this is a unique collection that will enhance any student's or practitioner's knowledge of sport management as a field of study.

The first part (Critical Approaches in Sport Management) provides several provocative calls for sport management scholars to engage with epistemologies and methodologies associated with cultural studies and sociology. All of the authors in Part I advocate for a more interdisciplinary approach to the field—one which addresses issues of race, gender, feminism, globalization, cultural capital, power relations, and postmodernism. These essays provide valuable overviews of some complex theoretical concepts and research traditions from outside of sport management which can be used to redefine the conceptual frameworks of the field. The six chapters collectively demonstrate some of the ways through which sport management research can benefit from casting a wider theoretical net.

Moving from the broader conceptual issues discussed in Part I to more narrowly focused research, Part II features an applied case studies approach. Readers will encounter critically informed research focused within three key topical areas of sport management: marketing and sponsorship, consumption, and governance and policy development. These thirteen case studies provide wide-ranging examples of research on the *global* sports industry through which students, professors, and professionals alike can form cross-cultural analyses. For example, Simon Chadwick and Nick Burton suggest that as players emerge as brands in their own right new problems emerge for brand managers as well as sporting franchises. Which "brand" should predominate? How much symbiosis of interest is possible? Can a global brand overrun a local brand? How much should the local bow down to the global? Or as Giulianotti suggests, are new age fans merely becoming *flâneurs* willing to follow fashion and trend more than substance? Several high profile sports have adopted the notion of "league speak" or "league think," whereby the goal is to create fans of a particular sport rather than of specific teams. The NFL is a prime example of this and has been highly successful. The Australian Football League has tried this approach as well but has struggled with traditional fans who flatly refuse *flânery*. These are pivotal issues and questions for 21st century sport managers that are addressed collectively in this collection.

Finally, we are keen to examine the *broader social consequences* of sport, be they economic or environmental or issues related to human rights. Who gets to play? who gets to watch? and how? are questions we should always have at the forefront of planning and programming in sport management. In this sense, Part III presents work that might be characterized as a socio-cultural approach to sport management. We believe that the emergent themes addressed here — economic development, human rights, media culture, and sports tourism — establish a new and fundamentally different research and policy agenda. We hope that this section will inspire students, researchers, and managers to think more critically about the wider implications of managing sport in the 21st century.

As we have suggested, we hope that this volume forms the basis for wider discussion and debate and for further reading in creating a renewed focus for the field of sport management. *The New Sport Management Reader* calls into question the dominant orthodoxy in sport management — particularly as it has been practiced in North America and which has taken hold in other regions of the world, notably parts of Europe and in Australia and New Zealand — and urges sport management professionals to critically examine the range of sport programs and policies with which they are actively engaged on a daily basis and to constantly ask "why" and "for whom" is sport being played? As Robert Rinehart reminds us, we are "players all"[25] in this game we call sports and there are certainly social, political, economic, cultural, environmental, and many other consequences of how we "do" sport individually and collectively.

Notes

1. Ziegler, E. (2007). Sport management must show social concern as it develops tenable theory. *Journal of Sport Management, 21*, 297–318.

2. The journals launched by these organizations are: *Journal of Sport Management, Sport Marketing Quarterly, European Sport Management Quarterly*, and *The Sport Management Review*.

3. Some of the key sport studies journals include the *Journal of Sport History, International Journal of the History of Sport, Sport History Review, Sociology of Sport Journal, International Review of the Sociology of Sport, Journal of Sport and Social Issues, Sporting Traditions*, and *Sport in Society*. In addition to the vast periodical literature in sport studies there is an expansive body of specialized monographs, edited collections, and invaluable reference books dealing with the social and historical development of the global sports industry.

4. Amis, J., & Silk, M. (2005). Rupture: Promoting critical and innovative approaches to the study of sport management. *Journal of Sport Management, 19*, 355–366.

5. Pitts, P. (2001). Sport management at the millennium: A defining moment. *Journal of Sport Management, 15*, 3–4.

6. Despite its broader, transnational moniker — the North American Society for Sport Management — the US model of sports development, especially its professionalized "amateur" sport, does not resonate in neither Canada nor Mexico.

7. Raymond Williams maintained that the term "culture" is one of the most complex and confusing words in the English language. Williams famously shifted the dominant view of "culture" as a privileged space of artistic production and specialist knowledge (e.g., "high cul-

ture") toward a broader understanding that "culture is a whole way of life." Culture is ordinary—it is "the lived experience of the everyday" (to use Ann Gray and Jim McGuigan's phrase). Williams, R. (1958). Moving from high culture to ordinary culture. In N.McKenzie (Ed.), *Convictions*. London: McGibbon and Kee. See also Gray, A., & McGuigan, J. (Eds.). (1997). *Studying culture: An introductory reader*. London: Edward Arnold.

8. See Girginov's invitation for a 2010 special issue on "sport management cultures" for the *European Sport Management Quarterly* at http://www .tandf.co.uk/journals/cfp/resmcfp.pdf (accessed on 07/06/09).

9. See also Henry, I., Amara, M., Al-Tauqi, M., & Lee. P. C. (2005). A typology of approaches to comparative analysis of sports policy. *Journal of Sport Management, 19*, 480–496. They note the very limited awareness and reflexivity of comparative work within the field of sport management.

10. North American Society for Sport Management Website (www.nassm.org).

11.The editors have ruminated on NASSM's decision not to provide thematic sessions at the annual conference. Unlike most other academic conferences wherein papers are grouped into identifiable topical blocks, the NASSM annual conference has lacked discernible conceptual scaffolding.

12. Pope, S. (1998). Sport history: Into the 21st century. *Journal of Sport History, 25*, i–x.

13. See for example Phillips, M. (Ed.). (2006). *Deconstructing sport history: The postmodern challenge*. Albany: State University of New York Press.

14. See Pope, S. (1997). *The new American sport history: Recent approaches and perspectives*. Urbana: University of Illinois Press.

15. The most comprehensive single volume survey of sport history published to date is Guttmann, A. (2005). *Sport: The first two millenia*. Amherst: University of Massachusetts Press. For a detailed examination of the development of methodology within sport history, see Booth, D. (2005). *The field: Truth and fiction in sport history*. London: Routledge; and Pope, S., & Nauright, J. (Eds.). (2009). *The Routledge companion to sports history*. London: Routledge.

16. One of the key works in this tradition was Gruneau, R. (1984). *Class, sports, and social development*. University of Amherst Press. See also his influential work: Gruneau, R. (1988). Modernization or hegemony: Two views of sport and social development. In J. Harvey & H. Cantelon (Eds.), *Not just a game: Essays in Canadian sport*

sociology (pp. 9–32). University of Ottawa Press. An incisive statement of this work's legacy is provided by Gruneau ("A postscript 15 years later") in the second edition of the book published by Human Kinetics in 1999.

17. Ingham, A., & Donnelly, P. (1997). A sociology of North American sociology of sport: Disunity in unity. *Sociology of Sport Journal, 14*, 364–395.

18. For more on this see Andrews, D. (2008). Kinesiology's inconvenient truth and the physical cultural studies imperative. *Quest, 60*, 45–62.

19. Ryba, T. V., & Schinke, R. J. (2009). Decolonizing methodologies: Approaches to sport and exercise psychology from the margins. *International Journal of Sport and Exercise Psychology* (special issue) *7*(3); and Ryba, T. V., Schinke, R. J., & Tenenbaum, G. (2009). *The cultural turn in sport psychology*. Morgantown: Fitness Information Technology.

20. Ibid.

21. Zeigler advocates the need for a more critical definition of "sport" that would enable sport management to make the important, interdisciplinary connections within sport studies as well as the wider social scientific disciplines.

22. On a personal note, I'd like to acknowledge that Trevor Slack identified these basic shortcomings within the field even prior to the recent ("emergent") critique to which we point (expressed in private correspondence with Pope as early as 1998).

23. See Frisby, W. (2005). The good, the bad, and the ugly: Critical sport management research. *Journal of Sport Management, 19*, 1–12, *passim*. Frisby notes how with their "focus on organizations and managerial activities, sport management scholars are well position to question how structures and practices related to policy development." In the same 1995 special issue of the *JSM*, Robert Rinehart—a sociologist and cultural studies scholar—champions the use of personal narratives within sport management research methodology that would enable researchers to uncover the "stories, from the point of view of the participants, or the stories of others in order to better understand attitude, context and values within a given setting or setting." See Rinehart, R. E. (2005). "Experiencing" sport management: The use of personal narrative in sport management studies. *Journal of Sport Management, 19*, 498.

24. Amis & Silk, *op cit*, 355–356.

25. Rinehart, R. E. (1998). *Players all: Performances in contemporary society*. Bloomington: Indiana University Press.

PART I

CRITICAL APPROACHES IN SPORT MANAGMENT

1

RUPTURE: PROMOTING CRITICAL AND INNOVATIVE APPROACHES TO THE STUDY OF SPORT MANAGEMENT

John Amis and Michael Silk

We would like to be clear on one point. We are not calling for a total regermination of sport management. To do so, to leave behind the insights, theoretical development, impacts, and contributions brought to bear on the field would be, of course, nonsensical. We do, however, want to suggest that what currently holds the center in sport management research is a somewhat narrow definition of the field that, in many ways, blinkers sport management scholars in their ability and potential to provide a critical examination of the operations and machinations of sport-related industries and institutions. We are sure not all will agree, and we expect a welter of criticism; in fact, we encourage it. Rather than discarding that which currently holds the center, however, we echo Wendy Frisby's recent call in her 2004 Zeigler Award address for paradigmatic plurality (Frisby, 2005). We envision a set of not necessarily complementary vectors—a messier, challenging environment in which competing ontological, epistemological, and political positions exist alongside one another. This, we believe, will expand our intellectual horizons and offer the additional theoretical and practical insights that our rapidly developing field requires.

We are at an interesting time, a time in which debates across the social sciences are forcing the type of reflection that we are extolling here. There is little doubt that some related disciplines—such as education, cultural studies, leisure studies, and the sociology of sport—have progressed more rapidly than sport management in their acknowledgment of the value of different ideological, epistemological, and methodological approaches. A perusal of the major journals associated with these fields will reveal that the positivist and post-positivist approaches—along with their associated research designs, methods, and writing styles—that have long dominated the social sciences have been challenged by a diverse array of scholars keen to supplement, or supplant, existing knowledge bases through alternate modes of inquiry.

Now, with that said, it is worth making two points. First, we are not advocating any one paradigmatic, epistemological, or methodological approach over any other. Although we have our own preferences of course, "no specific method or practice can be privileged over any other" (Denzin & Lincoln, 2005, p. 7). Second, sport management is not alone in its need to embrace a wider array of approaches. Indeed, there is no doubt that *Journal of Sport Management, European Sport Management Quarterly*, and *Sport Management Review*, in particular, have published research that embraces a variety of political and epistemological positions. If one examines the leading management and marketing journals, for example, it is certainly not difficult to argue that sport management provides a greater diversity of approaches than these "parent" disciplines (see, for example, recent articles in *Administrative Science Quarterly* [Hinings & Greenwood, 2002] and *Academy of Management Journal* [Gephart, 2004] that have advocated similar disciplinary reexaminations of the type we call for here). It is apparent that as sport management scholars, however, we can go further in our efforts to embrace a wider variety of questions, approaches, and methods. For example, our representation of others and ourselves, our moral and political responsibilities as researchers, and how we express, present, and represent our work to various communities are issues that we have spent insufficient time addressing within our discipline. Too often our work in sport management has been presented as neutral and value free, with little regard for the historical, social, political, and cultural context in which the work takes place (see Frisby, 2005). In this respect, as Hinings and Greenwood (2002, p. 413, emphasis in original) argued in their critique of organization theory, the major research questions pursued by scholars tend to stress *"how to understand and thus design efficient and effective organizations. . . .* The question of consequences, i.e., efficient and effective *for whom?* is usually left unasked."

On Decentering

In 1989 Francis Fukuyama ignited a smoldering debate by controversially arguing that we had reached the "end of history." Grounded in a solidifying global hegemony of Western liberalism ushering in the protracted conclusion to the Cold War, Fukuyama (1989, p. 3) foretold the "total exhaustion of viable systematic alternatives" and, hence, predicted the "end of history as such: that is, the end point of mankind's ideological evolution and the universalization of Western liberal democracy as the final form of human government." Fukuyama's position is of course far from incontrovertible, yet it does offer a useful heuristic in our consideration of the field of sport management. Like the sports industry itself — dominated by brazenly hypercommercial enterprises and spectacles that make no effort to disguise their cardinal objective of delivering entertaining products designed to maximize profit margins (Andrews, 1999) — the discipline of sport management is, in a Fukuyamian sense, positioned at the end of history. Approaches to sport management that critique or oppose the industry are disappearing from our popular consciousness (if they were ever present) or are farmed off to our colleagues in other disciplines. Furthermore, the rise and rise of the corporate university in which higher education becomes increasingly commercialized and vocationalized as a source of profit for corporate interest — what Bauman (1999) calls the latest rendition of a society that has stopped questioning itself—legitimates and essentially concretizes a form of sport management that serves the industry yet ignores, for the most part, the most pressing social problems of our time and produces a politics that offers nothing but more of the same (Giroux, 2001). Frisby (2005) offers a similar analysis in her call for a more critical sport management that goes beyond the traditional search for ever more efficient modes of design and strategizing, that instead empowers individuals by confronting injustices and promoting social change. In so doing, she echoes Hinings and Greenwood's (2002) call for work on organizations that challenges the consequences of managerial and policy-making practice; we concur.

This forces us to reflect on the connections that exist between our classrooms and the challenges faced on the streets and in organizations (see, for example, Bartunek, 2002; Frisby, Reid, Millar, & Hoeber, 2005; Rynes, Bartunek, & Daft, 2001; Singer, 2005). We must provide spaces within our classrooms, within our texts, our academic journals, and our conferences for discussion of personal injuries and private terrors that we can translate into public considerations and struggles (Giroux, 2001). We need to understand sport management in its wider political, economic, and ideological context and be concerned with exposing patterns of inequality and intervening in local communities.

We would like to think that as a discipline we already do these things—and a few of our colleagues do—yet this is a position that clearly does not claim the center in the discipline of sport management. Rather, such work is perceived as marginal, taken on by stand-alone avant-garde figures who exist on the periphery of the field and often stand counter to "legitimate" forms of sport management, the norm against which everything else is judged. However, these are professionals and academics not acting alone, they are critical citizens whose collective knowledge and actions presuppose specific visions of public life, community, and moral accountability (Giroux). These are researchers who place sport management within the material contexts of everyday life and use it as an important site for critical conversations about cultural politics and multiracial, economic, and political democracy. These individuals spark conversations with their students and colleagues that address the imperatives of consumption, the dynamics of the marketplace, commercial space, the sweeping reach of neoliberal ideology, power and influence, the production of knowledges and identities, nation-states, globalization, freedom, and community (Denzin & Lincoln, 2000a; Giroux, 2001).

The potential of such work is evidenced in the stream of research that has emanated from Wendy Frisby and her colleagues that has explored the provision and uptake of community-based recreation opportunities for low-income women in British Columbia. Frisby, Reid, Millar, and Hoeber (2005) have presented a succinct analysis of their experiences carrying out feminist participatory action research (FPAR). To gain experiential knowledge, participatory action research (PAR) of all types is characterized by researchers entering into interactive relations with research participants in some or all phases of the research. Clearly eschewing many of the last vestiges of positivism, the co-participation and co-construction of knowledge can take place throughout the research process, including: collectively deciding on relevant research questions, determining appropriate data collection methods, collaboratively analyzing the results, and communicating the findings. Although there have been several calls for PAR, in general (and FPAR in particular), across the social sciences, accounts that deal with the paradoxes, ethical dilemmas, and practicalities of carrying out such work, particularly in sport and leisure organizations, have been lacking.

In keeping with a field that is inherently multidisciplinary in nature, we envision an academic landscape that is not dominated by any single overarching metanarrative that marginalizes and obfuscates alternative approaches. This is a sport management that can engage in concrete steps that will "change situations" and potentially "bring new value to identities and experiences that are marginalized and stigmatized by the larger culture. [This] will demonstrate how particular commodities or cultural objects negatively affect the lives of specific people." (Denzin, 2002, p. 486). This is a sport management that, alongside those concerns that have been central to this point, can, and should, "take sides" (Denzin, p. 487).

For example, rather than simply viewing sport sponsorship investments as neutral or inherently positive, as most research has done, we also need to consider who might be disadvantaged by such investments. Consider, for example, the rise of school sport sponsorship agreements and the exposure of emotionally vulnerable children to carefully contoured marketing campaigns. For those interested in facility construction and management, consider where new arenas and stadia are located and why, whose voices are excluded from the accompanying debates, and which populations are forcibly displaced to accommodate a city's new crown jewel. Though such issues are not new, they have been virtually ignored by those of us in sport management.

In addressing these types of issues—or indeed any organizationally based problem—an understanding of the context in which the research takes place is vital. Thus, though we certainly do not wish to downplay the role of quantitative research, we contend that we cannot obviate the need for an understanding of history and context by hiding behind terms such as reliability, validity, and generalizability. We advocate for more longitudinal research that can provide insight into the dynamic phenomena that characterize the existence of most organizations. In short, we would like to see more work—qualitative and quantitative—that can usefully detail the everyday realities of organizational life. One quantitative approach that appears useful in this regard is hierarchical linear modeling (HLM). In assisting the capture of the multidimensionality of most organizational phenomena, HLM offers the promise of revealing more accurate associations than might otherwise be possible.

Todd, Crook, and Barilla illustrate the potential of HLM for sport management scholars (Todd et al., 2005). In providing detailed methodological explanations and a comparison between HLM and regression analysis, Todd and his colleagues demonstrate the utility of HLM as a tool for examining a number of theoretical and empirical problems in which individuals are nested in teams, subunits, organizations, and even industries. In keeping with the theme of this special issue, the work of Todd et al. should help to expand the frontiers of understanding within the sport management discipline by demonstrating how HLM can help address previously ignored, or at least downplayed, research problems. Likewise, and as we continue to press for the ongoing development of research strategies that have existed at the margins of sport management, Skinner and Edwards (2005) have provided insight into the potential for sport management through the application of critical and postmodern thought to ethnographic practices. In particular, they have proposed that the field of sport management, through a considered reflection on the reasons for undertaking research, can gain the role of the self in the research process, the coparticipation of "the researched," and the facilitation of voice, stories, and solutions beyond those of the researcher.

Clearly, such developments do not disregard the managerial issues that have traditionally dominated the discipline, but they do place an emphasis on a wider consideration of the history, context, location, and implications of both the issues at hand and the research designs appropriate to investigate them. In so doing, for example, we are calling for a legitimate space for revealing the multifarious forms of the shifting structures of global and local capitalism and the ways in which the (sporting) media reproduce gender, race, sexual orientation, and social class stereotypes and even contribute to consumer practices that are harmful to personal health and the environment (Denzin, 2002). This in turn will help us counter the growing belief that today's culture of investment and finance makes it impossible to address major social problems such as inadequate health care, education, housing, inequality of wealth distribution, and the racial apartheid of inner cities.

From a managerial perspective, addressing such issues inevitably involves a consideration of the part played by organizations in altering or furthering the status quo. Nevertheless,

> answering questions that focus on the role and effect of organizations in society requires long-term perspectives, a grasp of history, and a focus on understanding so that the complexities of political and social movements are not reduced to dummy variables in a regression equation and an interest in speculation. Yet there is a sense in which organization theory has become without history, without context, and without time. The focus is thoroughly on being contemporary, being generalizable, and building causal models. (Hinings & Greenwood, 2002, p. 417)

If we are to realize a sport management that operates much more directly in the public good, recognizes that academic labor is a social endeavor, uses theory as a resource to think and act, critiques the extant distributions of resources and power, and offers opportunities to mobilize instances of collective action against glaring material inequalities (Giroux, 2001), we need an accepted plurality of epistemology and method that currently does not exist. In this spirit, and alongside the work of Frisby, Cara Aitchison (2005) argues that the relationship between structure and culture, revealed at the "social– cultural nexus," illuminates inequalities that have become ingrained in organizational structures and policies. Drawing on primary and secondary data collected from the U.K., Australia, New Zealand, Canada, and the U.S., Aitchison offers a revised epistemology that seeks to integrate social and cultural perspectives to highlight and better theorize gender–power relations in sport and leisure organizations. Markula and Friend (2005) complement this line of research by discussing the contributions that memory-work can bring to the knowledges produced in sport management. Already employed in marketing, they highlight the insights that memory work can bring to our understandings of sport consumers' and sport producers' behaviors, as well as the ways in which the method breaks down the hierarchical structure of the research process. There is little doubt that, important as the issues covered by these articles are, the logic could be extended to expose other inequities. It is this type of thinking that is required if sport management is to continue its advance as an academic discipline capable of significant theoretical and practical impact.

A Sport Management Bricolage?

As stated previously, it is our contention that sport management is a field blinkered by disciplinarity. That is, it is—as are other social science disciplines— dominated by quite fixed and rigid boundaries (see Clegg, 2002). In many ways this is the strength of the field at present; a range of models has been exhibited for engaging in a methodical, persistent, and well-coordinated process of knowledge production and model of expertise (Kincheloe, 2001), which for the most part has embraced the doctrines and standards of logical positivism. As we have consistently stated, we do not suggest discarding such advances, yet we do oppose parochialism and domination and the ways in which the conventions of this particular approach become accepted as the natural way of producing knowledge and viewing a particular aspect of the world. Indeed, following Kincheloe, we perceive that any single research perspective is laden with assumptions, blindness, and limitations; produces a naïve overspecialization; and is often imbued with elitist dimensions of dominant cultural knowledge techniques. Rather, to avoid such one-sided reductionism, there is a need for a variety of ways of seeing and interpreting in the pursuit of knowledge; the more one applies, the more dimensions and consequences of the field can be illuminated. It is in this sense that we embrace an expansion of knowledge, of ways of seeing and interpreting through engagement with alternative ontological, epistemological, ideological, political, and methodological approaches to the study of sport management.

For Denzin and Lincoln (1994; 2000a, 2000b; 2005), the concept of the bricoleur can be applied to the practice of research in which the "jack-of-all-trades" researcher draws on a variety of different tools, methods, and techniques of interpretation and representation dependent on the task at hand. As Grossberg suggested, the researcher

> can and should use any and every kind of empirical method, whatever seems useful to the particular project. Use them as rigorously and as suspiciously as you can. . . . I do not think that ethnography, or any other methodology, has a privileged status. . . . Nor do I think that any one methodology has a greater claim to being somehow more empirical than another. Use anything, including surveys and statistics, if it seems useful, but consider how they are themselves rearticulated (and their practice changed) by the theoretical and political commitments . . . of one's own project. (Wright, 2001, p. 145)

Recognizing the limitations of a single method and the discursive strictures of one disciplinary approach, bricolage can offer a multifaceted, "crystallized" view (see Richardson, 2000a) of what is missed by traditional practices of validation, the historicity of certified modes of knowledge production, the inseparability of the knower and the known, and the complexity and heterogeneity of all human forms (Kincheloe, 2001). Yet, though bricolage can avoid the parochialism of a unitary approach, we might well open ourselves to the superficiality of methodological breadth in which scholars, researchers, and students fail to devote sufficient time to understanding the disciplinary fields and knowledge bases from which particular modes of research emanate. Inhabiting the world of the bricoleur is far from an easy option; it requires knowledge—if not deep comprehension—of multiple worlds, methodological approaches, theoretical perspectives, and disciplinary assumptions (cf. Kincheloe, 2001; Lincoln, 2001; McLaren, 2001). As a field, however, we cannot ignore the benefits of an interdisciplinary approach. We are ensconced in a scholarly moment in which disciplinary boundaries are increasingly being crossed, analytical frames of more than one discipline are employed by researchers, and the empirical is understood in relation to a variety of contexts, is subject to new forms of rigor, and produces new challenges to researchers to push methodological and interpretive envelopes (Kincheloe, 2001). Though we might not all have the capacity or desire to be bricoleurs, our research needs to open elastic conversations about the ways in which bricolage can be developed—as individuals contributing to a more democratic whole, as teams, or as a field contributing to wider societal debates. At the very least, as individuals, we need to be open to competing discourses and viewpoints. The need for this at a time when there is an apparent political, ideological, and paradigmatic retrenchment among several influential institutions, such as the National Research Council (see, among others, Denzin & Lincoln, 2005), is vitally apparent. We are at a time—Denzin and Lincoln's (2005, p. 20) "eighth moment"—in which we must confront "the methodological backlash associated with 'Bush science' and the evidence-based social movement." We must ensure that the methodological and paradigmatic pluralism that promises expanded understandings of social phenomena is not lost in a chase for ever-declining research dollars from funding institutions (and by extension, university administrators that press for externally funded research) that narrowly define what constitutes an acceptable scholarly contribution.

Singer (2005) challenges us to think about epistemology as a system of knowing, asking important questions about the ways in which Eurocentrism is manifest in knowledge production and acquisition. Embracing a critical race theory that places racialized and ethnic epistemologies alongside those that currently hold the center, Singer encourages sport management scholars and students to think beyond and recognize the limits of the research paradigms and epistemologies that are presently legitimized in education, the academy, and society. Singer's article raises difficult challenges and questions for the field, calling for a scrutiny of our present, for meaningful dialogue, and for expanding the horizons of the knowledges produced in sport management. We, of course, embrace such debates. The alternative is that we simply regurgitate existing modes of thought and reproduce the comfortable and logical status quo. These points are of course exacerbated when we consider the influence that we have on students who are likely to reflect their graduate experiences in their own teaching and advising assignments. We thus advocate a sport management that is "unembarrassed in its effort to *rupture* particular ways of functioning in the established disciplines of research," an approach that subverts the stability of the field and fragments the impulse to fold its methodologies and the knowledge they produce neatly into disciplinary draws (Kincheloe, 2001, p. 687, emphasis added).

Paradigmatic Plurality:
Expanding the Horizons of Sport Management

But, what does this mean for sport management? Does all work have to be held against such criteria? We think not. We do argue for such work in sport management to be valued, however, to coexist alongside that which currently holds the center, and for such (uneasy) coexistence to stir, create debate, and push the boundaries of the field. Somewhat modifying Andrews (2002), we envisage a sport management that nurtures a broad-ranging interpretive vocabulary, theorizes the social, cultural, economic, political, technological, and ideological relations within contemporary existence, and critically engages with whichever theories and methodological strategies are useful within a particular empirical context. This is a sport management that will not provide answers that are known in advance, a sport management that will require an expansive and flexible methodological arsenal as a way to understanding, that will fashion new possibilities for the field in contributing to a multiracial, economic, and political democracy, and will ensure an open and vibrant space for scholars of all ideological, epistemological, and/or methodological persuasions. Perhaps most importantly, this is a sport management in which those working within the discipline engage with and reflect on how they want to live the life of the social inquirer (Schwandt, 2000).

We will all, of course, have our preferences; this does not mean that we need to reflexively oppose other's methodological choices or epistemological positions. There is great scope for interweaving viewpoints, for the incorporation of multiple perspectives, and for borrowing (or bricolage; Kincheloe, 2001; Lincoln & Guba, 2000). We are, however, arguing for a plurality of paradigms and perspectives that can coexist within sport management and push at the boundaries of the knowledges that "count" in the field. That is, cutting across our paradigmatic stances are issues concerning how to define what understanding actually means and how to justify claims to understand; the social and scientific purposes of our research; how to envision and occupy the ethical space in which researchers and researched relate to one another on the sociotemporal occasion or event that is research; and, consequently, how to determine the role, status, responsibility, and obligations the researcher has in and to the society he or she researches (Denzin & Lincoln, 2000a, 2005; Schwandt, 2000). As we push for a more open, embracing, and flexible sport management, these issues assume great importance as a narrative space for thinking through what Lincoln and Guba term as the most important issues in research today: axiology, commensurability, action, control, foundations of truth and knowledge, validity, voice, reflexivity, and textual representation.

Such reflection should also sensitize us to the various ways in which we write, present, represent, or indeed express our work. Such issues concern the hierarchies of the researched and the researcher, calling for us to reflect on that relationship as we minimize status difference, show our human side, perhaps answer questions raised in the field instead of hiding behind a cloak of anonymity, and recognize that our research products are co-produced accomplishments (see Fontana & Frey, 2000; Harrison, MacGibbon, & Morton, 2001). Further, we are not only referring to getting good data, we are enjoined to move beyond a concern for more and better data to think about how we can work to empower the researched. This requires a rethinking of the traditional criteria of validity, generalizability, credibility, and believability of our research—as assessed by the academy, our communities, and our participants—as we consider how we serve the interests of those who are researched, and how those research participants have more of a say at all points of the project (Denzin, 2002; Harrison et al., 2001; Madiz, 2000). There is a need to recognize that all of our work establishes a relationship with readers to convince them of the status of "findings" and to deal with issues surrounding the integration of participants, the positioning of the author, and how people are written in and written out. In this sense, all of our work is what Sparkes (1995) termed persuasive fiction, even those pieces that offer a stripped down, abstracted, detached form of language, an impersonal voice, a conclusion of propositions, or formulae involving a realist or externalizing technique that objectify through depersonalized and supposedly inert representations of the disengaged analyst (Sparkes, 1995). Clearly, not all work in sport management can be characterized in this way, where the author is everywhere and nowhere at the same time (Sparkes, 1995). There is a need, however, for more self-conscious texts that struggle with a whole set of claims related to authorship, truth, validity, and reliability, and that bring to the fore some of the complex political/ideological agendas hidden in our writing (Richardson, 2000b, 2000c). This parallels recent developments that have seen "messy," uncertain, multivoiced texts, cultural criticism, and new alternative works displacing classic forms of representation as the "only" legitimate form (see e.g., Altheide & Johnson, 1994; Atkinson, 1992; Clifford & Marcus, 1986; Clough, 2001; James, Hockey, & Dawson, 1997; Richardson, 2000a, 2000b, 2000c; Sparkes, 1992; 1995). Reflecting this movement into more reflexive forms of fieldwork, analysis, and intertextual representation (Tedlock, 2000), Rinehart (2005) discusses how personal narrative can be a form through which knowledge *and* understanding of personal experiences can inform structural changes in, among others, human resource management, marketing, advertising, policy studies, and leadership training for practitioners of sport management. Innovative approaches such as those suggested by Rinehart and others clearly contribute to a sport management committed to understanding and engagement, a sport management that embraces difference, plurality, and interdisciplinarity in a continual quest to render "a sensible understanding of the social world" (Gephart, 2004, p. 459).

There is a fledgling literature representing the types of epistemological approaches, research strategies, and methodologies that can (uncomfortably) coexist within a more flexible, fluid, and chewy center. Such works speak to challenging issues, take these concerns further, force reflection on the paradigmatic assumptions of the field, and address how different (or reconceptualized) approaches can expand the knowledge produced within sport management. They grapple with issues of reciprocity, with textual positivism, with interdisciplinarity, with methodological plurality, and the mechanisms through which research can have a progressive impact on the array of communities that sport management can potentially serve.

References

Aitchison, C. C. (2005) Feminist and gender research in sport and leisure management. *Journal of Sport Management, 19*(4), 497–522.

Altheide, D., & Johnson, J. (1994). Criteria for assessing interpretive validity in qualitative research. In N. Denzin & Y. Lincoln (Eds.), *Handbook of qualitative research.* Thousand Oaks, CA: Sage.

Andrews, D. (2002). Coming to terms with cultural studies. *Journal of Sport and Social Issues, 26*(1), 110–117.

Andrews, D. (1999). Dead and alive: Sports history in the late capitalist moment. *Sporting Traditions, 16*(1), 73–83.

Atkinson, P. (1992). *Understanding ethnographic texts.* Newbury Park, CA: Sage.

Atkinson, P., Coffey, A., & Delamont, S. (1999). Ethnography: Post, past, and present. *Journal of Contemporary Ethnography, 28*(5), 460–471.

Bartunek, J. M. (2002). The proper place of organizational scholarship: A comment on Hinings and Greenwood. *Administrative Science Quarterly, 47*(3), 422–427.

Bauman, Z. (1999). *In search of politics.* Stanford, CA: Stanford University Press.

Clegg, S. R. (2002). "Lives in the balance": A comment on Hinings and Greenwood's "Disconnects and consequences in organization theory?" *Administrative Science Quarterly, 47*(3), 428–441.

Clifford, J., & Marcus, G. (Eds.). (1986).

Writing culture: The poetics and politics of ethnography. Berkeley, CA: University of California Press.

Clough, P. (2001). On the relationship of the criticism of ethnographic writing and the cultural studies of science. *Cultural Studies ↔ Critical Methodologies, 1*(2), 240–270.

Denzin, N. K. (2002). Cultural studies in America after September 11th, 2001. *Cultural Studies ↔ Critical Methodologies, 2*(1), 5–8.

Denzin, N. K., & Lincoln, Y. S. (1994). Introduction: Entering the field of qualitative research. In N.K. Denzin & Y.S. Lincoln (Eds.), *Handbook of qualitative research.* Thousand Oaks, CA: Sage.

Denzin, N. K., & Lincoln, Y. S. (2000a). Introduction: The discipline and practice of qualitative research. In N. K. Denzin & Y. S. Lincoln (Eds.) *Handbook of qualitative research* (2nd ed., pp. 1–28). Thousand Oaks, CA: Sage.

Denzin, N. K., & Lincoln, Y. S. (Eds.). (2000b). *Handbook of qualitative research* (2nd ed.). Thousand Oaks, CA: Sage.

Denzin, N. K., & Lincoln, Y. S. (2005). Introduction: The discipline and practice of qualitative research. In N. K. Denzin & Y. S. Lincoln (Eds.) *The Sage handbook of qualitative research* (3rd ed., pp. 1–32). Thousand Oaks, CA: Sage.

Fontana, A., & Frey, J. (2000). The interview: From structured questions to negotiated text. In N. K. Denzin & Y. S. Lincoln (Eds.), *Handbook of qualitative research* (2nd ed., pp. 645–672). Thousand Oaks, CA: Sage.

Frisby, W. (2005). The good, the bad, and the ugly: Critical sport management research. *Journal of Sport Management, 19,* 1–12.

Frisby, W., Reid, C., Millar, S. & Hoeber, L. (2005). Putting "participatory" into participatory forms of action research. *Journal of Sport Management, 19*(4), 367–386.

Fukuyama, F. (1989, Summer). The end of history? *The National Interest,* 3–18.

Gephart, R. P. (2004). From the editors: Qualitative research and the Academy of Management Journal. *Academy of Management Journal, 47*(4), 454–462.

Giroux, H. (2001). Cultural studies as performative politics. *Cultural Studies — Critical Methodologies, 1*(1), 5–23.

Harrison, J., MacGibbon, L., & Morton, M. (2001). Regimes of trustworthiness in qualitative research: The rigors of reciprocity. *Qualitative Inquiry, 7*(3), 323–345.

Hinings, C. R., & Greenwood, R. (2002). Disconnects and consequences in organization theory? *Administrative Science Quarterly, 47*(3), 411–421.

James, A., Hockey, J., & Dawson, A. (Eds.). (1997). *After writing culture: Epistemology and praxis in contemporary anthropology.* London, UK: Routledge.

Kincheloe, J. (2001). Describing the bricolage: Conceptualizing a new rigor in qualitative research. *Qualitative Inquiry, 7*(6), 679–692.

Lincoln, Y. S. (2001). An emerging new bricoleur: Promises and possibilities — a reaction to Joe Kincheloe's "Describing the bricoleur." *Qualitative Inquiry, 7*(6), 693–700.

Lincoln, Y. S., & Guba, E. (2000). Paradigmatic controversies, contradictions, and emerging confluences. In N. K. Denzin & Y. S. Lincoln (Eds.), *Handbook of qualitative research* (2nd ed., pp. 163–188). Thousand Oaks, CA: Sage.

Madiz, E. (2000). Focus groups in feminist research. In N. K. Denzin & Y. S. Lincoln (Eds.), *Handbook of qualitative research* (2nd ed., pp. 835–850). Thousand Oaks, CA: Sage.

Markula, P. & Friend, L. (2005). Remember when . . . ? Memory-work as an interpretive methodology for sport management. *Journal of Sport Management, 19,* 442–463

McLaren, P. (2001). Bricklayers and bricoleurs: A Marxist addendum. *Qualitative Inquiry, 7*(6), 700–705.

Richardson, L. (2000a). Writing: A method of inquiry. In N. K. Denzin & Y.S. Lincoln (Eds.), *Handbook of qualitative research* (2nd ed., pp. 923–948). Thousand Oaks, CA: Sage.

Richardson, L. (2000b). New writing practices in qualitative research. *Sociology of Sport Journal, 17*(1), 5–20.

Richardson, L. (2000c). Evaluating ethnography. *Qualitative Inquiry, 6*(2), 253–255.

Rinehart, R. (2005) Experiencing sport management: The use of personal narrative in management studies. *Journal of Sport Management, 19*(4), 497–522

Rouse, M. J., & Daellenbach, U. S (1999). Rethinking research methods for the re-source-based perspective: Isolating sources of sustainable competitive advantage. *Strategic Management Journal*, *20*(5), 487–494.

Rynes, S., Bartunek, J. M., & Daft, R. L. (2001). Across the great divide: Knowledge creation and transfer between practition-ers and academics. *Academy of Management Journal*, *44*(2), 340–356.

Schwandt, T. (2000). Three epistemological stances for qualitative inquiry: Interpre-tivism, hermeneutics, and social construc-tionism. In N. K. Denzin & Y. S. Lincoln (Eds.), *Handbook of qualitative research* (2nd ed., pp. 189–214). Thousand Oaks, CA: Sage.

Singer, J. N. (2005). Addressing epistemo-logical racism in sport management re-search. *Journal of Sport Management*, *19*(4), 464–479.

Skinner, J., & Edwards, A. (2005) Inventive pathways: Fresh visions of sport manage-ment research. *Journal of Sport Management*, *19*(4), 404–421.

Sparkes, A. (1992). Writing and the textual construction of realities: Some challenges for alternative paradigms in physical edu-cation. In A. Sparkes (Ed.), *Research in physical education and sport: Exploring alter-native visions*. London, UK: Falmer.

Sparkes, A. (1995). Writing people: Reflec-tions on the dual crises of representation and legitimation in qualitative inquiry. *Quest*, *47*(2), 158–195.

Tedlock, B. (2000). Ethnography and ethno-graphic representation. In N. K. Denzin & Y. S. Lincoln (Eds.) *Handbook of qualitative research* (2nd ed., pp. 455–486). Thousand Oaks, CA: Sage.

Todd, S. Y., Crook, T. R., & Barilla, T. (2005). Hierarchical linear modeling of multi-level data. *Journal of Sport Management*, *19*(4), 387–403.

Wright, K. H. (2001) "What's going on?" Larry Grossberg on the status quo of cul-tural studies: An interview. *Cultural Val-ues*, *5*(2), 133–162.

2

HOCKEY CAPITAL:
APPROACHES TO THE STUDY OF THE SPORTS INDUSTRY

J. Andrew Ross

Sports industries evince several unique characteristics—relating to firm organization, labor relations, and markets—that highlight an alternative path of industrialization that has not been adequately examined. Indeed, the very concept of sport being considered an industry is culturally contested, which draws historians into a discussion of the part that business and industry play in the creation, production, and propagation of culture. With reference to the National Hockey League, I examine the various methodological approaches used by economists, sport historians, business historians and sociologists to study the sports industry and propose that a synthesis of these approaches using capital theory may provide additional insights into the cultural connections of industrial organization.

Only he (the innocent) did wonder just what a professional hockey-match, whose purpose is to make a decent and reasonable profit for its owners, had to do with our National Anthem. What are we afraid of? Is it our national character of which we are so in doubt, so fearful that it might not hold up in the clutch, that we not only dare not open a professional athletic contest or a beauty-pageant or a real-estate auction, but we must even use a Chamber of Commerce race for Miss Sewage Disposal or a wildcat land-sale, to remind us that liberty gained without honor and sacrifice and held without constant vigilance and undiminished honor and complete willingness to sacrifice again at need, was not worth having to begin with?

—William Faulkner[1]

Appearing in *Sports Illustrated* in 1955, Faulkner's essay "An Innocent at Rinkside" describes the Nobel Prize-winning author's impressions of a National Hockey League (NHL) contest between the Montreal Canadians and New York Rangers at Madison Square Garden in New York City.[2] In the piece, Faulkner brings a depth of visual imagery that is, needless to say, unusual in sports writing, and he suggests a profound lyrical connection of the sport to American life and values. Unlike a sports writer, he views the sport with a more disinterested gaze, and levels a critical eye on the need to associate the game with the national anthem—a commonplace characteristic of post-war professional contests that would have been unremarkable to most observers.[3] For Faulkner, this hockey game is emblematic of the overuse of national symbols by commercial interests. His identification of a discrepancy between the goals of the nation and the goals of business is somewhat paradoxical. Indeed, in "An Innocent at Rinkside," Faulkner sees sport as a metaphor for American life, yet at the end (as the quotation shows) he is not willing to include business in this metaphor. He iterates the notion that commerce and culture are somehow distinct and separable, and thus speaks to a profound widespread societal discomfort with the relationship between the commercial and the non-commercial.[4]

That a professional sporting match brought out this critical point is not surprising. The United States and Canada had no national car, or national movie, or national dish soap, but they did have national sports: baseball and hockey. There was popular acceptance of the concept, even if there was not always acceptance of the content.[5] It is obviously a mistake to identify these national sports entirely with commercial enterprises (amateur organizations as well as informal games have always made up a great deal of their cultural mass), but the role of the major professional leagues has become increasingly dominant over the last century. Yet, while commercialization has succeeded, there has been continual contesting of the process for over a century, both in the struggles among and within professional, amateur, and college leagues, and in public, where cries of "It's just a business now" are implicitly negative comments on the capitalist content of sport. In addition, this contest for the social identity of sport off the field has had a profound effect on firm organization, labor relations, and many other facets of the sports industry, leading to a pattern that is both highly successful and quite different from most other industries.

While they have existed since the mid- to late-nineteenth century, the cultural profile of sports industries has far exceeded their economic size. However, even as their economic importance has grown, sports industries still get only scant attention from scholars.[6] Indeed, the primary view of sports leagues, clubs, and players is through the lens of popular culture, which has so dominated the discourse that it that has also dimmed awareness and appreciation of the singular characteristics that distinguish sports industries from other mainstream commercial enterprises.[7]

Sports production has followed a distinctive industrial pattern. First, the contesting of the industry's transition from the non-commercial to the commercial sphere provoked public debate on the social value of sport. One reflection of this debate is in the nomenclature, which maintained the terms of the non-commercial sphere and downplayed the commercial enterprise: "leagues" rather than cartels, "commissioners" not presidents, "clubs" or "teams" not corporations, and "players" instead of laborers. The industry was a "game". Initially the conflicts over the legitimacy of sports laborers (that is, players) illustrated this best. Simply put, while steel workers never had to fight to justify being paid, the status of athletes was a longstanding issue arising out of the British amateur tradition, which limited sport participation on particular socio-economic, racial, and gender lines. Even with the transition from amateur to formal paid play in the late-nineteenth and early-twentieth centuries, other restrictions on labor mobility remained. The reserve clause bound a player to a particular team at the team's option. In situations where one league attained a virtual monopoly on the highest level of professional sport (a major league, such as baseball) this effectively allowed monopsony in the labor market. The league was the only supplier of major league competition, and therefore the only buyer of major league talent. Furthermore, while unionization was growing in this era, attempts to unionize athletes failed to prosper. The state abetted many of these characteristics by not applying anti-trust laws and other statutes, or giving explicit waivers, particularly in the case of baseball.

Another specialized feature of the sport industry was its organization. While early examples of single-ownership leagues did exist, the preeminent organization was the multi-owner cartel, an association of club owners with limits on multiple team ownership. The NHL was an unincorporated, non-profit organization, and used this non-profit façade to style itself foremost as the protector of Canada's national game, and not as a commercial organization. In many ways, this calls into question the boundaries and role of the corporate firm as the primary organizational unit of successful twentieth-century industries. The firm-market structure of sports industries has remained consistent over the last century, even with changes in scale, size, and cultural importance. Supply chain integration was also achieved outside the walls of the firm or cartel. By means of rule standardization and sponsorship agreements, but usually without formal ownership, major hockey leagues subordinated amateur, minor, college, and semi-pro leagues to their business model. By the 1950s, NHL teams had a great deal of influence over the education of minor-age players.

These and many other characteristics beg for an adequate examination, and the industries that call themselves "games" and their patterns of industrialization clearly require methodological approaches that can accommodate both commercial and cultural natures. Scholars may need to stretch and modify beyond common definitions of the firm, the market, and the border of the commercial world. In addition, the methodology must provide a framework for the integration of industry, economics, and culture in historical time.

Sport Historians

Scholarly investigation of sport industry has primarily been the purview of sport historians, who, to some degree, have marginalized it. The roots of the sport history sub-discipline are in physical education, and thus show a preference for amateur sport and sport education. When studying sport commercialization, this has often led to analytical frameworks that stress Marxian class conflict and unequal power relations.[8] Within this discipline, only a handful of scholars deal explicitly with the behavior of individual sport businesses and industries, although there are excellent broader studies of the social context of commercial sports.[9] Even so, they can remain tied to traditional Marxist approaches to commercialization.[10]

In general, these studies often bring to light many important insights into the historical relationship between sport and society, but they often do so at the expense of a nuanced treatment of commercial organizations and entrepreneurs.[11] Indeed, Stephen Hardy called for the need for more attention to sports entrepreneurs and the market, believing that the product of historical analysis of the sport industry is not limited to sports and business history, but offers special insights into North American consumer culture and society. Few have taken up the challenge.[12] In particular, there has been little historical academic study of the most prominent structures of modern sports era, the major professional leagues.[13] Sport management scholarship is a developing field, but it has yet to make its mark on historical issues, and usually promotes the short-term horizon of many management scholars.[14]

Economists

Economists have better served sport industries. Over the last three decades, economists have brought many of the tools of their trade to the sports arenas, and produced some important studies of franchises, labor relations, and other elements distinct to the industry.[15] However, these decades have also seen a devaluation of economic history in the economics discipline, and thus it is no surprise that the historical experience has been given short shrift. Many studies do not address the period before the era of free agency (i.e., pre-1970s). If they do, they tend to be discrete studies that trace a theme (for example, the reserve clause), but without a full consideration of historical context. We see the promise of a historically informed approach in the work of Eric Leifer, who shows how the organization of professional sports markets and business entities are determined by a dynamic interaction between league organizers and customers. Teams and leagues responded to demographic change, new technology, and fan demand by pursuing particular strategies for attaining competitive balance, managing failure (losing), and creating the civic and national markets that went beyond a mere market relationship and contributed to customers' identity formation.[16]

Leifer calls his field of inquiry economic sociology, and mainstream economic historians have not addressed the industry at all, focusing rather on financial history and longer-term economic trends that led themselves to the tools of cliometrics. However, the common refrain at the gathering of economic historians is that, after all is said and done, the answers to many of their problems lie in the realm of an economy's institutions, and therein lies the potential for a promising analysis. Douglass North defined institutions as "the humanly devised constraints that structure human interaction" made up of both formal constraints (rules, laws, constitutions) and informal constraints (norms of behavior, conventions, and self-imposed codes of conduct).[17] Simply put, cultural constraints on sport industry are certainly worth investigating. In particular, we must investigate the idea that the industry and its entrepreneurs are not only subject to institutional "constraint," but that they actively realign and adapt to the changing borders of the institution-market relationship.

Business Historians

One would expect that business historians would be prominent in sports industry study, but, in fact, very few researchers have studied the industry explicitly within the context of business history.[18] However, business historians do have the tools. As part of a disciplinary tradition of synthetic history represented most prominently by the works of Alfred D. Chandler, Jr., business historians have been prominent in addressing the gap between economics and history methodologies.[19] A focus on big business/core/traditional industries is a legacy of the Chandlerian approach, although attempts to address the nature of the newer dominant industries such as computers and batch production techniques have produced alternate frameworks.[20] Those industries under study have also facilitated this analysis. The story of large mass production firms lends itself to Chandlerian meta-narrative, while the other historians' treatment of smaller batch production firms led to identification of alternative paths of industrialization.[21] Furthermore, the firm as unit of study is limiting. Franco Amatori and Geoffrey Jones also note the value of moving beyond the focus on the firm as unit of analysis to include "in the historical analysis not only the internal organization and strategies of firms, but also the national culture in which they operate, along with their legal and political environment."[22] Kenneth Lipartito stresses the importance of this cultural context in particular, emphasizing that by ignoring culture, a strictly rational approach that reduces business behavior to the pursuit of profit, growth, and stability creates "an untenable abstraction of human action."[23] For him, we must consider the cultural influences on decision-making—how entrepreneurs create culture—and we must seriously consider general cultural factors as missing pieces of the puzzle.[24]

Capital Theory

In pursuit of a satisfactory theoretical underpinning for the necessary integration of culture and business, I am exploring the relevance of *capital theory*, from which cultural and social capital are derived. As developed by several sociologists and business management researchers, *social capital* is an acknowledgement that we can mobilize non-tangible resources such as the relationships among people that facilitate collective action and access to resources for economic use.[25] As envisioned by Pierre Bourdieu and others, *cultural capital* comprises the use of social status and family connections to attain educational goals. Economists such as Gary Becker and Theodore Schultz operationalized what they called *human capital*—showing the achievement of productivity increases through skill development and education.[26]

Management analysts have used social capital, but their studies remain restricted to the field of intra- or inter-firm network relationships, and are generally ahistorical in approach, preferring to deal with recent phenomena.[27] The other major use of social capital theory does step beyond the corporation, but for different reasons. Robert Putnam, Francis Fukuyama, and others use the concept to study civic engagement and voluntarism, drawing popular attention to social capital in the context of declining public participation in voluntary organizations and increasing mistrust of formal institutions in the United States.[28] However, the sociologist Nan Lin cautions that a social capital theory cannot simply become "merely another trendy term to employ or deploy in the broad context of improving or building social integration and solidarity." Rather it must be distinguished from collective assets and goods such as culture, norms, trust, and so on.[29] In his focus on the discrete individual interactions and networking, Lin makes the case for quantification of social capital. In contrast, James Coleman questions if social capital will become a useful quantitative concept and stressed that its current value is qualitative.[30] Lin is concerned that the broadening of the concept—as with the definition of "culture"—leads to a watering down of its utility and blurring of cause and effect resulting in tautology.[31] This is the methodological downside of social capital theory. The quest for broad application takes the study beyond the networks of firm and inter-firm, and out into society, threatening to subsume any useful observations in a sea of data. Historians are generally comfortable with such methodology, which depends on qualitative evaluation rather than quantitative measurement and conclusions crafted with metaphor rather than statistics.[32]

That said, a theory is needed which can accommodate the social, cultural, economic, and political resources that are activated and turned into capital by the sports industry model. It needs also to help explain the complex social and commercial identity that sport represents. My tentative approach is to "unload" the expectations of social capital theory and the implications of Bourdieu's cultural capital theory, by referring to a new framework as *sport capital*, and more specifically, as *hockey capital*, acknowledging the specificity of the phenomena I am seeking to define.[33] I propose to take a more empirical approach and adduce a broad range of material for the assessment of the relationship between hockey industry and its culture, from basic financial statements to the popular perceptions of the hockey industry. I will examine two processes: a) the way in which hockey entrepreneurs, organizations, and laborers function, and b) how these "players" use the meanings, identities, and institutions of hockey as a capital input in their business model. At the very least, the notion of hockey capital should serve as a metaphor for developments particular to the hockey industry.[34]

Conclusion

The sport historian Alan Metcalfe has suggested that:

> . . . sport is one of the sub-systems of culture that transcends socio-economic, educational, ethnic, and religious barriers. As well, it has the ad-

vantage of being a free-time activity, regarded as "frivolous" and thus "not important." As a result, these activities reflect the attitudes and values an individual holds rather than those one is "expected" to hold.[35]

While it is intriguing to think that a sub-system can be isolated from its system and profound insight derived thereby, the very suggestion that sport should be seen in isolation from industry plays into the false dichotomy that drives much of sport history—and business history— research. One sees conflict between the social and the commercial, the other studies business without proper attention to cultural interplay. In fact, the study of sport—however "not important" or "frivolous"—must be married to that of industry (arguably the most important and least frivolous activity in a capitalist society). The interaction promises to be a fascinating nexus of investigation that will speak to the fundamental cultural meanings of business activity. In so doing, we may attempt to fill in the conceptual gaps between culture and economy, and perhaps, then, be less innocent when the national anthem plays at rinkside.

Endnotes

1. William Faulkner. (24 Jan. 1955). An Innocent at Rinkside, *Sports Illustrated*. Text taken from Faulkner's typescript printed in James B. Meriwether, ed., *Essays, Speeches & Public Letters by William Faulkner* (New York, 1966), 51. For an examination of the context of this piece in Faulkner's writing, see Robert W. Hamblin, "*Homo Agonistes*, or, William Faulkner as Sportswriter," *Aethlon: The Journal of Sport Literature* 13 (Spring 1996): 13–22.

2. Editor Sidney James commissioned Faulkner; striving for a literary angle for his new magazine, James had enticed not just Faulkner, but Robert Frost, Ernest Hemingway, and John Steinbeck to contribute articles.

3. The NHL had initiated the regular playing of the "'national" anthem before each game early in the Second World War, and the practice spread to baseball, persisting after the war. See Richard C. Crepeau, "The Sports Song of Patriotism,"http://www.poppolitics.com/articles/2003 -02-28-flagprotest.shtml, accessed 3 March 2004).

4. Note that that Faulkner did not question the commercialization of the sport itself, admitting that commercial sport's "purpose is to make a decent and reasonable profit." However, the overt use of the symbols of the nation was undesirable.

5. Though baseball held the U.S. title, football and basketball also have their "national" characteristics. In Canada, lacrosse had a longstanding claim to "national status."

6. William S. Kern, ed., *The Economics of Sports* (Kalamazoo, Mich., 2000). For the purposes of this paper, "sports industries'" refer to those concerned with the production and sale of athletic contests broadly defined.

7. Robert E. Weems Jr., commented that "In recent decades it has become crystal clear that professional sports, notwithstanding fans' never-ending preoccupation with the on-field (on on-court) heroics of gifted athletes, must be viewed in the context of business enterprise." See Robert E. Weems Jr., "Review of Neil Lanctot, *Negro League Baseball: The Rise and Ruin of a Black Institution*," *Enterprise & Society* 6 (March 2005): 189.

8. See Bruce Kidd, *The Struggle for Canadian Sport* (Toronto, 1996).

9. See Melvin L. Adelman, *A Sporting Time: New York City and the Rise of Modern Athletics, 1820–70* (Urbana, Ill., 1986); Stephen Hardy, *How Boston Played: Sport, Recreation, and Community, 1865–1915* (Boston, 1982).

10. See Kidd, *The Struggle*, ff.

11. Jules Tygiel shows the potential of this marriage of sport, culture, and business in historical context; Jules Tygiel, *Past Time: Baseball as History* (New York, 2000).

12. Stephen H. Hardy. "Entrepreneurs, Organizations, and the Sports Marketplace," *Journal of Sport History* 13 (Spring 1986): 14–33. Hardy also uses a broad definition of entrepreneurship and organization that dilutes the easy dichotomies of amateur and professional, and includes purveyors and organizations of both commercial and associative sports activities. Regrettably, this article was reprinted 11 years later

without the need for updating in S. W. Pope, ed. *The New American Sports History: Recent Approaches and Perspectives* (Urbana, Ill., 1997): 342–365. In general, industry specific studies using the tools of business historian are rare.

13. John Wong is to cover the National Hockey League in *The Lords of the Rink* (Toronto, forthcoming 2005). Based on his doctoral dissertation, in which he applied a rudimentary business history methodology to the history of the league, Wong generally follows the amateur-professional dialectical approach of the sport history mainstream; John Wong "The Development of Professional Hockey and the Making of the National Hockey League" (Ph.D. diss., University of Maryland, College Park, 2001).

14. Although Daniel Mason has worked in both sport management and historical problems, his work as yet has not attempted to bridge the gaps.

15. Representative examples include: James P. Quirk and Rodney D. Fort, *Pay Dirt: The Business of Professional Team Sports* (Princeton, N.J., 1992); Paul D. Staudohar, *Playing for Dollars: Labor Relations and the Sports Business* (Ithaca, N.Y., 1996); and Paul D. Staudohar and James A. Mangan, eds., *The Business of Professional Sports* (Urbana, Ill., 1991). It can be argued that sports are treated relatively well by economists, a characteristic seen more clearly when compared to industries with a more explicitly "cultural" content. Richard Caves comments that economists study many industries for their "special or distinctive features" but that those industries that supply "goods and services that we broadly associate with cultural, artistic, or simply entertainment value" have generally been missed, and economists "have largely ignored questions about why those activities are organized the way they are." We see creative industries as "'frivolous' activities [that] can hardly exert the intellectual pull of serious industries such as steel, pharmaceuticals, and computer chips." Indeed, Caves postponed his own project for two decades until his "reputation for professional seriousness could more comfortably be placed at risk." Richard E. Caves, *Creative Industries: Contracts Between Art and Commerce* (Cambridge, Mass., 2000), vii, 1.

16. Eric Leifer, *Making the Majors: The Transformation of Team Sports in America* (Cambridge, Mass., 1996).

17. Douglass C. North, "Economic Performance through Time," Lecture to the memory of Alfred Nobel, 9 Dec. 1993 (accessed 11 April 2005 at http://nobelprize.org/economics/laureates/1993/north-lecture.html).

18. Exceptions that show the promise of a fully contextualized historical treatment of commercial sport include Neil Lanctot's *Negro League Baseball: The Rise and Ruin of a Black Institution* (Philadelphia, Pa., 2004). Wray Vamplew is one of the few scholars to bridge sport history and economics; see "The Economics of a Sports Industry: Scottish Money-gate Football, 1890–1914," *Economic History Review* 35 (Nov. 1982): 549–567; and *Pay Up and Play the Game: Professional Sports in Britain, 1875–1914* (Cambridge, U.K., 1988).

19. In particular, Alfred D. Chandler, Jr., *The Visible Hand: The Managerial Revolution in American Business* (Cambridge, Mass., 1977). Chandler's debt to the functional sociological theory of Talcott Parsons is well known; see Richard R. John, "Elaborations, Revisions, Dissents: Alfred D. Chandler, Jr.'s *The Visible Hand after Twenty Years*," *Business History Review* 71 (Summer 1997): 151–206.

20. See for example, the debate in the Sept. 2004 issue of *Enterprise & Society* (Vol. 5) between Richard N. Langlois ("Chandler in a Larger Frame: Markets, Transaction costs, and Organizational Form in History," 355–375), Naomi R., Lamoreaux, Daniel M.G. Raff, and Peter Temin ("Against Whig History," 376–387) and Charles F. Sabel and Jonathan Zeitlin ("Neither Modularity nor Relational Contracting: Inter-Firm Collaboration in the New Economy," 388–403.

21. See in particular the work of Philip Scranton, especially, *Proprietary Capitalism: The Textile Manufacture at Philadelphia, 1800–1885* (Cambridge, U.K., 1983).

22. Franco Amatori and Geoffrey Jones, eds., *Business History around the World At The Turn of the Twenty-First Century* (New York, 2003), 7.

23. Kenneth Lipartito, "Culture and the Practice of Business History," Business and Economic History 24 (Winter 1995), 33.

24. Lipartito, "Culture and the Practice," 2. Louis Galambos views cultural approaches in business history with cautious optimism. The organizational synthesis that he envisioned as the heir to Chandler's work did not survive the linguistic turn in the social sciences and the ensuing attack on meta-narratives. Yet, the move to studies on class, gender, and race do not provide the potential for synthetic history that Galambos would probably like; see Louis Galambos, "Identity and the Boundaries of Business His-

tory" in *Business History around the World At The Turn of the Twenty-First Century*, ed. Franco Amatori and Geoffrey Jones (New York, 2003), 26.

25. For a discussion of social capital theory and its antecedents, see Nan Lin, *Social Capital: A Theory of Social Structure and Action* (New York, 2001).

26. Gary Becker, *Human Capital: A Theoretical And Empirical Analysis, With Special Reference to Education* (New York, 1964); Theodore Schultz, *Investment in Human Capital: The Role of Education and of Research*, (New York, 1971). We can distinguish human capital from Bourdieu's cultural capital by its lack of a class-based analysis. Bourdieu's capital is tied to class interest and power structures, while Becker and Schultz allow capital to be developed universally through education and skill development. This dimension of capital was first acknowledged by Adam Smith in *An Inquiry into the Nature and Causes of the Wealth of Nations* (1776) Book 2, Chapter 1, when he wrote that national fixed capital included "the acquired and useful abilities of all the inhabitants or members of the society."

27. See for example, Don Cohen and Laurence Prusak, *In Good Company: How Social Capital Makes Organizations Work* (Boston, 2000); Robert Burt, "The Network Structure of Social Capital," http://gsbwww.uchicago.edu/fac/ron ald.burt/research/NSSC.pdf. Accessed April 12, 2005; Janine Nahapiet and Sumantra Ghoshal, "Social capital, Intellectual Capital, and the Organizational Advantage," *Academy of Management Review*, 23 (April 1998): 242–266; Wenpin Tsai, "Social Capital, Strategic Relatedness and the Formation of Intraorganizational Linkages," *Strategic Management Journal* 21 (Sept. 2000): 925–939; Tom Schuller, "The Complementary Role of Human and Social Capital," *Canadian Journal of Policy Research* 2 No. 1 (Spring 2001): 18–24.

28. Robert Putnam, *Bowling Alone: The Collapse and Revival of American Community* (New York, 2000); Robert Putnam, *Making Democracy Work: Civic Traditions in Modern Italy* (Princeton, N.J., 1993); Francis Fukuyama, *The Great Disruption: Human Nature and the Reconstitution of Social Order* (New York, 1999); Jane Jacobs, *The Death and Life of Great American Cities* (New York, 1992); Jenny Onyx and Paul Bullen, "Measuring Social Capital in Five Communities," *Journal of Applied Behavioral Science*, 36 (March 2000): 23–42.

29. Lin, *Social Capital*, 26.

30. James C. Coleman, "Social Capital in the Creation of Human Capital," *American Journal of Sociology* 94 Supplement (1988): S95–S120. Coleman's broader approach — seeing social capital in terms of culture, norms, trust, etc. — is followed by Burt, "The Network Structure," and others.

31. Lin, *Social Capital*, 28.

32. With reference to creative industries, which share several characteristics with sport industries, Richard Caves notes that although systematic data may be scarce, "If one settles for information that is heterogeneous and largely qualitative, but nonetheless abundant, a great deal can be learned of the economic organization and behavior of these sectors." Caves, *Creative Industries*, vii).

33. Ideally, extrapolation to the broader category of sport capital will be feasible at the conclusion of my study, but even then, the addition of other sports to the concept will be tentative.

34. Professional hockey offers particular advantages to such a study of cultural capital, because it transacts business over several different geographic and cultural regions. Additionally, it provides an opportunity for comparing the dynamics of cultural and economic interaction, which is relevant to theories of globalization and borderlands.

35. Alan Metcalfe, *Canada Learns to Play: The Emergence of Organized Sport 1807–1914* (Toronto, Ont., 1987): 13-14.

Note: The author acknowledges comments from Ben Forster and the participants of the Business History Conference in Minneapolis, May 2005. A Social Science and Humanities Doctoral Fellowship, Ontario, Graduate Scholarships, and a Canada-United States Fulbright Research Award provided funds for this research, which is part of a business history of the National Hockey League from 1924 to 1967.

3

FEMINIST AND GENDER RESEARCH IN SPORT AND LEISURE MANAGEMENT: UNDERSTANDING THE SOCIAL–CULTURAL NEXUS OF GENDER–POWER RELATIONS

Cara Carmichael Aitchison

The last decade has given rise to unparalleled growth in the literature on gender and sport with much of the body of published research adopting explicit feminist perspectives. It is important at the outset, however, to speak of the plurality of feminist perspectives because it is the contested nature of feminist epistemology, as much as debates between feminist and nonfeminist research, that has contributed to recent developments within this subfield of sport research. Whereas the 1980s came to be dominated by structuralist–feminist accounts of gender relations across social science, including sport studies and management studies, the 1990s gave way to the "cultural turn" and the increasing influence of poststructural and postmodern feminist theories. The developing discourses of poststructural and postmodern feminism have become increasingly evident in sociological studies of sport but rather less so within management studies of sport in which feminism, poststructuralism, and postmodernism have all remained under-theorized. This article seeks to evaluate the different trajectories of structural analysis and cultural theory and to explore the neglected interface between these two seemingly polarized social and cultural perspectives. In doing so, the article advocates the expansion of our current research horizons by exploring the social–cultural nexus of gender relations in research on sport and leisure management. Rather than focusing on either organizational structures or cultures, the article calls for feminist and gender research that acknowledges and investigates further the lineage and linkages between structural and poststructural perspectives and the complexities of gendered power inherent in these mutually informing social and cultural relationships.

It is difficult to overstate the impact of poststructural and postmodern theories on gender theory and methodology in recent social science research. Increasingly, gender studies, sociology, social and cultural geography, social policy, and, more recently, leisure, sport, and tourism studies have engaged with poststructural and postmodern analyses of gender–power relations, albeit with varying degrees of acceptance. Within business and management studies, too, there has been a growing recognition of the need to examine organizational cultures to supplement and complement previous analyses of organizational structures. Notwithstanding these developments, the research of gender–power relations in sport and leisure management remains limited in volume and predominantly structuralist in approach. Consequently, cultural representations of gender–power relations in sport and leisure management have remained largely under-theorized (Aitchison, 2000).

The general critique offered here draws on materialist, structuralist, poststructuralist, and postmodern accounts of gender, sport, and management in recognition of the interconnections between material, social, cultural, and symbolic relations. The central focus of the article is the development of a theoretical critique that further integrates social and cultural perspectives. This accommodation of the social and the cultural is articulated here through the conceptualization of the social–cultural nexus. The social–cultural nexus is explained as both a site and process of construction, legitimation, reproduction, and reworking of gender relations. In this way, the article engages with structural and poststructural theories to explore the social and cultural workings and reworkings of gender–power relations in everyday life. Simultaneously, however, the article acknowledges the value of materialist analyses of patriarchy and capitalism or patriarchal capitalism in shaping the power relations that construct, legitimate, and reproduce gender and management relations, often on a global scale. The article therefore seeks to offer a more critical and comprehensive analysis of gender relations in sport management. For example, although equal-opportunities policies are now enshrined in the legislation of many countries and implemented within many organizational structures and policies, legacies of previous inequity often remain ingrained in the management cultures and practices of organizations. Moreover, it is argued here that the relationship between materialities or structures and symbols or cultures, revealed at the social–cultural nexus, often serves to perpetuate both structural and cultural inequality. This theoretical analysis has been constructed inductively after the analysis of empirical data gathered in a national study of *Gender Equity in Leisure Management* conducted by the author in 1998/99 (Aitchison et al., 1999). Deductive analysis was then applied to similar research undertaken in Australia, New Zealand, Canada, and the United States, demonstrating that gender–power relations in sport and leisure management are frequently produced, legitimated, reproduced, and reworked at the intersection of the social and cultural, or in the social–cultural nexus of organizations.

The thesis outlined in this article builds on previous work by management theorists such as Oerton (1996) and Acker (1990, 1992) who have called for both structural and cultural analyses of gender–power relations. Acker (1990, 1992), for example, has advocated analyses of gender and organizations that address both the structural and the symbolic representations of gendered power across four intersecting processes: (a) the construction of gender divisions and hierarchies within organizations represented by horizontal and vertical sex segregation identified through distributive research; (b) the symbolism related to such divisions and distinctions; (c) the inter- and intra-actions between men and women; and (d) the nature of gender and sexuality in the construction of the self and individual identity in relation to, and in response to, such an organizational culture. The approach advocated by Acker stresses the need to examine material and symbolic interactions and the role of structures and cultures at the site and process of the social–cultural nexus within organizational management. Such a research agenda requires a broadening of epistemological perspectives as much if not more than the adoption and implementation of a wider range of methodological perspectives or research techniques.

In relation to sport and leisure management research, including feminist and gender research, current management research is conducted in what is still an emerging profession. Witz (1992, p. 39) advocates analyses adopting a critical perspective of the structures of gender–power relations within organizations when she contends that "the relationship between gender and professionalization is a neglected one." Part of the explanation for this neglect, she suggests, rests in the lack of recognition of the gendered nature of the professions themselves, and she argues, "It is necessary to speak of 'professional projects,' to gender the agents of these projects, and to locate these within the structural and historical parameters of patriarchal capitalism" (Witz, p. 39). In relation to the sport and leisure management profession, research undertaken in the U.S. by Henderson (1992), Bialeschki and Henderson (1984), and Henderson and Bialeschki (1993, 1995) examining the status of women and their career development in sport and leisure management also drew attention to structural constraints. In their earlier research, Bialeschki and Henderson (1993) found that women reported a number of material factors related to gender that made competition for senior management posts problematic. These factors included low pay, inadequate childcare, and family conflicts. By the 1990s, however, feminist researchers in sport and leisure management were beginning to recognize the presence of cultural power relations in addition to material constraints. Frisby and Brown (1991) then indicated the presence of organizational cultures, as well as structures, in their research that found that women had lower aspirations for career progress than did their male colleagues. Later research by Henderson and Bialeschki (1993) concurred with this finding, with over half of women respondents stating that they perceived that they had fewer opportunities for career advancement than their male colleagues. Many of these findings were again reiterated in the *Gender Equity in the Leisure Services Field* research conducted by Shinew and Arnold (1998), as well as in recent research by Bialeschki and Henderson (2000). What these more recent research findings appear to indicate is the presence of more complex combinations of constraining influences that require a more nuanced research approach capable of understanding structural constraints, cultural influences, and the interplay between the two.

In the sport and leisure management sector, the Institute of Leisure and Amenity Management (ILAM) defines itself as "the professional Institute for the leisure industry." Together with the Institute of Sport and Recreation Management, ILAM aims to represent the broad spectrum of management services and managers across the leisure industry in the UK. ILAM was formed in 1983 after the amalgamation of four leisure and recreation associations/institutes: the Association of Recreation Managers, the Institute of Municipal Entertainment, the Institute of Park and Recreation Administration, and the Institute of Recreation Management. In 1998, ILAM commissioned a research project titled *Gender Equity in Leisure Management*. The research formed part of the work program of ILAM's Equal Opportunities Working Party, formed in 1995 with a broad remit of recommending further research and initiatives designed to enhance gender equity within the Institute and the wider leisure industry. The Equal Opportunities Working Party was established four years after ILAM's first piece of commissioned research into gender equity in leisure management (Bacon, 1991). For the 1998 research, a combination of quantitative and qualitative data-capture methods was employed. These included a self-administered postal questionnaire provided to all 1,151 women members of ILAM (which achieved a response rate of 30.1%), collation and analysis of data from the returned questionnaires, secondary research relating to leisure management, secondary research relating to gender equity in other service-sector industries, and qualitative research in the form of individual interviews with middle and senior women leisure managers outside of the membership of ILAM, as well as former members whose memberships had lapsed. The primary data cited in this article are drawn from the questionnaire survey of women members of ILAM.

Although there was an increase from 568 women members in 1991 to 1,151 in 1998, the respondents to the ILAM survey still testified to isolation, discrimination, and harassment within the organizational culture of sport and leisure management. Moreover, in spite of the increasing number of women entering junior management, evidence remained of a "glass ceiling" in the industry. Whereas many of the structural inequalities identified in the 1991 research had been addressed, the glass ceiling appeared to have been maintained by cultural constraints or the interplay between the remaining structural constraints and cultural constraints that had yet to be recognized and/or addressed. At the time of the 1991 research, women in leisure management reported discrimination and harassment in relation to four aspects of their work. These were identified as: (a) inequality in working conditions experienced by women and men; (b) unfavorable treatment for women attempting to balance paid work and domestic responsibilities; (c) negative perceptions about women as managers; and (d) the use of sexist language and behavior by male colleagues. By 1998 female membership of ILAM had increased to 1,151, or over 20% of the total membership. That was up from 568, or less than 10%, in 1991, and by 2003, female membership of ILAM had increased to just over 27%. More detailed scrutiny of these total membership figures for 2003 continues to reveal distinct levels of gender inequity at different levels within the organization. At each successive level of membership status, the representation of women decreased significantly (i.e., 45% of Student Members were women, 37% of Associate Members were women, but only 18% of those with Full Member status were women) thus indicating that men continue to dominate the senior ranks within the Institute. In fact, only 4 of the 93 members holding the prestigious rank of Fellow were women (ILAM 2003).

From the opening paragraphs outlined above, it should be evident that this article is as much, if not more, concerned with expanding epistemological horizons in relation to research perspectives as it is in expanding methodological horizons in relation to research techniques. The relationships among epistemology, methodology, and methods are of central importance in the construction of both knowledge and power.

This article focuses on epistemology as the underpinning theoretical perspective or way of knowing that, in turn, influences the researcher's approach toward research methodology and research methods. After an introduction to epistemological approaches in feminist and gender studies, this article explores both structuralism and poststructuralism in more depth. Attention then turns to feminist and gender research in sport and leisure management and the influence of feminism in developing new insights into gender–power relations within organizations.

Drawing on data from a study, *Gender Equity in Leisure Management*, conducted by the author on behalf of the UK's leading professional body in sport and leisure management, three specific aspects of gender–power relations in sport and leisure management organizations are discussed: perceptions of gender (in)equity within sport and leisure management; evaluations of policies and practices designed to address inequity; and career appraisal and progression opportunities designed to achieve equity. These themes were the three most significant to emerge from the data captured by the study and also reveal the interconnectedness of social and cultural relations. This discussion therefore seeks to illustrate the utility of the social–cultural nexus as a new conceptual framework for developing a deeper understanding of gender–power relations within sport and leisure management.

The intention is neither to negate the validity of findings from previous research examining gender relations in sport and leisure management nor to criticize the epistemological or methodological approaches adopted by previous studies. Rather, the purpose of this article is to move beyond the useful descriptive data provided by previous studies that have adopted a feminist standpoint in explaining *what* and *where* particular manifestations of inequity take place and to offer a theoretical critique that explains *why* and *how* such sites and practices are constructed, legitimized, reproduced, and reworked. It is through the development of this deeper understanding of gender–power relations that further research, policy-making, and management practice can effect the changes required to bring about gender equity thereby contributing to more effective working practices for all engaged in the production and consumption of sport and leisure.

Epistemological Approaches in Feminist and Gender Research

Extensive debate has taken place in feminist circles about the nature of feminist epistemology or epistemologies; the relationships among epistemology, methodology, and methods; and the existence of feminist research methods (Dyck, 1993; Gray, 1997; Harding, 1987; Jackson & Jones, 1998; Jackson & Scott, 2002; Oakley, 1998, 2000; Roberts, 1981; Stanley & Wise, 1993). It is important to review these debates at the outset so that the reader can make informed judgments about the epistemological and methodological underpinning of research discussed in this article and in the wider literature relating to sport and leisure management. The contested nature of feminist epistemology has already been clearly documented elsewhere (Jackson & Jones, 1998; Letherby, 2003; Stanley, 1990; Stanley & Wise, 1983, 1993). Stanley and Wise contend that previous criticism of feminist research is founded largely on a semantic misconception whereby many academics have assumed that feminist researchers have been calling for a radical change to research *methods* rather than research *epistemologies*. For example, feminist research has erroneously been confused and/or conflated with qualitative research, and assumptions abound relating to feminists' alleged unwillingness to engage with quantitative research methods. Such criticism has merely served to exacerbate the already established and unhelpful false dichotomy of qualitative and quantitative methods (Oakley, 1998).

Instead of providing a partisan focus on particular types of research methods, the contribution of feminist research is much more evident in revealing the partisan nature of knowledge construction prior to the stage of selecting appropriate research methods. If research methods are simply the means by which research questions are answered, then the real task is not in selecting the right methods but in asking appropriate questions. More so than in the natural sciences, the way in which we frame our social research questions reveals our theoretical "take" on the social world around us. Feminist, poststructural, and postmodern research are all more concerned with a re-evaluation of our supporting models of the world, ways of knowing, or epistemologies than with methodology or methods per se. Here, epistemology refers to ways of knowing, seeing, and believing what we understand to be the realities of the world around us. A continuing assertion throughout this article is that particular social and cultural policies and practices, including those relating to sport and leisure management, are the outcome of equally particular perspectives and philosophies. In other words, our epistemology, or preconceived model of the world, shapes the ways in which the management of sport and leisure is produced and understood within that worldview. Stanley and Wise, in relation to more generic social science, explain the need to revisit and re-evaluate epistemological issues as follows:

> An "epistemology" is a framework or theory for specifying the constitution and generation of knowledge about the social world; that is, it concerns how to understand the nature of "reality." A given epistemological framework specifies not only what "knowledge" is and how to recognize

it, but who are the "knowers" and by what means someone becomes one, and also the means by which competing knowledge-claims are adjudicated and some rejected in favor of another/others. The question of epistemology, then, is crucial, precisely fundamental, for feminism, for it is around the constitution of a feminist epistemology that feminism can most directly and far-reachingly challenge non-feminist frameworks and ways of working. (Stanley & Wise, 1993, pp. 188–189)

A feminist epistemology can be defined as a set of concepts that rejects traditional epistemological theories for their empiricism and rationalism (Coward, 1977). This emphasis on empiricism and rationalism is associated primarily with post-Enlightenment thinking, with modern science, and with positivism. Such an approach is also manifest in research that has been constructed to explain social phenomena in which men's experiences are viewed as the "norm" and women's experiences are viewed as secondary, deviant from the norm, or Other. Feminists have rejected these interpretations of their lives because they have been made by undertaking research within a patriarchal framework that neglects or negates women's experiences. Feminist research therefore acknowledges the significance of the researcher or writer in shaping the research process and written outcomes. Moreover, the relationship between the researcher and the research subject(s) has been scrutinized by a number of feminist researchers (Farran, 1990; Gilligan, 1982; Oakley, 1981; Seller, 1994; Stanley & Wise, 1983, 1993). From here on, this article will refer not to research subjects but to research participants or respondents. This attempt to create a less hierarchical relationship within the research process is in line with what Morris, Woodward, and Peters (1998, p. 221) see as the "third tenet of feminist methodology which is the rejection of hierarchical relationships within the research process by making those being researched into partners or collaborators." The other tenets of feminist methodology outlined by Morris et al. (pp. 220–222) include: a "commitment to feminist principles" in the purpose, conduct, and reporting of the research; a commitment "to doing feminist research *for* women, and not just *on* them"; and a "commitment to reflexivity, based on notions of openness and intellectual honesty."

Feminist research is therefore research undertaken from a particular perspective or epistemology: a feminist perspective or feminist epistemology. Just as it is difficult to separate epistemological and philosophical issues from methodological issues in feminist research, so it becomes difficult to separate philosophical issues from political issues. Feminist research has an explicit political purpose, and distinct schools of thought within feminism have placed political significance on different power relations that are seen to subordinate women. This can be seen in all three "waves" of feminism, from "first wave" feminism—informed by the suffragette movement at the turn of the 19th and 20th centuries, to "second wave" feminism—informed by liberal, radical, and socialist feminism in the 1960s and 1970s, to the current "third wave" of feminism—influenced by poststructuralism, postmodernism, and postcolonialism. For example, whereas liberal feminism sees the lack of equality of opportunity within organizations and institutions such as education and work as being a major cause of inequality, socialist and Marxist feminism view the very structure of such institutions as inherently patriarchal. Radical feminism, in a further contrast, directs attention toward the institution of the family, sexuality, and the oppression of women through unpaid domestic labor and reproduction as being the primary cause of inequality. Poststructural and postmodern feminism(s) would view such a perspective as essentialist and overly homogenizing of women through its neglect of cultural difference and the myriad ways in which sexuality is experienced in the workplace in addition to the home. Similarly, postcolonial and Black feminism(s) might also emphasize the cultural diversity of women and the legacy of colonial power in shaping gender relations in both objective and subjective spheres. Although there is insufficient scope within this article to explore each of these perspectives in more detail, it is worth outlining the main features of structuralism and poststructuralism. Such a discussion will enable the reader to make the connections between the social and the cultural as outlined within the thesis advocating the utility of a theoretical framework that explores the social–cultural nexus of gender–power relations in all spheres of life, including sport and leisure management. (For a fuller discussion of the range of feminist theoretical perspectives highlighted above and their relationship to leisure and sport relations, see Aitchison, 2003).

Structuralism, Poststructuralism, and Social Research

During the period of second-wave feminism in the 1960s and 1970s, feminist analyses were informed by structuralist perspectives. Structuralism can be divided into two broad approaches derived from distinct disciplinary perspectives. On the one hand, neurolinguistics, anthropology, and psychology, respectively, have engaged in research positing structures as linguistic, social, and psychological constructs. On the other hand, sociology has modified its previously dominant Marxist analyses of structures as material constructs to view structures as social processes. Although these represent two very different approaches, they both seek explanations for observed phenomena in general structures that underpin all phenomena but are not necessarily identifiable within them. The distinction between the two approaches lies in the degree to which individuals are accorded human agency and the extent to which they can realize this agency. With the structures-as-constructs theory, observed phenomena, evident as a form of essential logic in the actions of human subjects, are seen as representations of deep structures genetically imprinted on human consciousness. The literary and linguistic theories of Chomsky (2003), the social anthropological theories of Lévi Strauss (1968), and the psychological theories of Piaget (1958), thus, have a fixity about them that leaves little scope for change and intervention made as a result of human agency or historical development.

This article is less concerned with this form of linguistic "structure as construct" but more with the sociological concept of "structure as process." Here, it is the transformation of structures at societal and individual level, rather than neural level, that is significant. Such theory has formed the basis of the structural Marxism of Althusser (1971), the Marxian humanism of the Frankfurt School, the critical theory of Habermas (1989), and Giddens' theory of structuration (1984). Although differing in the degree to which they accord agency to individuals, each of these structure-as-process perspectives seeks to overcome the fixity of the structure-as-construct perspectives developed by the early linguistic and literary theorists. Moreover, the structuralist sociology of the 1970s and 1980s, although informed by Marxism, sought to move beyond the rigidity of the materialist perspective of Marxist structuralism that came to be seen as offering limited scope for individual action, contestation of power relations, and the creation of social change. Thus, structuralist perspectives can be viewed as forming a continuum from total domination by society or genetics at one end to the other end in which individual agency is accorded the same status as societal structure. On one side of this continuum range are Marxist, materialist, and radical feminist perspectives emphasizing the inflexible nature of structures, and on the other side are phenomenological and postmodern perspectives emphasizing the power of human agency and individualism. Throughout this article, reference is therefore made to structuralism in the sociological structure-as-process sense. As the next section will illustrate, the contribution of linguistic and literary theorists to the article is in their development of poststructural theory rather than the structural theories of "structure as construct."

Poststructuralism is commonly conflated and confused with postmodernism, and the two terms are frequently used interchangeably. It is important to acknowledge, however, that although they are overlapping and mutually informing, they are also differentiated by their objects of study. Postmodernism is concerned with the critical study of modernity, whereas poststructuralism is concerned with the critical study of the power relations inherent in, and resulting from, the structures and structured order of modernity. Thus postmodernism seeks to deconstruct the metanarratives and grand theories of modernist society, whereas poststructuralism seeks to reveal the power relations on which the construction, legitimation, and reproduction of modernist society depends. This difference in object and method of study has resulted in postmodern accounts remaining largely within the realms of the humanities, whereas poststructural critiques have crossed into the social sciences in which critical engagement with theories of social, economic, and cultural power is already established.

Heavily influenced by French philosophy, much of poststructural theory draws on the psychoanalytic, linguistic, and cultural theories of male writers such as Derrida, Lacan, Lyotard, and Foucault, but it has been articulated more recently in feminist poststructural theory by feminist writers such as Cixoux, Kristeva, and Irigary. Language and communicative practices are central to poststructural critiques, which often employ discourse theory and discourse analysis to read between the lines of social and cultural relations to identify and make sense of the power relations inherent in social and cultural processes. Poststructural theory is thus deeply indebted to the structural linguistic theories advanced by those proponents of the structure-as-construct thesis outlined above. Poststructuralism, however, has also drawn on theories of "structure as process," and the work of Foucault is perhaps the most widely recognized for illustrating the ways in which power is exercised within everyday structures and discourses in order to maintain regimes of truth. Flax (1990) has emphasized this point by stating:

> [These] discourses are all deconstructive in that they seek to distance us from and make us skeptical about beliefs concerning truth, knowledge, power, the self, and language that are often taken for granted within and serve as legitimation for contemporary Western culture. (Flax, p. 41)

Hughes (1990), for example, has stated:

> Meaning is profoundly to do with language considered not as a system of grammatical or syntactical rules but as social interaction. To adapt a statement from Austin: language does not merely report on the world but is itself performative of action in that world. (Hughes, p. 117)

Hughes' use of the term *performative* alerts us to the poststructural discourse of Butler (1990, 1993) and others, in which meaning and identity are seen as fluid and enacted processes. This focus on language and meaning also resonates with many of the theories of phenomenology, including ethnomethodology and interpretive sociology. While some parallels can be drawn between postmodernism and phenomenology, "postmodernists have gone beyond earlier historicist claims about the inevitable 'situatedness' of human thought within culture to focus on the very criteria by which claims to knowledge are legitimised" (Nicholson, 1990, p. 3). One of the main concerns of poststructuralism is therefore to refute the notion of one single theory or "grand narrative" capable of explaining social, cultural, and power relations throughout time and across space. In particular, poststructuralism denies the existence of one single truth or logical reason — logocentric constructs that have been so important in Western philosophy since the Enlightenment.

This acknowledgment of the uncertainty of truth renders regimes of truth unstable and modern bureaucracies and economic systems open to question. According to Foucault (1979, 1980), power therefore has to be exercised in everyday discourses to maintain such regimes of truth. In addition to exercising power through punitive and penal social codes and practices evident in the material realities of our social institutions, power is also exercised in cultural practices "dispersed throughout society, and exercised at a micro-level" (Bryson, 1999, p. 37). Foucault's identification of Bentham's panopticon provides an insightful illustration of the way in which macro-level social structures can be maintained through micro-level cultural practices. The panopticon was a prison designed to afford the prison guards views into all the prison cells but without enabling prisoners to see which cells were being watched at any one time. This form of surveillance resulted in a corresponding form of self-surveillance as prisoners policed their own behavior for fear of being seen and therefore caught if they behaved in any way deemed to be outside the behavioral codes enforced within the prison. The concept of self-surveillance therefore emphasizes the relationship between structural power, in the form of the prison and prison guards, and cultural power, in the form of self-surveillance and self-policing.

Surveillance can also serve to influence our behavior in everyday life: as sport and leisure participants or providers, we are subject to the gaze of others, and we can also be "Othered" by that gaze. The fundamental fear of being Other, of being marginal, an outsider, or just different is played on from the playground to the workplace in order to encourage conformity to the dominant codes and behaviors of society (Lorde, 1984). According to a structuralist perspective, the dominant codes of society are generally constructed, legitimated, normalized, and reproduced by and in the interests of those with power. Poststructural theory, however, provides a lens through which to view the potential for the reworking, disruption, contestation, transgression, and transformation of the dominant codes and behaviors of society such that change is possible over periods of time and across different spaces.

McKay (1996) has offered insight into the gendered workings of such cultural codes and discourses in sport and leisure management. In his research of gender equity in sports organizations in Australia, New Zealand, and Canada, he found that 90% of men believed their organizations promoted the "best person for the job" and that "sex was irrelevant to gatekeepers." In contrast, "only about ten per cent of women identified their organization as looking like this, and most reported intense feelings of exclusion and isolation." Their use of language employed a variety of metaphors to describe their situation: "glass ceilings," "brick walls," "hoops," "blockages," "hurdles," "ghettos," "on the outside looking in," "passing the ball but never having it passed back," "frozen out," "kept in the dark" (McKay, p. 64). McKay's references are to intangible barriers and constraints that reflect an organization's culture as much as its structure, and the cultural critiques or discourse analysis advocated by poststructural theory serves to provide insight into the symbolic nature of exclusion in addition to the structures of exclusion revealed by materialist analyses.

Researching Gender and Management in Sport and Leisure

Previous structural research has demonstrated that many service-sector industries are "dominated by women but managed by men" (Brockbank & Traves, 1996). Such levels of gender inequity in management are exaggerated within sport and leisure services in which the legacy of male-dominated provision relative to other service sectors is more pronounced. Moreover, in the UK during the 1970s and early 1980s, when there was increasing recognition of the importance of public-sector leisure provision, local authority sport and leisure services were most likely to be formally organized within male-dominated Technical Services Departments rather than forming part of local education services or youth and community services in which women were more visible both as employees and service users. In spite of a shift toward autonomous leisure services departments in the UK during the 1980s, the impact of Compulsory Competitive Tendering (adopted in 1986) meant that many separate leisure services departments disappeared or were subsumed within environmental services or economic development departments that, again, tended to be rather male-dominated areas of local government. Bacon (1991), in his research of women in leisure management, commented that the dominant culture of the leisure industry, in both public and commercial sectors, served to exacerbate gender inequity identified in other sectors of the service industry. The characteristics of sport and leisure services included their association with informality, sociability, alcohol, and different states of dress and undress. Indeed, from all areas of leisure services, sport was singled out in Bacon's research as the area in which women experienced most discrimination and harassment as a result of what sport sociologists have termed "corporate masculinity" (McKay, 1996) and the "locker room culture" of masculinity prevalent in sport (Messner, 1998).

McKay and Messner have thus gone beyond the confines of the dominant body of distributive research accounts of gender inequity in management structures to relational research addressing the interface of gendered cultures and management structures. As Hearn, Sheppard, Tancred-Smith, and Burrell (1989, p.10) point out in relation to organizational theory, "gender has either been ignored, treated implicitly as male, considered an organisational 'variable,' reduced to relative stereotypes, or been analysed in a blatantly sexist way." Hearn et al., in attempting to shift the focus of debate from the macro-level of the structural bureaucracy or professional institution to the micro-level of the cultural relationships and processes within the organization, have sought to focus on the ways in which sexuality and its associated power constructs organizational relationships and processes. This shift in focus from structural to cultural constraints in management research is reflective of the increasing accommodation of poststructuralist perspectives in what had previously been a largely structuralist-dominated research field. In common with the developing discourse of poststructural management theory in the mid-1990s, Alvesson and Billing (1997, p. 41) argued that, "to the extent that men and women are of interest to study, it is the discourses in which they are constituted that are relevant to explore" with discourses being defined as "a set of statements, beliefs, and vocabularies that is historically and socially specific and that tends to produce truth effects — certain beliefs are acted upon as true and therefore become partially true in terms of consequences" (Alvesson & Billing, p. 40).

The final section of the article therefore adopts an integrated analysis informed by materialism, structuralism, poststructuralism, and postmodernism in order to explore the findings of the *Gender Equity in Leisure Management* research project. Three themes are examined in some detail within a discussion that progresses from inequity to equity: perceptions of (in)equity within sport and leisure management; evaluations of the policies and practices designed to address inequity; and career appraisal and progression opportunities intended to achieve equity within the workplace.

Perceptions of Gender (In)Equity Within Sport and Leisure Management

In the *Gender Equity in Leisure Management* research project questionnaire, respondents were presented with a series of statements about specific aspects of gender equity within their organization and asked whether they agreed or disagreed with each. The statements and responses can be seen in Table 1.

When asked about their knowledge and experience of sex discrimination within their organization, 16.3% of women claimed to know of someone in their organization who had been discriminated against, and 14.7% claimed to have personal experience of sex discrimination within their organization.

Table 1. Respondents' Perceptions of Gender (In)Equity Within Leisure Management

Statement	Percent that agree	Percent that disagree
Women work harder than men to achieve equal recognition in my organization.	52.3	18.8
Men treat women as their equals in my organization.	37.5	50.2
There are enough women mentors for female staff in my organization.	24.9	50.8
What my organization needs is more women managers.	44.4	14.2
Women in my organization do not need more female role models.	23.3	42.2
Men get ahead more easily than women in my organization.	41.3	47.4
Women with family responsibilities are disadvantaged in my organization.	33.3	51.7
Women in my organization eventually hit a "glass ceiling."	32.3	32.0
Women in my organization have adequate informal networks.	31.8	30.8
The rules of behavior in my organization are more relaxed for men.	13.3	53.3
Prejudice against gays and/or lesbians in my organization is common.	12.9	45.5
Sexual harassment of women is uncommon in my organization.	60.9	11.4

Note. N = 346; response rate = 30.1%.

Rather than identifying discriminatory structures within their organizations, many respondents referred to their organizational cultures as supporting discriminatory practices:

> I've had difficulties with male colleagues who have been in post for years, coping with a female of equal standing but a lot younger. (Survey respondent)

> Discrimination is difficult to identify in a "recruitment, selection, and promotion" situation, as there are many reasons which could be "smoke screens." I feel that discrimination takes place in a more informal day-to-day manner, such as in attitudes of (usually elderly) males to women in more senior positions. Respect is often slow in coming—you are likely to be treated as "fluff." There is often an underlying attitude of "don't worry your pretty little head about it." (Questionnaire survey respondent)

> Assertive, confident male candidates are more likely to be considered for parks posts than diffident or "too assertive" female counterpart. (Questionnaire survey respondent)

> Many councillors expect a male to work in sport and have limited understanding of female sporting structures. (Questionnaire survey respondent)

> The Assistant Director did not want a "woman as manager" of the leisure center. (Questionnaire survey respondent)

In spite of the identification of working cultures that contravened equal opportunities structures, the most common response to personal experience of sex discrimination was for the complainant to make an informal verbal complaint to her manager(s). The least common response was to make a formal written complaint to a manager. These actions (or inactions) could be seen as indicating a lack of confidence in the structural procedures designed to enforce equal opportunities legislation and organizational policy thereby pointing to deeper cultural constraints within organizations.

Evaluations of Policies and Practices Designed to Address Inequity

In an attempt to address inequalities, many local authorities have been eager to implement equal opportunities policies. The research found that 86.6% of respondents stated that their employing organization had an equal opportunities policy. Only 55.7% of these respondents, however, felt that their policy was effective. Reasons for thinking the policy was effective centered on material or quantitative evidence of change: workforce statistics showing equal numbers of male and female employees, evidence that management took the policy seriously, and evidence that awareness of equal opportunities had been raised. Reasons given for thinking that their organization's policy was ineffective were more likely to be related to organizational culture: lack of value and respect for the policy within the organization, lack of visibility of the policy, and minimal implementation of the policy, for example, "I have never seen a copy and doubt that anybody else has so it's unlikely that anyone abides by it" (Questionnaire survey respondent).

Women were asked whether their organizations employed a series of work-related practices that were sympathetic to the needs of women employees. The presence of these measures in the respondent's organization can be seen in Table 2.

The responses outlined in Table 2 indicate that, although the majority of employers provided education and training designed to enhance women's career prospects, only a minority of employers provided the practical or structural support required to enable women, particularly women with children, to progress in their careers. Even when employers provided support for some women, this was often at the expense of favorable working conditions for other women: "My employer provided flexible hours to help part-time staff with children but this meant longer hours for the manager, as she had to cover late starts and early finishes" (Survey respondent).

One third of the respondents agreed that their organization had a "glass ceiling." Women, however, were optimistic that their situation in the workplace would improve, and they suggested a range of additional measures that their employers could take in order to enhance their prospects of career progression. First, women suggested that cultural change was needed, and this change should involve greater recognition and allowance for family commitments, better consultation and communication, more respect and recognition for women employees from senior management and local authority councilors, more encouragement to women returners, more encouragement for personal

Table 2. Presence of Flexible Employment Practices Within Respondent's Organization

Flexible employment practices	Respondents stating practices present (%)
Funding for out of house training	72.7
In-house training for professional development	69.7
Flexible working hours	67.4
In service training (provided by external organization)	64.6
Job share opportunities	47.7
Mentoring	21.5
Career breaks	19.4
Creche/childcare facilities	18.8
Term-time employment	13.1

Note. N = 346; response rate = 30.1%.

development, and greater opportunities for informal networking. Second, women suggested a series of training-related measures to enhance their career prospects. These measures included: mentoring, training for women managers, awareness training for men, more information on training opportunities, and more help with career planning. Third, a series of measures related to improving working conditions for women were suggested. These included employment of more women managers, more flexible working conditions with more opportunities for working from home, flextime, job-sharing, workplace childcare, career breaks and flexible contracts, the identification of role models through teamwork, workplace job shadowing and secondments, a greater focus on job specifications rather than person specifications, and the restructuring of bonus schemes.

Career Appraisal and Progression Opportunities Designed to Achieve Equity

When asked about the issue of annual staff development appraisals or performance reviews, 67.3% of respondents stated that their organization employed such a scheme. Only 40.5% said that they were satisfied with the operation of the scheme. Women highlighted a series of experiences that reflected both good practices and bad practices in relation to annual appraisals and performance reviews. These positive and negative experiences were highlighted in relation to social support and procedural matters, with more good practice identified in relation to procedural factors and more bad practice identified in relation to social factors. Thus, although adequate structures might be in place, social and cultural practices appeared to produce less positive results than could or should be possible. Good social support included having a supportive line manager, having plenty of time to undertake the review, experiencing two-way communication, placing the emphasis on the employee being reviewed, and being given a chance to achieve. Good procedural practice included being part of the Investors in People program, having links between the review and pay, identifying training needs and being linked to training opportunities, experiencing the review as both detailed and regular, and seeing links between the review and promotion. Poor social support included lack of knowledge on the part of the reviewer, poor organization of the review process, poor communication, reviews being hurried, agreements from the review not being implemented, and having to remind line managers about the need for the review and the need to implement agreed upon outcomes. Poor procedures included irregular and unstructured reviews, lack of documentation relating to the review, and a lack of clear goals emanating from the review process.

Women placed a high emphasis on education and training to achieve promotion. Of the respondents, 90% stated that one of the reasons they had joined ILAM was "to receive information about job opportunities," 80% said "to improve my career prospects," and 70% indicated "to make use of training opportunities." Similarly, the most important aspect of ILAM membership was seen as "information on job opportunities/careers" (contained within ILAM's weekly publication, *Leisurenews*). Less than one third of respondents stated that "information on leisure issues" was an important aspect of their membership. Women's desire to receive training did appear to be met by many employers. At least 70% of employers provided funding for both external training opportunities and in-house training for professional development. In contrast, less than half of the respondents' employers provided job-share opportunities, and less than 20% provided career breaks, crèche facilities, or childcare provision. Although the majority of respondents' employers provided education and training opportunities designed to enhance women's career prospects, only a minority of employers provided the support required to enable women, particularly women with children, to progress in their careers once they had taken advantage of such education and training.

Over 60% of respondents stated that their career plan for the next 3 to 5 years was to secure promotion. One third of respondents were looking externally for promotion, and a quarter of respondents had their sights on internal promotion opportunities. When asked to identify multiple reasons for seeking a change in employment, the responses indicated an overwhelming enthusiasm and optimism for the leisure industry. "To gain more experience," "to gain a higher salary," "to have a more challenging job," and "to have more responsibility" were all cited as explanations by more than half of the women seeking a change in their job. "I don't like my job," "I want to spend more time with my family," "I don't get on with my superiors," "my current job is too stressful," and "to get away from sexual harassment and discrimination" were each cited by less than 10% of respondents as reasons for seeking change. Notably, sexual harassment and discrimination, although experienced by 15% of respondents, was only cited by 2.8% as a reason for seeking a change of job. In other words, the majority of women who experienced sexual harassment in their current jobs seemed resigned to tolerating this type of behavior in the workplace. The responses indicate clearly that women were seeking change for career enhancement reasons and were optimistic about their career paths. Very few women were seeking change because of negative conditions at work. Rankings of responses as to why respondents were seeking a change to their current employment position can be seen in Table 3.

In spite of the high percentage of women of child-bearing age but without children, only 1.2% stated that they intended to leave their organization temporarily during the next 3 to 5 years for any purpose, including having children. If respondents were not seeking a change to their current employment position, when asked why they stated that they were either satisfied with their current position or that they needed more qualifications and experience to gain promotion. Very few women stated that they were not seeking promotion because of family circumstances such as childcare or partner's jobs. Again, the responses indicate optimism about the industry and women's roles within it. There was clear evidence, however, that many women were deferring starting a family in order to further their management career. Although almost 80% of respondents were between 21 and 40 years of age, only 21% of all respondents

Table 3. Reasons for Seeking Change in Employment

Reasons	Percent
To gain more experience	65.7
To gain a higher salary	65.6
It is the next logical step in my career path	61.7
To have a more challenging job	60.9
To have more responsibility	54.5
To spend more time with my family	8.8
I don't like my job	5.6
I don't get on with my superiors	4.7
My current job is too stressful	4.7
To get away from sexual harassment or discrimination	2.8

Note. Respondents could give more than one reason; N = 346, response rate = 30.1%.

had children under the age of 18, and only 13% of all respondents had children less than 5 years of age. The combination of career and family was seen by many women to be both incompatible and unsustainable.

Previous research on both organizational behavior and employee relations has demonstrated that

> the degree to which women accept, conform to or challenge gendered patterns of organisational segregation and gender politics within their organisation will depend on a balance between their consciousness of discrimination and career barriers; their reading of organisational politics and their willingness to adopt individualist, collectivist and/or separatist strategies. (Ledwith & Colgan, 1996, p. 23)

In sport and leisure management, Yule (1997a, 1997b, 1998), drawing on the work of Connel (1987) and Sheppard (1989), has pointed to a four-fold typology of subcultural strategies employed by women and ranging from "compliance" to "resistance." The ILAM survey results demonstrated that the dominant strategy in leisure management was one of "compliance" or "blending in" (Sheppard, 1989) but with some women adopting an "individual strategy of resistance" (Yule, 1998).

Conclusion

This article has sought to identify and explain the origins and nature of materialist, structuralist, poststructuralist, and postmodern feminist and gender research in social science generally and in sport and leisure management research specifically. In doing so, the article has called for the expansion of our current research horizons to include new epistemological approaches in feminist and gender research. This article advocates an epistemological approach that engages with both structural and cultural analysis as a theoretical framework capable of providing more rigorous critical insights into the complex workings of gender–power relations. Such an approach highlights the significance of the social–cultural nexus as both a site and process in the production, legitimation, reproduction, and reworking of sport and leisure management.

The research findings from the ILAM project titled *Gender Equity in Leisure Management* (Aitchison et al., 1999) were introduced to illustrate not only the presence of structural and cultural constraints but the interconnectedness of the structural and the cultural in determining progress toward gender equity in sport and leisure management. Three specific aspects of the research findings were discussed: perceptions of gender (in)equity within sport and leisure management; evaluations of policies and practices designed to address inequity; and career appraisal and progression opportunities designed to achieve equity. In each case the analysis demonstrated that gender (in)equity was the outcome of the interconnected workings of both structural and cultural influences. In other words, it is at the social–cultural nexus that gender (in)equity is produced, legitimated, reproduced, and reworked. The findings of this research also echo those of comparative data from recent international studies of gender equity in sport and leisure management. Of particular note here are the study of gender equity in sports organizations in Australia, New Zealand, and Canada conducted by McKay (1996), the work of Henderson and Bialeschki (1993, 1995), which examined the status of women and their career development in leisure management in the U.S., and Shinew and Arnold's (1998) study of *Gender Equity in the Leisure Services Field*, again in the U.S.

Across all of the research studies cited, there was strong evidence to demonstrate that women's experience of sport and leisure management was shaped by both material and cultural factors. Indeed, there was evidence to show that the interrelationship between materialities, in the form of organizational structures, procedures, and policies, and those of cultures, in the form of discourses, attitudes, and appearances, was often what consolidated or maintained the social–cultural nexus of gender inequity within leisure management organizations. Although each of these studies generated new quantitative data relating to women's positions in sport and leisure management, and each also used wide-ranging qualitative research techniques to explore women's experiences of sport and leisure management, the findings highlight the need for new epistemological perspectives as much as new methodological approaches and techniques. By offering acknowledgment of the complexities of gender–power relations in the workplace together with recognition of the interconnectedness and mutually informing nature of structural and cultural power, a more sophisticated understanding of gender equity in sport and leisure management can be produced. In future gender studies of sport and leisure management it would therefore be appropriate to explore organizational structures and cultures from an integrated feminist perspective that seeks to accommodate both structuralist and poststructuralist critiques that investigate the social–cultural nexus as a significant site and process in the making and remaking of gender–power relations.

Acknowledgments

I would like to acknowledge the support and generosity of spirit of three anonymous referees who provided extensive and insightful comments on an earlier draft of this article. I would also like to thank Dr. John Amis and Dr. Mike Silk for their extensive feedback and support.

References

Acker, J. (1990). Hierarchies, jobs, bodies: A theory of gendered organisations. *Gender and Society, 4*(2), 139–158.

Acker, J. (1992). New perspectives on an old problem: The position of women academics in British higher education. *Higher Education, 24*(1), 57–75.

Aitchison, C. C. (2000). Women in leisure services: Managing the social–cultural nexus of gender equity. *Managing Leisure, 5*(4), 81–91.

Aitchison, C. C. (2003). *Gender and leisure: Social and cultural perspectives.* London: Routledge.

Aitchison, C. C., Brackenridge, C., & Jordan, F. (1999). *Gender equity in leisure management.* Reading, UK: Institute of Leisure and Amenity Management.

Althusser, L. (1971). *Lenin and philosophy and other essays.* London: New Left Books.

Alvesson, M., & Billing, Y. D. (1997), *Understanding gender and organizations.* London: Sage.

Bacon, W. (1991). *Women's experiences in leisure management.* Reading, UK: Institute of Leisure and Amenity Management.

Bialeschki, D., & Henderson, K. (1984). The personal and professional spheres: Complement or conflict for women leisure service professionals. *Journal of Park and Recreation Administration, 2*(1), 45–54.

Bialeschki, D., & Henderson, K. (2000). Gender issues in recreation management. In M. T. Allison & E. Schneider (Eds.), *Diversity and the recreation profession* (pp. 73–97). State College, PA: Venture.

Brockbank, A., & Traves, J. (1996). Career aspirations — women managers and retail-ing. In S. Ledwith & F. Colgan (Eds.), *Women in organisations: Challenging gender politics* (pp. 78–98). Basingstoke, UK: Macmillan.

Bryson, V. (1999). *Feminist debates: Issues of theory and political practice.* Basingstoke, UK: Macmillan.

Butler, J. (1990). *Gender trouble: Feminism and the subversion of identity.* London: Routledge.

Butler, J. (1993). *Bodies that matter.* London: Routledge.

Chomsky, N. (2003). *On nature and language.* A. Belletti & Luigi Rizzi (Eds.). Cambridge: Cambridge University Press.

Connell, R. W. (1987). *Gender and power.* Oxford: Polity.

Coward, R. (1977). *Language and materialism.* London: Routledge and Kegan Paul.

Dyck, I. (1993). Ethnography: A feminist method. *The Canadian Geographer, 20*(4), 410–413.

Farran, D. (1990). "Seeking Susan": Producing statistical information on young people's leisure. In L. Stanley (Ed.), *Feminist praxis: Research, theory and epistemology in feminist sociology* (pp. 262–273). London: Routledge.

Flax, J. (1990). Postmodernism and gender relations in feminist theory. In L. Nicholson (Ed.), *Feminism/Postmodernism* (pp. 39–62). London: Routledge.

Foucault, M. (1979). *Power, truth and strategy.* M. Morris & P. Patton (Eds.). Sydney, Australia: Feral.

Foucault, M. (1980). *Power/knowledge: Selected interviews and other essays 1972–1977.* Brighton, UK: Harvester.

Frisby, W., & Brown, B. (1991). The balancing act: Women leisure service managers. *Journal of Applied Recreation Research, 16*(4), 297–321.

Giddens, A. (1984). *The construction of society: Outline of a theory of structuration.* Cambridge: Polity.

Gilligan, C. (1982). *In a different voice.* Cambridge, MA: Harvard University Press.

Gray, A. (1997). Learning from experience: Cultural studies and feminism. In J. Mc-Guigan (Ed.), *Cultural methodologies.* London: Sage.

Habermas, J. (1989). *The new conservatism: Cultural criticism and the historians' debate.* Cambridge: Polity.

Harding, S. (Ed.). (1987). *Feminism and methodology.* Milton Keynes, UK: Open University Press.

Hearn, J., Sheppard, D. L., Tancred-Sherrif, P., & Burrell, G. (1989). *The sexuality of organisation.* London: Sage.

Henderson, K. A. (1992). Being female in the recreation and park profession in the 1990s: Issues and challenges. *Journal of Park and Recreation Administration, 10*(2), 15–30.

Henderson, K. A., & Bialeschki, D. (1993). Professional women and equity issues in the 1990s. *Parks and Recreation, 28*(3), 54–59.

Henderson, K. A., & Bialeschki, D. (1995). Career development and women in the leisure services profession. *Journal of Park and Recreation and Administration, 13*(1), 26–42.

Hughes, J. (1990). *The philosophy of social research* (2nd ed.). London: Longman.

Institute of Leisure and Amenity Management. (2003). *Breakdown of ILAM membership by grade and gender* (ILAM Information Service). Reading, UK: Institute of Leisure and Amenity Management.

Jackson, S., & Jones, J. (1998). Thinking for ourselves: An introduction to feminist theorising. In S. Jackson & J. Jones (Eds.), *Contemporary feminist theories* (pp. 1–12). Edinburgh: Edinburgh University Press.

Jackson, S., & Scott, S. (2002). *Gender: A sociological reader.* London: Routledge.

Ledwith, S., & Colgan, F. (1996). *Women in organisations: Challenging gender politics.* Basingstoke: Macmillan,

Letherby, G. (2003). *Feminist research in theory and practice.* Buckingham: Open University Press.

Lévi Strauss, C. (1968). *Totemism.* London: Penguin.

Lorde, A. (1984). *Sister outsider.* New York: The Crossing.

McKay, J. (1996). *Managing gender: Affirmative action and organisation power in Australian, Canadian and New Zealand sport.* Albany: State University of New York Press.

Messner, M. (1998, July). *The triad of men's violence: Sport as pedagogy.* Article presented at Leisure Studies Association International Conference, Leeds Metropolitan University, Leeds.

Morris, K., Woodward, D., & Peters, E. (1998). "Whose side are you on?" Dilemmas in conducting feminist ethnographic research with young women. *Social Research Methodology, 1*(3), 217–230.

Nicholson, L. (1990). *Feminism/postmodernism.* London: Routledge.

Oakley, A. (1981). Interviewing women: A contradiction in terms. In H. Roberts (Ed.), *Doing feminist research* (pp. 30–61). London: Routledge.

Oakley, A. (1998). Gender, methodology and people's ways of knowing: Some problems with feminism and the paradigm debate in social science. *Sociology, 32*(4), 707–732.

Oakley, A. (2000). *Experiments in knowing: Gender and method in the social sciences.* Cambridge: Polity.

Oerton, S. (1996). *Beyond hierarchy: Gender, sexuality and the social economy.* London: Taylor and Francis.

Piaget, J. (1958). *The child's construction of reality.* London: Routledge and Kegan Paul.

Roberts, H. (Ed.). (1981). *Doing feminist research.* London: Routledge.

Seller, A. (1994). Should the feminist philosopher stay at home? In K. Lennon & M. Whitford (Eds.), *Knowing the difference: Feminist perspectives in epistemology* (pp. 230–248). London: Routledge.

Shinew, K. J., & Arnold, M. (1998). Gender equity in the leisure services field. *Journal of Leisure Research, 30*(2), 177–94.

Stanley, L. (1990). *Feminist praxis: Research, theory and epistemology in feminist sociology.* London: Routledge.

Stanley, L., & Wise, S. (1983). *Breaking out: Feminist ontology and epistemology.* London: Routledge.

Stanley, L., & Wise, S. (1993). *Breaking out again: Feminist ontology and epistemology.* Routledge: London.

Witz, A. (1992). *Professions and patriarchy.* London: Routledge.

Yule, J. (1997a). Engendered ideologies and leisure policy in the UK, Part 1: Gender ideologies. *Leisure Studies, 16*(2), 61–84.

Yule, J. (1997b). Engendered ideologies and leisure policy in the UK, Part 2: Professional ideologies. *Leisure Studies, 16*(3), 139–54.

Yule, J. (1998). Sub-cultural strategies in patriarchal leisure professional cultures. In C. Aitchison & F. Jordan (Eds.), *Gender, space and identity: Leisure, culture and commerce.* Eastbourne, UK: Leisure Studies Association.

4

ADDRESSING EPISTEMOLOGICAL RACISM IN SPORT MANAGEMENT RESEARCH

John N. Singer

Introduction

In recent years sport management scholars have insisted on the need for scholars and students in our field to reconsider and reexamine their methods and assumptions when conducting research (see Chalip, 1997; Frisby, 2005). There is a specific need to do so, however, when studying and conducting research with individuals from racial and ethnic groups that have historically been marginalized (e.g., Blacks or African Americans) in Western civilization. In posing the question, "are our research epistemologies racially biased," Scheurich and Young (1997) introduced the concept of epistemological racism and acknowledged many prominent scholars of color who have suggested that the epistemologies currently legitimized in the academy might be racially biased ways of knowing (e.g., Banks, 1993, 1995; Gordon, Miller, & Rollock, 1990; Stanfield, 1985, 1993). Epistemological racism emerged out of civilizational racism, which encompasses the deepest, most primary assumptions about the nature of reality (ontology), the ways of knowing that reality (epistemology), and the disputational contours of right and wrong or morality and values (axiology) — in short, presumptions about the real, the true, and the good (Scheurich & Young, p. 6). Essentially, Scheurich and Young contend that scholars in the academy have, for the most part, lived, understood, worked, thought, and acted within the social history and perspectives of the dominant White race in Western civilization (while excluding the epistemologies of other racial and ethnic groups).

Ladson-Billings (2000) argued that an epistemology is not only the nature, status, and production of knowledge and the way one knows and understands the world, but it is also a "system of knowing" (p. 257) that is linked to worldviews based on the conditions under which people live and learn; and she asserted that schools, society, and the structure and production of knowledge have been designed to create individuals who internalize the dominant worldview (i.e., Eurocentric perspective) and knowledge production and acquisition processes. In essence, not only has racism (i.e., White supremacy) historically manifested itself in the very educational system that has trained scholars in our discipline and in other academic disciplines (see Fredrickson, 2002; Ladson-Billings, 1994; Shujaa, 1994; Stanfield, 1985; Teo & Febbraro, 2003; Watkins, 2001; Woodson, 1933/1990), but it is also evident in other social institutions and cultural practices within society (e.g., religion, media, sport). Therefore, it is my contention that scholars of all racial and ethnic backgrounds, including the dominant group (i.e., Euro-American, European, Caucasian, White), can benefit from a sincere discussion and dialogue that challenges sport management scholars and students to think beyond the research paradigms and epistemologies that the dominant White race has legitimized in the academy and society.

The primary purpose of this article is to challenge sport management scholars and students by arguing that critical race theory (CRT), which emerged as a challenge to the positivist and legal discourse of civil rights (Ladson-Billings, 1998), serves as a viable and legitimate means for conducting certain kinds of research in our field. The CRT movement is rooted in the social missions and struggles of the 1960s and, from its beginning, sought justice, liberation, and the empowerment of people of color in this society (Tate, 1997). It is important to note, however, that the seminal writings of historians and scholars of color such as W.E.B. DuBois (1903/1953) and Carter G. Woodson (1933/1990) provided the foundation for this epistemological framework. And as a result, scholars in the academy have been able to embrace the CRT research approach to address some of the salient research issues within the various academic disciplines. For example, a special issue of *Qualitative Inquiry* (Volume 8, Number 1, 2002) employed multidisciplinary frameworks in addressing the historical, methodological, and epistemological issues related to the scope and trajectory of educational research in the 21st century (Lynn, Yosso, Solo'rzano, & Parker, 2002). And more recently, articles in a special issue of *Race, Ethnicity, and Education* (Volume 8, Number 1, March 2005) attempted to explain the progress and future directions of critical race research in education (Dixson & Rousseau, 2005).

In essence, scholars in the field of education (see Ladson-Billings, 1998; Ladson-Billings & Tate, 1995; Tate, 1997) have established CRT as a powerful tool for understanding and addressing issues of race and racism in the field. In discussing the question, "What can critical race theory, a movement that has its roots in legal scholarship, contribute to research in education," Roithmayr (1999, p. 4) argued:

> The use of critical race theory offers a way to understand how ostensibly race-neutral structures in education—knowledge, truth, merit, objectivity, and "good education"—are in fact ways of forming and policing the racial boundaries of white supremacy and racism.

Our colleagues in education have provided us with a road map for conducting critical, race-based research in sport management. The sections to follow will briefly highlight the multiple paradigms present in the social sciences, as well as offer a rationale for why there is a need for CRT to be considered in sport management research. I will include a description of CRT and its epistemological and methodological bases, explain how CRT applies to sport management research, outline some of the challenges associated with CRT and qualitative research in sport management, and discuss the implications it has for sport management research and education.

A Need for Race-Based Epistemologies in Sport Management Research

We live in a world of multiple competing discourses and ways of knowing, and as Usher and Scott (1996) remarked, "Researchers speak through particular discourses, paradigms, and traditions which understand and 'close' the world in particular ways" (p. 179). A researcher's paradigmatic assumptions, whether they are based on positivism, interpretivism, critical social science (CSS), post modernism, or a combination of these assumptions (for a more detailed discussion of these paradigms, see Habermas, 1971, and Sipe & Constable, 1996), influence the research questions they ask, the research designs and methods they use, and ultimately the impact the research will have on society (Frisby, 2005). Although the majority of research in sport management has gravitated toward and continues to embrace positivism (Boucher, 2000; Frisby, 2005; Olafson, 1990; Slack, 1997), sport management scholars have acknowledged that interpretivism (e.g., Inglis, 1992) and CSS (e.g., Chalip, 1997; Frisby, 2005) are important to sport management research.

Although the use of CSS in sport management research has become a topic for discussion and issues of diversity are recognized as being important to sport management scholars (e.g., the forthcoming special issue on diversity in the *Journal of Sport Management* bears witness to this), there is still a specific need for us to consider alternative race-based epistemologies, especially because the epistemological frameworks and research concerns of scholars of color and other people of color have not been legitimized in the academy and continue to be muted (Jones, 2000, 2002; Stanfield, 1993), and because there is potential for the use of the positivist, interpretivist, and even the CSS research traditions to distort the lives and realities of racial and ethnic minority groups (Andersen, 1993).

The section to follow will discuss how CRT is a legitimate attempt to elucidate the potential of an alternative race-based epistemology to reconceptualize the present disciplinary-based system of knowledge that has traditionally been legitimized in the academy in general and the sport management field in particular. It is important to note, however, that the intent of this discussion is not to devalue those research paradigms (e.g., logical positivism, interpretivism, CSS) that have been embraced and promoted by the dominant group or to impose any particular racial and ethnic epistemology on sport management research and education. Instead, as Ladson-Billings (2000) explained:

> The point of working in racialized discourses and ethnic epistemologies is not merely to "color" the scholarship. It is to challenge the hegemonic

structures (and symbols) that keep injustice and inequality in place. The work is also not about dismissing the work of European and Euro-American scholars. Rather, it is about defining the limits of such scholarship. (p. 271)

Critical Race Theory

According to Gloria Ladson-Billings (2000, p. 263), "One research paradigm in which racialized discourses and ethnic epistemologies . . . may be deployed is critical race theory (CRT)." Richard Delgado (1995), a CRT pioneer, credits scholars Derrick Bell (a Black male) and Alan Freeman (a White male) with the establishment of the CRT movement. These scholars' and others' (e.g., Kimberle Crenshaw, 1988; Patricia Williams, 1988) work serves as a foundation for this epistemological and theoretical approach to research that is intended to challenge "the scholarship that would dehumanize and depersonalize" (Ladson-Billings, 2000, p. 272) people and communities of color.

As its name implies, CRT views "race" as a most important social construct to consider in the analysis of social, political, and educational problems of people in society. Ladson-Billings (1996) attempted to reposition race on the multicultural agenda because she wanted to

> examine the ways that race, a social construct with powerful social and political implications, has been muted in the current multicultural paradigm or pitted against other subjectivities — particularly class and gender — to render it "undiscussable" as a difference or a site of struggle. (p. 249)

In a more recent writing, Ladson-Billings (1998) insisted that although attempts have been made to marginalize race in public (political) discourse (e.g., D'Souza, 1995; Wilson, 1978), it continues to be a powerful social construct. Others scholars such as Cornell West (1994) agree with Ladson-Billing's assessment that "Race Matters" when it comes to understanding the problems of marginalized racial and ethnic groups in American society.

CRT scholars have asserted that any examination of race and racism must begin with an understanding that "Whiteness" has been positioned as the optimal status criterion in this society. That is, in the present social order, Whites (i.e., people of a Caucasian and/or European background) have created a system of human domination or a "constellation of institutions, ideas, and practices" (Morris, 1993, p. 20) that has successfully enabled them to achieve and maintain power and privilege over other racial and ethnic groups (i.e., people of color). This ideological hegemony is a process by which the White dominant group (particularly White males) controls the content and nature of ideas permeating a society and its social institutions (Morris). As a result, the folkways, mores, values, attitudes, and beliefs of the dominant White race have become the norm or standard upon which other racial and ethnic groups in society are judged and evaluated.

CRT scholars have discussed the advantages and privileges associated with being White (e.g., McIntosh, 1990, 1997). Delgado and Stefancic (1997) described White privilege as "the invisible bundle of expectations and courtesies that go along with membership in the dominant race" (p. xvii). CRT scholars insist that the omnipresence of racism provides material and psychic benefits to White people, both the economic elite and the working class, to such an extent that they are not likely to voluntarily end it (Broido & Manning, 2002). It is for this reason that CRT becomes an important tool for scholars to implement in their research. As Ladson-Billings (1998) stated:

> It is because of the meaning and value imputed to whiteness that CRT becomes an important intellectual and social tool for deconstruction, reconstruction, and construction: deconstruction of oppressive structures and discourses, reconstruction of human agency, and construction of equitable and socially just relations of power. (p. 9)

Tate (1997) outlined the defining elements of CRT. First, CRT recognizes that racism is endemic in U.S. society—deeply ingrained legally, culturally, and even psychologically. In essence, racism is a normal part of society and its many social institutions, including sport. It is important to note that although CRT advances a strategy to foreground and account for race and racism in social institutions, it works toward the elimination of racism as part of a larger goal of opposing or eliminating other forms of subordination based on gender, class, language, and so forth (Matsuda, 1991).

Second, CRT crosses epistemological boundaries, borrowing from several traditions such as liberalism, feminism, Marxism, poststructuralism, cultural nationalism, critical legal studies, and so forth in order to provide a more complete analysis of "raced" people. This element of CRT, according to Tate (1997), forces scholars to question the appropriateness and potential of their theoretical and conceptual frameworks. This explains why sport management scholars should not only look to CSS in addressing the "bad and ugly sides of sport" (Frisby, 2005) but should also consider race-based epistemologies such as CRT when analyzing and studying the unique experiences of people of color in sport and sport organizations.

Third, CRT reinterprets civil rights law in light of its limitations, suggesting that laws designed to remedy racial inequality (e.g., Title VII of the Civil Rights Act of 1964) are often undermined before they can be fully implemented. CRT insists on the critique of liberalism, arguing that liberalism has no mechanism for the sweeping changes that are needed to appropriately address racism. This suggests that progress has been much too slow. The movement by the Black Coaches Association (BCA) and prominent Black lawyers (e.g., Johnnie Cochran, Cyrus Mehri) to legally force the National Football League (NFL) and big-time college sport programs to strongly consider Blacks and other people of color for upper management and head coaching positions during the hiring process is indicative of this point (see, for example, Cochran & Mehri, 2002).

Fourth, CRT challenges the dominant legal claims of neutrality, objectivity, color blindness, and meritocracy and posits that these claims are camouflages for the self-interests of the powerful entities in society. The CRT pioneers have argued that White elites will tolerate or encourage racial advances for people of color only when they also promote White self-interest (Bell, 1987, 1992). Some people might point to the progress that has been made in the sport industry to argue that sport is one institution in society where people of color (particularly Blacks/African Americans) have benefited from civil rights legislation. Examples of this progress could include: the significant increase in organized sport participation among women and people of color (Coakley, 2004); the record number of Black head coaches in the National Basketball Association (NBA) in recent years (Nance, 2002); Robert Johnson (a Black male) becoming the first majority owner of an NBA franchise (i.e., Charlotte Bobcats); major sport organizations' (e.g., NASCAR, PGA Tour, NFL) focus on "diversity" initiatives; the Southeastern Conference's (SEC) recent hiring of the first Black head football coach in its history (i.e., Sylvester Crooms at Mississippi State University); and Tyrone Willingham being hired (only to be fired 3 years into his 5-year contract) as the first Black head football coach at Notre Dame University (he was the first and only Black head coach of any sport in the history of the university; see Whiteside, 2004; Wieberg, 2004). Despite this progress, CRT scholars would still argue that White people's (those with power) realization that it was to their advantage (e.g., financially) to allow talented Blacks into their sport organizations (mostly as athletes, but a few in positions of "power") is what motivated them. Richard Lapchick's (2003) most recent racial and gender report card provides some empirical evidence that the "playing field" is still not level in the sport industry.

Finally, and perhaps most importantly, CRT challenges ahistoricism and insists on a contextual/historical examination of the law and acknowledgment of the experiential knowledge of people of color in analyzing the law and society. Donnor (2005) highlighted the need to combine the legal literature with narrative methodologies in order to provide a rich context for explaining the experiences of people of color. Moreover, storytelling and narratives allow people of color to not only engage in dialogue that can help them more deeply reflect on their condition and what can be done to improve it but also to uproot the dysconscious racism or uncritical and distorted ways of thinking about race that have led to tacit acceptance of the dominant White norms and privileges (King, 1997). Storytelling can encourage self-introspection on the part of the oppressed, and it has the potential to prick the consciousness of the oppressor. The aim of storytelling, counterstorytelling, and naming one's own reality is to illuminate the "voice" of the marginalized and dispossessed in efforts to eventually effectuate positive social change (Ladson-Billings, 1998). As Ladson-Billings (1998) stated, "the voice component of CRT provides a way to communicate the experience and realities of the oppressed, a first step in understanding the complexities of racism and beginning a process of judicial redress" (p. 16).

Although there is no particular set of research methodologies that all CRT scholars subscribe to (Ladson-Billings, 1998), there are some research approaches that are particularly suited to the CRT epistemological framework.

For example, Parker and Lynn (2002) discussed how educational researchers could use storytelling and CRT to conduct case study research. According to Parker and Lynn (p. 11):

> Thick descriptions and interviews, characteristic of case study research, not only serve illuminative purpose but also can be used to document institutional as well as overt racism. The interviewing process can be pulled together to create narratives that can be used to build a case against racially biased officials or discriminatory practices.

In my qualitative case study research with Black male football players in a big-time college sport program, I incorporated a focus group and individual interviews in an attempt to understand and document these Black males' perceptions of racism and to collaborate with these individuals in efforts to create strategies for improving their developmental experiences (see Singer, 2002).

As a research approach that combines interpretivist movements in anthropology and sociology and neomarxist and feminist theory, critical ethnography is also an appropriate methodology to use with CRT because the overriding goal of critical ethnography is to use oral history methods, informant narratives, and collaborative research to empower research participants to free themselves from sources of domination and repression (Anderson, 1989). Carrington's (2002) ethnographic case study research with Black males in an English cricket club, and McDonald's (2002) anti-racist activism and research in English cricket are examples of how our colleagues in sport sociology have successfully incorporated elements of CRT into their research.

CRT is also congruent with action research, a form of research that "aims to solve pertinent problems in given contexts through democratic inquiry in which professional researchers collaborate with local stakeholders to seek and enact solutions to problems of major importance to the stakeholders" (Greenwood & Levin, 2000, p. 96).

In particular, participatory action research (PAR) has emerged as a viable research approach in sport management (see Frisby, Crawford, & Dorer, 1997; Frisby, Reid, Millar, & Hoeber, 2005). According to Frisby and colleagues, this approach to research calls for the active involvement of both the beneficiaries and providers of sport services in defining research problems, executing interventions, interpreting results, and designing strategies to change existing power structures. This focus on empowering and emancipating research participants renders PAR compatible with CRT.

Phenomenological qualitative research is another approach that reflects CRT as these researchers revisit and rewrite history from the perspective of the respondents' experience rather than an "objective" record of reality (Broido & Manning, 2002). Wiggins and Miller's (2003) attempt to evoke the meanings of the Black experience in sport from the perspectives (through written narratives) of Black participants, observers, and commentators serves as an example of how scholars in other disciplines have successfully utilized this research approach.

And finally, a content analysis research design is also compatible with CRT because the purpose of this approach to research is to systematically examine the contents of a particular body of material (e.g., newspapers, television, speeches, legal cases) to identify patterns, themes, and biases. Davis' (1993) critical analysis of *Sports Illustrated* is an example of a case study that supports the argument that the sport media helps to create, reproduce, and legitimate relations of domination in racist, sexist, and capitalist societies by placing affluent White Western males in the ideal subject position. The section to follow will attempt to explain how CRT could inform and be applied to research in areas within sport management.

Critical Race Theory and Sport Management Research

Because very few attempts have been made to conduct critical race qualitative research in the field of sport management (Singer, 2002, and Bruening's 2000 dissertation research are rare exceptions), it is not within the scope of this article to provide an in-depth and detailed account of how CRT and qualitative research is actually (or has been) carried out in sport management research. The primary purpose is to provide sport management scholars and students with some basic insight into how CRT's epistemological and methodological bases could be applied to research in our field. For instance, there are several research issues and problems within sport and sport organizations that sport management scholars could use CRT and qualitative research techniques to address: the lack of gender, racial, and ethnic diversity in leadership and upper management (Fink & Pastore, 1999; Fink, Pastore, & Reimer, 2001; Lapchick, 2003); discrimination based on race, ethnicity, and gender (Brooks & Althouse, 2000; Brown et al., 2003; Cunningham, 2004); the marketing of sport to people of color (Armstrong, 1998); depictions, images, and roles of athletes and people of color in the sport media (Andrews & Jackson, 2001; Chideya, 1995; Davis, 1993); and the stereotypical images of American Indians in sport organizations (Beca, 2004).

Frisby (2005) discussed how, as sport management scholars, our focus on organizations and managerial activities positions us to question how structures and practices related to policy development, human resource management, marketing, the media, and so forth perpetuate and contribute to the many issues and problems that sport managers face today. In this regard, CRT should be seen as a framework or set of basic insights, perspectives, and methods that could help sport management scholars identify, analyze, and change those structural and cultural aspects of sport that maintain subordinate and dominant racial positions in and out of various sport organizations. CRT and qualitative research could allow us to better understand how these structures and practices negatively impact people of color in sport organizations, and what needs to be done to ameliorate the social conditions of these individuals.

Solo'rzano and Yosso (2002) advanced a "critical race methodology" and argued that it provides a tool for CRT scholars to counter majoritarian stories (i.e., stories that carry layers of assumptions that persons in positions of racialized privilege bring with them to discussions of racism, sexism, classism, and other forms of subordination) and deficit storytelling (i.e., storytelling that upholds deficit, racialized notions and negative stereotypes about people of color), and a space for CRT scholars to conduct and present research that is grounded in the experiences and knowledge of people of color. There is a need for sport management scholars to implement the critical race methodology into our study of diversity, policy development, human resource management, marketing, and the media by incorporating the voices and perspectives of those individuals who are victims of racial and other discriminatory practices into the research process. Sport management scholars could use the various qualitative approaches that were discussed in the previous section (i.e., case studies, critical ethnography, PAR, phenomenology, content analysis) to create the practical knowledge (i.e., knowledge that result from research participants' actual understanding and interpretation of social conditions), and ultimately, emancipatory knowledge (i.e., knowledge that empowers and challenges research participants to engage in the change process) that is absolutely necessary if we are serious about addressing the research issues mentioned here. We must begin to move beyond the important technical knowledge (i.e., knowledge that enhances prediction in order to control the environment) that has been produced by scholars in our field (see Kershaw, 1992 for information on technical, practical, and emancipatory knowledge).

Although it has been suggested that the use of critical race qualitative research has the potential to address racism and other forms of discrimination in the sport industry, its utility in conducting research designed to bring about social justice and change in sport organizations has not yet been demonstrated. I have attempted to provide some insight into how we might incorporate CRT into sport management research by looking to the research that scholars in other fields (e.g., special issues of *Qualitative Inquiry* and *Race, Ethnicity, and Education*) have successfully carried out in proposing alternative ways of knowing and knowledge building. We certainly should be mindful of this important work that our colleagues in other fields have done and, when appropriate, use it as an example and blueprint for some of the research that we do in our own field of study. The remainder of this article will discuss the major challenges involved with conducting critical race qualitative research in our field and the implications this research approach has for the sport management academic discipline.

Discussion

Challenges of Conducting Critical Race Qualitative Research

As sport management scholars and students begin to contemplate and think about conducting critical race qualitative research, it is important for us to acknowledge some of the key issues, challenges, and obstacles that lie ahead. First, because many Whites, as well as some people of color, have embraced the "color-blind" and race-neutral perspective, constructs such as CRT that are built on the premise that racism is a normative cultural behavior in American society will be resisted, if not outright rejected. Duncan (2002) discussed the problems that emerge when people of color are socialized to embrace the perspectives of members of the dominant group. According to Duncan (2002), "people of color who, socialized in the various institutions that certify them to assume positions of responsibility in society, uncritically accept or identify with the values that inform these institutions, to the destruction of communities of color" (p. 91). In essence, it is very challenging to conduct emancipatory research with people of color who have had "favorable" or "successful" experiences in this society and, as a result, think and feel that racism is a thing of the past. Sport management scholars and activists might find it difficult to convince most athletes, coaches, employees, and managers of color to engage in research studies that are designed to critically analyze and dismantle the cultures and structures of sport organizations in which these individuals work, play, and make a living.

Second, the essentialist argument has also emerged as a critique of CRT. Critics assert that people of color have a myriad of experiences that shapes who they are and what they know, and they are uncomfortable with CRT because they feel that it treats all members of a racial and ethnic group the same (Delgado Bernal, 2002). Critics of essentialist notions of race and identity are correct to point out that individuals within a particular racial and ethnic group do not necessarily think and act in monolithic, predicable, and homogeneous ways. These critics, however, must also recognize that CRT scholars acknowledge and understand that one's identity is not based solely on the social construction of race but rather is multidimensional and intersects with various experiences (e.g., gender, class, language, migration, immigration; Delgado Bernal, 2002). Therefore, although race is the central component of CRT, it is but one of many components that are woven together, and they certainly are not static. Sport management scholars who are interested in exploring the appropriateness of CRT in studying issues of racial and ethnic diversity in various organizational contexts must be mindful of this.

Third, the use of storytelling and narratives as a methodological framework in CRT has become the focus of criticism (see, for example, Farber & Sherry, 1995, 1997). The argument against the use of personal stories and narratives is a critique against alternative ways of knowing and understanding and is "basically an argument over subjectivity versus objectivity" (Delgado Bernal, 2002, p. 119). Critics such as Farber and Sherry contend that narratives fail to meet the standards of traditional legal scholarship because they fail to explicate through the usual methods of fact, logic, and linear reasoning, and they fail to rely on universality and typicality. CRT scholars, however, do not position the debate between objectivity and subjectivity; instead, they acknowledge that all stories are subjective and the production of knowledge is situated (Delgado Bernal, 2002). Sport management scholars working from a CRT perspective need to understand that it is important not only for dominant ways of knowing (e.g., positivistic research) to be embraced and acknowledged but also for other ways of knowing and understanding — particularly stories and narratives of those people of color who have experienced and responded to discrimination and oppression — to be embraced and acknowledged.

Fourth, central questions surrounding voice(s) and who speaks for whom have become critical issues in qualitative research and CRT (Parker & Lynn, 2002). Sport management scholars and students who are concerned with conducting critical race-based research with people of color in sport organizations must acknowledge this tension. This "crisis of representation" (i.e., researchers struggle with how to locate themselves and their participants in reflexive texts) is something that all researchers must grapple with in telling the stories of research participants (Denzin & Lincoln, 2000). But more specifically, because CRT argues that White privilege is an integral part of this society, sport management scholars from the dominant group who are concerned with conducting race-based emancipatory research must especially be cognizant of this tension. Andersen (1993) argued that in order for White scholars to generate research with people of color as research participants they must be reflexive by acknowledging and challenging White privilege and how it might shape the research experience and process. Bruening's (2000) research provides an excellent example of how a White female sport management researcher followed Andersen's advice by using a reflexive personal journal throughout her research with African American female student-athletes in an attempt to acknowledge her biases and privilege, as well as the limitations this placed on her study.

On a final note, other factors such as the need for researchers to carefully negotiate their stance as critical race researchers (i.e., ask who stands to benefit from the research being conducted; see Fine, Weis, Weseen, & Wong, 2000), the challenge of negotiating access to the power brokers (e.g., upper management) and other stakeholders (e.g., athletes, coaches) within sport organizations, and the tremendous amount of time that it takes to conduct critical race qualitative research are some things that sport management scholars must be cognizant of when engaging in the research process. Despite all of the challenges involved with conducting critical race qualitative research and the concerns raised by critics of CRT and qualitative research, it remains a powerful research tool for scholars to consider when conducting emancipatory research with people of color in sport management.

Implications for Sport Management Research and Education

In her Earle F. Zeigler Award address over a decade ago, Dr. Joy DeSensi (1994) stressed the "tremendous need for our sport management programs to make a commitment to reflect and directly address multicultural issues and education toward that end" (p. 63). Here, we are concerned with the issue of epistemological racism and the negative impact that it could have on theory, research, and practice in sport management. Moreover, in the foregoing sections, CRT was advanced as a viable epistemological tool for addressing this problem. Again, the point of this discourse was not to dismiss other approaches to research that have traditionally been embraced by scholars in our field; but rather, the purpose was to expose sport management scholars, educators, and students to this growing and important body of race-based theoretical and epistemological work and to challenge us to think beyond the Eurocentric worldviews that have permeated the education and training of scholars and students in our field. The remainder of this article offers some suggestions for scholars, educators, and students in the field of sport management to consider if we are to successfully address the issue of epistemological racism in our sport management educational programs, our individual and collective research agendas, and ultimately, in how sport organizations are managed.

The future of sport management depends to a great extent on the quality of our doctoral programs (Costa, 2005) because the doctoral students who matriculate through these programs must stand on the shoulders of the pioneers and current faculty to elevate the sport management discipline to greater heights. Therefore, sport management doctoral programs could benefit by strongly encouraging students to take research methods courses in other disciplines such as Black/African American Studies, education, and sociology in which discourses on CRT and other race-based epistemologies have emerged. Perhaps this will provide our students with alternative perspectives to bring into the seminars and courses (e.g., organizational theory, organizational behavior, research colloquiums) that doctoral students are required to take. This could result in some lively discussions that not only challenge the paradigmatic assumptions of the students but also those of the faculty who teach these courses.

Sport management doctoral students are not the only stakeholders who stand to benefit from exposure to alternative approaches to research. The professional development of sport management faculty is as equally important to the future success of sport management research, education, and practice. Moreover, if sport management scholars and educators are to encourage, teach, and challenge doctoral students to adopt or consider alternative research epistemologies, as well as challenge their masters level and undergraduate sport management students (the future leaders and managers in the sport industry) to think outside of the traditional Eurocentric paradigms that have been embedded within the cultures and power structures of sport organizations, these scholars could benefit if they exposed themselves to the various discourses on alternative race-based epistemologies by reading academic journals (e.g., *Qualitative Inquiry, Educational Researcher, Western Journal of Black Studies*) that have embraced this work.

Finally, collaborative research across disciplines, as well as within sport management, is a very important strategy for scholars and students in our field to pursue (Costa, 2005). In particular, the disciplines of education, sociology (sport), ethnic studies (e.g., Black/African American studies), history, humanities, law, and women's studies provide fertile ground for sport management scholars to pursue collaborative relationships with critical race scholars in other fields. These relationships would expose sport management scholars and students to some of the literature on race-based epistemologies that, in turn, could help to expand the research agendas in our field. For instance, the academic quarter that I spent as a doctoral student in a Black/African American studies research methods class not only exposed me to CRT and other race-based epistemologies, but it also allowed me to establish a relationship with the professor (he became one of my committee members for my comprehensive exams) that would eventually lay the foundation for both my dissertation research (see Singer, 2002) and this article, which originally appeared in a special issue of the *Journal of Sport Management*. It is my hope that this article can be used as a departure point for productive research relationships with scholars in our field, as well as other fields within the academy.

Conclusion

This article used Scheurich and Young's provocative article published in *Educational Researcher* in 1997 to bring the concept of epistemological racism into the sport management research dialogue, as well as to argue that CRT is an appropriate research tool for addressing this problem. Furthermore, it was suggested that we must begin to recognize people of color as holders and creators of knowledge (Delgado Bernal, 2002). Sport management scholars and practitioners must not devalue, omit, or misinterpret and misrepresent the histories, experiences, cultures, and languages of people of color in sport (e.g., athletes, coaches, spectators, employees, citizens, managers, and administrators) when studying the impact that the cultures and structures of sport organizations have on their experiences. Therefore, this article provided sport management scholars with an explication of the critical race theoretical framework as a starting point for demonstrating the significance of race and ethnicity as viable epistemological considerations in some of the research that is done in our dynamic and interdisciplinary field of study. A focus on CRT, however, will require—as Ladson-Billings (1998) suggested to her colleagues in education—sport management scholars and students to take more time to study and understand the legal literature from which this epistemological and theoretical framework is derived, as well as to begin to carefully rethink and re-examine the relationship between race and sport management. This article challenges sport management scholars to expand their horizons and engage in an intense study of CRT, meaningful dialogue, and eventually, action that could improve sport management research, theory, and practice.

References

Andersen, M. L. (1993). Studying across difference: Race, class, and gender in qualitative research. In J. H. Stanfield, II, & R. M. Dennis (Eds.), *Race and ethnicity in research methods* (pp. 39–52). Newbury Park, CA: Sage.

Anderson, G. L. (1989). Critical ethnography in education: Origins, current status, and new directions. *Review of Educational Research, 59*(3), 249–270.

Andrews, D. L., & Jackson, S. J. (Eds.). (2001). *Sport stars: The cultural politics of sporting celebrity*. London and New York: Routledge.

Armstrong, K. L. (1998). Ten strategies to employ when marketing sport to Black consumers. *Sport Marketing Quarterly*, 7(3), 11–18.

Banks, J. A. (1993). The canon debate, knowledge construction, and multicultural education. *Educational Researcher*, 22(5), 4–14.

Banks, J. A. (1995). The historical reconstruction of knowledge about race: Implications for tranformative learning. *Educational Researcher*, 24(2), 15–25.

Beca, L. R. (2004). Native images in schools and the racially hostile environment. *Journal of Sport & Social Issues*, 28(1), 71–78.

Bell, D. (1987). *And we are not saved: The elusive quest for racial justice*. New York: Basic.

Bell, D. (1992). *Faces at the bottom of the well: The permanence of racism*. New York: Basic.

Boucher, B. (2000, April 26). *Methodological diversity in sport management research: Decade in review*. Paper presented at The Ohio State University, Research Colloquium in Sport Management, Columbus, OH.

Broido, E. M., & Manning, K. (2002). Philosophical foundations and current theoretical perspectives in qualitative research. *Journal of College Student Development*, 43(4), 434–445.

Brooks, D., & Althouse, R. (Eds.). (2000). *Racism in college athletics: The African American athlete's experience* (2nd ed.). Morgantown, WV: Fitness Information Technology, Inc.

Brown, T. N., Jackson, J.S., Brown, K. T., Sellers, R. M., Keipers, S., & Manuel, W. J. (2003). "There's no race on the playing field": Perceptions of racial discrimination among white and black athletes. *Journal of Sport and Social Issues*, 27(2), 162–183.

Bruening, J. E. (2000). *Phenomenal women: A qualitative study of silencing, stereotypes, socialization, and strategies for change in sport participation of African American female student-athletes*. Unpublished doctoral dissertation. The Ohio State University, Columbus, OH.

Carrington, B. (2002). Sport, masculinity and black cultural resistance. In J. Sugden & A. Tomlinson (Eds.), *Power Games: A critical sociology of sport* (pp. 267–291). London: Routledge.

Chalip, L. (1997). Action research and social change in sport: An introduction to the special issue. *Journal of Sport Management*, 11, 1–7.

Chideya, F. (1995). *Don't believe the hype: Fighting cultural misinformation about African-Americans*. New York: Plume.

Coakley, J .J. (2004). *Sports in society: Issues & controversies* (8th ed.). Boston: McGraw-Hill.

Cochran, J. L., & Mehri, C. (2002, September 30). *Black coaches in the national football league: Superior performance, inferior opportunities*. Retrieved December 3, 2004, from http://www.findjustice.com

Costa, C. A. (2005). The status and future of sport management: A Delphi study. *Journal of Sport Management*, 19(2), 17–42.

Crenshaw, K. W. (1988). Race, reform, retrenchment: Transformation and legitimation in anti-discrimination law. *Harvard Law Review*, 101, 1331–1387.

Cunningham, G. B. (2004). Already aware of the glass ceiling: Race-related effects of perceived opportunities on the career choices of college athletes. *Journal of African American Studies*, 7(1), 57–71.

Davis, L. R. (1993). Critical analysis of the popular media and the concept of ideal subject position: Sports illustrated as a case study. *Quest*, 45, 165–181.

Delgado, R. (1995). Introduction. In R. Delgado (Ed.), *Critical race theory: The cutting edge* (pp. xiii–xvi). Philadelphia: Temple University Press.

Delgado Bernal, D. (2002). Critical race theory, Latino critical theory, and critical raced–gendered epistemologies: Recognizing students of color as holders and creators of knowledge. *Qualitative Inquiry*, 8(1), 105–126.

Delgado, R., & Stefancic, J. (Eds.). (1997). *Critical White studies: Looking behind the mirror*. Philadelphia: Temple University.

Denzin, N. K., & Lincoln, Y. S. (2000). Introduction: The discipline and practice of qualitative research. In N.K. Denzin & Y.S. Lincoln (Eds.), *Handbook of Qualitative Research* (2nd ed., pp. 1–28), Thousand Oaks, CA: Sage

DeSensi, J. T. (1994). Multiculturalism as an issue in sport management. *Journal of Sport Management*, 8, 63–74.

Dixson, A. D., & Rousseau, C. K. (2005). And we are still not saved: Critical race theory in education ten years later. *Race, Ethnicity, and Education*, 8(1), 7–27.

Donnor, J. K. (2005). Towards an interest-convergence in the education of African-American football student athletes in major college sports. *Race, Ethnicity, and Education, 8*(1), 45–67.

D'Souza, D. (1995). *The end of racism.* New York: Free Press.

Du Bois, W. E. B. (1953). *The souls of Black folk.* New York: Fawcett. (Original work published 1903).

Duncan, G. A. (2002). Critical race theory and method: rendering race in urban ethnographic research. *Qualitative Inquiry, 8*(1), 85–104.

Farber, D., & Sherry, S. (1995). Telling stories out of school: An essay on legal narratives. In R. Delgado (Ed.), *Critical race theory: The cutting edge* (pp. 283–292). Philadelphia: Temple University Press.

Farber, D., & Sherry, S. (1997). *Beyond all reason: The radical assault on truth in American law.* New York: Oxford University Press.

Fine, M., Weis, L., Weseen, S., & Wong, L. (2000). For whom? Qualitative research, representations, and social responsibilities. In N. K. Denzin & Y. S. Lincoln (Eds.), *Handbook of qualitative research* (2nd ed., pp. 107–131). Thousand Oaks, CA: Sage.

Fink, J. S., & Pastore, D. L. (1999). Diversity in sport? Utilizing the business literature to devise a comprehensive framework of diversity initiatives. *Quest, 51,* 310–327.

Fink, J. S., Pastore, D. L., & Riemer, H. A. (2001). Do differences make a difference? Managing diversity in Division 1A intercollegiate athletics. *Journal of Sport Management, 15,* 10–50.

Fredrickson, G. M. (2002). *Racism: A short history.* Princeton, N.J.: Princeton University Press.

Frisby, W. (2005). The good, the bad, and the ugly: Critical sport management research. *Journal of Sport Management, 19*(1), 1–12.

Frisby, W., Crawford, S., & Dorer, T. (1997). Reflections on participatory action research: The case of low-income women accessing local physical activity services. *Journal of Sport Management, 11,* 8–28.

Frisby, W., Reid, C., Millar, S. & Hoeber, L. (2005). Putting "participatory" into participatory forms of action research. *Journal of Sport Management (Special Issue on Critical and Innovative Approaches to Research), 19*(4), 367–386.

Gordon, E. W., Miller, F., & Rollock, D. (1990). Coping with communicentric bias in knowledge production in the social sciences. *Educational Researcher, 19*(3), 14–19.

Greenwood, D. J., & Levin, M. (2000). Reconstructing the relationships between universities and society through action research. In N. K. Denzin & Y. S. Lincoln (Eds.), *Handbook of qualitative research* (2nd ed., pp. 85–106). Thousand Oaks, CA: Sage.

Habermas, J. (1971). *Theory and practice.* Boston: Beacon Press.

Inglis, S. (1992). Focus groups as a useful qualitative methodology in sport management. *Journal of Sport Management, 6,* 173–178.

Jones, L (Ed.). (2000). *Brothers of the academy: Up and coming Black scholars earning our way in higher education.* Sterling. VA: Stylus.

Jones, L (Ed.). (2002). *Making it on broken promises: Leading African American male scholars confront the culture of higher education.* Sterling, VA: Stylus.

Kershaw, T. (1992). Afrocentrism and the Afrocentric method. *The Western Journal of Black Studies, 16*(3), 160–168.

King, J. E. (1997). Dysconscious racism: Ideology, identity, and miseducation. In R. Delgado & J. Stefancic (Eds.), *Critical White studies: Looking behind the mirror* (pp. 128–132). Philadelphia: Temple University.

Ladson-Billings, G. (1994). *The dreamkeepers: Successful teachers of African American children.* San Francisco: Jossey Bass.

Ladson-Billings, G. (1996). "Your blues ain't like mine": Keeping issues of race and racism on the multicultural agenda. *Theory Into Practice, 35*(4), 248–255.

Ladson-Billings, G. (1998). Just what is critical race theory and what's it doing in a nice field like education? *Qualitative Studies in Education, 11*(1), 7–24.

Ladson-Billings, G. (2000). Racialized discourses and ethnic epistemologies. In N. K. Denzin & Y. S. Lincoln (Eds.), *Handbook of qualitative research* (2nd ed.; pp. 257–277). Thousand Oaks, CA: Sage.

Ladson-Billings, G., & Tate, W. F. (1995). Toward critical race theory of education. *Teachers College Record, 97,* 47–68.

Lapchick, R. (2003). Racial and gender report

card. University of Central Florida. Orlando, FL: The Institute for Diversity and Ethics in Sport.

Lynn, M., Yosso, T. J., Solo'rzano, D. G., & Parker, L. (2002). Critical race theory and education: Qualitative research in the new millennium. *Qualitative Inquiry, 8*(1), 3–6.

Matsuda, M. (1991). Voices of America: Accent, antidiscrimination law and a jurisprudence for the last reconstruction. *Yale Law Journal, 100*, 1329–1407.

McDonald, I. (2002). Critical social research and political intervention: Moralistic versus radical approaches. In J. Sugden & A. Tomlinson (Eds.), *Power games: A critical sociology of sport* (pp. 100–116). London: Routledge.

McIntosh, P. (1990, Winter). White privilege: Unpacking the invisible knapsack. *Independent School*, 31–36.

McIntosh, P. (1997). White privilege and male privilege: A personal account of coming to see correspondences through work in women's studies. In R. Delgado & J. Stefancic (Eds.), *Critical White studies: Looking behind the mirror* (pp. 291–299). Philadelphia: Temple University.

Morris, A. (1993). Centuries of black protest: Its significance for America and the world. In H. Hill & J. E. Jones, Jr., (Eds.), *Race in America: The struggle for equality* (pp. 19–69). Madison: The University of Wisconsin Press.

Nance, R. (2002, February 14). NBA out front on black coaches: Russell's success paved way for a record 13 calling shots. *USA Today*, C3.

Olafson, G. A. (1990). Research design in sport management: What's missing, what's needed' *Journal of Sport Management, 4*, 103–120.

Parker, L., & Lynn, M. (2002). What's race got to do with it? Critical race theory's conflicts with and connections to qualitative research methodology and epistemology. *Qualitative Inquiry, 8*(1), 7–22.

Roithmayr, D. (1999). Introduction to critical race theory in educational research and praxis. In L. Parker, D. Deyhle, & S. Villenas (Eds.), *Race is . . . race isn't: Critical race theory and qualitative studies in education* (pp. 1–6). Boulder, CO: Westview Press.

Scheurich, J. J., & Young, M. D. (1997). Coloring epistemologies: Are our research epistemologies racially biased? *Educational Researcher, 26*(4), 4–16.

Shujaa, M. J. (Ed.) (1994). *Too much schooling, too little education: A paradox of Black life in White societies*. Trenton, NJ: Africa World Press, Inc.

Singer, J. N. (2002). *"Let us make man": The development of Black males in a big-time college sport program*. Unpublished doctoral dissertation. The Ohio State University, Columbus, OH.

Sipe, L., & Constable, S. (1996). A chart of four contemporary paradigms: Metaphors for the modes of inquiry. *Taboo: The Journal of Culture and Education, 1*, 153–163.

Slack, T. (1997). *Understanding sport organizations: The application of organization theory*. Champaign, IL: Human Kinetics.

Solo'rzano, D. G., & Yosso, T. J. (2002). Critical race methodology: Counter-storytelling as an analytical framework for education research. *Qualitative Inquiry, 8*(1), 23–44.

Stanfield, J. H., II. (1985). The ethnocentric basis of social science knowledge production. *Review of Research in Education, 12*, 387–415.

Stanfield, J. H., II. (1993). Epistemological considerations. In J. H. Stanfield, II & R. M. Dennis (Eds.), *Race and ethnicity in research methods* (pp. 16–36). Newbury Park, CA: Sage.

Tate, W. F. (1997). Critical race theory and education: History, theory, and implications. In M. Apple (Ed.), *Review of Research in Education 2* (pp. 191–243). Washington, DC: American Educational Research Association.

Teo, T., & Febbraro, A. R. (2003). Ethnocentrism as a form of intuition in psychology. *Theory & Psychology, 13*(5), 673–694.

Usher, R., & Scott, D. (1996). Afterword: The politics of educational research. In D. Scott & R. Usher (Eds.), *Understanding Educational Research* (pp. 175–180). London: Routledge.

Watkins, W. H. (2001). The white architects of black education: Ideology and power in America, 1865–1954. New York: Teachers College Press, Columbia University.

West, C. (1994). *Race matters*. New York: Vintage.

Whiteside, K. (2004, December 1). Willingham out at Notre Dame: Coach fired after three seasons for lack of "progress on the field." *USA Today*, C1.

Wieberg, S. (2004, December 1). Willingham's dismissal frustrates black coaches group. *USA Today*, C2.

Wiggins, D. K., & Miller, P. B. (Eds.). (2003). *The unlevel playing field: A documentary history of the African American experience in sport*. Urbana, IL: University of Illinois Press.

Williams, P. J. (1988). Reconstructing ideals from deconstructed rights. In J. Lobel (Ed.), *A less than perfect union: Alternative perspectives on the U.S. constitution* (pp. 56–70). New York: Monthly Review.

Wilson, W. J. (1978). *The declining significance of race*. Chicago: University of Chicago Press.

Woodson, C. G. (1990). *The mis-education of the Negro*. Trenton, NJ: Africa World Press. (Original work published 1933).

5

URBAN REGIMES AND SPORT IN NORTH AMERICAN CITIES: SEEKING STATUS THROUGH FRANCHISES, EVENTS, AND FACILITIES

Gregory H. Duquette and Daniel S. Mason

Introduction

Competition has intensified as North American cities clamor to gain access to foreign investment, corporate headquarters, and a burgeoning market for tourism (Hall, 2005; Loftman & Nevin, 1996; Sassen, 2002). As a result, a number of local institutions such as the arts (theatres, symphonies, museums), sport (teams, events, stadiums), and tourist attractions (theme parks, landscapes, monuments) come to play an influential role in promoting the city (Bianchini, 1990; Dunn & McGuirk, 1999; Logan & Molotch, 2002). The competitive market of places has led today's cities to increasingly closer links and partnerships with the private sector, due also to declining financial support from higher levels of government (Logan & Molotch, 2002; Schimmel, 2002; Squires, 2002). Development projects such as Harbor Place in Baltimore, MD, the Riverwalk in San Antonio, TX, or Fisherman's Wharf in San Francisco, CA, are examples of public-private partnerships that involve local elites engaged in strategic local development in the promotion of place, and are a product of a complex network of local elites involved in local development.

For many cities, sport-related strategies have taken the form of the construction of sports facilities, the staging of mega-sporting events, and, in the case of North American cities, the hosting of local professional sports teams (Baade, 1996; Chalip & Leyns, 2002, Euchner, 1993; Friedman & Mason, 2004; Hinch & Higham, 2003; Quirk & Fort, 1999; Rosentraub, 1999). Such projects typically represent an example of development initiatives deemed to have both economic and cultural value to the community. This is significant in that it highlights a shift of the city into non-traditional areas such as branding and marketing, in addition to material production.

It has been stated that a city bent on competing for capital must be entrepreneurial (Harvey, 1989a). In the context of rapid change within cities, sport has, if anything, increased its profile as a tool for civic promotion, development, and branding. Prominent examples where sport has been used as a catalyst for local development include such North American cities as Calgary, AB, Atlanta, GA, and Salt Lake City, UT, cities that have hosted the largest sport event of them all — the Olympic Games (Deccio & Baloglu, 2002; Ritchie, 2000). In addition, cities such as Baltimore, MD, Cleveland, OH, and Indianapolis, IN, have openly incorporated local sport facilities into broader local/ urban redevelopment projects, often under the banner of regeneration and reinvention (Cagan & deMause, 1998; Judd, 1995; Rosentraub et al., 1994). Further, the incorporation of local sport in development initiatives extends to major league sports franchises. Cities such as Columbus, OH, and Nashville, TN, have specifically targeted the hosting of professional sport teams as a means of re-branding the community (Curry et al., 2004; Friedman & Mason, 2005).

A key question remains however: Who are the individuals involved in creating sport-related civic strategies and why have they chosen to use sport? This paper explores the networks of business and political elites that comprise the strategic core of cities. In doing so, we provide an explanation of why cities have become more entrepreneurial, how the networks/partnerships among business and political elites have operated, and why sport has figured so prominently in their strategies. The paper is organized as follows: first, a brief overview of the competitive context between contemporary cities is provided. We then examine the dialectic in urban regimes between private sector and public sector interests that has emerged to govern and lead cities strategically, and review how they have used sport in three specific contexts: the hosting of sports teams; the staging of sporting events; and the construction of sport-specific facilities. We conclude with an overview of the implications of our discussion.

Competition between Cities

It could be argued that, at the start of the 21st century, cities are competing more than ever to attract different consumers — generally focusing on the unique characteristics, meanings, and practices possessed by the city and community (Ashworth & Voogt, 1990; Held & McGrew, 2000). Cities are competing to gain access to foreign investment, to attract corporate headquarters, and to expand local institutions in an effort to draw economic capital, a skilled workforce, and increased tourism. The competition between cities within a globalized economy has led to rapid change in virtually all aspects of the city — its development, its governance, its identity (Appadurai, 1996; Borja & Castells, 1997; Sassen, 2002).

In this sense, our political economic view of the globalized economy — also commonly described as a key component of the process of globalization — is the deregulated expansion of capital into new markets (Ritzer, 1996; Robertson, 1995; Robins, 1997). Greater market access means that the competitive environment between places has changed in which capital (i.e., economic, cultural, social) flows more freely (Bourdieu, 1998). While it has been stated that cities have been competing against one another for centuries and even longer (Held & McGrew, 2000), what characterizes the current globalization is the speed with which capital can flow. As a result there is a sense of urgency in cities, as local stakeholders act upon a perceived threat of globalization (Fainstein & Judd, 1999; Kelly & Grieder, 2003; Schimmel, 2002). Cities continue to shift away from traditional industrial, production-based economies toward non-traditional, service-oriented industries. As a result, there is greater emphasis placed on consumption rather than production within cities (Hannigan, 1998; Judd, 2003). In order to navigate this competitive global climate, networks between different local stakeholders involved in managing place as a product have emerged (Wolfson & Frisken, 2000).

As mentioned above, a key strategic course of action for cities has been the emergent initiatives involving sport. Sport's utility in this scenario is due, in part, to the way in which sport is consumed, participated in, organized, and experienced. Local sport is unique to specific contexts, and therefore represents a possible point of differentiation between cities. In other words, it represents a potential source of competitive advantage for cities. Thus for cities competing for capital, sport represents a valued local resource, and has implications for economic development (Crompton, 1995; Friedman & Mason, 2004; Smith, 1994), tourism (Gibson, 2003; Higham & Hinch, 2003; Hinch & Higham, 2001), and marketing or branding the city (Chalip et al., 2003; Chalip & McGuirty, 2004; Whitelegg, 2000).

The role of sport in North American cities has been examined from a number of different angles (Baade & Dye, 1988; Hall, 1992; Johnson, 1993; Ritchie et al., 2002; Whitston & Macintosh, 1993). Some of this research has focused on local sports franchises and community (Danielson, 1997; Euchner, 1993; Quirk & Fort, 1999). Other research has focused on sporting events (Burbank, 2002; Chalip & Leyns, 2002; Green, 2001) and/or sports facilities such as stadiums, arenas, or ballparks (Baade, 1996; Jones, 2002; Noll & Zimbalist, 1997). It is these three areas—franchises, events, and facilities—that represent the core of local sport as a tool for civic competition, and are a focus of our discussion below.

The prominent role of local sport in attracting tourists, and in shaping perceptions of status, suggests that how sport is managed may be related to the identity or brand of the city (Chalip & McGuirty, 2004; Palmer, 2002; Rowe & McGuirk, 1999). Unfortunately, there has been little research that focuses specifically on those individuals, groups, and the corresponding networks or linkages involved in local development strategies related to sport, at least in terms of viewing the city as a strategic entity in competition with other cities. In order to examine the network of organizations and stakeholders that act on behalf of cities in greater detail, we borrow from the urban studies literature and the concept of urban regimes.

City and the Urban Regime

Urban regime theory has emerged as a way of examining those individuals and groups responsible for the management of cities (Logan & Molotch, 1987; Stone, 1989). Urban regimes consist of an elite group of individuals involved in local development, and represent informal but often enduring and stable coalitions of civic and corporate elites that make key policy decisions for the local community (Stoker & Mossberger, 1995; Stone, 1989). The processes by which the coalition of stakeholders in the urban regime unite to influence the economic, social, and cultural conditions of communities—local development—represent an important example of the local policy creation process (Jones & Fleming, 2003). Seen in this way, the regime's urban policies are pursued by those individuals and organizations involved in "managing" places (Philo and Kearns, 1993).

It is this group of elites that has access to, and control over, civic resources critical to local development. The theory's greatest contribution is that it identifies the coalition(s) of key individuals in the urban policy process (Elkin, 1985; Logan & Molotch, 2002). In other words, urban regime theory seeks to identify those individuals and organizations with interest in places and how those interests may affect use and exchange values (Logan & Molotch, 1987). Logan and Molotch (1987, p. 62) describe members of the urban elite as: "people who use their time and money to participate in local affairs . . . the ones who—in vast disproportion to their representation in the population—have the most to gain or lose in land-use decisions."

At the same time, urban regime theory does not ascribe all local power solely to the private sector. Rather, regime theory holds that local public sector officials make genuine choices in response to the economy and do not simply follow the commands of business (Stone, 1989). Thus, regime theory emphasizes the politics of urban development, especially the importance of the public sector who, in their role as coalition leaders, manage development policies to induce growth and sustain electoral support. The ways in which this has occurred is shaped principally by the strategies of political leaders, especially by their use of the resources of local government. Therefore, it might be argued that regime theory views private sector elites as shaping city politics, and public sector elites as setting the rules under which local stakeholders act.

Regardless of sector, it has been stated that pro-growth strategies are generally stratified in favor of the interests of different local elites (Logan & Molotch, 1987; Mills, 1956; Zukin, 1995). In managing the pro-growth city, this group of elites has seen greater involvement from the private sector and a more entrepreneurial approach to local development initiatives. Thus, pro-growth strategies are also symbolic of branding the community as an attractive place to live and work, and also an attractive place-product to be consumed.

Urban Regime and "The Local": Public Sector versus Private Sector

An increasing emphasis on nurturing political, economic, social, and cultural life in cities has brought greater attention to those individuals who manage the city (Borja & Castells, 1997). In identifying the coalitions involved in the local policy creation process, one must view the urban regime as the network of coalition-builders and the informal arrangements through which public office-holders have to come to terms with private interests in the governing of the city (Stone, 1989). According to Stoker and Mossberger (1994), there are five categories of participants in the urban regime:

1. business leaders
2. locally elected politicians
3. trade unions
4. local technocrats (i.e., government, development corporations)
5. members of community organizations.

Among these participants, urban regimes include public and private actors (Elkin, 1987; Stone, 1989). In the case of cities, the distinction between private and public sector has been a long-standing dialectic of competing interests, especially in terms of urban governance (Agger et al., 1964). For example, the private sector has generally been interested in generating profits for specific interests, while the public sector's responsibility is in providing welfare. In this dialectic, members of the urban regime from the private sector might include individuals such as corporate CEOs, local developers, and local franchise owners. Depending on the size of the regime, it may also include other corporate managers, local entrepreneurs, and construction contractors.

Conversely, members of the urban regime from the public sector might include such individuals as mayors, city councilors, commissioners, bureaucrats, and state/provincial legislators. As direct representatives of place, these individuals typically wield political power with respect to the operations of the city. Yet in the case of each sector, these individuals represent the urban regime responsible for managing place. What is a critical common denominator is that, in the growing competition between cities, each of these members above also has a unified interest in promoting place.

However, there is a lack of research that examines those in power who manage places, specifically as it relates to sport and local development (Green et al., 2003; Paul & Brown, 2001; Swindell & Rosentraub, 1998). In terms of the private sector, the corporate naming of stadiums, the sponsorship of events, and the corporate ownership of teams illustrate the increasing influence of business interests in managing place.

However, the fact that we see the taxpayer funding of stadiums, the level of citizen support for hosting events, and the pursuit of community-owned professional sport teams strengthens urban regime theory's claims that management of place requires the presence of political elites as well as business elites.

Urban Regimes and Sport

It is the role of the urban regime — those individuals with the power to use sport as a strategy in community development — that ultimately shapes the ways in which cities use sport. What emerges in looking at the involvement of the urban regime in sport is the presence of a local sport triad — franchises, events, and facilities. The following describes these three general areas in which regimes have actively pursued pro-growth local sport strategies in North America.

Urban Regimes and Sport Franchises in North America

Historically, professional baseball teams served as representatives of their communities as early as the 1880s (Pope, 1993). As the continent's cities grew from colonial outposts to prosperous centers of industrial production, economic growth was dependent on place-making, migration, and capital investment. Traditionally in North America, local sports teams were owned and operated by local elites with the economic resources to support a team and the civic-minded goal of giving something back to the community. Team nicknames, local stadiums, and uniform colors often represented links with local culture, local geography, and local politics. In the case of baseball, teams such as the Cincinnati Red Stockings and the Pittsburgh Pirates served as representative of this new urbanism and the economic expansion of cities beyond the Atlantic seaboard. Teams in these cities were competing with teams in established cities such as New York, Boston, and Philadelphia. Consequently, the value of sport teams in promoting cities such as Pittsburgh and Cincinnati was established.

Generally speaking, it is those in the urban regime that come to view the city as capable of being managed as a business that are most focused on place status, and teams can allegedly provide a means of differentiation between competing cities. Following this logic, the urban regime in a city with a sports franchise, all things being equal, is able to promote their city as having more status than one without a team. Thus, a team means a degree of status for the community. This can occur across all levels or sizes of communities. For example, having a minor professional baseball team might confer status to a medium sized, midwestern city in the USA, over a city of similar size and industry that lacks one (cf. Johnson, 1993).

Sports Franchises and the Private Sector

At the same time, the urban regime's involvement in local sports teams has diffused. With the escalation of franchise values in major and minor-league sports in North America, fewer and fewer teams are owned by one owner and team owners and operators are less likely to be residents of the community in which the team is based. Thus, while community support for the local team through boosterism can be good for different local businesses, local communities can no longer rely on any one local individual to bear the civic responsibility of ownership.

In terms of the private sector, one key group in the urban regime that actively promotes local sport is the media. For example, the success of professional baseball teams in the late 1880s or hockey teams in the 1900s in various communities was related to the role of the media in covering, promoting, and sponsoring professional sport teams (Mason & Duquette, 2004). Thus, media elites (such as station CEOs/Presidents, newspaper/magazine editors, broad-casters) serve as powerful members of the urban regime (Friedman & Mason, 2004). Their powerful role in shaping the local public discourse is comple-mented by their prominence in serving on various local stakeholder groups such as boards of directors. The significance of the media in local sport grows with their greater role in team ownership (e.g., Ted Turner/CNN, Rupert Mur-doch/Fox/BSkyB, ABC/Walt Disney). Thus, in promoting a local team, the media are typically serving their economic interests under the banner of com-munity pride. An example of where this occurred is when the NHL's Win-nipeg Jets were on the verge of being sold and relocated to Phoenix, Arizona. Local community groups rallied around the team, which was lead by the local media: "In the period May 15–21, 1995, the *Winnipeg Free Press* ran sixty-eight stories on the Jets, exclusive of editorials and letters to the editor. No more than six of the sixty-eight stories could even remotely be considered to be jour-nalistically balanced" (Silver, 1996, p. 140). Thus, in the case of Winnipeg, ac-cording to Silver (1996, p. 140), the media "fed the emotional frenzy that roared like a tidal wave over the city. They parroted the [pro-team and arena] line, shut down the critics."

Sports Franchises and the Public Sector

In the public discourse, a sports franchise is generally viewed as a positive as-set to community members. As such, local politicians are generally very sup-portive of the team. One is increasingly aware of the tradition of mayors of cities with teams in the Super Bowl making wagers on the game as a means of demonstrating their local pride. Also common are various local politicians campaigning to save a team or bring a team to the city. In cases where teams have threatened to leave for another host community, "saving" the team can re-sult in a positive legacy for local politicians. As explained by Riess (2000, p. 23):

> Keeping a franchise or bringing in a new team enhanced a mayor's per-sonal image, demonstrated his community spirit, and made points for him with urban boosters, contractors, the construction trades, and the tourist industry. On the other hand, a politician who opposed expensive new parks and arenas ran the risk of being labeled an unprogressive killjoy who let a beloved team leave town or failed to bring in a much-de-sired sports franchise.

Meanwhile those politicians governing during a team's departure or campaign-ing against the presence of a sports team are rarely rewarded. To many voters, sport teams represent a local institution which provides a source of status. Thus, the status of the community and the status of those governing the com-munity are enhanced by positive associations between team and place.

Urban Regimes and Sporting Events in North America

The urban regime's involvement in local sport has extended beyond sports franchises. Increasingly, a successful entrepreneurial city is also one capable of hosting large-scale events such as conventions, concerts, and, in the case of this paper, sporting events. For the growing number of cities seeking to attract consumers, staging a sporting event is increasingly associated with the status of an attractive place to live and/or to visit (Chalip et al., 2003; Jago et al., 2003). For example, a city like Atlanta, GA, has hosted such well-known sporting events such as the Olympic Games and the Super Bowl. A city like Calgary, AB, has hosted the Olympic Games and the Grey Cup (Canadian Football League) Championship.

In addition, less prominent communities seek the place-status associated with hosting events, albeit on a smaller scale. The key here is that the event is large-scale for the city that is hosting — the goal is to improve status in relation to competitors and to move up in pecking order in a larger order of cities. For example, the city of Grande Prairie, Alberta, hosted the Canada Winter Games in 1995. The event featured 3500 athletes and coaches competing in 22 events, along with 200 artists participating in cultural activities organized around the Games. Most notably, Grande Prairie, with a population of just 30,298 in 1995, had less than half the population of most cities that had previously hosted the event. As explained by the head of the athlete's village, "At that time, I think they were legitimately called the best Games ever and I think that certainly has had an impact on people seeing Grande Prairie as a place that could do this sort of thing" (Seymour, 2005).

A sporting event usually falls somewhere between two ends of a continuum, being either participatory or spectator-driven. Events can be held periodically or can be a one-time occurrence, attracting participants, spectators, and volunteers, and ideally an influx of capital to the community. Moreover, a sporting event provides a contained, mediated forum through which place marketers can actively promote the community. Therefore, from a tourism perspective, a major benefit sought by organizers of events is increased awareness and an enhanced image for the host region in a broader marketplace of cities (Hall, 1992; Ritchie & Smith, 1991), while at the same time attracting consumers to the city and spurring overall consumption.

It is important to note here that those involved in attracting the event to the community may be different than those in charge of operating or promoting the event (Chalip, 2005). For example, promoters of an event may be primarily interested in attracting positive awareness of the community while operating an event has typically required the work of volunteers, primarily local citizens with a passion for the sport. Typically, regime members will be more involved in the initial stages of bidding and attracting the event, which will then be turned over to other stakeholders in the city and sporting community. In addition, it is critical to recognize that different groups and members within the stable coalition that comprises the regime will emerge and involve themselves variously in different events. Thus, their level of involvement can and will change according to circumstances, over time. An example might be where hosting one type of sporting event is in the interests of a stakeholder, but hosting another event is not, which ultimately determines their willingness to support the event and the extent to which they become involved.

Seen in this manner, there is not always consensus within the regime. The result is a more diverse group of urban regime elites involved in sport events. However, as part of local pro-growth strategies, it remains true that many of the same local stakeholders discussed earlier (politicians, corporations, and media) are equally supportive of most sporting events, just as they are of sports franchises. Generally speaking, hosting sporting events is viewed positively for urban regimes interested in promoting their community; however, as mentioned above, an individual regime member's level of involvement will vary based on their own interest in any one specific event.

Sporting Events and the Private Sector

Private sector interests such as owners of restaurants, lodgings and businesses located in the geographic proximity of the event are afforded the opportunity to benefit from the hosting of sporting events. Local small businesses are provided with the opportunity to leverage the event (Chalip & Leyns, 2002), while local business elites serve on boards of local chambers of commerce, economic development organizations, and tourism agencies. The primary goal of these local business, development, or tourism organizations is promoting the local as an attractive place. In an entrepreneurial city, these individuals represent a key part of the growth machine (Molotch, 1976). They help to link pro-growth associations and government. Their pro-growth agenda is based on attracting as much capital and exposure to the community as possible. This explains why business elites seek to be involved in strategic decisions involving the hosting of sporting events within their respective communities.

Sporting Events and the Public Sector

From the perspective of a place-manager within the public sphere, a sporting event is self-contained, providing a quick and mediated forum for place managers to pursue their case-specific strategic development agendas. Most local politicians, councilors, and bureaucrats generally support events that attract any degree of positive attention to the community. However, the degree of their role in hosting the event is dependent on the infrastructure requirements for staging the event and the level of financial support the event requires from the local government. In other words, a city is unlikely to object to hosting an event if the successful hosting of the event requires little involvement and resources from the city, and fits with the city's desired image. However, events still require policing, zoning, and other infrastructure responsibilities typically the responsibility of the public sector. As is often the case, public funds are also required for facilities; here their role in the event becomes even more prominent.

As mentioned earlier in many cases, the responsibility of operating a sporting event often falls on the shoulders of the managers of different local sport

organizations. The influence of the urban regime is seen through its representation on regional and municipal sports commissions and authorities, or economic development corporations. Once the right to host the event is granted,
and the resource streams are in place, the actual hands-on delivery of the event
is then turned over to experts in event hosting. However, while some place
managers view the hosting of different sporting events in the community as a
means to promote the city as an attractive place to live, to do business and/or
to visit, sport managers who put on the event might view the aims of the event
through a different light. They are typically passionate about their sport and
active within the community in promoting their sport. As a representative of a
local sport organization, these managers have a vested interest in staging a
successful event. Ancillary benefits (i.e., the promotion of the community) are
simply the by-product of a job well done.

Urban Regimes and Sports Facilities in North America

While many in the urban regime are likely to benefit from having a sports
team or hosting a sporting event, the city must possess the infrastructure where
the team can play or the event can occur. Thus, the final component of the local sport triad is the sport facilities required to host local sport franchises
and/or sport events. It has been argued that the degree of place status associated with the construction of new sport facilities able to host such teams and
events has increased (Altshuler & Luberoff, 2003; Schimmel, 2002). For cities
competing as place-products, a new sport facility portrays the image of 'open
for business' while often increasing development directly around the stadium,
arena, or ballpark. Thus a new, state-of-the-art facility is showcased as a symbol of the city's new (or renewed) urban landscape.

In numerous cases, the potential for local development, urban regeneration,
and/or job growth around these sports facilities has been a focal point in the urban regime's arguments to invest in such strategies. The urban regime's desires
for growth are inevitably linked to local development initiatives with the greatest
public approval and the ability to make the greatest "splash." Thus, in order to
host sports teams and sporting events, a city's urban regime has to become heavily involved in local policies and development strategies involving local sports facilities such as stadiums, ballparks, arenas, and other sports infrastructure.

For example, in the city of Cleveland, OH, three new major-league sports
facilities have opened since 1994. The primary tenants for these three facilities
are the Cleveland Browns (NFL), the Cleveland Cavaliers (NBA) and the
Cleveland Indians (MLB). All these facilities were promoted as part of local
economic development initiatives designed to stimulate development in the
downtown core and rebuild/sustain the community's image. Yet the justifications made for the construction of each specific facility were different. Gund
(now Quicken Loans) Arena was constructed to attract the Cleveland Cavaliers to a downtown site from its previous home in suburban Richfield. After
years of deliberations, Jacobs Field was constructed to ensure the Cleveland
Indians did not follow through on repeated threats to leave the city. Perhaps

most significantly (and most costly), Cleveland Browns Stadium was built as part of the regime's attempt to regain an NFL team after the original Browns franchise relocated (to rival Baltimore). Most estimates have projected an overall cost of these facilities well exceeding $US1 billion (Rosentraub, 1999).

Sports Facilities and the Private Sector

Not surprisingly, members of the urban regime most heavily involved in supporting local sports facilities include local developers, construction companies and real estate brokers. Prominent members of urban regimes that also stand to directly benefit from facility construction, based on their financial interests, include lending agents, or even law firms that see construction to fruition. These majestic facilities are designed with professional teams as their prime long-term tenants, and represent a select resource capable of hosting sporting events such as international and national/league championships.

Decisions regarding the geographical location of the sport facility within the city are often influenced by the visions of local developers. For example, the proposed site of Baltimore's baseball stadium, Oriole Park at Camden Yards, just happened to abut against a warehouse purchased by a group of investors that included then-governor William Don Schaeffer's leading fundraiser (Euchner, 1993). For construction companies, with the opportunity to build a facility comes the promise of jobs and standing in constructing a prominent local landmark. In selling the stadium as a catalyst of urban regeneration, real estate brokers are able to capitalize on the subsequent rise in surrounding property values. In addition, banks and law firms profit from bonds issued to finance construction, which Petersen (2001) estimates to be approximately $2 million for a $250 million dollar facility.

The role of corporate interests in facilities is often associated with their role in the place in which they are headquartered. For example, the city of Columbus, Ohio's NHL arena, Nationwide Arena, is named after the insurance company headquartered there. However, unlike other corporations with facilities naming rights agreements, Nationwide Insurance not only owns the naming rights to the facility, it actually built the facility itself (Curry et al., 2004). This corporate involvement with teams also extends to the purchase of corporate boxes or other form of corporate sponsorship through advertising and signage. For corporate interests, a strong corporate identity in the community is linked to perceptions of their commitment to the city. Thus, corporate support for the local team can make sound business sense.

In addition, those corporations most heavily involved in sports teams are more likely to enjoy greater prominence in cities through stadium advertising, naming rights, and other sponsorships. A corporation may also view sport as an additional cultural amenity that makes it easier to attract prospective employees. While this occurs in larger cities, it also takes place in smaller urban centers. For example, Prospera, a regional credit union, has the naming rights to the 6000-seat arena in Kelowna, British Columbia. Prospera Place is the home arena of the Kelowna Rockets, a hockey franchise that competes in the

Western Hockey League, a feeder league to the National Hockey League. Associating with the highest caliber of sporting competition in the most prominent public facility in that city reaffirms Prospera's position within that community.

Sports Facilities and the Public Sector

Sport facilities represent a highly visible symbol of local progress, and therefore confer significant capital to political elites. The sight of cranes and construction translates into an image of growth. Sports facilities represent the type of flagship development required in which policymaking, development planning, and regeneration strategies can originate. For example, Rich (2000) has hinted that sports stadium development is so attractive to local politicians because securing a sports franchise is one of the few things the elite or urban regime desire; they often show less enthusiasm for other needs of the city. In this case, the construction of a sport facility and development properties around the sport facility are viewed as symbols of local prosperity. It also explains why stadium proposals are privileged over other less glamorous local infrastructure development projects, such as road improvements.

As with the media exposure generated through teams and events, local politicians gravitate to facility ground breaking, ribbon-cutting ceremonies, in order to associate with facility construction. Politicians are able to promote their leadership in getting these facilities constructed (Paul & Brown, 2001). A 20,000-seat arena or a 70,000-seat stadium represents a prominent flagship development in the local landscape. For many in the public sector, it provides the opportunity to establish themselves as part of a community's legacy.

Local Sport and the Urban Regime: A Discussion

Within the entrepreneurial city, "place managers" are increasingly concerned with developing the local as an attractive place-product to consumers (Perry, 2003; Philo & Kearns, 1993). Yet, as Logan and Molotch (1987) have suggested, a city's growth strategies are highly tilted in favor of the interests of local elites — the urban regime. Unfortunately, there has been minimal research that critically examines the urban regime and local development, specifically those elites involved in sport and local development (Chalip, 2004; Owen, 2002; Paul & Brown, 2001; Pelissero, 1991).

In the entrepreneurial city, it is typically members of the local urban regime that view the establishing of a local identity or local "brand" as critical for success in a global market (Brown et al., 2002; Robins, 1997; Sklair, 2001), and many cities have incorporated sport into a variety of local economic development initiatives (Abbott, 1981; Colclough et al., 1994; Euchner, 1993; Jones, 2002). Local sport has been integrated into overall development strategies designed to promote cities (Johnson, 1998; Whitson & Macintosh, 1996), to raise their media profile (Chalip, 2005; Hannigan, 1998), and to increase tourism within and around cities (Hinch & Higham, 2003; Ritchie et al., 2002). As we have shown in this paper, urban regime theory provides a useful framework in identifying local coalitions that comprise key individuals in the urban policy process (Elkin, 1985; Logan & Molotch, 2002), and explaining how inter-organizational linkages are formed around sport-specific growth initiatives within cities. However, the nature of these relationships are becoming more opaque, in that relationships are such that traditional divisions between the public and private sector are increasingly blurred, especially as it relates to sport in the community. The example of local sport reaffirms the growing linkages between public and private interests in the management of the 21st century city.

In addition, the integration of public and private sectors via sport-related local development strategies remains problematic. For example, in the case of Sydney, Australia and the 2000 Olympic Games, Searle (2002, p. 858) questioned the value of public-private partnerships to the city. He stated:

> The overall outcomes of public-private infrastructure projects in Sydney range from those which are very profitable (the motorways) to those which have made large losses (the airport rail line and the Olympic stadiums). One possible conclusion is that infrastructure which has a steady stream of revenue under monopolistic conditions, such as urban motorways, is a surer bet than infrastructure operating under oligopolisitc conditions [such as sports facilities].

Traditionally, those whose primary goals involve rapid social and economic growth tend to see community development as a means to mobilize mass support for their own goals. According to Logan and Molotch (2002, p. 200), "[a]lthough [elites] may differ on which particular strategy will best succeed, elites use their growth consensus to eliminate any alternative vision of the purpose of local government or the meaning of community." This is the nature (and power) of the urban regime in many communities. In city after city that comes to view sport as a catalyst for local development, it becomes critical to understand the role of the urban regime in these debates as more and more questions about strategies that promote the city as a place for leisure, tourism, and consumption are raised (Booth & Loy, 1999; Burbank, 2002; Chalip & Leyns, 2002; Rosentraub et al., 1994).

This becomes even more critical in light of concerns that have been raised about the overall benefits that teams, events, and facilities offer in community development (Quirk & Fort, 1999; Whitson & Macintosh, 1996). Proponents of local sport have long argued that its presence in the community attracts business, improves the quality of life, and increases civic status. In some cases, it has become a matter of economic necessity for places to commodify local attributes such as local sport, which then become assets to be capitalized and exploited in a rush for growth (Judd, 2002; Logan & Molotch, 2002). Many communities have felt pressured to offer additional incentives to keep up with competitor cities and provide symbolic assurance that they offer a healthy economic climate (Squires, 2002).

As a result, some researchers have hinted that many cities are not effectively managing the sport-city relationship (Chalip, 2004; Danielson, 1997; Judd,

1995; Rosentraub, 1999; Weed, 2003). In other words, while we have identified those individuals and groups involved in sport-related civic development,
and the benefits that they receive, it would appear that these groups receive
disproportionate wealth effects, and may not even be maximizing the potential
that sport has within their given communities. Combined with the fact that independent research has not supported claims of the economic development
benefits of local sport (Nunn & Rosentraub, 1995; Rosentraub, 1996; Shropshire, 1995), the following question must be raised: What are cities really doing by pursuing local sport initiatives?

Maximizing Status

We argue here that the fundamental driver of sport-related growth initiatives,
in cities of all sizes, is status. In addition to the aforementioned benefits, urban
regimes within communities consider the presence of sports franchises, events,
and facilities in their communities as sources of status that allow them to differentiate their cities from their perceived competitors. Thus, in terms of the
local sport triad, success in the competition between cities through franchises,
events, and facilities results in perceptions of increased city status. Traditionally, this has referred to the presence of major-league sport(s) in the community. In North American sport, major-league has typically referred to the presence of a MLB, NHL, NBA or NFL team in the community (Shropshire,
1995; Danielson, 1997; Noll & Zimbalist, 1997). It has been suggested that the
presence of a major-league sports team translates into a so-called major-league
status for cities and those that live there (Rosentraub, 1999; Shropshire, 1995).

However, we argue that the concept of major-league status also extends to
cities that host sporting events with international, national, or even regional
relevance (Burbank, 2002; Chalip & McGuirty, 2004), or feature minor league
franchises (Johnson, 1993; Kraus, 2003). As the competition between cities intensifies, the concept of major-league status has grown to include the presence
of a premier sport facility in which the sports team is likely to play (Friedman
et al., 2004; Rosentraub et al., 1994) or in which the sport or other cultural
event is likely to be held (Altshuler & Luberoff, 2003). The concept of status is
ideally viewed through the urban regime's involvement in the local sport triad.

Franchises and Status

In the case of sport teams, civic boosters continue to argue that the most important benefits of a major sports franchise are intangible and therefore impossible to measure solely in economic terms (Judd, 1995). According to Logan and Molotch (2002), sport teams provide an important ideological use
within the city by helping to instill civic pride in business through jingoistic
logic. However, the degree to which major-league status as a city is reflected
by the presence of a sports team remains ambiguous.

In the current globalized economy, North American franchises are increasingly mobile. Quirk and Fort (1999) have highlighted the powers of professional sport leagues which have allowed them to pressure communities into

publicly subsidizing sports facilities, often regardless of cost. Baade (1996) contends that the primary beneficiaries of any taxpayer subsidies are the team owners and players, and not the community at large. When cities are threatened with losing a team, it is the strategies of the urban regime which dictate the local course of action. In the case of the decisions made by the city of Cleveland's urban regime during the 1990s, it is evident that reactive local management strategies, based on "'keeping up" with competitors, are generally not a position of strength for any urban regime. Accommodating the demands of the Indians, Cavaliers, and Browns resulted in increased taxes as well as highly publicized battles among the urban regime's leaders. In spite of this, the city does lay claim however to maintaining its status as a major league sport city.

Status remains an important argument, as it is difficult for cities to measure the economic benefits from having a major-league team (Zimbalist, 1992), and independent studies have hinted that major-league teams have little positive economic impact on their host communities (Rosentraub, 1999). Despite a lack of economic support, clearly cities that have teams and lose them can encounter an image problem (Zimbalist, 1992), depending on the level of competition and the importance of a given sport within a community or region.

For urban regimes actively seeking to improve the status of their cities, the discourse surrounding the city's image or identity through a local professional franchise can be substantial. Place managers operating within the public-private dialectic come to view status as a critical component of place promotion. Media coverage of sport teams often serves to re-enforce local, national, and even international perceptions of status among competing cities. For tourists, the development of a regional image is related to the exposure the region received from people watching games or from viewing media coverage about the local team (Higham & Hinch, 2003).

Events and Status

City status as an attractive place to live and/or to visit is also associated with staging a sporting event (Chalip et al., 2003; Jago et al., 2003). The hosting of sporting events (which can range in scope from the Olympic Games to regional championships/tournaments) is promoted in marketing the city as a desirable place-product. A number of North American cities have designated positions in place management whereby the primary responsibility is to procure events for the city, including Edmonton, AB, Cleveland, OH, and Indianapolis, IN.

The scope of the event generally dictates the exposure generated in marketing the host city (Green, 2003). Thus, larger, spectator-oriented events provide a greater audience for place promotion than do smaller sporting events. In hosting large scale events, the city is able to cultivate an image of being a player in a global landscape of cities, one that extends to a local, regional, and international audience (Whitelegg, 2000).

Yet many cities have also pursued hosting strategies that target smaller-scale events to compliment larger ones (Gibson et al., 2003). Smaller events typically do not require new facilities and they do not garner the media exposure that mega-events are able to. In terms of status, the ability to host a variety of events allows cities to present themselves as an attractive and liveable destination for employers, investors, or tourists (Kearns & Philo, 1993; Whitson, 1998). The ways in which sport events, large and small, are coordinated by members of the urban regime is critical to strategies promoting destination or place status (Chalip & McGuirty, 2004). In this sense, achieving the status of a major league city refers more to the city's capabilities in hosting sporting events of all types than simply mega-events. In addition, this can occur in smaller communities where hosting a smaller scale event can still confer a degree of status on a host community.

Facilities and Status

In North America, place status has also become increasingly associated with the construction of sport facilities that are able to host teams and events (Altshuler & Luberoff, 2003; Friedman & Mason, 2004; Rosentraub, 1999). Sport facilities require generous land, infrastructure, and direct public subsidies because, from an operations perspective, many lose money (Judd, 1995); however, many public officials and civic boosters do not seem concerned that sport, recreation, and tourist infrastructure rarely generate revenue (Judd, 1995). Cagan and deMause (1998) have even suggested that cities incur significant economic and social costs regardless of whether sport facilities are privately or publicly funded.

Yet cities continue to invest in sport facilities as part of local development strategies. Antiquated sport facilities are viewed to be on the wrong side of pro-growth agendas (Pelissero, 1991). Cities that choose not to invest in new sports facilities are threatened by team owners with the team relocation. Similarly, cities without the necessary facilities, or an unwillingness to build new ones, are bypassed in the selection process for hosting sporting events. In most cases, the goal of the urban regime is to "sell" new sport facility development as an economic engine for local development (Searle, 2002). Pagano and Bowman (1995, p. 3) have argued that public officials' views toward local development projects often have less to do with profits and "far more to do with the vision or image officials share about the overall direction a city is taking."

Since research has shown that most facilities, as independent economic development endeavors, do not make sound financial sense (Johnson & Sack, 1996; Paul & Brown, 2001), it stands to reason that cities are viewing sport facilities as a means of attaining (or maintaining) place-based status. As place managers tout urban regeneration around the sport facility as a symbol of local progress, this status is influenced by media coverage of new facility construction. Place promoters highlight prominent sport facilities as being part of the local experience. Therefore sport facilities are increasingly positioned as sites of progress and prosperity. It is the never-ending pursuit of this status that appears to be driving the urban regime's strategic decision-making in many North American cities.

Conclusion

Globalization research has theorized that cities are operating with closer ties to the private sector (Logan & Molotch, 1987; Squires, 2002), that cities are shifting to become centers of consumption (du Gay, 1997; Fainstein & Judd, 1999), and that cities are competing more than ever to attract capital to the community (Hannigan, 1998; Kelly & Grieder, 2003). The city-as-place-product is often described as a "bundle" of services and experiences (Ashworth & Voogt, 1990). In order to compete, the post-modern city has become more entrepreneurial (Harvey, 1989b), and sport has emerged as a key resource, or point of differentiation in many entrepreneurial cities (Cagan & deMause, 1998; Jones, 2002; Noll & Zimbalist, 1997; Quirk & Fort, 1999).

In this paper, we demonstrate that local development initiatives to achieve place-based status are related to the presence of franchises, events, and facilities that bestow a new or heightened level of status on a given city. In this case, perception of what constitutes a major league city is dependent on who the regime views as its competitors and how its competitors view the city. More specifically this is associated with local development strategies intended to promote the local "brand" as a major-league one, or at least one that is superior to that of its rivals, which can occur at any point in a larger hierarchy of cities. According to Brown et al. (2002), local sport contributes to a destination's image and brand as attributes of the destination.

This paper has described those individuals involved in the management and strategic positioning of local sport as a civic resource. In focusing specifically on urban regimes and local sport—in this case, sports franchises, sporting events, and sports facilities—the overlapping interests in the management of place and the management of sport are highlighted. The next step in this process is to examine urban regimes in specific cities to see how sport has been used in unique contexts, to examine how sport fits into broader development initiatives, and how members of local sporting communities network and interact with a city's broader business and political community. Future research thus needs to explore the urban regime and its attempts, via sport-related local development strategies, to attract tourism, investment, and media coverage. In doing so, a greater understanding of how elites in the urban regime see themselves, collectively as a community and/or as a place-product, can be ascertained. While some research has already explored this in a North American context (Friedman & Mason, 2005), a greater understanding of the status-seeking strategies of urban regime elites is required.

From a sport management perspective, this suggests more extensive research on urban regimes, specifically those in the urban regimes that are implicitly involved in the management of place through local sport.

Acknowledgment

The authors would like to thank the Social Sciences and Humanities Research Council of Canada for supporting this research.

References

Abbott, C. (1981) *Boosters and businessmen: Popular economic thought and urban growth in the antebellum Middle West*. Westport, CO: Greenwood Press.

Agger, R. E., Goldrich, D., & Swanson, B. E. (1964). *The rulers and the ruled: Political power and impotence in American communities*. New York: Wiley.

Altshuler, A. A., & Luberoff, D. E. (2003). *Mega-projects: The changing politics of urban public investment*. Washington: Brookings Institute Press.

Appadurai, A. (Ed.). (1996). Playing with modernity: The decolonization of Indian cricket, *Modernity at large: Cultural dimensions of globalization* (pp. 89–113). Minneapolis: University of Minnesota Press.

Ashworth, G. J., & Voogt, H. (1990). *Selling the city*. London: Bellhaven.

Baade, R. (1996). Stadium subsidies make little economic sense for cities: A rejoinder. *Journal of Urban Affairs, 18*(1), 33–37.

Baade, R., & Dye, R. (1988). Sports stadiums and area development: A critical review. *Economic Development Quarterly, 2*(3), 265–275.

Bianchini, F. (1990). *Urban renaissance? The arts and the urban regeneration process*. Liverpool: University of Liverpool.

Booth, D., & Loy, J. (1999). Sport, status and style. *Sport History Review, 30*, 1–26.

Borja, J., & Castells, M. (1997). *Local and global: Management of cities in the Information Age*. London: Earthscan.

Bourdieu, P. (1998). The state, economics and sport. *Culture, Sport, and Society, 1*(2), 115–121.

Brown, G., Chalip, L., Jago, L., & Mules, T. (2002). The Sydney Olympics and brand Australia., In N. Morgan, A. Pritchard, & R. Pride (Eds.), *Destination branding: Creating the unique destination proposition* (pp. 163–185). Oxford: Butterworth-Heinemann.

Burbank, M. J. (2002). Mega-events, urban development, and public policy. *The Review of Policy Research, 19*(3), 179–202.

Cagan, J., & deMause, N. (1998). *Field of schemes: How the great stadium swindle turns public money into private profit*. Monroe, ME: Common Courage Press.

Chalip, L. (2004). Beyond impact: A general model for sport event leverage. In B. W. Ritchie & D. Adair (Eds.), *Sport tourism: Interrelationships, impacts, and issues* (pp. 226–252). Clevedon, UK: Channel View Publications.

Chalip, L. (2005). Marketing, media, and place promotion, In J. Higham (Ed.), *Sport tourism destinations: Issues, opportunities, and analysis* (pp. 162–176). Oxford, UK: Elsevier Butterworth-Heinemann.

Chalip, L., & Leyns, A. (2002). Local business leveraging of a sport event: Managing an event for economic benefit. *Journal of Sport Management, 16*(2), 132–159.

Chalip, L., & McGuirty, J. (2004). Bundling sport events with the host destination. *Journal of Sport Tourism, 9*(3), 267–282.

Chalip, L., Green, B. C., & Hill, B. (2003). Effects of sport event media on destination image and intention to visit. *Journal of Sport Management,17*(3), 214–234.

Colclough, W. G., Daellenbach, L. A., & Sherony, K. R. (1994). Estimating the economic impact of a minor league baseball stadium. *Managerial and Decision Economics, 15*, 497–502.

Crompton, J. L. (1995). Economic impact analysis of sports facilities and events: Eleven sources of misapplication. *Journal of Sport Management, 9*(1), 14–35.

Curry, T. J., Schwirian, K., & Wolduff, R. A. (2004). *High stakes: Big time sports and downtown redevelopment*. Columbus: The Ohio State University Press.

Danielson, M. (1997). *Home team: Professional sports and the American metropolis*. Princeton, NJ: Princeton University Press.

Deccio, C., & Baloglu, S. (2002). Non-host community resident reactions to the 2002 Winter Olympics: The spillover impacts. *Journal of Travel Research, 41*(4), 46–56.

Du Gay, P. (Ed.). (1997). *Production of culture/ cultures of production*. London: Sage.

Dunn, K. M., & McGuirk, P. M. (1999). Hallmark events. In R. Cashman & A. Hughes (Eds.), *Staging the Olympics: The event and impact* (pp. 18–32). Sydney: University of New South Wales Press.

Elkin, S. L. (1985). Twentieth century urban regimes. *Journal of Urban Affairs, 7*(2), 11–28.

Elkin, S. L. (1987). *City and regime in the American Republic*. Chicago: University of Chicago Press.

Euchner, C. C. (1993). *Playing the field: Why sports teams move and cities fight to keep them*. Baltimore: Johns Hopkins University Press.

Fainstein, S., & Judd, D. R. (1999). Global forces, local strategies, and urban tourism. In D. R. Judd & S. Fainstein (Eds.), *The tourist city* (pp. 1–17). New Haven, CT: Yale University Press.

Friedman, M. T., & Mason, D. S. (2004). A stakeholder approach to understanding economic development decision making: Public subsidies for professional sport facilities. *Economic Development Quarterly, 18*(3), 236–254.

Friedman, M. T., & Mason, D. S. (2005). Stakeholder management and the public subsidization of Nashville's coliseum. *Journal of Urban Affairs, 27*, 93–118.

Friedman, M. T., Andrews, D. L., & Silk, M. L. (2004). Sport and the façade of redevelopment in the postindustrial city. *Sociology of Sport Journal, 21*(2), 119–139.

Gibson, H. J. (2003). Sport tourism: An introduction to the special issue. *Journal of Sport Management, 17*(3), 205–213.

Gibson, H. J., Willming, C., and Holdnak, A. (2003). Small-scale event sport tourism: Fans as tourists. *Tourism Management, 24*(2), 181–190.

Green, B. C. (2001). Leveraging subculture and identity to promote sport events. *Sport Management Review, 4*, 1–19.

Green, B. C. (2003). Marketing the host city: Analyzing exposure generated by a sport event. *International Journal of Sports Marketing and Sponsorship, 4*(4), 335–353.

Green, B. C., Costa, C., & Fitzgerald, M. (2003). Marketing the host city: Analyzing exposure generated by a sport event. *International Journal of Sports Marketing and Sponsorship, 4*, 335–352.

Hall, C. M. (1992). *Hallmark tourist events: Impact, management and planning*, London: Belhaven Press.

Hall, C. M. (2005). Selling places: Hallmark events and the reimaging of Sydney and Toronto. In J. Nauright & K. S. Schimmel

(Eds.), *The political economy of sport* (pp. 129–151). Basingstoke: Palgrave Macmillan. Hannigan, J. (1998). *Fantasy City: Pleasure and profit in the postmodern metropolis*. London: Routledge.

Harvey, D. (1989a). From managerialism to entrepreneurialism: The transformation in urban governance in late capitalism. *Geografiska Annaler, 71B*, 3–17.

Harvey, D. (1989b). *The urban experience*. Oxford: Blackwell.

Held, D. & McGrew, A. (Eds.). (2000). *The global transformation reader*. Cambridge: Polity.

Higham, J., & Hinch, T. (2003). Sport, space and time: Effects of the Otago Highlanders franchise on tourism. *Journal of Sport Management, 17*(3), 235–257.

Hinch, T., & Higham, J. (2001). Sport tourism: A framework for research. *International Journal of Tourism Research, 3*, 45–58.

Hinch, T., & Higham, J. (2003). *Sport tourism development*. Clevedon, UK: Channel View Publications.

Jago, L., Chalip, L., Brown, G., Mules, T., & Ali, S. (2003). Building events into destination branding: Insights from experts. *Event Management, 8*(1), 3–14.

Johnson, A. T. (1993). *Minor League Baseball and local economic development*. Urbana, IL: University of Illinois Press.

Johnson, A. T. (1998). Home team/major league losers. *Urban Affairs Review, 33*(4), 579–581.

Johnson, A. T., & Sack, A. (1996). Assessing the value of sports facilities: The importance of non-economic factors. *Economic Development Quarterly, 10*(4)369–381.

Jones, C. (2002). The stadium and economic development: Cardiff and the millennium stadium. *European Planning Studies, 10*(7), 819–829.

Jones, M. T., & Fleming, P. (2003). Unpacking complexity through critical stakeholder analysis: The case of globalization. *Business and Society, 42*(4), 430–454.

Judd, D. R. (1995). Promoting tourism in US cities. *Tourism Management, 16*(3), 175–187.

Judd, D. R. (2002). Promoting tourism in US cities. In S. Fainstein & S. Campbell (Eds.), *Readings in urban theory* (2nd ed., pp. 278–299). Malden, MA: Blackwell.

Judd, D. R. (2003). *The infrastructure of play. Building the tourist city*. Cleveland: M. E. Sharpe.

Kearns, G., & Philo, C. (1993). *Selling places: The city as cultural capital, past and present*. Oxford: Pergamon Press.

Kelly, M., & Grieder, W. (2003). *The divine right of capital: Dethroning the corporate aristocracy*. San Francisco: Barrett-Koehler.

Kraus, R. S. (2003). *Minor League Baseball: Community building through hometown sport*. Binghamton, NY: The Haworth Press.

Loftman, P., & Nevin, B. (1996). Going for growth: prestige projects in three British cities. *Urban Studies, 33*(6), 991–1019.

Logan, J. R., & Molotch, H. L. (1987). *Urban fortunes: The political economy of place*. Berkeley: University of California Press.

Logan, J. R., & Molotch, H. L. (2002). The city as a growth machine. In S. Fainstein & S. Campbell (Eds.). *Readings in urban theory*, (2nd ed., pp. 199–238). Malden, MA: Blackwell.

Mason, D. S., & Duquette, G. H. (2004). Newspaper coverage of early professional ice hockey: The discourses of class and control. *Media History, 10*, 157–173.

Mills, C. W. (1956). *The power elite*. London: Oxford University Press.

Molotch, H. L. (1976). The city as a growth machine. *American Journal of Sociology, 82*, 309–332.

Noll, R., & Zimbalist, A. (1997). Sports, jobs, and taxes: Are new stadiums worth the cost? *The Brookings Review, 15*(3), 35–39.

Nunn, S., & Rosentraub, M. (1995). *Sport wars: Suburbs and center cities in a zero sum game*. Center for Urban Policy and the Environment, Indiana University, Indianapolis.

Owen, K. A. (2002). The Sydney 2000 Olympics and urban entrepreneurialism: Local variations in urban governance. *Australian Geographical Studies, 40*, 323–336.

Pagano, M. A., & Bowman, A. O. (1995). *Cityscapes and capital: The politics of urban development*. Baltimore: Johns Hopkins University Press.

Palmer, J. P. (2002). *Bread and circuses: The local benefits of sports and cultural businesses*. Ottawa: C.D. Howe Institute.

Paul, D., & Brown, C. (2001). Testing the limits of elite influence on public opinion: An examination of sports facility referendums. *Political Research Quarterly, 554*, 871–888.

Pelissero, J. P. (1991). Urban regimes, sports stadiums, and the politics of economic development agendas in Chicago. *Policy Studies Review, 10*(2–3), 117–129.

Perry, D. C. (2003). Urban tourism and the privatizing discourses of public infrastructure. In D. R. Judd (Ed.), *The infrastructure of play*, Armonk, NY: M.E. Sharpe.

Petersen, D. C. (2001). *Developing sports, convention, and performing arts centers* (3rd ed.). Washington, DC: Urban Land Institute.

Philo, C., & Kearns, G. (Eds.). (1993). Culture, history, capital: A critical introduction to the selling of places. *Selling places: The city as cultural capital, past and present* (pp. 1–32). Oxford: Pergamon Press.

Pope, S. W. (1993). Negotiating the "folk highway" of the nation: Sport, public culture, and American identity, 1870–1940. *Journal of Social History, 272*, 327–340.

Quirk, J., & Fort, R. (1999) *Hard ball: The abuse of power in pro team sports*. Princeton, NJ: Princeton University Press.

Rich, W. R. (Ed.). (2000). *The economics and policies of sports facilities*. Westport: Quorum.

Riess, S. A. (2000). Historical perspectives on sports and public policy. In W. C. Rich (Ed.), *The economics and politics of sports facilities* (pp. 13–52). Westport, CT: Quorum Books.

Ritchie, B., Mosedale, L., & King, L. (2002). Profiling sport tourists: The case of super 12 rugby union in Australian capital territory, Australia. *Current Issues in Tourism, 5*(1), 33–44.

Ritchie, J. R. B. (2000). Turning 16 days into 16 years through Olympic legacies. *Event Management, 6,3*, 155–165.

Ritchie, J. R. B., & Smith, B. H. (1991). The impact of a mega-event on host region awareness: A longitudinal study. *Journal of Travel Research*, Summer, 3–10.

Ritzer, G. (1996). *The McDonaldization of society*. Thousand Oaks, CA: Pine Forge Press.

Robertson, R. (1995). Globalisation: Time-space and homogeneity-heterogeneity. In M. Featherstone, S. Lash, & R. Robertson (Eds.), *Global modernities* (pp. 25–44). London: Sage.

Robins, K. (1997). What in the world's going on? In P. D. Gay (Ed.), *Production of culture/cultures of production* (pp. 11–66). London: The Open University.

Rosentraub, M. (1996). Does the emperor have new clothes? A reply to Robert A. Baade. *Journal of Urban Affairs, 18*1, 23–31.

Rosentraub, M. (1999). *Major League losers: The real cost of sports and who's paying for it*, 2nd ed. New York: Basic Books.

Rosentraub, M. S., Swindell, D., Przybylski, M., & Mullins, D. R. (1994). Sport and downtown development strategy: If you build it, will jobs come? *Journal of Urban Affairs, 16*3, 221–239.

Rowe, D., & McGuirk, P. (1999). Drunk for three weeks: Sporting success and city image. *International Review for the Sociology of Sport, 34*(2), 125–141.

Sassen, S. (2002). Cities in a world economy. In S. Fainstein & S. Campbell (Eds.) *Readings in urban theory* (2nd ed., pp. 32–56). Malden, MA: Blackwell.

Schimmel, K. (2002). The political economy of place: Urban and sport studies perspectives. In J. Maguire & K. Young (Eds.) *Theory, sport, and society* (pp. 335–351). London: Elsevier Science.

Searle, G. (2002). Uncertain legacy: Sydney's Olympic stadiums. *European Planning Studies, 10*(7), 845–860.

Seymour, S. (2005). Its legacy lives on, 1995 Canada Winter games forged grand Prairie's sporting community. *Grande Prairie Daily Herald Tribune*, 18 February. Retrieved 29 March from: http://www.canadagames.ca/Content/NewsHome.asp?ItemID=14514&LangID=1.

Shropshire, K. L. (1995). *The sports franchise game: Cities in pursuit of sport franchises, events, stadiums, and arenas*. Philadelphia: University of Pennsylvania Press.

Silver, J. (1996). *Thin ice: Money, politics and the demise of an NHL franchise*. Halifax: Fernwood Publishing.

Sklair, L. (2001). *The transnational capitalist class*. Oxford: Blackwell.

Smith, H. (1994). *Marketing the city: The role of flagship developments in urban regeneration*. London: E&FN Spon.

Squires, G. D. (2002). Partnership and the pursuit of the private city. In S. Fainstein & S. Campbell (Eds.), *Readings in urban theory* (2nd ed., pp. 239–259). Malden, MA: Blackwell.

Stoker, G., & Mossberger, K. (1994). Urban regime theory in comparative perspective. *Environment and Planning C—Government and Policy, 12*(2), 195–212.

Stoker, G., & Mossberger, K. (1995). The post-Fordist local state: The dynamics of its development. In J. Stewart & G. Stoker (Eds.), *Local government in the 1990s* (pp. 210–227). London: Macmillan.

Stone, C. N. (1989). *Regime politics: Governing Atlanta 1946–1988*. Lawrence, KS: University Press of Kansas.

Swindell, D., & Rosentraub, M. S. (1998). Who benefits from the presence of professional sports teams? The implications for public funding of stadiums and arenas. *Public Administration Review, 58*1, 11–20.

Weed, M. (2003). Why the two won't tango! Explaining the lack of integrated policies for sport and tourism in the UK. *Journal of Sport Management, 17*(3), 258–283.

Whitelegg, D. (2000). Going for gold: Atlanta's bid for fame. *International Journal of Urban and Regional Research, 24*(4), 801–817.

Whitson, D. (1998), Circuits of promotion: Media, marketing, and the globalization of sport. In L. Wenner (Ed.), *Mediasport* (pp. 57–72). London: Routledge.

Whitson, D., & Macintosh, D. (1993). Becoming a world-class city: Hallmark cents and sport franchises in the growth strategies of western Canadian cities. *Sociology of Sport Journal, 10*, 221–240.

Whitson, D., & Macintosh, D. (1996). The global circus: International sport, tourism, and the marketing of cities. *Journal of Sport and Social Issues, 20*(3), 278–297.

Wolfson, J., & Frisken, F. (2000). Local responses to the global challenge: Comparing local economic development policies in a regional context. *Journal of Urban Affairs, 22*(4), 361–384.

Zimbalist, A. (1992). *Baseball and billions: A probing look inside the big business of our national pastime*. New York: Basic Books.

Zukin, S. (1995). *The cultures of cities*. Cambridge, MA: Blackwell.

6

SPORT AND THE REPUDIATION OF THE GLOBAL

David Rowe

Introduction: Conceptions of Globalization

The phenomenon of sport is consistently presented as a prime instance of the gathering force of globalization, especially by extending and reconfiguring national cultural practices as global phenomena. As a result, "What may at first seem a national preoccupation takes on global implications" (Wenner, 1998, p. 3). While there can be no doubt that the vast expansion of sport and its associated institutions does, indeed, resonate at the global level (Maguire, 1999), the precise character of these "implications" is nonetheless highly contestable. Not least among the reasons for this analytical uncertainty is the mutability of sport itself as a cultural form and the mantra-like status of the concept of globalization, which is compulsively invoked with varying meanings in different discourses.

In this article, I want to raise the question of whether sport, despite appearances and, especially, the spectacular instances of global mega-media sports events like the Olympics and the football World Cup (not forgetting the more routine forms of mediatized sport circulated around the globe), may be constitutively unsuited to carriage of the project of globalization in its fullest sense.[1] This is a stronger, perhaps more provocative position that goes beyond an apparently emerging consensus in the sociology of sport that cultural nationalism and (g)localism resist globalizing processes, and also that the progress of globalization is unevenly developed across space and time. It suggests, more radically, that the social institution of sport is so deeply dependent on the production of difference that it repudiates the possibility of comprehensive globalization while seeming to foreshadow its inevitable establishment. The first analytical task in canvassing this argument is briefly to secure the "floating signifier" of globalization.

The master concept of globalization has, in less than two decades, passed from a technical term circulating among a limited number of academic economists, political scientists, and sociologists to an all-purpose buzz-word deployed by bank economists, politicians, and "lay" social commentators (Waters, 1995). As I (with co-authors) have argued elsewhere, globalization has also largely supplanted "postmodernity" in sociology (and, indeed, in cultural studies) as an omnibus concept used to explain transformations and to describe their outcomes in totalizing fashion (Miller et al., 2001, pp. 6–7). The analytical utility of the concept of globalization is similarly compromised when it is used, mechanically and teleologically, to describe all manner of developments from growing homogeneity to fragmentation.

At an abstract level, globalization can be regarded as a long-standing tendency within modernity that compresses time and space, and so links, in new and accelerated ways, localities that hitherto had little direct connection (Giddens, 1990). Such a synoptic approach leaves open the task of teasing out the manifold, directional complexities of globalization as it is played out "at ground level," and the multiple permutations of, in the case of sport, its impacts on reception, interpretation, organization, and practice. These developments have unfolded through complex intrication with the processes of governmentalization, Americanization, televisualization and commodification operating in the context of a developing new international division of cultural labor in sport and other cultural forms (Miller et al., 2001).

Hence, not only are there competing theories of globalization, but also contending accounts of how this process interacts with others — and, indeed, the extent to which it is separable from them. At one end of the theoretical spectrum, globalization is a technical term describing the greater economic, political, technological, and communicative connectivity that has been evolving for centuries. While this enhanced connectivity is seen as imposing new constraints on individual societies (in relation to trade barriers, the cost of labor and so on), its cultural consequences can be regarded as indeterminate and, indeed, as capable of liberating local people from their inherited cultural particularities in new, unpredictable, "unscripted" ways. At the other end of the spectrum, globalization is figured as a transformative process at every level, accelerating rapidly since the late 20th century, systematically eroding locally specific structures and practices, and imminently ushering in a common global culture. In both accounts, the entity standing between the local and global spaces is the nation, conceived as both a politico-juridical organization and as a representational focus of culture that may or may not overlap with it.

In this article I will focus on the cultural dimensions of globalization as they apply to the idea of nation, threading some reflections on the 2002 FIFA Korea/Japan World Cup through the discussion by way of illustration. While recognizing the inseparability of culture from other components of the social formation, it is the cultural nation that, in the case of sport (especially that of an international, competitive kind), is simultaneously problematized and mobilized by globalization. The nature and durability of this dynamic tension needs to be assessed in the light of claims that sport is a key agency of globalization.

Globalization and the National Cultural

Alan Bairner (2001, p.1) notes at the commencement of his book *Sport, Nationalism, and Globalization* that, while many tentative propositions can be presented concerning sport, identities and social practices:

One theory, however, that is put forward with a greater degree of confidence suggests that, as a result of the process known as globalization, the relationship between sport and *national* identity is self-evidently unravelling to reveal an increasingly global sporting culture.

This is a powerful and persuasive theoretical position that appeals both to commonsensical observation and empirical evidence. Bairner's book, however, repays some close attention in revealing the theory's limitations through its seven national case studies drawn from Europe and North America, laying bare the invented traditions of many competing, contradictory "ethnic" and "civic" nationalisms in the process. These include the sporting practices and affiliations of those Protestants of Northern Ireland who are loyal subjects of the British monarchy and hostile to the Irish republic, but who are also involved in "all-Ireland" sports like golf, tennis, cricket, field hockey, and rugby union, some of which have "national" representative status.

The sporting nation, then, has deep historical roots that may cross nation-state boundaries and divisions of identity influenced by class, culture, education, gender, religion, and politics, creating here "a tripartite distinction between British, universal, and Gaelic games" (Bairner, 2001, p. 28) that marks out different relations to such sports as rugby, soccer, basketball, and hurling. These distinctions and permutations are multiplied by international representative sport regulations that can see citizens of different countries playing as teammates, while in other cases competing against each other. In addition, there are distinct affiliations of the nationalist and Catholic minority in the Six Counties, historic religion-based connections with Scotland, and some support for the more glamorous English and continental European football teams and African American-led basketball teams in the USA.

In examining Scotland and Ireland, traditional Gaelic games are shown to be limited for the former by region and by their incapacity to play the Old Enemy (England) in asserting Scottish national identity, whereas in Ireland, Gaelic games like handball and *camogie* have been of greater national significance through the encouragement of the Gaelic Athletic Association (Cumann Lúthchleas Gael). Yet Protestants (some of whom were Irish nationalists) are shown to have been instrumental in the formation of the Association (which still operates in the North). While football has made considerable inroads into the Irish sporting formation (with, for example, considerable support evident for its well-performing team in the 2002 World Cup), it is by no means an "open market" for imported sports. Bairner, for example, observes that "with the exception of basketball, American sports have had a negligible impact in Ireland" (2001, p. 89). The case of Sweden displays both similarities and differences, with a historical rejection of "excessive" sporting nationalism and celebration of an anti-competitive ethos favored by the Swedish Sport Confederation (Riksidrottsförbundet), counterbalanced today by vigorous displays of support by Swedish football and tennis fans, their faces painted with the national flag. Here there is evidence of support for both a traditional sporting ethos within the nation and an aggressive assertion of national identity in the arena of global sport.

In Bairner's North American case studies, ice hockey is shown to be even more crucial to the maintenance of Canadian identity (see also Miller et al., 2001, pp. 74–78) as franchises and players migrate south and Canadian dominance has been threatened by other nations. At such moments, key sporting figures like "Number 99" Wayne Gretzky become bearers of "Canadianness" (Jackson, 2001). The USA, in contrast, so routinely regarded as culturally imperialist (often in the name of globalization), is shown to be culturally protectionist in the mobilization of myths of nation through sports such as American football and baseball (Juffer, 2002). Bairner's case studies demonstrate, then, neither the successful insulation of national sporting culture nor its obliteration by sporting globalization. Among its many complexities, however, is a clear pattern that perceptions of external threat—mainly the erosion of the national by a malign combination of Americanization and globalization—provoke defensive responses that may be effective through strategic adaptation and new combinations of sporting forms, practices, and personnel in national contexts.

Such close and reflexive analysis indicates the necessity of going beneath the surface sheen of globalization rhetoric and media sport economics to the sociocultural sphere that reveals sport's less-than-smooth accommodation to the disciplines of global production, consumption, mythology, and identity. Certainly, from the case of the 2002 Korea/Japan World Cup Final between Brazil and Germany, with an estimated global audience of 1.5 billion collectively exposed to the corporate logos of such global brands as Nike, adidas, Yahoo!, McDonalds, Budweiser, Philips, and Fujifilm, it appears self-evident that sport is globalization's most attentive handmaiden. Such sporting megaevents are especially dramatic presentiments of a fully developed global culture of the future, in which the "whole world is watching" (in an ironic echo of the civil rights slogan of the 1960s) the same thing at the same time. Viewed in a negative light, sport emerges here as the social institution that has taken over the function analogous to that of the school as characterized by Ivan Illich (1971, p. 48), with its ideological and organizational diffusion making it "eminently suited to be the World Church of our decaying culture."

Less apocalyptically, sports mega-events are, as Maurice Roche (2000, p. 227) argues, important constituents of an "evolving global cultural economy." Within this framework of "interconnected political, economic and cultural institutions, systems and processes" (2000, p. 226), sport interpellates "the world," requiring more countries to invest in professionalized participation in selected sports, and inducing more people to consume the paraphernalia of sports culture (like Chicago Bulls and Manchester United shirts) circulating as cultural capital in previously unlikely places. Again, in the 2002 World Cup, television images were generated of a potentially postnational sports fandom, with some Japanese fans (although especially after the Japanese team had been eliminated) adopting the stylistic inscriptions and accoutrements of selected elements of a distantiated English football culture. So, where sport can be detached from strong, spatially limited identities, the prospect of global sport—and so of global society, culture, economy, and polity—comes into clearer view.

Yet this picture may be deceptive, and sport seen as stubbornly resistant to the "harder" forms of globalization because of its dependency on the robustness of the *idea* of the sporting nation. Sport certainly has manifest advantages for the project of globalization: it is a cultural practice that, at the elite level at least, takes place according to standardized rules in delimited time and space with a ready-made "on-site" audience. It is readily amenable to televisualization—or if it is not it can be modified to make it so—allowing a massive inflation of audience size for the purposes of exposure to advertising of a heavily branded kind. But at the heart of sport's ethos is the idea of competition. This is what provides sport with its drama, but its affective force derives directly from the connotative attachment of competition to identity.

The Sport and Identity Paradox

Sports events and their outcomes become most meaningful and powerful—and so most amenable to capital accumulation and political exploitation—where there can be an extrapolation of sociocultural significance from the action on and around the field of play. This split discourse of sport is produced in the interplay of tensions between "noble" universalism and "base" partisanship. Sport's reliance on passionate national differentiation and celebrity is so thoroughgoing as to question its suitability as an exemplar of global culture. In this sense, sport is rather less sympathetic to globalization than other cultural forms, such as music (Rowe, 1995) or film, which may be more easily communicated as universal in nature and, even when deeply connected to notions of identity, do not necessarily foreground the idea of hierarchically based, competitive national performance.

The history of sport in modernity is conventionally written as a process of cultural diffusion from Victorian Britain, with rationalized and regulated physical play either directly exported as part of the apparatus of imperialism and/or absorbed through the unfolding process of (post)colonialism. The commodification of sport, perfected in the United States, then produced second and successive waves of sports diffusion, as much through appropriation and advocacy by the state as by the market. The development of the apparatus of sport in each country varies according to the specific character of its historical social formation, but there are few sports that have not—either voluntarily or under duress—been aligned with some conception of nation. This is because international sporting competition functions so effortlessly as metaphor for the state of the nation at the popular political level, while at the level of cultural economy "indigenous" sports are less tradable within the burgeoning "media sports cultural complex" in all but the largest and most affluent sports markets (Rowe, 1999). In fact, despite the success of sport in the institutionalized diffusion of the framework for regulated, competitive physical play, the record of the actual "export" of national sports is much less impressive. Truly international sport consists only of a relatively small set of games that are regularly and readily translatable as the "Esperanto" of mediatized entertainment. Nonetheless, any sport can claim to be "international" even where contested by a limited set of territories marked by geopolitical and/or sporting systems of governance (for example, rugby league), or where it is dominated by one country while attracting overseas fan interest and foreign labor (as in the case of US baseball and its domestic World Series).

This structural importance of the nation persists despite the increasing circulation of sportspeople around the globe as part of the new international division of cultural labor. For example, more association football players operate outside their countries of origin than ever before, and their clubs complain of the loss of, and potential damage to, their labor power caused by international demands (while frequently threatening to set up rival, cross-national club competitions such as a European Super League). Football more than any sport can lay claim to be the "global game" (Giulianotti, 1999). Yet the clubs still retain a "national" brand irrespective of the composition of their playing and coaching staff and of their shareholder register, and their players are still expected to return to "home base" in their respective continents for peak international sports tournaments like the World Cup. Furthermore, as Patrick Mc-Govern (2002) has recently noted in analyzing patterns of recruitment of foreign players[2] to the English football leagues between 1946 and 1995, labor-market trends have been international rather than global in nature, and the range of supply countries highly limited. His study (albeit one that stops just before the crucial 1996 Bosman European Court of Justice ruling that deregulated footballer movement within the European Union)[3] shows that:

> . . . the changes that are taking place do not suggest that a single, global labor market either has, or is, emerging. Rather, markets are expanding along different international patterns that have national elements as the English case suggests. (McGovern, 2002, p. 39)

In particular, a preference is shown for players who socially, culturally, and linguistically resemble those who are hiring them — a case of "homosocial reproduction" (Kanter, 1997).

The nation, therefore, is never far below the surface of sports discourse, always threatening to assert itself and to circumscribe the free circulation of sports personnel and the meanings that can be derived from its operation (see e.g., Duke & Crolley, 1996; Stevenson, 2002). As Dayan and Katz (1992) note, media sports events generate "contest" narrative forms that are perfectly suited to articulations of nation. Sport's dependency on the nation, therefore, always reinserts the restrictive framework of modernity into the fluid workings of post-modernity. In so doing — and in a highly emotional manner — sport operates as a perpetual reminder of the social limits to the reconfiguration of endlessly mutable identities and identifications.

This does not have to be the literal invocation of the nation state. As noted above, the sporting nation is not coterminous with the sovereign, legal nation. In events like the football World Cup, the non-existent English nation, as symbolized by the flag of St. George, can materialize in international sporting competition (see following discussion), just as Catalan nationalists strategically capitalized on the opportunities afforded by the 1992 Barcelona Olympics (Hargreaves, 2000). International sport can, then, be a key marker of national fantasy or aspiration, but above all it is generative of a symbolic entity that comes into being by affixing a notion of identity that is likely to be an impediment to the free-floating cosmopolitanism so crucial to the ethos of globalization.

It could be objected that, in an adaptation of a classical Marxist economic base–cultural superstructure model, sport's fixation on the nation functions as cover for more profound changes occurring at the political economic level. Sport can, therefore, be seen as a sop to sovereignty and difference, masking the creeping control of global institutions. On screen, the world secular religion of football might appear to fuse with branded transnational capitalist consumption, leading the football teams of nations to resemble just so many niches in a global market. Mega-media sports events do, indeed, reflect the domination of the North America–Europe–Japan triad in trade and foreign direct investment (Hirst and Thompson, 1999). Of the 15 partners (that is, major sponsors) of the Korea/Japan 2002 World Cup, 14 came from the Triad (six from the USA, two from Europe, and six from Japan), with the remaining partner coming from co-host Korea, in a tournament organized by FIFA (the acronym for the Fédération Internationale de Football Association), the historically Francophile peak governing body (Tomlinson, 1986).

Of course, the restricted scope of globalization in such examples provides its own questioning of the globalization thesis, but even if global power were to be more widely dispersed, a left functionalist perspective reduces sport's complex workings within the popular sociocultural sphere to that of a mechanical effect of capitalist ideology. While the potential for ideological manipulation of sport and the tendency towards conservatism of sporting organizations and personnel is readily apparent, the ideological complexion of the institution of sport cannot be so neatly classified, just as expressions of nationalism do not in all instances operate as ideological cement preserving the unity of class-ridden societies for the benefit of their ruling class. Here globalization might be said to have its progressive side as a counterweight to ultra-nationalism.

The rhetoric of globalization does, however, in practice predominantly reflect the drive of global capital to extend and deepen its dominion. But even if its dynamic impulses were more benign, sport's constant evocation of the nation as its anchor point and rallying cry makes for an uneasy relation to globalization advocacy. It is improbable that sport can be reconfigured as postnational and substantially stripped of its "productive" capacity to promote the forms of identity (local, national, geopolitical, racial and so on) because these are, simultaneously, the source of its affective power and the potentially activated resistive impediments to the globalization process. This paradox was evident in global sport's most recent and spectacular festival.

Reflections on the Korea/Japan World Cup, 2002

Observation of the recent Korea/Japan World Cup from three different vantage points illustrates how the nation, imagined or real, is so central to sport as to present a constant potential interruption to the smooth passage of globalization. This was not a rigorous methodological exercise, but an attempt to trace elements of national cultural formations during a mega-media global sports event. "La Coupe du Monde," as the peak spectacle of the self-described "world game," generating massive broadcast rights fees (although somewhat problematic in the light of the collapse of KirchMedia, which had purchased the rights from FIFA) and recruiting major corporate partners, seems to represent globalization in and through sport par excellence.

But there are limits even to the cultural portability of association football. In countries where it is known as "soccer," like Australia, Canada, New Zealand, and the US, the linguistic marker signifies that it is not the dominant code of football. This word choice may also have an explicitly political edge, as in the case of the Irish nationalist preference for the term "soccer" to demarcate it more effectively from "indigenous" Gaelic football. Korea/Japan 2002, it could be argued, nonetheless represented a substantial step toward the globalization of football with the appearance for the first time of China, the world's most populous nation. China's involvement, however, also raised the stakes of the nationalist rivalry in east Asia that was so starkly revealed in the difficult relationship between the co-hosts, whose deep historical enmity is well known, and between whom there is continuing tension over the Japanese educational erasure of culpability for Second World War atrocities, and reluctance to make reparation (Horne & Manzenreiter, 2002). Ironically, furthermore, as Korea met Turkey in the play-off for third place, North Korea (recently pronounced part of the Axis of Evil by the US government) and its southern neighbor were involved in a naval engagement resulting in several fatalities on both sides, and placing the militaries of both nations on full alert. This failure of the World Cup's equivalent of the *Pax Olympia* (the cessation of hostilities during the ancient Olympics) dramatically revealed the limitations of sport as a global pacifier and, in this case, the potential of the World Cup to exacerbate regional national resentment (see Sugden & Tomlinson, 1998).

Mega-media sports events like the World Cup and the Olympics take place at particular sites, and what occurs is relayed to differentiated audiences in customized fashion (de Moragas Spà et al., 1995). Watching the World Cup from the vantage point of three countries with different historical and contemporary experiences of football (as I did fleetingly during the 2002 competition) demonstrated how the same spectacle mutates according to national context and viewing position. The main focus here is on the UK, where interest in the event was (understandably, given England's participation) more intense, with brief observations of contrasting national cultural milieu.

In Australia, the World Cup could be watched on television in prime time as the tournament was taking place in the Asia-Pacific region for the first time. Australia, however, has only once qualified for the World Cup (in 1974), and failed to do so again in 2002. This meant that football spectators in Australia had a wider repertoire of viewing positions than those of participating nations. These included the universalist appreciation of the world game; "adoption" of a favorite team (on some grounds of affinity, glamour, and so on); the finding of Australian connections (such as an Italian player who had lived in the country as a child); and (as would have often occurred irrespective of Australia's involvement) support for a team of the viewer's national-ethnic origin, such as Italy, England, Turkey, China, and South Africa. In the case of Australia, therefore, the *absence* of direct national representation opened up more diverse viewing spaces than would have been possible had the national team qualified, which would have immediately mobilized an intense, nationalist discourse. The nation, present or absent, is then still crucial to the experience of the World Cup. The location, geopolitical position, history and demography of the nation will, in turn, condition responses to the event at the various points of intersection with global forces.

This observation was borne out in a different country visited briefly during the World Cup (not counting the credit card advertisements and screened games in the quasi-postnational space of the airport transit lounge). Holland, unlike Australia, usually reaches the World Cup but also did not qualify for Korea/Japan 2002. Association football is the dominant winter sport in that country (rather than the "poor cousin" as it is in Australia), thereby seeming to create greater resentment at non-participation. Far distant from the site of the tournament, "Europeanness" came to the fore in Holland, with a greater concentration on and identification with Dutch- and Europe-based players and teams. Some supporters of the Dutch team were able to express negative identification in the form of the teams that they didn't want to win (and, contra European unity, this seemed mainly to be France or Germany).

In cabled European televisual space, however, British, German, Belgian, French, and other nation's viewers could watch their team as presented by their own national broadcasters. Touristic spaces were created for viewing the World Cup, some of which had the quality of postmodern pastiche, as in the cases of the English and Irish theme pubs promising "All World Cup Games Live." At a time when the most conspicuous political issue in the European Union (signaled by a turn to the right in France, Italy, Denmark, Austria, and Holland itself) was immigration and asylum seekers, there was visible support on Dutch streets for the various nations of origin that comprise the contemporary Netherlands, such as Tunisia, Brazil, and Nigeria. As might be expected of viewers of an international tournament, the emblems of nation were everywhere to the fore, and few seemed to take the opportunity to adopt a position of neutrality in the role of global cultural citizen.

This role was even less visible in the next nation state visited — the UK — and, within it, the sporting nation of England. "Britishness" had been much fore-grounded during recent golden jubilee celebrations of the reign of Queen Elizabeth II as a constitutional monarch, although the flag of St. George, as an emblem of England, supplemented and often replaced the Union Jack (the sign of the nation state in a now post-Scots, Welsh, and Northern Irish devolution Britain) in bedroom and shop windows, and other publicly visible sites. The World Cup offered an even more compelling opportunity for the aggressive assertion of "Englishness" through the flag of St. George and licensed a temporary, symbolic secession from Great(er) Britain (mirrored, it might be noted, in pre-tournament debates in Scotland concerning the "traitorous" tendency there to support any team playing against England). As in earlier tournaments (see e.g., Carrington & McDonald, 2001, and Garland & Rowe, 1999, on jingoism during Euro '96), the participation of a team, extracted from the nation state and invested with a specific national character for the purposes of sport, activated conceptions of the nation that were the antithesis of "progressive" global cosmopolitanism. While it is necessary to be cautious in naively ascribing cultural and ideological representativeness to the tabloid press, the popular media amplified strong, nostalgic, and inevitably fantastical myths of nation in and through football.

To take a small number of examples, *The Sun* opened its front-page text with the anticipatory statement that "All of England will get up for the Cup tomorrow to see our heroes tackle Nigeria . . . at half past Sven [the given name of the England's Swedish-born manager]" (Clench, 2002, p. 1), while the back-page headline recorded the "Beckham Battle-Cry" to "FINISH THE JOB LADS" (Howard, 2002, p. 56). For the next game, *The Sun* promised that, "ENGLAND'S soccer heroes will inflict pain on the Danes today by booting them out of the World Cup" (2002b, p. 1). As a game against Brazil approached, the wrap-around front and back page consisted of only player and manager headshots and the headline "YOU CAN DO IT LADS" (*The Sun*, 2002d, p.1), while inside stories included "One Flies Flag for the Lads" carrying a fake Internet photograph of the queen in an England shirt with her face painted with the flag of St. George (*The Sun*, 2002c, p. 3). The story "BEAT 'EM FOR MY GRANDAD, Says Bobby Moore's [the late, World Cup winning England captain] grandson" (*The Sun*, 2002a, p. 6) was one of many nostalgic references to England's solitary World Cup tournament win in 1966. The *Daily Mirror* (2002a, p. 1), for example, on the same day listed 12 reasons "WHY WE'LL WIN" on its front page, adding that these were all precedents from 1966.

On the day of the game, the front page of the *Daily Mirror* (2002b, p. 1) consisted of white space, a small flag of St. George and the small, centered headline, "This page is cancelled. Nothing else matters." Its World Cup supplement noted that, while the "loyalties" of Japanese fans (we might note, in global postmodern style terms) were "split": "The whole of England has been brought together with a dream of victory. We want it, we need it, we crave it. The country is speaking with one voice: DO IT FOR US!" (*World Cup Mirror*, 2002, p. 1). The next day, after England's loss, the *Daily Mirror*'s (2002c, p. 1) black wrap-around carried a front-page picture focusing on distraught England goalkeeper David Seaman, accompanied by the headline "Anyone for tennis," while the back page carried an image of a controversial German victory in the same round with the statement "AND JUST WHEN YOU THOUGHT IT COULDN'T GET ANY WORSE . . ." Within a few days, *The Sun* (2002e, p. 1) rearticulated football and monarchy with the emphasis on the latter, carrying a prominent front-page image of Prince William in jeans juggling a football.

This brief snapshot of English tabloid media discourse during the 2002 World Cup illustrates the ways in which international sport compulsively reactivates and recirculates long-standing and emergent myths of nation. Constant homages were paid to "our lads" and "our heroes," with frequent cross-references to serving military personnel in Afghanistan such as the Royal Marines, who were "hunting Taliban" while monitoring the progress of the World Cup during their tour of duty (Crossie et al., 2002, p. 2). Interpellations of the national "us" (despite the fact that the national "we" is an effect of sporting governmentality — and incorporates "citizens" who are not football supporters of any kind) constitute the kind of discourse that is inimical to globalization rhetorics. For example, in Britain, confronted with the prospect of a referendum on the replacement of the national currency (sterling) in favor of the multinational Euro, the World Cup fostered a political and cultural climate that was unlikely to be favorable to changes seeming to infringe national sovereignty by replacing the heavily symbolic pound in the name of cross-border exchange rate efficiency. The cultural atmosphere in early 21st-century England was close to the kind of discourse reflected in much earlier representations of sport and nationhood, such as Geoffrey Green's famous reflections in the London *Times* on the significance of the English national team's first home defeat at (the now controversially under renovation) Wembley Stadium by "communist" Hungary in 1953: "England at last [were] beaten by the foreign invader on solid English soil" (quoted in Miller et al., 2001, p. 43).

During the 2002 World Cup, the English nationalist fetishization of David Beckham's hair and left foot, and of Michael Owen's groin; the continuing reference to the Falklands/Malvinas War on the eve of its 20th anniversary in the lead-up to the game against Argentina; and the anxiety about a possible German tournament win, were all examples of the foregrounding of local, idiosyncratic rivalries and identifications. On a wider stage, the victory of first-time participants Senegal over world champions France in the opening match (the country in which most team members regularly play their football) was open to (post)colonial interpretation, just as the first-time hosting of the World Cup in Asia provoked interpretive narratives of the rising nations of the Orient challenging the established hegemony of the Occident (Larmer, 2002). Spectacular expressions of South Korean nationalism (an estimated four million Koreans publicly celebrated their quarter-final win) and the more general carnivalesque presentations of national culture that football generates problematize the meanings and effects of sport. The sport carnival's turning of the "world upside down" by celebrating the (legal or imagined) nation may be interpreted in functionalist terms as a safety valve for resistance to globalization. But, less automatically, it can clearly operate as a force that provides considerable cultural reinforcement for those who wish to preserve older structures and boundaries — and, indeed, to (re)construct new ones.

Conclusion: Repudiating the Global?

This article has had one principal aim — to interrogate conventional claims that sport, especially in the shape of mega-media events, is a harbinger of globalization, especially at the cultural level. While the discourses presented display a range of potential applications to the concepts of globalization and of nation, it appears that international sport's fundamental reliance on localized, nationally inflected forms of identity inevitably also offers resources for the mobilization of conscious and unconscious anti-globalization perspectives. This position does not mean ignoring the development of a global cultural economy in which sport is a central player, or romanticizing the nation as an inherently virtuous bearer of positive human values. But it does question whether sport's primary organizational framework valorizing identity-based competition, despite its many variations, will inevitably assist the completion of cultural globalization in its most advanced sense.

Thus, perhaps the project of globalization will have to look elsewhere for an ideal sociocultural institution that is not likely to trigger, with considerable intensity, the kind of cultural nationalism evidenced by sport. There is certainly no immediate prospect of the uncoupling of the sport–nation nexus. As has been argued, such a reconceptualization of sport would simultaneously erode (if not destroy) a key component of the affective power that is translatable into economic capital. As David L. Andrews and C. L. Cole (2002: 123) argue in a recent issue of the *Journal of Sport and Social Issues* devoted to "The Nation Reconsidered," the "nation remains a virulent force in everyday lived experience" despite the current "global moment." Under these circumstances sport may not, ultimately, be so much a repudiation of the idea of the global in the fullest — that is, comprehensively cultural — sense, as something of a disappointment to it.

Thus, sociologists of sport need to go beyond the current accumulation of evidence of the resilience of the national, the local, and the particular. While useful, this growing body of empirical knowledge tends to be furnished as an indication of the limits to globalization arising from unwillingness or inability to translate global prescriptions into local structures and practices. In this regard, sport is little different from other cultural forms bearing the imprint of globalizing pressures alongside the signs that they have not been completely accommodated. Deeper consideration might be given to the lineaments of the institutional formation of sport itself, and to the analytical possibility that sport may do more than exhibit and resist different elements of globalization. Sport's compulsive attachment to the production of national difference may, instead, constitutively repudiate the embrace of the global.

Notes

I would like to thank two anonymous reviewers for their constructive and helpful suggestions that have improved the final version of this article.

1. It is important to be precise about the "mega" concepts analyzed here without becoming too deeply immersed in expository debate. The "global level" is regarded as the supra-national stratum of institutional operation that, at least ideationally, transcends particularist institutions and relations. The "project of globalization" is proposed as the discursive logic of such "postparticularism" rather than the desired outcome of any specific set of elite individuals or institutions. For the purposes of the argument globalization is being construed in its strongest, most totalizing sense. It has, of course, been variously argued that the global and the local interpenetrate, conceptually and empirically, as Roland Robertson's (1995) often-cited neologism "glocalization" reveals. Here, however, the full discursive logic of globalization — which is commonly mobilized in a range of academic and other contexts — is countenanced. The "nation" in its various formulations here ("cultural," "sporting," "sovereign," "legal," "imagined") is understood not as a fixed empirical object, but as a mutable concept applied to a diverse range of symbolic and material relations invoking an identified "people" and their variously construed distinctive institutions, practices and values.

2. It should be noted that by far the largest "foreign" source in footballing terms came from the same nation state — Scotland.

3. Jonathan Magee and John Sugden (2002: 421) note that, by the 1998–9 season, over 500 "overseas" players operated in the English leagues, comprising 45 percent of squad players in the elite Premier League. They, however, use a more conventional core–periphery model than a globalization model per se.

References

Andrews, D. L., & Cole, C. L. (2002). The nation reconsidered. *Journal of Sport and Social Issues 26*(2), 123–124.

Bairner, A. (2001). *Sport, nationalism, and globalization: European and North American perspectives*. Albany: State University of New York Press.

Carrington, B., & McDonald, I. (Eds.). (2001). *"Race," sport and British society*. London and New York: Routledge.

Clench, J. (2002). Up for the Cup: Clock it to 'em Becks, *The Sun* (11 June), 1.

Crossie, P., Thompson, P., & Kay, J. (2002). Eggs and Beckham: Millions lap up big breakfast and footie feast, *The Sun* (11 June), 2.

Daily Mirror (2002a). Why we'll win: The year was . . . 1966 (20 June), 1.

Daily Mirror (2002b). This page is cancelled: Nothing else matters (21 June), 1.

Daily Mirror (2002c). Anyone for tennis? And just when you thought it couldn't get any worse . . . (22 June), 1.

Dayan, D., & Katz, E. (1992). *Media events: The live broadcasting of history*. Cambridge, MA: Harvard University Press.

de Moragas Spà, M., Rivenburgh, N. K., & Larson, J. F. (1995). *Television in the Olympics*. London: John Libbey.

Duke, V., & Crolley, L. (1996). *Football, nationality and the state*. Harlow: Longman.

Garland, J., & Rowe, M. (1999). "War minus the shooting? Jingoism, the English press, and Euro 96," *Journal of Sport and Social Issues, 23*(1), 80–95.

Giddens, A. (1990). *The consequences of modernity*. Cambridge: Polity.

Giulianotti, R. (1999). *Football: A sociology of the global game*. Cambridge: Polity.

Hargreaves, J. (2000). *Freedom for Catalonia? Catalan nationalism, Spanish identity and the Barcelona Olympic Games*. Cambridge: Cambridge University Press.

Hirst, P., & Thompson, G. (1999). *Globalization in question* (2nd ed.). Cambridge: Polity.

Horne, J., & Manzenreiter, W. (Eds.). (2002). *Japan, Korea and the 2002 World Cup*. London: Routledge.

Howard, S. (2002). Finish the job, lads: Beckham battle-cry, *The Sun* (11 June), 56.

Illich, I. (1971). *Deschooling society*. New York: Harper & Row.

Jackson, S. J. (2001). Gretzky nation: Canada, crisis and Americanization. In D. L. Andrews & S. J. Jackson (Eds.), *Sport stars: The cultural politics of sporting celebrity* (pp. 164–86). London and New York: Routledge.

Juffer, J. (2002). Who's the man? Sammy Sosa, Latinos, and televisual representations of the "American pastime." *Journal of Sport and Social Issues, 26*(4), 337–59.

Kanter, R. M. (1977). *Men and women of the corporation*. New York: Basic Books.

Larmer, B. (2002). An empty feeling. *Newsweek* (17 June), 36–41.

McGovern, P. (2002). Globalization or internationalization? Foreign footballers in the English League, 1946–95. *Sociology, 36*(1), 42.

Magee, J., & Sugden, J. (2002). "The world at their feet": Professional football and international labour migration. *Journal of Sport and Social Issues, 26*(4), 421–37.

Maguire, J. (1999). *Global sport: Identities, societies, civilizations*. Cambridge: Polity.

Miller, T., Lawrence, G., McKay, J., & Rowe, D. (2001). *Globalization and sport: Playing the world*. London: Sage.

Robertson, R. (1995). Glocalization: Time–space and homogeneity–heterogeneity. In M. Feather-stone, S. Lash, & R. Robertson (Eds.), *Global modernities* (pp. 25–44). London: Sage. Roche, M. (2000) *Mega-events and modernity: Olympics and Expos in the growth of global culture*. London and New York: Routledge.

Rowe, D. (1995). *Popular cultures: Rock music, sport and the politics of pleasure*. London: Sage.

Rowe, D. (1999). *Sport, culture and the media: The unruly trinity*. Buckingham: Open University Press.

Stevenson, D. (2002). Women, sport and globalization: Competing discourses of sexuality and nation. *Journal of Sport and Social Issues 26*(2), 209–25.

Sugden, J., & Tomlinson, A. (1998). *FIFA and the contest for world football: Who rules the people's game?* Cambridge: Polity.

The Sun (2002a). Beat 'em for my grandad, says Bobby Moore's grandson" (15 June), 6.

The Sun (2002b). Danish quakin': We'll stuff Hagar's boys" (15 June), 1.

The Sun (2002c). One flies flag for the lads" (20 June), 3.

The Sun (2002d). You can do it, lads" (20 June), 1.

The Sun (2002e). World Cup Willie (24 June), 1.

Tomlinson, A. (1986). Going global: The FIFA story. In A. Tomlinson & G. Whannel (Eds.), *Off the ball: The Football World Cup* (pp. 83–98). London: Pluto.

Waters, M. (1995). *Globalization*. London: Routledge.

Wenner, L. A. (1998). Playing the mediasport game. In L. A. Wenner (Ed.), *MediaSport* (pp. 3–13). London and New York: Routledge.

World Cup Mirror (2002) Divided nation, united nation" (21 June), 1.

PART II

CASE STUDIES IN THE NEW SPORT MANAGEMENT

7

THE FOUR DOMAINS OF SPORTS MARKETING: A CONCEPTUAL FRAMEWORK

Sam Fullerton and G. Russell Merz

Introduction to Sports Marketing

The concept of "sports marketing" is ambiguous in its meaning for both practitioners and academicians. Discussions about its application in the popular press and in many textbooks include categories ranging from tickets to spectator sports to sport-related wagers in legal gambling establishments (Shannon, 1999). Some tend to take a narrow view about what the discipline of sports marketing encompasses. To them, the primary task is one of selling tickets and putting fans in the seats at organized sports events (Sports Marketing Surveys, 2002), thereby equating the sports product to tickets for spectator sports. This definition, broadly applied, may include the sale of tickets for minor events such as high school sports and minor league ice hockey, but the prevailing thinking focuses on major sports properties such as an NCAA Division IA (FBS) college football game, a NASCAR event, the Super Bowl, and the Olympics. Undoubtedly, this perspective reflects the vast marketing expenditures for these major properties.

With the 2008 Summer Olympics fast approaching, Du Wei, the Vice Chairman of the "Institute of Beijing Olympic Economy," recently stated in comments directed to Chinese companies that "sports marketing has become one of the most effective of all marketing strategies" (Anonymous, 2006). However, Wei was not narrowly referring to the tasks associated with the selling of tickets to Olympic events. Rather he was using a broader definition by suggesting that marketers of nonsports products can benefit by becoming more involved with the 2008 Olympic Games. But since these firms are not selling sports products, how are their actions characterized as sports marketing? In order to fully appreciate and understand the dynamics and differing perspectives of sports marketing, it is imperative that the task of *marketing through sports* also be accepted as an integral component of the industry. Coca-Cola has been associated with the Olympic Games since 1928; however, this relationship was not focused on demand creation for one of the world's premier sporting events. Clearly, it focused on the sale of Coca-Cola products. Many marketers use a sports platform as the basis for appeals to consumers across a vast array of products, the majority of which have little or nothing to do with sports. The *marketing through sports* component of sports marketing tends to be overlooked by some texts (Pitts & Stotlar, 1996). This is unfortunate because it is in this domain where many marketing practitioners are employed and use their skills to implement sports marketing strategies. A comprehensive review of recently published sports marketing textbooks reveals inconsistencies in the definitions of *sports marketing* (Van Heerden, 2001). This conceptual weakness illustrates the need for including both the *marketing of sports* and *marketing through sports* in a broader sports marketing platform that encompasses the entire realm of sports marketing practice. It is the purpose of this article to propose a broadened framework built upon this conceptual dichotomy.

A "Veritable Plethora"[1] of Definitions

Exactly what does the practice of sports marketing encompass? In other words, how can we define sports marketing? The reality is that there exists a veritable plethora of definitions of sports marketing. In fact, some spokespersons seek to differentiate between "sport" marketing and "sports" marketing. Much like any other business concept, the realm of sport(s) marketing has continued to evolve while encompassing a broader array of business activities. The disparity clearly indicates a need to re-conceptualize the construct. Consider the following definitions.

The genesis of the term "sport marketing" can be attributed to a story in a 1978 issue of *Advertising Age*. In that venerable publication, sport marketing was characterized as "the activities of consumer and industrial product and service marketers who are increasingly using sport as a promotional vehicle" (Gray & McEvoy, 2005). In their recent contribution to a compilation of sports marketing literature, Gray and McEvoy noted that this set of activities is best characterized as "marketing *through* sport; that is using sport as a promotional vehicle or sponsorship platform for companies that market consumer, and to a lesser extent, industrial products" (p. 229). Gray and McEvoy further noted a perceived shortcoming of that definition by calling attention to the absence of any reference to the "marketing *of* sport." The implication is that there is a second major dimension of sports marketing, one entailing "the application of marketing principles and processes to market goods and services directly to sports participants and spectators" (p. 229). The amalgamation of *marketing through sport* and the *marketing of sport* provided the foundation for Gray and McEvoy's broad-based definition: "the anticipation, management, and satisfaction of consumers' wants and needs through the application of marketing principles and practices" (p. 229). Presumably, this definition encompasses both major dimensions. Some organizations market sport products to a targeted set of consumers, while others market an array of nonsports products to market segments that have a "personal investment" in sports entities such as athletes, events, and teams (Merz & Fullerton, 2005).

Similarly, Mullin, Hardy, and Sutton (2000) characterize sports marketing in a way that encompasses either dimension, or thrusts, as they describe them.

Their resultant definition is based on the premise that: "sport marketing consists of all activities designed to meet the needs and wants of sports consumers through exchange processes. Sport marketing has developed two major thrusts: the marketing of sport products and services directly to consumers of sport, and the marketing of other consumer and industrial products or services through the use of sports promotions" (p. 9). This definition was subsequently embraced in a contribution by Gladden and Sutton (2005) in the text edited by Masteralexis, Barr, and Hums (2005). Yet readers may question the concept of "sports promotions." Exactly what actions comprise this activity? Is it limited to sponsorship or would an advertisement featuring a generic sports theme fit within this thrust of sport marketing? A second question concerns the exclusive province of sport promotion. Can strategic initiatives other than promotion be used to create a sports overlay that would fit within the realm of marketing through sports?

Questions such as these were addressed by Blann and Armstrong (2003) when they articulated the point that the term sport marketing has been used in many contexts thereby leading to confusion as to exactly what the term really means. Not only do they incorporate both dimensions, but they also expand one of the earlier perspectives by stating that marketing through sports encompasses far more than just advertising and public relations.

Schlossberg's (1996) early book on sports marketing did not specifically define the concept; however, it focused on the efforts of marketers who use sports as a marketing platform for nonsports products. More specifically, Schlossberg states that "sports has become a marketing medium in and of itself with the ability to target, segment, promote, and cast products and services in heroic lights. More and more companies you'd never think of being remotely attached to sports are using sports to enhance and embellish their marketing" (p. 6). In describing the efforts of companies such as Coca-Cola and Visa, Schlossberg's reference seems to be directed toward sponsorship activities.

With their focus on sports products, Pitts and Stotlar (1996) offer a different perspective of the practice of sport marketing. In their text, sport marketing is defined as "the process of designing and implementing activities for the production, pricing, promotion, and distribution of sport product to satisfy the needs or desires of consumers and to achieve the company's objectives" (p. 80). This definition was reiterated in Stotlar's (2001) later book that delineated the process of developing "successful sport marketing plans." Of note is the inclusion of pricing, distribution, and promotion—three traditional elements of the marketing mix. This inclusion represents a meaningful extension of the assertion by Gladden and Sutton (2005) that sport marketing was based solely upon promotional efforts by the marketer.

Similarly, while stating that "sports marketing does not have a single, consistent definition," Moore and Teel (1994) offer a definition that focuses on the marketing of sports products as a basis for the generation of revenue for sports entities while developing marketing plans that will lead to the maximization of revenues accruing to the sports entity. Yet they still incorporate marketing through sports by referring to sports entities such as athletes, teams, and programs in the firm's marketing plan. Sponsorships such as Lenovo's involvement in "the Olympic Partner (TOP)" program for the cycle that included the 2006 Winter Olympics in Torino and the 2008 Summer Games in Beijing would fit within the parameters of their definition of sports marketing. Their early work offers a forward-looking perspective via their assessment that "attention to marketing tools is long overdue" in the marketing of sports products.

This brings us to two of the most recent entries into the sports marketing textbook arena. Shank (2005) defines sports marketing as the "specific application of marketing principles and processes to sports products and to the marketing of nonsports products through association with sports" (p. 3). Finally, Fullerton (2007) provides no specific definition of the term, yet the book is divided into the two aforementioned dimensions: *marketing through sports* and the *marketing of sports*.

Purpose of the Paper

While there continues to be no single, universal definition of the concept of sports marketing, one key consideration is evident. As articulated earlier, the practice of sports marketing is generally recognized as consisting of two fundamental thrusts. However, while recognition of this dichotomy in sports marketing practice is a necessary part of conceptualizing a sports marketing framework, it is insufficient for clearly distinguishing among the multitudes of sports marketing practices that exist today. It is the objective of this article to refine and extend this dichotomy into more detailed constituent components based on actual sports marketing activities in the environment. The authors adopt a grounded theory building approach (Glaser & Strauss, 1967) based upon numerous observations of actual sports marketing activities to develop a preliminary conceptualization of the field of sports marketing.[2] The resulting framework provides a more comprehensive classification of sports marketing practices than has heretofore been advocated, and is suggestive of sports marketing decision-making guidelines. In the remainder of this article two important distinctions that underlie sports marketing practices are identified and discussed. These two distinctions are then combined to form a new sports marketing framework consisting of four categories of sports marketing domains. The article provides support for the framework by discussing and illustrating each domain with examples of actual sports marketing activities.

Identifying Domains within the Sports Marketing Environment

Two important product-related aspects of the sports marketing environment are noteworthy. First is the strategic focus aimed at the marketing of pure sports products. Less evident is the marketing of nonsports products while using a sports platform as the foundation of the firm's marketing efforts. Therefore, two prominent initiatives in sports marketing are identified. They are the *marketing of sports products*, and the *marketing of nonsports products through sports*. Some universities offering sports marketing programs have opted to offer courses using this nomenclature. This is particularly evident when the program is offered through a Business or Management School. However, even with the acknowledgement of these two broad initiatives, the question of exactly what constitutes a sports product still begs to be answered.

Sports Products versus Nonsports Products

In developing a model that depicts the sports marketing environment, an essential distinction is the difference between sports products and nonsports products. Making this distinction is not as simple as it may sound. The following overview is provided in an effort to clarify the difference.

Sports Products

Sports products have been described in many studies. In fact, an early article that sought to estimate the gross domestic sports product (GDSP) in the United States went so far as to include agent services, sports law services, golf course construction, and pari-mutuel betting receipts (Meek, 1997). While some readers may agree with the breadth of this eclectic array, others will view it as having no real focus. The latter view is shared by the authors of this article. For the purpose of describing the sports marketing environment, three categories of sports products have been identified. They are spectator sports, participation sports, and a third eclectic category that is comprised of sporting goods, apparel, athletic shoes, and sports-related products.

1. Spectator Sports

From college sports, to minor league sports, to the highest level of professional sports, and for international events such as the Olympics, one key marketing objective is that of selling tickets. Yet, it is not only those who purchase tickets to a game or event who are important; sports marketers also work to increase viewership and listenership on a variety of broadcast media. This includes television options such as free-to-air TV, premium cable and satellite networks, pay-per-view for special events, enhanced access to a sport's broadcasts (such as DIRECTV's NFL Sunday Ticket), and devoted networks such as the Rugby Channel and the Golf Channel that are dedicated to an array of programming germane to a single sport. Other media include traditional radio, satellite radio, audio/video streaming on the Internet, and an emerging emphasis on mobile technology such as the cellular phone and podcasts.

With this in mind, the spectator sports product can be viewed from two perspectives. First is the sale of access to events; that access may legitimately be viewed as the product. Second is the reality that access has no value without the competition on the field of play. Thus, whether audiences are live or media-based, it is the game or event that represents the product in the spectator sports market.

2. Participation Sports

The category of participation sports rightfully includes an array of activities that might not normally be perceived as sports. While organized soccer leagues, golf, and tennis are recognized as participation sports, other activities that are done on an individual basis are not always acknowledged as sports. The absence of competition that identifies a winner and loser may be the basis for this reluctance. Individuals who jog around the neighborhood or who lift free weights at home or at the health club are not typically characterized as athletes. There is yet another tier of activities that represent participation and competition although only the most liberal definition would permit them to be classified as sports. The most recent addition to this category is poker; even sports networks such as Fox Sports and ESPN have begun to broadcast "Texas hold 'em" poker tournaments. Other activities such as darts, fishing, competitive eating, and billiards are also noteworthy from a participation perspective.

In many cases, marketing's role is to increase the number of participants and the frequency of participation in a specific activity. For example, golf courses want to attract new golfers while at the same time inducing current golfers to play even more. The primary benefit to these sports marketers is that increased participation keeps facilities such as golf courses, tennis clubs, swimming pools, and health clubs busy. A secondary benefit is that it creates demand for more sports equipment and apparel. This leads us to the third and final category of sports products.

3. Sporting Goods, Apparel, Athletic Shoes, and Sports-Related Products

The final category of sports products is somewhat more difficult to define. While sporting goods such as snowboards, apparel such as skiwear, and athletic shoes such as a pair of "Air Jordans" are easy to understand, the final component, sports-related products, is very diverse. It includes sports souvenirs, publications, lessons, and a diverse assortment of products that can be purchased at event venues.

Sporting goods include tangible products specific to a participation sport or activity. These products may be sold to casual participants as well as those who take part in organized activities. The 55 million Americans who participate in bowling (Anonymous, 2003c) create a demand for bowling equipment. Golfers throughout the world have fueled a tremendous increase in the sale of clubs, balls, bags, and gloves on a global basis.

Apparel is clothing that falls into one of two categories. First and foremost, it may be purchased to facilitate participation. The annual start of a new season for many sports creates demand for new uniforms. Style changes may induce golfers to abandon last year's clothing in favor of new styles so that they look good on the golf course. The second category is based on the acknowledgement that sports apparel can be fashionable within certain market segments. These buyers may be fans who wear clothing that features the logos of teams that they support. Others may buy the same apparel, not because they support the team, but because the clothing is in vogue among their peers.

The third component of this category is *athletic shoes*. While these were once primarily devoted to the participant market, this has changed significantly since the advent of Nike's Air Jordan shoes. Today, athletic shoes are an integral part of almost everyone's wardrobe. For participants, there are designs that are deemed appropriate for specific activities such as racket sports, basketball, running, walking, and cross training. No longer are athletic shoes combined into the generic category of tennis shoes.

The final component consists of a broad array of *sports-related products*. These include souvenirs that may be purchased at event venues as well as a number of other official retailers. Consumers often purchase sports magazines. These may feature sports in general, but many focus on a single sport or even a specific team. Lessons to improve one's skill at sports like tennis or golf fit best within this category as well. But the broadest set of products in this category is comprised of venue-specific products. While these products are not tied to a sport per se, they are purchased by spectators in attendance. So, while we might be reluctant to classify beer as a sports product, the reality is that it represents an important revenue stream for teams and stadium operators.

Nonsports Products

In contrast to the various sports products, marketers of *nonsports products* have used sports platforms or themes as part of their marketing strategy as well. Examples of nonsports products that have used sports platforms include automobiles, medical services, fast food, consumer electronics, and beverages such as milk, water, and colas. Yet, even this group of products has some gray areas. When beer or fast food is sold at a sports venue, is it a sports product or not?

The above discussion (see Table 1) summarizes the array of products that are sold within some domain of the sports marketing industry. Sports marketers

Table 1. Products Sold by Sports Marketers

Sports Products	

Spectator Sports Products	• The game or event itself
	   Tickets for attendance
	   Viewership and listenership on electronic media

Participation Sports Products	• Organized participation (leagues & tournaments) • Casual participation • Access to public and private athletic facilities
Sporting Goods, Apparel, Athletic Shoes, & Sports-Related Products	• Sports equipment (skis, golf clubs, and soccer balls) • Sports apparel (hunting clothing, swimwear, and team uniforms) • Athletic shoes • Sports-related products (souvenirs, lessons, and refreshments)
Nonsports Products	
Goods and services not directly related to a sport	

must understand which products are important to their target markets and develop a strategy that meets those needs. Furthermore, the product strategy must be consistent with the other elements of the marketing mix. Only then can the sports marketer take full advantage of the opportunities that exist.

Level of Integration:
Traditional versus Sponsorship-Based Strategies

In addressing the marketing of products through sports, the degree of integration with the sport is the second key consideration. Here the choices are broad but can be classified into two categories—traditional and sponsorship-based.

Traditional Integration

The first category represents the use of sport as part of the marketing program and typically involves the basic components of a marketing strategy: a target market and a corresponding marketing mix. As such, these strategies involve no official relationship with a sports entity such as a league, team, or player. Using a *traditional* marketing strategy, the marketer identifies target markets and develops corresponding product, distribution, pricing, and promotion strategies that are designed to appeal to those target markets. A traditional strategy using a sports overlay may simply involve an advertisement that features actors or models playing a sport; it may involve the placement of an ad in a sports publication that reaches the same target market, or it may utilize graphics on the packaging that feature a sports setting. Each component of the marketing strategy can be integrated within the marketer's effort to incorporate a sports theme.

Sponsorship Integration

In contrast to the traditional approach for integrating sport into the marketing of products, *sponsorship* involves an array of activities whereby the marketer attempts to capitalize on an official relationship with an event, a team, a player, or some other sports organization such as the NCAA, the IOC, or FIFA. One article recently referred to sponsorship as having a "fairly loose meaning in sport" (p. 24). In other words, the concept goes beyond the traditional sponsorship arrangement that most readily comes to mind (Felt, 2003). But it is essential to understand that a sponsorship involves two entities, the sponsor and the sponsee.

The most readily acknowledged sponsorship can be characterized as the traditional sponsorship. The traditional sponsorship generally involves the acknowledgement of the sponsor by the sports property and the ability of the sponsor to use the property's trademarks and logos in its efforts to leverage the sponsorship and reinforce the relationship in the minds of members of the sponsor's target market. During the 2006 post-season games in MLB, each sponsor was recognized with a display on the scoreboard and through virtual advertising for those watching on TV. The traditional sponsorship can involve title rights; for example the Accenture Match Play Championship leaves no doubt as to whom the primary sponsor is. In a somewhat more subtle implementation, a marketer might be recognized as the presenting sponsor. Two noteworthy examples are "the Rose Bowl Presented by Citi" and "Chicago Bears Football Presented by US Bank." In addition to these approaches for the implementation of a traditional sponsorship, three special cases of sponsorship are used by today's marketers. These include (1) venue naming rights, (2) endorsements, and (3) licensing. Some readers might question the designation of these three strategies as being sponsorship-based. However, the following review of the literature finds ample support for this premise.

Venue naming rights have often been characterized as *building sponsorships*. The Edmonton Oilers play their home games in the Skyreach Centre. In a recent article, the relationship between the team and the marketer (Skyreach Equipment, Ltd.) was specifically characterized as a "building sponsorship" (Zoltak, 1998, p. 1). A more recent article in *Brandweek* referred to "building sponsors" and the evolution of that type of strategy over the past few years (Green, 2002). Even the venerable publication, *Advertising Age*, concurs with this characterization. In its review of stadium naming rights, it noted that there are "more than 50 corporations involved in major *sponsorships* of U.S. sports facilities" (Lippe, 2002). Similarly, the International Events Group (IEG) referred to venue naming rights as "title sponsorship deals" (Ukman, 2002). A.C. Nielsen recently added a service called "Sponsorship Scorecard" with the express purpose of developing a better understanding of "the value that sponsors receive from stadium naming rights" (Anonymous, 2004a). The important conclusion that can now be drawn is that venue naming rights do represent a special form of sponsorship. Therefore, when Pepsi-Cola paid to have its name attached to a sports facility in Denver, it was reasonable to presume that the company was implementing a sponsorship-based strategy to sell its nonsports products through sports.

Endorsements have been referred to as "personal (or personality) sponsorships" (Anonymous, 2003a, p. 70). Furthermore, when referring to endorsement opportunities for the NHL's first selection in the 2005 draft, Sidney Crosby, one Canadian publication stated that these personal "sponsorships could prove huge for Crosby's pocketbook" (Anonymous, 2005, p. 14). Another publication referred to Tiger Woods' significant earnings from "sponsor endorsements" (Kedrosky, 2005, p. 17). David Beckham is perhaps the most famous soccer player in the world, and his endorsement power is staggering. *The Economist* magazine specially referred to his deals with Pepsi and adidas as *personal sponsorships* (Anonymous, 2003a). Additional anecdotal support for the premise that endorsement deals fall within the realm of the sponsorship environment can be found on the *SportBusiness International* Web site. Nike's signing of LPGA golfer Grace Park was touted as a sponsorship deal (Barrand, 2003a), and in a separate posting, *SportBusiness International* referred to Yao Ming's endorsement of Pepsi-Cola as a "sponsorship agreement" (Barrand, 2003b). It should now be evident that the general consensus within the sports marketing industry is that endorsements are indeed a form of sponsorship.

Of the three special cases, licensing may be the most debatable as to whether or not it represents a sponsorship-based strategy. Yet, there is ample support for this assertion in the practitioner-oriented literature. Also noteworthy is the fact that many traditional sponsorship deals provide the marketer with the right to use the sport property's logos and trademarks in its own marketing endeavors. One common sponsorship category is that of "official supplier." These sponsors are often granted the right to produce and sell logo apparel and a variety of other licensed products. The NHL recently announced the signing of Reebok as its *official apparel supplier* at the beginning of the 2005–06 season. A recent report out of the UK discussed "sports licensing" within the context of "kit sponsorships" (Barrand, 2005). The report went on to state that licensing provides sponsors with the opportunity to maximize the value of their sponsorship rights.

In another example that ties the concept of licensing to that of sponsorship, a recent report indicated that Reebok has an arrangement that allows for the use of the logos of MLB's 30 teams in the marketing of a special line of footwear (Anonymous, 2004b). Until 2008, Sears used a traditional sponsorship with NASCAR with the specific goal of driving the sale of its Craftsman brand of tools. Beyond that relationship, Sears also sold a broad array of NASCAR-licensed merchandise in many of its retail stores (Anonymous, 2003b). EA Sports recently signed a seven-year contract with NASCAR providing the marketer with exclusive rights to use the organization's logos in the video game market (Hein, 2003). The importance of this form of sponsorship was noted by Felt (2003) who observed that "Nike and Adidas now have intellectual property rights whose value far exceeds that of the products through their association with leading sports teams and events." It is also noteworthy that each venue selected to host the Olympic Games is now required to implement a new stringent set of rules that protect this class of sponsors. Clearly, the literature bears witness to the co-mingling of the terms "sponsors" and "licensing." Given this fact, it seems reasonable to assume that licensing can be classified as a special form of sponsorship. Thus the marketer has a wide array of options available when the decision to implement a sponsorship-based strategy is made.

If the marketing decision maker wishes to integrate a sports theme into the marketing strategy there are two choices. The marketer either opts to use a traditional marketing strategy approach based on the selection of target markets and the development of a corresponding marketing mix for each target, or alternatively the decision maker may integrate sports in a more formal manner by employing one or more of the four sponsorship strategies described on the preceding pages (traditional sponsorships, venue naming rights, endorsements, and licensing agreements).

Basic Principles of Sports Marketing

From the previous discussion three principles are relevant for the assessment and understanding of today's sports marketing industry. They are:

- The nature of the sports marketing focus (marketing of sports or marketing through sports);
- The nature of the product being marketed (sports or nonsports); and,
- The level of integration of sports within the marketing strategy (traditional or sponsorship-based).

A summary of the basic components for each area is presented in Table 2. The latter two are used in the development of a detailed framework that extends the previous broad approaches of "marketing through sports" and the "marketing of sports" into a more strategic conceptualization of the four domains of sports marketing.

Table 2. The Basic Principles of Sports Marketing

Nature of Sports Marketing Focus	• Marketing of Sports
	• Marketing through Sports
Products	• Sports Products Spectator Sports Participation Sports Sporting Goods, Apparel, Athletic Shoes, and Sport-Related Products
	• Non-Sports Products
Level of Integration	• Traditional Target Market Selection Marketing Mix Decisions
	• Sponsorship-Based Traditional Venue Naming Rights Endorsements Licensing

The Four Domains of Sports Marketing

As illustrated in Figure 1, the four domains that comprise the sports marketing environment are identified as *theme-based* strategies, *product-based* strategies, *alignment-based* strategies, and *sports-based* strategies. An explanation and rationale for each proposed domain, along with illustrations of actual sports marketing strategies, is provided in the following sections.

Theme-Based Strategies

Theme-based strategies can be defined as the use of *traditional marketing strategies* that incorporate a sports theme into the marketing program for *nonsports*

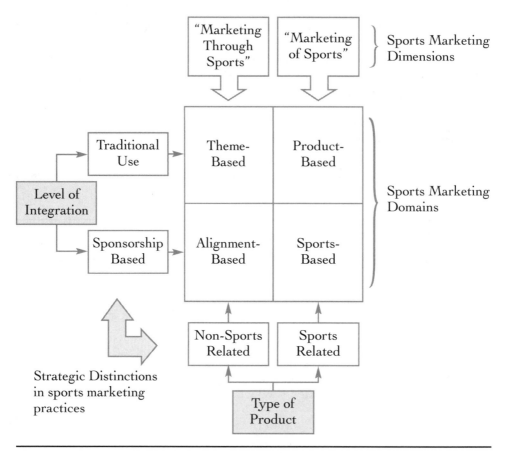

Figure 1. The Four Domains of Sports Marketing

products. The marketer might opt to use a sports-related copy platform or advertise products in sports-related media to effectively reach customers. A key aspect of theme-based strategies is that the marketer's efforts are not predicated upon an official relationship with any specific sports property in its effort to create the sports overlay for its marketing efforts. A bank that advertises in a sports magazine or during a TV broadcast of a sports event has incorporated sports at a rudimentary level. As such, this domain represents the lowest level of integration of sports within the sports marketing environment. There is plenty of anecdotal evidence that illustrates how sports marketers have used theme-based approaches in the implementation of target market access, as well as product, promotion, pricing and distribution strategies.

Implementation of a theme-based strategy may be achieved by placing advertisements in vehicles that appeal to one or more of their sports-oriented target markets. It is important to note that the advertisements used in this type of strategy will not necessarily have a sports theme. Marketers of nonsports products often reach different target markets by objectively selecting their media vehicles.

The use of a theme-based strategy is also evidenced by the incorporation of sports into the other elements of the marketing mix. A well-conceived marketing mix will be tailored so as to coincide with the characteristics of a particular target market. To accomplish this, the marketer must consider the specific initiatives that are used in the task of defining its product, promotion, pricing, and distribution strategies. Thus the task is one of utilizing one or more of these components in such a way so as to create a sports overlay that will appeal to its own target markets.

Product strategies can incorporate sports themes as a way to provide resonance with customers. Sports bars use the promise of televised sports programming as a way to sell food and beverages; fashion labels create clothing that features a sports motif such as polo or golf; and credit card marketers may provide access to member-only sporting events as part of their product offering. Most marketers accept the premise that packaging represents part of the product strategy, so packaging will frequently feature a sports design or motif.

It is common that sports overlays are incorporated into promotional efforts for a variety of nonsports products. For example, tie-ins with sports event through the use of hospitality tents at the event; TV advertisements that feature kids being treated to a trip to a favorite fast-food restaurant after winning their game; and commercials suggesting that viewers get more enjoyment from watching televised sports when they watch it on a particular brand of high definition TV all illustrate the use of a theme-based approach.

Technology has also increased the tie-in capabilities of theme-based marketers. Virtual advertising technology can be used to place computer-generated signage at strategic locations during the broadcast of a sports event. During the recent Major League Baseball post-season games, TV viewers were exposed to a sign for a new Gillette razor whereas the fans in the stands simply saw a blank green surface. An advantage of virtual signage is that it can be changed during the broadcast. The Gillette sign that TV viewers first saw became a sign for State Farm Insurance later in the broadcast. It can also be used to display different signage to viewers in different geographic markets.

In each of the aforementioned examples, the intent was not to sell a sports product; rather it was to sell a marketer's nonsports offering. The list of theme-based efforts that feature a sports overlay through promotion is almost endless—no doubt a testament to the popularity and perhaps the effectiveness of this type of strategic initiative.

Strategies involving the pricing variable and a sports overlay are a bit more difficult to implement. However, one common strategy is for casual restaurants and bars to offer discounts to patrons who are wearing their uniforms from a participation sport such as softball. Another similar strategy is for hotels, restaurants, and bars to offer reduced prices for patrons holding a ticket to a particular sports event. By coupling this action with effective promotion, the marketers are able to create the sports overlay that can be used to appeal to one or more meaningful target markets.

The final element of the marketing mix is the distribution (or place) strategy. The food service industry has been effective and profitable by virtue of its ability to achieve a distribution point at a number of sports venues across the globe. One of the more notable efforts of this type involves the presence of a Hard Rock Café at the Rogers Centre in Toronto, Canada. Similarly, there is a Big Boy Restaurant located inside Detroit's Comerica Park. Not all of these providers are readily recognizable retailers. For example, Levy Restaurants are present at many sports venues across the United States; however, the Levy brand is not emphasized. Marketers of alcoholic beverages have also sought to have their products available at sports venues. In an interesting distribution strategy, FedEx negotiated for the right to have a temporary shipping point located on the Oakland Hills Golf Course during the 2004 Ryder Cup. The strategy provided convenience for the spectators who bought souvenirs as well as incremental revenue for FedEx. Finally, marketers will consider the geographic aspects of their distribution strategy. Budweiser's distribution of 8-packs of beer (in recognition of Dale Earnhardt, Jr. when he was still driving the number 8 car) was initially confined to major NASCAR hotbeds such as Charlotte, Darlington, and Atlanta.

Table 3 summarizes the array of examples delineated in this section on theme-based strategies. It is important to remember that the intent of a theme-based strategy is to use traditional elements of a marketing strategy to create a sports overlay in an effort to sell nonsports products; it is not based upon any type of sponsorship relationship between the marketer and any sports entity. It is also important to note that the five elements of marketing strategy are not mutually exclusive; rather they are integrated in such a way so as to create a synergistic effect. Thus the question is not which element to use; instead, it is how can the firm develop and integrate target marketing, product, promotion, pricing, and distribution strategies so as to capitalize on the opportunities presented by the sports environment while simultaneously avoiding the high fees associated with an actual sponsorship. In answering this question, it is important to note that many firms have adopted strategies that are referred to as ambush marketing. These efforts involve a non-sponsor developing a strategy that creates the false impression that it is an official sponsor of some sports property. Ambushing has become more common as the rights fees for premier properties have continued to escalate. Companies such as Wendy's Hamburgers, American Express, Pepsi-Cola, and Telecom New Zealand have been noted over the years for their effective use of ambush marketing initiatives.[3]

Product-Based Strategies

Efforts to market *sports products* using *traditional marketing strategies* when the marketer has no official relationship with the sports entity being used in its marketing efforts are classified as product-based strategies. These strategies may or may not involve a sports theme beyond the product offering. Consider the marketer of athletic shoes who drops prices and provides incentives for the retailers. It is apparent that these specific strategic decisions are independent from the sports environment; however, since the product is sports-related, the strategy still falls within the realm of sports marketing. Within this product-

Table 3. Overview of Theme–Based Strategies (Traditional Strategies for Nonsports Products)

Target Marketing	Budweiser Using Sports Media to Reach Consumers (Super Bowl; Sports Illustrated) Cadillac Using Golf Magazine to Reach Upscale Segment Cadillac Appealing to Target Market Based on Ability to Fit Four Sets of Clubs in the Trunk
Product	Sports Bars Feature Sports TV Programming as Part of their Product Assortment Clothing Featuring a Sports Motif (Men's Underwear and Tie Featuring Golf Graphics) Kodak Film Packaging Featuring Generic Sports Images M&M Packaging Featuring Checkered Flag Graphic and Racing Team Labeling Crunch 'n Munch Packaging Featuring a Young Boy Playing Basketball Tag Heuer's Invitational Golf Tournament for Buyers of an Expensive Model of Its Watch Visa Signature Credit Card Providing Access to Exclusive Properties (Pebble Beach GC)
Promotion	Detroit Newspaper's Hospitality Facility at Ryder Cup Competition McDonald's Advertisement Featuring Kids After Winning a Sports Competition Sony Advertisement — You Can Enjoy Sports More on a Sony High Definition TV New Zealand Radio Station — 99 FM — "Breakfast with Balls" Theme Panasonic Laptop Computers and Football — Toughness and Performance Gillette and State Farm Insurance Using Virtual Advertising during MLB Broadcasts Kraft's Game Day Cake Recipe during Time Period Preceding the Super Bowl Ambush Marketing (Wendy's, American Express, Pepsi-Cola, and Telecom New Zealand)
Pricing	Bars Offering Discounts to Recreational Sports Participants (softball players) Hospitality Industry Offering Discounts to Ticket Holders of Select Sports Events
Distribution	Hard Rock Café at Rogers Centre in Toronto Big Boy Restaurant at Detroit's Comerica Park Levy Restaurants at Sports Venues (Wrigley Field, Comerica Park) Alcoholic Beverages at Sports Venues (Mike's, Cuervo, & Bass Ale) FedEx at Ryder Cup Venue (Oakland Hills) Budweiser Distribution in NASCAR Geographic Markets (i.e., Darlington)

based domain, it is logical for the marketer to implement strategies that incorporate sports themes. It is also important to understand that such strategies are not achieved solely by virtue of a marketer's promotional efforts.

The NHL changed its rules at the beginning of the 2005–06 season in an effort to make the game more appealing. This effort does not represent a sponsorship-based strategy because it fails to meet the litmus test of having a sponsor and a sponsee involved in an integrated marketing endeavor. A second example is the sporting goods retailer who chooses to give away free caps at a baseball game in an effort to create awareness of its brand. If this strategy is the result of the retailer providing compensation for the right to distribute the caps and not on the basis of an official sponsorship, then it can be classified as a product-based strategy. Clearly, there are varying levels of involvement of sports for strategies within the product-based domain. Since efforts within this domain are implemented using the traditional elements of the marketing mix, it is worth reiterating the point that traditional strategies involve the selection of the target market and the development of a corresponding marketing mix. So the question becomes one of how a marketer of sports products can use its target marketing, product, promotion, pricing, and distribution strategies to influence purchase behavior. How can they get consumers to purchase more of their sports products?

The assessment of the product-based strategies begins with descriptions of how marketers of sports products use traditional strategic initiatives in their efforts to appeal to designated target markets. As an example of an effort on the part of one marketer of sports products to reach a key target market, consider an ad that was placed by the PGA for its "Tour Partners" club in *Golf for Women* magazine. It is important to note that while the PGA used another sports entity (in this case, a sports magazine) to reach a key target market (female golfers), that is not a condition of this domain. For instance, had the advertisement been placed in *USA Today* or *BusinessWeek* magazine, the effort would have still qualified as a product-based strategy. The key distinction in this case is the absence of any type of sponsorship relationship between the PGA and the publication. In a somewhat controversial target marketing strategy, the WNBA's Los Angeles Sparks made an overt effort to target the gay and lesbian segment and supported that initiative by staging a pep rally at an area bar that is frequented by gay and lesbian consumers. Less controversial in nature, MLB has targeted the Hispanic segment while the NBA has tried to capitalize on the emergence of Yao Ming by targeting the Chinese-speaking segment of the sports market. Many sports organizations have implemented relationship marketing programs designed to appeal to their most avid fans; one example is the Real Madrid soccer team that featured David Beckham. In the aftermath of the 2006 World Baseball Classic, MLB decided to nurture the interest that had emerged in several European markets. As one component of that strategy, the MLB Road Show, an exhibit that allows "fans" to experience the game of baseball by hitting in batting cages and pitching in an environment that allows the speed of their pitches to be measured, traveled to "new" geographic target markets such as Germany. Target marketing may also involve B2B efforts. For example, in one effort to reach sports business professionals, adidas placed an advertisement in *SportBusiness International* magazine.

It should now be apparent that any alteration in the organization's target marketing strategy is typically supported by other changes in its marketing mix. The product is tweaked; the promotion is altered; the price is modified; or the distribution strategy is changed so as to better work in harmony with the efforts to reach a new target market.

There are numerous examples for product decisions. The San Diego Padres provide a Spanish-language broadcast for its aforementioned Hispanic target market. This modification of the team's product provides a better fit for some members of its media-based audience. Marketers of spectator sports often target large business accounts; the product that has become a prominent part of every new sports venue built in the past 15 years is the luxury box. There are few individual fans who would be interested in purchasing this product; in fact, even the few "super-wealthy" fans who can afford a luxury box would prefer to spend their money on the expensive premium seats at the venue. TV viewers will frequently see actor Jack Nicholson in the front row of Lakers games, director Spike Lee in the front row of Knicks games, and singer Kid Rock in the front row of Pistons games.

Some sports have opted to change the rules that govern their game. As mentioned above, after losing a season because of the inability to reach an agreement with the players association, the NHL introduced substantial modifications to its rules beginning with the 2005–06 season. Similarly, in an effort to speed up its football games, the NCAA introduced rules changes that governed the starting and stopping of the clock at the beginning of the 2006 season. Virtually every major sport has changed its core product in some meaningful way over the past 20 years. Marketers of spectator sports must carefully consider any decision to modify the way their game is played or officiated as any changes will inevitably be met with resistance by some segment of the fan base. Yet, such changes are often viewed as an improvement to the product that will enhance its appeal among members of one or more key target markets. Another key product decision for team management concerns the players who are on the field. A team may sign a new star play in order to improve the quality of play and to induce a more positive perception of the team on the part of fans and the media.

Sports equipment is often altered in an effort to create brand preference. Even though they violate the official rules of the game, golf balls that float or travel too far are sought by some golfers. Golf clubs have been modified in an effort to provide players with the opportunity to hit the ball further and straighter; tennis rackets have larger sweet spots; and bowling balls have stronger hooking characteristics. The sale of basketballs has been enhanced by modifying its dimensions. A slightly smaller ball is used by women who play organized basketball (such as the WNBA). This smaller ball is also more likely to be purchased by women who participate informally as a form of recreation and exercise.

There are many promotions used to sell sports products. Examples abound from the use of TV ads by New Balance; the use of the Internet by FIFA, the New York Yankees, the Plymouth Whalers, and Nike; direct mail campaigns by the Chicago Bears; and local newspaper ads by the PGA and the NBA's Memphis Grizzlies. Sports teams often use sales promotion as a marketing tool; one of the more popular techniques is the giveaways that are designed to encourage attendance and to nurture relationships. For MLB's Los Angeles Dodgers, one of the more popular giveaways is the infamous bobble-head doll. In another example, for the 2007 tour of the Harlem Globetrotters, anyone purchasing a minimum of six tickets could enter a special code in the Internet ticketing service dialog box and receive a free basketball. Sales promotions like these reflect many people's narrow perspective of sports marketing, one that focuses on the question: how can we put more fans in the seats?

Spectator sports are not the sole province for sports marketers who utilize promotion as a means of implementing a product-based strategy. Marketers of participation sports products and the varied array of sporting goods, apparel, shoes, and other sports-related products also rely extensively on promotion as an important component of their strategies. For example, Bowflex uses TV advertisements, the Internet, and a CD-ROM that is sent to prospects in their efforts to nurture demand. The popular women's fitness center, Curves, has used two-for-one coupons while Bally's Fitness Centers have used 30-day free trial membership periods to get customers through the door. A bowling center in Westland, Michigan, sent coupons to all of the registered league bowlers in its database providing them with the opportunity to bowl a free game during the late summer, a notoriously slow period for bowling centers nationwide. Marketers everywhere acknowledge that trial is often the prelude to adoption, so manufacturers and retailers of golf clubs often stage "Demo Days" at local pro shops; this promotion is designed to get prospects to try new equipment in a risk-free environment. Finally, some marketers will provide premiums for buyers much the way that the marketers of spectator sports use the giveaway strategy. The example in this case is for subscribers of *Golf* magazine to receive a dozen new Titleist golf balls.

In regard to pricing, many MLB teams work with local organizations and provide their members with discounts. Examples include a team's decision to sell discounted tickets to members of AAA and AARP. Another is the group sales strategy that provides discounts for employee groups and students at certain schools. Many marketers of spectator sports have begun to use bundling strategies as a mechanism for providing discount pricing. During the 2007 season, MLB's Atlanta Braves offered fans their Grand Slam Ticket Pack that included four game tickets, four hot dogs, four Coca-Colas, four team bucket hats, one game program, and parking at prices starting as low as $59.

One interesting strategy for a participation sport involves the task of making golf affordable. The USGA and its "First Tee" program have sought to reach kids, especially inner-city kids who generally do not have the financial resources required to play a round of golf. The marketing of athletic shoes has long been marked by controversy as the high prices often led to robberies and even murders by kids who simply could not afford to pay $150 for a pair of desirable sneakers (Telander & Ilic, 1990). Some marketers have begun to offer new shoes at greatly reduced prices.[4]

In an interesting example that illustrates potential pitfalls in establishing prices that benefit the organization, the Chicago Cubs were recently sued because of the team's decision to sell highly desirable tickets through its Wrigley Field Premium Tickets service. The result was that prices escalated far beyond the face value printed on the ticket. When the team was absolved of any legal violations, it was stated that this tactic would likely become more prevalent in situations where the demand for tickets exceeds the supply (Rovell, 2003). In fact, some teams and events (as well as other entertainment events such as concerts) have begun to offer the best seats through auctions in an effort to maximize revenue. The Detroit Tigers auctioned off some of the front row seats at the team's on-deck circle during the final days of its run to the 2006 MLB playoffs. Similarly, the organizers of a boxing match between Lennox Lewis and Kirk Johnson sold 300 VIP ringside tickets to the highest bidders.

From these examples, it should be evident that pricing decisions do not always involve discounted prices. While the focus has been on ticket prices for spectator sports, those marketers also have to think about the prices for access by the media-based audiences — those using TV, radio, the Internet, and mobile technology to watch or listen to the event. Pricing decisions can also be a key part of the strategy for marketers of participation sports, sporting goods, apparel, and athletic shoes.

The final area to consider in the product-based quadrant is distribution. How can the marketer implement distribution strategies that assist in the marketing of sports products? For marketers of spectator sports, this involves access to the event and efforts to distribute tickets to the fans. For the live audience, consideration must be given to the location of franchises. The NHL engaged in an aggressive expansion program that resulted in the location of new franchises in warm weather locations such as Phoenix and Miami. Leagues must also evaluate opportunities involving the relocation of struggling franchises. One of the most recent moves involved the relocation of MLB's Montreal Expos to Washington, DC. Many marketers of spectator sports have begun to reach out to new international markets; the non-defunct NFL-Europe is one example of this phenomenon. The location of special events often involves a series of difficult decisions. The Super Bowl, the Olympics, and the World Cup of Soccer evaluate the infrastructure of candidate cities as part of the decision-making process.

Tickets for most sporting events are now available through a variety of outlets; no longer is the fan limited to the traditional box office. Teams and events offer tickets through independent agencies such as Ticketmaster and Stub-hub.com. Fans can purchase tickets over the Internet; in fact, they can even print their tickets on their own computer.

The media-based audience has become increasingly vital to the well-being of every marketer of spectator sports. We have seen the emergence of numerous TV options including team-dedicated networks (Manchester United Network), general sports networks (ESPN), specific sport networks (the Rugby Channel), sports tiers (NBA League Pass), free-to-air TV (Fox), and pay-per-view (PPV for boxing matches). The growth of satellite radio has also provided another distribution outlet. For example, NASCAR broadcasts many of its races on Sirius Radio. Perhaps the most significant innovation of the past few years has been the ability to use the Internet for audio and video streaming. Major League Baseball was quick to capitalize on this emerging source of revenue with its MLB TV programming. An emerging application is the distribution of sports programming through mobile technology such as cellular phones and Blackberry PDA units.[5]

In the distribution of participation sports facilities, the emphasis is on supply and demand. Brunswick once evaluated each geographic area on the basis of the number of bowling lanes that it could support. Then, based on the number of existing lanes in that area, Brunswick would calculate the surplus or deficit and use that statistic as the basis for determining whether or not a new facility should be built. In the absence of this type of objective assessment, the golf industry has overbuilt; as a result, decisions have had to be made regarding the closure of many courses (Fullerton, 2007).

For the marketing of sporting goods, apparel, and shoes, consider Reebok's distribution strategy; it is quite different from that of most of its key competitors. While most marketers of athletic shoes seek to use channels that emphasize large retailers, Reebok has historically focused on small specialty stores that provide an enhanced level of customer service (Rohm, 1997). The final example to consider is that of Callaway's marketing of golf clubs. It uses the Callaway Golf Tour Fit Van to go to remote locations and reach out to consumers. The van reaches golf enthusiasts who are given easy access to the marketer's products.

From these preceding examples, it is evident that marketers of each category of sports products will seek to implement traditional strategies that will allow them to take advantage of the opportunities that the marketplace presents. These actions may or may not result in a competitive advantage to the marketer. In many cases the actions taken are quickly imitated and thus become *points of parity*. However, an interesting research question to answer might be the extent to which marketing innovations in the sports marketing arena are sustainable and provide competitive advantages. Marketers are acutely aware of the need to identify viable target markets and to develop a series of corresponding marketing mixes that will appeal to each target market. Table 4 provides an array of examples that illustrate the traditional strategic initiatives employed in the implementation of product-based strategies.

Table 4. Overview of Product–Based Strategies (Traditional Strategies for Sports Products)

Target Marketing	PGA Focus on Women (through Golf for Women Magazine Ad) WNBA's Los Angeles Sparks Targeting the Gay & Lesbian Segment MLB Targeting the Hispanic Market NBA Targeting Chinese-Speaking Fans Adidas' Advertisement in SportBusiness International to Reach Sport Business Professionals Real Madrid's Relationship Marketing Program Targeting Avid Fans MLB Road Show in 13 Cities in Germany
Product	NHL Changes in Rules to open up the Game and Eliminate Ties MLB's San Diego Padres' Spanish Language Radio Broadcast Luxury Boxes for Large Corporate Customers Expensive Premium Seats for Wealthy Fans NCAA Football Rules Changes to Speed up the Game Signing Star Player to Improve Product (Chicago Bulls Signing of Ben Wallace) Sporting Goods with Performance Characteristics (golf clubs, golf balls, tennis rackets, bowing balls) Sporting Goods Tailored to Target Market (Smaller Basketball for Female Players)
Promotion	Creative Appeals in Advertising (New Balance – "for the love of the game") Internet Site for Dissemination of Information (FIFA, New York Yankees, Plymouth Whalers, Nike) Direct Mail (Chicago Bears Season Ticket Renewal Solicitation) Newspaper Advertising (Teams and Events (Memphis Grizzlies and the PGA Championship)) Sales Promotion – Giveaways (Los Angeles Dodgers Bobblehead Dolls; Harlem Globetrotters Ball) CD-ROM (Bowflex Mails to Prospects Identified through Direct Response Advertising) Free Trial (Bally's 30-Day Complimentary Membership; Golf Products "Demo Days") Discount Coupons (Curves 2-for-1 Offer) Free Participation (Coupon for Free Game for Registered League Bowlers) Premiums (Golf Magazine Giving a Dozen Titleist Balls to Subscribers)
Pricing	Discounts for Member of Recognized Groups (AARP & AAA) Group Discounts for Informal Groups (Parties, Students) Bundling of Tickets, Food, Beverages, and Other Products (Atlanta Braves Grand Slam Ticket Pack) Bundling of Events (Ford Field College Football Package) Programs to Make Participation Affordable (USGA's "First Tee" Program) New Lines of Athletic Shoes Selling at Lower Prices

(continued on overleaf)

Table 4. *Continued*

Pricing *(continued)*	Premium Tickets Sold at Premium Prices (Chicago Cubs Wrigley Field Premium Ticket Service) Auction – Price Determined by Bidding (Lennox Lewis Fight; Detroit Tigers On-Deck Seats)
Distribution	NHL Expansion to Warm Weather Locations (Miami, Phoenix, Atlanta, Tampa Bay) MLB Relocation Decision (Move Montreal Expos Team to Washington, DC)1 Location of Special Events (2010 World Cup of Soccer in South Africa) Competitions in International Markets (NFL Europe) Internet Ticket Procurement (Ticketmaster, Stubhub.com, Print-at-Home) Alternative TV Distribution (i.e., NFL Sunday Ticket, ESPN, the Golf Channel, Pay-Per-View) Satellite Radio (NASCAR on Sirius Radio) Audio and Video Streaming on Internet (i.e., MLB.TV) Distribution via Mobile Technology (i.e., Mobile ESPN) Construction of Participation Facilities Based on Supply and Demand (Brunswick Bowling Centers) Mobile Retail Facility Going to the Customer (Callaway Golf Tour Fit Van)

Alignment-Based Strategies

Many marketers of *nonsports products* officially align themselves with sports properties via one or more of the four forms of *sponsorship* previously described (traditional sponsorships, venue naming rights, endorsements, and licensing agreements). The nature of this sponsorship-based relationship reflects a higher level of integration of sports within the sports marketing environment. A common strategy involves a sponsor who uses an association with sports to market nonsports products; this combination emphasizes initiatives that are classified as alignment-based strategies. In an effort to sell more fast food, McDonald's advertising and packaging feature its official partnership with the Olympic Games. Volvo uses its sponsorship of a high-profile sailing event to strengthen the public's perception of the carmaker as one that exudes prestige while concurrently emphasizing safety and technology. While the strategic initiatives that augment the sponsorship are important, the foundation for the resultant strategy is the fact that the marketer, by virtue of its official sponsorship, is highly integrated within the sports environment. Thus, the task for these marketers of nonsports products is one of implementing strategic initiatives that allow them to capitalize upon their position within this realm of the sports marketing environment. Such initiatives are alternatively characterized as leveraging or activation.

Examples using traditional sponsorship abound; however, two of the most noteworthy examples are Coca-Cola's relationships with the World Cup of

Soccer and the Olympics. Other noteworthy Olympics sponsors include McDonalds, Lenovo Computers, and John Hancock Life Insurance (see Table 5 for several examples).

In addition to traditional sponsorship, there are three special forms of sponsorship that are available to today's marketers. The professional teams in Denver provide excellent examples of how marketers of nonsports products use venue naming rights (or "building sponsorships") as a platform for creating demand. MLB's Denver Rockies play their home games in Coors Field. The NHL's Avalanche and the NBA's Nuggets both play their home games in the Pepsi Center. In this same vein, the NBA's Memphis Grizzlies play in the FedEx Forum while MLB's San Diego Padres play their games in Petco Park. Significant growth has also occurred in the American collegiate market and in minor league professional sports; consider Ohio State's Value City Arena and the Memphis Redbirds in AutoZone Park. Virtually every major venue in the United States now has a naming rights sponsor; as a result, much of the recent growth in this type of sponsorship activity has taken place in international markets. A few examples are Allianz Arena in Munich, Germany; Lexus Centre in Melbourne, Australia; Coca-Cola Stadium in Xi'an, China; T-Mobile Arena in Prague, Czech Republic; and DeBeers Diamond Oval in Kimberly, South Africa.

Venue naming rights inevitably provide benefits far beyond that of simply putting a corporate moniker on the façade of some sports facility. For example, the Pepsi Center serves Pepsi Products, and all of the ATMs in Comerica Park belong to Comerica Bank. Thus, venue naming rights can be an integral component of a marketer's strategy in its efforts to influence consumer attitudes and preferences as well as the purchase of its nonsports products by members of the organization's target markets.

A second special form of sponsorship is that of the implementation of an endorsement strategy or what has been referred to as a "personality sponsorship" (Gillis, 2005, p. 4). One can seldom watch a TV program or read a magazine without seeing at least one effort to use an athlete's endorsement as a means of cutting through the clutter. These celebrity endorsers are generally easily recognized, in part because they have achieved a high standard of performance. While there are many types of personalities who can perform in the role of a celebrity endorser, within the realm of sports marketing, the focus is on athletes. Indianapolis Colts' quarterback, Peyton Manning, has become a popular endorser. Among his recent spate of endorsements is one for Sony High Definition TV. It is worth noting that no NFL trademarks or logos are used in these advertisements because another marketer, Samsung, is the official high definition TV sponsor for the NFL. Some critics may actually refer to Sony's effort as ambush marketing

The final special form of sponsorship involves the use of licensing to sell nonsports products. Consider the relationship between Mattel and NASCAR. By using select NASCAR trademarks, Mattel is able to capitalize on the sport's popularity and sell more of its Hot Wheels toy cars. Consumers may also purchase a slow cooker from Rival; the marketer's "Crock Pots" bear the likeness of one of several NASCAR drivers including Jeff Gordon and Dale Jarrett. Major credit card companies have entered into licensing agreements with virtually every major sports league and their teams. The resultant affinity credit cards can represent an attractive offering for fans. Two examples are the Visa "NFL Extra Points" card and the MasterCard that features MLB's St. Louis Cardinals.

It is important to reiterate the fact that each of the examples delineated represents a marketer's effort to sell nonsports products. However, the efforts reflect a higher level of integration of sports within the marketing strategy than is in evidence with theme-based strategies. This is achieved through the use of some form of sponsorship that ties the marketer to some important sports entity. Table 5 provides a compendium of examples of alignment-based strategies.

Sports-Based Strategies

The final domain, sports-based strategies, is characterized by *official sponsors of a sports property* who are selling other *sports products*. Because of the role of sports in both the product and integration dimensions, this domain may reflect the greatest reliance on sports-oriented initiatives. It may also represent the least common type of strategy employed by today's sports marketers. Within this domain, the most common strategy features the marketer of sporting goods or sports apparel in a traditional sponsorship of a sports team or a sporting event. Strategies in this domain can be very effective when appealing to customers who are excited by the sports that are used in the implementation of the specific strategic initiatives (Fullerton, 2007). For example, adidas sells sporting goods and it uses advertising that complements its traditional sponsorship of FIFA and the World Cup of Soccer. This consistency produces the synergy that is characteristic of the sports-based domain.

An example that features a traditional sponsorship is Adams Golf and the PGA. The maker of the "Tight Lies" brand of clubs sponsors a lower level regional series of golf tournaments that comprise the Tight Lies Tour. Another example is the traditional sponsorship for adidas and the New Zealand All Blacks (New Zealand Rugby Football Union). While this is similar to the sponsorship of the World Cup of Soccer by adidas, the difference lies in the type of property with which the sponsor is aligned. In the former case, adidas is sponsoring an event; in the latter case, the marketer is sponsoring an organization and its famous team. While each of these examples best fits within the realm of traditional sponsorship, the sponsors' contracts typically provide them with opportunities to sell officially licensed merchandise and to gain the services of key players for endorsements. Thus, there is often an overlap in the types of sponsorships used by any marketer that is operating in the sports-based domain.

The three special forms of sponsorship can also be employed by marketers operating in the sports-based quadrant. For example, Reebok has venue naming rights for a soccer stadium in Bolton, England; the Reebok Stadium is the

Table 5. Overview of Alignment-Based Strategies (Sports Sponsorship-Based Strategies for Nonsports Products)

Traditional Sponsorship	Olympic Sponsorships (McDonald's, Lenovo, & John Hancock Life Insurance Volvo's Sponsorship of the Ocean Race World Cup Sponsorships (Google!, Coca-Cola, McDonald's) NASCAR Sponsorships (DeWalt, DuPont, Best Western, Budweiser & Pepsi-Cola) Weetabix Women's British Open PGA Tournament Title Sponsors (FedEx) NFL "Official" Products (Coors Lite, Samsung HDTV) Official Energy Bar of the New Zealand All Blacks (Moro) Official Energy Source of the PGA Tour (Nature Valley Granola Bars) Barclay's Premiership League MLB's Chicago White Sox sponsorship by 7-11 Red Bull Sponsorship of MLS Team (New York Red Bulls)
Venue Naming Rights	Denver Sports Facilities (Coors Field, Pepsi Center) Memphis Sports Facilities (FedEx Forum and AutoZone Park) San Diego MLB Facility (Petco Park) Detroit MLB Facility (Comerica Park) College Venues (Ohio State's Value City Arena) Minor League Sports (Memphis Redbirds' AutoZone Park) International Venues (Allianz Arena, Lexus Centre, Coca-Cola Stadium) Other International Venues (T-Mobile Arena, DeBeers Diamond Oval)
Endorsements	Sony High Definition TV and Peyton Manning "Got Milk?" and Peyton, Eli, & Archie Manning Prilosec and Brett Favre Tag Heuer Watches and Tiger Woods and Michelle Wie Buick and Tiger Woods Accenture and Tiger Woods Arnold Palmer and Invacare Menard's Home Improvement and Dale Earnhardt, Jr. Old Spice Fragrances and Tony Stewart
Licensing	Mattel "Hot Wheels" Cars and NASCAR Rival "Crock Pots" and NASCAR Monogram Lunch Meats and NASCAR Visa and the NFL MBNA and MLB's St. Louis Cardinals Van Dillen Asiatech and FIFA World Cup Hawthorne Village and the NHL York Heating and Air Conditioning and NCAA Sports Teams (U of Michigan) Danbury Mint (Watches) and NCAA Teams (University of Michigan) Glidden Paint and an Array of Sports Entities (i.e., NFL, NCAA, NBA, & USOC) Oak Grove Caskets and NCAA Teams (i.e., Ohio State University)

result. While this strategy has seldom been chosen as an appropriate sponsorship endeavor by marketers of sports products, it may become more common as new stadia are built with a focus on revenues from the marketers holding the naming rights for each venue.

Endorsements for sports products that use athletes as spokespersons represent the best examples of the sports-based domain. Nike's personal sponsorship of Michelle Wie is one of the most recent and most noteworthy efforts of this type. Early in Tiger Woods' career, Nike was criticized for its substantial payment for the golfer's endorsements of Nike's new line of golf products. Given the terms of their new contract, it is evident that Nike felt like the world's number one golfer contributed to its sales in a positive way, much the way that Michael Jordan did throughout his illustrious NBA career. Marketers of spectator sports can also implement endorsement-based strategies. Most often, these involve spokespersons who are still active in the sport. The PGA has long run a "these guys are good" campaign that features current golf stars. Similarly, the National Basketball Association has relied on its "the NBA is FANtastic" advertising theme that features current NBA stars such as Dwayne Wade and Yao Ming. Because of their potential impact, endorsements are a commonly employed strategy within the sports-based domain.

Finally, we turn our attention to licensing. It is important to reiterate the earlier point that the other forms of sponsorship may convey to the sponsor the right to produce and sell an array of merchandise that features the trademarks, logos, and likenesses of the sponsee. Nike has licensing deals with a number of top tier university athletic programs. Among the most noteworthy are the University of North Carolina, Duke University, and The Ohio State University. Upper Deck uses a licensing agreement with professional sports leagues and players such as those in Major League Baseball as the foundation of its efforts to sell collectable trading cards. It is important to understand that the licensee is using its relationship with a sports property to influence demand for its own sports products.

For each of the aforementioned examples, the synergy emanating from the two sports entities should be evident. As noted earlier, this domain represents the one with the greatest overall immersion into the world of sports; therefore, it can be extremely effective when the target market is comprised of fans of the sports entity with which the marketer has an official relationship. Clearly, the marketing of sports products can be impacted in a positive manner via the incorporation of the sponsorship of a recognizable sports property within an integrated marketing communications strategy. Table 6 provides a summary of the sports-based strategies that were cited in this section.

Conclusions

The purpose of this conceptual paper is to provide a grounded theory-based framework for classifying activities that comprise sports marketing strategies. It begins with the recognition that there are two distinct dimensions within the sports marketing industry: the marketing of sports products and marketing

Table 6. Overview of Sports-Based Strategies (Sports Sponsorship-Based Strategies for Sports Products)

Traditional Sponsorship	Adidas and FIFA (World Cup of Soccer) Adams Golf and the PGA (Tight Lies Tour) Adidas and the New Zealand Rugby Football Union (New Zealand All Blacks) Adidas and National Soccer Teams (e.g., Germany and Argentina) Quiksilver and the X Games Real Madrid Soccer Team and a Formula 1 Race Team
Venue Naming Rights	Reebok Stadium in Bolton, England Fila Forum in Milan, Italy Pro Player Stadium in Miami, Florida, USA (contract terminated)
Endorsements	Nike and Michelle Wie, Tiger Woods, and Michael Jordan Adidas and David Beckham Burton Snowboards and Shaun White Storm Bowling Balls and Pete Weber Callaway Golf and Arnold Palmer PGA Golf and Star Players ("These guys are good") NBA and Star Players ("The NBA is FANtastic") MLB and International Star Players (World Baseball Classic)
Licensing	Nike and Major Universities (e.g., North Carolina, Duke, and Ohio State) Upper Deck and MLB (collectable trading cards) Reebok and NHL (apparel and equipment) Gilbert and Super 14 Rugby (balls) Wilson and the NFL (balls)

through sports. Thus, sports marketing is not solely focused on how to get more fans in the seats at a specific sports venue. By taking the type of product sold and the level of sports integration into account, four strategic domains have been identified. The types of products have simply been identified as sports products and nonsports products. The marketers' level of integration concerns its involvement with some sports entity in some form of official sponsorship. As such, the two broad areas for integration have been designated as traditional and sponsorship-based. Using these dimensions, the two-by-two matrix shown in Figure 1 emerges. This matrix provides the foundation for the definition and description of the four domains of the sports marketing industry.

At the most fundamental level, theme-based strategies use the traditional components of a marketing strategy—target market and marketing mix decisions—to sell nonsports products. This can be differentiated from the product-based strategies that represent the use of traditional marketing mix and target marketing decisions in an effort to sell sports products. Representing a higher level of integration, many marketers have aligned themselves with sports properties via some form of sponsorship. The sponsorship-based strategies are represented by the alignment-based and sports-based strategies. Alignment-based strategies use sponsorship in the efforts to sell nonsports products; it is the fact that the marketer is aligned with some sports entity that qualifies this type of strategy as one of the sports marketing domains. Conversely, sports-based strategies involve some form of official sponsorship of a sports property in the task of marketing one of the many sports products that crowd the marketplace.

The classification of recent examples within the sports marketing industry provides evidence and further documents the fact that these four domains are mutually exclusive and collectively exhaustive, thus meeting a basic test for the usefulness of this proposed framework. In addition, the broadened set of sports marketing domains articulated herein provides a method for classifying the many strategies that have recently evolved in the practice of sports marketing. This classification system is an initial first step for the development of theory in a field, it allows for the development of testable hypotheses to guide the development and execution of research, and finally it provides guidance to decision-makers in the field.

Directions for Future Research

The classification framework presented herein gives rise to a number of interesting and potentially fruitful research topics related to sports marketing. We mention several here.

A key question is the relative performance of these various sports marketing approaches in the accomplishment of business objectives. The performance characteristics should consider the advantages and disadvantages of each approach. For instance, there is some evidence that sponsorship strategies may stimulate negative societal attitudes toward the practices in particular and sports in general (Merz, Fullerton, & Taylor, 2006).

In addition, the development of descriptive research to document the relative costs associated with each of the four domains and the identification of contingencies for choosing one approach over another would help establish useful decision-making guidelines. For instance, strategy research can identify conditions under which it is more advantageous for a marketer of non-sports related products to use a theme-based versus an alignment-based strategy.

Finally, the practice of sports marketing strategies internationally is another area of fruitful inquiry. As many of the examples used in this paper reveal, while the underlying framework as a theory possesses face validity, clearly how the approaches are executed varies dramatically in a cross-cultural context. Marketers engaged in global activities need guidelines about how best to use sports marketing strategies in the international arena.

Notes

1. Howard Cosell first uttered the expression "veritable plethora" in a sports context during the broadcast of a Monday Night Football game in the 1970s. That phrase seems to be an appropriate description of the current state of sports marketing.

2. A grounded theory approach has as goals the identification of concepts, categories and propositions. Concepts and categories are the basic units of analysis and the starting point for most grounded theory applications. It is the conceptualization and categorization of observed

events (the data) that establishes the bases and means for integrating the emerging theory. In its formation the grouping of concepts into categories is supported by examples (samples of data) observed by the researcher.

3. For example Qantas Airway's ambushing of Ansett Australia during the Sydney Olympics, and Nike's ambushing of the official adidas sponsorship of the World Cup of Soccer.

4. Grabbing much of the headlines in recent days is the pricing strategy used by Steve and Barry's University Sportswear store to sell its new basketball shoe for $14.98. In light of Payless Shoe Source's marketing of its successful $35 Amp running shoe, one sports marketing firm issued a stern warning that "if I were a branded athletic company right now, I'd be reconsidering my whole approach" (Holmes 2007).

5. ESPN attempted to provide this type of service, but it was met by general disinterest by American consumers.

References

Anonymous (2006, September 19). *Experts urge Chinese companies to back Beijing Olympics*. Retrieved November 18, 2007, from http://www.sportbusiness.com/news/160453/experts-urge-Chinese-companies-to-back-Beijing-Olympics

Anonymous (2005, August 15). Sidney Crosby: Already an NHL endorsement superstar. *Marketing, 110*(27), 14.

Anonymous (2004a,). *Nielsen expands sports arm*. Retrieved April 27, 2004, from http://www.sportbusiness.com/news/index

Anonymous (2004b, May). News Briefs. *Sporting Goods Business, 37*(5), 12.

Anonymous (2003a, July 5). Business: Branded like Beckham; Sporting endorsements. *The Economist, 368*(8331), 70.

Anonymous (2003b, July). Sears maximizes tools of the NASCAR trade. *Retail Merchandiser, 43*(7), 44.

Anonymous, (2003c). *SGMA sports participation trends*. Retrieved August 28, 2004, from http://www.SGMA.com

Barrand, D. (2005, June). Why brands are banking on sport. *Promotions & Incentives*, 13–14.

Barrand, D. (2003a). *Nike signs up first female golfer*. Retrieved July 14, 2003, from http://www.sportbusiness.com/news/index?news_item_id=150250

Barrand, D. (2003b). *Yao and Coke resolve image row*. Retrieved October 20, 2003, from http://www.sportbusiness.com/news/?news_item_id=152825

Blann, F., & Armstrong, K. (2003). Sport marketing. In J. Parks & J. Quarterman (Eds), *Contemporary Sport management* (2nd ed.). Champaign, IL: Human Kinetics.

Felt, J. (2003, December/January). How sponsorship can help your brand. *Managing Intellectual Property, 125*, 24.

Fullerton, S. (2007). *Sports marketing*. New York, NY: McGraw-Hill/Irwin.

Gillis, R. (2005). Harnessing the power of personality. *Sponsorship Works*, (2), London, UK: SportBusiness International, 4–6.

Gladden, J., & Sutton, W. (2005). Marketing principles applied to sport management. In L. Masteralexis, C. Barr, & M. Huns (Eds), *Principles and practice of sport management*. Sudbury, MA: Jones and Bartlett Publishers.

Glaser, B., & Strauss, A. (1967). *The discovery of grounded theory*. Chicago: Aldine.

Gray, D., & McEvoy, C. (2005). Sport marketing strategies and tactics. In B. Parkhouse (Ed.), *The management of sport: Its foundation and application*. New York, NY: McGraw-Hill Inc.

Green, P. (2002, December 9). Sponsorship with no booths or logos. *Brandweek, 43*(45), 16.

Hein, K. (2003, September 22). EA drives into the action as NASCAR's solo gamer. *Brandweek, 44*(34), 9.

Holmes, S. (2007, January 22). Changing the game on Nike: How budget sneakers are tripping up its basketball business. *Business Week*, 80.

Kedrosky, P. (2005, March 14). Tiger, tiger burning bright. *Canadian Business, 78*(6), 17.

Lippe, D. (2002, October 28). Inside the stadium-rights business. *Advertising Age*. Retrieved November 13, 2002, from http://www.adage.com/news.cms?newsID=36406

Masteralexis, L., Barr, C., & Hums, M. (Eds.). (2005). *Principles and practice of sport management*. Sudbury, MA: Jones and Bartlett Publishers.

Meek, A. (1997). An estimate of the size and

supported activity of the sports industry in the United States. *Sport Marketing Quarterly, 6*(4), 15–21.

Merz, G. R., & Fullerton, S. (2005, March 24–26). Developing a personal investment measurement scale for sport spectator behavior. In J. Chapman (Ed.), *Expanding marketing horizons into the 21st Century; Proceedings Association of Marketing Theory and Practice* (pp. 394–399). Jekyll Island, GA.

Merz, G. R., Fullerton, S., & Taylor, D. (2006, March 23–25). An exploratory study of societal attitudes in the United States and New Zealand toward sport sponsorship: Differences, structure and effects. In J. Chapman (Ed.), *Enriching theoretical and practical understanding of marketing; Proceedings Association of Marketing Theory and Practice* (pp. 69–70). Hilton Head, SC.

Moore, E., & Teel, S. (1994). Marketing tools for sports management. In P. Graham (Ed.), *Sport business: Operational and theoretical aspects*. Dubuque, IA: Brown & Benchmark.

Mullin, B., Hardy, S., & Sutton, W. (2000). *Sport marketing*. Champaign, IL: Human Kinetics.

Pitts, B., & Stotlar, D. (1996). *Fundamentals of sport marketing*. Morgantown, WV: Fitness Information Technology.

Rovell, D. (2003, November 24). *Judge decides business is legit*. Retrieved October 14, 2005, from http://www.sports.espn.go.com/mlb/news/index?news_item_id=1670041

Rohm, A. (1997). The creation of consumer brands within Reebok Running. *Sport Marketing Quarterly, 6*(2), 17–25.

Schlossberg, H. (1996). *Sports marketing*. Cambridge, MA: Blackwell Publishers, Inc.

Shank, M. (2005). *Sports marketing: A strategic perspective*. Upper Saddle River, NJ: Pearson Education, Inc.

Shannon, J. R. (1999). Sports marketing: An examination of academic marketing publication. *The Journal of Services Marketing, 13*(6), 517–34.

Sports Marketing Surveys (2002, October 7). *Insights Newsletter*, 1–3.

Stotlar, D. (2001). *Developing successful sport marketing plans*. Morgantown, WV: Fitness Information Technology.

Telander, R., & Ilic, M. (1990, May 14). Senseless: in America's cities, kids are killing kids over sneakers and other sports apparel favored by drug dealers: Who's to blame? *Sports Illustrated, 72*(20), 36–42.

Ukman, L. (2002, February 21). *Naming rights: Not just for stadiums anymore*. Retrieved February 22, 2002, from http://www.sponsorship.com/learn/namingrights.asp

Van Heerden, C. R. (2001, September 9). Factors affecting decision-making in South African sport sponsorships. *Doctoral Thesis* (etd-11072001–165433). University of Pretoria, South Africa.

Zoltak, J. (1998, October 12). Skyreach Equipment Ltd. purchases naming rights at Edmonton. *Amusement Business, 110*(49), 1.

8

SPORTING SIGN WARS: ADVERTISING AND THE CONTESTED TERRAIN OF SPORTING EVENTS AND VENUES

Jay Scherer, Michael Sam, and Richard Batty

Introduction

> Sponsoring is a tradition that goes back to Ancient Greece, where wealthy Athenians would contribute financially to expenses related to culture, defense, the state and sports, in order to make them more accessible to all citizens. In return, the state honored them by engraving their names on marble tablets. This tribute was a mark of respect, value, and high appreciation by the city. (Sponsoring, 2004, para. 1)

"To remain faithful to this heritage," the Athens 2004 Sponsoring Department, in conjunction with the Greek state, have implemented an unprecedented level of clean venue policies to prevent ambush marketing and "guarantee the greatest possible return for Sponsors and develop strong bonds with the business community" (Sponsoring, 2004, para.2). To bond with the multinational business community, an estimated 750,000 euros have been spent clearing 10,000 billboards from buildings and rooftops in Athens while the remainder have been preserved for official partners of the Olympic movement who have paid over $US1 billion for exclusive advertising rights to have their brands associated with the Athens 2004 Summer Olympic Games. These restrictions are not exclusive to Athens, but also apply to provincial towns and the areas alongside national motorways while additional restrictions have been imposed on bus-side advertising and billboards on bus stops (Gibson, 2004). Meanwhile, the local business community in Athens has been subject to daily surveillance and legal intimidation by a corporatist policing network involving numerous state bodies and the Olympic Games Organizing Committee (OGOC).[1] Even citizens and spectators are being encouraged to document and report evidence of ambush marketing that will withstand the scrutiny of the courts through a "Brand Protection Incident Report Form" available on the Athens 2004 website. Moreover, strict regulations have been implemented by OGOC to ensure the removal of spectators who do not comply with a lengthy list of restricted items and actions including: ambush marketing, pirate

"Athens 2004" products, unauthorized signs and labels, and any food or drink including water. Athens 2004 is without a doubt, the advertising Olympics (Jay, 2004).

Such unparalleled levels of surveillance are the cumulative effects of at least two decades of ambush marketing at the Olympic Games and the IOC's utmost dedication to provide sponsors, who now account for up to 32% of the IOC's total revenue, with exclusive rights and opportunities to associate with the Olympic movement.[2] For example, companies in The Olympic Partner Programme (TOP), who from 1997 to 2000 provided the IOC with revenue of US$579 million, not only receive exclusive marketing rights and opportunities within their designated product category and use of Olympic imagery, but are also guaranteed ambush marketing protection (*Sydney 1997–2000*, 2001). However, the increasing levels of brand protection afforded to sponsors and their most valuable assets, their corporate brands, place extraordinary pressures on local organizing committees, sport managers, local businesses, and spectators, who despite paying for tickets must comply with increasingly stringent terms and conditions of admission or risk being refused entry. Moreover, the transformation of public spaces into restricted corporate zones raises important questions for local taxpayers who will pay an estimated US$12 billion to host the Athens 2004 Olympics, plus an ongoing fee of up to $100 million per year to maintain more than a dozen Olympic sites (Murphy, 2004). Such contemporary issues speak to the extent to which local sporting spaces, public landscapes, and by extension the bodies of spectators are produced, regulated, and constituted by a range of power relations (Bale, 1994; van Ingen, 2003), in this instance the maintenance and protection of the interests and sign values of multinational corporate sponsors. Indeed, while global mega-sporting events represent important flexible promotional platforms for multinational corporations to reach transnational audiences, they remain dependent on local stadia, urban places/spaces as vehicles for their commercial messages and, by extension, the vast amounts of public funds that are used to bid for and subsidize mega-sporting events.[3]

In this paper, we examine a range of local issues pertaining to ambush marketing and the brand protection/clean venue policies employed by local organizing committees and sport managers in two case studies: the 2000 Sydney Olympics and the 1999 FIFA Under-17 World Soccer Championships in New Zealand. While the 2000 Sydney Olympics represents a typical mega-event (Roche, 2000), even smaller-scale sporting events such as the 1999 FIFA Under-17 World Soccer Championships held in locales such as Dunedin, New Zealand, have emerged as important promotional spaces and platforms from which commercial representations are communicated. These local sporting spaces exist as contested terrains where corporate sign wars (Goldman & Papson, 1996) and other broader power relations are effectively played out at the global-local nexus. What follows is a brief discussion of the significance of sports advertising and sponsorship in the context of globalization and corporate sign wars, and an outline of the growing body of literature pertaining to ambush marketing. We then present our two case studies drawing attention to the similar themes and strategies employed at both sporting events to protect official sponsors. We conclude by discussing some of the local implications of sporting sign wars on sports managers and the lived experiences of spectators attending sporting events and citizens who are inevitably connected to the wider structures of power operating within and through these local sporting spaces.

Sports Advertising and Corporate Sign Wars: Branded

In the context of globalization, corporate brand images have emerged as flexible capital assets whose equity, or sign value, can quickly dissipate if left unattended or unprotected. For example, Nike's CEO Phil Knight has referred to the multinational sporting corporation as a marketing company as opposed to a production-oriented company (Willigan, 1992) highlighting the substantial amount of equity value aligned with Nike's brand image. However, as a result of the unprecedented presence of corporate brands within contemporary promotional culture (Wernick, 1991), a voracious competition has emerged between corporations for sign/brand visibility, market share, and by extension corporate valuation on the equity markets.[4] These "war[s] of images" (Morley & Robins, 1995), or "sign wars" (Goldman & Papson, 1996), frequently "spill over into the legal arena where the ownership rights to images, logos, and signs are contested and enforced" (Goldman & Papson, 1996, p. 44). While the most prominent sign wars occur between rival corporations (e.g., Nike vs. Reebok, Coke vs. Pepsi), it has become commonplace for corporations to compete against all other brands in the mediascape; arguably the most prominent battleground has been the commercial medium (Goldman & Papson, 1996). For example, as part of the cola wars in the 1980s and early 1990s, Pepsi routinely took aim at Coke's brand image in several television commercials that insinuated Coke's inferiority. In a similar vein, the sneaker wars of the same time period stimulated a commercial evolution that tied brand images to celebrity endorsements, while broader marketing strategies attempted to denigrate and diminish the brand equity of rival corporations.

In conjunction with the cluttered image-economy and broader climate of corporate sign wars, it has become commonplace for corporations to produce spectacular and entertaining commercials to differentiate their corporate signs and increase brand equity. These commercials simultaneously appeal to alienated and media savvy audiences who are increasingly disenfranchised with commercials and the clutter of the spectacle of media culture (Kellner, 2003). For example, clothing company Benetton has consistently challenged traditional boundaries between advertising, politics, and profanity in their advertisements that are frequently produced to shock and disturb viewers (Goldman & Papson, 1996). However, as the advertising industry readily acknowledges (Nava, 1997), even the most visually entertaining, shocking, and profane commercials can never be guaranteed to reach target markets and viewers who are constantly bombarded with commercial messages. Consequently, it is not surprising that corporations have increasingly turned to sponsorship, and in particular sporting sponsorships as relatively impervious promotional platforms for their marketing aspirations.[5] Whereas creative or innovative advertisements can potentially secure visibility, controlling the spaces and sites where brand images and corporate signs are delivered is often regarded as a more effective means of brand communication.

Clearly, many mega-sporting events such as the Olympic Games represent high profile and fertile sporting sites to cultivate and communicate brand images and attitudes (Goldman & Papson, 1996) to a global audience through the medium of television. For example, the IOC explicitly recognizes the importance of offering sponsors exclusive rights and privileges to associate with a globally recognizable sporting event and the Olympic's five-ring logo. The IOC somewhat misleadingly advertises "its" local sporting landscapes and telecasts as clean and secure for a deliberately controlled number of major corporate sponsors. As the IOC explains: "No venue advertising is permitted. The Olympic Games are the only major sporting event in the world where there is no advertising in the stadium or on the athletes" (IOC, 2004, para. 1). Beyond the attraction of uncluttered and clean sporting landscapes and broadcasts, present-day sport holds enormous appeal to corporations which are anxious to procure ample returns on their often-sizeable sponsorship investments. Major global sporting competitions such as the Summer or Winter Olympics, World Cup Soccer or Rugby, the Champions League, the Super Bowl, the World Series, or the Stanley Cup playoffs have become regular features on our emotional calendars that consistently produce newsworthy events. As Clarke and Clarke (1982, p. 64) note, "sport has become a significant international currency" and an ideal vehicle for capturing "massive and/or committed audiences with consumption profiles attractive to advertisers/sponsors" (Arundel & Roche, 1998, p. 60).

According to Singer (1998, p. 36), "Only sports has the nation, and sometimes the world, watching the same thing at the same time, and if you have a message, that's a potent messenger." Beyond this, sport is highly desirable to advertisers because as Jackson et al. (2004) note, it:

- Attracts large and often passionately devoted global audiences.
- In a relative sense it is cheaper to produce than many other types of programming.
- Is human drama at its finest providing a stimulus and an acceptable arena for the full range of human emotion.
- Reveals real people demonstrating the limits of the body.
- Is sexy and erotic (Guttmann, 1996).
- Provides us with carefully crafted narratives of heroes and villains (Whannel, 2002).
- Is associated with positive images of health and nationhood (Rowe, 1996).

In combination, all of these factors provide insights into what makes the sporting landscape a unique and highly valued cultural commodity. They also help explain why sport sponsorship and advertising have risen from $US0.5 million to $20 billion annually in the past 30 years (Marqusee, 2000). However, despite the extensive endeavors by sporting organizations to provide clean venues and broadcasts for sponsors, there are never any guarantees that corporate brands and logos will be immune from attack from rival corporations at sporting events. In fact, as a result of the sheer amount of money corporations expend to be official sponsors of sporting events, a particularly hostile version of sign wars entitled ambush marketing has become increasingly prevalent over the past 20 years. The ethics of ambush marketing has, not surprisingly, been extensively debated within the business and academic communities.

Ambush Marketing: Battle of the Brands

Ambush marketing is arguably the most contentious and visible corporate sign war (Goldman & Papson, 1996). However, despite the term's widespread use and its frequent association with copyrighting, trade marking, and passing off, ambush marketing is not a legal concept in its own right.[6] Rather, it is a popular label loosely applied to identify attempts by nonsponsors to benefit from the official sponsorship of another company (Crow & Hoek, 2003). That is, ambush marketing (also referred to as "parasitic" or "guerrilla" marketing) is "a planned effort by an organization to associate itself indirectly with an event in order to gain at least some of the recognition and benefits that are associated with being an official sponsor" (Sandler & Shani, 1989, p. 11). The terms *ambush* or *parasitic* emerge from the propensity for these campaigns to undermine consumer awareness of the existing and sanctioned promotions of official sponsors while simultaneously promoting the products and brands of nonsponsors (Meenaghan, 1996). In other words, ambush marketing needs to be understood as an attempt to disrupt and diminish the sign value and brand equity of official sponsors, while creating visibility and interest in the brands of unofficial sponsors.

Given its contested and controversial nature, there exists a growing body of literature that addresses a variety of issues pertaining to ambush marketing. We identify three recurring issues and themes that are emblematic of the debates surrounding ambush marketing. The first relates to the contentions of official sponsors who argue that sponsorship agreements and brand equity are devalued as a result of ambush marketing attempts. For example, in some consumer recall studies, survey respondents have failed to link official sponsors with the events (McCarthy & Lyberger, 2001) and there is evidence to suggest that nonsponsors can often be perceived to be official sponsors (Shani & Sandler, 1999). Moreover, there have been additional suggestions that the rebel and often highly visible activities of unofficial sponsors may become more memorable than those of official sponsor (Coulson, 2004). However, to the dismay of sponsors, the possibility also exists that given the constant bombardment of corporate signs, audiences may simply be ambivalent to or uninterested in sponsorship issues (D'Alessandro & Owens, 2002). As one marketer points out: "the most important thing for any official sponsor to keep in mind is that the average fan does not understand the differences between a title sponsor, associate sponsor, or ambush marketer—nor do they care" (cited in Gemma, 2003, p. 43).

A second and closely related argument is that sport and sporting organizations will ultimately suffer if the commercial interests of sponsors are jeopardized by ambush marketing. Specifically, critics claim that ambush marketing erodes the benefits of official sponsors, effectively threatening the sponsorship revenue that sustains sporting events and organizations. For example, Billy Payne, CEO of the Atlanta Olympic Games Organizing Committee, suggested that ambush marketers were doing "damage to the very people who made it all possible—the sponsors" (Shell, 1994, p. 11) and that ambushing "devalues the sponsorship investment and jeopardises the continued health of the Olympic movement" (Shell, 1994, p. 11). Payne's frank remarks offer an enlightening commentary on the priorities and central concerns of the increasingly commercialized Olympic movement. Nevertheless, while these dire predictions are frequently repeated (Meenaghan, 1994), they have failed to materialize; if anything, the values of sponsorship rights have increased substantially for major sporting events.

Finally, the very ethics of ambush marketing is often brought into question. Indeed, opponents of ambush marketing suggest it is essentially a negative tactic describing it as: "unethical," "cheating" (Shell, 1994), "stealing," and "outright robbery" (Brewer, 1993; Ettore, 1993). The IOC, for example, routinely labels corporations that engage in ambush marketing as parasites. However, opinions are also divided over the ethical implications of ambush marketing. Jerry Welsh, former head of worldwide marketing for American Express and the man who coined the term "ambush marketing," argues that claims of unethical marketing practice represent a "weak minded view that competitors have a moral obligation to step back and allow an official sponsor to reap all the benefits from a special event" (Meenaghan, 1996, p. 108). He further argues that competitors have "not only a right, but an obligation to shareholders to take advantage of such events" and that "all this talk about unethical ambushing is . . . intellectual rubbish and posturing by people who are sloppy marketers" (Meenaghan, 1996, p. 108).

As Welsh explains:

People think ambush marketing hurts the Olympics? Good. Who cares? Are the Olympics going to disappear from the planet? I don't think so. This isn't religion or virginity here, it's business. Marketing is a form of warfare, and the ambush is a helluva weapon. (Brewer, 1993, p. 74)

Despite the contention surrounding such issues and debates, ambush marketing remains a relatively common strategy for rival sponsors to disrupt the marketing activities and sign values of official sponsors during sporting events. Not surprisingly as ambush marketing strategies have evolved, so too have sponsor defenses.

Ambushing Sport: Strategies and Defenses

In the past two decades, various nonsponsors have employed a range of ambush marketing activities to imply an association with a sporting event (McKelvey, 1994; Meenaghan, 1994; Townley et al., 1998).[7] Meenaghan (1996), for example, identifies five common ambush marketing strategies. First, nonsponsors can legally sponsor media coverage of a sporting event thereby gaining access to potential global audiences. In what was arguably the first case of ambush marketing (Sandler & Shani, 1989), Fuji, an official worldwide sponsor of the 1984 Summer Olympics in Los Angeles was effectively ambushed by competitor Kodak who became the sponsor of ABC's coverage of the Games (Meenagham, 1994). Second, nonsponsors can sponsor a subcategory within a sporting event including teams and individual athletes. To a large extent, the former has become justifiable because of legislation protecting athletes' rights to seek their own endorsements while the latter has gained legitimacy simply because the media encourage competitors to purchase advertising time (Crompton, 2004). Kodak, for example, also became a sponsor of the US track team in 1984 further disrupting Fuji's visibility as an official sponsor. However, if Fuji was a victim of ambush marketing in 1984, it is widely accepted that it enacted revenge in 1988 (Crow & Hoek, 2003). While Kodak secured the worldwide category sponsorship for the 1988 Olympic Games, Fuji aggressively promoted their sponsorship of the US swim team. In another visible instance, while Reebok was the official sponsor of the 1996 Atlanta Olympics, Nike achieved visibility through its association with Michael Johnson who wore distinctive gold Nike running shoes in his victories in the 200- and 400-meter races.

Third, nonsponsors can purchase advertising time around sporting event broadcasts to achieve visibility and an indirect association with the event. For example, at the 1998 World Cup of soccer, Nike purchased a large amount of television advertising slots to promote their sponsorship of the Brazilian team. As a result, Nike achieved a higher awareness rating for the World Cup than the official sponsor which was Adidas (Crompton, 2004). Fourth, nonsponsors can deploy promotional activities to coincide with a sporting event including the use of billboard advertising in close proximity and within sporting venues. At the 2003 Rugby World Cup in Sydney, for example, Vodafone, an official sponsor of the Australian Wallabies but a nonsponsor of the Rugby World Cup, launched a number of promotional activities that included handing out branded flags and hooters during games while controversially placing giant inflatable Vodafone dolls outside of the venues. Other promotions by rival nonsponsors can include branded t-shirts, leaflets, coupons, product giveaways, cellular phone updates, and the presence of rogue banners. Equally contentious are attempts by nonsponsors to recruit groups of spectators to attend sporting events and display distinctive brand-related clothing and corporate signs. For example, Reebok recently branded the foreheads of 500 US college students with temporary tattoos to ambush Adidas's sponsorship of the

Boston Marathon (Thomaselli, 2003). Fifth, nonsponsors are increasingly adopting other creative and inventive strategies to imply an association with a sporting event. The NCAA is currently taking the Coors Brewing Company to court because Coors attempted to imply an association with the NCAA Final Four Basketball Tournament by conducting a ticket sweepstakes and offering tickets to the final three games of the tournament run annually in March and April (McKelvey, 2003).

In light of such attacks on official sponsors and their brands, a number of strategies have been employed by sponsors, sporting organizations and host cities/local governments to counter ambush marketing practices (Ettore, 1993; Payne, 1998; Shani & Sandler, 1999; Townley et al., 1998). Much of the literature suggests that a combination of preemptive counter-measures is most effective (Meenaghan, 1996). Take for example Townley et al.'s (1998) recommendations for cities bidding to host major sporting events. According to these authors, a trinity of commercial rights protection should be employed:

- control of intellectual property,
- control of event partners,
- and control of the event environment.

Controlling intellectual property is accounted for primarily by legally enforceable contracts which can include anything from exclusivity clauses or obligations on teams to cover up rival logos, to conditions for the use of participants' images in media. For example, in 1998 the US government passed amendments to the Olympic and Amateur Sports Act of 1978 which enabled the USA Olympic Committee to sue companies that attempted to illegitimately associate with the Salt Lake City Winter Olympics (Crompton, 2004). Meanwhile, sponsors and sport organizations can also limit the nature of subcategory sponsorships or dictate how tickets can be disbursed to prevent ambushers from using event tickets as prizes (McKelvey, 2003).

However beyond these contractual remedies, the most combative and arguably controversial strategies against ambush marketing relate to the nonnegotiable provision and maintenance of clean sporting venues (the third part of the rights protection trinity). Few in New Zealand will forget the failure of the New Zealand Rugby Union (NZRU) to secure co-hosting rights to the 2003 Rugby World Cup. After announcing their decision to award the Australian Rugby Union the sole rights to host the Rugby World Cup, the International Rugby Board noted that its decision was grounded on the inability of the NZRU to guarantee clean venues (Crow & Hoek, 2003). As Crow and Hoek (2003) explain, the NZRU's "bid for hosting rights foundered in part because of the IRB's determination to close promotion loopholes that rivals of official sponsors might exploit" (p. 3). Nevertheless, although sponsors build into their contracts the "right to control all commercial activity in and around the venue" (Dowse & Rafferty, 1995), a clean stadium can only be assured through the deployment of brand protection units to remove all additional advertising and monitor any ambush marketing attempts. Event management companies such as International Management Group (IMG) are marketing their services as anti-ambushers (Dowse & Rafferty, 1995) who scour sporting venues and spectators for any sign of nonsponsor brands and products. IMG recently represented the International Rugby Board for the 2003 Rugby World Cup in Australia and reported up to 500 marketing irregularities during the event which ranged from intellectual property misuse to instances of perceived ambush marketing (Lyons, 2003).

The following two case studies, the 2000 Sydney Olympic Games and the 1999 FIFA Under-17 World Soccer Championships, illustrate the increasingly aggressive nature of the defenses that event organizers, often in conjunction with sporting governing bodies and local governments, employ against the pervasive threat of ambush marketing. To some extent, we suspect that the similarity of the defenses in these two cases can be partially explained by the legacy of the involvement of global marketing and promotions company ISL-ISMM (ISL) in both organizations. The Swiss-based marketing company represented the IOC until they were replaced by the partly IOC-owned Meridian Management in 1996, while ISL was FIFA's marketing partner for almost 20 years until the marketing company spectacularly and controversially collapsed in 2001. Nevertheless, the types of ambush defenses outlined in these examples are by no means uncommon. Indications are that such tactics have become commonplace at a growing number of major international sporting events.

The Sydney 2000 Olympics

The Games of the XXVII (27th) Olympiad were held in Sydney, Australia, in September 2000. Almost all of the 34 different sports were staged at venues in the Sydney area with several events taking place in public areas including the harbor (for yachting and windsurfing) and the streets of Sydney (for the cycling road race and triathlon). Throughout the 1980s and 1990s, the IOC willingly embraced commercialism and has since witnessed substantial increases in revenue from the sale of worldwide television rights and the fusion of the Olympic five-ring symbol to the products and services of various multinational corporations.[8] Despite the confirmation of long alleged corruption and scandals within the IOC (Jennings, 1996; 2000; Simson & Jennings, 1992), 11 worldwide TOP sponsors contributed close to US$550 million to associate themselves with the Olympic movement and the Sydney Olympics. Additionally, the Sydney Organizing Committee (SOCOG) generated a substantial amount of further income from 13 Domestic Millennium Olympic Partners, 18 Sydney 2000 Supporters, and 38 Sydney 2000 Providers who supplied everything from beer, biscuits, dairy, and indoor sports surfaces to metal detectors and sunscreen (Landler, 2000). Meanwhile, the IOC negotiated over US$1.3 billion for total world television rights for the Sydney Games with the largest fees paid by the National Broadcasting Company (US$705 million) and the European Broadcasting Union (US$350 million) (Barney et al., 2002).

The defenses employed to protect official sponsors against ambush marketing in Sydney were developed from the IOC's experiences with previous Olympic Games and in particular the commercial debacle (Barney et al., 2002) of the 1996 Atlanta Summer Olympics where efforts to protect sponsors against ambushing were less than effective.[9] Ironically, Nike, one of the most aggressive and detested ambush marketers in Atlanta (Nike leased a parking garage near Centennial Park and constructed a gigantic tent city entitled "Nike Town" to promote its athletes and products) was warmly welcomed back into the Olympic family as an "Australian Sponsor" for the Sydney Olympics. Nevertheless, as a result of the proliferation of ambush advertising in Atlanta, a number of specific initiatives were undertaken well before the Sydney Games to protect official sponsors from ambush marketing. For example, shortly after Australia was awarded the 2000 Olympic Games in September 1993, the Australian Senate Legal and Constitutional References Committee conducted an inquiry into the protection of Olympic Insignia and sponsorship for the Sydney Games (Kendall & Curthoys, 2001). As a result of the committee's final report, the Sydney 2000 Games (Indicia and Images) Protection Act 1996 was enacted to regulate the commercial use of the indicia and images associated with the Games to ensure exclusivity for official Olympic sponsors (Kendall & Curthoys, 2001). The legislation prohibited commercial use of the words "Olympics," "Sydney 2000" "Sydney Games" and any images that would suggest a connection to the Sydney 2000 Olympics by unlicensed users. SOCOG would eventually license approximately 3000 different consumer products bearing official Olympic marks and symbols for sale in 2000 closely monitored outlets across Australia (Barney et al., 2000).

The value of this legislation was visible over a year before the start of the Olympics. For example, leading up to the Olympics, SOCOG compelled the National Australia Bank to remove Olympic Rings on display in its branches or face legal consequences (Tolhurst, 2000). Meanwhile, prior to the Olympics, SOCOG was sending as many as a dozen letters a week threatening legal action against companies who had misused branding, such as reproducing the Olympic rings or the Sydney 2000 logo (Dabkowski, 2000). Additionally, the IOC and SOCOG launched public relations campaigns to outline restricted items and examples of ambush marketing to communications agencies and television and radio stations in Australia. As Michael Payne, the IOC's marketing director from 1989 to 2003, has noted, "Public relations is becoming one of the best ways to control ambush marketing and even deter it from happening in the first place" (Payne, 1998). Following the IOC's cue, SOCOG unveiled an additional AU$3 million advertising campaign in July 2000 featuring Olympic gold medalist Herb Elliot to educate and warn Australians about the "dangers" of ambush marketing while focusing on the positive aspects of Olympic sponsorship (Tolhurst, 2000).

Closer to the Olympic Games a raft of legislation was "pushed through the NSW (New South Wales) parliaments to protect the brand rights of Sydney 2000 and sponsors who have paid to use them" (Dabkowski, 2000, p. 55). In March 2000, amendments to Sydney's Olympic planning laws were instituted to protect the Sydney Games image which restricted outdoor advertising in and around all Olympic venues, along designated routes and at specific locations across Sydney including Sydney Harbor. As the Minister for Urban Affairs and Planning noted, the amendments were publicly promoted as security for Olympic sponsors, but also as protection for the image of Sydney specifically, and Australia in general, to facilitate tourism and transform Australia's Olympic profile into investment opportunities (Morris, 2000). In other words, the vast legal protection afforded to the interests of multinational corporations and industry was camouflaged under the populist mantra of urban boosterism and nationalism.[10] As a result of the restrictive legislation, only official sponsors were allowed advertising space in or around all Olympic venues, including six sites around the city where giant screens broadcast the Games, with fines as high as AU$250,000 for any breach of advertising restrictions (Stravropoulos, 2000). According to IOC marketing director, Michael Payne, the IOC worked with public authorities in Sydney to control a three-mile area around Olympic venues (Payne, 1998) and the public areas around the six local sites where the Games were televised. Such conditions were sanctioned by the New South Wales government through the introduction of the controversial Olympic Arrangements Act (OAA) which according to the IOC "successfully plugged all the major loopholes" (Ambush Advertising, 2000, para.6). As Olympic Coordination Authority Chief David Richmond noted, the OAA granted a substantial amount of power to protect SOCOG and the Olympic sponsors: "The intention is very clearly there to make sure there is as much legislative power as is reasonably possible in a democratic society to protect the operations of the Games and the interest of SOCOG" (Salom, 2000). Besides covering everything from security to parking, the OAA allowed authorities to control airspace above Olympic venues from flying billboards, balloon advertising, or skywriting (Morris, 2000). Moreover, the OAA provided additional financial penalties for unsanctioned advertising in any form within designated distances of Olympic venues, and permitted authorities to remove and demolish any unauthorized advertising (Landler, 2000). Thus, the OAA controlled and restricted vast amounts of public space to preserve the rights and interests of SOGOC and the multinational sponsors of the Sydney 2000 Olympics; its reach extended well beyond Olympic stadia and involved various levels of government.

Prior to the Games, and in conjunction with the host city agreement, one of the first steps in the defense against ambushers was to cleanse all Olympic venues and eliminate existing advertising messages. It is important to note here that such efforts were not only undertaken to cleanse venues, but to monitor and control all forms of commercial activity "including concessions, franchises, and type of food sold in restaurants" (Payne, 1998, p. 329). The IOC and SOCOG extensively monitored all commercial activities during the Games, ensuring that spectators ate only officially endorsed foods and only used Visa, the official credit card of the Olympic movement, to purchase Olympic tickets and many other retail items at venues. Even computers and equipment of media from companies other than those of official partners IBM or Panasonic were required to be covered with tape at security check points (Many games, 2000). The extent of the levels of brand surveillance during the Games arguably verged on paranoia and some extreme instances were reported and circulated by the media generating some controversy for both SOCOG and the IOC. In Sydney, for example, a café inside the Olympic complex was asked to remove a bacon and egg roll known as a "damper" from its menu on the orders of "SOCOG's food police" (Anthony, 2000). The suspect bacon and egg roll was deemed to closely resemble the "Egg McMuffin" sold by McDonald's, a worldwide partner of the Olympic movement. Moreover, while SOCOG initially banned spectators from taking any food and drink into Olympic venues, a public outcry forced the organizing committee to allow small packages of homemade food and drinks (Stravropoulos, 2000). However, food and beverages were only permitted without any brand identification and up to a minimal size thereby forcing spectators to purchase sustenance from official caterers and sponsors who marked up prices by at least 100% (Stravropoulos, 2000). Meanwhile, security at venue-checkpoints, while also checking for dangerous items such as guns and knives, were asked to ensure that spectators were not carrying cans of Pepsi to appease Coca-Cola, one of the IOC's Worldwide Olympic Partners (Chaudhary, 2000).[11] According to newspaper accounts, spectators who refused to surrender their cans or bottles of Pepsi were refused entry to the Games (Anthony, 2000).

The IOC, however, is well aware that the presence of legislation and security checkpoints alone are not enough to deter willing ambush marketers. Consequently the IOC polices and monitors all venues through special "ambush hit squads" (Payne, 1998, p. 329). At the Sydney Olympics, SOCOG employed a brand-protection manager and utilized a team of 60, including specialist trademark and intellectual property advisors, to monitor corporate developments during the Games (Dabkowski, 2000). SOCOG also recruited large ambush hit squads to patrol Olympic venues and grounds to monitor commercial or unauthorized signage, including signage on spectators' clothing during the Games. A volunteer group known as the Brand Name Protection Unit (BNPU) which consisted of over 100 volunteers, mostly local university law students (Stravropoulos, 2000), were the "eyes and ears of SOCOG during the Games" (Dabkowksi, 2000, p. 5). The BNPU enforced sponsorship rights by asking spectators to turn any nonsponsor clothing inside out or have it removed, while explaining to spectators that ambush marketing limits SOCOG's ability to generate revenue (Stravropoulos, 2000). Meanwhile, outside the Olympic venues teams of "logocops" scanned Olympic souvenir items in shops and market stalls around Sydney to stop pirated goods by locating holograms that were embedded in official merchandise (Stravropoulos, 2000).

While such examples and tactics are by no means exhaustive, they are indicative of some of the measures organizing committees, sporting organizations and host local governments are taking to preserve and monitor sponsor rights and privileges. Issues surrounding the incursions of multinational signs into public spaces and the privileging of corporate rights are particularly important in this case given that the estimated total public cost of hosting the Sydney 2000 Olympics was US$1.3 billion (Waitt, 2003). It is also important to note that while the privileging of sponsor rights and the supposed resulting economic impacts of hosting the Games were promoted as benefiting the entire community, several studies have raised critical questions surrounding Aboriginal injustices, environmental issues, and the urban inequalities including housing and real-estate impacts on low-income populations that resulted from the Sydney Games (Hall, 2001; Hall & Hodges, 1998; Lenskyj, 2000). Indeed, while Australians were invited to "Share the Spirit" (Hall and Hodges, 1998) of the Games by massively subsidizing the Olympic movement and its sponsors, the benefits of hosting the Games were certainly not shared equally.

Similar ambush marketing defenses were employed at another global, although admittedly less high-profile and less controversial, sporting event: the 5th FIFA Under-17 World Soccer Championships held in New Zealand. Many of the details described in the following section stem from personal observations of one of the authors who attended planning meetings, and helped the Venue Organizing Committee (VOC) organize student volunteers who assisted with the tournament. The author attended all games played in Dunedin, New Zealand.

The 5th FIFA Under-17 World Soccer Championships

World soccer governing body FIFA, much like the IOC, has gone to extensive lengths to guarantee exclusivity for a limited number of Official Partners, Suppliers, and Licensees for each of FIFA's events. Moreover, FIFA has established a closely controlled and regulated marketing program to protect the rights and interests of their multinational sponsors. Since the conclusion of the 1998 FIFA World Cup in France, FIFA has been increasingly concerned with eliminating the manufacturing of unauthorized goods and preventing ambush marketing attempts by any unauthorized individuals or corporations to associate with FIFA events. For example, prior to the 2002 FIFA World Cup in Korea and Japan, FIFA organized a specialized anti-ambush team, comprised of trade mark specialists, commercial lawyers and sports marketing specialists based in Switzerland as well as in the two host countries, to monitor and control all commercial and sponsorship arrangements. While such protective measures are increasingly common at grandiose mega-events such as the FIFA World Cup, it is important to note that FIFA is similarly stringent with respect to their efforts to protect multinational sponsors from ambush marketing at their substantially low-profile global soccer events.

Take for example the 5th FIFA Under-17 World Soccer Championships held in New Zealand in November, 1999. Sixteen nations from six continents were divided into four groups with the top two teams in each group advancing to the quarter-finals. Dunedin, New Zealand's fifth largest city, hosted one of the tournament's four pools and a quarter-final game; other games were played in Auckland, Napier and Christchurch. A total of seven games were played in

Dunedin between Pool D members Paraguay, Qatar, Burkina Faso, and Jamaica at Carisbrook, a multi-sport venue that primarily hosts rugby matches and is known locally as the "House of Pain." The winner of Pool D, Paraguay, progressed to meet the eventual tournament winners, Brazil, in the quarter-finals. The event was broadcasted to an estimated audience of over 300 million in 60 countries around the world. The tournament, which received a subsidy of NZ$200,000 from the Hillary Commission (New Zealand's sporting governing body at the time of the tournament), was organized by a Local Organizing Committee in Auckland (NZ Under 17'99 Ltd)[12] and by Venue Organizing Committees based in each of the four urban centers. In Dunedin, the committee was comprised of local soccer officials, Carisbrook management, and business and tourism interests who worked together with City Councilors, and Dunedin City Council's Economic Development Unit and Events Coordinator. Dunedin was predicted to benefit from NZ$5 million in direct expenditure, with $3 million in trickle-down effects according to the local organizing committee while the global television coverage of the event was predicted to significantly boost the local tourism industry (Dunedin Expects, 1999).

Notably, the 1999 Under-17 Championships was organized under the regular supervision of FIFA officials who were frequently consulted during the planning stages while a large contingent of FIFA officials attended the event. For example, FIFA's official inspection party carefully scrutinized Carisbrook, local training venues, and local accommodation in June 1999. This was the third inspection by FIFA officials who, after having substantial trepidations with the planning and organization of the World Under-20 Youth Championships in Nigeria earlier that year, were concerned about the quality of stadia and accommodation. Moreover, representatives from FIFA's marketing company, ISL, and a local assistant were based at each of the venues prior to and throughout the tournament. The roles of the ISL marketing staff included managing venue advertising, ensuring client-sponsor servicing, and protecting sponsors against any form of ambush marketing. In terms of sponsors, the tournament had one "Presenting Partner," global electronic company JVC, and five "Official Partners," Coca-Cola, Fuji Film, Hyundai, Mastercard, and McDonalds, as well as a number of additional official suppliers. FIFA's emphasis on protecting the exclusive rights and privileges for their valued multinational sponsors was evident prior to the event. For example, Carisbrook features a number of semipermanent advertising boards belonging mainly to local companies. To comply with FIFA's clean venue policies, it was necessary to remove all competing signage from Carisbrook well before the tournament began. Interestingly, rather than entrusting local organizers with the job of covering these signs (a task that seemingly would not require a high level of skilled labor), a team of five professional advertisement-removers was flown from Europe to New Zealand over a week before the first pool game at Carisbrook (Carisbrook advertisements, 1999). London-based *Estadio Publicidad* is used by FIFA at events throughout the world in order to guarantee local consistency with respect to FIFA's clean venue policies. Even a small and relatively isolated locale such as Dunedin would be no exception to FIFA's stringent guidelines. Consequently, each advertising board at Carisbrook was painstakingly covered or removed by FIFA's advertisement-removal team which also set up and installed officially approved signage from sponsors at ground level.

One would presume that much of ISL's ambush marketing protection efforts would have focused on ensuring clean television coverage of the event; after all, it is the global coverage of the event that effectively communicates corporate brands around the world. Surprisingly, however, in Dunedin the ISL marketing representative paid a great deal of attention to detail that seemingly had very little to do with ensuring a clean broadcast for the tournament's multinational sponsors. For example, prior to the event a small article appeared in a free local Dunedin community newspaper (Dewy Deposits, 1999) outlining how the team from Burkina Faso was adapting to the local conditions. A photograph accompanying the article showed two of the Burkina Faso players lying on the grass. Conspicuous in the photograph is a Pump water bottle (a brand distributed by the New Zealand manufacturer of Coca-Cola, one of the event sponsors) from which one of the players is drinking. Meanwhile, on the left sleeve of one of the player's tracksuits a strip of masking tape can be clearly seen. Just visible above and below the tape are the familiar tail and hind leg of the Puma logo, covered, albeit not completely, to preserve multinational sporting corporation Adidas's sponsorship rights.

With Carisbrook in a relatively clean state, the anti-ambush team targeted several signs and logos that were noncamera visible and in most instances difficult, if not impossible, for local spectators and the global television audience to detect. For example, a number of small speakers had been strategically placed behind advertising boards around the venue for spectators to hear announcements and the national anthems of the respective countries taking part in the championships. On the side of each speaker was a small nameplate (no more than an inch in height and three inches in length) featuring the brand name of a company other than the tournament's principal sponsor, JVC. Shortly before the first pool game at Carisbrook, ground staff could be seen covering the nameplates with masking tape, apparently at the request of the ISL representative. Meanwhile, ISL staff also ensured that Carisbrook's luxury boxes were clean by carefully taping over the brand names of all microwave ovens and refrigerators.

Once Carisbrook had been cleansed according to FIFA's required standards, the efforts of the ISL marketing staff focused on carefully monitoring team officials and spectators attending the matches. Team officials were closely scrutinized by ISL staff since they were allowed to enter the playing area and could consequently be viewed by the global television audience. For example, at one point during the tournament a member of the coaching staff of one of the participating teams was asked by the ISL marketing representative to wear his jacket inside-out to conceal a logo from a rival brand, Kappa. Spectators received similar attention. During the tournament, for example, a member of the VOC approached local volunteers with instructions to monitor spectators as they entered Carisbrook to ensure that snack-food products other than official tournament supplier Bluebird were not consumed within the venue. Volunteers were explicitly told to direct spectators to either discard or consume rival products before entering the stadium. It is notable that the local volunteers felt uncomfortable with this directive, and the only child who approached the stadium with an offending bag of potato chips was allowed to pass freely. Another brand security measure employed by the ISL representative to protect and preserve the exclusive rights of sponsors to associate with the 1999 Under-17 World Soccer provides a useful, if extreme, example of FIFA's stringent brand protection policies. In an effort to attract local spectators to Carisbrook to watch the championships, the VOC initiated a variety of promotions, one of which included a banner competition for local schools. Surprisingly, even the presence of hand-crafted banners in the crowd during matches drew considerable attention from the ISL representative. One banner from a local girl's high school featured a cartoon soccer character which was surrounded by the logos of the presenting partner and the tournament's official partners. While the banner was ultimately allowed to remain, the ISL representative stapled pieces of cardboard over the logos to minimize any confusion between official sponsor logos and their hand-drawn counterparts. Such relatively minor case studies are exceedingly important to highlight the significance of even small locales/sporting spaces as global promotional platforms for corporate brands. In a similar vein as larger scale mega-events, local stadia such as Carisbrook and those spectators in attendance effectively become the canvas upon which commercial representations are transmitted and are increasingly being carefully controlled, structured and monitored in relation to the interests of corporate sponsors.

Conclusion

The case studies of the Sydney 2000 Olympics and the 5th FIFA Under-17 World Soccer Championships illustrate the increasingly prominent defensive strategies employed by sporting organizations, local organizing committees, and local governments to control sporting spaces and protect the interests of multinational sponsors from ambush marketing. In both cases, with the Sydney Games being the most extreme, the organizing committees employed numerous tactics to effectively create a hermetically sealed brand/consumption sporting environment: a legally enforced local product community/brand cocoon in which everyone drinks the same beverages and eats the same food while under the surveillance of brand protection hit squads and marketing representatives. It is also important to note that these are neither isolated nor unique incidents. For example, in September 2002, the South African government passed "draconian legislation" to prevent ambush marketing at the Cricket World Cup (Alvavy, 2003, p. 14). According to one report, a family was evicted from a match for drinking Coca-Cola because the official sponsor was Pepsi (Alvavy, 2003), while two school teachers escorting 34 children were initially barred entrance to a match because they were wearing shorts with an Adidas logo. The two primary teachers were eventually allowed entrance after they put their shorts on inside-out (Teachers Barred, 2003).

It is altogether not surprising that such heavy-handed tactics, which inevitably disregard the notion of a competitive free market, are often promoted as safeguarding and sustaining the interests and economic stability of sporting organizations and their global mega-events. Indeed, these issues simultaneously highlight the dependency of major international sporting organizations on revenue streams accrued from exclusive sponsorship deals with primarily multinational corporations. Consequently, with respect to the Olympics, local organizing committees and the IOC are increasingly attempting to steer public discourses and perceptions of ambush marketing through various public relations and advertising campaigns. Such strategies also serve, perhaps more importantly, as promotional notices to sponsors of the Olympic movement who demand reassurances that their brands will be protected from rival corporations. The IOC routinely vilifies ambush marketing as parasitic and unethical (Payne, 1998), while presenting sponsors and by extension the Olympic movement as the victims of ambush marketing and economic sabotage. However, such commentary is emblematic of a particular paradox embodied by the IOC. While the IOC clings to an ethos of amateurism and promotes its movement as a celebration of humanity, the Olympics are heavily commercialized and explicitly aligned with the interests of global capital, and have been scandalized with the recent confirmation of long suspected allegations of extensive corruption and fraud.

Such issues are particularly relevant as urban centers anxiously compete to host sporting mega-events and are increasingly willing to cede to the growing demands of sporting organizations to transform stadia into controlled, monitored, and branded environments (Hall, 2001). It is also notable that sporting sign wars extend well beyond the camera angles destined for global television audiences and take place within stadia (luxury boxes, media stations, food vendors) and beyond sporting boundaries. That is, sign wars are increasingly encroaching on broader urban landscapes (along transport routes, local communities outside urban centers, and, controversially, the skies above venues) which are being carefully monitored in relation to corporate interests. For example, in 2001 a US farmer who pruned a cornfield maze into the shape of the interlocking Olympic rings and a logo of an official sponsor was quickly instructed by the Salt Lake Organizing Committee's brand protection department to plough the corn under or alter the crop so it no longer resembled the Olympic logo (Amazed by reaction, 2001). In this respect, there is much need for a broad critical analysis that illuminates the geography of social relations (van Ingen, 2003) and how urban sporting and non-sporting spaces are being structured by particular political-economic and socio-cultural practices associated with the hosting of sporting mega-events. While the Olympics are promoted as a celebration of humanity, or in FIFA's case as the "beautiful game," there exist many unattractive and corporatist trends with respect to control, restriction, and surveillance of public spaces and citizens alike.

However, by treating spectators and citizens as potential accomplices to ambush marketing, it is increasingly likely that mega-sporting events such as the Olympics will lose considerable appeal and generate resistance and a deliberate desire to challenge and transgress the rules and regulations designed to protect and preserve sporting spaces for sponsor interests in the first place. This is particularly so as paying spectators and even citizens are being recruited by the IOC to participate in brand protection squads and to act as informants on any suspicious marketing activities. For example, a Greek sports fan recently questioned the privileging of corporate interests in Athens: "I don't see why, after all the money that Greek taxpayers will end up paying to host the games, McDonald's should dictate what I can eat in my own city" (Franchetti, 2004). Indeed, as multinational sponsor interests are continually privileged there is a greater chance that local spectators and taxpayers will choose to resist the Orwellian nightmare of hosting mega-sporting events and the appropriation of public spaces in the interests of global capital.

Notes

1. The state bodies include the Financial Crime Body, Hellenic Police, Customs, Prefecture Trade Services, and the Municipal Police. In the two months prior to the start of the Olympics, over 100 businesses and shops throughout Greece were patrolled and over 100,000 pirated items confiscated; over 20,000 products were seized through monitoring of all imposts. Athens 2004 performs daily checks on ambush marketing (2004), retrieved August 16, 2004, from http://www.athens204.com/athens2004/page/new slist?cid=3f797ae4be659f00VgnVCMServer281 30b0aRCRD&lang=en&oid=fc805bac4dbfdf00V gnVCM4000002b130c0aRCRD.

2. Total sponsorship revenues for the TOP program have increased from US$376 million from 1993–1996 to US$579 million from 1997–2000 (*Sydney 1997–2000*, 2001).

3. Such an understanding is grounded in contemporary conceptualizations of globalization processes as paradoxically compressing (Harvey, 1989) spatial and time constraints, while remaining dependent on local spaces, places, and labor (Morley and Robins, 1995).

4. Since 1970 more brands have been launched than throughout the entire history of marketing (Brierley, 2002), while brand images and their symbolic value have become the closest thing to an international language and are recognized in many more places than English (Klein, 2001).

5. Corporate sponsorship has grown from a US$7 billion-a-year industry to a US$19.2 billion one in 1999 (Klein, 2001).

6. For a company to establish "passing off," it must show that its rival has misrepresented its association with the event or sport and that this misrepresentation has caused damage to the official sponsor.

7. Due to space limitations, we are unable to review all of the detailed typologies of ambushing tactics and their counter-measures. For greater detail see: Crompton (2004); Crow and Hoek, (2003); Dowse and Rafferty, (1995); Meenaghan (1994; 1996; 1998).

8. Following the continued burden of the 1976 Montreal Olympics on taxpayers, the city of Los Angeles amended its charter to prevent the use of public funds to host the 1984 Summer Olympics. In fact, the Los Angeles Olympic Games were the first to be organized by a private, for-profit organization and relied heavily on the private sector, notably television money and corporate sponsorship, marking the dawn of the sponsorship age of the Olympic Games.

9. Conflicts between the Atlanta Olympic Games Organizing Committee (ACOG), municipal officials, and the USA Olympic Committee resulted in an "avalanche of Olympic commercialism" (Barney et al., 2002, p. 3) and a plethora of ambush marketing. This resulted in the IOC stipulating "clean city" agreements with local authorities in host cities.

10. For example, at one point during the games, Quantas was accused of being "un-Australian" by rival, and official Olympic sponsor Ansett, for newspaper advertisements that featured Cathy Freemen (Burbury, 2000). Ansett, the "official" airline of the Olympics took national rival Quantas to court for using the word "Olympics" in a newspaper advertisement which also featured a photograph of athlete Cathy Freeman. The case was settled out of court and just before

the start of the Games all Quantas advertising featuring athletes was removed and replaced with by a new campaign that carried the disclaimer "Quantas is not an Olympic sponsor" (Burbury, 2000).

11. SOCOG had the right to search clothing, baggage, and containers, and even conduct body searches (Stravropoulos, 2000).

12. NZ Under 17'99, Ltd., a separate legal entity from New Zealand Soccer, was set up specifically to run the tournament. While having a New Zealand Soccer representative on the board of directors and operating out of the New Zealand Soccer offices in Auckland, NZ Under 17'99 was officially separate from the national body.

References

Alvavy, K. (2003). Cricket sponsorship will have to adapt to survive. *Marketing Week*, *26*, 14.

Amazed by reaction. (September 8, 2001). *Otago Daily Times*, p. 28.

Ambush Advertising. (2000). *Ambush Advertising Targeted by Organizers*. Retrieved August 28, 2004, from http://archive.showmenews.com/2000/Jul/20000709Spor024.asp

Anthony, T. (September 14, 2000). Marketing war in Sydney, it's all about the sponsors. *The Harrisburg Press*, p. C01.

Arundel, J., & Roche, M. (1998). Media sport and local identity: British rugby league and sky TV. In M. Roche (Ed.), *Sport, popular culture, and identity*. (pp. 59–91). Aachen: Meyer and Meyer Verlag.

Bale, J. (1994). *The landscapes of modern sport*. Leicester: Leicester University Press.

Barney, R., Wenn, S., & Martyn, S. (2002). *Selling the five rings: The International Olympic Committee and the rise of Olympic commercialism*. Salt Lake City: The University of Utah Press.

Brewer, G. (1993). Be like Nike? *Sales and Marketing Management*. 66–68.

Brierley, S. (2002). *The advertising handbook* (2nd ed.). London: Routledge.

Burbury, R. (September 28, 2000). Ambush! All's fair in adland wars. *Australian Financial Review*, p. 34.

Carisbrook Advertisements. (October 19, 1999). Carisbrook advertisements to go. *Otago Daily Times*, p. 10.

Chaudhary, V. (September 19, 2000). Olympics ban guns, knives . . . Pepsi, to protect official sponsors. *Knight Ridder Tribune Business News*.

Clarke, A., & Clarke, J. (1982). Highlights and action replays—ideology, sport and the media. In J. Hargreaves (Ed.), *Sport, culture and ideology* (62–87). London: Routledge & Kegan Paul.

Coulson, N. (2004). Ambush marketing. *Brand Strategy*, *179*, 32.

Crompton, J. L. (2004). Sponsorship ambushing in sport. *Managing Leisure*, *9*, 1–12.

Crow, D., & Hoek, J. (2003). Ambush marketing: a critical review and some practical advice. *Marketing Bulletin*, *14*, 1–14.

Dabkowski, S. (June 3, 2000). Games will protect its brand. *Sydney Morning Herald*, p. 55.

D'Alessandro, D.F., & Owens, M. (2002). *Brand warfare: Ten rules for building the killer brand: Lessons for new and old economy players*, New York, London: McGraw-Hill.

Dewy Deposits (November 2, 1999). Dewy deposits cause a dose of distraction. *Dunedin Star*, p. 12.

Dowse, L. and Rafferty, L. (1995). Legal issues in sports marketing. In M. Fewell (Ed.), *Sports law: A practical guide*. North Ryde, NSW: LBC Information Services. 32–77.

Dunedin Expects. (1999). *Dunedin expects to benefit by $8 million*. Retrieved September 1, 2004, from http://global.factiva.com/en/arch/print_results.asp

Ettore, B. (1993). Ambush marketing: Heading them off at the pass. *Management Review*, *82*(3), 53–57.

Franchetti, M. (2004). *Olympic struggle: Fans face boot for eating or drinking wrong brands at games*. Retrieved August 16, from http://www.herald.ns.ca/stories/2004/08/08/f202.raw.html

Gemma, C. (2003). Sneaking in. *Marketing Week*, *26*(14), 43–44.

Gibson, O. (2004). *Olympics battles against "ambush marketing."* Retrieved August 6, from http://sport.guardian.co.uk/olympics/story/0,10308,1266558,00.html

Goldman, R., & Papson, S. (1996). *Sign wars: The cluttered landscape of advertising*. New York: Guilford Press.

Guttmann, A. (1996). *The erotic in sport.* New York: Columbia University Press.

Hall, C. M. (2001). Imaging, tourism and sports event fever: The Sydney Olympics and the need for a social charter for mega-events. In C. Gratton & I. Henry (Eds.), *Sport in the city: The role of sport in economic and social regeneration* (pp. 166–183). London: Routledge.

Hall, C. M. & Hodges, J. (1998). The politics of place identity in the Sydney 2000 Olympics: "Sharing the spirit of corporatism." In M. Roche (Ed.), *Sport, popular culture, and identity* (pp. 95–111). Aachen: Meyer and Meyer Verlag.

Harvey, D. (1989). *The condition of postmodernity.* Oxford: Blackwell.

IOC. (2004). *Uniqueness of the Olympic Games.* Retrieved August 12, 2004, from http://www.olympic.org/uk/organisation/facts/introduction/objectives_uk.asp

Jackson, S., Andrews, D., & Scherer, J. (2004). Introduction: The contemporary landscape of sport advertising. In S. Jackson & D. Andrews (Eds.), *Sport, culture, and advertising: Identities, commodities and the politics of representation* (pp. 1–23). London: Routledge.

Jay, M. (2004). *Sponsors, too, are going for gold at the Olympics.* Retrieved August 28, from http://news.scotsman.com/index.cfm?id+904802004

Jennings, A. (1996). *The new Lords of the Rings.* London: Simon and Schuster.

Jennings, A. (2000). *The great Olympic swindle: When the world wanted its games back.* London: Simon and Schuster.

Kellner, D. (2003). *Media spectacle.* London: Routledge.

Kendall, C., & Curthoys, J. (2001). Ambush marketing and the Sydney 2000 games (Indicia and Images) protection act: A retrospective. *E Law-Murdoch University Electronic Journal of Law, 8*(2).

Klein, N. (2001). *No logo.* London: Flamingo.

Landler, M. (September 29, 2000). Sponsors guard their investments at Olympics. *The New York Times,* p. 1.

Lenskyj, H. (2000). *Inside the Olympic industry.* Albany: State University of New York Press.

Lyons, K. (November 11, 2003). Slap on the wrist for RWC ambushers. *B & T Weekly, 53,* p. 6.

Many Games. (September 30, 2000). Many games spectators need to be fit too. *Otago Daily Times,* p. 10.

Marqusee, M. (2000). Sport as apocalypse. *Frontline, 17,* pp 1–10.

McCarthy, L., & Lyberger, M. (2001). An assessment of consumer knowledge of, interest in, and perceptions of ambush marketing strategies. *Sport Marketing Quarterly, 10*(2), 130–137.

McKelvey, S. (April 18, 1994). Sans legal restraint, no stopping brash, creative ambush marketing. *Brandweek,* p. 20.

McKelvey, S. (2003). Unauthorized use of event tickets in promotional campaign may create new legal strategies to combat ambush marketing: NCAA v. Coors. *Sport Marketing Quarterly, 12*(2), 117–118.

Meenaghan, T. (1994). Point of view: ambush marketing—immoral or imaginative practice. *Journal of Advertising Research,* September–October, 77–88.

Meenaghan, T. (1996). Ambush marketing—a threat to corporate sponsorship. *Sloan Management Review,* Fall, 103–113.

Meenaghan, T. (1998). Ambush marketing: Corporate strategy and consumer reaction. *Psychology and Marketing, 15*(4), 305–322.

Morley, D. & Robins, K. (1995). *Spaces of Identity: Global media, electronic landscapes, and cultural boundaries.* London: Routledge.

Morris, L. (March 17, 2000). Ads ban protects games sponsors. *Sydney Morning Herald,* p. 8.

Murphy, B. (August 31, 2004). What now for Athens venues?: If new or refurbished sports facilities built for the Olympic games become idle, Greek taxpayers will be hit hard. *The Hamilton Spectator,* p. SP08.

Nava, M. (1997). Framing advertising: Cultural analysis and the incrimination of visual texts. In M. Nava, A. Blake, I. MacRury, & B. Richards (Eds.), *Buy this Book: Studies in advertising and consumption* (pp. 34–50). London: Routledge.

Payne, M. (1998). Ambush marketing: The undeserved advantage. *Psychology and Marketing, 15*(4), 323–331.

Roche, M. (2000). *Mega-events and modernity: Olympics and Expos in the growth of global culture.* London UK: Routledge.

Rowe, D. (1996). The global love-match: Sport and television. *Media, Culture, and Society, 18*(4), 565–582.

Salom, T. (March 1, 2000). Calling in the ad busters/sponsors protected. *Daily Telegraph,* p. 11.

Sandler, D. M., & Shani, D. (1989). Olympic sponsorship vs "Ambush" marketing: who gets the gold? *Journal of Advertising Research,* August–September, *11,* 9–14.

Shani, D., & Sandler, D. (1999). Ambush marketing: Is confusion to blame for the flickering of the flame? *Psychology and Marketing, 15*(4), 367–383.

Shell, A. (1994). Ambush marketers will win no medals. *Public Relations Journal,* January, *50,* 11.

Simson, V., & Jennings, A. (1992). *The Lords of the Rings: Power, money, and drugs in the modern Olympics.* London: Simon and Schuster.

Singer, T. (1998). Not so remote control. *Sport,* March, 36.

Sponsoring. (2004). *Sponsoring.* Retrieved August 16, 2004, from http://www.athens2004.com/ en/Sponsors

Stravropoulos, P. (2000). *Sydney reorganized to benefit Olympic games corporate sponsors.* Retrieved August 8, from http://www.wsws.org/articles/2000/sep2000/olypi-s09_prn.shtml

Sydney 1997–2000. (2001). *Sydney 1997–2000 Games of the Olympiad: Facts and figures.* Retrieved August 14, 2004, from http://www.multimedia.olympic.org/pdf/en_report_682 .pdf

Teachers barred. (2003). *Teachers barred entry to oval for wearing shorts with logo.* Retrieved September 12, 2004, from http:www.witness.co.za/showcontent.asp?id=13199&action=full

Thomaselli, R. (2003). Reebok's Terry Tate set to play dirty ball. *Advertising Age, 74*(16), 4–5.

Tolhurst, C. (July 26, 2000). Beware of the ambush. *Australian Financial Review,* p. 18.

Townley, S., Harrington, D., & Couchman, N. (1998). The legal and practical prevention of ambush marketing in sports. *Psychology and Marketing,* 15(4), 333–348.

Van Ingen, C. (2003). Geographies of gender, sexuality, and race. *International Review for the Sociology of Sport,* 38(2), 201–216.

Waitt, G. (2003). Social impacts of the Sydney Olympics. *Annals of Tourism Research,* 30(1), 194–215.

Wernick, A. (1991). *Promotional culture: Advertising, ideology, and symbolic expression.* Newbury Park: Sage.

Whannel, G. (2002). *Media sports stars: Masculinities and moralities.* London: Routledge.

Willigan, G. E. (1992). High performance marketing: An interview with Nike's Phil Knight. *Harvard Business Review,* July–August, 91–101.

9

EXPRESSING FENWAY: MANAGING AND MARKETING HERITAGE WITHIN THE GLOBAL SPORTS MARKETPLACE

Michael T. Friedman and Michael L. Silk

> The ballpark is the star. In the age of Tris Speaker and Babe Ruth, the era of Jimmie Foxx and Ted Williams, through the empty-seats epoch of Don Buddin and Willie Tasby, and unto the decades of Carl Yastrzemski and Jim Rice, the ballpark is the star. A crazy-quilt violation of city planning principles, an irregular pile of architecture, a menace to marketing consultants, Fenway Park works. It works as a symbol of New England's pride, as a repository of evergreen hopes, as a tabernacle of lost innocence. It works as a place to watch baseball. (Nolan, 1999, p. 27)

The success of the 92-year-old Fenway Park, home to the Major League Baseball (MLB) organization Boston Red Sox, flies in the face of the contemporary logic underpinning baseball stadium design, which, within the context of the global economy, seems to demand the production of spectacular consumption environments. As one of two "early modern stadiums" remaining in use and also a key design influence for the recent, retro-style "postmodern stadiums" (Bale, 1994; Ritzer & Stillman, 2001), Fenway Park seemingly lacks sufficient consumption-oriented amenities such as the large number of luxury suites and concessions points-of-sale common in Fenway's recently-built competitors, yet it generates more revenue than any other MLB facility (MLB Valuations, 2004). Indeed, the cultural intermediaries responsible for contouring Fenway Park's future have struggled over the last decade with this paradoxical situation as they face the challenge of ensuring that the Red Sox organization continues to thrive within an increasingly cluttered and competitive global sports marketplace.

The processes of globalization have enabled an unprecedented degree of economic, political, and cultural interaction; complex connectivity; and interdependence as technology has helped to overcome the geographic barriers that had once restricted flows of trade, information, and populations (Harvey, 1990; Keohane & Nye, 2000; Tomlinson, 1999). With increasingly dense networks trafficking in capital, goods, images, ideas, and people, the global marketplace has emerged as the logics of late capitalism promoting global expansion in the search for new sources of supply and labor and markets for finished goods (Appadurai, 1990; Castells, 1989; Jameson, 1991). Globalization has then resulted in once geographically-bound local markets being flooded with distantly-created products ranging from manufactured hard goods to ephemeral media presentations and individual experiences (Albrow, 1996; Robins, 1997). Consumers, whose choices were once relatively limited to locally produced goods, now have to differentiate products from a dizzying assortment in which functional differences are minute, if they exist at all (Olins, 2000).

As global processes have broadened consumer choice, they have also challenged producers to identify and create features that will differentiate their products from those of their global competitors; and in so doing, the producers develop resources enabling them to acquire a sustainable competitive advantage over their rivals (Barney, 1991; Peteraf, 1993; Wernerfelt, 1984). Furthermore, producers of goods, experiences, and services are required to neutralize any advantage that competitors may gain, usually through the acquisition of similar resources. This means that competitive advantage is often short-lived, especially if resources are easily imitable (Amis et al., 1997; Grant, 1991; Wright, 1994). Therefore, within a global context, organizational fields are subject to contradictory pressures toward homogenization and heterogeneity—organizations are both attempting to differentiate themselves from each other, yet are, at the same time, attempting to mimic those whom are perceived as successful within the organizational field. These contradictions are most clearly manifest through competitive and institutional processes.

The competitive pressures from the global sports marketplace clearly form the context within which the Red Sox management operates. Following the success of the first retro ballparks and fearing the insufficiency of Fenway Park's revenue-generating capacity, in 1999, Red Sox President John Harrington proposed the construction of a virtual replica with contemporary amenities—a polemic that caused much antagonism between owners and fans. Harrington's plans ultimately failed, and under the new ownership of John Henry since 2002, the Red Sox have taken a different route toward maximizing Fenway's revenue streams—by making several aesthetic and physical improvements to the ballpark (which are somewhat ironically based on the Fenway-inspired new-old ballparks) that emphasize selected historical elements.

While some of the changes to Fenway Park, both proposed and made, were designed to address the stadium's perceived structural deficiencies, their primary purpose has been to enhance the consumer experience. In the strategies employed under Harrington and Henry, the Red Sox management has sought to utilize the team and stadium's unique histories as symbolic resources in a global marketplace in which many contemporary scholars (e.g. Hannerz, 1996; Lash & Urry, 1987; Morley & Robins, 1995; Sassen, 2000) suggest that products are consumed for their cultural meanings rather than for their physical attributes and functional uses. Within this "symbolic marketplace" (Schultz et al., 2000, p. 5), meanings, emotions and symbols combine to establish brand image, which helps organizations separate their products from those of their

competitors. The product is thus far more difficult to imitate than tangible resources (Amis, 2003; Olins, 2000; Robins, 1997; Smart & Wolfe, 2000). As
such, "the battle for market share becomes articulated as a struggle for the
imagination of the consumer" (du Gay, 2000, p. 71), often expressed through
the production of consumption environments (Ritzer, 1999).

This "expressive" (Schultz et al., 2000) turn provides the focus for our critical interrogation of the place of Fenway Park within the contemporary global
sports marketplace. Capitalizing upon its storied past as the home of the Red
Sox (Shaughnessy, 1996), those responsible for "expressing" Fenway seek to
differentiate themselves and gain a competitive advantage over producers of
other leisure experiences by creating a heritage environment that functions
not only to draw tourist spending, but also to provide settings for entertainment, relaxation, and consumption (Apostolakis, 2003; Chhabra et al., 2003;
Poria et al., 2003; McIntosh & Prentice, 1999; Waitt, 2000; Wang, 1999). However, and emblematic of the manufacture and management of heritage under
the dictates of corporate capitalism, expressing Fenway invokes the commodification of "pastness," producing an emphasis of style over substance and an
interpretation of the past manipulated in the interests of capital or dominant
social norms (Apostolakis, 2003; Ashworth & Larkham, 1994; McIntosh &
Prentice, 1999; Waitt, 2000).[1, 2]

Therefore, within the balance of this paper, we address the ways in which
those cultural workers at the Boston Red Sox organization have addressed
and responded to the complex environment within which they are operating.
In particular, we focus on how these perceived pressures have impacted upon
the struggles over Fenway Park, since over the last 15 years, heritage has become a central component in the production of MLB venues and baseball entertainment experience.

Locating Fenway Park

> The seats are small and hard. There is no legroom. When a row is full, it's
> nearly impossible to get to a center seat . . . And like a 1950s kitchen,
> with bad paneling and lumpy linoleum, Fenway is almost impossible to
> clean. Even when it's thoroughly washed and vacuumed, it looks dirty.
> (Shaughnessy, 1996, p. 226)

Located in the Fenway neighborhood of Boston, Fenway Park occupies an
eight-acre parcel of land bounded by five city streets. Similar to other stadiums from the early-modern era of ballpark construction (Ritzer & Stillman,
2001), Fenway Park can be seen as "the unique product of its circumstances
and of the architectural dialogue between two existing forces: the diamond,
the outfield, and the stands pushing outward, and the surrounding streets and
structures containing them" (Neilson, 1995, p. 41). As such, Fenway Park is
integrated into the neighborhood alongside office buildings, residential apart-
ments, two schools, and various retail and entertainment establishments. In
turn, the neighborhood has become part of the Fenway Park experience, with

food vendors and fans gathering on the public Yawkey Way before games. According to one Red Sox fan, "it's not a game if you don't go into the Souvenir Shop at least once and look at a new hat, or get a sausage on Yawkey [Way]" (Mattson, 2002).

Those groups seeking to preserve Fenway Park have identified five historic districts in proposing the said ballpark for landmarks designation under National Park Service guidelines (although the Red Sox are opposed to such a designation): the playing field, the main grandstand, the right field grandstand, the left field grandstand and the left field wall, which is also known as "the Green Monster" (Decker, 2000, personal interview). Of these five areas, the best known is the Green Monster, which is described as one of the most iconic structures in US sports (Bale, 1994; Gershman, 1993; Ritzer & Stillman, 2001).

The stadium is MLB's smallest, with a capacity of just over 37,000 and "boasts" of just one deck. Built in an era long before night games, television, suburbanization and corporate boxes, Fenway Park lacks many of the amenities that have become familiar in the late capitalist consumption environments. Moreover, the experience from having many seats could be considered as poor because support posts obstruct the view, while others are poorly oriented (Campbell, 2002). Yet over 92 years, a variety of changes have been made to meet the functional requirements and revenue demands of the moment. Each decade has seen major structural changes such as a full renovation in 1934, the addition of lights in the 1940s, and the construction of a new press box and luxury club seats in the 1980s. There were also more mundane alterations such as the addition of bullpens or the changing of the composition of the left field wall (Shaughnessy, 1996). While the changes were necessary for its continued operation, trends in stadium design and development have substantially diverged from Fenway's seemingly more organic evolution, leaving Fenway Park to compete somewhat uncomfortably within the era of the postmodern ballparks.

In the decades following World War II, Fenway Park's contemporaries from the early-modern period of ballpark construction (such as Brooklyn's Ebbets Field, Pittsburgh's Forbes Field, and Philadelphia's Shibe Park) were replaced with "late-modern facilities" (Ritzer & Stillman, 2001). Stadiums of this era were generally unadorned, circular, multi-purpose, concrete structures that were virtually identical to one another (Bale, 1994; Ritzer & Stillman, 2001). Where early modern ballparks were distinctive, these late-modern facilities can be described as "characterless, other than the purity of their form and the amusement of looking at them from 10,000 feet up" (Janet Marie Smith, Boston Red Sox Vice President of Planning and Development; personal interview). These overly rationalized structures often detracted from the baseball experience as seats were poorly angled and (are/were) too far from the field, and the environment was fairly "antiseptic" (Raitz, 1987; Ritzer & Stillman, 2001).

The construction of Oriole Park at Camden Yards (OPCY) was the break from the late-modern design style — a physical manifestation of baseball's shift from the trammels of nation building to a spiraling existence within the vectors of global capitalism. According to Smith, who held the same position with the Baltimore Orioles at the time Camden Yards was designed and built, "(Orioles President Larry Lucchino) was just looking [at how] to make the home of the Orioles as spirited a place as it could be and as much like the ballparks that he'd grown up loving in Pittsburgh" (personal interview). Seeking "to have a modern stadium, yet retain[ing] the warmth and intimacy of an old-fashioned ball park," (Maryland Stadium Authority, 1987, p. 10), Camden Yards aesthetically produced an idealized baseball environment by mining the sport's history for design elements. Coexisting with a variety of decontextualized baseball signifiers are a plethora of revenue-enhancing amenities including luxury seating, specialized food concessions and a variety of shopping choices.

As the first retro stadium, Camden Yards was designed to gain a competitive advantage within the symbolically-oriented global sports marketplace through the manufacture and marketing of heritage. Indeed, heritage, as a cultural product, is clearly an economic resource "in which very selective material artifacts, mythologies, memories, and traditions become resources for the present" (Graham, 2002, p. 1004), and is manifested in the production of consumption spaces. As such, organizations can utilize heritage to fashion narratives that can attract consumers and direct their gaze toward a (limited) range of interpretations (Waitt, 2000). However, heritage critically goes beyond the function of representing the brand image: it can function internally as a locus of community affect and identity, and it can reproduce the concept of a spatially constructed, localised, imagined unity—a redefinition of place in the mind of external and internal consumers (Graham, 2002; Rowe & McGuirk, 1999; Silk, 2002).

Camden Yards, in particular, sought to utilize heritage as a resource in its use of aesthetic elements to weave symbolic meanings into the environment. Through a "random cannibalization of all the styles of the past" (Jameson, 1991, p. 18), Camden Yards' designers hoped to transfer the meanings associated with early modern ballparks into a new consumption space that would create a spectacular environment, providing consumers with a distinctive experience enticing additional consumption (see also Ritzer, 1999; Van Ingen, 2003).

Within Camden Yards, Smith and Lucchino (along with architects from HOK Sport) created this spectacular environment in a number of ways. First, in order to emulate the look of the early-modern ballparks, they chose to use exposed structural steel and brick facades rather than display reinforced concrete. Other architectural signifiers from baseball history and the surrounding city were utilized throughout Camden Yards as well, with the incorporation of the historic Camden Yards Warehouse, the use of ivy on the centerfield batter's eye (reminiscent of Wrigley Field), and the construction of a sun shade above the upper deck similar to that of Forbes Field. Specifically borrowing from Fenway Park, Camden Yards attempted to recreate Yawkey Way by incorporating Eutaw Street into the ballpark and by featuring a tall right field wall similar to the "Green Monster."

Yet in this production of heritage, what is marketed as "history" is often just one version of the past—a version that can bear only partial resemblance to histories (Ashworth, 1990; Ashworth & Tunbridge, 1990; Kearns & Philo, 1993; Waitt, 2000). As suggested above, this commodification of "pastness" provides an emphasis of style over substance—an interpretation of the past manipulated in the interests of capital or dominant social norms, pointing to the relative power of certain organizations to control and disseminate historical knowledge (McLean, 1995).

This commodification and depthless representation of pastness in postmodern ballparks is evident through comparing the Green Monster with Camden Yards' tall right field wall. The Green Monster did not even exist when Fenway opened in 1912. It only came to being during the ballpark's life. With Lansdowne Street just 315 feet from the home plate, the left field was originally a ten-foot wall atop a ten-foot hill known as "Duffy's Cliff," named for the Red Sox left fielder of the era. In the 1934 renovation, owner Tom Yawkey sought to purchase Lansdowne St. from the City in order to expand the ballpark. But as he was unsuccessful, he instead had a 37-foot wall built (Shaughnessy, 1996, personal interview). Initially, the wall featured advertisements; and eventually, it was painted completely green in 1947 (Gershman, 1993). Since its construction, the Green Monster has been associated with great Red Sox players such as Ted Williams and Carl Yastrzemski, and great baseball moments such as the home runs of Red Sox catcher Carlton Fisk that won the 6th game of the 1975 World Series, as well as that of Bucky Dent for the New York Yankees in the 1978 American League East Playoff (Sporting News, 2003).

In contrast, the right field wall at Camden Yards was an aesthetic choice on a blank tableau of urban space, upon which the Orioles and HOK Sport could determine a stadium's parameters within broad guidelines. The wall's height serves no real functional purpose other than to evoke pastness and to provide a contrived quirkiness. Just as there was no architectural or legal necessity to retain the Warehouse, the Orioles could have chosen other uses for that space, including placing seats behind a wall with more of a conventional height. Yawkey had no such option when he had the Green Monster built on the property border of Fenway Park. Moreover, the Green Monster has attained its iconic status and sense of pastness as a result of the events and activities with which it is directly associated.

The contrived nature of Camden Yards' aesthetics was not a barrier to its success, as the Orioles have drawn more than 85% of its capacity in its first nine years (Baltimore, 2003). With Camden Yards' variety of revenue enhancers, team revenues escalated significantly and the value increased from $70 million to $173 million between 1988 and 1993 (Friedman et al., 2004). With these increased revenues, the Orioles were able to increase their payroll and attract top free agents, aiding the team in making the playoffs in 1996 and 1997. Subsequently, each of Major League Baseball's 16 facilities that have opened have heavily utilized nostalgic tropes (Ritzer & Stillman, 2001; van Rooij, 2002) in order to make the new stadiums "look and feel like what fans think the old-time fields must have looked like and felt like" (Epstein, 1996, p. A13), and to create "a sense of place that didn't exist [in] those parks of the '70s", according to Boston Preservation Alliance's Executive Director Albert Rex in a personal interview. Indeed, as Ritzer and Stillman (2001) proposed, these postmodern stadiums attempt to "reenchant" the consumption experience by copying the physical elements from baseball's past in an attempt to tie this consumption experience into the game's historic meanings.

The proliferation of nostalgia-laden retro stadiums is exemplary of the tendency toward homogenization (or "isomorphism") within increasingly complex organizational fields (which consist of similar services or products) through mimetic, normative, and coercive processes (DiMaggio & Powell, 1983). Mimetic isomorphism entails the development of products and adoption of practices similar to their successful competitors much, if not more, for their legitimacy than for their perceived ability to improve performance (DiMaggio & Powell, 1983). This legitimacy is particularly important in moments of uncertainty intensified by the perceived pressures of globalization, as failure to properly adapt to changing conditions can be potentially devastating. In normative isomorphism, professionalized workers and networks diffuse dominant ideas within an industry (DiMaggio & Powell, 1983). As globalization is marked by increasing interconnectedness, concepts of best practices are easily, rapidly, and broadly communicated (Mavima & Chackerian, 2001). In coercive isomorphism, organizations react to formal and informal pressures from legal requirements and cultural expectations to conform to certain standards of behavior (DiMaggio & Powell, 1983). While globalization presents a diverse legal and cultural patchwork, organizations seeking acceptance within a particular area often need to conform to local legal and cultural standards in order to be successful (Cousens & O'Brien, 2004).

With imitation at their core, postmodern facilities demonstrate mimetic isomorphism as their designers conscientiously attempt to copy the past as well as each other in order to appeal to consumer imaginations, enabling them to remain competitive for consumption spending. Indeed, Smith (in a personal interview) described the design process for Camden Yards as "art imitating life in looking at Fenway and Ebbets and others to do [this ballpark]", while architectural elements throughout the Baltimore stadium allude to early-modern facilities. Subsequent postmodern stadiums have attempted to replicate the perceived successful elements of Camden Yards with their heavy utilization of retro elements (with a degree of contrived quirkiness) and similar spatial configurations (with broad concourses, allusions to team history, specialty-themed food stands, and locally inspired design elements). However, there has been a tendency toward homogenization, as Smith alludes to when he said that "after a while, you may have 20 new ballparks built within a ten-year period, and they all may learn from each other . . . but at some point, they do start to look alike" (personal interview).

Such tendencies toward isomorphism are perhaps not surprising, given that since the mid-1980s, there have only been three architectural firms in the US primarily responsible for designing major league sports facilities — HNTB Sports, Ellerbe Becket, and HOK Sports — all based in Kansas City, the last two of which were started by former HNTB architects (Provoost, 2000a). HOK Sport has been particularly active in the design of retro baseball stadiums, starting with Camden Yards (Provoost, 2000b). Moreover, many of the subcontractors in these projects follow these patterns of normative isomorphism. For example, Ronnie Younts of David Ashton and Associates has designed signage in nine various sporting venues (personal interview). Smith's role is also particularly instructive. In addition to Camden Yards, she served as project manager for Atlanta's Turner Field and has consulted on several other retro stadiums, and is thus able to offer a unique perspective on the construction of these postmodern ballparks. In considering the isomorphic pressures within the contemporary environment, she suggests, "on the one hand, the advantage of having a firm that specializes in something is that you're not starting from scratch . . . [But] the flip side of that is that it's hard for a new idea to emerge out of a repeated approach to the same thing" (personal interview).

Faced with varying competitive pressures, those responsible for Fenway Park in the late 1990s were uncertain about the future. Therefore, they initiated plans to construct a replacement. In May 1999, Red Sox President John Harrington proposed the construction of a new Fenway Park, with home plate just 206 yards compared with that of the original (Harrington, 1999). Describing Fenway Park as physically and economically obsolete, Harrington (1999) proposed a "design that preserves all that is good about baseball in Boston," and stated that "the new ballpark will be modeled on Fenway and will provide affordable family entertainment, conveniences, and the community benefits of a Camden Yards" (p. A19).

In its design, the new Fenway attempted to recreate many aesthetic elements of the original, to which would be added the most profitable elements of retro stadiums. The HOK design featured a replica of the Green Monster complete with a manual scoreboard, in-play ladder and an identical view of the distant Citgo sign. The new stadium would also have virtually identical outfield dimensions and outfield bullpens; and, transferred from the original, the same right field foul pole named for '40s second baseman Johnny Pesky. In addition, the new stadium would have broad concourses (to allow for increased concession points-of-sale), more than 5000 club seats and 100 luxury boxes, and a capacity exceeding 45,000 (Macero & Myers, 1999). The original Fenway Park would be memorialized with remaining portions of the outer façade, and the infield and Green Monster symbolically marked where they once stood (Krupa & Vaillancourt, 1999, personal interview). The project's cost was initially estimated at $545 million and required land-takings from 24 property owners for the 14-acre site (Vaillancourt & Cassidy, 1999).

Harrington's proposal was rooted in the uncertainty of increased competitive pressures. Although Harrington's plan implicitly recognized the importance of Fenway Park to the Red Sox brand image, the original was perceived as a source of aesthetic elements rather than as a source of competitive advantage for the organization. Instead, Fenway Park's age meant that it lacked amenities, its intimate size constrained revenues, its neighborhood required re-development, its history was transportable, and its quirkiness was little more than an aesthetic touch. With these limitations, Fenway Park left the Red Sox ill-equipped to compete for consumption spending, especially as competitive pressures were perceived to come from three primary sources: comparison with the experience provided in other baseball venues, national and global labor markets, and the local market.

First, the increasing spectacularization of space (Belanger, 2000) has rede-fined consumer expectations such that the Red Sox management believed that fans would consider the Fenway experience inadequate, as they were exposed to newer facilities through travel and the media. The management feared that, as Fenway lacked comparative amenities and was perceived to be deficient in terms of cleanliness and comfort, fans would stop coming to the games. Ac-cording to Harrington, the new Fenway would "provide the fans with a better experience, no obstructed views, comfortable seats, easier access and egress, and even a decent number of rest rooms for women and families" (qtd. in Krupa & Vaillancourt, 1999, p. A1).

Second, with retro stadiums having superior amenities, it was feared that other franchises would generate revenues far in excess of what the Red Sox could realize from Fenway Park. With this revenue disparity, the Red Sox would be at a competitive disadvantage in the global baseball labor market in terms of attracting and retaining talented players (Save Fenway Park!, 2002a). This inability to compete in labor markets would lessen the team's ability to challenge for championships, which would further erode consumer support due to a less attractive on-the-field product.

Third, given that the majority of revenues were derived from local consumers and corporations, increasing competition for sports-related spending within Boston made the need for a New Fenway seem particularly urgent. In 1995, the Fleet Center arena opened, and one month prior to the Red Sox formally proposing the New Fenway, plans for a new football stadium were announced. In total, these two state-of-the-art facilities offered 8000 club seats and 200 luxury boxes, while the Red Sox could provide only 600 club seats and 31 suites of inferior quality (see Cafardo, 1999; Vennochi, 1990).

In combination, these factors could have potentially undermined the organi-zation's long-term viability, as it was believed that fans and corporations would not pay to see an inferior product within an antiquated facility. Harrington's response to this possibility demonstrated both normative and mimetic isomor-phism, as HOK Sport was hired to build a retro stadium similar to Fenway and other facilities.

However, consistent with Ritzer's (1999) observation (that consumers be-come easily bored with the spectacular elements of consumption environments and require new spectacles to keep them engaged), retro stadiums have be-come less successful in attracting fans as the former have aged and become in-creasingly commonplace (Save Fenway Park!, 2002b). As expressed by Stuart Rosenberg, Political Director for Boston City Councilor Michael Ross, this is particularly evident in the case of the Fleet Center, which has replaced the Boston Garden. In a personal interview, Rosenberg described that although he frequently receives phone calls from out-of-town friends asking for tickets to Fenway Park, "[he is] not getting a lot of calls for the Fleet Center"—a situation he attributes to the Fleet Center's lack of distinctiveness.

In addition to the overly exaggerated revenue potential of such stadiums, it is important to remember that the social transformations of space and place are neither neutral nor innocent with respect to power. Rather, as Raymond Williams (1988) reminds us, they are fundamental framing decisions replete with multiple possibilities, which govern the conditions (often oppressively) over how lives can be lived. That is, the transformation of such spectacular spaces is imbued with power relations—in this case, a social struggle around the (re)production and/or maintenance of Fenway Park.

Not surprisingly, given that the proposed transformations to the ballpark were in the interests of capital accumulation for a small few, opposition emerged from groups of fans, preservationists, and neighborhood residents to challenge the New Fenway. One such group was Save Fenway Park!, who was clear in its opposition to Harrington's plan for a retro stadium that utilized historic tropes to evoke nostalgia for a still-operational building. Dan Wilson, research director of Save Fenway Park!, said, "We don't want the 14th replica of Camden Yards" (qtd. in Farrey, 2000, p. 4).

Wilson's comment points to the polemic between eliminating competitive disadvantages by replicating the physical elements of retro stadiums (and, thereby maintenance of the Red Sox competitive advantage by manufacturing heritage through copying the aesthetics of the original Fenway) and the importance of "authenticity" within ever homogenizing sporting spaces. Harrington seems to have underrated the value of authenticity and was willing to discard it, believing that Red Sox consumers would readily (if not eagerly) embrace a different narrative of heritage abstracted from its original space. However, many Red Sox consumers were not willing to accept a "nostalgic" environment produced to entertain them with the purpose of realizing revenue. As Rex suggested, such environments offer a faux historicity that border on the "Disneyesque." Furthermore, Save Fenway Park! Board Member Erika Tarlin described these ballparks as "plasticky" [sic], adding that in visiting Camden Yards, "[she] saw so many links to Fenway that [she] didn't feel like [she] was in an authentic place" (personal interview).

Where Fenway Park developed "organically" over decades as a result of incremental changes within a constrained urban space, postmodern facilities are purely contrived spaces with flexible boundaries. As a result, according to Save Fenway Park! Chairman Steve Wojnar (in a personal interview), the postmodern stadium is "nowhere nearly as charming [as the originals]. It doesn't have the depth. It doesn't have the history. It can imitate, but it cannot replace." The goals of Save Fenway Park! may well have been achieved in the wake of homogenizing corporate capitalism. However, and perhaps as a result of this resistance, the management of heritage has become increasingly important for the Red Sox organization in the expression of organizational identity and the sustenance of competitive advantage within the global marketplace. As such, to express the intangible, the Red Sox are increasingly looking to imagine, define, articulate, and exploit the past within their capital accumulation strategies.

The Fenway Factor: The Camdenization of Fenway Park

> Fenway has provided fans with a uniquely wonderful baseball experience for 90 years, drawing baseball lovers in droves from around the country and the world to experience its excitement, traditions, and intimate embrace. As time passes, fans from across the country will value more and more the treat of watching a ballgame at this magical place that connects fans with their own childhood and with the golden age of baseball's past. (Shannon & Wilson, 2002, Directors, Save Fenway Park!)

The Harrington plan ultimately failed due to the combination of organized resistance by Save Fenway Park! and neighborhood groups, the inability to secure financing, and a soaring price tag. As such, the Yawkey Trust, which owned the Red Sox, put the team up for sale in 2001. Outbidding several other groups, a group led by John Henry and Tom Werner (and included former Orioles President Larry Lucchino) recognized the value of enhancing and possibly renovating Fenway Park. As Lucchino stated, "We were trying to imitate Fenway when we designed and built Camden Yards . . . So it seemed the height of irony not to make an effort to preserve the model" (Greenberger, 2002, p. A1). Since 2002, the Red Sox have made several physical and aesthetic transformations to Fenway Park under the direction of Janet Marie Smith, who said in a personal interview, "We've tried very hard to identify what is special about historic Fenway and [to] improve on it without changing its basic look." In each of their three seasons, the Red Sox have unveiled a series of changes designed to enhance team revenues by improving the Fenway experience. In 2002, the Red Sox began renting Yawkey Way from the city for several hours on game days, essentially privatizing the street during games and transforming it into an entertainment and concessions area with themed stands. In 2003, seats were added atop the Green Monster and between the dugouts, and the area under the bleachers was transformed into the "Big Concourse." For Red Sox co-owner Tom Werner, the Green Monster seats were a particular achievement: "They showed that we could add revenue and still be sensitive to the history of Fenway Park. I think we created revenue there by accenting, rather than diluting, any of that history" (as qtd. in King, 2003). In 2004, a party deck was built atop the right field roof, the third base concourse was expanded by tearing down a wall between two Red Sox properties, and two gates (B and E) were expanded and made more attractive. Aesthetically, these new additions have been designed to maintain the visual character of the ballpark. According to Tarlin in a personal interview, "The Monster Seats look like they've always been there, and the right field roof's seats all blend right in."

Where Harrington saw Fenway Park as economically obsolete and a source of competitive disadvantage, Henry and Lucchino have recognized that much of Fenway Park's potential has been untapped. According to Schoenfeld (2002), since the purchase, the new Red Sox management has been able to "exploit fans' love affair with Fenway, which not so incidentally helps position the ballpark as a profit center even when the Red Sox aren't playing." The creation of the "Legends Suite" demonstrates one way in which the Red Sox have been able to utilize heritage toward increasing revenues. Removing one $175,000 suite from its inventory, the Red Sox spent a "few" thousand dollars to improve its amenities. But by offering the opportunity for suite buyers to be hosted by a former Red Sox player, the organization (in 2003) charged $10,000 per game and expected to quadruple that suite's revenues (King, 2003). Through similar strategies that have accentuated the ballpark and the team's history and developed heritage (the organization's primary symbolic resources), Red Sox owners have been able to increase their revenues, which were derived directly from the ballpark's ticket sales, advertising, concessions, and other uses (concerts, special events, tours); and secondarily, from more aggressive licensing of the Fenway image through souvenirs (King, 2003; Schoenfeld, 2002).

While Smith may claim that the changes have made "a more gracious Fenway, a more commodious and welcoming Fenway, but . . . still the same old Fenway" (Greenberger, 2003, p. A1), the ballpark is being redesigned in ways mimicking retro stadiums. Lucchino has described this process as "the Camdenization of Fenway Park" (Buckley, 2003, p. 82), while Smith described the changes as "life imitating art," as the Fenway Park-inspired Camden Yards is now inspiring elements within Fenway Park itself (personal interview). In particular, the renting of Yawkey Way is similar to Camden Yards' use of Eutaw Street, while the Orioles' use of the Warehouse as a center for many stadium functions is being copied in Fenway Park's "Laundry Building" (which borders the Big Concourse with a line of fully-equipped concession stands and new bathrooms, and into which the Red Sox have moved Aramark's central concessions kitchen from the concourse behind the home plate).

Additionally, Fenway Park has copied the extensive use of old-style motifs found within the retro stadiums — the difference being that in emphasizing the ballpark's heritage, the Red Sox are utilizing "the palette of what was [there] at Fenway" (Smith, personal interview) with styles and materials from the ballpark's history. In designing the signage for the new concourses, graphic designer Ronnie Younts scrutinized old photographs of Fenway Park and mimicked the typefaces, styles, frames, and even the manner in which the original signage was hung, although according to a personal interview with Smith, "it was a hard decision whether to go with the 1912 look or the 1934 look." Even some of the materials used in the additions have been recovered from older parts of the ballpark. As Tarlin describes in a personal interview, "In an incredibly charming and true Janet Marie Smith gesture, they took the wood from the bowling alley [located in Fenway Park] . . . and the wood was incorporated into the bar that's up there [on the right field roof]." Furthermore, the bricks on the bar's base were from the walls torn down to expand the two concourses—embellishments that are emblematic of the commodification of the past that manufactures a sense of style over substance.

While mimetic processes are the most evident, normative and coercive pressures are also present in the "Camdenization" of Fenway Park. As President of the Orioles and San Diego Padres, Lucchino has been responsible for the construction of two retro ballparks: Camden Yards and Petco Park. Moreover, Lucchino hired Smith as Vice President for Planning and Development precisely because of her experience on Camden Yards and other stadium projects. Similarly, Ronnie Younts' presence on the project also demonstrates the homogenizing influence of a professionalized field as he has worked on several other stadium and arena projects. In terms of coercive pressures, and despite being exempt due to its age from the guidelines of the Americans with Disabilities Act (ADA), the changes have been made with ADA compliance in mind because "if something is ADA accessible, it means it is easier for every fan to walk through" (Smith, personal interview).

While Harrington and Smith have produced what could be termed as the "official" expressions of Fenway Park over the last decade, the raw materials of history can be produced into a multitude of heritage narratives. With over 92 seasons of play, there have been more than 6500 games played within the confines of Fenway Park, which have been experienced by more than 115 million spectators, players, ballpark employees, Red Sox staff, and residents of the Fenway neighborhood. These games have a definitive result in terms of wins and losses, which have been comprised of great feats, terrible failures and predominantly mundane plays. Each year, the accumulation of victories and defeats has combined with fan expectations to create seasons remembered for greatness, mediocrity, or disappointment. Among the millions of people directly and tangentially involved with Fenway Park, there have been innumerable moments of human interaction. Each of these people has the ability to develop their own narratives of Fenway Park as they selectively choose and recombine these raw materials.

However, as Waitt (2000) reminds us, the management and manufacture of heritage involves the construction of a limited range of interpretations in which only certain histories, memories, emotions, and symbols are drawn upon and used within by powerful groups for particular interests. In this way, as part of the intangible expression of the Red Sox organization, only certain memories are remembered while others are actively forgotten, and those which predominate become part of a carefully constituted, authorized, and legitimate past conjured up in the present in the interests of capital. The presently preferred narrative positions Fenway Park as an authentic and enchanted setting that is derived from five characteristics: its small and intimate size, its quirkiness, its iconic feature, its urban setting, and its historical nature for both the events that have taken place and the nostalgia inspired by the architecture and built environment (Ritzer & Stillman, 2001). In a personal interview, Janet Marie Smith highlighted similar themes, stating that:

> There is something so gritty and authentic and real about a place that has been here since 1912. That very original, couldn't-dream-it-up-if-you-tried touches from the Green Monster to the single level facility to its sort of dark concourses. It's got its own personality.

Save Fenway Park! (1998) have termed this narrative the "Fenway Factor," consisting of a combination of the "park's unique history, physical features, and 'sense of place' " (p. 1).

As such, Fenway Park is often expressed through particular moments (e.g., Fisk's and Dent's home runs), entire seasons (individual: Ted Williams hitting .406 in 1941; or collective: the "Impossible Dream" American League championship team of 1967), or players. (According to Tom Farrey (2000), Fenway Park is "the place where Babe Ruth once tossed fastballs, where Ted (Williams) and Yaz (Carl Yastrzemski) once played the carom.") Fenway Park becomes inextricably linked to these defining elements of team history, and therefore, has become the spiritual center for the team's fans, who are collectively known as "Red Sox Nation" (Shaughnessy, 1996) — a term which in and of itself raises numerous questions with regard to categories of inclusion and exclusion, belonging, and inequality within and across the local, national, and transnational expressions of "nation." This construction of the Red Sox and Fenway Park's heritage may obscure many of the less laudatory policies and practices from the organization's history as well as the exclusionary practices more broadly evident within Boston.[3]

Those responsible for articulating the "Fenway Factor" to position the ballpark as an inimitable and sustainable source of competitive advantage for the Red Sox have reaped financial gain. Although Fenway Park has the fewest seats, is the oldest structure and charges the highest ticket prices in MLB, the Red Sox set an organizational record in 2004 by selling more than 2.5 million seats before opening day (almost 85% of the entire inventory) and selling out the entire season, while organization revenues from stadium operations are the highest in the sport.

Yet as Save Fenway Park! Chairman Steve Wojnar seems to suggest, the ability to charge these prices is because of, rather than in spite of, Fenway Park's size and age, as the public has responded "with its pocketbook to the two remaining classic ballparks and that happen to be the homes of the two most storied, cursed franchises" (personal interview). Nonetheless, the ability to enjoy Fenway Park is becoming increasingly limited to upper class and corporate patrons, which are the primary targets for both Harrington's ill-fated New Fenway plan and the present ownership's "Camdenization." Yet, while the organization may bask in its economic accomplishments and while Save Fenway Park! can be satisfied with its role in helping to ensure the longevity of the ballpark, multiple concerns surround the hawking of heritage within the trammels of global capitalism.

Coda: History and Heritage in the Symbolic Expression of Fenway Park

The use of the physical and imagined spaces of Fenway Park within the maintenance and sustenance of global competitive advantage is emblematic of the "expressive" response to the homogenizing tendencies of transnational capital on the production and consumption of sports. Fenway Park serves as a key symbolic space through which the Red Sox organization becomes imagined, marketed, and expressed. Through amassing symbolic sporting capital and accumulating marks of distinction, history, and heritage (or through revising, performing, or selecting these) as signature architectural embellishments, the Red Sox organization is able to redefine the extant stadium in relation to the logic of global capital. Of course, while the physical and social landscape of Fenway Park (and indeed the production and consumption of sporting space per se) is shaped according to distinctively capitalist criteria, we should not forget that social space could be the site for resistance. Of particular note within this example is the politics of resistance that surrounded the proposed pastiche of the New Fenway Park. While the Save Fenway Park! organization may have been an important part of a small victory in the face of corporatism, this very "victory" may well have functioned as a locus of affect in the homogenization of sporting space. That is, through mobilizing the "authentic," the original Fenway Park is itself embroiled within the trappings of global capital.

Through recourse to an "authentic" and mythical past, the Red Sox organization has appropriated certain histories as a central intangible marketing resource. However, this commodification of pastness is just one version of the past that speaks to style and simulation over substance, "depthlessness" over depth, partiality over wholeness; and one version of the space in which powerful groups can train or entertain us in our historicity (Healey, 1997). These are but interpretations of the past that are manipulated in the interests of capital (McLean, 1995). In this sense, the selected histories, signifiers, and bricks and mortar as well as the representative subjectivities of the Boston Red Sox become disseminated in the interests of capital accumulation, and are likely (although certainly not preordained to be) weaker, less palpable, and superficial reconstructions of the past. This distortion or staging of the "authentic" in the name of capital (Chhabra et al., 2003) is imbued with social relations. It is a knowledge that is "accompanied by a complex and often conflicting array of identifications and potential conflicts, not least when heritage, places, and objects are involved in issues of legitimation of (corporate) power structures" (Graham, 2002, p. 1006).

For the Red Sox, this involves a focus on and mobilization of selected elements of baseball's history—selections that emphasize the storied, mythical and somewhat quirky past of Fenway Park and indeed of baseball itself. Yet simultaneously, these depictions have the possibility of trivializing, if not masking and ignoring, the histories of the marginalized (those marginalized in the past when baseball has been embroiled within a series of gendered, sexualized, ethnic, local, national, transnational, and racial struggles) and of those sections of the population—"the unemployed, the underemployed, women, the racialised or otherwise discriminated against—who are institutionally excluded from the high table of global feast" (Brah, 2002, p. 37). In this way, the management and manufacture of heritage at Fenway Park is imbued with a series of processes that redefine sporting space in relation to the logic of capital, thereby reproducing an established hierarchy of cultures that "consolidates hegemonic relations without challenging the hierarchy of the majority and the minority" (Banjeree & Linstead, 2001, p. 704).

Notes

1. Frow and Morris (2000) proposed a number of discourses that a cultural studies analysis should, at least partially and necessarily incompletely, engage. These "discourses" (although we prefer the word "contexts") include the political, the aesthetic, the economic, the gendered, the historical, the textual, and the ethnographic. In this paper, we articulated our site (Fenway Park) with this context in an effort to locate or articulate this particular cathedral of sporting consumption as an element of the cultural terrain within a wider cultural politics. Thus, our approach is a qualitative inquiry of the sporting empirical, where we can begin to understand sports as a site through which various discourses are mobilized in regard to the organization and discipline of daily life in the service of particular political agendas (Andrews, 1995; Giroux, 2001; Grossberg, 1992, 1997). In this sense, our engagement with the sporting empirical becomes a component of a wider ideological critique that critically interrogates a range of sites in which the production of knowledge and identities takes place (Giroux, 2001).

2. In an effort to get at the particularities of the space under investigation, we employed a variety of strategies of inquiry that included ethnographic observations and analysis of the Boston Globe and Boston Herald newspapers. However, for the most part, our analysis is based on a series of elite interviews with participants selected for their unique knowledge of and involvement in the changes surrounding Fenway Park (see Amis, 2005). Four semi-structured interviews (ranging from 45 to 75 minutes) were conducted over a two-day period in Boston in April 2004, with five individuals (including a simultaneous interview of two individuals) each of whom understood that they would not be anonymous, signing an informed consent allowing the use of their names. Participants included Boston Red Sox Vice President of Planning and Devel-

opment Janet Marie Smith, Save Fenway Park! board members Erika Tarlin and Steve Wojnar, Boston Preservation Alliance Executive Director Albert Rex, and Stuart Rosenberg, Policy Director for Boston City Council member Michael Ross, whose district includes the Fenway neighborhood. Anonymity was not maintained because their identities added to the validity of the data. Nevertheless, all participants have the right to review and edit the interview transcripts and to reject material for attribution or use. Fortunately, all participants approved their transcripts.

3. Klein (2000, p. 406) suggested that the "friendly confines of Fenway" is "anything but friendly to people of color both on and off the field." A disturbing history surrounding the Red Sox—being the last team to integrate the racist epithet "get these niggers of the field" (15 years after Jackie Robinson broke the color line) offered by Red Sox General Manager in 1945 (when the Boston Red Sox offered a brief trial to African-Americans), the jeers thrown at Boston's first African-American player Plumpsie Green in 1959, the racism at the clubs' spring training facility in 1986, the racial indignities thrown at Oakland A's Dave Stewart in 1991, the sluggish recruitment of Latin American talent, and the many unreported incidents—have meant that the Red Sox are associated with a folklore of racism that has kept many minorities away from Fenway Park (Klein, 2000). Indeed, despite recent advancements in the growing numbers of Latinos/Latinas, Asians and African-Americans on and off the field, Klein (2000) proposed that this folklore of racism dies hard and that significant numbers of minorities perceive the team and the city as racist—the anglo-response to the increased presence of Dominican nationals at Fenway following the pitching of Pedro Martinez only exasperates the racial bigotry within the "storied" vaults of Fenway Park

References

Albrow, M. (1996). *The global age*. Stanford, CA: Stanford University.

Amis, J. (2003). "Good things come to those who wait": The strategic management of image and reputation at Guinness. *European Sport Management Quarterly. 3*, 189–214.

Amis, J. (2005). The art of interviewing for case study research. In D. Andrews, D. Mason, & M. Silk (Eds.), *Qualitative research in sports studies*, forthcoming. Oxford: Berg.

Amis, J., Pant, N., & Slack, T. (1997). Achieving a sustainable competitive advantage: A resource-based view of sport sponsorship. *Journal of Sport Management, 11*, 80–96.

Andrews, D. (1995). Excavating Michael Jordan: Notes on a critical pedagogy of sporting representation. In G. Rail & J. Harvey (Eds.), *Sport and postmodern times: Culture, gender, sexuality, the body, and sport*. Albany, NY: State University of New York Press.

Apostolakis, A. (2003). The convergence process in heritage tourism. *Annals of Tourism Research, 30*(4), 795–812.

Appadurai, A. (1990). Disjuncture and difference in the global cultural economy. *Public Culture, 2*(2), 1–24.

Ashworth, G. (1990). The historic cities of Groningen: Which is sold to whom? In G. Ashworth & B. Goodall (Eds.), *Marketing tourism places* (pp. 138–155). London: Routledge..

Ashworth, G. & Larkham, P. (Eds.). (1994). *Building a new Europe: Tourism, culture, and identity*. London: Routledge.

Ashworth, G., & Tunbridge, J. (1990). *The tourist-historic city*. London: Belhaven.

Bale, J. (1994). *Landscapes of Modern Sport*. London: Leicester.

Baltimore, O. (2003). *Orioles Information and Record Book 2003*. Baltimore, MD: Author.

Banjeree, S., & Linstead, S. (2001). Globalization. Multiculturalism, and other fictions: Colonialism and the new millennium. *Organization, 84*, 683–722.

Barney, J. (1991). Firm resources and sustained competitive advantage. *Journal of Management, 17*(1), 99–120.

Belanger, A. (2000). Sport venues and the spectacularization of urban spaces in North America: The case of the Molson Center in Montreal. *International Review for the Sociology of Sport, 35*(3), 378–397.

Brah, A. (2002). Global mobilities, local predicaments: Globalization and the critical imagination. *Feminist Review, 70*, 30–45.

Buckley, S. (August 19, 2003). Baseball: New course at Fens. *Boston Herald*. Retrieved September 15, 2003, from LexisNexis Academic Database.

Cafardo, N. (May 11, 1999). Bonus points ahead; patriots anticipating fringe benefits from new stadium. *Boston Globe*, p. C5.

Campbell, R. (2002). *Architecture: Change it? Save it? Make your Fenway pitch*, June 9, retrieved September 15, 2003, from Lexis-Nexis Academic Database.

Castells, M. (1989). *The informational city*. Oxford: Basil Blackwell.

Chhabra, D., Healey, R., & Sills, E. (2003). Staged authenticity and heritage tourism. *Annals of Tourism Research, 303*, 702–719.

Cousens, L., & O'Brien, D. (2004). Beyond boundaries: A comparative investigation of change in the organizational fields encompassing North American and Australian professional sport organizations. *Paper Presented at North American Society for Sport Management Conference*, June 5.

Decker, H. (2000). *The Future Fenway*. Retrieved June 28, 2004 from http://www.savefenwaypark. com/sfp/preserve/slide01.shtml

DiMaggio, P., & Powell, W. (1983). The iron cage revisited: Institutional isomorphism and collective rationality in organizational fields. *American Sociological Review, 48*(2), 147–160.

Epstein, E. (March 18, 1996). Giants' stadium architects sell high-tech nostalgia: Designs go for comfort and native flair. *San Francisco Chronicle*, p. A13.

Farrey, T. (November 8, 2000). *Historic Fenway faces uncertain future*. Retrieved December 12, 2003, from http://espn.go.com/mlb/s/2000/1031/849361.html

Friedman, M., Andrews, D., & Silk, M. (2004). Sport and the façade of redevelopment in the postindustrial city. *Sociology of Sport Journal, 21*, 119–139.

Frow, J., & Morris, M. (2000). Cultural studies. in N. Denzin & Y. Lincoln (Eds.),
Handbook of Qualitative Research (2nd ed.,
pp. 315–346). Thousand Oaks, CA: Sage.

Du Gay, P. (2000). Markets and meanings:
Re-imagining organizational life. In
M. Schultz, M. Hatch, & M. Holten
Larsen (Eds.), *The expressive organization:
Linking identity, reputation and corporate brand*
(pp. 66–74). Oxford: Oxford University
Press.

Gershman, M. (1993). *Diamonds: The evolution
of the ballpark from Elysian Fields to Camden
Yards*. Boston, MA: Houghton Mifflin.

Giroux, H. (2001). Cultural studies as performative politics. *Cultural Studies — Critical
Methodologies, 1*(1), 5–23.

Graham, B. (2002). Heritage as knowledge:
Capital or culture? *Urban Studies, 39*(5–6),
1003–1017.

Grant, R. (1991). The resource-based theory
of competitive advantage: Implications for
strategy formulation. *California Management Review, 33*(3), 114–135.

Greenberger, S. (July 1, 2002). New Fenway
push by former owners called into question. *Boston Globe*. Retrieved September 15,
2003, from LexisNexis Academic Database.

Greenberger, S. (August 19, 2003). Sox offer
new lure under the stands. *Boston Globe*.
Retrieved September 15, 2003, from LexisNexis Academic Database.

Grossberg, L. (1992). *We gotta get out of this
place: Popular conservatism and postmodern culture*. London: Routledge.

Grossberg, L. (1997). *Bringing it all back home:
Essays on cultural studies*. Durham, NC:
Duke University Press.

Hannerz, U. (1996). *Transnational connections:
Culture, people, places*, London: Comedia.

Harrington, J. (May 15, 1999). Why Red Sox
need a new park. *Boston Globe*. Retrieved
December 13, 2003, from LexisNexis Academic Database.

Harvey, D. (1990). *The condition of postmodernity: An enquiry into the origins of cultural
change*, Oxford: Basil Blackwell.

Healey, C. (1997). *From the ruins of colonialism:
History as social memory*. Cambridge: Cambridge University Press.

Jameson, F. (1991). *Postmodernism or the cultural logic of late capitalism*. Durham, NC:
Duke.

Kearns, G., & Philo, C. (1993). *Selling Places:
The city as cultural capital, past and present*,
Oxford: Pergamon.

Keohane, R. O., & Nye, J. S. (2000). Globalization: What's new? What's not? (And
so what?). *Foreign Policy, 118*, 104–119.

King, B. (April 28, 2003). Sox owners honor
new tradition: Innovation. *Sports Business
Journal*. Retrieved October 29, 2004 from
www.sportsbusinessjournal.com

Klein, A. (2000). Latinizing Fenway Park: A
cultural critique of the Boston Red Sox,
their fans and the media. *Sociology of Sport
Journal, 17*, 403–422.

Krupa, G. ,& Vaillancourt, M. (May 16,
1999). Proposed $545m ballpark to retain
cherished details. *Boston Globe*, p. A1.

Lash, S., & Urry, J. (1987) *The end of organized capitalism*. Wisconsin: University of
Wisconsin Press.

Macero, C., & Myers, J. (May 15, 1999).
Fenway charm intact in new park; plan
preserves look, adds 10,000 seats. *Boston
Herald*, p. 1.

Maryland Stadium Authority (1987). *Request
of the Maryland Stadium Authority to final
competitors for the design and planning contract
for the State of Maryland's Twin Stadium Project*. Baltimore: Author.

Mattson, J. (2002). Fans, activists defend
Fenway legacy, tradition. *The Daily Free
Press*. Retrieved September 15, 2003, from
LexisNexis Academic database, Boston
University.

Mavima, P., & Chackerian, R. (2001). Administrative reform adoption and implementation: The influence of global and local institutional forces. *Perspectives on Global
Development and Technology, 17*(2), 91–110.

McIntosh, A., & Prentice, R. (1999). Affirm-
ing authenticity: Consuming cultural heritage. *Annals of Tourism Research, 263*,
589–612.

McLean, F. (1995). A marketing revolution in
museums? *Journal of Marketing Management, 11*, 601–616.

MLB Valuations (April 26, 2004). *Forbes Magazine*. Accessed on-line, June 28, 2004 at
http://www.Forbes.com/free_Forbes/2004/
0426/066tab.html

Morley, D., & Robins, K. (1995). *Spaces of
Identity: Global media, electronic landscapes, and
cultural boundaries*. London: Routledge.

Neilson, B. (1995). Baseball. In K. Raitz (Ed.), *The theater of sport* (pp. 1–29). Baltimore, MD: Johns Hopkins University Press.

Nolan, M. (1999). A ballpark, not a stadium. In C. Smith (Ed.), *Our house: A tribute to Fenway Park* (pp. 27–31). Lincolnwood, IL: Masters Press.

Olins, W. (2000). How brands are taking over the corporation. In M. Schultz, M. Hatch, & M. Holten Larsen (Eds.), *The expressive organization: Linking identity, reputation, and corporate brand* (pp. 51–65). Oxford: Oxford University Press.

Peteraf, M. (1993). The cornerstones of competitive advantage: A resource-based view. *Strategic Management Journal, 14,* 179–191.

Poria, Y., Butler, R., & Airey, D. (2003). The core of heritage tourism. *Annals of Tourism Research, 30*(1), 238–254.

Provoost, M. (2000a). *The stadium: The architecture of mass sport.* Rotterdam: NAI Publishers.

Provoost, M. (Ed.) (2000b). Interview with HOK sports facilities group. *The stadium: The architecture of mass sport* (pp. 101–103). Rotterdam: NAI Publishers.

Raitz, K. (1987). Perception of sport landscapes and gratification in the sport experience. *Sport Place, 1*(1), 5–19.

Ritzer, G. (1999). *Enchanting a disenchanted world: Revolutionizing the means of consumption.* Thousand Oaks, CA: Pine Forge Press.

Ritzer, G., & Stillman, T. (2001). The postmodern ballpark as a leisure setting: Enchantment and simulated De-McDonaldization. *Leisure Sciences, 23,* 99–113.

Robins, K. (1997). What in the world is going on? In P. du Gay (Ed.), *Production of culture/cultures of production* (pp. 11–67). London: Sage. Rowe, D., & McGuirk, P. (1999). Drunk for three weeks: Sporting success and the city image. *International Review for the Sociology of Sport, 34,* 125–142.

Sassen, S. (2000). Whose city is it? Globalization and the formation of new claims. In F.J. Lechner (Ed.), *The globalization reader* (pp. 70–76). Malden, MA: Blackwell.

Save Fenway Park! (1998). *Our field of dreams: An economic and planning analysis.* Boston: Author.

Save Fenway Park! (2002a). SFP! Vigilance critical to replacing fiction with fact. *Save enway Park! Newsletter, 4*(4), p. 1.

Save Fenway Park! (2002b). *Home field advantage: Why renovating Fenway Park makes sense.* Retrieved December 1, 2003, from http://www.savefenwaypark.com/Homefield.html

Schoenfeld, B. (July 8, 2002). New owners playing to Boston fans. *Sports Business Journal.* Retrieved October 29, 2004 from www.sportsbusinessjournal.com

Schultz, M., Hatch, M., & Holten Larsen, M. (2000). Introduction: Why the expressive organization. In M. Schultz, M. Hatch, & M. Holten Larsen (Eds.), *The expressive organization: Linking identity, reputation, and corporate brand* (pp. 1–7). Oxford: Oxford University Press.

Shannon, P., & Wilson, D. (July 7, 2002). Renovating Fenway will blend tradition with modern comforts. *Boston Herald.* Retrieved September 15, 2003, from LexisNexis Academic Database.

Shaughnessy, D. (1996). *At Fenway: Dispatches from Red Sox Nation.* New York: Three Rivers Press.

Silk, M. (2002). Bangsa Malaysia: Global sport, the city, and the refurbishment of local identities. *Media, Culture, and Society, 246,* 775–794.

Smart, D., & Wolfe, R. (2000). Examining sustainable competitive advantage in intercollegiate athletics: A resource-based view. *Journal of Sport Management, 14,* 133–153.

Sporting News. (2003). *The Sporting News: Baseball's 25 greatest moments.* Accessed on-line, December 12, retrieved from www. sportingnews.com/baseball/25moments/list.html

Tomlinson, J. (1999). *Globalization and culture.* Chicago: University of Chicago Press.

Vaillancourt, M., & Cassidy, T. (May 15, 1999). Red sox to unveil plans for new ballpark today. *Boston Globe.* Retrieved December 13, 2003, from LexisNexis Academic Database.

Van Ingen, C. (2003). Geographies of gender, sexuality, and race. *International Review for the Sociology of Sport, 38,* 201–216.

Van Rooij, M. (2000). Stadium fever. In M. Provoost (Ed.), *The stadium: The architecture of mass sport* (pp. 122–136). Rotterdam: NAI Publishers. Vennochi, J. (November 30, 1990). Garden developers seek $140m from hub firms. *Boston Globe,* p. 1.

Waitt, G. (2000). Consuming heritage: Perceived historical authenticity. *Annals of Tourism Research, 27*(4), 835–862.

Wang, N. (1999). Rethinking authenticity in the tourism experience. *Annals of Tourism Research,* 26(2), 349–370.

Wernerfelt, B. (1984). A resource-based view of the firm. *Strategic Management Journal,* 5(2), 171–180.

Williams, R. (1988). *Second generation.* London: Verso.

Wright, R. (1994). The effects of tacitness and tangibility on the diffusion of knowledge-based resources. *Academy of Management Best Paper Proceeding,* 52–56.

10

FROM BECKHAM TO RONALDO—ASSESSING THE NATURE OF FOOTBALL PLAYER BRANDS

Simon Chadwick and Nick Burton

When Manchester United toured South East Asia in the summer of 2007, many of its players were mobbed by local fans eager to see some of the stars of European football. Most notable among these was Cristiano Ronaldo, the Portuguese international winger. Such attention marked a major turnaround for Ronaldo, who little more than 12 months earlier had been cast as a pantomime villain following his infamous clash with United teammate, Wayne Rooney, during a FIFA World Cup quarter-final game in 2006. During the 2006/2007 Premier League season, Ronaldo overcame the taunts and chants of hostile English crowds to pick up a host of national "best player" awards. Indeed, such has been his recent renaissance that some commentators are now claiming Ronaldo, or "Brand Ronaldo" as they are calling him, is fast becoming the heir apparent to David Beckham and his global brand. While this in part may be attributable to careful and astute management by Ronaldo's agent, as it has been in the case of Beckham, it is also due to the associations that players such as these have with other products, particularly through endorsement deals, that bring the players to the attention of a wider market. This paper contends, however, that Beckham and Ronaldo, among others, are becoming brands in their own right: transcending their other product associations and club affiliations. As such, this paper sets out to examine what player brands are and from where they derive characteristics, features, and strengths.

It is interesting that Ronaldo's emergence as a global football brand has coincided with Beckham's move to Major League Soccer (MLS) in the USA. Beckham has been one of the stars of European football over the last decade, despite not being an especially strong football player (in, say, the same way as Ronaldinho, Henry, or Zidane). Such has been Beckham's fame that he has actually become something of a global superstar, with iconic status and a profile that is more "rock star" than "East London-born footballer." Much has been written about the factors that led the former Manchester United and Real Madrid star to join an MLS club (LA Galaxy): a fallout with Real Madrid manager, Fabio Capello; pressure to move from his wife, Victoria; a friendship with Tom Cruise; and so on. There is one indisputable fact, however: such is the power of Beckham and his brand that the player and his advisors felt the time was right to move to the USA, the last uncharted football (or should that be soccer?) market in the world. Clearly there are immense opportunities open to Beckham in the world's largest and most strongly established sport market. His contract with LA Galaxy is a lucrative one, his deals with companies such as Adidas will enable him to generate income and create profile across the USA, and his soccer camp business is likely to flourish in one of the biggest markets in the world for such services. The question is, if the US market for soccer is so important, why is it that US soccer franchises have thus far only been able to attract players of the caliber of Terry Cooke (ex-Manchester United) and Jaime Moreno (ex-Middlesbrough)?

The answer is that Beckham, and indeed Cristiano Ronaldo, have certain characteristics and embody particular qualities that mark them out as being different from other football players. This has led to them both being referred to as brands, a term that in itself is interesting because it implicitly asserts that the stars of sport are no longer just on-field performers, they are also valuable off-field commercial properties. This is not necessarily a new or a surprising phenomenon: footballers have always been associated with business and commerce (for instance, how many readers remember Kevin Keegan advertising Brut aftershave back in the 1970s?) and many still are. Beckham's association with global brands such as Pepsi, Police, and Gillette created the conditions from which his brand began to derive power in the first place. What is different about more recent developments is that players have become products and brands themselves, not just "faces and names" with which other products and brands can be associated. This raises some important questions: what is a football player brand? Are football players the same as or different to other brands? Why is it that some players become successful brands but others do not? What factors will players and their commercial advisers consider when undertaking the branding process?

A brand is normally signified by a name (such as Coca-Cola), a design (such as an Apple computer) or a symbol (such as the McDonald's Golden Arches). Some corporations additionally use colors as part of their brand (such as Ikea), while a number of brands (such as Mercedes-Benz) are currently thought to be working on brand smells. The reason for trying to "mark" a company and its products clearly is really threefold: first, to make them instantly recognizable to potential and actual consumers such that they become automatic purchase choices; secondly, to persuade and reassure consumers that a particular purchase choice is an appropriate one that will confer certain benefits upon them; and, thirdly, to differentiate a company's products from its competitors' rival product offerings. A brand can be an important part of the tangible product, the functional or psychological part of a product that consumers can see or touch. In the case of Coca-Cola, for example, this is the brown liquid in the red can that people drink to quench their thirst. It can also be that brands are a vital element of the intangible part of a product, in other words, the functional or psychological part of the product that it is difficult specifically to identify, see or touch. Again, in the case of Coca-Cola, this could be the sense of fashionability one feels when drinking it or the comfort one might derive from being seen to consume a branded product that other people know and like. The consequent effects will be that a particular brand will foster awareness and become instantly recognizable to consumers, create a stimulus, image or expectation in their minds, and help to create a sense of trust that helps to facilitate consumers' purchase decisions.

So where do football players fit into this? Leaving smell aside (although a range of Beckham or Ronaldo fragrances is certainly part of this), clearly their names are important and will evoke certain images in the minds of consumers. In the case of "Becks" and "Ronnie," both are athletic, good-looking, skillful players. It is also no coincidence that both have played for leading teams, the names of which are equally as well known and respected. When each started playing football neither name was known and most if not everyone would have had trouble attributing any qualities or characteristics to them. This implies that football itself has played an important role, not only in bringing them to prominence but also in helping to establish the features of their brands. As for design, clearly players cannot be artificially designed or created (at least not yet). One could argue that their physical features are an aspect of their brand's design, however, as are the clothes they wear and the cars they drive when they are not playing football.

As for symbols, like the symbol of pop star Prince which springs to mind, these are one way of identifying a player brand (some readers may also recall the recent alphanumeric incarnation of ex-player Paul Gascoigne). To the authors' knowledge, this approach is yet to be employed by a current footballer. More realistically, symbols are more likely to be something like Beckham's famous array of tattoos or Ronaldo's slick hairstyle.

Taken together, one can begin to see what a football player brand is comprised of. In Beckham's case, the teams he has played for, the type of football he plays, the way he looks, how he dresses and not forgetting who he is married to have all been important influences on his brand.

Some of what has been described above is clearly a tangible part of the brands in question. Beckham's hairstyles have been groundbreaking and iconic; fans know what they look like and many will still be able to recall how his hair was cut (remember the "Mohican" at World Cup 2002?). Some may even have been to a hairdresser to have the same haircut, no matter how wild the style, because Beckham gave it credibility and made it socially acceptable for people to have such styles. In turn, this clearly illustrates the more intangible aspects of a football player brand; fashion is a subjective, indeed a cultural, concept, and what people may feel about his tattoos is likely to differ greatly across different sections of the globe's population. As for Victoria, his sarong, his houses, his jewelry and his cars, quite what they mean to people is difficult to say and individual feelings about them are certainly the more intangible parts of his brand: is he a metrosexual archetype? A role model for 21st century men? A fashion icon? Whatever his brand represents, it appears to have transcended gender, age, cultural boundaries, and geography, to the extent that Beckham is no longer just an English footballer or a European citizen, he has become a global sports brand. Which is why Ronaldo has suddenly become such a hot property: great player, playing for a successful team, known all over the world, good-looking . . . a sexy guy!

What this discussion therefore calls for is a different interpretation of what a football player brand actually is, as most of the standard textbook definitions of brand are not really appropriate for describing what is known about players. Moreover, rather than simply being a name or a symbol, because these brands are human beings, they are rather more multi-faceted and complex than other brands. As such, a football player brand might be defined as:

> A unique, distinctive combination of unplanned and planned factors that mark out a player as being different to other players thus enabling the immediate identification of the player and the activities in which they are involved.

Unlike other products and brands, individual human beings are unique and the distinctiveness that characterizes people, such as Beckham and Ronaldo, cannot easily be achieved by others. Each football player brand is therefore a one-off, never to be repeated again. Moreover, unlike other brands, some of which have tremendous longevity, humans age and get old. Footballers in particular have a relatively short "shelf life." The destiny of these young people is therefore foretold and so the life cycle and nature of their brands can be predicted with some degree of ease. What happens with these talented, good-looking people in the relatively short commercial lives they have as players thus far and in the main has been the profile, reputation, and success of unplanned. When Beckham made his debut in 1996, few would have thought that he would become such a global phenomenom. When he married former Spice Girl Victoria Adams in 1999, however, it was rather more certain that he would become a focus for the world's media. In the same year as his marriage, Beckham also won a sporting treble (Premier League, FA Cup and UEFA Champions League), thus cementing his position as a successful, top-level sports star. At this point, the unplanned and planned components of his brand began to interact. Beckham's clothing became more fashionable and daring, his hairstyles became the source of intense media attention, he began signing lucrative endorsement deals with major global corporations, collaborative deals with organizations such as Marks and Spencer were established and he agreed to contracts for books about his life. All of these things, unplanned and planned, made Beckham different, something that could not be copied or replicated by anyone else. Although he may not have been the first football player to wear a sarong or to sport a mohican haircut, they became synonymous with him and were an immediate identifier across the world, alongside his tattoos and wife, of the the Beckham brand. Ten years later and people still know him as a celebrity, an icon, a global brand, and a valuable commercial property.

The unique, distinctive set of planned and unplanned factors mentioned above would therefore appear to encapsulate a large number of characteristics that can be classified according to the following mnemonic: TOPSTAR.

Team—the team(s) that a player plays for or has played for; the associations a player has with a particular team; the profile, reputation, and success of the team; the player's role within the team.

Off-field—where the player lives; who the player socializes with and where; who the player is married to or dating; the type of house the player lives in, the car they drive, the clothes they wear.

Physical characteristics, mentality, and values—the facial appearance and physique of the player; other distinguishing features such as hairstyle, tattoos, etc; the way a player thinks and the views they hold.

Success—the player's on-field record; the number of trophies, medals, and prizes the player has won; the winning teams and games in which the player has been involved.

Transferability—the extent to which the player appeals to males and females, young and old, followers and non-followers of football; the extent to which the player and their image are culturally and geographically transferable; language(s) spoken.

Age—the stage at which a player is in their career (viewed in product life cycle terms, this will have an impact on the profile, characteristics, and longevity of the brand as well as influencing how the brand is managed).

Reputation—the player's reputation as a footballer; style of play; disciplinary record; the player's reputation outside of football; the way in which the player deals with public and media attention.

Using this mnemonic, one can start to see how and why the Beckham brand emerged, but also begin to understand why Cristiano Ronaldo is rapidly becoming a brand in his own right. Moreover, it helps to explain why Ronaldinho, Shevchenko, and Kaka are important football player brands but not as established, acceptable, or successful as Beckham.

One other issue that needs to be addressed by players and their advisers is brand positioning. For instance, Beckham is fashionable, stylish, married to a pop star, and so on. Compare this with Zinedine Zidane and one sees that the latter is more cerebral, quieter, and less likely to seek the media spotlight. Indeed, although the Zidane brand was not as actively or strategically managed as Beckham's; nevertheless, one can see that Zidane is much more likely to have appealed to a different group of consumers than Beckham. With this and the issue of positioning in mind, this paper now takes a closer look at each element of TOPSTAR in turn to identify some of the decisions that players and their advisers will have to consider in seeking to establish and build a player brand.

Team

In terms of global brand potential, signing for one of the world's leading clubs would appear to be essential. This is one of the reasons why Beckham's brand was so successful, especially as he signed for Real Madrid during the "galactico" era. Cesc Fabregas playing for Arsenal would seem to mark him out as a potentially strong brand, particularly at this time: a young vibrant player playing for a young vibrant team. The reputation and success of a player's team is actually very important to their brand: it makes them globally recognizable and highly appealing. Successful player brands need to play for teams that are consistent with a player's positioning and image. Unless positioned as some kind of tough guy or maverick, someone who plays for a team with a poor disciplinary record is unlikely to attain the level of brand success to which they and their advisers might aspire. At the same time, one would expect to see a player being acknowledged as essential to a club and an integral part of a team, rather than a perpetual substitute or squad player, if they are to become a strong brand. In turn, when playing for the team, one would expect to hear the player being referred to as a "defensive rock," "creative genius," or "goal machine" for their brand to realize full potential. It is interesting that Beckham, when he first signed for Real Madrid, was somewhat dismissively referred to as "Forest Gump" due to his endless running. Yet, when he left the club, this is one of the qualities he had become best known for: tireless running and a "never say die" attitude in his commitment to the team.

Off-Field

In different countries, the extent to which the off-field activities of players are scrutinized will vary hugely. The scrutiny is partly based on the role and power of the media in different countries, the rise of celebrity culture and the public's desire to know more about famous people. The reporting of a player's off-field life is therefore becoming just as important a part of their brand as their on-field performances. Where a player lives can be significant—consider Thierry Henry. Unlike many English players who often live in newly constructed houses on exclusive estates, when Henry lived in London he resided in Hampstead (with its mix of Victorian and Georgian villas), a haven for free-thinking, liberal intellectuals in North London. This minor detail added to many people's perceptions of Henry as a more thoughtful player than most in the Premier League. Beckham meanwhile has just acquired a house in a private, gated community in Los Angeles. Beckham and his wife, Victoria, count actors Tom Cruise and Katie Holmes among their good friends. While the friendship between the two couples provides fertile ground for newspaper gossip, the more subtle interpretation of it is that "Brand Beckham" is truly global, also transcending geography and, indeed, industrial sectors. As a counterpoint to such brands, it is interesting that, when Jurgen Klinsmann played for Tottenham Hotspur, he drove an old Volkswagen Beetle, rather than a Ferrari or a Porsche. Klinsmann has often explained that he did so because of the London traffic; however, what this actually did was to send out some subtle messages about him, his mentality and his values. As an individual among his fast car driving peers, he clearly differentiated his brand from those of other players at the time.

Physical Characteristics, Mentality, and Values

At one level, it would be easy to say that a good-looking player is more likely to become a successful brand. To an extent this is true, although in the case of someone like Beckham it is much more besides because he has added to his appearance over time by acquiring new tattoos and hairstyles. For younger players like Cristiano Ronaldo, it is more likely that physical conditioning will play a part in how consumers perceive them. As players get older and their aging physique gradually diminishes their performance, the cerebral side of a player's game and how they think about football will play a much larger part in a player brand. Mentality too is important, therefore, with the interplay between physical characteristics and mentality being most aptly demonstrated by Ronaldinho. Seemingly someone who really enjoys playing football, this is apparent in the smile he often displays when taking part in games. In turn, this is an important identifier that differentiates him from other players and has led some to suggest that he is currently the most valuable football player brand in the world. One assumes from Ronaldinho's smile that he loves football, believing it is fun and a privilege to play. These values are important, especially when a player brand is involved in activities aimed at, say, children. Values can be the way in which players approach the games in which they are involved, but it is also intended to include their personal values, allied to their views on, say, family, poverty, crime, the environment, and so on. Beckham is often referred to as a devoted family man, while England goalkeeper David James is increasingly known for his outspoken views on the future of the planet, something that very clearly differentiates him from most other players in the Premier League.

Success

One of the reasons why people consume one branded product instead of another is that it will be thought to deliver superior benefits to them. They can feel confident therefore in purchasing and consuming a product, believing that it is better for them than the alternatives. Among other things, people like to bask in reflected glory, meaning they like to be associated with the success of others, hence many people's desire to be associated with players like Beckham et al. A successful player in a successful team would appear to be the optimum state for a successful brand to flourish. Even so, a high-scoring striker in a less successful team, for example, will also have brand potential. At game level therefore, individual performances, the number of goals scored, and so on will be important. At the level of the club, the number of games won, league position, and the number of trophies secured will be important. Otherwise, the achievement of player awards will be an important signal to consumers of the success and quality of a player brand. For instance, it is notable that Cristiano

Ronaldo, having progressed from being a "troublesome foreigner' to winning several annual player awards in England, started being referred to as "Brand Ronaldo." If this particular is to become a major global one, however, such successes will have to be forthcoming on an international basis, both for his club and for his country.

Transferability

Some brands perform very well when positioned and targeted at specific groups, but in Beckham's case he was able to transcend gender, age, cultural, and geographic boundaries. As a white, Anglo-Saxon, English-speaking male, he has inevitably been popular in markets where consumers display similar characteristics. But such has been his status that, in places such as China, South Korea, and Japan, he has been perceived as an aspirational figure, a fashion icon, and a luxury brand. Clearly therefore, his unique combination of features have enabled his brand to be successful in a range of different market-places. Being able to speak English is an advantage for any football player, especially given the dominance over world sport of English-speaking nations. In football, however, the global profiles of Spanish, French, Italian, and German teams, allied to the colonial, cultural, and political influences of these countries, mean that players either from these countries or playing in them are likely to exhibit global brand potential.

Age

When Zinedine Zidane announced his retirement from professional football in 2006, the Zidane player brand effectively ceased to exist. Actually, the Zidane brand became something different: a global campaigner for good causes rather than a footballer. In Beckham's case, rather than reinventing the brand in a related industrial category, he decided to extend and diversity his brand by moving to the USA. In the case of both players, each had to confront the reality that, unlike other brands, the very essence of their brands rapidly begins to deteriorate and that this is entirely predictable and completely avoidable. As such, player brands have a highly concentrated life cycle, the stages of which will be defined by age, maturity, and experience. For someone like Roy Keane, formerly of Manchester United, this saw him make the transition from being a young firebrand to a trusted leader and heartbeat of his team. In cases like this, therefore, branding opportunities change, just as they do when a player starts to become less attractive, a slower runner, or adopts a more reflective approach to the game. Brand managers and advisers therefore should be aware of how such changes effectively impose certain restrictions on player brands. Rather than being market driven, they actually originate internally and cannot be avoided, although they can still be managed. In the case of Pele, the brand lives on, even if the player does not. He is still associated with exciting football, the Brazilian national team, and Mexico 1970, but is now perhaps better known by some people for his work with corporations and products such as Viagra.

Reputation

In most cases, the managers of other product brands will seek to associate with particular player brands because of the possible association they believe consumers have with certain players. In cases where players behave badly or inappropriately, this will undermine such associations and so brands managers will be less inclined to work with them. For example, McDonald's terminated an agreement with Wayne Rooney because the company felt he was an unsuitable role model for young people, largely due to his disciplinary record. Such behavior clearly diminishes the value of brands, thus placing a strong onus on players to conduct themselves in a particular way, on the field of play and also off it. This is exacerbated by the media scrutiny that players are subject to, even in situations such as press conferences and charitable activities. Allied to this aspect of a player's reputation, the nature and effectiveness of a brand will draw on consumers' associations with the player as, say, a "hard man," "goal poacher," or "magnificent leader." Similarly, the number of fouls committed, bookings received, or sending offs may serve to diminish brand strength, although clearly, in the case of some like Eric Cantona, this actually added to the brand rather than detracting from it.

The Downside

As Alexander Pope once wrote, "to err is human, to forgive divine."[1] Despite Brand Beckham's iconic status, its luster has been threatened periodically. Most notably, when Beckham first arrived in Madrid, allegations abounded that he was having an affair with his personal assistant, Rebecca Loos. For a brand strongly founded on family, this was incredibly problematic. To add to Beckham's woes at this time, his arrival at Real Madrid was cynically received by some fans of the club who dubbed him "Forrest Gump" for his tireless running but lack of imagination. That Beckham subsequently was able to address both difficulties provides some interesting lessons for brand managers. The Loos allegations are essentially still just that, with claims of Beckham's infidelity remaining publicly unsubstantiated. Moreover, the portrayal of Beckham as a loyal family man has seemingly strengthened, rather than diminished, in the wake of the scandal. In the main, this has been down to careful tactical management and good public relations, both very important tools in preserving the brand. The response to comparisons with Gump was rather more unplanned but no less effective. Beckham's arrival at Real coincided with a decline in the club's fortunes as its "galacticos" strategy first stuttered, then began to age and ultimately failed. Yet throughout, Beckham grew in stature, his Gump-like performances reinforcing the brand as one underpinned by passion and commitment. The unintended consequences of Beckham's play were nevertheless leveraged to the full by personal and club managers who were apparently responsible for actions including the Beckham ritual of staying on the field after a game, stripping his shirt off, and handing it to a member of the crowd. Such clever orchestration ultimately proved to be a shrewd way of leveraging value out of Beckham's playing style in order to reinforce the nature of the brand.

As David Beckham signed for Real Madrid in 2003, Brazilian footballer Ronaldinho signed for Barcelona, also of La Liga, from Paris Saint Germain. At the time, the Brazilian was seen as a player of potential but something of a wayward young man with a flamboyant lifestyle. Three years on and, according to Germany's BBDO, Ronaldinho had toppled David Beckham as the world's most valuable football player brand.[2] Thereafter, however, the brand seemingly lost its luster and some even argue that the player is in decline. In managerial terms, the Ronaldinho case is therefore an interesting one, especially compared to Beckham. Rather than being based on family, fashion, and sexuality, the Ronaldinho brand has been more about the pure joy of playing football, attributable especially to the Brazilian's skill. Conversely, this has been what has made his brand so fragile in many ways because, as the player's on-field performances have diminished, it has eroded the power of his brand. While Beckham was able to transcend sustained criticism because of the features his brand has exhibited, a poor World Cup in 2006 and a couple of mediocre seasons at Barcelona have put Brand Ronaldinho under serious threat (a fact not helped by concerns about his off-field lifestyle). Moreover, while Beckham appeared to relish the challenges facing his brand, both in the short and long term, Ronaldinho and his advisers do not seem to have taken any remedial action, or certainly none that has been especially effective. The key issue here is that, if a player brand is based solely on on-field performance, the inevitable decline of a player's prowess can, in an instant, erode a brand's value. This reinforces how important off-field activities are to a player's brand, but also highlights the inextricable and two-way link between on-field performance and off-field activities.

In the same vein, brand shocks in football are an inevitability rather than a possibility. While no brand can necessarily plan for its "Dasani moment," football players will get injured and spend time away from the core activity that gives their brand so much power in the first place. Take the example of Brazilian international, Ronaldo: a young protege, a World Cup winner, and a multiple award-winning player of the year. Yet a mixture of injury, disaffection, weight problems, and loss of form have prevented Ronaldo taking his place alongside Beckham and Ronaldinho as a global brand icon. With his latest injury, suffered in a recent game for AC Milan, the maintenance and possibly even the resurrection of his brand are effectively at an end. For players such as Ronaldo's Portuguese namesake and his advisers, the message is stark: there will be difficult times in a player's career and a player therefore will have to be engaged in a portfolio of activities that provide the brand with sustenance when they are away from the field of play. Maintaining brand prominence, and thereby power, will therefore require advisers not to manage the brand as a transitory sporting celebrity, but as a commercial and strategic asset with a potentially finite life. Hence, there should be clear thinking about how to preserve and protect value through remedial activities in the event of, say, serious injury or off-field indiscretion.

So, after Beckham and Ronaldo, who can spot the next big brand? Messi, Pato, Nasri, Walcott, or Podolski? Or, do others who have already been playing for a while have some, as yet unleashed, potential? Torres? Ribery? Quagliarella? For such players, the appeal of actively seeking to build and promote their brands is clear: it creates opportunities for boosting profile, associating with other brands, transferring to one of the world's leading teams and generating revenue outside one's playing career. But it is worth noting finally that not everyone can be a worldwide global brand. Some brands remain local but nevertheless enjoy a high level of distinctiveness and popularity. Lee Trundle, formerly of Swansea City—an English League One club—is something of a case in point. Despite being almost unknown outside the UK, he was a local phenomenon and even had his own range of branded clothing. The point is, because of what they do, football players enjoy unique advantages over other brands (and brand managers). It is therefore likely that the continuation of Beckham-like brands will be seen in the future, the key questions about them being: who will these players be, what will their brands be like, how powerful will their brands be, and where will they be successful?

Notes

1. Pope, A. (2004). *An essay on criticism*. Whitefish, MT: Kessinger Publishing.

2. BBDO (2006) Ronaldinho is footballer with world's highest brand value. Retrieved April 30, 2008, from http://www.bbdo.de/de/home/presse/aktuell/2006/30_30_06_soccer-ranking.html

11

DANGEROUS LIAISONS: HOW CAN SPORTS BRANDS CAPITALIZE ON THE HIP HOP MOVEMENT?

Barbara Manivet and Andre Richelieu

Introduction

With the exception of music, cinema, and religion, teams generate an emotional response from their fans, one that is stronger than that in any other field of activity (Underwood et al., 2001). Unfortunately, this potential emotional attachment is still underexploited by sports teams (Bobby, 2002). A strong brand can help a team capitalize on the emotional attachment with its fans, in order to instill trust and trigger fan loyalty. In return, this trust and loyalty can help the sports team generate additional revenues through the sale of a variety of goods and services, within and beyond the sports arena (Gustafson, 2001; Richelieu, 2004). Although the level of success on the field of a professional team has an impact on brand development (Waltner, 2000), ultimately, strong brand equity should transcend the team record through the establishment of a strong identity (Couvelaere & Richelieu, 2005).

Beyond traditional sports fans, the Hip Hop movement represents an axis for growth that contains significant potential for the development of a club's brand equity, since Hip Hop has itself drawn on apparel and symbols associated with major league professional sports teams and some equipment makers (e.g., New Era and Reebok). It started with NBA merchandise, thanks to the popularity of basketball on inner-city streets, soon followed by MLB, NFL, and, to a lesser extent, NHL merchandise.

The Strategic Management and Leadership Group (SMLG) estimates that 45.3 million consumers in North America spend approximately US$12.6 billion on Hip Hop media and merchandise (Marketing Week, 2004). Of those aged between 13 and 34 years, 80% are Caucasians and have a total buying power of US$1000 billion (Devaney, 2004). Furthermore, merchandise sales for sports teams in North America in 2008 will exceed ticket sales for the first time in history, reaching more than US$19 billion (PWC, 2004). However, given current attitudes toward Hip Hop, how could such a niche be developed without alienating long-time sports team fans? In the present paper, we intend to provide preliminary guidelines in this regard, through an exploratory research that will help pave the way for future empirical work.

We will start by underlining the major principles of Hip Hop. Secondly, we will review the literature dealing with the diffusion and adoption processes of a product and of a new or marginal phenomenon, which will contribute to a better understanding of useful approaches. Thirdly, we will focus on the consequences a professional sports team or an equipment maker may face when they establish an association with Hip Hop. Lastly, this exploratory overview, the first step in our work on the Hip Hop segment in sports, will be the source of some guidelines for sports teams and equipment makers on ways to capitalize on the Hip Hop market. We will end the paper with a conclusion and some avenues for future research.

Hip Hop

The Hip Hop movement originated in the 1970s in New York with the launch of the first controversial albums dealing with the oppression of Blacks and rejection of the established order: GrandMaster Flash and The Furious Five, Sugarhill Gang, and Kurtis Blow (Devlin, 2004; La Presse, 2005). It was not expected to last very long but grew significantly in importance, influencing fashion, technology, and culture. Hip Hop became a cultural epicenter within the "arts and fashion communities, ethnic subcultures, professional communities and consumption communities" (Holt, 2002, p. 84).

The Principles of Hip Hop

Hip Hop is made up of four elements: *Break Dancing*, *Graffiti*, *DJing*, and *Rapping* (Hornsey, 2003). It is the culture of urban ghettos and the lifestyle of young street people who use music, dance, graphic arts, and fashion to express their self-image. Coexistent with this culture are the deeply felt fears toward it on the part of the general population, fears that are reinforced by highly mediatized suburban gang wars in major cities. The gangs take for their own use apparel associated with professional sports teams; as Sternbergh (2002) notes, Hip Hop fans wear baseball caps as a sign of belonging to a particular group. On the one hand, the caps represent a geographic community, and on the other, they identify street gangs with the colors of a particular team. In some instances, symbols have such a strong connotation that they are banned in schools and colleges in the USA to avoid fights, as is the case with the Oakland Raiders merchandise (the team has a very mean and tough image).

The main values expressed by this culture can be identified as revolt, anti-globalization, and denunciation of the past, values expressed through violent behavior, fiery songs and the choice of apparel (Friede, 2003; Spiegler, 1996). The expression of the individual as a unique human being constitutes a motivation for adopting the style. However, the core value in Hip Hop is authenticity, a quintessential value for the new generation of echo boomers (Salzman et al., 2003). Through the media, rap stars have become the new models for young people. A rap star has to be credible and reliable, with an underlying consistency between his attitude, his words, and his troubled past, a symbol of the American Dream (Zivitz, 2004) who remains an imperfect human being with a close connection to his fans (*The Windsor Star*, 2004).

Today, although Hip Hop still advocates rebellion and rejects the established social order, the message has been toned down compared to its earlier forms of expression (Ogunnaike, 2004). Hip Hop has led a number of the movement's current stars to become more involved in social action, rather than simply denouncing injustice in their songs (Hornsey, 2003). Puff Daddy/Diddy, for example, has established a Foundation aimed at providing shelter to homeless children (Ogunnaike, 2004).

The Characteristics of Hip Hop "Fashion" Fans

Hip Hop seems to be today's "blackest" culture (Gilroy, 1997). Defining a typical profile for a Hip Hop supporter is increasingly harder to do as the movement spreads more widely and embraces different forms of cultural expression. The profile that follows applies to the USA and the majority of countries that have adopted its style, but some differences do exist (Devaney, 2004; Friede, 2003; Ogunnaike, 2004; Parnes, 2000):

- Demographic profile: Aged between approximately 12 and 34, Hip Hop fans are either young people or those who are older and who are looking for ways to convey youthfulness.
- Political profile: The feelings of revolt expressed by the Hip Hop movement are present in capitalist societies and are taken up by opponents of the system.
- Ethnic profile: Hip Hop fans are primarily Blacks but this characteristic tends to disappear, especially with the arrival of Caucasian male rappers: Eminem, Pee Zee, etc.

The degree to which individuals feel the need to express or denounce ideas or opposition to them is reflected in a Hip Hop culture that is more or less violent, and more or less acceptable to the society (Valencia, 2002). For example, Japan has developed its own version of Hip Hop with a very mild character, not synonymous with violence. It is expressed solely through choices in clothes by people of all ages and income (Takatsuki, 2003).

Review of Literature

To understand how Hip Hop has penetrated society and how sports teams might approach it, we will now review the literature on the diffusion and adoption processes of both an innovative and marginal phenomenon.

Indeed, because Hip Hop started as a marginal phenomenon, which is now spreading throughout society, we believe that the diffusion and adoption processes represent relevant theoretical foundations to help explain why and how Hip Hop has gained in popularity and is now becoming more and more mainstream.

The Diffusion Process

The diffusion process is a concept originally described by Rogers (1983, p. 5): "Diffusion is the process by which an innovation is communicated through certain channels over time among the members of a social system. It is a special type of communication in that the messages are concerned with new ideas." Rogers (1962) shows that communication is most effective between individuals with shared values, culture, beliefs, or status. From this perspective, the rapid spread of Hip Hop over the past few years can be explained by the growing tendency for the values of revolt that characterize that culture to coincide with public opinion. Four elements characterize the diffusion process of ideas: innovation, communication channels, time, and the social system. It is the inherent characteristics of an innovation that can either foster its adoption or hinder it (Tomatzky & Klein, 1982). These characteristics establish its relative advantages; demonstrate its compatibility with existing values, past experiences, or with the needs of individuals or organizations; suggest its perceived complexity; and show whether it might be tried out and the consequences observed.

Osumare (2001, p. 171) finds that Hip Hop has spread due to mass media; he characterizes this phenomenon as "technology-mediated global youth culture." However, the existence of a new product can also be communicated by word of mouth (Morin, 1983), through rumors (Hume, 1987), or urban legends (Donovan et al., 1999). The effect of the information can be reinforced when the source is more similar to the communications target (Rogers, 1995). The fact that the Hip Hop movement has become less strident in the course of the past few years (Ogunnaike, 2004) has undoubtedly influenced its wider appeal through music and clothing, transcending its original clientele to seduce more mainstream consumers. At the same time, because Hip Hop has been disseminated through society and accepted by a larger audience, it takes on a mainstream image, which favors its adoption by the masses.

Strang and Soule (1998) and Rogers (1995) show that practices are more likely to be adopted when they are culturally consistent with local conventions or frames of reference and as such make them familiar and attractive. Watson (2002) and Guillén (2001) find, however, that adopters and agents of change in the social system possess a different kind of political, social, and cultural power and, in the long term, have a positive influence on the diffusion of an innovation.

Rogers (1962, 1976) differentiates the adoption process from the diffusion process in that the diffusion process occurs within society, as a group process; the adoption process pertains to an individual. In 1962, Rogers broke adopters of innovations down into five distinct groups based on their degree of innovation: innovators (venturesome), early adopters (opinion leaders—a critical category in the adoption process), the early majority (longer reflection time and strong interaction with the social system), the late majority (acts under peer pressure), and the latecomers (purchase after seeing demonstrable benefits).

This theory has been the subject of some criticism. Boyd and Mason (1999) believe that it is more advantageous to directly target the majority rather than focus efforts around early adopters. Goldsmith and Hofacker (1991) consider that the theory is unproductive in predicting future behavior. Kirton (1976) argues that the Rogers classification is less appropriate than a classification that takes into account an individual's tendency to innovate, based on the cognitive style applied to the adoption of new technologies.

The model proposed by Bass (1969) is recognized as being extremely effective in predicting the adoption curve for a new technology. In this model, two influences have an impact on the adoption curve, one with no connection to preceding adopters and the other positively influenced by them. They are also described as external and internal influences (Lekvall & Wahlbin, 1973). Bass' model implies exponential growth of initial purchases to a peak and then exponential decay (Bass, 1969).

The Adoption Process of Fashion

Fashion is defined as a temporary way of behaving, adopted by an identifiable proportion of the members of a social group because it is considered appropriate by that society for the moment and the situation (Sproles, 1979).

Although the different authors agree on the fact that there are several stages in the adoption process, they characterize them differently. For Rogers (1962, 1976), the adoption process or innovation-decision process is a mental process. More precisely, Rogers (1962, 1976) defines five stages in the process to adopt or reject the innovation, the first three being mental exercises: awareness of the innovation, formation of an attitude to it, decision, implementation, and confirmation.

Rogers (1962) notes that elements such as an earlier trial of the innovation, needs and problems experienced, a propensity to innovate, and conventions within the social system can all influence the decision process when it comes to innovation. Rogers (1962) also presents prior conditions that affect the innovation-decision process (previous practice, needs or problems felt, innovativeness, and norms of the social systems). Moreover, Rogers (1962) states that awareness and knowledge of an innovation could be made more efficient through mass media. As he points out, an innovation may be rejected during any stage of the adoption process or may suffer from discontinuance. On one hand, there is disenchantment discontinuance, which is the decision to reject an idea as a result of dissatisfaction with its performance; on the other hand, there is replacement discontinuance, which is the decision to reject an idea in order to adopt a better one.

For Dodgson and Bessant (1996), success in innovation is more than a matter of moving a resource from a part to another but rests on the ability of recipients to use it or innovate effectively. Dodgson and Bessant also recognize that innovation is a temporal but not instantaneous process and break it down into six stages: awareness of an opportunity or need, research, comparison, selection, acquisition, implementation and long-term use.

As for fashion, consumer emotions seem to define the major trends (Cho and Lee, 2005), as they do for anti-fashion, a trend widely promoted and exploited by designers since the 1990s. This trend is closely akin to Hip Hop, defined as a means to express identity by representing values opposed to social conventions and rules. In the post-modern era, fashion establishes a connection between fans and their idols (Cova, 1997), and enables the fans to express their identity and their authenticity, a value central to what is advocated by the generation of echo boomers (Salzman et al., 2003). New Era baseball caps are a good illustration of this phenomenon, having become the caps of reference for the Hip Hop movement that uses the symbol as a fashion statement or to show loyalty to an artist, music group, or street gang (Richelieu & Boulaire, 2005).

The relationship to fashion varies from one country to another. The desire to be in style or not can vary with an individual's financial situation (Parker et al., 2004), and the motivation to adopt a style may be influenced by the level of individualism in a culture (Wong & Ahuvia, 1998) or the degree of materialism in a society (O'Cass, 2004).

Miller et al. (1993) have conceptualized the individual adoption process of a fashion trend. Adoption of a style at the individual level is a continuing and iterative process, since the assessment of other people's styles is influenced both by the weight of *a priori* preferences and by the desire to be in style. Individuals, driven by their own assessments and selective influences, develop an image of what is appropriate or not if they want to achieve their goal of expressing their difference from, or conformity with, a group (e.g., Rogers' conventions within the social system; Rogers, 1962). These elements, and individuals' attitudes to change, lead them to choose a particular style.

The Adoption of the Hip Hop Phenomenon

Bourdieu (1986) argues that cultural capital, made up of items with symbolic value, plays a large role in the creation of individual and group identities. On the basis of this theory, as applied to the field of Hip Hop, Clay (2003) shows that cultural capital is used to establish a hierarchy between individuals, distinguish between what is legitimate or authentic and what is not, and proscribe the latter. Several different authors have studied the ongoing struggle for identity within the Hip Hop community (Binder, 1999; Collins, 1990; McLeod, 1999; Rose, 1994) and its focus on what is or is not authentic, with the goal of establishing a convincing identity that, in return, defines the community (Clay, 2003). This continuing struggle is particularly evident in Hip Hop culture, especially through the use of apparel as symbols, because, as Clay (2003, p. 1349) points out, "an element such as skin color no longer seems to constitute proof of racial identity or authenticity. Ethnic groups establish their own status symbols to delineate limits and build the community around the group".

When faced with the threat of assimilation, subcultures are driven to look for new ways of distinguishing themselves from imitators and use new symbols to preserve cohesion and uniformity in their identity (McLeod, 1999). This principle explains the evolution of Hip Hop fashion since the 1990s, borrowing from sports symbols, which it alters to fit with its own image of uniqueness and authenticity (McLeod, 1999; Miller et al., 1993). A good example of the latter point is represented by sports team merchandise (caps, shirts, jackets, etc.) that are produced with colors others than the official ones. As the General Manager of New Era Canada points out, "When Spike Lee asked for a red New York Yankees cap, it changed headwear in the 1990s. Indeed, it started the trend for new colors, material and designs" (interview with Wayne Best, 5 March 2004, Toronto).

Referring to the importance of symbols, Brian Povinelli, VP Global Integrated Marketing for Reebok, underlines that "It's about putting out a message that resonates and is relevant to today's youth. If your brand isn't connecting [with consumers] on an emotional level, it's hard [for them] to make the conversion standing at the shoe wall" (Sanders, 2005, p. 5).

The Conceptual Framework of the Adoption Process of the Hip Hop Phenomenon

The conceptual framework that can be established from this literature review is in part a restatement of the model developed by Miller et al. (1993). This model illustrates the individual adoption process of a fashion trend, the environment being broadly defined as a factor influencing how other people's styles are observed (economic view — Shama, 1981; ecological view — Boisvert, 2000; social view — Haynes, 2003; political view — Hornsey, 2003), and the value system particular to each individual, an extremely important factor in the adoption of the phenomenon. "The observation of styles adopted by others that appears in the original model proposed by Miller et al. (1993) has been replaced by the process of readjustment of symbols of a subculture (see Figure 1), thereby enabling us to use the diagram to illustrate the internal process characterizing Hip Hop supporters.

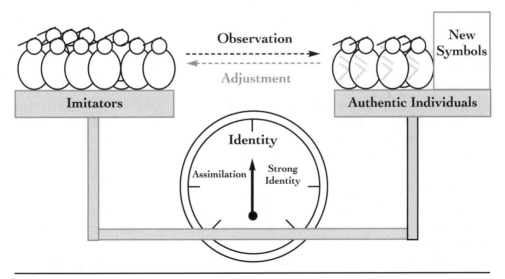

Figure 1. The rebalancing process used by subcultures to preserve their identity (adapted from McLeod, 1999, and Miller et al., 1993)

Every individual, whether or not he or she belongs to the movement, observes Hip Hop style (which is in a state of constant change) and forms an opinion on what is appropriate or not, based on his or her values, preferences, the environment, and desire to be in style. Depending on an individual's desire for individuality or conformity with the group observed and the opinions this person has developed, he or she will choose to adopt or reject a particular style, and so the process starts over again.

A parallel can be made between this model and the stages of adoption identified by Pereira (2002): awareness, persuasion, decision, implementation, and confirmation (underlined in Figure 2). Awareness and understanding of the phenomenon are thus determinants of the effects that values, the environment, and the desire for being in style can have on later impressions; understanding is the first step toward acceptance (Faure, 2001). The persuasion stage is shown in parallel with the formation of impressions on what is appropriate or not, depending on the desire for differentiation or conformity with the group of individuals. The decision stage corresponds to the selection of the style, while confirmation corresponds to the stage where the process begins again, based on observations of how the style evolves. This is also in line with the steps identified by Rogers (1962) and by Dodgson and Bessant (1996), which we presented in section 3.2.

Establishing an Association with the Hip Hop Movement: Consequences for Professional Sports Brands

Any association with Hip Hop style must be planned with a full understanding of the issues, opportunities, and requirements it carries with it. But why study sports brands in relation with the Hip Hop segment? Because sports, fashion, and music (Hip Hop) mix up well and as underlined earlier, in the post-modern era, fashion establishes a connection between fans and their idols (Cova, 1997) and enables the fans to express their identity and their authenticity (Salzman et al., 2003). As stated in a recent interview, Snoop Dogg mentions that "Hip Hop draws the biggest amount of business to anything . . . I'm seeing Hip Hop now in all the commercials because it's what's driving people to the store. Even if you don't like the product you'll get it because Snoop represents it" (Hein, 2005, p. 9). Undoubtedly, entertainment artists and sports stars have a powerful force of attraction for consumers who want to associate themselves with popular figures; the latter act as emotional anchors and give both legitimacy and meaning to a brand (Cassidy, 2004; Holt, 2002).

Furthermore, not only have sports brands been espoused by Hip Hop, but sports are also becoming more popular, especially among women, and sports gear is seen as fashionable. Says Ms Grossman from Nike: 'The growth [of woman apparel] reflects increasing numbers of women working out and the acceptance of sport-influenced looks as fashionable" (Kang, 2006, p. B4).

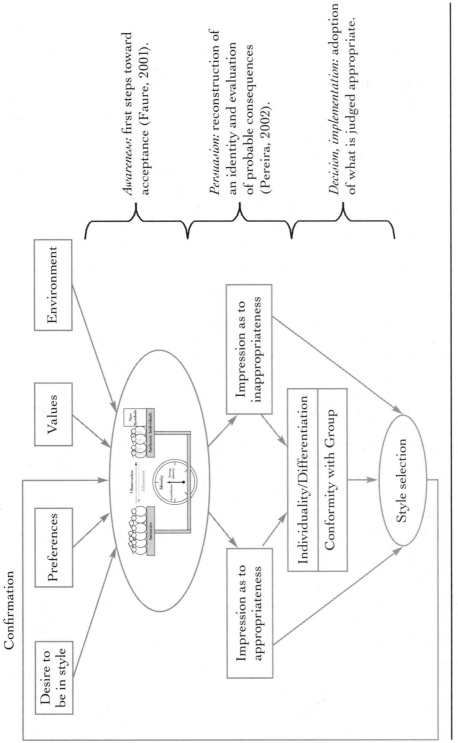

Figure 2. Individual process of adoption of Hip Hop style and of evolution of fashion

Issues

Professional sports teams and equipment makers cannot afford to ignore the potential represented by the Hip Hop market. They would find in it a significant source of revenue to support the development of their brands. The stakes are extremely high, as previously mentioned. On the one hand, in 2003, Hip Hop accounted for over US$12 billion in the USA (Marketing Week, 2004); on the other hand, in 2008, merchandising revenues will represent more than US$19 billion in North America, a higher figure than that for ticket sales, and will be over US$7 billion in Europe (PWC, 2004).

To tap the potential of this marketing niche would mean that sports teams need to develop an offer aimed at a category of "fashion" fans (Pons & Richelieu, 2004), without forsaking their regular fans; the latter continue to be a core group crucial to the survival of a team (Mullin et al., 2000). Pons and Richelieu (2004) identify four categories of fans in their model:

- "Affective" fans are those that consistently attend games and have a high degree of loyalty to a team. They associate a team's success with their own success and want an experience that takes them outside their daily lives; they perceive sports as an art that generates strong emotions. They feel the need to belong to a group of fans, and identify with this group. They want to experience a symbiosis between the atmosphere in the stands and that on the field. These are the most valuable of all fans in terms of the survival and success of a team (Mullin et al., 2000); they are part of the "Super Fan" category, as presented by Pimentel and Reynolds (2004).

- "Cognitive" fans find self-satisfaction in the skills they can demonstrate to possess through their knowledge of game statistics, strategies, and tactical choices, as seen in sports-related bets, for example. These fans see themselves as belonging to a community of experts. They put particular emphasis on the quality of play and on the possibility of having access to an environment (real or virtual) for discussion where they can demonstrate their know-how in the company of other cognoscenti. They are loyal to the sport, not necessarily to a particular team.

- "Relational" fans want to be part of a social group, so they can enhance their self-esteem. What is especially important for these individuals is their interaction with other people, since they feel the value of their experience is inextricably linked to the quality of their interactions with others.

- "Fashion" fans find their source of self-esteem in fads and fashion. Their need is to identify with a group that is not normally associated with the sports sector (like an artist, music group, or street gang, for instance). As a result, their level of involvement with a team is almost non-existent, their only connection being the fact that they are consumers of club merchandise. As a matter of fact, caps of certain baseball teams become very popular after a singer has worn the cap during a video clip or a concert; for instance, the Philadelphia Phillies cap was worn by Will Smith during one of his recent video clips, which was played at Foot Locker stores around the world.

As a parallel to this model, Mahony et al. (2000) identify a segmentation break-down based on the degree of fan loyalty, assessed on two axes: psychological involvement and consistency of attitudes (i.e., frequency of attendance at games). Extremely loyal fans should be encouraged to identify with their team through a well-developed merchandising strategy. This group resembles the affective fans of Pons and Richelieu (2004). The group characterized by false loyalty (high levels of attendance at games but low psychological attachment) needs a justification for buying team merchandise and has to be sold on its benefits; these fans are similar to fans in the relational or cognitive categories, fans whose attendance is motivated by factors other than the team itself (Pons & Richelieu, 2004). Latent loyalty (strong psychological attachment but low levels of attendance at games) calls for actions that eliminate potential barriers to game attendance; this group resembles the affective fans, a group strongly affected by barriers. Non-existent team loyalty (low level of psychological at-tachment and low tendency to attend games) calls for choosing between either an aggressive action strategy that is sustained and costly or no action at all; fashion fans in the Pons and Richelieu (2004) typology would fall into this category.

Figure 3 shows the links an association with Hip Hop would create. Com-mitted fans of a professional sports team are connected to the team by shared values. If Hip Hop were to become part of the team image, this could influ-ence their sense of ownership in two ways. First, if these fans do not want to be associated with Hip Hop, they could distance themselves from the team, and secondly, the image and values of the team would become unclear. Misap-prehension and confusion about the new values could also compromise sports fans' identification with the team. Very popular teams, such as the New York Yankees, which draw different types of fans and consumers, are more exposed to this risk and to the potential dilution of their brand than others (Keller & Sood, 2003) because the brand loses its uniqueness and authenticity; even one of the terrorists involved in the 2005 London bombings wore a Yankees cap.

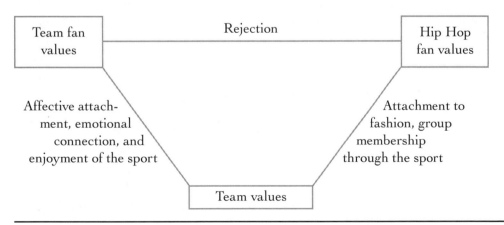

Figure 3. Connections between a team, team fans, and Hip Hop

The critical challenge in the development of a Hip Hop marketing niche for a professional sports team is to build up the number of fashion fans while retaining the loyalty of the affective fans. To avoid the risk of alienating sports fans, particularly the affective fans, it is important to be fully aware of the effect an association with Hip Hop could have on these latter fans' feelings of identification with the team, so that informed choices can be made in this regard.

Development Opportunities

Distinctions within the Profiles of Hip Hop Fans

Riddle (2005) identifies a scale of attitudes in relation to a marginal phenomenon. The different positions are repulsion/condemnation, pity, tolerance, acceptance, support, admiration, appreciation, and nurturance. In Figure 4, we propose a graphic diagram where public attitudes to the phenomenon could be quantified; we combine Riddle's model with Rogers' groups of adopters (innovators, early adopters, early majority, late majority, and latecomers; Rogers, 1962).

When attitudes of the general public are identified along this continuum, it becomes possible to predict the psychological effect that an association with the movement would have on affective fans of a sports team. Ogunnaike (2004) claims that the Hip Hop movement has become less harsh, but public attitudes toward it remain somewhat blurred. The diagram implicitly suggests that there is no stage more favorable to a culture than nurturance, and none more harmful than condemnation (Riddle, 2005). An imaginary line has been added (shown in dotted form), simply as an illustration; it is not based on any hard data yet.

Individuals that adopt Hip Hop fashion are not always authentic rappers; in fact, they are relatively small in number compared to the overall rap market (Spiegler, 1996). To fall into the rapper category, individuals, in addition to adopting the clothing style, must be able to break dance and rap, do *Graffiti* or engage in *DJing*. Moreover, McLeod (1999) emphasizes that true members of the Hip Hop culture feel threatened by the risk of mass-driven assimilation, with the softening up of the movement given its increase in popularity since the 1990s. The initial values of Hip Hop as a brutal expression of popular revolt in the New York subculture now seem to have dissipated as the movement has become successful, which helped the diffusion and adoption of Hip Hop by mass consumers. Today, well-known rap artists communicate messages of peace and non-violence themselves (Ogunnaike, 2004). In light of the way the movement has evolved, we can identify two kinds of Hip Hop fans:

- *Authentic individuals*: they are leaders in Hip Hop fashion. They establish and define how it develops as a way to find new symbols for their identity. They rap, practice *Break Dancing* and *Graffiti*, and see Hip Hop as a tool for voicing their frustrations about the established order and creating their own distinctive identities.
- *Imitators*: these are the individuals that adopt the characteristics of Hip

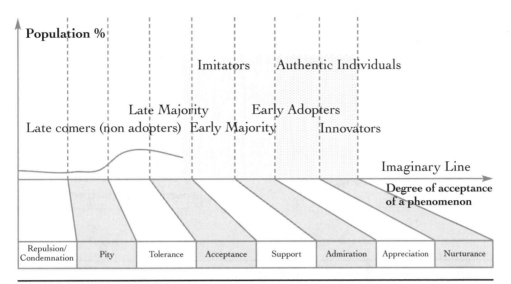

Figure 4. Distribution of the population based on the scale of attitudes toward a marginal phenomenon versus imitators and authentic individuals classification (Riddle, 2005; Rogers, 1962)

Hop culture in order to be identified with it, not to demarcate themselves from others as a way of expressing discontent. In many cases, they use the fashion style only as a symbol of their identification with Hip Hop.

The characteristics of those that adopt the Hip Hop phenomenon are neither well understood nor quantified but it would be useful to differentiate between *authentic individuals* and *imitators*. The Figure 4 we propose here should make it possible to identify what is in the particular nature of imitators and authentic individuals and as such draw conclusions as to implications for team management. It might be assumed that there will be an interrelation between imitators and authentic individuals and where they fall on the continuum of attitudes. Additionally, the diagram shows the range of attitudes pertaining to the adoption of a marginal phenomenon; it is similar to the classification of segments of adopters used by Rogers (1962); the more advanced levels in the adoption scale could be correlated with the more favorable attitudes to the phenomenon.

Hip Hop fans can be broken down into specific categories (Richelieu et al., 2005), as illustrated in Figure 5. Each of the circles of Figure 5 represents one type of Hip Hop fan, characterized by a certain level of authenticity and attachment to the movement and the channel through which they adopt a particular fashion style. The inner two circles represent the most authentic individuals. The first circle corresponds to rap singers that create the fashion and embody the fashion standards: they are consumers of expensive "designer" products. The second circle group (early adopters) is strongly influenced by the core users and follows their standards to the letter; they adopt the same fashion standards (designer apparel) and influence those represented in the

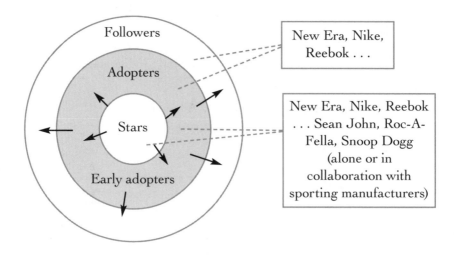

Figure 5. Schematic diagram of influences on Hip Hop consumption (Richelieu et al., 2005)

third circle, the "followers." Individuals in this latter group, who want to be part of that broad social circle but purchase less expensive goods, tend to go more for the style than the brand (Marketing Week, 2004; Spiegler, 1996), although the brands they buy are still always sanctioned by the Hip Hop fraternity (e.g., Nike, Puma, or Reebok; Kates, 2004).

Motivations for Adopting Hip Hop

When a brand is used by a movement, the company involved needs to identify the values inherent in this choice in order to adapt its marketing strategy (Beverland & Ewing, 2005). Osumare (2001) argues that the adoption of this marginal phenomenon can be attributed to the social feedback particular to expressive "Black" culture through its historical political connections with other nations. In concrete terms, motivations to connect with Hip Hop culture are many and varied. As mentioned in an earlier section (O'Cass, 2004; Parker et al., 2004; Wong & Ahuvia, 1998), we can underline the culture itself (Jamaica and Cuba), social class (North Africans in France), historical oppression (native Hawaiians in Hawaii) or simply the construction of a youth class status in defiance of parents (Japan) (Osumare, 2001).

Spiegler (1996) notes that motivations of Whites and Blacks in adopting the Hip Hop style are not the same. The motivation on the part of Whites is to enter an unfamiliar world they had been fearful of: "the attraction is part admiration, part fascination, and part fear" (Spiegler, 1996, p. 31). For young Blacks, it is a means of expressing the reality of their lives, their past and present frustrations, and their search for strength in numbers. They make no distinction between skin colors; by adopting the style, individuals are looking for ways to express their own personality, which is consistent with Clay's comments, underlined in section 3.3 (Clay, 2003).

"Moderating" Elements

An Authentic Culture that Cannot Be Managed

"The most successful crossovers don't try" (Spiegler, 1996, p. 34). Some brands, taken up by Hip Hop culture without their prior knowledge (Kangol and New Era), have been able to capitalize on that situation. New Era, a manufacturer of baseball caps, succeeded in developing its image of authenticity with the Hip Hop public by adopting its slogan, its website, and particular models of caps, and by developing partnerships with rap stars (e.g., Walé Adeyemi, Trevor Andrew, and Dizzee Rascal; Richelieu & Boulaire, 2005). These stars collaborate with the manufacturer's designers in the production of exclusive, limited edition caps. New Era has become a brand of reference in the Hip Hop segment because it carries value and authenticity through the slogans of the brand, depicting the consumer as rebellious, engaged, proud, and victorious through the cap he or she wears.

The example of the Kangol Company is also an illustration of the difficulties inherent in managing the phenomenon (Beck & Hop, 1997, p. C): "We were hijacked, to our benefit, by Hip Hop." Beverland and Ewing (2005) discuss the issues arising from the adoption of a brand by consumers without a company being aware of it and make a number of recommendations on how to contribute to the rapid diffusion that is already in progress or, on the contrary, how it can be slowed down. Their analysis concludes that a strategy aimed at establishing long-term value for the brand calls for slowing down the diffusion process by identifying the value system that led to the adoption of the brand and adapting the marketing strategy to this system. New Era and Kangol are examples of brands that were able to capitalize on a market segment they did not initially target, and re-align their strategy accordingly.

If rappers feel that they are being manipulated, they will not want to adopt a brand and it is here that the greatest challenge lies: maintaining an image of authenticity for Hip Hop fans, while carrying out actions to secure the market, without this being too obvious. Authenticity (Cova & Cova, 2001), the central value of the way the business strategy must be developed, seems to have become increasingly important since 1990 with the adoption of this fashion by a growing number of users (McLeod, 1999; Salzman et al., 2003). Because they live in fear of losing this aspect of their identity, fans attach significant importance to indicators of authenticity (Sternbergh, 2002) and reassert them. Authenticity in Hip Hop fashion is seen as a fundamental characteristic in adopting new symbols of the culture and emerging styles.

Image and Values of Hip Hop

The traditional perception of Hip Hop is that of a violent movement (Osumare, 2001) and this will continue to weigh heavily in the coming years, in spite of the fact that the movement has evolved toward milder forms of expression (Ogunnaike, 2004). The widespread nature of this image at the international level further increases the challenges involved (Haynes, 2003; Rodriguez,

2004; Valencia, 2002), due to the risk of diluting the brand image and lack of consistency. The values associated with Hip Hop constitute an additional risk in the retention of affective team fans, when Hip Hop values are not shared by the sports fans. Table 1 provides a direct comparison between Hip Hop and sports values.

Sports Brands Associated with the Hip Hop Movement

Considering the stakes at issue here, the opportunities for development and the factors calling for moderation, we have developed the following preliminary orientations for capitalizing on the Hip Hop market for professional major league sports team brands and equipment makers.

Avoid Alienating the Team's Affective Fans

Benefits a sports team could derive from its association with Hip Hop should ideally lead the team to undertake a bidirectional strategic marketing ap-

Table 1. Comparison of Hip Hop and sports values and how they are expressed

	Hip Hop	Sports
Values	Rebellion, rejection of social conventions	Winning and winners
	Expression of a unique identity	Excellence
	Violence	Youthfulness and good health
	Sexism	Team spirit
	Authenticity	Fair play
	Tough life experience, oppression of Blacks	Comradeship (Perraudin, 2005)
	The American Dream	
Expression of values	Custom-made symbols; dress differently from others	Team rallying cries or fan chants
		Mascots
	Violent attitudes, in-your-face language	Community involvement
		Wearing team colors
	Use of words that put down women and society (Rap and *DJing*)	In general, pilgrimages, rituals, use/wearing of team merchandise/colors (Pimentel and Reynolds, 2004)

proach. The ultimate goal is to succeed in getting two lucrative markets (Hip Hop and committed sports fans) to coexist in two parallel worlds where their values, expectations, and consumer preferences can be very different but where they both want to be consumers of the same product. Strategically, an approach based on these two axes involves differentiating between what is to be offered to each market and how each one will be approached.

A potential danger of being associated with Hip Hop is ending up having no clear brand identity that consumers can grasp and understand. This could become the case of the Montreal Canadians hockey club, when they introduce bright orange and yellow caps with a black logo in the official team store at the arena, which is incoherent with the sacredness of tradition and the blue, white, and red colors associated with the club.

Reebok is also exposed to this danger: "Underground buzz is great, but where does the buzz come from, and does the buzz translate to enduring brand success?" (Sundhaman et al., 2005, p. 17A). Truly, a brand can tie up with Hip Hop, but it should not forget about the fundamentals of brand equity, namely defining the identity (attributes or values of the brand), positioning the brand and developing marketing actions that will strengthen the identity and positioning of the brand (Kashani, 1995).

Adopting an Operational Marketing Approach for the Hip Hop Market

Operational marketing has to reflect the development strategy at two different levels. A sports team or an equipment maker needs to have one product offer and a specific approach for its affective fans (Richelieu & Pons, 2005), and a separate approach adapted to the Hip Hop market. This distinction must be made in order, on the one hand, to ensure that actions undertaken are most effectively adapted to the target group, and on the other hand, to minimize negative reactions by affective sports fans to a team's association with Hip Hop. The distinction between the two market segments is not always as clear as it might seem. Some consumers will in fact fall right between the two groups: Hip Hop "imitators," for example, with values that are not entirely characteristic of the movement; team fans on the outside of the committed fan group (e.g., relational or cognitive fans; see Pons & Richelieu, 2004); or other kinds of consumers looking to find in their product purchases values that fall between those of Hip Hop and those of sports. Figure 6 shows the potential areas for development in terms of these two axes, including the "buffer" zone to which "ambivalent" fans can be assigned. We can use the examples of both Nike and Reebok.

Nike is now targeting women fitness dancers. The company has created shoes and apparel designed for women attracted to aerobic activities, such as fitness dance: "The high energy workout was born out of a rising interest in Hip Hop and upbeat dance music typically found in music videos starring Beyonce and Jennifer Lopez" (Kang, 2006, p. B4).

Nike's latest fitness-dance line includes tissue-thin tank tops, low-rise baggy

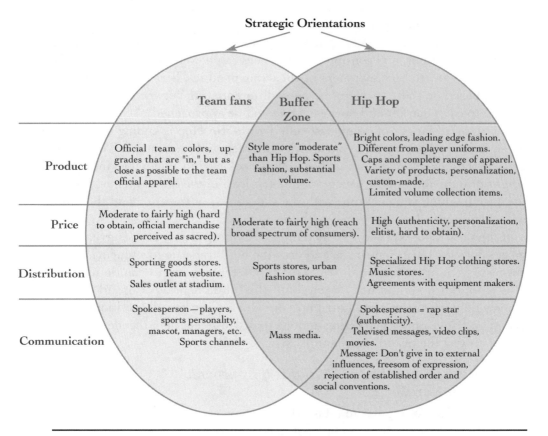

Figure 6. Potential areas for development, based on two strategic orientations and four operational strategies

pants and flirty short skirts that are good for both the gym and the nightclub. Today, Nike focuses on activities women do, even if, in this case, it moves them away from the traditional competitive sports (Kang, 2006).

Reebok, for its part, has tried to broaden its associations beyond sports figures, since 2002, by featuring pop culture stars such as 50 Cent and Jay-Z in TV ads and signing them up for limited edition footwear collections. Reebok's goal is to reach males and females in urban and suburban locales (Sanders, 2005). Reebok has carved out a niche, which gives the company a strong legitimacy with young adults. Says Reebok CMO, Dennis Baldwin: "We also saw a trend where entertainers and musicians in particular were having as much or more influence on young consumers than athletes had in the last decade" (Cassidy, 2004, p. 22).

Reebok's global platform, "I am what I am," builds on Reebok's strong links to celebrities and sports stars. It connects to its target by demonstrating an understanding of their issues (Sanders, 2005). Even better, it can be said that Reebok has "defined relevancy in [such a way] that we now absolutely are manufacturing pop culture" (Cassidy, 2004, p. 23).

This is because Reebok looked at the key interests of youth, namely sports, music, and fashion, that play a major role in their lives, then tried to represent this combination to the youth consumer and become their brand of choice (Cassidy, 2004).

Conclusion

By examining the literature on diffusion and adoption processes (e.g. Bass, 1969; Rogers, 1962, 1983, 1995; Sproles, 1979; Strang & Soule, 1998), this paper stresses the ongoing adjustment of Hip Hop culture (Clay, 2003; McLeod, 1999), the challenges, opportunities and constraining factors a professional sports team should consider when approaching Hip Hop. These are preliminary guidelines in our work on Hip Hop and sport; truly, some empirical work is needed in the next stage.

The world of Hip Hop carries an extremely significant financial potential, but penetrating this market is difficult, delicate, complex, and risky (Devaney, 2004; Osumare, 2001), all of which illustrate how success in such an environment is well earned. The level of risks taken (the loss of affective fans, a change in image and a repositioning) corresponds to the level of the potential rewards. We propose a preliminary approach based on two strategic orientations and four operational strategies to minimize undesirable effects on the sports team fan base or on an equipment maker's clientele. This approach involves the use of distinct operational marketing strategies for the different market segments: a specific offer for sports fans, another specific offer for authentic Hip Hop fans, together with an intermediate approach for "ambivalent" fans, now that Hip Hop is becoming more mainstream and being espoused by mass consumers (Figure 6). Each one of these groups has its own preferences, values, and motivations driving the choices of its members as consumers of team merchandise.

However, not all brands are equal in terms of their values and reputations. Some brands have a good fit with Hip Hop, while others do not. Indeed, some sports brands are positioned as more family-focused, such as the Ottawa Senators hockey club, which tries to build its fan base with younger fans after a 60-year absence of NHL hockey in Canada's capital. Some other sports brands are positioned as tough and aggressive, such as the Oakland Raiders or some NBA teams. Truly, the former type does not have as good a fit with the Hip Hop movement as the latter.

This preliminary study paves the way for further research on the Hip Hop phenomenon, a field that heretofore has not been the subject of much academic study; this explains some of our non-scientific references. The next phase shall involve undertaking an empirical study focused more precisely on the structure of the Hip Hop target market, in order to develop a better understanding of what leads imitators and authentic individuals to adopt the style, by interviewing sports team managers, equipment makers, store managers, and customers. This would provide sports team managers with tools for choosing the approach best suited to the Hip Hop market, depending on the sport (basketball, baseball, football, hockey, soccer, etc.) and the region of the world (North America, Europe, and Asia).

References

Bass, F. M. (1969). A new product growth model for consumer durables. *Management Science, 15*, 215–227.

Beck, E. K. & Hop, p. (April 18, 1997). Kangol's Kangaroo makes jump to high style due to Rap fans. *Wall Street Journal*, p. C.

Beverland, M. T., & Ewing, M. (2005). Slowing the adoption and diffusion process to enhance brand repositioning: The consumer driven repositioning of Dunlop Volley. *Business Horizons, 48*, 385–391.

Binder, A. (1999). Friend or foe: Boundary work and collective identity in the Afrocentric and multi-cultural curriculum movements. In M. Lamont (Ed.), *The cultural territories of race: Black and White boundaries* (pp. 221–248). University of Chicago Press, Chicago.

Bobby, D. (2002). Can a sports club be a brand?. *Sport Business International*. April 2002. Accessed September 2002, http://www.wolff-olins.com/sportsclub.htm.

Boisvert, D. (2000). La simplicité volontaire, pour quelles raisons. *Revue Notre Dame.* March 2002, 1–3.

Bourdieu, P. (1986). The forms of capital. In J. G. Richardson (Ed.), *Handbook of theory and research for the sociology of education* (pp. 241–258). Greenwood, Westport, CT. (original work published in 1983).

Boyd, T. C., & Mason, C. H. (1999). The link between effectiveness of "extrabrand" attributes and the adoption of innovations. *Journal of the Academy of Marketing Science, 27*, 306–319.

Cassidy, H. (2004). When "bad" rap is good brand. *Brandweek, 45*(41), 22–23.

Cho, H. S., & Lee, J. (2005). Development of a macroscopic model on recent fashion trends on the basis of consumer emotion. *International Journal of Consumer Studies, 29*(1), 17–33.

Clay, A. (2003). Keepin' it real: Black youth, Hip-Hop culture, and Black identity. *The American Behavioral Scientist, 46*(10), 1346–1358.

Collins, P. H. (1990). *Black feminist thought.* Routledge, New York.

Couvelaere, V., & Richelieu, A. (2005). Brand strategy in professional sports: The case of French soccer teams. *European Sport Management Quarterly, 5*(1) 23–46.

Cova, B. (1997). Community and consumption. *European Journal of Marketing, 31*(3), 297–316.

Cova, V., & Cova, B. (2001). *Alternatives marketing.* Dunod, Paris.

Devaney, P. (June 24, 2004). Hip-Hop's "bling" culture is wooing corporate America: Despite the violent associations with "gangstar" rappers, Hip-Hop music and their bling-bling culture are a sure-fire moneyspinner. *Marketing Week*, p. 38.

Devlin, M. (January 22, 2004) Rock n' roll, A to Z, A guide to music genres. *Star—Phoenix*, p. B1.

Dodgson, M., & Besssant, J. (1996). *Effective innovation policy: A new approach.* London: International Thompson Business Press.

Donovan, D. T., Mowen, J. C., & Chakaborty, G. (1999). Urban legends: The word of mouth communication of morality through negative story content. *Marketing Letters, 10*(1), 23–34.

Faure, L. (2001). L'acceptation du transsexualisme: La prochaine évolution?. *Nand-Iris.* Accessed June 2005, http://www.nand-iris.com/publication/author/document.php 3?document=47.

Friede, E. (September 5, 2003). Fashion, music strongly linked. *Northern Daily News*, p. 11.

Gilroy, P. (1997). After the love has gone: Biopolitics and and etho-poetics in the Black public sphere. In A. McRobbie (Ed.) *Back to reality? Social experience and cultural studies* (pp. 83–115). Manchester, UK: Manchester University Press.

Goldsmith, R. E., & Hofacker, C. F. (1991). Measuring consumer innovativeness. *Journal of the Academy of Marketing Science, 18*(3), 209–221.

Guillén, M. F. (2001) *The limits of convergence: Globalization and organizational change in Argentina, South Korea, and Spain.* Princeton, NJ: Princeton University Press.

Gustafson, R. (April 5, 2001). Product brands look set to gain new advantage. *Marketing*, p. 20.

Haynes, M. (2003). Watching celebs a popular pastime. *Daily News*. December 2003, p. 25.

Hein, K. (2005). Snoop Dogg rides Hip Hop advertising wave in style. *Brandweek, 46*(38), p. 9.

Holt, D. B. (2002). Why do brands cause trouble? A dialectical theory of consumer culture and branding. *Journal of Consumer Research, 29*, 70–90.

Hornsey, C. (April 2003). Hip Hop's power play, fans of free form style carry political influence, artists suggests. *The Windsor Star*, p. B3.

Hume, S. (August 3, 1987). Corona fights bad beer rumors. *Advertising Age*.

Kang, S. (February 15, 2006). Nike targets women with new Hip Hop line; fitness-dance gear, moves go from gym to night-club; a sweat-wicking corset. *The Wall Street Journal*, p. B4.

Kashani, K. (1995). Comment créer une marque puissante?. *Les Échos*. Accessed February 2003, http://www.lesechos.fr.

Kates, S. M. (2004). The dynamics of brand legitimacy: An interpretive study in the gay men's community. *Journal of Consumer Research, 31*(2), 455–464.

Keller, K. L., & Sood, S. (2003). Brand equity dilution. *MIT Sloan Management Review, 45*(1), 12–15.

Kirton, M. J. (1976). Adaptors and innovators, description and measure. *Journal of Applied Psychology, 61*, 622–629.

La Presse. (December 11, 2005). Les racines du Rap. *Cahier Oups*, p. 7.

Lekvall, P., & Wahlbin, C. (1973). A study of some assumptions underlying innovation diffusion functions. *Swedish Journal of Economics, 75*, 362–377.

Mahony, D. F., Madrigal, R. & Howard, D. (2000) Using the psychological commitment to team (PCT) scale to segment sport consumers based on loyalty. *Sport Marketing Quarterly, 9*(1), 15–25.

Marketing Week. (June 24, 2004). Hip-Hop's "bling" culture is wooing corporate America. *Marketing Week*, p. 38.

McLeod, K. (1999). Authenticity within Hip-Hop and other cultures threatened with assimilation. *Journal of Communication, 49*(4), 134–151.

Miller, C. M., McIntyre, S. H., & Mantrala, M. K. (1993). Toward formalizing fashion theory. *Journal of Marketing Research, 30*(2), 142–158.

Morin, S. P. (February 28, 1983). Influencials advising their friends to sell lots of high tech gadgetry. *The Wall Street Journal*, p. 30.

Mullin, B. J., Hardy, S., & Sutton, W. A. (2000) *Sport Marketing* (2nd ed.). Champaign, IL: Human Kinetics.

O'Cass, A. (2004). Fashion clothing consumption: antecedents and consequences of fashion clothing involvement. *European Journal of Marketing, 38*(7), 869–882.

Ogunnaike, L. (January 12, 2004). Eyeing mainstream success, rappers clean up their act and cultivate their philanthropy. *New York Times*, Section E, Page 1, Column 5.

Osumare, H. (2001). Beat streets in the global hood: Connective marginalities of the Hip Hop globe. *Journal of American and Comparative Cultures, 24*(1–2), 171–181.

Parker, R. S., Hermans, C. M., & Schaefer, A. D. (2004). Fashion consciousness of Chinese, Japanese, and American teenagers. *Journal of Fashion Marketing and Management, 8*(2), 176–187.

Parnes, F. (June 6, 2000). Hip-Hop Puff Daddy up for serious fashion award. *The Gazette*, p. F3.

Pereira, R. E. (2002). An adopter-centered approach to understanding adoption of innovations. *European Journal of Innovation Management, 5*(1), 40–49.

Perraudin, M. (President, World Federation of the Sporting Goods Industry) (April 2005) What do brands want from sports? *Conference SportAccord*, Berlin.

Pimentel, R. W., & Reynolds, K. E. (2004). A model for consumer devotion: Affective commitment with proactive sustaining behaviours. *Academy of Marketing Science Review, 5*, 1–45.

Pons, F., & Richelieu, A. (2004). Marketing Stratégique du sport. Le cas d'une franchise de la Ligue Nationale de Hockey. *Revue Française de Gestion, 30*(150), 161–175.

Price Waterhouse Coopers (PWC). (2004). Global outlook for the sports market. *Global Entertainment and Media Outlook: 2004–2008*. New York.

Richelieu, A. (2004). Building the brand equity of professional sports teams. In B. Pitts (Ed.), *Sharing best practices in sport marketing* (pp. 3–21). Morgantown, WV: Fitness Information Technology Inc.

Richelieu, A., & Boulaire, C. (2005). A postmodern conception of the product and its application to professional sport. *International Journal of Sports Marketing and Sponsorship*, *7*(1), 23–34.

Richelieu, A., & Pons, F. (2005). Reconciling managers' strategic vision with fans' expectations. *International Journal of Sports Marketing and Sponsorship*, *6*(3), 150–163.

Richelieu, A., Manivet, B., & Boulaire, C. (2005). *Le mouvement Hip-Hop: Axe de développement du capital de marque des équipes de sport professionnel?*. Administrative Science Association of Canada Conference, Ryerson University, Toronto, May 2005.

Riddle, D. (2005). *Niveaux d'attitude vis-à-vis de l'homosexualité*. Tucson, AZ, accessed June 2005, http://www.lambda-education.ch/con tent/menus/doc/homophobie3.html.

Rodriguez, J. (January 2004). Montreal's curious geo-psychic position. *CanWest News*, p. 1.

Rogers, E. M. (1962). *Diffusion of innovations*. New York: The Free Press.

Rogers, E. M. (1976). New product adoption and diffusion. *Journal of Consumer Research*, *2*(4), 290–301.

Rogers, E. M. (1983). *Diffusion of innovations* (3rd ed.). New York: The Free Press.

Rogers, E. M. (1995). *Diffusion of innovations* (4th ed.). New York: The Free Press.

Rose, T. (1994). Black noise: Rap music and Black culture in contemporary America. Hanover, NH: University Press of New England.

Salzman, M., Matathia, I., & O'Reilly, A. (2003). *Buzz: Harness the power of influence and create demand*. New York: John Wiley and Sons.

Sanders, L. (2005). How Reebok resuscitated its connection with youth market. *Advertising Age*, *76*(32), 5.

Shama, A. (1981). Coping with stagflation: voluntary simplicity. *Journal of Marketing*, *45*, 120–135.

Spiegler, M. (1996). Marketing street culture. *American Demographics*, *18*(11), 28–32.

Sproles, G. (1979). *Fashion: Consumer behavior toward dress*. Minneapolis, MN: Burgess Publishing.

Sternbergh, A. (2002). The secret meaning of baseball hats. *National Post Online*. Accessed September2005, http://www.nation alpost.com/scripts/printer/printer.asp?f=/s tories/20020518/238261.html.

Strang, D., & Soule, S. (1998). Diffusion in organisations and social movements: From hybrid corn to poison pills. *Annual Review of Sociology*, *24*, 265–290.

Sundhaman, A., Guerrero, D., & Zhang, H. (January 14, 2005). Mixed signals could hit Reebok's return. *Media*, p. 17A.

Takatsuki, Y. (December 17, 2003). Japan grows its own Hip-Hop. *BBC Tokyo*.

The Windsor Star. (January 6, 2004). Music inspires ex-Spit. *The Windsor Star*, p. D1.

Tomatzky, L., & Klein, K. (1982). Innovation characteristics and innovation adoption-implementation: A meta-analysis of findings. *IEEE Transactions of Engineering Management*, *EM-29*, 28–45.

Underwood, R., Bond, E., & Baer, R. (2001). Building service brands via social identity: Lessons from the sports marketplace. *Journal of Marketing Theory and Practice*, Winter, 1–13.

Valencia, D. (2002). Global noise: Rap and Hip Hop outside the USA. *Library Journal*, *127*(1), 106.

Waltner, C. (August 28, 2000). CRM: The new game in town for professional sports. *Informationweek*, pp. 112–116.

Watson, J. (2002). Transnationalism, localisation, and fast foods in East Asia. In G. Ritzer (Ed.), *McDonaldization: The reader* (pp. 222–232). Thousand Oaks, CA: Pine Forge Press.

Wong, N. Y., & Ahuvia, A. C. (1998). Personal taste and family face: Luxury consumption in confucian and western societies. *Psychology and Marketing*, *15*(5), 423–441.

Zivitz, J. (January 22, 2004). Much searching finds. *The Gazette*, p. D1.

12

SUPPORTERS, FOLLOWERS, FANS, AND FLÂNEURS: A TAXONOMY OF SPECTATOR IDENTITIES IN FOOTBALL

Richard Giulianotti

No one would deny that world football (or soccer, as it is sometimes known) has undergone a fundamental structural transformation. At the elite level, football's finances have grown exponentially, while there have been major changes in the cultural organization of the game as experienced by players, spectators, and media commentators. The United Kingdom (particularly England) has perhaps witnessed the most dramatic change in football's social and economic standing, because in the mid-1980s the English game was synonymous in the global public imagination with spectator violence and an entrenched infrastructural decline.

One area of substantial discussion over the past decade has concerned the impact of football's new political economy on its grassroots custodians, the football spectators. In the United Kingdom, there have been persistent criticisms of this boom on the basis that established (but relatively poorer) football spectators are being squeezed out of any stakeholder position within their clubs, most notably the biggest ones, in exchange for wealthier new spectators.[1] *The Guardian* newspaper described these disenfranchised spectators as "football's new refuseniks."[2] Football's burgeoning popularity, its increasingly serpentine ties with corporations and other business institutions, the reduction of stadium capacities to create high-priced seating, and the advent of pay-per-view television are four key ingredients identified in this process of commodification. A government-appointed football task force, with a mandate to identify and recommend on spectator interests, produced two rival, concluding reports and has had a negligible effect beyond promoting antiracist work within the game. Nevertheless, concern with the impact of this commodification remains strong in the public sphere, notably in the United Kingdom and also in Spain, Germany, Italy, and France.

In this brief article, I seek to examine the impact of football's commodification on spectator identities relative to their association with professional football clubs. The article is divided into two broad sections. First, I consider in some detail the major arguments advanced by UK sociologists Ian Taylor and Chas Critcher during the 1960s and 1970s to explain the growing commercialization of football at that time. Second, I set out a model of four ideal-type spectator identities that may be found in the contemporary football world. In doing so, I seek to redefine more precisely and sociologically four particular spectator identities, and these are supporters, followers, fans, and flâneurs.

The analysis mapped out here applies principally to professional football clubs, particularly those whose corporate structures are owned or controlled on market principles by individuals or institutions. These privately owned clubs are most apparent across Western Europe (with the partial but declining exception of some clubs in France, Germany, Scandinavia, Spain, and Portugal) and increasingly in Eastern Europe. Similar processes of commodification look set to affect other football societies and other sporting codes. In Latin America (as in Iberia), clubs have traditionally existed as private associations, under the ownership and political control of their many members (socios). However, there are signs, notably in Brazil, that future legislation will enable single investors or institutions to buy a controlling interest in football clubs. In North America, elite baseball, basketball, American football, and, to a lesser extent, ice hockey have all undergone extensive commodification and remarketing, resulting in different and new kinds of spectator relationships to clubs.[3] In Australia, there have been intensive attempts in recent years to construct national leagues for elite level clubs in Australian Rules Football (AFL), rugby league, and soccer (A-League). The AFL appears to have been most successful in constructing a popular, lucrative national profile for its sport and in the process generating new kinds of spectator identification, which have experienced resistance from more traditional supporters (Hess & Stewart, 1998). This apparent trend toward a homogenization of the corporate structures of professional sports suggests that the arguments presented here do not just pertain to football but, instead, have a cross-code and cross-cultural purchase.

The article develops critical sociological and normative arguments presented elsewhere on the nature of football's commodification (Giulianotti, 1999; Giulianotti & Gerrard, 2001a; Walsh & Giulianotti, 2001). Following earlier work, I take commodification to mean that process by which an object or social practice acquires an exchange value or market-centered meaning. Commodification is not a single process but an ongoing one, often involving the gradual entry of market logic to the various elements that constitute the object or social practice under consideration. As I argue below, the marked intensification of this process in recent years is of a different order to that which was experienced up until the late 1980s, and so might now be described as a period of hypercommodification.

Envisioning the Football Consumer: Taylor, Critcher, and Others

The earlier work of sociologists Ian Taylor and Chas Critcher provides a crucial starting point for any analysis of football's commodification from the 1960s onward. Writing separately, they marshaled a set of Marxist arguments to explain the apparent problems besetting English football during the 1960s and 1970s (notably spectator hooliganism, but also declining attendance). Generally, it was submitted that football support was being commodified, most obviously through a pursuit of wealthier audiences to attend games, a process underpinned by the attempts of the game's controlling forces to reinvent its social relations. Ian Taylor (1971a, 1971b) identified a corporate-driven transformation of football that had been under way since the early 1960s. The old working-class supporters—with their subcultural "soccer consciousness" that centered on the local team, masculinity, active participation, and victory—were being squeezed out, to be replaced by the "genuine," middle-class spectators and their presumed interest in family football, spectacle, skill, and performative efficiency (Taylor, 1971a, pp. 359, 364). Working-class fans during the 1930s might have seen themselves as members within a participant culture at football clubs, but after the war, club directors perceived a need to repackage their "product" to challenge other cultural sites of conspicuous consumption in the emerging "society of leisure" (Taylor, 1971b, pp. 145, 147–148).[4] Concomitant to this "bourgeoisification" of football culture were the processes of internationalization and professionalization, involving more fixtures with overseas teams and the growing socioeconomic and cultural gulfs between local supporters and celebrity players (Taylor, 1971a, pp. 356–357; 1971b, p. 149). Critcher (1979) developed Taylor's themes and drew on Raymond Williams (1961) to elucidate the changing cultural relationships of spectators to football clubs. Williams identified three kinds of historical relationships that individuals or social groups hold toward institutions: members, customers, and consumers. With Taylor, Critcher (1979, p. 170) stated that traditional fans viewed themselves as club "members," an identity rooted in the unbreakable reciprocal relationship between fan and club, and which is structured through obligations and duties, with the supporter holding some "representative" status for the club. Taylor had described this arrangement as an informal "participatory democracy" within local clubs. The customer, however, has fewer fixed loyalties; club involvement is relatively more instrumental, being rooted in "the satisfaction of public wants." If these wants are not secured, the customer will probably take his or her money and emotional investments elsewhere. Conversely, the consumer has no brand loyalty but is instead a sporting variant of economic man, an exemplar of rational choice. The consumer maximizes information about the plurality of market alternatives before calculating which product will bestow the greatest personal benefits. Critcher was less explicit as to how the customer and consumer models might be applied to football spectators. One might speculate here that the customer will follow the local club so long as it meets some associative purposes and its players can "do the job" on the pitch; otherwise, match attendance and interest in the club becomes irregular. The consumer supporter is very likely to switch clubs or follow those that offer winning teams or which are more socially suited to advancing the spectator's social and economic mobility. Nevertheless, Critcher is critical of the market-driven approach of club directors and football officials in their attempts to replace traditional spectators with consumers.

Both Taylor and Critcher used their analyses of changing club-spectator relationships, which are rooted in the commodification of football, to explain the growing phenomenon of football hooliganism (rooted in class and generational forms of cultural alienation) from the early 1960s onward.[5] I have argued elsewhere that to explain football hooliganism in this way may be rather economically reductive and pay too little attention to the internal subcultural dynamics and empirical complexity of violent spectator groups (Giulianotti, 1999, pp. 40–42). In addition, in elucidating the identity of spectators, both Taylor and Critcher were cautious to qualify their validation of the traditional spectators' claim to a "membership" status. Such a self-perception among spectators could be "wrongly" or "illusorily" inferred (Critcher, 1979, p. 145; Taylor, 1971b, p. 145). One might speculate that working-class spectators who have lived through the deeply disempowering realities of the postwar British class system would consider themselves to have a real membership status or to operate within a participatory democracy that is really owned and controlled by a handful of local businessmen.

The focus of Taylor and Critcher is, understandably, on British (in truth, English) football culture and therefore has nothing to say on developments across the European and South American games. However, their arguments do find a long echo in Alt's (1983) critical historical analysis of North American sports. Alt argued that television has "dissolved" local team identification, such that North American sports viewers "shop around the franchise marketplace for that team which embodies the necessary winning traits" (p. 100). The old ritual sublimations that served to bind sports fans to their club and community have been replaced by the mass consumption of televised, market-driven sport. Shadowing Critcher's anticipation of consumer fans, Alt noted that those teams that hit a losing streak are also quick to lose the empathy of television viewers. We may forward empirical instances of cross-cultural exchange to reflect Alt's theoretical continuities with British football sociologists. Spectators living through English football's commodification during the 1960s and 1970s were confronted by some features of cultural Americanization, such as cheerleaders and pre-match entertainment associated with the razzamatazz and gimmicks of North American sports events.

Hypercommodification and Disorganized Capitalism: Football's Postmodern Political Economy

There is little doubt that Taylor and Critcher served to rearticulate many public observations and criticisms that have surrounded postwar developments in football. Sports journalists like Arthur Hopcraft, Hugh MacIlvanney, and Brian Glanville were writing in the late 1960s of the new business figures, celebrity players, and spectator identities that were asserting their influence over a financially driven game. Nevertheless, as I argue further below, Taylor and Critcher did adumbrate some important spectator categories, with constituent features, to assist a theorization of the game's commodification. Yet, football's contemporary commodification — its hypercommodification — does have some striking differences to the condition that these sociologists and journalists had described some 30 years earlier. Since the late 1980s, this hypercommodification has been driven by extraordinary and different volumes of capital that have entered the game from entirely new sources: satellite and pay-per-view television networks, Internet and telecommunications corporations, transnational sports equipment manufacturers, public relations companies, and the major stock markets through the sale of club equity. I have argued elsewhere that if the commodification of football up until that time can be classified as modern, then this ongoing transformation of the game's political economy may be termed a postmodern one (Giulianotti, 1999). Concomitantly, a new set of social and cultural relations have arisen in this period, notably featuring the greater migration of elite labor, a gradual proliferation of continental and global competitions, astronomical rises in elite player salaries, new media outlets for football (for example, satellite television, club television stations, the Internet, and in future, mobile telephones), and new forms of cultural encoding of football through these media.

These transformations have been symptomatic of the contemporary condition of "disorganized capitalism" identified by Lash and Urry (1987, 1994), that is postindustrial, postmodern, and post-Fordist in its structural and cultural forms, and highly reflexive in its social manifestations. Disorganized capitalism emerges after the epochal shifts that Taylor and Critcher chronicled. It is characterized by the genesis of intensified flows between individuals, social groups, objects, and institutions across an increasingly globalized terrain, rather than through a more organized chain of relations within national boundaries (cf. Lash & Urry, 1994, p. 10). Part of this transformation involves the increased social and sociological relevance of communication flows, not merely in the electronic media, but also in terms of the aestheticization of consumer culture and the semiotic expression of social identity within an information age (cf. Castells, 1996). The old institutions and organizations that had regulated economic and cultural relations throughout the 20th century entered what may be a terminal decline toward the new millennium (Lash, 1994, pp. 213–214). Within football, that transformation may well be illustrated through the rising power and influence of transnational corporations (TNCs) and the political and economic decline of some national or continental associations. Among the rising TNCs, we might certainly list major media corporations and sports merchandise corporations, but increasingly top football clubs such as Manchester United, Real Madrid, and Juventus possess transnational characteristics in consumer profile, flexible labor recruitment practices, and the global diffusion of corporate symbolism. The most powerful of these "superclubs" have formed an organization called (with some statelike irony) the

"G14." Following warnings of an impending breakaway from established football structures, Union des Associations Européennes de Football (UEFA — European football's governing body) agreed in 1999 to amend Europe's top club tournament (the Champions League) to suit G14 demands for more lucrative fixtures. Reflecting the disorganized political structure within European football, continuing speculation has surrounded the future format of top club tournaments, as a range of institutional actors (old and new) jockey for positions that are most advantageous economically to their respective owners, shareholders, and officials. Finally here, as I have indicated, these transformations are all constituent of the broader, immensely complex process that is the contemporary globalization of football. I do not have the space to deal with these issues with any degree of adequacy. However, as a basic statement on the subject, I would follow the positions of Robertson (1992) and Scholte (2000, p. 239) in arguing that there is nothing inherently divisive within globality or "supraterritoriality" per se. The problem arises through the specific hegemony of neoliberal policies and ideologies in underwriting the structural textures of global disorganized capitalism and its differentially experienced, socially divisive, everyday consequences (cf. Walsh & Giulianotti, 2001).

Critcher and Taylor advanced a modern sociological analysis that addressed football's modern commodification during the 1960s and 1970s, and so they were unable to comment substantively on the consequences of more recent political economic trends within the game. In what follows, I concentrate on one critical social relationship that has undergone transformation throughout football's modern and postmodern eras of hypercommodification. I refer to the identities of spectators and their relationships to football clubs.

Contemporary Spectator Identities: The Principles Behind the Taxonomies

I argue that there are four ideal-type categories, into which we may classify spectators. The main criterion for classifying spectators relates to the particular kind of identification that spectators have toward specific clubs.

As Figure 1 demonstrates, the four spectator categories are underpinned by two basic binary oppositions: hot-cool and traditional-consumer. Thus, there are four quadrants into which spectators may be classified: traditional/ hot, traditional/cool, consumer/hot, consumer/cool. The four quadrants represent ideal-type categories, through which we may map the historical changes and cultural differences experienced by specific spectator communities in their relationships with identified clubs.

The traditional/consumer horizontal axis measures the basis of the individual's investment in a specific club: traditional spectators will have a longer, more local and popular cultural identification with the club, whereas consumer fans will have a more market-centered relationship to the club as reflected in the centrality of consuming club products. The traditional-consumer spectator opposition is clearly indebted to the initial spectator categories generated by Tay-

HOT

		TRADITIONAL		CONSUMER	
THICK SOLIDARITY	*Topophilic Spaces*	*Product-mediated distances*	THICK/THIN SOLIDARITY		
Supporter			**Fan**		
Grounded Identity	*Subcultural relations*	*Non-reciprocal Relations*	Market Identity		
Nested Identity	*Symbolic exchange relations*	*Virtual Relations*	Cosmopolitan Identity		
Follower			**Flâneur**		
THICK/THIN SOLIDARITY	*Instrumental spaces*	*Simulation spaces* / *Non-places*	THIN SOLIDARITY		

COOL

Figure 1.

lor and Critcher in the 1970s, and over the past decade at least, those terms have been central to the critical debates that have surrounded football within the broader public domain.

The hot-cool vertical axis reflects the different degrees to which the club is central to the individual's project of self-formation. Hot forms of loyalty emphasize intense kinds of identification and solidarity with the club; cool forms denote the reverse. The hot-cool opposition is indebted to at least two sources. First, theorists of the mass media, such as Marshall McLuhan (1964) and Jean Baudrillard (1990), have employed this opposition to explain the cool social relations that structure the communicative processes involving the electronic media. Second, the hot-cool distinction is also derived from an essay by Bryan Turner (1999) on the changing historical and cultural meanings of body marks.

Turner argued that in more traditional societies, body marks were relatively obligatory and employed to designate hot forms of loyalty to the collective. Conversely, in postmodern societies, identification with the collective is voluntary and transient, reflecting cooler, postemotional forms of personal identity. Thus, tattoos in Western societies have traditionally demarcated the individual's hot and permanent masculine loyalty toward a specific social entity (such as the nation, family, female partner, military unit, football club, etc.). Latterly, postmodern tattoos have emerged that are impermanent, are unisex in bearer, are heavily aesthetic (often borrowed from Eastern cultures in design), and reflect a cool or nonexistent association with a specific social group. Turner also employed the binary distinction between thick and thin forms of solidarity. These latter categories tend to be congruent with his earlier binary, so that hot loyalties reflect "thick" forms of social solidarity, whereas cool identification produces "thin" forms of social solidarity.

When reapplied to the sports context, I will argue that Turner's model does assist in explaining forms of identification and participation among sports spectators. Ironically, however, it is worth noting that one weakness in Turner's analysis centers on those occasions in which he uses sports-related communities to illustrate his generalizations. His reading of sports-related communities (especially football crowds) is a little dated and reliant on commonsense knowledge that can be empirically refuted. He makes the unfortunate, rather stereotyped error of discussing the "local solidarity" of football clubs in connection with fascism and overt hostility to economic globalization.[6] More seriously, in reaching for generalizations on contemporary corporeal culture, Turner left us to piece together a rather confused portrait of bodily relations within specific cultural forms. In the case of football, he argued that clubs are "emotive communities," conforming to Maffesoli's "neo-tribal" category in constituting sites for "Dionysian affective and orgiastic experiences" (Turner, 1999, p. 48). Yet even these working-class clubs are still seen as subject to market colonization, being "quickly incorporated into financial interests" (Turner, 1999). Meanwhile, the authenticity of the supporters' local solidarity is punctured by Turner (1999, p. 46), in being described as "partly simulated forms of traditional communalism." In sum, this leaves us with a somewhat fragmentary, confusing reading of spectator identities: given to orgiastic pleasures, comprehensible in relation to fascistic tendencies, subject to commodification, and a simulation of prior forms of community.

In turn, by way of redeveloping Turner's model, it is important to return to the cultural form and to the social relations surrounding the game itself to map out the spectator identities. Each of the four spectator categories shows a distinctive synthesis of hot, cool, traditional, and consumer qualities. Each category displays distinctive kinds of identification with a specific club and a particular motivation for such a personal association. Each category evidences a particular form of spatial relationship to the club. As ideal types, these categories do allow for degrees of empirical variation and difference among their constituents, for example in their relative manifestations of thick or thin solidarity.

Traditional/Hot Spectators: Supporters

The traditional/hot spectator is defined here as a supporter of the football club. The classic supporter has a long-term personal and emotional investment in the club. This may be supplemented (but never supplanted) by a market-centered investment, such as buying shares in the club or expensive club merchandise, but the rationale for that outlay is still underpinned by a conscious commitment to show thick personal solidarity and offer monetary support toward the club. Showing support for the club in its multifarious forms (including market ones) is considered to be obligatory, because the individual has a relationship with the club that resembles those with close family and friends. In South America, supporters talk of their respective clubs as "mothers," whereas they are its "sons" or "children." More routinely, whereas the players at the club may change, the ground is always "home." Renouncing support or switching allegiances to a rival club is impossible; traditional supporters are culturally contracted to their clubs.

Traditionally, the club is an emblem of its surrounding community, from whence it draws its core supporters. To establish themselves, clubs may have "raised the banner of town chauvinism, and prospered under it" (Hopcraft, 1968, p. 186), but the social and cultural impact of a club is always more relevant to local supporters than its unstable economic impact. Localist solidarity is strong, although some clubs with ethnic traditions might retain the deep affections of diasporic supporters. To continue the Durkheimian metaphor, the club might be seen as a totemic representation of the surrounding community. Thus, the various supporter rituals surrounding match day (not least the chanting of the club's name and the oldest supporter songs) coalesce to become a ceremony, through which the supporters worship themselves. The body becomes a key vehicle for communicating these hot and permanent forms of solidarity with club/community: Club crests are tattooed onto arms and torsos; club colors are worn perennially; during matches, the supporter corpus comprises hands, arms, and bodies that move in unison as part of the various supporter chants.

Supporters habitually have a "topophilic"[7] relationship toward the club's core spaces, primarily the home ground (Bale, 1994). Supporters attend regularly, coming to know the ground's nooks and crannies in a very familiar, personal manner. The ground enhances their thick solidarity with fellow supporters, crowds of whom generate an atmosphere on match days that is considered to be special or unique. Supporting the club is a key preoccupation of the individual's self, so that attending home fixtures is a routine that otherwise structures the supporter's free time.[8] Supporting the club is a lived experience, rooted in a grounded identity that is reflected in an affectionate relationship to the ground that is regularly revisited. Moreover, the supporter's emotional investment in the club is reciprocated in several ways. The club might be seen to repay that faith by winning some matches or even some trophies, but less instrumental elements of reciprocated affection are at least as crucial. The club's players might play in a style that is favored by the supporters and the club's traditions (whether this is flamboyant, fluent, tough, or efficient), perhaps even reflecting some distinctive local values. Outwith match day, supporters may enjoy some community benefits through use of club facilities or social engagements with officials and players.[9]

Supporters themselves husband these strong senses of hot, traditional identification in a subcultural manner. Following Taylor, we may state that the cultural history and identity surrounding the club, its community, and its supporters might be considered sufficiently specious for these to be considered as subcultural in the sociological sense, at least when contrasted with those traditions and identities holding sway in other football clubs and nations. New generations of supporters are socialized into the core subcultural values by their parent groups or by older peers. Key forums for the debating of local club questions and the reproduction of subcultural values emerged through the creation of specific supporter associations, or latterly through the production of "fanzines" that are sold on the streets outside the ground. Yet within the support, there are inevitably various status gradations. To borrow from Thornton's (1995, pp. 8–14) development of Bourdieu (1984), some supporters seek to display greater volumes of "subcultural capital" to authenticate their support to the extent of claiming greater status over their fellow supporters. In the United Kingdom, subcultural capital is really reserved for those supporters who continued to attend and to live through those periods when their clubs were unsuccessful rather than become part-time supporters; distinction is also acquired by those football spectators who did not emerge during the post-1990 boom in the sport's fashionability.[10] The embodiment of key values is also accorded status, such as dedication to the club or vocal appreciation of the aesthetics behind the team's playing style. Moreover, the supporters' commitment to the team's cause does not preclude a deep interest and understanding of the various qualities and subcultural values of other clubs and their players. Supporters are both custodians of football qua game and hot participants in active rivalries with other clubs, notably those from neighboring communities (Armstrong & Giulianotti, 2001). For traditional/hot supporters, one cannot acquire subcultural capital in a purely market manner simply by purchasing the latest club commodities.

Traditional/Cool Spectators: Followers

The traditional/cool spectators are followers of clubs, but they are also followers of players, managers, and other football people. The follower is so defined not by an itinerant journey alongside the club but, instead, by keeping abreast of developments among clubs and football people in which he or she has a favorable interest. The follower has implicit awareness of, or an explicit preconcern with, the particular senses of identity and community that relate to specific clubs, to specific nations, and to their associated supporter groups. But the follower arrives at such identification through a vicarious form of communion, most obviously via the cool medium of the electronic media.

Traditional/cool followers may evince either thin or thick forms of solidarity toward their favored football institutions. In its thin solidarity form, the follower might be drawn to a particular club because of its historical links to his or her favored club, such as in one club hiring the other's players or manager. The distant club might have ideological attractions for specific individual followers, such as the anarcho-leftist St. Pauli club in Hamburg, the ethno-national culture of Barcelona, or the fascistic subcultures at clubs such as Lazio, Verona, Real Madrid, or some clubs from the former East Germany. In its thick form of solidarity, groups of followers might establish friendship relationships with the traditional hot supporters at these clubs. In Italy, for example, there are complex, subcultural lineages of friendship and strong rivalry that exist across club supporter groups, which might, for example, encourage Sampdoria supporters to be Parma followers.[11] In the United Kingdom, there are friendships that link club supporter groups through religious-ethnic sentiments.[12] Among some hooligan groups in particular, there are signs of informal transnational friendship networks, such as those between English firms and hooligans in the Benelux countries, or Scottish groups with ties to some English club hooligans and some ultras in southern Europe. (It is worth pointing out here that rarely, if ever, do these subcultural affinities between club supporters carry a commercial raison d'être. Italian ultras, for example, manufacture their own attire and, if surplus value comes to prevail in its exchange, the group's membership can be fatally undermined.) Informal communities are ritually cemented through the symbolic exchanges of football paraphernalia and the generous hosting of visiting friends. In its fullest sense, very thick senses of social solidarity might be reproduced through the club in a nationalist sense, enabling the "imagined community" to be socially realized—such as when Turkish clubs visit Germany and find that the local "guest workers" are in massive attendance, magically recreating their national identity whereas their actual identification with the specific club is typically a cool, instrumental one.

In both thick and thin versions of solidarity, we have a set of noneconomic, symbolic exchange relationships involving the follower and the favored club. The latter is accorded the interest or backing of the follower, but the favored club does offer something in return that accords with the follower's habitus or established football interests, such as in terms of employing a favored player or in the club's cultural politics. The follower may seek to authenticate in normative terms this association with the club by appealing beyond principles of mere football success to more abstract social and cultural values. Typically, these values harmonize with those associated with the follower's other, more established focus for support. Followers may define themselves against consumer values to authenticate their traditionalist motives, such as through a stylized denial of the role of team success or "fashionability" in inspiring their club allegiance (as one finds among Scandinavian followers of such unlikely football teams as Cowdenbeath or Stenhousemuir in Scotland).

To borrow from Cohen (1978), the notion of a set of "nested identities" might help to explain how the self seeks to integrate these different objects of allegiance.[13] There may be no simply ranked pyramid set of affiliations that the follower has for organizing his or her allegiances. Instead, these affiliations may be composed in a rather complex manner, with no obvious way of determining which identification is favored when different favored entities rub up against one another (such as when a favored manager comes up against a favored team). Nested identities instead function to provide the follower with a range of favored clubs and football people in different circumstances, ensuring that the follower's football interest is sustained when his or her supported true team is no longer competing. The proliferation of televised football now means that, to sustain the traditional spectating habit of favoring a particular team, the viewer must become a follower of some clubs. But, the follower is suitably inured with the cultural politics of football to know that certain elements cannot combine to construct a viable nest: Only flâneurs (see below), for example, would declare a penchant for both Liverpool and Manchester United, or Fiorentina and Juventus.

Moreover, the follower lacks the spatial embedding of the supporter within the club and its surrounding communities. For followers, football places may be mere practical resources with few symbolic meanings: a stage upon which favored players and officials might pitch up to perform before moving on. In circumstances of thicker solidarity, the public geography surrounding the favored club may be respected by followers, but from a distance, typically with no deep personal knowledge or engagement within this particular lifeworld.

Hot/Consumer Spectators: Fans

The hot/consumer spectator is a modern fan of a football club or its specific players, particularly its celebrities. The fan develops a form of intimacy or love for the club or its specific players, but this kind of relationship is inordinately unidirectional in its affections. The fan is hot in terms of identification; the sense of intimacy is strong and is a key element of the individual's self. But, it is a relationship that is rather more distant than that enjoyed by supporters. Football's modern move into the market and its more recent hypercommodification have served to dislocate players and club officials from supporters, particularly in the higher professional divisions. The individual fan experiences the club, its traditions, its star players, and fellow supporters through a market-centered set of relationships. The fans' strength of identification with the club and its players is thus authenticated most readily through the consumption of related products. Such consumption might take the direct form of purchasing merchandise, buying shares, or contributing to fundraising initiatives. More significantly in future, more indirect forms of consumption come into play, particularly purchasing football magazines and pay-per-view or other subscription rights to the club's televised fixtures. The consumer relationship to the club is thus at its strongest among the wealthiest of football clubs.

The hot/consumer spectator can incline toward relatively thicker or thinner versions of social solidarity. In its thicker manifestation, bordering on the supporter identity, the fans' consumption practices are orientated toward enhancing the collective consciousness, intensifying the rituals of support. If large groups of fans attend matches in club shirts or other trademarked colors, then this striking display of visual solidarity may energize the players during matches. Thinner forms of solidarity are evinced from a greater distance. In its more extreme manifestation, buying into club regalia or shares becomes one of the few means by which fans scattered across the world may continue to signify their deep allegiance to a local team.

The fan recognizes that in contemporary professional sport, the amoral free market dominates, consequently the club's survival and successes are dependent upon greater financial contributions from all kinds of backers relative to the wealth of other clubs. Purchasing shares in clubs may be investments in football's boom time, but fans are reluctant to sell in the interests of personal profit. The brand loyalty and inelastic demand of fans for club shares and merchandise are consciously intended to provide the club with financial stability, typically to enable the purchase of better players (Conn, 1997, p. 155). But in promoting the transformation of its spectators into rather consumer-centered fan identities, the club tends to generate a set of utilitarian conditions for its consumers to continue attending. If the club fails to deliver on its market promises (such as "brand improvement" of the team), then the fans may drift into other markets (other leisure activities, other football leagues, though probably not supporting rival teams) in the deculturalized pursuit of "value for money." If solidarity is rather thicker, then fans may collectivize and agitate to unseat the incumbent controllers, such as by sacking the board or forming independent shareholder associations. Most typically, the club's fans are politically passive, strong in their affections for club and players, probably geographically removed from the club's home, and especially separated from the entertainment "star system" in which the players circulate.

Consequently, football fans resemble the fans of leading musicians, actors, and media personalities, through their largely unidirectional relationship toward these household names. Thompson (1997) described this social framework in terms of "non-reciprocal relations of intimacy with distant others" (pp. 220–222). Fans refer to stars by first name, discuss their private lives and traits, collect biographical snippets, surround the family home or workplace with their images, and perhaps even fantasize about a loving, sexual relationship with their objects of affection. Star footballers, like other celebrities, are rarely in a position to reciprocate. Football matches before live audiences only afford a temporary break in the distance between stars and fans, but in any case, the divisions are symbolically retained. Football players at matches, or even when signing autographs or visiting sick children in hospital, continue to play the star role. Their "work with the public" is a form of emotional labor, necessitating a form of professional "deep acting," which Hochschild (1983) has previously documented. Thompson viewed fan identity as a strategy of the self, a deliberate entry into a relationship that is fundamentally different from those founded on face-to-face interaction. Consequently, we may add that such a relationship is dependent on specific media that allow for a continuous and multifarious flow of star-related signs toward the fan. In the West particularly, this must mean capital-governed signifiers, through product endorsement, television interviews, and even forays into other realms of popular culture, such as pop music. Again, for such public relations, football players and club officials are trained to draw upon an ever-expanding reservoir of clichés and dead metaphors to confirm typified public constructions of their personality. These more shallow, mediated forms of acting help to preserve the highly profitable, parallel football universe that has been constructed to supply the fan market.

The commodity-centered mediation of football qua entertainment intensifies, so the fan identity comes under pressure to enter the realm of the flâneur, the unreconstructed cool consumer. This process is most apparent as market representations of football are increasingly telescoped onto playing stars and their celebrity lifestyles (rather than what they do on the field of play). The process first appeared in the United Kingdom with the public identity of George Best, but it has reached a new category of representation with Beckham, whereas in global terms, Ronaldo is the tragic exemplar.[14] As commodity logic comes to prevail, we encounter a redoubled fetishizing of the star's exchange value, beyond merely transfer worth and club wages, but into the highly unstable environment of general marketability, fashion, and exposure in popular media. Thus, football stars are quickly nudged out of the limelight by new performers and are liable to experience a decline in their "rating" among distant fans to a degree that far outstrips their continuing regard among supporters or those within the game. The hot identification that fans once attached to stars embarks upon a categorical decline, as fans generally learn to cool their affections, in expectation that the next player qua commodity sign will arrive sooner than ever.

Cool/Consumer Spectators: Flâneurs

The cool consumer spectator is a football flâneur. The flâneur acquires a postmodern spectator identity through a depersonalized set of market-dominated virtual relationships, particularly interactions with the cool media of television and the Internet.

The flâneur constitutes a distinctive urban social type first chronicled and characterized by Baudelaire in the mid-19th century, remolded sociologically by Simmel, expounded upon more critically by Walter Benjamin (1973, 1999) during the 1930s, and latterly the flâneur has been the subject of substantial debate among cultural theorists.[15] In its original sense, the flâneur was a modern urban stroller: male and bourgeois, typically in full adulthood, he would promenade through boulevards and markets. For the true flâneur, "kaleidoscopic images and fragments whose novelty, immediacy and vividness, coupled with their fleeting nature and often strange juxtaposition, provided a range of aesthetic sensations and experiences" (Featherstone, 1995, p. 150). Benjamin's (1999) flâneur is understood in part as an idler and traveler, a student of physiognomy and character among the passing throng, essentially semidetached in his engagement with the crowds and commodities of the labyrinthine metropolis.

In its contemporary manifestation, I would suggest the flâneur is less gender specific. Class differences must remain, because the flâneur has the economic, cultural, and educational capital to inspire a cosmopolitan interest in the collection of experiences. In addition, compared to Baudelaire's initial version, the contemporary flâneur is increasingly detached from the experiences that are collected, for at least three reasons: first, following Foucault, the rise of a self-regulating, panoptical self that gazes on objects and bodies (including one's own); second, the rise of virtual forms of communication that increasingly replace face-to-face, intersubjective exchanges and experiences; third, the growing commodification of social relationships and objects, such that there are fewer forms of public interaction or elements of material culture that appear without a market-centered motive. Accordingly, the flâneur's social practices are increasingly oriented toward consumption.

The football flâneur may tend to be more male than female, but not by definition. The flâneur is more likely to be bourgeois and thus in pursuit of a multiplicity of football experiences. The flâneur adopts a detached relationship to football clubs, even favored ones. A true football flâneur, the cool consumer belongs only to a virtual community of strollers who window-shop around clubs. In the most extreme manifestation, national allegiances may also be exchanged on the grounds of competitive successes or mediated identification with superstar celebrities. The adornment of a team's attire is in tune with a couture aesthetic, drawn to the signifier (the shirt color, the shirt design, its crest, even its sponsor logo) rather than to what is signified conceptually (the specific, grounded identity of the club or the nation). The flâneur thereby avoids any personal consumption by the appended signs but instead consumes these signifiers in a disposable and cliché-like fashion, as if adopting a temporary tattoo. Moreover, the football flâneur's natural habitat is increasingly the virtual arena, seeking the sensations of football as represented through television, Internet, or perhaps in the future, the audiovisual bodysuit. Thus, television presentation of football is tailored toward a flâneur-type experience. Television compresses time-space differences, distilling entire matches or tournaments into 100-second transmissions of blinding, aestheticized action, to an accompanying backbeat that drifts between techno and opera.

The cool/consumer seeks relatively thin forms of social solidarity with other fellow fans. Within the context of a postemotional panoply of social relations, the flâneur is definitively low in genuine collective affect. Nevertheless, there are occasions when flâneurs congregate and thus come to simulate in a playful manner the football passion that they have witnessed in prior media representations of those who appear to be true supporters.[16] The cool consumer is a cosmopolitan, but not in the classical sense whereby constant perambulations produce a worldly merchant in ideas. Rather, this cosmopolitan has relatively little biographical or strategic interest in discerning an underlying meta-narrative from the medley of football signifiers around which the flâneur dances, save for the instrumental identification with an avant-garde, winning brand. Flâneurs evidence the "transferable loyalties of the postmodern passenger" (Turner, 1999, p. 48); accordingly, they are liable not only to switch a connection with teams or players, but also to forsake football for other forms of entertainment. And the true cosmopolis, the cultural setting, for the community of strollers is the non-place, such as the airport departure lounge or the most contemporary shopping mall (Augé, 1995). Such locations are devoid of topophilic meaning, are emptied of any sense of home, but house instead the cool and ungrounded circulation of football's commodity ephemera.

Some of the largest world clubs have provided the flâneur with an increasingly welcoming shop window in which to gaze, thereby creating a quasi-community of cosmopolitans. And thus, relatively more committed, regular forms of engagement with these clubs (so long as they continue to win or to be chic) encourages the germination of a proxy form of narcissistic self-identity for the cool consumers. Invariably, association with winning is particularly favored, but so too are cosmopolitan signifiers of conspicuous wealth, European sophistication (French, Italian), or an avant-garde setting (high-tech stadium). Clubs thus become appendages, selected for what they may say about the flâneur's personality.

Flâneurs may seek to authenticate their cosmopolitan identity through direct and unfavorable representation of spectators that possess traditional or hot characteristics. Traditionalists are constructed as regressive figures from the past — chauvinists, romanticists, xenophobes — in sum, truculent locals who refuse to reconcile themselves to the ineluctable hegemony of neoliberal principles within football. Flâneurs might try to depict hot spectators as emotionally driven and thus intellectually incapable of appreciating the fineries of the game. Yet as we have noted, the real identity of the flâneur is rooted in persistent motion, classically in material terms but increasingly in virtual terms, through switching affiliations like television channels. Thus, the flâneur who endeavors to authenticate a stable football identity relative to other spectators is something of a contradiction in terms.

Motives, Landscapes, and the Paradoxes of Cross-Category Relationships

The four spectator categories examined above have been distinguished according to their different football identities and the distinctive, underlying relationships that they have toward the game. I shall avoid treating the reader as a flâneur and providing a highlighted recapitulation of arguments, but it is useful to elucidate briefly these categorical differences by reference to two analytical heuristics — the specific motivations and the spatial relationships of these spectator identities.

In terms of motive, supporters give their support to clubs because they are obligated to do so. The club provides the supporter not simply with an element of personal identity but a complex and living representation of the supporter's public identity. Followers forward various allegiances to clubs because it helps to sustain and spread their personal senses of participation in football. This diffusion of allegiances is structurally facilitated by an increasingly complex, mediated networking of football information and images. Fans are motivated to produce nonreciprocal relationships with distant others, which are qualitatively different to face-to-face relationships and which promote a consumption-oriented identity to bridge symbolically the socio-spatial divide. Finally, flâneurs are motivated to seek sensation, excitement, and thus to switch their gaze across clubs, players, and nations. The greater commodification of football, and emphasis on association with success, structures the flâneur's peripatetic pursuit of winning or chic teams.

In terms of their relationship to the material environment, supporters have inextricable biographical and emotional ties to the club's ground, which is a key cultural emblem of the surrounding community. Similarly, followers are cognizant of the symbolic significance of the ground to the club, but their dependency on mediated representations of favored clubs reflects their circumscribed ties to this other community. Fans experience a distant socio-spatial relationship to favored clubs and their stars. Consumption of star-focused products might affirm and demonstrate fan loyalties, but the communicative divisions remain even in face-to-face interludes as stars consciously reaffirm their celebrity identity. Finally, the flâneur's preferred habitat is replete with audiovisual stimulation, such that high-tech electronic media are particularly favored. As a mobile cosmopolitan, the flâneur lives in a cosmopolis of consumption and thus has no capacity to secure personal alignment with a club qua locally defined institution. Instead, club signifiers are adorned in a cool, market-oriented style, such that the most congruous landscapes for these displays must be the character-free non-places of what Augé would prefer to term "supermodernity."

Evidently, this model of spectator identities displays significant continuities with the categories advanced by Taylor and Critcher, but major differences are also apparent. The supporter and consumer categories have been reworked. I have tried to provide a less politically empowered vision of the supporter but accept their principal claims regarding the historical, cultural, and existential bonds of supporter to club. In addition, although inevitably accepting their market-centered definition of the consumer spectator, I seek to advance a dichotomous model that recognizes differing degrees of club affection between the hot and cold consumer.

The model forwarded here suggests a different structural relationship between the various spectator categories. Fans and followers share some primary, paradoxical qualities in their basic constitution. As hot/consumers and traditional/cool spectators, their dichotomous identities border on oxymoron. Followers have a traditional position in regard to the game's culture, but that is tempered by a cool relationship toward the clubs followed. Fans possess a hot sense of loyalty to players and to clubs, but that is tempered by a market-centered approach toward surmounting symbolic distances. Consequently, this synthesis of apparently conflicting qualities ensures that followers and fans can display relatively thick and thin forms of social solidarity. Historically, we may also view these spectator categories as intermediary retreats, as part of a strategy of negotiation and accommodation, whereby gradually the traditional/hot properties of the supporter are dissolved into the cool/consumer practices of the flâneur, although this does point toward a deeper social paradox.

As presented here, supporters and flâneurs are literally in diametrical opposition to one another, but they do appear to be dependent on each other for different reasons. In an increasingly neoliberal financial environment, local supporters practicing realpolitik come to recognize that the club must attract the custom of cosmopolitan flâneurs to preserve its status and perhaps push on for more successes. But can the same be said of the wealthy cosmopolitan who flits over the locals? After all, the contemporary structures of football are geared toward global consumption. Football is dominated by transnational corporations, particularly the merchandise companies (Nike, Reebok, Adidas), the world's governing bodies (notably the Fédération Internationale de Football Association and UEFA), and the largest football clubs. Unquestionably, the football flâneur is the cultural consumer that these transnational corporations are committed to seduce; their overtures are motivated by the rather hazardous aim of securing the flâneur's attention and thus securing his or her conversion into a warmer (more regular) consumer. Such a fundamental transformation in football, as in other sports or other realms of popular culture, threatens a Pyrrhic victory for the neoliberal agenda. As the political philosopher Michael Walzer has argued in a broader context, "There is a sense in which the cosmopolitan is parasitic on people who are not cosmopolitans...you could not exist if there were not people who sat still and created the places that you visit and enjoy" (as cited in Carleheden & Gabriëls, 1997, p. 120).

Otherwise stated here, if supporters become flâneurs, then the spectacle that is created by the spectators themselves will be threatened. There will be no more curious displays of football tribalism past which to stroll or on which to gaze.[17]

Acknowledgments

My thanks to the two anonymous referees for their constructive and helpful suggestions regarding improvements on an earlier version of this article. I am indebted to Adrian Walsh for encouraging me to consider a Walzerian approach to sport sociology and to Mike Gerrard for putting up with my initial ideas on spectator categories in an earlier coauthored paper.

Notes

1. See, for example, Conn (1997), Horton (1997), Fynn and Guest (1994), Giulianotti (1999), Lee (1998), Perryman (1997), Dempsey and Reilly (1998), and the more accommodative work by Szymanski and Kuypers (1999). At least two separate editions of the British Broadcasting Corporation's Panorama series have also assessed, with strong criticism, the affect of football's financial boom on its established grassroots spectators and players.

2. In highlighting the abandonment of match attendance by an architect and his wife, the relevant article pointed out that the poorest spectators were not alone in feeling financially and culturally marginalized from football (*The Guardian*, August, 22, 1999, http://www.guardian.co.uk/Archive/Article/0,4273,3894685,00.html).

3. There is a reasonable range of literature in this area. On North American sports generally, see Alt (1983); on Canadian sports and North American ice hockey, see respectively Gruneau (1983) and Gruneau and Whitson (1994); on basketball, see Andrews (1995).

4. Taylor (1971b) was presented originally in 1968. He pointed out that, in writing the paper, his greatest debt is to his parents for an "incom-

parable education" in the "subcultural values" of their local football team (Taylor, 1971b, p. 372n).

5. Similarly, Hargreaves (1986,p.136) argued that selling sport to consumers as entertainment, coupled with the breakdown of social ties between football players and the audience, can lead to greater expectations and tensions within the audience, which may result in violence.

6. I have argued elsewhere against the rather lazy connection drawn by some commentators between working-class forms of football fandom and fascist political tendencies (Giulianotti, 1999). See also the work of Robson (2000).

7. Topophilia involves an intense emotional attachment to a particular part of the material environment; otherwise stated, it is a love of place.

8. As one football journalist explained, "It is difficult for those who care about their game and, more particularly, care about their team, to comprehend life without this obsession" (Allsop, 1997, p. 95).

9. In South America, most clubs remain private member associations, so that their swimming pool, gym, and other recreation facilities are all available to members in return for a modest annual fee.

10. By far the most successful text on UK football during the 1990s was Nick Hornby's *Fever Pitch*, which became a major bestseller, acquiring numerous awards before being turned into a stage play and film. Hornby's book is a kind of autobiography, in which the author claims that his football obsession has determined his life course. However, the "subcultural capital" of Hornby as genuine football man has been revalued; for example, some critics point disparagingly to his abandoning of Arsenal as a supporter during his time at university. More generally, some traditionalist supporters also refer critically to spectators who came into football during its 1990s boom as "post-Hornby fans."

11. For example, in Italy during the early 1990s, Sampdoria's ultras were "friendly" with Verona, Inter, Atalanta, Cremonese, and Parma fan groups; they were strongly opposed to fans from the lineage linking Genoa, Torino, Bologna, and Pisa (cf. Roversi, 1992, p. 58).

12. For example, there are the pro-Irish nationalist sentiments of some fans of Celtic and Manchester United, or the "Blues Brothers" network of Unionist fan groups (Chelsea, Glasgow Rangers, and Linfield of Northern Ireland).

13. I am indebted to Bea Vidacs for the first application of this concept to football identity and to her provision of the reference to Cohen.

14. For a discussion of how specific football players appear to fit into traditional (Stanley Matthews), modern (George Best), and postmodern (Paul Gascoigne) identity categories, see Giulianotti and Gerrard (2001b).

15. See, for example, Tester (1994), Featherstone (1995), and Weinstein and Weinstein (1993).

16. This is increasingly apparent at major tournaments such as the World Cup, when the carnival atmosphere before and during matches is often a strikingly sanitized, simulated version of supporter passion. The most extreme illustrations occur when a dead atmosphere among thousands of fans suddenly changes into highly animated collective behavior when the television cameras come into view.

17. Nor should one assume that an attempt to protect the interests of traditional supporters is an act of xenophobia toward those who want to join the football spectator community. There is no credible a priori argument that states that other spectator categories, including flâneurs, are incapable of harboring deeply intolerant attitudes towards some other communities. In addition, as Walzer (in Carleheden & Gabriëls, 1997, p. 129) himself argued, one may quite easily identify those genuinely intolerant communities and seek to remove such traditions, but all the while encourage the community members to adapt to the new conditions, to redefine their values.

References

Allsop, D.(1997). *Kicking in the wind: The real life drama of a small-town football club*. London: Headline.

Alt, J. (1983).Sport and cultural reification: From ritual to mass consumption. *Theory, Culture and Society, 1*(3), 93–107.

Andrews, D. L. (1995, September 7–9). *The [trans]national basketball association: American commodity-sign culture and global-local conjuncturalism*. Paper presented at the First Annual Conference for Popular Culture, Manchester, UK.

Armstrong, G., & Giulianotti, R. (Eds.). (2001). *Fear and loathing in world football*. Oxford, UK: Berg.

Augé, M. (1995). *Non-places: An introduction to the anthropology of supermodernity*. London: Verso.

Bale,J.(1994).*Landscapes of modern sport*. Leicester, UK: Leicester University Press.

Baudrillard, J. (1990). *Seduction*. London: Macmillan.

Benjamin, W. (1973). *Charles Baudelaire: A lyric poet in the era of high capitalism*. London: NLB.

Benjamin, W. (1999). *The Arcades Project*. Cambridge, MA: Belknap.

Bourdieu, M. (1984). *Distinction*. London: Routledge and Kegan Paul.

Carleheden, M., & Gabriels, R. (1997). An interview with Michael Walzer. *Theory, Culture and Society, 14*(1), 113–130.

Castells, M. (1996). *The network society*. Oxford, UK: Blackwell.

Cohen, R. (1978). Ethnicity: Problem and focus in anthropology. *Annual Review of Anthropology, 7*, 379–403.

Conn, D. (1997). *The football business*. Edinburgh, Scotland: Mainstream.

Critcher, C. (1979). Football since the war. In J. Clarke, C. Critcher, & R. Johnson (Eds.), *Working class culture: Studies in history and theory* (pp. 161–184). London: Hutchinson.

Dempsey, P., & Reilly, K. (1998). *Big money, beautiful game: Saving soccer from itself*. Edinburgh, Scotland: Mainstream.

Featherstone, M. (1995). *Undoing culture*. London: Sage.

Fynn, A., & Guest, L. (1994). *Out of time: Why football isn't working*. London: Simon & Schuster.

Giulianotti, R. (1999). *Football: A sociology of the global game*. Cambridge, UK: Polity.

Giulianotti, R., & Gerrard, M. (2001a). Cruel Britannia? Glasgow Rangers, Scotland and "hot" football rivalries. In G. Armstrong & R. Giulianotti (Eds.), *Fear and loathing in world football* (pp. 23–42). Oxford, UK: Berg.

Giulianotti, R., & Gerrard, M. (2001b). Evil genie or pure genius? The (im)moral football and public career of Paul "Gazza" Gascoigne. In D. L. Andrews & S. Jackson (Eds.), *Sport stars: The politics of sport celebrity* (pp. 124–137). London: Routledge.

Gruneau, R. (1983). *Class, sport and social development*. Champaign, IL: Human Kinetics.

Gruneau, R., & Whitson, D. (1994). *Hockey night in Canada*. Toronto, Canada: Garamond.

Hargreaves, J. (1986). *Sport, power and culture*. Cambridge, UK: Polity.

Hess, R., & Stewart, B. (Eds). (1998). *More than a game: An unauthorised history of Australian Rules football*. Melbourne, Australia: Melbourne University Press.

Hochschild, A. R. (1983). *The managed heart: Commercialization of human feeling*. Berkeley: University of California Press.

Hopcraft, A. (1968). *The football man*. London: Simon & Schuster.

Horton, E. (1997). *Moving the goalposts*. Edinburgh, Scotland: Mainstream.

Lash, S. (1994). Expert-systems or situated interpretation? In U. Beck, A. Giddens, & S. Lash, *Reflexive modernization* (pp. 198–215). Cambridge, UK: Polity.

Lash, S., & Urry, J. (1987). *The end of organized capitalism*. Cambridge, UK: Polity.

Lash, S., & Urry, J. (1994). *Economies of signs and space*. London: Sage.

Lee, S. (1998). Grey Shirts to grey suits: The political economy of English football in the 1990s. In A. Brown (Ed.), *Fanatics!* (32–49). London: Routledge.

McLuhan, M. (1964). *Understanding media*. London: Routledge.

Perryman, M. (1997). *Football United: New Labour, the task force and the future of the game*. London: Fabian Society.

Robertson, R. (1992). *Globalization: Social theory and global culture*. London: Sage.

Robson, G. (2000). *No one likes us we don't care: The myth and reality of Millwall fandom*. Oxford, UK: Berg.

Roversi, A. (1992). *Calcio, tifo e violenza* [Football, the fan, and violence]. Bologna, Italy: Il Mulino.

Scholte, J. A. (2000). *Globalization: A critical introduction*. Basingstoke, UK: Macmillan.

Szymanski, S., & Kuypers, T. (1999). *Winners and losers: The business strategy of football*. London: Viking Press.

Taylor, I. (1971a). "Football mad": A speculative sociology of football hooliganism. In E. Dunning (Ed.), *The sociology of sport: A selection of readings* (pp. 352–377). London: Frank Cass.

Taylor, I. (1971b). Soccer consciousness and soccer hooliganism. In S. Cohen (Ed.), *Images of deviance* (pp. 134–163). Harmondsworth, UK: Pelican.

Tester, K. (1994). *The flâneur*. London: Routledge.

Thompson, J. B. (1997). *The media and moder-*

nity: A social theory of the media. Cambridge, UK: Polity.

Thornton, S. (1995). *Club cultures: Music, media and subcultural capital*. Cambridge, UK: Polity.

Turner, B. S. (1999). The possibility of primitiveness: Towards a sociology of body marks in cool societies. *Body & Society*, 5(2–3), 39–50.

Walsh, A., & Giulianotti, R. (2001). This sporting mammon: A normative analysis of the commodification of sport. *Journal of the Philosophy of Sport*, 28, 53–77.

Weinstein, D., & Weinstein, M. A. (1993). *Postmodern(ized) Simmel*. London: Routledge.

Williams, R. (1961). *The long revolution*. Harmondsworth, UK: Pelican.

13

A MODEL TO EXPLAIN SUPPORT IN SPANISH FOOTBALL

Angel Barajas and Liz Crolley

Introduction

The level of support for a football club is a key variable within the revenues of the club and, of course, determines most other revenues, either directly (via ticket sales, for example) or indirectly (such as merchandising, sponsorship, or even the sale of television rights in some countries). Taking Spanish professional football as reference, we are going to analyze the relationships between different kinds of variables and attendances. We acknowledge that there are many forms of support recognized by football clubs (for example, "consuming" football in other ways, such as via television or the Internet), but our focus here is on live attendances at football matches. We have chosen to examine average attendances over the course of a whole season (ATT). This allows us to seek factors which may be useful in order to estimate cash-flows for a club's valuation. The fact that the sample consists exclusively of Spanish professional clubs partly dictates, of course, the nature of the results obtained.

The conceptual model tested is shown in Figure 1. The methodology used is mainly the OLS (Ordinary Least Squares) regression. We have tested the relationship between different sets of variables and attendance, looking for those which best explain patterns of support. The three sets of variables analyzed have been called "socio-economic," "quality of product" (related to results) and "quality of the means of production" (quality of the team/squad). When several variables exist, we have also employed multivariate regression. The sample consists of all football teams in the Spanish First Division, and 13 from the Second Division during the season 1999/2000. The socio-economic variables analyzed vary only slightly from year to year so we might expect the results to be relevant over time.

The structure of the paper is derived from the conceptual model outlined in Figure 1. In the first section, the basic characteristics of football fans are described and the main features of their behavior explained. Then, we focus on those aspects that affect or are influenced by attendance.

The following three sections focus on the three main sets of variables: the influence that the socio-economic environment has on support, the extent to

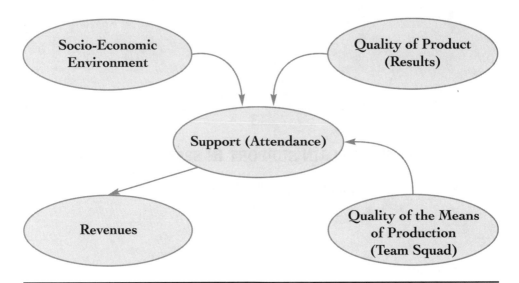

Figure 1. Support and influential factors

which the quality of the means of production (team squad) affects attendance, and how the quality of the product (results on the pitch — both current and historical) might explain attendances. Finally, the repercussions that the level of attendance has on a club's revenues will be analyzed.

The Concept of Support in Football

In Spanish the word for support is *afición*. This term comes from Latin *affection*, which means love, or affection. So, the Spanish word *afición* would represent loving feelings or affection toward someone or something. This Spanish expression perhaps differs from the English term "support": its connotations are more overtly affectionate though less actively supportive. Nevertheless, the Football Supporters Association[1] defines "support" as "a lifelong and unchangeable commitment" (FTF, 1999; 4.3). So, we are dealing with a concept that implies a loyal affection.

We have to differentiate between two levels within this love of football. Usually one will follow as a result of the other, but it is possible that one might exist without the other. First, we can talk about support for football in general, as a sport and a spectacle. Then, the supporter identifies with one particular team. However, it is possible to find people who support a club, without being attracted to football in general. There are also people keen on this sport who do not support a specific club. From the point of view of the economic value of a club, the most influential fans will be those who support a particular team, because they will provide the main revenue streams.

Football supporters are not consumers in a traditional sense because football support is an expression of passion and loyalty to the club. The relationship between a fan and his or her club belongs to a different order and magnitude than that of other brand loyalties. The decision to support a particular team is quite different from choosing to shop at one store or other. Sir John Smith, in an FA report,[2] affirmed that the football fan probably supported a club "almost from the cradle to the grave." (FTF, 1999)

Football support goes beyond loyalty. Football fans of a specific club, even without being shareholders or members, feel that the club belongs to them, that it is something of their property.

A fan's loyalty has an "irrational" component. The relationship between supporters and their club is exceptional because fans do not need success on the pitch. Victory is desirable but not a condition for their support. Fans do not normally change allegiance if their team loses or performs badly—or even if their support is exploited and abused. Nevertheless, short and long term components of this "irrationality" must be distinguished. Mellor (2001) explains how the success of great teams attracts fans. Historical sporting success helps to brings fans. At the same time, teams recruit new fans during their glory days. These supporters will probably continue to support the team through thick and thin. These factors are taken into consideration in our model.

However, not all fans have the same degree of elasticity in their support during bleak times on the pitch. Supporters like Atlético de Madrid have demonstrated a loyalty to their colors that could be qualified as admirable. In the 2000/2001 season when the team was playing in the Spanish Second Division, the average attendance at their matches was clearly higher than most First Division Clubs. Derbaix et al. (2002; 512) define the "good" fan as "the one who is faithful and supports his team even in bad times." However, there are other supporters, called "fickle" by Porter (1992; 64), who need good results in order for them to keep cheering their team on. From a marketing perspective, it is necessary to segment the fanbase in order to identify the types of supporters who will be the target of marketing objectives. Indeed, academics have segmented the football fanbase into categories in different ways, often according to patterns of supporting behavior (such as degree of loyalty, identification, method of "consuming" football). Tapp and Clowes (2000) segmented the fans into: fanatics, regulars, and casuals. In a later article, Tapp (2004) differentiates between four types of fans: fanatics, repertoire fans, season ticket holders, and casual fans. Giulianotti (2002) divides spectators into supporters, followers, fans, and flaneurs. These types of segmentation are now becoming widespread and more sophisticated as CRM (Customer Relationship Management) strategies are increasingly applied to football. While it is important to take these typologies into consideration, for the purpose of our study we do not need to work with these classifications. Rather we need to take into consideration the diversity of football fans: support is more inelastic for some than for others. The dichotomy is more complex than a simple division, as has often been made in the UK, between "old" fans (traditional, identity-driven) and "new" fans (consumer spectators). Importantly, for some fans their attendance at the ground might depend on variable factors. It is useful for clubs to understand what these factors are given, as was mentioned earlier, that the valuation of a club at least partially depends on the size of its fanbase.

It is also worth taking into consideration a clubs potential market size if we are going to regard the fan as a potential customer or a shareholder. While market size is significant in order to determine a club's revenues,[3] a team with a small market size can be competitive if its supporters have a sufficiently high elasticity with respect to the club's results (Vrooman, 1995; 975). This approach might be extended to the ability to obtain funds other than the usual revenue streams, via shareholders. Ruyter and Wetzels (2000) analyze precisely this phenomenon and they conclude that "the social rule of reciprocity," as well as the level of affect and the "perceived efficiency degree," stimulates fans to feel a duty to support their club financially by buying its shares. The FA Report on English Football (mentioned earlier) concludes that supporters are the main asset of a successful club because their support will become tickets, merchandising, television revenues, and so on. However, this is also the case for less successful clubs for the reason that, in times of financial difficulties, they organize and lead the club's fight for survival (FTF, 1999).

Support has an important local component, especially in Spain where medium and small cities typically have one football club which acts as its symbol and represents its flag. So, it is natural that a link exists between the football club and the local/regional population. It is difficult to imagine a European club moving to another city as the North American franchises do.[4]

On the other hand, it seems compulsory to point out that in a global market, when we talk about market size, we should not be to be limited to the population in close proximity to the football club.[5] Many clubs also look to extend their markets through success in international competitions, and other means such as pre-season tournaments abroad. However, for most Spanish clubs, attendances are largely drawn from within the region in which the club is located.

Normally, the support that fans give to their club represents an inelastic demand with respect to price because fans will continue attending the football or buying club products independently of the price. However, since attendances are not static, there must be variable factors which influence attendance. Some of these factors are now considered.

Socio-economic Environment and Attendance

Szymanski and Kuypers (1999; 41) outline the historical evolution of attendances at stadia in England. They describe the rise in attendances after the Second World War which coincides with a fall in ticket prices and a popularization of leisure activities. However, between 1953 and 1977, while the population grew wealthier, the average attendance dropped. This phenomenon contrasts with Veblen's well-known ideas (1966) about the "leisure classes" described for the first time in 1899. According to him, sports, and games in general, were something more or less set aside for the most powerful classes. We cannot forget that we are talking about more than a century ago and that since then sport has become popularized. However, for many sport is still a commodity which is accessed when basic needs are covered. McElgunn (2002) highlights this point. He states that when fans' income rises while the price of basic products decreases relatively, then they have more money to spend on attending matches or buying sports products and they like to spend more free time attending or watching the available supply of sport live or on television. Hoehn and Szymanski (1999; 208) go further when they claim that football has become essentially the working class distraction offered at affordable prices for middle-class entertainment.

Cocco and Jones (1997) maintain that the support for a particular club, measured by attendance at specific home matches, depends on the underlying demand within that city — specifically factors relating to its location such as income, population, etc. — as well as on characteristics specific to the club.

Falter and Perignon (2000) develop a multivariate model[6] that explains attendance at a particular match using socio-economic, football-related, and what they call "incentive" variables (including the time of year and whether or not the match is televised). García and Rodríguez (2002) employ a similar model. They break down the football variables into those which consider the expected quality of the match and those which measure the uncertainty of the result. In their model, the variables called "incentives" by Falter and Perignon are designated as the "opportunity cost" variables of attending a match. Indeed, uncertainty of outcome is deemed by many academics as one of the most fundamental factors in professional sport if competitive balance is to be achieved, and the interest of fans maintained (Morrow, 2001).

Baimbridge (1997) and Koning et al. (2001) work with analogous models for explaining the demand for international football competitions, using economic, demographic, and geographic variables.

The purchasing power of the population, its size, even other factors such as the educational level and tradition will have repercussions on the degree of support for a club. In the next two sections we are going to examine the relationships between the variable of attendance (ATT) and the socio-economic variables employed by academics. Although models concerning attendance are usually multivariate, we are going to build from a univariate analysis of each type of variable on attendance, and then end with a multivariate analysis.

Variables Relating to Support

There are different aspects of support. Depending on what is being examined, a range of variables have been used by researchers, and measurement methods also differ. Palomino and Rigotti (2000 a, b) consider demand in economic terms. They measure it through sports revenues. So, there is a financial approach to support.

The most frequent approach to measuring support, however, is made through the attendance variable (Baimbridge, 1997; Guijarro et al., 2000; Koning et al., 2001; Garcia and Rodriguez, 2002). Due to the exponential nature of the attendance function, some authors use the logarithm of attendance at each match (Falter and Perignon, 2000). Guijarro et al. (2000) look for a hierarchical criterion of clubs in their model for determining the club's brand value. They carry out an initial estimate through the number of "brand clients."

This would be equivalent to the fanbase. So, they explain that the fanbase — the number of customers — can be measured by calculating the number of season ticket holders or average match attendances. However, they reject the validity of the first variable (the number of season ticket holders) because of the existence of other consumers (club members, etc.). They do not consider the second (average attendances) to be valid either. The reason for this is that in any particular match there might be opposition fans, attracted by the appeal of the away team and, as a consequence, not interested in the brand of the home team. Finally, Bambridge (1997) suggests measuring support through the percentage of stadium utilization.

We are going to utilize average attendances at league matches (ATT). Firstly, in order to make a valuation of a club, which is the context chosen for this paper, the capacity to generate revenues from its support is highly relevant. So, apart from the variables mentioned above, generic aspects such as the appeal of competition, competitive balance, and so on, should be considered. These factors are incorporated within our variable of average attendance (ATT). Secondly, since we are working with average attendances throughout the season, the effect of matches played against less attractive opposition will be balanced against those with more attractive clubs.

We appreciate the advantages of working with data of average attendances in all competitions. However, the data available only deal with league attendances. Nevertheless, we do not believe this represents serious limitations because it is probable that the team performance in all competitions reflects on league match attendances. For example, a team with good performances in international competitions creates expectations that will generate the desire to watch it at every home game.

Socio-economic Variables

Ticket prices might be the first socio-economic variable to be included in an analysis of attendances (Garcia and Rodriguez, 2002), although authors such as Falter and Perignon (2000) do not include it in their model as they consider it to be an endogenous variable (meaning that price is affected by attendance). We are not going to employ it either. Firstly, because we agree to some extent with Falter and Perignon, but also because we propose a study which focuses on average attendances. Pricing policies comprise a wide range of ticket prices according to location within the stadium, the type of match, as well as discounts for season ticket holders, and so on. This would complicate considerably the choice of price to use as a measure.

Market size is another variable to take into consideration. For the purposes of this investigation, market size relates to the size of the surrounding population. Baimbridge (1997) studies a competition at international level. In his paper, he takes the variable to be the population of the country divided by the distance, in air miles, between the capital of the country in question and London. Baimbridge (1997) uses size of population as one of the variables in his study of an international football competition. Garcia and Rodriguez (2002) use the population of the province[7] in which the club is based. Finally, Cocco and Jones (1997), Falter and Perignon (2000), and Blasco et al. (2002) choose the number of inhabitants of the city in which the club is located. The former two articles employ a logarithmic form of the variable and the latter divides the population in those cities with more than one club according to the number of season ticket holders at each club.

We are going to work with both measures: city and provincial populations. We will then choose the most appropriate measure for later stages of the research. We have adjusted the population of cities or provinces with more than one team following the same criterion as Blasco et al. (2002) to produce the adjusted population of province (APP) and adjusted population of town (APT). In order to make that adjustment, we assume that teams located in smaller towns and cities might attract spectators from their own towns but that it is more difficult to draw fans in from more developed cities. So, in the case of Madrid, where Getafe and Leganes have their respective teams, we have subtracted the population of these two towns from the overall province and we have distributed the remainder among the other three teams of the capital (Real Madrid, Atlético de Madrid, and Rayo Vallecano) according to the number of respective season ticket holders. In the province of A Coruna, we have subtracted the population of Santiago de Compostela from the rest of the province in order to estimate the population relating to Deportivo de La Coruna. Finally, for Asturian clubs, we have followed the criterion of number of season ticket holders for dividing the population.

Another set of factors that seem relevant following the market size approach are those related to the purchasing power of potential "customers." For example, the gross income per capita reflects the purchasing power of the population and it may be an influential factor when deciding whether or not to go to a match (Baimbridge, 1997; Cocco and Jones, 1997; Koning et al., 2001; and Garcia y Rodríguez, 2002). Falter and Perignon (2000) prefer the average wage as an indicator of purchasing power. We have opted to include as variables: the economic level of the province, the industrial, commercial, tourism and catering, economic activity indices,[8] and the adjusted market share (AMS).[9]

If we assume that sport is a product that is only demanded when the basic necessities are covered, then factors such as high unemployment in a particular city or region might affect football match attendances negatively. Falter and Perignon (2000) use the rate of unemployment as a socio-economic variable. We also will employ the unemployment rate[10] of the town in order to establish its relationship with attendance.

Relationship between Socio-economic Variables and Attendance

The hypothesis that we are going to test in this section is that *socioeconomic*[11] *features of the local population influence football match attendances.*

In order to analyze the effect that different socio-economic variables have on attendance, we have opted for an Ordinary Linear Squared (OLS) regression model. Most researchers (Baimbridge, 1997; Cocco and Jones, 1997; Falter and Perignon, 2000; and Garcia y Rodriguez, 2002) use this kind of model. The data for the population of towns and provinces, as well as economic data, are extracted from "Fundacion La Caixa" reports (2002, 2003). The variation from year to year of this type of data, especially those referring to population, is not considerable. Therefore, we have opted to focus our analysis on data from the 1999/2000 season. The sample consists of 33 teams. We aimed to work with all professional Spanish football clubs, but this was impossible because some clubs, even some which are companies, do not allow the public to view their accounts. However, we consider the sample to be representative: all First Division clubs and 13 of the Second Division clubs allow relevant conclusions to be drawn.

From the results of the regressions between attendance and each of the independent variables explained in the previous section, it is clear that the variable which best explains attendance is the adjusted population of the province (APP) which is statistically significant and explains 78.5 percent (this its R2) of attendance. The adjusted population of the town (APT) is also statistically significant with a high explanation power (R2= 0.722). Finally, the last variable which presents a good performance is the adjusted market share (AMS)12 (statistically significant, R2 = 0.732).

The industrial, commercial, catering, tourism and economic activity indexes have little explanation power. Their R2 vary between 0.288 and 0.337.

So, we found that the unemployment rate and the results for the levels of economic activity were not statistically significant. Nevertheless, the AMS variable, that measures the effect of population wealth, explains attendances well, and suffices to prove the existence of a relationship between attendances and socio-economic factors.

Once the regressions between the distinct independent variables and attendances were carried out, we proved, by means of a bivariate correlation analysis, that multicollinearity exists between the explicative variables. This is the reason why the regression analysis was performed step by step, in order to determine whether or not it is possible to use a socio-economic multivariate model which explains attendances better than the univariate models.

The result is a model of only one variable in which the independent variable is the adjusted province population (APP) excluding the other variables. The expression of that model — with an explanation degree of 78.5 percent and being statistically significant — is thus:

(1) ATT = 4784.136 + 0.017·APP + e

To summarise, then, in this section the relationship between attendance and several socio-economic variables has been tested. The adjusted population of the province (APP), the adjusted population of the town (APT), and adjusted market share (AMS) are statistically significant and with a high explanation power (all of them above 70 percent). The other variables used are not significant and are of low explanation power. In a second stage, a multivariate regression was analyzed in order to identify the variable or variables that best explain attendance avoiding multicollinearity problems. The outcome is a model in which there is only one significant independent variable (APP) and its R2 is 78.5 percent. Therefore, this variable subsumed all the information of the rest of the variables we have employed.

Quality of Squad and Attendance

Cocco and Jones (1997) include in their model of matchday attendances a co-efficient that considers changes in demand as a response to specific features of the home team. Palomino and Rigotti (2000 a, b) consider the wealth of a club (which is linked to its quality) as one of the variables that explain the demand for football.

Falter and Perignon (2000) explain attendance based, at least partially, on a series of purely football-related variables. They include the budget of the club within this. Garcia and Rodriguez (2002) work with a similar model. They utilize the budget in real terms. Furthermore, they clarify that this budget depends on salaries. We agree with Gerrard (2001) that budget is a finance proxy variable for the quality of the squad.

We understand that it is relevant to introduce into the model a variable which relates to the quality of the team squad. It seems obvious that a team with many stars is more likely to attract fans than a team without "big name" players. In fact, it is striking the expectation that a signing of a new player can awaken (Stead, 1999). Nevertheless, in Europe usually the fans' feelings are linked more closely to their club than to a particular football player.

Financial approaches to quality of squad include considering budgets (Falter and Perignon, 2000; Garcia and Rodriguez, 2002; Lucifero and Simmons, 2003) and the wealth of the club (Palomino and Rigotti, 2000 a, b). Barajas (2004) demonstrates that the variable most appropriate to the Spanish case is the sum of the wages of sports-related staff and the depreciation of rights on players (W+D). For this reason, we chose to contrast the relationship between attendance and quality of the squad using this financial approach.

So, the hypothesis that we are going to test is that *the higher the quality of the squad, the higher the attendances*.

In order to test this hypothesis, the "support" variables described in the previous section and the quality variables suggested by Barajas (2004) are employed. The same model of analysis as before is employed; that is, a univariate linear regression model.

The result is that indeed a positive and statistically significant relationship exists between the average attendance at football stadia over a season and the squad quality estimated by calculating its annual cost—the sum of wages and depreciation (W+D). The explanation degree of the dependent variable is high (R^2 = 0.745). The resultant model is expressed thus:

(2) ATT = 7,258.374 + 0.001·(W+D) + e

In this section, using a financial approach to determine the quality of the squad, we have proven that attendance can be explained well by the chosen variable of the quality of the squad.

Incidence of Sports Performance on Attendance

Szymanski (2001) claims that the utility of fans depends on the sporting success of their team. We may agree in general terms with this, but some nuances may be drawn. It is reasonable to distinguish short-term influences and a broader perspective. In the first case, the club may count on fans' loyalty and on keeping their support. However, new supporters will be attracted to the most successful teams of the moment. Also we may assert that clubs with a larger quantity of supporters at the present time have been those who have been more victorious in the past.[13]

Falter and Perignon (2000) only use result variables relating to current team performances. In this way, they draw on league positions, average goal differences, and results of the last match. They, along with Garcia and Rodriguez (2002), focus on determining an attendance function from weekly results. This is a more volatile perspective than we are pursuing. We are concerned with influences on the economic value of a club. So, we are looking for a smoother, longer-term relationship. Therefore, we will work with annual results and also with other variables that we call "historical" or to do with *prestige*. Below, we explain the current and historical result variables that shall be used in this paper.

Variables of current results examined here are the *compound index* (CIND)[14] which includes results of all the competitions in which a club participates over the course of the 1999/2000 season, and the *league position* (LPOS)[15] at the end of the season. The more matches played in the First Division the more tradition and ability the club has to consolidate its fanbase. The historical results we have worked with for each club date from the start of the national Spanish league championship. Logically, the higher the *number of matches won* (MW) the more positive the effect will be. We have created another variable which represents the *number of matches not won* (MNW), that is, the number of matches in First Division minus matches won. We understand also that the number of *goals for* (GF) in the First Division is a positive factor for generating fans. *Goals against* (GA) may constitute a dissuasive factor for attending matches; nevertheless, goals against may have less importance when the *goal difference* (GD) was positive. In fact, if that goal difference is positive, conceding goals may become an incentive to attending matches because it implies an attacking style of play, inspired by scoring more goals than the opposition. It is worth remembering FC Barcelona when it was coached by Johan Cruyff (1988–96): the team had a great ability to score goals without paying too much attention to defending.

We have calculated the univariate regressions between attendance and each of the enumerated variables of current and historical results. From that analysis, it is remarkable that all variables of results present a positive and statistically significant relationship with the stadia attendances. That link is greater or lesser depending on the independent variables.

The variable of current results which best explains attendance is the compound index (CIND) with an R2 of 0.698. Considering that this index includes results of all competitions in which the club participates and that the attendance only refers to league matches, it may be concluded that the good performance of the club in different competitions contributes to a higher attendance at league matches due to the expectation created by the good results.

Regarding prestige variables, which consider historical results, those with a greater explanation degree are goals for (GF) and matches won in the First Division (MW) with R2 of 0.736 and 0.755, respectively.

Contrary to expectations, both goals against (GA) and matches not won (MNW) also have positive coefficients. Two factors may explain this phenomenon. On the one hand, both variables refer to seasons when the clubs have remained in First Division, which contributes to increase the number of fans. Furthermore, promotion and relegation both have a positive effect on attendances (Noll, 2002). Teams with worse results will be more easily implicated in the fight to avoid relegation, so more spectators turn up. On the other hand, especially in the case of goals against, we might expect a better spectacle or even that part of the public come to watch the rival team, if it is talented.

We have sought also to explain attendance through a multivariate regression model. The result of this is that the independent variables which explain the attendance are matches won (MW), matches not won (MNW), and the league position variable (LPOS). In this model, the variable matches not won (MNW) has a negative coefficient. In this analysis we had to exclude Real Betis from the sample due to its anomalous behavior regarding attendances. We may affirm that the popular saying, "Viva er Betis man que pierda"[16] is statistically corroborated. Every coefficient and the intercept are statistically significant. The model has an explanation degree of 93.2 percent and can be represented by the following expression:

(3) ATT= 11,736.952 + 55.108·MW − 25.816·MNW + 2,866.577·LPOS + e

Therefore, in a first stage of analysis, the relationships between attendance and the different variables of current and historical results have been tested. All the independent variables tested are statistically significant. The compound index (CIND) which reflects the performance of the team in all competitions is the variable of current results which best explains attendance. In a second stage of analysis, a multivariate model explains attendance. This model includes historical variables (MW and MNW) and the league position variable (LPOS) of the previous season. This model, statistically significant, has a high explanation power (93.2 percent).

Explanation of the Whole Model of Support

Falter and Perignon (2000) draw their model of attendance from socioeconomic, football-related, and "incentive" variables. They assume a linear relationship that could be expressed as:

(4) $ATT_i = \alpha + \beta_1 \cdot E_i + \beta_2 \cdot F_i + \beta_3 \cdot I_i + \varepsilon_i$

Where ATT_i is the logarithm of attendance at match i; E_i represents the whole of the group of socio-economic variables where unemployment rate, population, average wage, and transport costs are included; F_i symbolizes those football-related variables (league position, goal difference, budget, and last result); and, finally, I_i signifies the "incentive" variables such as the time of the year when the match is played and whether or not it is televised.

The model we propose takes into account the contributions of Falter and Perignon (2000), Barajas (2004), and Garcia and Rodriguez (2002). We assume that attendance is conditioned by socio-economic factors, quality of product (results), and quality of the means of production (squad). As we do not analyze attendance of individual matches, the "incentive" variables which the former authors use are not relevant to us. Neither are the "opportunity cost" variables employed by the Garcia and Rodriguez.

We have already seen how the quality of squad affects sports results. Now, we are concerned with whether it also has a direct effect on attendance, or whether it only influences it through sports results. We have checked this by mean of a trajectory analysis which tells us whether the effects are direct or indirect as shown in Figure 2.

Our model expresses the average attendances at stadia during a season and it is explained by socio-economic variables (E_i), variables related to quality of squad (P_j) and our football variables (F_l), which indicate the quality of product (results).

$$(5)\ ATT = \alpha_0 + \sum_{i=1}^{K_1} \beta_i E_i + \sum_{j=1}^{K_2} \gamma_j P_j + \sum_{l=1}^{K_3} \delta_l F_l + \varepsilon$$

We use a stepwise regression, after checking the existence of multicollinearity among variables that we tried to introduce into the model. Again, we have had to exclude Real Betis from the sample due to their abnormal behavior. The results are presented in the following model:

$$(6)\ ATT = -2{,}591.179 + 0.007 \cdot APP + 120.882 \cdot ACP + 7.715 \cdot GD + 7.516 \cdot MW + e$$

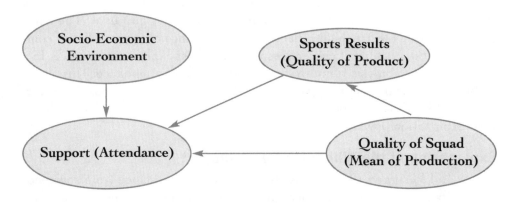

Figure 2. Factors Which Determine Attendance

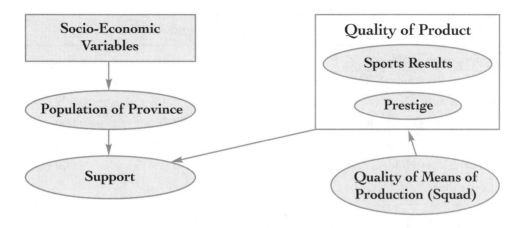

Figure 3. Schema of Model of Support

The dependent variable attendance (ATT) is explained to a high degree ($R2 = 0.956$) and is statistically significant. The quality of the squad variable has been excluded from the model. So, Figure 3 shows us the conceptual model of support.

Variables on information about the economic characteristics of the population do not appear either in this model. The reason for this is the presence of population of the province as an independent variable in the model. This variable has a strong correlation with market share (0.89 at two-tailed 0.01 level of significance).

With this model, it is demonstrated that the quality of squad in a financial approach only affects attendance through sports results, and that socioeconomic factors may be summarized in the potential market size measured by adjusted province population (APP).

Incidence of Attendance in Sporting Revenues

Until now, we have analyzed the factors which affect support as measured via attendances. Now we are going to focus the study on the influence that attendances have on sporting revenues. According to the Football Task Force, support is the main asset of a particular club because it is the origin of matchday, media, and commercial revenues (FTF, 1999). Directly or indirectly, the fan is the key to most of the club's revenue streams (Deloitte & Touche, 2000; 50).

So, we are going to test the hypothesis that attendances influence sporting revenues. In order to do this, we are going to employ the average attendance (ATT) as an independent variable and several revenue variables as dependent. These dependent variables relate directly to sporting activity following the criteria established in the specific accounting rules for the sports industry in Spain.[17] The variables that we are going to use are sporting revenues (SR; the sum of all the other revenues, though calculated differently for each club), matchday and pools monies (MDP), television rights (TVR), advertising (ADV), and number of season ticket holders (STH).

Table 1. Summary of Regression Between Attendance and Revenues

Dependent Variables	R2	t	sig.
Sporting Revenues (SR)	0,862	13,704	0,000
Matchday and Pools (MDP)	0,424	4,455	0,000
Television Rights (TVR)	0,890	14,752	0,000
Advertising (ADV)	0,748	8,944	0,000
Season Ticket Holders (STH)	0,874	13,954	0,000
Independent Variable: ATT			

We have excluded Real Betis again because they do not register any amount of money in the accounts that we use as variables in our study. This club hands over the revenues of its core business to companies that ensure a minimum amount to the club, plus a percentage of the additional incomes achieved.

A summary of the most remarkable output is shown in Table 1. First, it highlights the existence of a direct, positive, high—except on tickets and pools (MDP)—and statistically significant relationship between attendance and the different variables of revenues. The income from tickets (MDP) has the worst explanation power. The reason is the lack of information about this kind of revenues in some clubs.

Conclusions

Throughout the paper the main conclusions of the analysis have been highlighted. First, the relationships between attendances—as an approach to support—and socio-economic variables were tested. Attendance is highly explained by the adjusted population of the province (APP), or the adjusted population of the town (APT), or even by adjusted market share (AMS). However, the unemployment rate is not statistically significant, and other indices have a low explanation power. A great correlation exists between all the socioeconomic variables. This has been checked by the multivariate model. The outcome of this model is that only one independent variable remains (the adjusted population of province, APP) with an R2 of 0.785.

As result of the regression analysis of quality of the means of production (squad), analyzed via the sum of wages and depreciation (W+D), and support, approached by average attendance (ATT), we have found that the former explains the latter by 74.5 percent, being statistically significant. So we can affirm that a good squad will attract people to the stadium.

The third step leads us to obtain conclusions about the degree of relationship between success on the pitch and support. Again, the latter has been approached by attendance. After testing several variables of current and historical results, we found that all the variables tested are statistically significant. So, according to this, we can state that support is well explained by team performance on the pitch. Furthermore, we checked to find out if the model works better by including several variables of current and historical results. The outcome is a multivariate model which has an explanation power of 93.2 percent, being statistically significant. The matches won (MW) and the matches not won (MNW) in First Division throughout the history of the club and the ranking in the season are the factors which explain attendance.

Once we checked that the quality of the squad and results influence support, and considering that the better the squad of a team the better its performance is, we wondered whether the effect of squad quality on attendance is direct or if it only affects attendance through results on the pitch. We tested it and presented a multivariate model based on the conceptual schema shown in Figure 2. The outcome is that attendance is explained for a socio-economic variable, adjusted population of province (APP), the current results of the team — measured by the points that the team has obtained — and the historical results (GF and MW). So we can assert that all the influence of the quality of the squad on attendance comes through team performance. We have also found a model for explaining average attendance with a high power of explanation (95.6 percent). Finally, in order to test the initial schema (Figure 1), we have ended checking the influences of attendance on several sporting revenues. The main finding is that attendance has an important explanation degree on the whole of sporting income (86.2 percent).

Notes

1. The Football Supporters Association (FSA) was founded following the Heysel Stadium disaster in May 1985. It provided a strong and united voice for football fans to defend the game at a time when their image was tarnished by hooliganism. The FSA merged with National Association of Football Supporters Clubs (NAFSC) in 2002 to become the Football Supporters Federation.

2. Quoted in "Football, its values, finances and reputation," February 1998.

3. Budget, capacity of stadium, and number of season ticket holders are three elements which determine a club's size. The last two factors are more geographically limited. However, the budget might be higher even if the club is located in a relatively small town if, by playing well, it attracts television revenues and sponsors. TV deals in Spain are not negotiated centrally.

4. A useful introduction to this is the paper written by Cocco and Jones (1997). In Spain, Toledo F.C. was sold to a firm called Ivercom on 10 June 2003. Since then Toledo F.C. began to be known under the name of the owner company. The club moved to Murcia with the intention of taking the place of Cartagonova (another football club). The problem arose when the RFEF (the Spanish Football Association) objected to the move. Then Ivercom turned all its

efforts to trying to avoid the relegation of Cartagonova for the unfulfilment of administrative requirements (*Marca*, 13 August 2003, p. 27). In England, the case of London club Wimbledon moving to Milton Keynes in 2002 and becoming established as the Milton Keynes Dons (known as MK Dons) is unlikely to happen again.

5. For example, some estimates suggest that the number of Real Madrid CF fans around the world is 70 million (*Marca*, 21 June 2001).

6. It is a model which considers more than one variable. See expression (4).

7. The Spanish State consists of Comunidades Autónomas (Autonomous Communities) and these are divided into provinces although there are some Autonomous Communities with only one province such as Madrid, Rioja, Cantabria, Asturias. There are 52 provinces in Spain.

8. These entire indices are elaborated by "La Caixa" considering levels of income, industrialization, commerce, etc. in the province.

9. This index expresses the comparative consumer capacity of the different towns. This capacity is measured considering the importance of the population and its purchasing power taking into account the following variables: number of telephones, cars, lorries, branches of banks, and retail shops. Data employed here refers to January 2001 (Fundación "La Caixa," 2002).

10. We use the unemployment rate calculated by "La Caixa." It is estimated in a different way from the official government figures taken from the Survey of Working Population (EPA). In this case, it is calculated over Total Population instead of Active Population (Fundación "La Caixa," 2002; 11–12).

11. Although we speak about socio-economic features it would be more accurate speak only about potential market size because the characteristics not directly associated to it are not significant.

12. The adjustment has been applied to cities with more than one team (Madrid, Barcelona, Sevilla, and Valencia) taking into consideration the number of season ticket holders, as explained in the previous section.

13. Mellor (2000) explains how Manchester United became a "super club" with high levels of popularity and attendance thanks to its sporting success in the 1960s.

14. If P_i represents the points achieved in the i competition and a_i represents the weight of each competition considered (*Copa del Rey*, UEFA Cup, *Liga*, UEFA Champions' League) then the index may be expressed as:

$$IND = \sum_{i=1}^{4} \alpha_i P_i$$

This index needs a system to convert the cup competition into points. We use the weighting and the system of conversion proposed by Barajas (2004).

15. This variable has been estimated from Szymanski and Kuypers (1999, 187) but they work with 92 teams and we work with 42. So, the expression we employ is thus:

$$LPOS = -\log\left(\frac{p}{43-p}\right)$$

where p represents the ranking of a particular team at the end of the season.

16. Written in colloquial Spanish, it means "Hail Betis even if they lose!"

17. In Spain, sporting companies and clubs have to present their accounts following the General Plan of Accountancy adapted for sporting companies.

References

Baimbridge, M. (1997). Match attendance at Euro 96: Was the crowd waving or drowning? *Applied Economics Letters*, 4, 555–558.

Barajas, A. (2004). Modelo de valoración de clubes de fútbol basado en los factores clave de su negocio. Doctoral Thesis. Facultad de Ciencias Económicas, Universidad de Navarra.

Blasco Ruiz, A., Ribal Sanchis, F. J., & Rodriguez, J. A. (2002). Valoración de intangibles en las Sociedades Anónimas Deportivas en España. Jugadores y marcas. *Comunicación al I Congreso Internacional de Valoración y Tasación, Universidad Politécnica de Valencia*, 3–5 julio 2002.

Cocco, A. & Jones, J. C. H. (1997). On going south: the economics of survival and relocation of small market NHL franchises in Canada. *Applied Economics*, 29, 1537–1552.

Derbaix, Ch., Decrop, A., & Cabossart, O. (2002). Colors and scarves: The symbolic consumption of material possessions by soccer fans. *Advances in Consumer Research*, 29, 511–517.

Falter, J-M., & Perignon, C. (2000). Demand for football and intra-match winning probability: an essay on the glorious uncertainty of sports. *Applied Economics*, 32, 1757–1765.

FTF (1999). *Football: Commercial Issues. Report One*. A submission by the Football Task Force to the Minister for Sport.

Fundación "La Caixa": Anuario social de España. Barcelona (2003). From http://www.estudios.lacaixa.es/anuariosocial

Fundación "La Caixa": Anuario económico de España. Barcelona. (2002). From http://www.estudios.lacaixa.es/anuarioeconomico

Garcia, J., & Rodriguez, P. (2002). The determinants of football match attendance revisited: Empirical evidence from the Spanish Football League. *Journal of Sports Economics*, 3(1), 18–38.

Gerrard, B. (2001). A new approach to measuring player and team quality in professional team sports. *European Sport Management Quarterly*, 1(3), 219–234.

Giulianotti, R. (2002). "Supporters, followers, fans and flaneurs." *Journal of Sports and Social Issues*, 26(1), 25–46.

Guijarro, F., Blasco, A., Rival, F. J., & Rodriguez, J. A. (2000). Aplicacion de costes presupuestarios para la valoración de marcas de clubes de fútbol españoles. Comunicación al Congreso ACODI, October.

Hoehn, T., & Szymanski, S. (1999). The Americanization of European Football. *Economic Policy, April*, pp. 205–240.

Koning, R. H., Ridder, G., Koolhaas, M., &

Renes, G. (2001) Simulation model for soccer championships. University of Groningen, SOM Research Reports 01A66.

Lucifero, C., & Simmons, R. (2003). Superstar effects in sport: Evidence from Italian soccer. *Journal of Sports Economics*, *4*(1), 35–55.

McElgunn, J. (2002). The Sports Bubble. *Marketing Magazine*. 14 October 2002.

Mellor, G. (2000). The rise of the reds: An historical analysis of Manchester United as a super-club. *Singer & Friedlander. Review 1999–2000 Season*, pp.18–21.

Mellor, G. (2001). Can we have our fans back now? Football, community and the historical struggles of small-town clubs. *Singer & Friedlander. Review 2000–2001 Season*, pp. 34–37.

Morrow, S. (2003). *The people's game? Football, finance and society*. London: Palgrave Macmillan.

Noll, R. G. (2002). The economics of promotion and relegation in sports leagues: The cases of English football. *Journal of Sport Economics*, *3*(2), 169–203.

Palomino, F., & Rigotti, L. (2000 a). Competitive balance vs incentives to win: A theoretical analysis of revenue sharing. *Working Papers in Economics*. RePEc:ecm:wc2000 :0930.

Palomino, F., & Rigotti, L. (2000 b). The sport league's dilemma: Competitive balance versus incentives to win. *Working Papers in Economics*. RePEc:wpa:wwwpio:0012003.

Porter, P. K. (1992). The role of the fan in professional baseball. In Sommers, P. (Ed.), *Diamonds are forever: the business of baseball*. Washington: Brookings.

Ruyter, K. de, & Wetzels, M. (2000). With a little help from my fans — Extending models of pro-social behaviour to explain supporters' intentions to buy soccer club shares. *Journal of Economic Psychology*, *21*, 387–409.

Stead, D. (1999). The Bosman legacy. *Singer & Friedlander. Review 1998–1999 Season*, pp. 23–26.

Szymanski, S. (2001). Income inequality, competitive balance and the attractiveness of team sports: Some evidence and a natural experiment from English soccer. *The Economic Journal*, *111*, 69–84.

Szymanski, S., & Kuypers, T. (1999). *Winners and losers: The business strategy of football*. Penguin: Harmondsworth.

Tapp, A. (2004). The loyalty of football fans — we'll support you evermore? *Database Marketing and Customer Strategy Management*, *11*(3), 203–215.

Tapp, A., & Clowes, J. (2000). From "carefree casuals" to "professional wanderers": Segmentation possibilities for football supporters. *European Journal of Marketing*, *36*(11/12), 1248–1269.

Veblen, T. (1966). *Teoría de la clase ociosa*. México: Fondo de Cultura Económica (2nd ed.).

Vrooman, J. (1995). A general theory of professional sports leagues. *Southern Economic Journal*, *61*, 971–990. 20

14

EL REY DE LOS DEPORTES: BODIES, BUSINESS, AND BORDER IDENTITIES IN MEXICAN BASEBALL

Rich Schultz

Like most other countries in Latin America, Mexico is a place where soccer dominates the sport headlines, and where business generally grinds to a halt when the national team plays in World Cup qualifiers. Mexico's second sport, baseball, battles for attention on television and radio, and in newspapers. Yet, in the northwestern states of Sonora, Sinaloa, and Baja California Norte, baseball has "planted its seed," and enjoys dominance over soccer when it comes to professional organization.[1] While soccer is still popular in the northwest, it is baseball—*el rey de los deportes* or "the king of sports"—that has blossomed into the more significant source of regional pride and economic importance. Baseball's popularity in one of Mexico's most important regions reflects the distinctions between the northwest and the rest of the country, in large part due to the region's proximity to the United States.

Studying this difference between the popularity of one sport over another can inform our understanding of the ways in which local, regional, and national identities are formed, challenged, and constituted. In a border region such as northwestern Mexico, where individuals and families often live within two worlds— one on either side of the international border—people demonstrate that there is no one way to be Mexican or American, Sonoran or Sinaloan, male or female. These are, after all, socially constructed labels to attach to the ways of thinking about oneself, and about groups with whom one wishes to, and wishes not to, associate.

In the northwestern states, there is much local diversity; the region is not culturally or geographically homogeneous. Sinaloa, which does not border the United States, is a much different cultural environment than, say, the border cities of Tijuana or Mexicali. Nevertheless, Sinaloa, like Sonora and Baja California Norte and Sur can reasonably be considered a border region because both individually and collectively, their economies are so closely tied to the United States. Mazatlán and Cabo San Lucas rely heavily on the dollars spent by tourists, many of them Americans. In many interactions it is, in fact, dollars not pesos, which change hands in this part of Mexico. Hermosillo, the state capital of Sonora, is home to a large Ford manufacturing plant; the economic well-being of thousands of Sonorans depends on decisions made in the U.S. The border cities have even closer connections to the U.S., as many of the residents of those cities cross the border daily to work, study, and shop.

What is now the northwestern border region in Mexico was isolated from the country's more powerful central region until the construction of rail lines in the 1880s.[2] This coincided with the international promotion of baseball as a hallmark of American culture by U.S. businessmen, journalists, and politicians.[3] Even with the railroads, places like Culiacán and Hermosillo remained remote outposts.[4] Tijuana had less than one thousand residents at the beginning of the twentieth century.[5] American investors led many of the most important business ventures in states like Sonora. The United States and its entrepreneurs had substantial clout when it came to the economic development of the Mexican northwest in the six decades between the U.S.-Mexico War and World War I. Economic circumstances opened the door for American cultural influence in northern Mexico. Baseball is perhaps among the most visible forms of the American presence in the region. But the ways in which the game is played, staged, promoted, and discussed in northwestern Mexico illustrates how Mexicans have appropriated baseball for their own cultural needs and wishes.

The *Liga Mexicana del Pacífico* (LMP) is Mexico's highest level of professional baseball, and it operates in eight northwestern cities. Beyond providing the mechanisms for baseball players to earn a living, and to offer fans a few hours at the ballpark, the LMP provides a very public display of the sorts of struggles underway for a variety of individual and group identities in northwestern Mexico. The LMP is a window into Mexican society, one which illuminates the links between gender, race, politics, government, and business in the generation of a variety of self and group identities in a region struggling to compete in an increasingly globalized world. The trend toward widespread commercialization of the game, along with corporate ownership of some teams, manifests the workings of globalization. Teams may represent local communities, but players include Americans, and other non-Mexicans, and the league relies on foreign companies for advertising and television revenues.

Within Mexico, the difference in organizational sophistication between baseball in the northwest and soccer elsewhere illuminates a larger center-periphery phenomenon in the country. Mexico City has always been the center of national political decision-making in the country. But the regions have played a significant role as well. Sonora was home to some of Mexico's biggest mining operations in the late nineteenth and early twentieth century, and wages were highest in the north during that time.[6] It was the site of distinct revolutionary forces in 1910–11; its attitudes helped create a Catholic-based party, the PAN, in opposition to the official PRI; and two presidents, Alvaro Obregón and Plutarco Elias Calles, hailed from the state, forming the core of the "Sonoran dynasty" in Mexican politics.[7] Presently, it is the maquiladora-based economic growth in border cities like Tijuana, Mexicali, and Ciudad

Juárez which stimulates the northern border region economies. Yet, northern cities remain second-class locations for the "national" game, soccer. If anything the fact that one region of the country is responsible for producing the national league or always hosting the national team's games points to a rather fractured sense of unity. Cities like Tijuana, Mexicali, Hermosillo, and Mazatlán do not even have teams to compete for the highest national soccer trophy.[8] None of these cities have adequate facilities to play host to any World Cup qualifying games for the national men's team (most of these are held in Mexico City). The northwest, despite large population centers, is largely seen as a backwater for the national sport.

Conversely, because the winner of the *Liga del Pacífico* represents Mexico at baseball's most important Latin American event, the league provides a rare opportunity for cities like Culiacán, Ciudad Obregón, or Mexicali: to represent the entire nation state at an international event, of sports or of any other variety. Additionally, one of the league's teams plays host to the *Serie del Caribe* every four years, bringing tourist dollars and an international spotlight otherwise unthinkable for boosters in most of these cities, with the obvious exception of the beach resort Mazatlán. In 2009, Mexicali hosted its first *Serie del Caribe*, and images of the city and its remodeled stadium, Estadio Casas Geo, made their way to millions of television sets throughout the Americas on ESPN Deportes. Baseball allows northwestern Mexican cities to keep their communities "on the map" within Mexico and within the baseball world. All of this is a source of great pride in the region, and a factor in shaping local and regional identities in the shadow of the dominant capital city to the south.

In what follows here, I offer evidence of the ways in which baseball is tied to the formation of self and group identities in Mexico's northwest. Links between the state, private entrepreneurs, large corporations (including Major League Baseball), players, and those who buy tickets to watch the games in the stands generate these various and competing identities. While the global marketplace seems to have a dominant position in terms of the ways that baseball is organized in Mexico and other parts of Latin America, there are many ways that specifically local and/or regional interests, including the state, shape the game and its performance, acting as a counterbalance to any domination from outside.

Bodies and Borders

Edgar González was an obvious selection to represent Mexico at the *Serie del Caribe* in 2003. Among the most talented pitchers in Mexico, González dominated most of the statistical categories (8-1, 1.89 ERA) during the 2002–03 LMP season. Just twenty years old, González was picked by the league champion from Los Mochis to bolster the team that would represent Mexico in Puerto Rico. But, in a twist that illustrates the ambiguity of national identities in the globalized realm of modern professional sports, González was denied the opportunity to play for Mexico. The Arizona Diamondbacks, with whom he was under contract at the time, blocked his participation over fears that his body had already worked enough over the winter months. With the help of a contract signed between Latin American winter leagues and Major League Baseball, the Diamondbacks were able to keep González rested and injury-free for their own upcoming season.[9] With an opening on the roster, leaders of the Mexican delegation shopped around other teams in the LMP, and picked up Charles "Bubba" Smith, a thirty-one year old, 240-pound first baseman from North Carolina with several seasons experience playing winter baseball in Mexicali.[10] An aging American veteran, and not a bright young Mexican star, represented Mexico at the 2003 *Serie del Caribe*.

This very brief set of transactions, a seemingly microscopic incident in baseball history, illustrates the ways that the game is interconnected with notions of nationalism and global economics. The baseball industry, like other sports, demands that its participants choose between money and national pride. This is particularly the case in Latin America, where players leave their homes and families to play in culturally and linguistically different cities in the United States and Canada, in order to follow their dreams and earn a paycheck.[11] The González case demonstrates just one of many ways that identity formation plays out in Mexican winter baseball. Americans represent cities in northwestern Mexico; players wear uniforms advertising products they may themselves never purchase nor support, but which they nevertheless help to sell and promote. People connected to baseball—in whatever way—are engaged in continuous negotiations over ways to perceive themselves as individuals and as associated groups.

Baseball is, like other modern sports, essentially about public athletic display, a "contested terrain" where competing ideas about the human body collide. As Pierre Bourdieu argues, sport is part of the "larger field of struggles over the definition of the *legitimate body* and the *legitimate use of the body*."[12] Conflicts over how the body should be displayed, understood, and talked about are waged under pretexts of dominant religious beliefs, political ideologies, gender identities, the rules of the marketplace, and a number of other controls on morality. In short, every element of a given culture contributes to the struggle over the "legitimate body" and the "legitimate use of the body." This is "body culture," a term used by Susan Brownell to refer to everything remotely involved with what people do with and to their physical form:

> Body culture is a broad term that includes daily practices of health, hygiene, fitness, beauty, dress and decoration, as well as gestures, postures, manners, ways of speaking and eating, and so on. It also includes the way these practices are trained into the body, the way the body is publicly displayed, and the lifestyle that is expressed in that display. Body culture reflects the internalization and incorporation of culture. Body culture is embodied culture.[13]

Representations of the male and female body are on display at stadiums each night, open to whatever applause, laughter, or ridicule their appearances may generate. That which draws cheers at one game can be expected back for an encore the following night; that which is scorned and criticized may not return again. The physical appearance of male athletes and female cheerleaders, the clothing worn by spectators and performers alike — all of these aspects to a night at a Mexican baseball game are part of the process by which people think about themselves, their team, their city, and their country.

Dominant ideas about the public display of bodies in Mexico underwent significant changes in the late nineteenth century, during the same time that American traders, miners and railroaders introduced the game to Mexicans. Mexico's most influential men believed in the wonders of science and the doctrines of Positivism. The writings of two men in particular — Herbert Spencer and August Comte — had a profound impact on the intellectuals, journalists, and policy makers in the young Mexican state. In their linear concept of the development of humans, adherence to the laws of science was considered to be a final stage of human knowledge.[14] Those nations like the United States, which were rapidly industrializing, offered proof to Mexican elites of the supposed truths of Positivism. Porfirio Díaz, whose lengthy hold on the presidency between 1876 and 1910 was largely the result of economic development policies, believed that Mexico should follow American business practices and cultural norms if the nation was to "progress."[15] Baseball, with all of its statistics, measurements, and demands for on-the-field precision, fit perfectly in the minds of Díaz and other Mexican leaders who admired both the infallibility of science and the rapid economic growth of the United States. Baseball was a "civilized game" according to those of the "Porfirian persuasion" who enjoyed the "sense of sharing the same activities and attitudes of the international gentry."[16] To play or watch baseball was to be modern in late nineteenth-century Mexico.

Díaz was only one of many Latin American leaders eager to embrace this visionary link between baseball and progress. Not only did those who felt this way wish to copy American business policy and recreational activities, they had Americans like Albert G. Spalding willing to sell them guidebooks and equipment to perfect their imitations. Spalding realized the power of organized games to build friendly relationships between Americans and the people of different lands. The game was to "follow the flag" in American business, political, and military pursuits.[17] Baseball was also a convenient source of profits for go-getters such as Spalding, who were ready to sell Latin Americans and others however many bats, balls, gloves, and instructional booklets they could buy. From the outset, then, baseball carried connotations of American culture and the promise of profit for its promoters. The game was to be played by men, usually by foreigners, by members of social clubs, or by the employees of American-minded companies. The historical trajectory of soccer in Mexico follows a similar path with European connections. Imported forms of recreational activity were organized in a way that fostered the participation of a chosen few. Not all bodies were immediate candidates for civilization through sport.

The manifestation of body culture in organized Mexican baseball has evolved in a parallel process with Mexican political and economic history. The influence of the state, state-backed industries, and later, global trade economics has literally been stamped on players' bodies. In the 1930s, "PNR-Hermosillo" was one of the strongest semi-professional teams in the region. Their uniforms consisted of the colors of the *Partido Nacional Revolucionario*, the official party (now the *Partido Revolucionario Institucional*, or PRI) and its acronym.[18] This, during a decade when the party's aim was to "consolidate" the gains of the Mexican Revolution through the redistribution of land and the nationalization of the Mexican petroleum industry. Party officials realized that sponsoring a strong baseball team would exemplify its own strength. By the 1950s, teams in the northwest took on names still used today—*Naranjeros, Algodoneros, Tomateros*, and *Cañeros*—which represented the dominant export crop in their respective regions. Perhaps of less significance now, these team nicknames nevertheless conveyed an image to the public that made industry magnates in the orange, cotton, tomato, and sugar cane industries all the more powerful. Their commercial enterprises were represented on the bodies of the players, connecting wealthy local interests to physical strength on the baseball diamond. Today, teams of the *Liga del Pacífico* don uniforms with as many as eight corporate logos, advertising everything from Volkswagen and Nestle to local newspapers and Mexican beer. The male body on Mexican baseball diamonds is literally a walking billboard. This on-field commercialization reflects the concessions granted to corporations in a country so affected by neo-liberal economic reforms since the 1980s.

If, as Brownell argues, "body culture is culture embodied" then spectator sports offer examples of the ways in which gender, race, politics, and economics have not only penetrated, but constituted, the cultural realm in Mexico. Ideas about what represents Mexican culture—*lo mexicano*—are shaped by unequal social, political, and economic relations, within Mexican towns and cities, between Mexican regions, and between Mexico and other nation states. Through sports we can see how the "battle for control of the body" is being waged in societies.[19] Baseball reminds us of the prevalence of "male preserves" in Mexico, in which women are either paying spectators or dancing cheerleaders hired to increase attendance among males.[20] Player uniforms also aim to sell, whether the product is political ideology or consumer goods. The players themselves compete with one another to rise up the ranks, forever hopeful of a scout's eye and a bigger financial contract somewhere down the road. Other more sedentary bodies choose to spend their money and leisure time watching both the players and the other spectators at the stadium. As Janet Lever illustrates in her study of Brazilian soccer, sports are able to bring people from various social classes together on a regular basis.[21] The congregation of so many individuals in one place allows for the display of many bodies performing a variety of roles, among them the expression of identity and culture.

The "bringing together" quality of sports is vital to recognizing how organized games help mold local identities. The work involved before, during, and after the game that allows two groups of men to play their nine innings each night involves thousands of participants. Some of these—namely the players— are in fact outsiders, and other than their performance on the field they may contribute very little to the actual staging of the sport spectacle. Countless others make their living grooming the field, selling souvenirs, repairing lights, pouring beer, or cleaning bathrooms; outside the stadium, vendors sell tacos and drinks, cab drivers shuttle fans, and nearby taverns cash in on thirsty fans. Promotion of the game, whether by radio or television broadcast, on the internet, or in newspapers, involves a number of writers, technicians, and organizers. Visiting teams and their entourage of club officials and sports writers also provide work for hotel and restaurant workers. Finally, without spectators willing to pay money to watch the game, money would not circulate. These are very important economic links that make baseball a highly relevant component in daily lives in a given community.

The force connecting all of these participants in the baseball spectacle is the man willing to risk financial loss for the benefits of owning a local team. Team owners, when not large corporations, are usually local businessmen and/or government officials who wield substantial clout in the local community. The *Liga del Pacífico*'s most striking example of this figure is Juan Manuel Ley López, the owner of both the *Tomateros* in Culiacán and the grocery/department store chain "Ley"—the large signs of which are ubiquitous on the horizons of most cities in northwestern Mexico. Ley's family has long been a leader in local commerce, and his father started the *Tomateros* franchise in 1960.[22] Ley, like his counterparts in Major League Baseball, is willing to accept financial losses through baseball for the gains both to his prestige and to his other business interests.[23] He can be seen as a local philanthropist in a setting that disguises class differences by allowing all members of the community, in whatever way, to participate. Estadio General Angel Flores, where the *Tomateros* play their home games, is plastered with advertisements for the Ley stores, promoting both the business and the family name. These advertisements are not only in constant view to as many as 15,000 spectators inside the stadium, but to the thousands watching on television, who see the giant red lettered "LEY" signs as the backdrop for lofty fly balls and home runs. Ley's financial successes have been so great, in fact, that he also purchased another baseball team, the *Saraperos* of Saltillo, which plays in Mexico's summer league. Here emerges the figure of the regional strongman, a type common in the history of northwestern Mexico, who not only controls large sectors of the regional economy, but who also appears to "give back" to the community in a reciprocal relationship through his sponsorship of baseball teams.

Another influential team owner, Mario López Valdez, provided the clearest example of the ways that baseball is tied to local politics. For a few years at the start of the 21st century, López Valdez was both the president of the *Cañeros* in Los Mochis, and the *Presidente Municipal*, the most important political office in his city.[24] López Valdez operated the team as though it were, in fact, part of his responsibilities as the local political boss. In addition to assembling the team roster, staff members with the *Cañeros* work on a variety of "community outreach" projects, many of which resemble state education programs.[25] In 2003, the team produced an education program involving print materials aimed at "enhancing the image of Mexico" among 1,200 school children in northern Sinaloa.[26] The team's General Manager, Antonio Castro, describes as "true assimilation" the relationship between team and local government:

> Here the team consists of—fortunately for us—around forty percent players from here in the region. From here in Los Mochis and from nearby *ejidos* and towns. When the team gets together [in the weeks before the start of the season each October] we visit rehabilitation centers, we visit local jails, we visit senior citizen assistance homes. This is the social work we do. We go to schools, elementary schools, and when the American players arrive, to bilingual schools. We attend social events, inaugurations, and awards ceremonies for local youth baseball.[27]

The *Cañeros* are, perhaps, an exception. The *Aguilas* in Mexicali and the *Naranjeros* in Hermosillo also have publicly visible team presidents who are deeply involved in local business, but neither of these teams is so obviously integrated with local government.

The emerging form of team ownership is that of the corporation. That large corporations now run half of the LMP teams reflects a larger trend in Mexico over the past two decades. Corporate ownership allows what would otherwise be relatively small local businesses to operate with the necessary financial backing to keep up with the constantly rising costs associated with professional baseball, particularly player salaries. But like other corporate operations in Mexico, particularly since the inception of the North American Free Trade Agreement in 1994, there is a high degree of anonymity involved with team ownership. Rather than having an individual face to connect with the owner, fans now generally associate ownership of, say the *Yaquis* of Ciudad Obregón, with the Modelo brewery.[28] By bankrolling the local baseball team, the brewery has unrestricted access to the marketing of its products at the stadium and on all team merchandise. In this light, Ley López in Culiacán represents somewhat of an anomaly. As owner of both the team and of the Ley chain of stores, his image remains directly connected to the successes and failures of the *Tomateros*. For other team administrators, maintaining a high publicity post with the team depends in large part on one's ability to maneuver within corporate politics.

For fans, placing importance on the existence of an LMP team has little to do with respect for the owner. There is a belief among the communities of northwestern Mexico that it is important to have a team in the *Liga del Pacífico* to maintain a certain level of civic pride. As Ronald Frankenberg argued in his study of Welsh communities near the border with England, regional and national leagues are important entities for generating community identity and pride.[29] If "other villages have teams," he writes, "it is considered that each important village should be represented in its local league in order to maintain its prestige."[30] Juan Aguirre, an executive with the *Naranjeros* club in Hermosillo expressed this same point by comparing the difference between his city and

Guaymas, the latter having lost its *Liga del Pacífico* team during the years of the peso collapse of the early 1980s:

> Really, it [the *Naranjeros*] is very symbolic for the community. The *Naranjeros* aren't just the *Naranjeros*. It's a sense of pride, especially for the kids, to wear the hat of the *Naranjeros*. If they go to the United States they go around with their hats on, or to somewhere else, with their jackets on. It's a symbol, a symbol of the community. . . . We went to Guaymas last October to play some exhibition games — Los Mochis, Obregon, and us, the *Naranjeros*. And *damn* the people are hungry for baseball there. That's how I imagine Hermosillo without the *Naranjeros*. A lost city.[31]

Aguirre realizes the symbolic importance of baseball, and more specifically the *Naranjeros*, for the youths of Hermosillo, particularly when they are away from the city. Youngsters, he suggests, proclaim their identity as *hermosillenses* when they are physically elsewhere, whether that be in some other part of Mexico or in the United States. Without such a symbol Aguirre feels, and he is not alone, that Hermosillo would be "lost" or somehow taken off a map of important places, as he apparently considers Guaymas to be.

Although the baseball season is relatively short — four months from October to January — the *Liga del Pacífico* plays an important role in providing a form of affordable entertainment for the residents of the eight cities in which it operates. The bright lights of the baseball stadium on a brisk December evening are beacons to people for miles around, announcing that the spectacle is under way. Rural baseball *aficionados* can make the drive in from their small towns or villages to see a game in one of these cities to cap off a day of shopping or conducting other business. Ticket prices start as low as 10 pesos, or roughly one U.S. dollar in almost all of the stadiums. This is less than it costs to see a film at a local cinema, making it a cheaper option for couples with children, or for groups of friends. It is certainly more affordable than attending concerts or plays in places like Mazatlán and Mexicali where large venues exist for such events. If professional soccer is played in one of these cities it is, with the exception of Culiacán, of a lesser quality, and certainly without the historical local importance attached to baseball. For those children who play baseball, the *Naranjeros*, *Tomateros*, and other teams represent upward mobility. In the sense that the game is globalized — played and watched by millions — these teams also represent modernity as well. People form opinions about the places in which they live based upon the opportunities available or lacking there. Many residents of the cities of the *Liga del Pacífico* make the symbolic connection, as Juan Aguirre does, between baseball and the qualities of a culturally diverse, desirable place in which to live.

A Struggle for Regional and National Identity

Among narratives that suggest the more populated center of the country "has more" than do the hinterlands of the northwest, especially when it comes to cultural activities, baseball is a regional asset. Given the *Liga del Pacífico's* unique niche as the circuit that provides Mexico's national representative at the *Serie del Caribe*, baseball gives residents of the northwest something to claim that they *do* have—something which the more economically and politically powerful south, does not. In short, people in Mexico's northwest struggle with national narratives placing themselves at the periphery, and Mexico City at the center.

So, what role does sport play in fostering differences and/or similarities between center and periphery? The theory of sports as a national unifier has its practical limits. Lever's study on soccer in Brazil demonstrated that the state and the economically powerful supported the game because they realized its potential to bring the masses together for common national purposes.[32] Soccer's "divide-and-unify role" not only pits people of the same nationality against one another when their competing clubs meet on the field, it also allows people of similar backgrounds to come together for games and social events that accompany the operation of a club team in Brazil.[33] At the same time, all Brazilians, from all backgrounds, are able to enjoy the successes of the national team on the international stage.[34] But if we understand national integration to mean a more equal distribution of opportunities for education and health care, of employment, or of standards of living, then the daily realities of poverty and marginalization which manifest the differences between center and periphery will not be solved through sport.

The structure of professional baseball in Mexico suggests that the sport works to undermine a unified sense of national identity. In the northwestern states, attendance at baseball games dwarf those of soccer.[35] In most of the northwestern cities like Hermosillo and Mexicali, baseball is the only professional spectator sport of importance. This is not to say that soccer is not important in these communities, for the game is most certainly followed throughout all of Mexico. But baseball allows the northwest to set itself aside from the rest of the country when it comes to professional sports. Not only does the winner of the LMP represent all of Mexico at the *Serie del Caribe*, but a majority of the game's best players come from states in the border region. Baseball's unique place in the minds of northwestern Mexicans parallels the regional difference that has always existed between the center of the country and its northern periphery.

People in the northwest have adopted their own narratives about the differences between their region and the rest of Mexico, through sport. Having seen many newcomers to Ciudad Obregón over six decades, baseball writer Alfonso Araujo Bojórquez contends that people from Mexico City undergo a sort of sports transformation when they move to Sonora:

A lot of people that I know that have come here from the center of the country, they get here, and because there is no football, well, they have to go to baseball games. Then, they tell me, "Look, I didn't like baseball when I was there [Mexico City], but now that I'm here now I don't like soccer."

Or they'll say, "I like soccer as much as baseball." In other words, baseball gains followers here simply because it has always been the number one sport.[36]

The idea that baseball is somehow ingrained in the very fabric of society in the northwestern states — native to it — is evident in phrases like "has always been the number one sport." There are clearly two sides to the struggle over one's sports identities: football and its Mexico City connotations, or baseball and its ties to the northwestern states. Araujo maintains that once in the northwestern states, those from the capital and other parts of central Mexico recognize the merits of baseball when compared to soccer. They either prefer soccer or place it on even par with their newly adopted game, baseball. Regardless of that choice, Araujo (and apparently his friends too) make the distinction between the northwestern states and the center of Mexico through sports.

A distinct northwestern regional identity and the competing ideas about what constitutes Mexican national identity are further complicated by the region's proximity to the United States. The northwestern states are situated between two domineering cultural entities: the one that generates images of Mexican nationalism from Mexico City, and the English-speaking American colossus to the north. Essentially a globalized game, baseball has nevertheless served to reinforce regional interests and regional identities in northwestern Mexico. In large part this is due to the structure of the international baseball calendar, which has propelled Latin America's winter leagues to the forefront of non-U.S. baseball. By claiming the highest rank of winter baseball in Mexico, the northwest — as a region — has placed itself on par with three countries that compete for the annual *Serie del Caribe*. When people who attend this event refer to the Mexican team, they are talking about a city in Mexico's northwest. This may be of little significance to the Dominicans and Puerto Ricans, whose leagues tend to be spread out geographically over those island countries. But for those of northwestern Mexico, the *Serie del Caribe* represents a chance to display both their distinctly northwestern culture and their pride in representing the country as a whole. The Mexican delegation usually includes *banda* musicians and large *sombreros* and signs made for the television crews, bidding hello to friends and family in Sonora, Sinaloa, or Baja California.[37] National pride is on the line for the four countries participating in this international event, but for Mexico there is an added ingredient: a chance to parade regional pride.

The International Pastime

Baseball and other modern sports serve as useful venues to watch the processes of globalization. On a given day in 2009, a Japanese star will pitch for Boston, a Venezuelan will play in Japan, Americans will bat for Dominican teams, a Panamanian will take infield in Mexico, and Dominicans will play for a team based in Canada. Equipment is made in the United States, China, and Japan. Games are broadcast all over the world via satellite in a variety of languages. Players from one country are bought and sold through overseas phone conversations, faxes, and e-mail. The game exemplifies the dealings of the international marketplace and the generation of transnational ways of thinking and being.

Today, the LMP and other Latin American winter leagues operate under a set of rules and restrictions set forth by American baseball organizers. By maintaining leverage over its contracted players who take part in the Latin American winter leagues, Major League teams can dictate who can play in Latin American leagues. They are essentially protecting their investments abroad. The LMP operates with an "import rule" which determines how many foreign-born players each team can keep on its roster. Theoretically, only the teams themselves would lower the number. The percentage of import players in all professional sports in Mexico is regulated by the national government.[38] In baseball, these players are almost always Americans. The number of *extranjeros* in the LMP has fluctuated between no limits and the present level, six. Fans are acutely aware of the names and Major League contract status of the six foreign players on their teams.[39] However much league and team executives may want to increase the number of imports on each club to enhance the reputation of the league, they nevertheless adhere to state regulations and maintain their import limits as a way to protect space on Mexican teams for Mexican players.[40] The international quality of the sport is still guarded closely by American capitalists and Mexican government authorities who monitor and regulate the game.

The state, in fact, has found two ways to maintain an important role in Mexican baseball: stadium facilities, and control over players' contracts. When the *Liga del Pacífico* signed an agreement with Major League Baseball in the early 1970s to allow players under big league contracts to play in Mexico, teams found themselves scrambling to make stadium improvements mandated in the new contract. Local and state governments came to their collective rescue. In four cities, entirely new stadiums were built with government money.[41] At other stadiums, state governments paid for extensive renovations. Sonora's governor used the opportunity to promote the game statewide, not only building new facilities for the professional teams in Hermosillo, Ciudad Obregón, and Navajoa, but also building more than 100 new diamonds in towns and cities throughout the state.[42] Stadium construction and financial support for smaller local ball fields were promoted in terms of the positive qualities of baseball for communities in the state.

In terms of player contracts, the Mexican government has sided with team owners in Mexico's summer league to make it more unlikely that the country will lose all of its top players to Major League Baseball. Unlike in the Dominican Republic and Venezuela, where Major League teams have built training facilities and sign hundreds of teenagers per year, or in Puerto Rico, where young players are subject to the U.S. amateur draft, young Mexican players usually start their careers at the nation's player development academy near Monterrey.[43] Unless an American scout has found him before the age of 18, a player in Mexico reports to the national academy and is eventually distributed through a draft to one of Mexico's professional teams, which will then hold the rights to that player. Should a Major League team want to acquire him, it would have to buy the contract from his Mexican team. This arrangement has in turn led to the escalation of signing bonuses being demanded by Mexican players who are under the age of 18 and who do come into contact with U.S. scouts. José Carlos Campos, a baseball writer in Culiacán, claims that the average Mexican teenage recruit is asking for five times the signing bonus that a prospect from the Dominican Republic demands.[44] State support for this player contract scenario suggests that the state views baseball players as national commodities, not to be sold away easily. Even in the highly profitable world of baseball, the Mexican government has found ways to counter the powerful forces of the global marketplace.

Conclusion

Baseball stadiums are social gathering places in northwestern Mexico, and the teams that play in them are sources of both civic and regional pride. Team owners, large corporations, and other advertisers all recognize this quality. There is a bond between members of the community who choose to spend their time and money at the ballpark, and "the product" itself, the group of men who wear the uniform of the local team. Businessmen and large corporations in the northwestern states have capitalized on this bond, staking their investment dollars on promotion of professional baseball. By doing so, they exert high degrees of influence on local and regional culture, and the ways in which people think about themselves and their community through baseball.

The state, too, has recognized the significance of the game. Since the 1930s, when the ruling party in Mexico pinned its name on a local baseball team in Hermosillo, the state's involvement in baseball remained steady. Gone are the days of naming stadiums after the heroes of the Mexican Revolution, or after the Revolution itself. But the stadium construction and renovation boom of the early 1970s made it clear that the state was still involved. Government money paid for most of the construction costs, and it was obvious that team executives shared close relations with those politicians who made sure the money was available. In LMP cities, the state provides for baseball when local friendships and business relationships necessitate such involvement. There is, then, still a role for the state to play in the staging of professional baseball in countries like Mexico. State involvement fosters a sense of nationalism where it may be under threat, as in the Mexican northwest.

In many Latin American countries, namely Argentina and Brazil, soccer dominates the headlines of sports pages, leaving little room for the other professional sports that vie for attention in those countries. It is not this way in Mexico. A mix of geographic, political, and economic realities created two spheres: the larger one in which soccer *does* dominate, and a smaller regional one where baseball is "king." To complicate matters, and to make them that much more interesting, the region in question is essentially a border zone where ecologies, economies, cultures, and identities are shared. In Sinaloa, Sonora, and Baja California, not only are personal and local identities tied up in the act of playing or watching professional sports, but also an entire regional identity is expressed through the popularity of baseball vis-à-vis soccer in the rest of the country. This, in turn, undermines beliefs in an all-encompassing Mexican identity to which all Mexicans adhere. Deeply rooted in the political, economic, and cultural history of the area, baseball speaks to a series of identity formation processes. Like the country itself, all of these identities — personal, local, regional, national, border, consumer, gender, racial — are contested, often times contradictory, and in constant change.

Notes

1. Interview with Jose Carlos Campos, columnist with *El Debate de Culiacán* and Operations Manager with *los Tomateros de Culiacán*. Conducted at Culiacán, Sinaloa, 5 November 2003. Translations of all Spanish-language interviews, and primary and secondary sources, are the author's.

2. Ramon Eduardo Ruíz. *The People of Sonora and Yankee Capitalists*. Tucson: University of Arizona Press, 1988, pp. 7–25.

3. Alan M. Klein. *Baseball on the Border: A Tale of Two Laredos*. Princeton: Princeton University Press, 1994, pp. 6–7.

4. Sergio Ortega Noriega. *Breve Historia de Sinaloa*. México, D.F.: Fideicomiso Historia de la Américas, 1999, p. 257; Ramon Eduardo Ruíz. *Triumphs and Tragedy: A History of the Mexican People*. New York: W.W. Norton & Company, 1992, p. 283.

5. T. D. Proffitt, III. *Tijuana: The History of a Mexican Metropolis*. San Diego: San Diego State University, 1994, p. 153.

6. Ruíz, *Triumphs and Tragedy*, p. 281.

7. Michael A.J. Ard. *An Eternal Struggle: How the National Action Party Transformed Mexican Politics*. Westport, CT: Praeger, 2003, pp. 21–93.

8. Mexico's premier soccer league did not have a team located in the northwestern states until the summer of 2004, when the Culiacán *Dorados* advanced, only to be relegated the following season.

9. This refers to the "Winter League Agreements," a set of contracts between Major League Baseball and the Latin American winter leagues in Mexico, Puerto Rico, Venezuela and the Dominican Republic. The agreements, slightly modified each season if at all, have, since the early 1970s, regulated the participation of players under Major League contracts playing in Latin America during the U.S. off-season.

10. For a summary of the selection process for the Mexican team that participated in the 2003

Serie del Caribe see Notimex news story of 30 January 2003 at "Beisbol Professional" web site: <http://www.beisbolprofessional.net/bp0173.htm> Viewed 1 March 2003.

11. Cuba represents the extreme example of this. Cuban players who decide to leave the island to play in the Major Leagues do so with the understanding that they may very well be leaving Cuba for good. Cuba stopped participating in the Serie del Caribe shortly after the Castro Revolution in 1959, and has been excluded from organized American baseball ever since.

12. Pierre Bourdieu, "How can one be a sports fan?" In Simon During (Ed.), *The Cultural Studies Reader*. London: Routledge, 1993, pp. 339–356. Italics in original.

13. Susan Brownell. *Training the Body for China: Sports in the Moral Order of the People's Republic*. Chicago: University of Chicago Press, 1995, pp. 10–11.

14. August Comte, "The Positive Philosophy. In Carlos B. Gil (Ed.). *The Age of Porfirio Díaz: Selected Readings*. Albuquerque: University of New Mexico Press, 1977, pp. 45–48.

15. William H. Beezley. *Judas at the Jockey Club and Other Episodes of Porfirian Mexico*. Lincoln: University of Nebraska Press, 1987, p. 14.

16. William H. Beezley, "The Rise of Baseball in Mexico and the First Valenzuela." *Studies in Latin American Popular Culture*. v. 4, (1985), pp. 3–13.

17. Albert G. Spalding. *Baseball: America's National Game, 1839–1915*. 1911. Reprint. San Francisco: Halo Books, 1991, p. 9.

18. Angel Encinas Blanco. *El Beisbol en Hermosillo*. Hermosillo: Editora Voz de Sonora, 1999, pp. 87–88.

19. John Hargreaves. *Sport, Power, and Culture: A Social and Historical Analysis of Popular Sports in Britain*. Cambridge: Polity Press, 1986, p. 13.

20. Almost all of the Liga del Pacífico teams

have between-inning dances performed by provocatively dressed young women, usually in clothing that advertises beer, but sometimes in thematic style dress.

21. Janet Lever. *Soccer Madness*. Chicago: University of Chicago Press, 1983, pp. 8–9, 145–154.

22. Interview with José Carlos Campos, conducted at Culiacán, Sinaloa, 5 November 2003. See also "Historia de Tomateros de Culiacán" on the Tomateros web site: <http://www.tomater os.com.mx/historia/default.asp>. Viewed 9 October 2003.

23. Jesee W. Markham and Paul V. Telpitz. *Baseball Economics and Public Policy*. Lexington, MA: Lexington Books, 1981, pp. 26–27. Baseball owners maintain strict privacy about their supposed losses. Markham and Teplitz, whose work was commissioned by the U.S. government to offer lawmakers a reference guide for dealing with the economics of baseball, obtained information from only a handful of owners of Major League teams. See also Rich Schultz. *El Rey de los Deportes: A History of Baseball in Northwestern Mexico*. M.A. Thesis. La Jolla: University of California San Diego, 2004, pp. 141–144. Juan Manuel Ley López invokes Mexican privacy laws to keep him from stating what the Tomateros and his summer league team, the Saraperos actually earn or lose each season. The public in Mexico has no way of knowing whether his baseball franchises are money makers, or money losers.

24. Interview with Antonio Castro Chavez, General Manager of the *Cañeros* of Los Mochis. Conducted at Los Mochis, Sinaloa, 11 November 2003.

25. Interview with Antonio Castro Chavez, 11 November 2003.

26. Interview with Antonio Castro Chavez, 11 November 2003.

27. Interview with Antonio Castro Chavez, 11 November 2003.

28. Interview with Alfonso Araujo Bojórquez, columnist and baseball historian. Conducted at Ciudad Obregón, Sonora, 13 November 2003.

29. Ronald Frankenberg. *Village on the Border: A Social Study of Religion, Politics, and Football in a North Wales Community*. London: Cohen and West, 1957.

30. Ibid., p. 101.

31. Interview with Juan Aguirre, Public Relations Director for the *Naranjeros* of Hermosillo. Conducted at Hermosillo, Sonora, 13 November 2003.

32. Lever, *Soccer Madness*, pp. 8–9, 145–154.

33. Ibid.

34. Ibid.

35. Of cities in the LMP, only Culiacán enjoys high levels of fan support for both baseball and soccer. Crowds for both sports usually top 10,000 per game.

36. Interview with Alfonso Araujo Bojórquez, conducted at Ciudad Obregón, Sonora, 13 November 2003.

37. This is based on observations made by the author while watching television coverage of the Serie del Caribe from 2003, when the event was held in Puerto Rico, to 2009, when Mexicali hosted.

38. David G. LaFrance, "Labor, the State, and Professional Baseball in Mexico in the 1980s" in Joseph L. Arbena and David G. LaFrance, eds. *Sport in Latin America and the Caribbean*. Wilmington, DE: Scholarly Resources, Inc., 2002, pp. 89–115. See p. 109.

39. It is not unusual to enter into discussions with Mexican baseball fans who are highly aware of which Major League clubs had signed both foreign-born and Mexican players, not only on their local team, but also with regard to the players on other teams.

40. Interview with Oviel Dennis, General Manager of the Liga Mexicana del Pacífico. Conducted at Culiacán, Sinaloa, 10 November 2003.

41. Interview with Alfonso Araujo Bojórquez, conducted at Ciudad Obregón, Sonora, 13 November 2003.

42. "Reconocimiento del Beisbol Mexicano al Gobernador Faustino Felix Serna." *El Imparcial* (Hermosillo). 27 Feb. 1971, p. A4.

43. José Carlos Campos, "Justicia para los mas valiosos." *El Debate de Culiacán*. 5 Nov. 2003, p. 8-B; Interview with José Carlos Campos, conducted at Culiacán, Sinaloa, 5 November 2003.

44. Interview with José Carlos Campos, conducted at Culiacán, Sinaloa, 5 November 2003.

15

US AND THEM: AUSTRALIAN PROFESSIONAL SPORT AND RESISTANCE TO NORTH AMERICAN OWNERSHIP AND MARKETING MODELS

John Nauright and Murray G. Phillips

This chapter was written at a time of great turmoil in Australian sport as media companies competed for market share in the pay television market with varying degrees of impact on Australian sporting codes. The main features of Australian sport remain similar with the four football codes in winter and the sport of cricket in summer dominating the sporting landscape both in terms of spectators and television coverage. Women's sport has followed some of the trends in men's sport including the formation of a Trans-Tasman league in netball with teams from Australia and New Zealand competing. Women's sport is still marginal in comparison to men's, however.

Even though there have been shifts in the political economy of professional sport from the dominant platform of broadcast television to the Internet, the prediction that "Super League" would transfer ownership models in Rugby League has been fulfilled. News Limited, as a consequence of a merging "Super League" with the pre-existing competition to form the National Rugby League (NRL), has a controlling interest on the board of the NRL, ownership of at least three teams, and pay television rights for a quarter of a century, as well as print media and sponsorship in many aspects of the game. By contrast, Australian football largely has not been privatized and ownership overwhelmingly remains with the state-based institutions, clubs, and members in part to resist takeover by global media interests. Alternative models of organization and ownership do exist and these can in some instances preserve a greater sense of democracy in sport.

Australian Sport

When Rupert Murdoch's News Limited Corporation brought almost one half of the rugby league clubs in Australia in 1995, under the concept "Super League," it created the biggest turmoil in the game's 90-year history. The fight between the Australian Rugby League (ARL), the traditional organizers of the game, and Murdoch's "Super League" has been a battle that has pitted player against player, club against club, city against city, state against state,

Table 1. Attendance at Sports in Australia (1994–95)

Sport	Persons	Percentage of National Population Attending Particular Sports
Australian rules	1,874,200	13.3
Horse racing	1,701,100	12.1
Rugby league	1,462,100	10.4
Cricket	1,165,900	8.3
Basketball	691,600	4.9
Harness racing	599,700	4.3
Soccer	558,800	4.0
Motor sports	451,500	3.2
Tennis	431,700	3.1
Rugby union	358,400	2.5
Netball	312,300	2.2

Source: Australian Bureau of Statistics, *Sports Attendance*, March 1995, Commonwealth of Australia.

country against country, pay-television operator against pay television opera-tor, phone company against phone company, and media mogul against media mogul. Most important, it represents the largest challenge to the traditional organizational model of Australian sport. Australian professional sport con-sists primarily of cricket in the summer months along with an American minor league standard baseball competition. Cricket has a national competition that is played among six states in both forms of more traditional 4- and 5-day cricket and the immensely popular 1-day version of the game. From this structure, a national team competes against other nations—England, India, New Zealand, Pakistan, Sri Lanka, and Zimbabwe—in regular 5-day test match series, 1-day competitions, and a quadrennial World Cup played in the 1-day format. Traditional 5-day cricket is suffering in terms of attractiveness to television, sponsors, and spectators; 1-day cricket is excelling in all three market areas and provides the financial fillip for the game overall. Baseball, on the other hand, is structured slightly different from cricket with private franchises in most state capital cities and a national competition that promotes city-based parochialisms. Baseball has a long history in Australia, but the national com-petition is only relatively young and is struggling to mount a serious challenge to cricket as the premiere summer sport (Dabscheck, 1995). In fact, the game does not rank in the top 11 sports in Australia (see Table 1).

During the winter months, three football codes and basketball compete against each other in the spectator sport market. The winter football codes are known as Australian rules football; rugby league; and rugby union. Australia is unique in having four different football codes that are all viable spectator sports; however, soccer has switched its season to the summer in the hopes of attracting more spectators.

Historically, Australian rules football has been centered on the southern states of Victoria, South Australia, and Tasmania and the western state of Western Australia. Each state had major competitions in its capital city with the Victorian Football League (VFL) based in Melbourne conducting the most prestigious and successful competition in Australia. The VFL has expanded since the 1980s and now, as the Australian Football League (AFL), runs a competition with 5 single-city teams in addition to the 11 original clubs from Melbourne and surrounding areas (Linnell, 1995). Australian football attracts more spectators than does any other sport in the country (see Table 1). AFL Grand Finals always draw capacity crowds of nearly 100,000 to the Melbourne Cricket Ground.

Rugby league has some structural similarities with Australian football. Based in New South Wales and Queensland in two major separate competitions, the Sydney-based competition, like its Melbourne counterpart, has expanded since the 1980s. Two key differences with Australian football are that the rugby league competition is not truly national, with teams from only three states, but it has an international dimension. Since 1995, the Auckland Warriors club from New Zealand has competed in the domestic competition, and for most of this century international matches have been regularly held against Great Britain, New Zealand, and France. The game's international component, albeit limited, as well as an immensely popular interstate series that has television ratings comparable to those of the Super Bowl in the United States, has boosted league's marketing, merchandising, and sponsorship potential (Heads, 1992).

Ironically, soccer, the football code with a massive global following and the largest participation base in Australia, does not enjoy equivalent popularity in the domestic spectator market (see Table 1). There are competitions in major cities and at the state and at the national level, and Australian teams have been quite successful internationally, but the game has not displaced the cultural centrality of Australian rules and rugby league. Soccer's single most defining feature is the support provided by so-called ethnic communities, who principally arrived in Australia as part of the post-World War II migration program; and at the present time the game's administration, in order to widen appeal and increase sponsorship and marketing, has ordered clubs to remove all vestiges of their ethnic heritage (Mosely, 1994).

Rugby union is more international than rugby league, with the Rugby World Cup now rated as the fourth largest international sporting event in terms of estimated television audience, yet not on a scale anywhere comparable to soccer. Union, like league is seriously played only in the states of New South Wales, Queensland, and in the Australian Capital Territory surrounding the national capital of Canberra, and it has failed to gain major followings in the Australian rules states. In the southern hemisphere, however, rugby union has benefited from a large injection of finance from Rupert Murdoch's media interests, which purchased television rights in Australia as well as in South Africa and New Zealand in 1995. The consequence of Rupert Murdoch's investment is an expanded provincial series called the Super Twelve between the top provincial (state) teams in Australia, New Zealand, and South Africa and a new annual home-and-away Tri-Nation series among the national sides of these countries, each of which has captured one of the three Rugby World Cups held in 1987, 1991, and 1995. Almost overnight the game moved from "shamateur" to full professional status, and commercial sponsors have welcomed the increased profile offered by regular international contests (Fitzsimons, 1996).

Basketball is one of the fastest growing sports in Australia (Harris, 1992). From a low profile sport with city-centered competitions and small parochial followings up until 1980, when the National Basketball League was established, basketball in1995 was the fifth most attended sport in Australia (see Table 1). Its main appeal is that it is perceived to be a family activity, and—unlike the rugby codes, soccer, and cricket, where twice as many males attend as females—it is one sport, along with Australian rules football, in which as many females go to games as males (Australian Bureau of Statistics, 1995). Basketball is ideally suited for television but, it should be noted, the game has not attained the rating successes that characterized Australian rules and rugby league. Basketball will move to the summer season to lessen competition with the football codes and to link more closely with the National Basketball Association season in North America.

Women's sports suffer under the hegemony of the male professional sports culture. There are national competitions in basketball, hockey, and netball, which has a massive participation base superior to that of most football codes and a substantial spectator base (see Table 1); but television, sponsorship, and marketing cannot be compared to male counterparts. Olympic success in softball, basketball, and hockey and near-perennial world champion status in netball are starting to generate a positive economic cycle. Nevertheless, there are no female sports that regularly feature on commercial television; in fact, they are restricted to funding their own shows on the government-owned Australian Broadcasting Corporation channel, the largest commercial sponsors—alcohol, computers, and communication companies—are uninterested, and there is no merchandising on the scale that exists in male sports (Stell, 1991).

Public Verses Private Ownership

One common link among nearly all sports—male and female—in Australia is their organizational structure as they are predominantly based on a form of public ownership. Privatization has occurred in baseball, where clubs are aligned with North American major league teams, and to a lesser extent in basketball, but the majority of Australian spectator sports—cricket, soccer, Australian rules football, rugby league, rugby union, and netball—are organized around membership-based clubs. As a general rule members of clubs democratically elect officers who act, in many cases, on a voluntary basis and who hire the appropriate professionals such as marketers, accountants, and administrators to manage affairs. This system gives members some control over major decisions and ensures club committees and employees ultimately are accountable to their constituents. Beyond the clubs are leagues and associations that administer the competitions at local, state, national, and international levels. These organizations are staffed by professionals with the expertise to manage modern spectator-oriented sports. Integral to this professionalization of sport administration has been growing government involvement in sport since the 1970s (Cashman, 1995).

A more rare form of public ownership in Australia is a combination of membership and shareholding, such as the North Melbourne Australian Football club. In order to save this club from its financial demise, shares were floated in 1986. Although there were some problems with financing and the share float, the stipulation was that no shareholder or group of shareholders could own more than 10% of the shares (Linnell, 1995). Thus, the North Melbourne agreement has some similarities with that of the Green Bay Packers of the National Football league (NFL) in the USA. The Packers are the only publicly owned team in the NFL, and the club has 90% of its 1,800 shareholders who own the 4,700 shares of stock living in the Green Bay area. No shareholder may own more than 200 shares, thus ensuring broad public control of the team (Sage, 1990). The Green Bay model is one more closely aligned to Australian sport because the franchise is geographically fixed and fans have some financial and decision-making stake in the team. Beyond that shared trait, Green Bay functions no differently from the other franchises that rely on the NFL's administration to market and promote the game; local teams do very little marketing. In regard to Australian teams, local marketing is crucial, yet with varying degrees of applicability, sports administrators of national leagues promote at the national level. As a result, there is immense competition between teams in close geographical proximity to secure sponsors and capital, and to attract spectators.

In regard to both systems of public ownership of Australian sport—membership based and shareholders—there is an inbuilt mechanism of accountability and responsibility to members and fans. Two recent examples at the St. George Football Club (rugby league) and the Footscray Football Club (Australian rules) highlight this trait. The St. George Football Club was established in the southern suburbs of Sydney in 1921 and has a very proud tradition based on a remarkable record of success—11 straight championships from 1956 through 1966—in the premier competition in Sydney. In July 1995, the elected board proposed a merger with another Sydney club, the Sydney City Roosters, for a host of essentially economic reasons. There was very little consultation with members, and a group of supporters, appropriately named "Save Our Saints" (SOS for short), was established to fight the merger proposal. Ultimately, the merger ceased because the club committee was threatened with a no-confidence motion that would have required fresh elections and the likelihood of a new committee.

Although Footscray's history is very different from that of St. George — only one VFL championship in 1954 — it provides a classic example of supporter power in Australia. In early October 1989, the Footscray Bulldogs and Fitzroy Lions Boards, with AFL Backing, announced that the two historic clubs were to merge and become the Fitzroy Bulldogs. The Footscray board announced this without full consultation with club members. Some board members who were involved with the "Save the Dogs" Committee were also kept in the dark about merger details. Footscray was in deep financial trouble, and AFL officials intimated that they would not renew the club's operating license for 1990 unless it merged. The result was a massive campaign by Footscray supporters and those of other clubs to save the team. Footscray is the only AFL club located in Melbourne's western suburbs, an area with a population of around one million people. The Save the Dogs Committee took the league and the Footscray board to court and won a stay of execution. The AFL gave them 3 weeks to raise the $1.5 million needed for the 1990 season. Volunteers walked the streets hour after hour, some pensioners gave their last savings to help the club, and money poured in from all over Australia, ultimately saving Footscray from the merger.

The underlying principal in the Footscray case was that the board and the AFL had violated the concept of the fair go. The fair go concept basically means that it is socially unacceptable for any one person or group to openly undertake unfair actions against another group of people. Although the fair go, along with the concept of mateship, has served to gloss over many injustices in Australian society, these concepts nonetheless represent an almost sacred code of public behavior. In addition, Footscray represented a truly working-class community and club that was under attack from the suit-wearing, private-school-educated officials of the AFL. These cases (and others) show that, although it is important not to ignore power relationships within membership clubs, the elected committee is ultimately accountable, and members have some real controlled over shaping the future of their football teams (Nauright & Phillips, 1996).

Against this organizational backdrop, the football codes have experimented with private ownership. This is perhaps not surprising when placed in the wider societal context in Australia. First, such experimentation is in line with the general trend toward privatization of government utilities in Australia. Over the last two decades, federal, state, and local governments have increasingly sold major public assets like banks, financial institutions, airlines, and more recently, communication companies and airports. As much as both sides of government, conservative and labor, have embraced privatization, sport on the whole has not, though, many administrators make annual trips to North America to meet with marketers and managers of professional franchises and leagues. Second, Australian sport has adopted, and modified, many of the themes, principles, and strategies that typify American sport (McKay & Miller, 1991). Consider some of the recent trends in Australian sports consumption: Australians all over the country wear T-shirts displaying images of American teams, most notably the Chicago Bulls, Charlotte Hornets, and Orlando Magic from basketball; the San Jose Sharks from ice hockey (played by very few people in Australia); stars such as Michael Jordan and Shaquille O'Neal; and brand names with Nike and Reebok predominating. Three American practices that are becoming the most pronounced are the wearing of baseball caps, the selling of sports trading cards, and the adoption of American names like Magic, Heat, Flames, Giants, Blades, and even Cowboys for Australian teams (McKay, Miller, & Rowe, 1996). Cowboys is the most intriguing when there is an Australian equivalent, the jackaroo, yet the North Queensland rugby league chose the American version.

Show business formats that comprise live entertainment, displays of various forms, team mascots, and cheerleaders have become common practice, even now in the staid game of cricket. The impact on Australian sport has been substantial; most notably, Australian grand final matches in football codes resemble cheaper version of Super Bowl-style extravaganzas (McKay, Miller, & Rowe, 1993). The ARL's precursor, the New South Wales Rugby League (NSWRL), employed Tina Turner to promote the game to a wider audience in the late 1980s and early 1990s in campaigns that integrated Anglo-Celtic heritage with multicultualism, re-packaged masculinity, and portrayed footballers as dedicated professional athletes (Yeates, 1995). Similarly, American personalities such as George Burns, Carl Lewis, and John McEnroe have been used in marketing campaigns for Australian rules football. Although American cultural imperialism is not totally responsible for all these features, sports in Australia are also influenced by the process of globalization; there are local interpretations and adaptions that make advertising and marketing more palatable for Australian audiences (Rowe, Lawrence, Miller, & McKay, 1994). Cultural aspects of American sport have been replicated or adjusted to suit local conditions in Australia, but most importantly, economic components, like privatization, have met with little success.

Australian rules football dabbled at first with franchises as part of a process of developing business orientation within the VFL. From 1968 club members could not enter away matches for free, and reserved seating and private boxes began to appear. Sponsorships began with a clothing company's $40,000 deal with Collingwood in 1977, and in the 1980s, a commission replaced the old league administrative structures. By the early 1980s, the VFL looked to expand to other states. Sydney was targeted first. In order to get a team in Sydney (Australia's largest market with nearly 4 million people), however, the VFL chose to move the weakest of the Victorian clubs, South Melbourne. Pascoe (1995) argues that the VFL misread the nature of the Australian sporting market when they supported the South Melbourne move to Sydney to become a privately owned enterprise, the Sydney Swans.

The move to Sydney and the creation of the Sydney Swans have been a financial drain for the Australian Football League (AFL) and its predecessor, the VFL, as the league has poured much capital into the new venture. Furthermore, the Swans have been an organizational nightmare as the flirtation with private ownership has failed twice and damaged the credibility of the game in a non-Australian football market. Since the Sydney Swans, new teams have been added as the game has been deliberately decentered out of Melbourne and expanded into other Australian states. Only one of the expansion teams, the West Coast Eagles from Perth, was publicly floated on the stock market, and this club's subsequent success has negated some of the Swans' legacy (Linnell, 1995). The Brisbane Bears, established in 1987, however, had many of the same problems as the Swans. Its first owner went bankrupt, and the second lost $5 million before the league and the state government stepped in to relocate the team to a new ground and to revert the club's organizational model (Linnell, 1995). Both Sydney and Brisbane are now very successful under the new model.

Before the West Coast Eagles were established, however, many people in Perth opposed the entry of a Western Australian team into the VFL as they, quite rightly, felt that the Eagles would lead to a decline in attendances at Western Australian Football League matches (Mulcahy, 1993). In Brisbane, similar concerns were raised when the Brisbane Broncos joined the NSWRL in 1988. Local Queensland Rugby League matches, which drew over 30,000 fans for grand finals, now draw much smaller attendances. The national sporting league model was opposed for the effects it would have not only on local teams but also on the shift of local power to the larger centers of Sydney and Melbourne. Australia resisted the move to a national professional sports league model much longer than did other countries; thus, the process of nationalization and globalization have combined to dramatically alter Australian professional sport over the last decade.

The experiment with private ownership in rugby league was at least successful as the West Coast Eagles' experience in Australian rules football. The Brisbane Broncos, admitted in 1988, viewed and organized their affairs from a radically different standpoint than those of competing membership-based clubs. The Broncos are owned and organized by a small group of businessmen who employ people with expertise outside sport in the parent disciplines of management, advertising, and marketing. Bill Walker (1996), the Public Relations Manager of the Broncos, summarized the club's beginnings;

> It was agreed by the four owners that as a commercial venture, the Broncos organization should be run as a business, with a sound business plan in place and a vision for the future. The club had to be structured from the ground up; with no example to follow, we borrowed ideas from already existing franchises in the United States and England to help form

the basis of our operation. It was the American model that impressed us most; the USA leads the way in sports administration and the lessons we learnt from them were invaluable. Their aggressive marketing and promotion of the game we have concentrated on with great effect. (p. 211)

With these ideas in place the Brisbane NSWRL/ARL franchise prospered. The Broncos enjoyed a one-city monopoly for 7 years until 1995. They are serviced by a compliant and recipient local newspaper (owned by Murdoch's News Limited) that is also a major sponsor of the club, and they have parochial support based on a history of antipathy between two eastern coast states, New South Wales and Queensland. Not surprisingly, the Broncos are the most successful club in rugby league in terms of spectator support (drawing three to seven times the average of Sydney-based clubs) and financial backing, and they provide the best example of sport designed for capital accumulation in Australia.

Murdoch's "Super League"

The broncos brought the "Super League" idea to News Limited in 1994, though this has been obscured in the Australian media coverage that has viewed "Super League" as a Murdoch-led raid on an Australian institution. Ken Cowley, head of News Limited's Australian operations, met with Ken Arthurson of the ARL over possible sponsorship and argued that if they were going to spend $60 million on rugby league, News Limited wanted some control over the game. The ARL rejected the proposal (Mascord, 1996). The Brisbane approach happened to appear at the right time when enough clubs and players were disillusioned with the Sydney-based hierarchy and its control of the game. News Limited became convinced that rugby league was an ideal sport to generate subscriptions for their pay-television operations in Australia, Britain, and Asia.

The acquisition of popular sports, like league, for media interests is a common tactic. For example, Rupert Murdoch, who has a major share in BskyB, a satellite television in Britain, purchased the rights to televise English Premier League Soccer in order to boost the station's flagging fortunes. In addition, he successfully concluded a deal with the British Rugby League to establish "Super League" in Europe with BskyB and Murdoch's European stations showing matches. With similar objectives, Murdoch's Fox Broadcasting Company purchased the rights to televise the NFC Conference of the NFL in 1993 and then the rights to televise the National Hockey League and Major League Baseball. Rugby league, by virtue of pay television, has become part of the establishment of global media sports, and domestically league is inextricably bound to the struggle for dominance between two rival consortiums, Foxtel (an alliance between Newscorp and Telstra) and Optus Vision (an alliance between Optus Communications, Continental Cable Communications, and an Australian company, Kerry Packer's Publishing and Broadcasting, which also owns one of the three commercial television networks, Channel 9). Foxtel wanted league to help launch its service, but Optus, through its partnership with Packer's Channel 9, owned the rights until a fierce battle between these rival pay-television consortiums that has divided the game and its followers (Phillips & Hutchins, 1996). The ensuring struggle resulted in attendances declining sharply in late 1995 and in 1996. After one court case, that effectively outlawed "Super League," and then a subsequent successful appeal, "Super League" will run an alternative competition to the ARL from 1997.

In many ways, the media scuffle and the debate about the inflated wages of the players, the threatened existence of the historic clubs, the creation of new clubs, and the disruption of the Sydney power base have overshadowed some of the fundamental changes to sport organization that underpin Murdoch's assault. The "Super League" version of rugby league is essentially a model of privately owned franchises run for profit, a model that will streamline the competition by reducing the number of teams and, thereby, increasing the potential markets. In 1996 there was a 20-team rugby league competition with 11 teams from Sydney, 2 from urban centers close to Sydney, 2 from Brisbane, 1 from Canberra, 1 from the Gold Coast, 1 from Townsville, 1 from Perth and 1 from Auckland (New Zealand). In "Super League" there will be 10 teams constituting 4 from Sydney and 1 from other major Australian cities and New Zealand. Specific territory and market zones are devised so that clubs will maximize their profit. Additionally, "Super League" signed a $15-million-a-year deal with Nike to be the exclusive supplier of playing apparel and merchandise, similar to exclusive merchandising contracts in North America. As a result, individual teams will not compete against each other, but will jointly benefit from the sale of merchandise from all teams. Whereas under the current arrangements all clubs individually negotiate contracts with companies and advertise those companies on playing jerseys and on virtually every feature of the playing ground and surrounding areas, "Super League" will not feature sponsorship on jerseys, and presumably there will be far less advertising in general to make way for increased value for television. The commercial panoply that has been a defining feature of Australian sport since 1970s will be, under "Super League," vastly reduced and much more closely aligned to that evident in American professional sport.

Conclusion

The key to Murdoch's proposed "Super League" is the organizational model it mandates. Australian sport has been principally publicly owned, and although there has been privatization in baseball, and to a lesser extent in basketball, rugby league, and Australian rules, "Super League" will single-handedly transfer one of Australia's highest profile spectator sports from public ownership to the private model. Sports fans in Australia need to think long and hard about what this means and whether such an approach is beat for professional sports, the players, and themselves. The American-style model is seductively attractive with its maximization of profits, its slick marketing and merchandising, and its entertaining sporting spectacles. Sporting spectators should consider what is lost as well as what is gained in the transition and, perhaps, take note of the American scene where there are steps being taken in attempts to redress the imbalance between those who own and those who follow professional sport. In Australia, the fans, who in general have democratic control over the elected club officials, have been much more successful than North Americans at limiting the ability of managers and marketers to control professional sports and at limiting the removal of their historical sporting teams. As the lure of North American sporting models and the attraction of North American sporting team apparel affects the Australian market, it may be more difficult to hang on to traditional models of Australian sport; however, there is widespread resistance to the wholesale adoption of North American ownership and marketing structures.

References

Australian Bureau of Statistics (1995). *Sports attendance*. Canberra: Commonwealth of Australia.

Cashman, R. (1995). *Paradise of sport: The rise of organized sport in Australia*. Melbourne: Oxford University Press.

Dabscheck, B. (1995). Australian baseballers form a team of their own. *Sporting Traditions*, *12*, 61–102.

Fitzsimons, P. (1996). *The rugby war*. Sydney: Harper Collins.

Harris, B. (1992). *Boom! Inside the NBL*. Sydney: Sun.

Heads, I. (1992). *True Blue: The story of the NSW Rugby League*: Sydney, Ironbark.

Linnell, G. (1995). *Football Ltd: The inside story of the AFL*. Sydney: Ironbark

Mascord, S. (1996). The madness and sadness. In D. Headon & L. Marinos, (Eds.), *League of a nation* (pp. 230–236). Sydney: ABC Books.

McKay, J., Lawrence, G., Miller, T., & Rowe, D. (1993). Globalization and Australian Sport. *Sport Science Review*, *2*, 10–28.

McKay, J., & Miller, T. (1991). From old boys to men and women of the corporation: The Americanization and commodification of Australian Sport. *Sociology of Sport Journal*, *8*, 86–94.

McKay, J., Miller, T., & Rowe, D. (1996). Americanisation, globalization and rugby league. In D. Headon & L. Marinos (Eds.), *League of a nation* (pp. 215–221). Sydney: ABC Books.

Mosely, P. (1994). *Ethnic involvement in Australian soccer: A history 1950–1990*. Canberra: Australian Sports Commission.

Mulcahy, D. (1993). *Them and us: National League?* Northbridge, Western Australia: Access Press.

Nauright, J., & Phillips, M. (1996). A fair go for the fans?: Super leagues, sports ownership and supporters in Australia. *Social Alternatives* (in press).

Pascoe, R. (1995). *The winter game: The complete history of Australian football*. Melbourne: Text Publishing.

Phillips, M., & Hutchins, B. (1995). Issues in the technicolour sports process: A brief history of rugby league and television in Australia. Paper submitted to *Journal of Australian Studies*.

Rowe, D., Lawrence, G., Miller, T., & McKay, J. (1994). Global sport? Core concern and peripheral vision. *Media, Culture and Society*, *16*, 661–675.

Sage, G. (1990). *Power and ideology in American sport*. Champaign: Human Kinetics.

Stell, M. (1991). *Half the race: A history of women in Australian sport*. Sydney: Angus and Robertson.

Walker, B. (1996). The Bronco dream. In D. Headon & L. Marinos (Eds.), *League of a nation* (pp. 211–214). Sydney: ABC Books.

Yeates, H. (1995). The league of men: Masculinity, the media and rugby league football. *Media Information Australia*, *75*, 35–45.

16

MECHANISMS OF INTERNATIONAL INFLUENCE ON DOMESTIC ELITE SPORT POLICY

Barrie Houlihan

Explaining Policy Stability and Change

In the mid-1990s Cerny (1995) argued that domestic policy making was increasingly constrained by international economic, political, and cultural forces, and Coleman and Perl concluded that globalization had "destabilise[d] traditional divisions of labour between sub-national, national, regional and international authorities" (1999, p. 692). Despite the hyperbole that surrounds much of the debate over the nature and the significance of globalization, it remains a central explanatory variable in recent policy analysis. These arguments resonate powerfully with contemporary elite sport, which has a well-established infrastructure of global sports institutions focused on event-organizing (for example, the International Olympic Committee and the Commonwealth Games Federation) or, as in the case of international federations, focused on both event-organizing and governance. More recently, these institutions have been joined not only by a powerful set of global sport media businesses which increasingly treat the world as a single market for their range of sports events and competitions, but also by a growing number of international governmental organizations with either a primary (e.g., International Intergovernmental Consultative Group on Anti-Doping in Sport, IICGAD) or secondary (e.g., Council of Europe, the European Union and UNESCO) interest in sport. The emergence of this global infrastructure for sport has prompted greater investigation of the impact of international or non-domestic factors on domestic elite sport policy.

In a study of the elite sport development systems in the UK, Australia, and Canada, Green and Houlihan (2005) concluded that all three countries had, over the previous 10 years or so, experienced an increase in government intervention intended to establish and refine elite policy objectives. These objectives were to be achieved largely through the provision of substantial investment of public and lottery funds in dedicated elite-focused facilities, specialist coaching, sports science and sports medicine support. These countries also experienced the reshaping, by domestic federations, of the competition calendar to suit the requirements of elite performance at international competition, in particular the Olympic Games. These conclusions were reinforced by a number of other studies conducted around the same time (Abbott et al., 2002; Digel, 2002a, 2002b; Green & Oakley, 2001a, 2001b; Oakley & Green, 2001; UK Sport, 2006). Table 1 provides a summary of their findings and suggests that the characteristics of successful elite systems have many common features which could be grouped under three main headings: contextual, processual, and sport specific. Reflecting on the similarity between elite sport systems, Oakley and Green argued that the 10 characteristics that they identified represented "common approaches to the problem of enhancing elite sport rather than responses to the social, political and economic elements in each country," which indicated that "there is a growing trend towards a homogeneous model of elite sport development" (2001, p. 91). Oakley and Green's conclusion is broadly endorsed by Digel (2002a, 2002b) and more recently by Houlihan and Green, who found that all countries in their edited study, with the exception of the USA, exhibited many common characteristics and concluded that "the countries discussed . . . provide strong evidence of strategic approaches based increasingly around a homogenous model of elite sport development but with subtle domestic variations" (2008, p. 291).

However, while Houlihan and Green raised the issue of the mechanisms by which this homogeneous model might have been adopted, little recent research into sport globalization takes the mechanisms of international influences on domestic public policy for sport as its central concern. Consequently, the focus of this paper is the interface between national/domestic sport policy systems and the increasingly prominent and, arguably, extremely influential set of international/non-domestic policy influences. More specifically, the primary aim of this paper is to evaluate the utility, for the analysis of elite sport policy, of the mechanisms of international influence which have been identified in the wider policy analysis literature. This paper is divided into three sections: the first discusses briefly the nature and significance of international influences; the second section examines the character and importance of domestic institutionalized practices — the weight of history — which can either facilitate or constrain policy change; and the final section discusses a series of mechanisms by which the international and the domestic dimensions intersect, and by which international influences affect domestic elite sport policy.

International Influences and Domestic Policy

Throughout the 1990s much attention was focused on the impact of globalization on social processes, including those associated with policy stability and change. Unfortunately, the often inflated claims regarding the significance, both political and social, of globalization prompted a skeptical reaction against the paradigmatic status that the concept seemed to be assuming. Unease focused on the utility of the concept, its descriptive accuracy and its explanatory potential (Bauman, 1999; Rosenberg, 2005; Fitch, 1996). Thus, while there is acknowledgement of the significance of globalization, the concept suffers in its

Table 1. Factors contributing to elite success.

Factors	Oakley and Green	Digel	UK Sport (SPLISS Consortium)	Green and Houlihan
Contextual	An excellence culture	Support, especially financial, of the state	Financial support	Support for "full-time" athletes
	Appropriate funding	Economic success and business sponsorship	Participation in sport	
		A media-supported positive sports culture	Scientific research	
Processual	Clear understanding of the role of different agencies	Talent development through the education system	Talent identification and development system	
	Simplicity of administration	Talent development through the armed forces	Athletic and post career support	
	Effective system for monitoring athlete progress		Integrated approach to policy development	
	Talent identification and targeting of resources		Coaching provision and coach development	
	Comprehensive planning system for each sport			
	Lifestyle support			
Specific	Well-structured competitive programmes	Sports science support services	International competition	A hierarchy of competition opportunities centred on preparation for international events
	Well-developed specific facilities		Training facilities	Elite facility development
				The provision of coaching, sports science and sports medicine support services

Sources: Digel (2002a, 2002b), Green and Houlihan (2005), Oakley and Green (2001), *UK Sport* (2006).

application as an explanatory variable from vagueness and from casual and inconsistent usage (Hirst & Thompson, 1999; Houlihan, 2007). For example, Scholte (2003), in evaluating the utility of the concept of globalization, identifies five common uses of the term: internationalization, liberalization, universalization, westernization/Americanization and deterritorialization, with each term giving different weight to economic, political and cultural aspects.

The breadth of interpretation of the concept of globalization needs to be borne in mind when examining the impact on policy. In the mid 1970s Hechter noted that much current policy research still assumed that "the causes of [policy] development were located within units defined by political boundaries, such as sovereign states" (1975, p. 217). By the mid 1990s there was a clear acceptance that an increasing number of policy issues were now embedded in a series of supranational policy networks and that the problem for the policy analyst was to determine whether actors external to the domestic political system were participants in a national policy process, or whether the proper focus should be on the global policy arena to which national actors sought entry and influence (see for example, Andersen & Eliassen, 1993).

Deacon, in his analysis of welfare policy (1997), noted that the relative decline in the power of national governments as a result of globally mobile finance capital had altered the traditional approach to welfare policy analysis — a view which could be applied with equal force to elite sport policy. According to Deacon, supranational policy actors can no longer be ignored, especially in relation to the "globalization of social policy instruments, policy and provision" (1997, p. 20), which takes three distinct forms — supranational regulation, supranational redistribution, and supranational provision. Supranational regulation refers to "those mechanisms, instruments and policies at the global level that seek to regulate the terms of trade and operation of firms in the interests of social protection and welfare objectives" (Deacon, 1997, p. 2). The European Union provides the best illustration at a regional level, for example, in relation to rights at work (as evidenced in relation to sport in the Bosman case),[1] while examples at a global level in sport would include the regulation by international sports federations of the transfer market and eligibility rules for national teams, the role of the World Anti-Doping Agency in shaping national anti-doping policy, and the growing importance of the Court of Arbitration for Sport in settling sports-related disputes.

Examples of sport-related supranational redistribution policies are scarce, but would include the work of Olympic Solidarity and the sport-development initiatives of international federations, such as the International Association of Athletic Federations (IAAF) and the International Federation of Football Associations (FIFA), all of which involve some redistribution of income to poorer countries. Supranational provision refers, according to Deacon (1997, p. 3), "to the embryonic measures . . . whereby people gain an entitlement to a service or are empowered in the field of social citizenship rights by an agency acting at the supranational level." The Court of Arbitration for Sport is beginning to fulfill this role for elite athletes, and the UN, through its Convention on the

Rights of the Child, has the potential to protect the rights of child elite athletes (David, 2005).

Within the discussion of the impact of globalization, two more specific trends, commercialization and governmentalization, require comment. "Commercialization" refers to the rapid expansion of sport-related businesses (most notably sport media) and to the transformation of many aspects of sport into successful commodities and brands, and has generated considerable research interest (see for example, Slack, 2004; Amis & Cornwell, 2005; Silk et al., 2005). Commercialization has also had an impact on the ethos and management practices in public services associated with elite sport, perhaps most clearly in the UK, Australia, and New Zealand, although few developed economies have been immune. In the UK, the Labor government's modernization agenda, which is strongly influenced by commercial management practices, has introduced a series of principles (such as confidence in the market and the development of partnership, participation and stakeholding) and technologies (public service agreements, inspection, "naming and shaming," and audit) which reinforce the process of commercialization.

As a distinct aspect of globalization, "governmentalization" refers to the development of a state apparatus for the delivery and management of services that were previously the primary or sole responsibility of organizations of civil society. While the former communist countries have a relatively long history of state direction of elite sport, a similar pattern, if not quite depth, of involvement emerged in many economically developed noncommunist countries in the 1960s and accelerated from the early 1990s (Houlihan & Green, 2008). Although the expansion of government involvement has generally taken place in conjunction with voluntary organizations, there has also been a steady accrual of functions by the state with the consequent development of specialist administrative units and agencies at national and sub-national levels, and the allocation of responsibility for policy at ministerial level. By the early twenty-first century, elite sport has become so well established within the machinery of government and within the portfolio of government responsibilities that many governments are able to influence significantly the pattern of elite sport opportunities.

Clearly, the extent to which globalization in general and the particular aspects of commercialization and governmentalization are recognized as external to particular domestic policy processes will vary considerably. For a number of countries, especially the more neo-liberal, the international ideological environment will appear far less alien than for countries where the commodification of services is more limited, as in the Scandinavian countries, and where the capacity of government to expand its role is also limited, as in the United States. Consequently, external influences may, in some countries, be reinforcing national administrative patterns, dominant policy paradigms, and deep structural values, whereas in others there will be a higher level of conflict at some or all of these levels. The impact of non-domestic influences consequently depends not just on their specific characteristics, but also on the particular pattern of institutional arrangements, both organizational and cultural, at the domestic level. The next section therefore discusses the institutions at the domestic level that mediate international influences.

Domestic Level Institutional Mediation

In all countries factors such as the accumulation of previous policy decisions, the organization of the machinery of government, the history of relations with other countries, the political party structure, and the relationship between the legislature and the executive combine to provide a series of institutionalized variables which mediate the relationship between international influences and the domestic policy system. Although the concept of an institution is defined in a variety of ways, there are two broad orientations in the literature, one emphasizing the significance of institutions as organizational entities and arrangements (agencies, departments, federalism, parliaments, etc.), and the other, cultural institutionalism, which highlights shared values, norms and beliefs.

Institutions constrain choice through their capacity to shape actors' perception of both problems and acceptable solutions. As such, the emphasis on institutions is a valuable corrective to the tendency of much pluralist theory to treat organizations (government departments, committees of enquiry, and local councils, for example) as arenas in which politics takes place rather than as independent or intervening variables in the process. Cultural institutionalism, with its emphasis on values, norms and beliefs, emphasizes the social construction of meaning and "how interest groups, politicians, and administrators decide their policy preferences" (Fischer, 2003, p. 29).

Institutions develop at a variety of levels within the socio-political system. While the recursive relationship between agency and structure ensures that even institutions at the level of the deep structure (Benson, 1982) of society are not immune from change, it is at this level (of deeply rooted social values) and at the levels of core policy paradigm and service-specific policy paradigms that the strongest resistance to international influences for change will be encountered; unless, of course, there is a correspondence between domestic cultural institutions and the values promoted by international influences.

The most successful attempt to capture the significance of cultural institutionalism for domestic policy has been by Esping-Andersen (1990) who, in his well-known analysis of welfare states, distinguished between three welfare regimes: liberal, conservative, and social democratic, with the distinction based on the private-public mix, the degree of de-commodification and modes of stratification or solidarities. Esping-Andersen's research stimulated considerable debate (for example, Sairoff, 1994; Liebfried, 1990) and while there was some refinement of his typology, there has been broad support for its underlying premise: that forces for change are strongly mediated by deeply rooted cultural predispositions irrespective of whether the source of change is internal or external to the domestic policy system (see Blomqvist, 2004; Ozga & Lingard, 2007). It is this observation that has led to an increased concern to move beyond assertions about the strength of international influences for change and the robustness or weaknesses of domestic institutions, and which has focused attention on the mechanisms by which factors and pressures external to the domestic policy sector permeate the domestic policy process and influence policy choice.

However, of equal importance to the empirical specification of international factors and domestic mediating factors is how their inter-relationship is theorized and, importantly for this paper, how the particular mechanisms of international influence are theorized. The theorization of the inter-relationship of non-domestic and domestic factors will be discussed in the conclusion, as it is argued that the discussion of the operation of the various mechanisms provides valuable theoretical insight into the long-term nature of the relationship. As regards the theorization of the various mechanisms of international influence, one issue which needs to be borne in mind is whether the various mechanisms discussed should be granted a broad equivalence, but not mutual exclusivity, which would allow them to be used in a complementary fashion — a form of theoretical pluralism. The theoretical status of the various mechanisms and their compatibility will also be examined more fully in the conclusion.

Mechanisms of International Influence on Elite Sport Policy

Although it is generally acknowledged that international influences affect an increasing range of domestic policy sectors, there is still only a relatively modest body of research which examines how these influences are manifest at the domestic level; the *process* of influence is significantly under-explored. If it is accepted that, at the very least, globalization has resulted in an increasingly common set of stimuli for national policy systems, there is no guarantee that the stimuli will produce a uniform response. In other words, even if the "reach" of global influence is similar, the response may vary considerably. The variation in response might be due to the institutional constraints within national policy systems discussed above; it might also be the result of the mechanisms through which international influence is manifest: the mechanisms may constitute independent variables in the shaping of domestic policy. This section examines a series of mechanisms which operate at the interface between the domestic and the international. The mechanisms are summarized in Table 2, along five dimensions which have been adapted from work by Dale (1999). While the table fulfills a useful heuristic purpose, it must be borne in mind that the different mechanisms are not, in practice, so neatly compartmentalized. As will be clear from the following discussion, elements of some mechanisms can be found in others. Elements of path dependency may, for example, be identified in the empirical analysis of instances of policy learning and transfer.

The first dimension identified in Table 2 concerns the locus of initiative for interaction between the international and the domestic. In some mechanisms, such as policy learning and policy transfer, the locus is clearly domestic, as was the case in the UK when the then Minister of Sport, Ian Sproat, and senior civil servants visited the Australian Institute of Sport in 1994 when the government was considering establishing a similar high-performance training center. In contrast, the locus of initiative for the change in many domestic anti-

Table 2. Mechanisms of international and domestic interaction.

Discussion	Policy Learning	Policy Transfer	Path Dependency	Mimetic isomorphism	Policy determines politics	Harmonisation	Imposition
Locus of initiative	National	National	National/international	National	Intrinsic to policy	International/national	International
Likely lead actor/organisation	Government/interest groups	Government	Government	Government	Government	International policy regime	International policy regime
Basis of engagement	Voluntary	Voluntary	Constrained	Pressure to conform	Constrained	Voluntary or compulsion	Compulsion
Key relationships	Bi-lateral	Bi-lateral	None	Multi-lateral	None	Multi-lateral/policy regime lead agency	Multi-lateral/policy regime lead agency, but can be bi-lateral
Nature of power (explicit, agenda setting, ideological)	Explicit	Explicit	Agenda control	Explicit/ideological	Agenda control/ideological	Explicit/agenda control/ideological	Explicit
Sport (UK) Elite sport development	Pattern of regular contact through governments, professional organisations and academics	Investment in specialist training centres and in sports scientists	Focus on elite sport has led to a separation of elite sport policy from policy on mass participation due to power of elite interests	Adoption of many policies and management practices from Australia, former GDR and Soviet Union	It is argued that once the commitment to elite sport success has been made particular policies are inevitably adopted e.g. paying athletes, specialist facilities, investments in sport science	Doping control through the activities of the World Anti-Doping Agency	Attempted imposition of the UN Convention on the Rights of the Child to cover training of young elite athletes

Source: Adapted from Dale (1999).

doping policies lay with the World Anti-Doping Agency (WADA), an international organization. However, the mechanism which suggests the possibility that policy determines or overrides politics is less easy to categorize, it is argued that the particular properties of a problem generate their own momentum towards certain policy choices, creating, in effect, an institutional constraint on policy choice. The second dimension concerns the likely lead actor and varies between domestic government and/or interest groups and international transnational governmental or non-governmental policy regimes, and emphasizes the potential for agency in the relationship between the domestic and non-domestic policy spheres. However, as will be discussed in more detail below some theorists of policy change (Haas, 1992; Hajer & Wagenaar, 2003; Fischer, 2003) stress the capacity of ideas to constitute an independent variable in the policy process which has the potential to make the concept of a "lead actor" redundant. The third dimension focuses attention on the basis of engagement between the international and domestic levels and the degree of constraint involved in policy choice and relates, as did the previous dimension, to debates about agency and institutionalism in policy decisions. The fourth dimension seeks to identify the key relationship, if any, that characterizes the level of engagement. In many examples of policy transfer the relationship is bilateral, as the initiation of the process of policy review is often domestic, e.g., due to the acknowledgement of a problem. However, intervention in domestic policy processes by international regimes is often the embodiment of a multilateral initiative. The final dimension is perhaps the most important and concerns the nature of power exercised or embodied in the relationship; it is based loosely on Lukes' three "faces" of power, namely the explicit exercise of power, the use of power to control or constrain the policy agenda, or power as ideology (Lukes, 2005).

International Policy Regimes: State Power or the Power of Ideas?

Krasner defines regimes as "sets of implicit or explicit principles, norms, rules and decision-making procedures around which actors" expectations converge in a given area of international relations" (1983, p. 2). In attempting to operationalize this concept it is argued that successful regimes possess some or all of the following characteristics: first, they exhibit a degree of stability in the pattern of relationships between actors and, by implication possess some process by which voices/interests can be acknowledged or ignored; second, regimes possess the organizational capacity to fulfill maintenance functions, such as agenda-setting, policy-monitoring and review, verification of compliance and, in some, the enforcement of compliance; and third, regimes actively defend and promote their values. Many regimes therefore have an identifiable organizational capacity, such as a permanent secretariat, while others fulfill regime maintenance functions through the actions of one or more member states or organizations as, for example, does the United States in maintaining the regimes associated with the General Agreement on Tariffs and Trade (GATT) and nuclear non-proliferation. The organizational significance of the state may be balanced or replaced by that of non-governmental organizations such as the International Olympic Committee (IOC) and the international federations in relation to sport development regimes. It has also been suggested that direction and organizational capacity can be provided by an epistemic community, which Haas has described as "a network of professionals with recognised expertise and competence in a particular . . . issue area" (1992, p. 3). Arguing that "control over knowledge and information is an important dimension of power," Haas suggests that the potential of epistemic communities to exercise influence increases with uncertainty and particularly the uncertainty found in areas of policy where states are strongly dependent on the policy choices of other actors. Uncertainty and dependence are characteristics of aspects of elite development systems: there is, for example, considerable uncertainty about the most effective youth talent identification process and the optimal process for athlete development, and elite systems often operate in a complex pattern of interdependencies involving public, not-for profit, and commercial organizations.

The most common explanation for the formation of regimes and the mechanisms by which they exert influence is that they are the creatures, if not the products, of hegemonic self-interest, where "stronger states in the policy sector will dominate the weaker ones and determine the rules of the game" (Keohane & Nye, p. 1977). It is possible to argue that the global anti-doping regime fits this analysis, as the policy could be interpreted as seeking to eliminate "cheap science" (i.e., doping) from sport, thus allowing those countries with access to sophisticated and expensive science to exploit their advantage in order to maintain their place in the medal rankings.

An alternative, and less state-centered, explanation for the formation of regimes assumes that ideas matter: first, in creating a predisposition to co-operate and comply; and second, in explaining the content of regime rules and how they evolve. According to Nadelmann, in his study of global prohibition regimes, "moral and emotional factors related neither to political nor economic advantage but instead involving religious beliefs, humanitarian sentiments . . . conscience, paternalism, fear, prejudice and the compulsion to proselytise can and do play important roles in the creation and the evolution of international regimes" (1990, p. 480). Checkel (see also Risse et al., 1999) also emphasizes the importance of ideas as a source of influence and argues that international institutions are often effective in shaping national policy due to a process of socialization of key domestic policy actors in government, such that "sustained compliance [is] based on the internalisation of new norms" (2005, p. 804). Checkel argues: "There is growing empirical evidence to suggest that what starts as strategic incentive-based cooperation within international institutions often leads at later points to preference shifts" (2005, p. 814).

Within elite sport, two examples of regimes concern the Olympic Movement and anti-doping policy, and illustrate the interplay between organizational capacity and ideas. There are two ways in which one might regard the

Olympic Movement as a policy regime: first, in relation to its promotion of Olympism as a value system and second, as the cluster of organizations that define the scope of elite sport outside the major commercial sports. Olympism, articulated in the Olympic Charter, expresses a clear set of principles and norms which should impact on the operation of National Olympic Committees, the preparation of athletes for Olympic competition, and the behavior of athletes at the Olympic Games. While Olympism is undeniably vague and, arguably, increasingly symbolic, it has been an important point of reference for National Olympic Committees when framing bids to host the Games and has also been used as a justification for NOC decisions, for example, the decision of the British Olympic Association not to select for the British team any athlete who has been found guilty of a serious doping violation. The regime values of the Olympic Movement are also promoted through a network of National Olympic Academies and the International Olympic Academy at Olympia. Perhaps a more persuasive example of an Olympic policy regime is the impact of the Olympic Movement on the definition of what constitutes elite sport. Not only does the Olympic Games increasingly shape the competition structure and elite athlete preparation timetable in many domestic systems, but the inclusion or removal of a sport from the summer or winter Games has a clearly discernible impact on domestic government funding decisions. However, while the Olympic Movement actively seeks to promote Olympism and can therefore be accepted as an active, if not especially effective, regime, the impact of the Olympic Movement on domestic conceptualizations of elite sport and what sports are valued is largely indirect, as the sheer dominance of the Olympic Games is sufficient to affect policy in many countries. The exception might be in relation to the work of Olympic Solidarity which, through its development activities, does seek to promote the practice of the Olympic diet of sports and events.

An equally strong claim for regime status can be made in relation to anti-doping centered on the activities of the World Anti-Doping Agency (WADA). Since its establishment in 1999, WADA, jointly governed by states and international sports organizations, has obtained agreement from all Olympic sport federations and endorsement from 192 governments. At the heart of WADA's activity is the World Anti-Doping Code, which places a heavy emphasis on the values encapsulated in the phrase "the spirit of sport" to justify its policy position. The Code is supported by a system of monitoring and a compliance structure, and has been recently reinforced by UNESCO's preparation of an Anti-Doping Convention, which imposes legal responsibilities on member countries. Demonstrating compliance with the World Anti-Doping Code and the UNESCO Convention has required many countries to revise their domestic anti-doping regulations and procedures.

Ascribing influence to international policy regimes is, however, rarely straightforward, as evidence of a high degree of actor compliance may only indicate an association rather than a causal relationship. Furthermore, there is considerable disagreement whether regimes, as international institutions, are more than simply a camouflage for state power. It is not only theorists from the realist school of international relations, such as Strange (1983), who are skeptical about reducing the significance of the state; Keohane et al., for example, caution that "states maintain control: the institutions themselves are quite weak" (1993, p. 17). Even if a strongly independent role is ascribing too much authority to regimes, they may yet fulfill a secondary, but nonetheless important, aggregation or facilitation role on behalf of more substantial actors, such as states or possibly non-governmental organizations (NGOs), for example, the IOC in relation to anti-doping. But whether as independent or mediating variables, there is a powerful accumulation of evidence that regimes have the capacity to affect policy in important areas of elite sport, most notably in relation to anti-doping policy.

Policy Learning, Lesson-drawing, and Policy Transfer

Implicit in much of the discussion of the development of public policy at national level is the assumption that countries learn from each other and that a process of policy transfer is in operation. At a commonsense level, policy learning and policy transfer are attractive. For example, the UK's main comparators in relation to elite sport success include France, Italy, Australia, and Germany, and it would be unrealistic and surprising not to expect UK policymakers to find out what these countries do and at least ask the question whether their practices could be adapted to the UK context.

The cluster of related concepts of "policy learning," "lesson-drawing," and "policy transfer" has featured prominently in much recent analysis of policy change. Policy-learning is rooted in an Eastonian systems model of the policy process where the policy-making cycle is regularly energized by feedback on the impact of existing policy (Easton, 1965; Frohock, 1979). While the process of policy learning can therefore be largely domestic and insulated from experience in other countries, or even other policy areas in the same country, it is increasingly accepted that policy learning can and increasingly does involve analyses of similar policy areas and issues in other countries. More recent conceptualizations of policy learning have emphasized the intentional aspect of the process, which moves beyond feedback on existing policy and involves the systematic scanning of the environment for policy ideas (see Yamamoto 2008, who notes that scanning is an integral part of elite development policy in Japan). Often, this systematic scanning is undertaken as a routine activity by public officials and is a technical process rather than a political one. Extending DiMaggio and Powell's (1983) ideas about institutional isomorphism, it may be argued that the greater the level of uncertainty involved in a public policy problem and the fewer the alternative policy responses, the more likely countries are to exhibit a form of mimetic isomorphism with regard to policy selection.

Hall (1986) provides a valuable typology of policy change, identifying three levels or "orders" of policy change which result, potentially at least, from policy learning. First order changes are alterations to the intensity or scale of an existing policy instrument, an example of which in relation to funding would be the decision in March 2006 by the UK government to provide an additional £200m to help prepare athletes for the 2012 Olympic Games. Second order changes are those that introduce new policy instruments designed to achieve existing policy objectives: examples of which would include the many countries which have established dedicated elite sports training centers. Finally, third order changes are those that involve a change in policy goals of which the — short-lived — decision by the Canadian government in the 1990s to downgrade the pursuit of elite success would be an example (Green & Houlihan, 2005).

Policy transfer refers to the process by which the lessons learnt (see Rose, 2005, for a fuller discussion of lesson-drawing) are transferred: how lessons are internalized, how lessons are recorded and described, and how they are incorporated into a different organizational infrastructure and value system in the importing country or policy sector. Bearing in mind that policy can be variously conceptualized as aspiration, action (involving the commitment of resources), or inaction (Hogwood, 1987; Jenkins, 1978; Heclo, 1972, Rose defines policy transfer as "action-oriented intentional activity" (2005, p. 16). An awareness of the extent to which the transfer mechanism facilitates or constrains transfer is crucial. For example, the important role of the armed forces in South Korea in developing elite athletes for the Olympic Games or the role of the high school and especially the university sectors in the United States in talent identification and development may be lessons that are clearly understood and learned, but which are difficult to transfer to a country such as the UK which does not have the institution of military conscription and where the cultural values of the higher education system preclude such a heavy emphasis on sporting success at the expense of educational attainment. As should be clear the analysis of the transfer process is as important as an understanding of the process of policy learning and lesson drawing. Lessons may well be accurately learned but be imperfectly transferred or transferred to an unsupportive organizational infrastructure or an unsympathetic value system.

The attractiveness of the concepts of policy learning and transfer are not without problems, the most obvious of which are the difficulty of explaining how policy makers learn (Oliver, 1997), what constitutes learning (Bennett & Howlett, 1992), and how learning might be quantified (Pierson, 1993). In addition there are substantial concerns relating to the process by which lessons are communicated and transferred policies are recreated in the receiving country (see Dolowitz & Marsh, 1996, 2000). These concerns notwithstanding, it is clear that policy learning and transfer are well established practices within many governments and domestic policy areas, including elite sport development.

Path Dependency

Underlying much of the discussion about policy learning is the assumption that policy change will be affected by both past experience and new information. As Greener notes, policy learning "considers policy legacies to be one of the most significant elements in determining present and future policy" (2002, p. 162). As such, policy learning has much in common with the concept of path dependency, which suggests that initial policy decisions can determine future policy choices: that "the trajectory of change up to a certain point constrains the trajectory after that point" (Kay, 2005, p. 553). Path dependency is also connected to the broader policy analysis literature on the importance of institutions which, for Thelen and Steinmo, are seen as significant constraints and mediating factors in politics, which "leave their own imprint" (1992, p. 8). Whether the emphasis is on institutions as organizations or as sets of values and beliefs (culture), there is a strong historical dimension which emphasizes the "relative autonomy of political institutions from the society in which they exist; . . . and the unique patterns of historical development and the constraints they impose on future choices" (Howlett & Ramesh, 1995, p. 27).

The relevance of institutionalism within sport policy analysis is clear. A number of authors have identified the organizational infrastructure of UK sport as a significant variable in shaping policy (Houlihan & White, 2002; Green & Houlihan, 2005; Pickup, 1996; Roche, 1993; Henry, 2001). Krauss (1990) and Wilson (1994) drew similar conclusions with regard to the United States, as did Macintosh (1991) and Macintosh and Whitson (1990) in relation to Canada. Allocation of functional responsibility for sport, federalism, the use of "arms' length" agencies, and the presence of a minister for sport are all seen as having a discernible impact on sport policy and its implementation. Similar claims for the significance of cultural institutions are also widespread. Beliefs, norms and values associated with social class (Birley, 1996), gender (Hargreaves, 1994), disability (Thomas, 2007), and ethnicity (Carrington & Macdonald, 2000) have all been demonstrated to have had, and indeed to continue to have, a marked impact on the character of UK sport policy.

Past decisions need to be seen as institutions in relation to current policy choices with path dependency capturing the insight that "policy decisions accumulate over time; a process of accretion can occur in a policy area that restricts options for future policy-makers" (Kay, 2005, p. 558). In a hard application of the concept of path dependency, one would argue that early decisions in a policy area result in current policy being "locked in" and also, perhaps, locked on to a particular policy trajectory. A softer application of the concept would suggest that early decisions do not lock a policy on a specific trajectory, but do significantly constrain subsequent policy options (Kay, 2005). This softer version of path dependency would be compatible with the argument underpinning Esping-Andersen's regime typology and indeed, with many other mechanisms discussed in this article. For example, the adoption of a policy designed to maximize Olympic medals has proved to be a slow and difficult process in some Scandinavian countries due to the cultural value of universalism of access to sport and the perception of Olympic elite sport as disengaged from everyday life (Augestad et al., 2006). The pursuit of Olympic medals has been made more culturally palatable by arguing that the sporting elite is the product of an extensive policy of mass participation rather than the outcome of a system of scientific talent identification.

In summary, it may be hypothesized that once a government takes the decision to value elite sport success (or to acknowledge the value given it in civil society), it is locked on to a predictable policy path usually involving the investment in specialist training facilities, cash payments to athletes, and the development of sport science capacity.

While it is not impossible to "devalue" elite sport success, few countries have attempted to do so, suggesting a prima facia case for further investigation of the path dependency hypothesis.

Does Policy Determine Politics?

Extending and, to a degree, contrasting with the discussion in the previous section one of the most significant insights from some, often large *n*, comparative policy studies was that nationally distinct political characteristics were only very weakly correlated with particular policies and that the dominant developmental process in advanced industrial countries was one of convergence. Freeman summarized the challenge as follows:

> The idea that distinctive and durable national policymaking styles are causally linked to the policies of states asserts that "politics determines policy." The policy sector approach argues, in contrast, that the nature of the problem is fundamentally connected to the kind of politics that emerges as well as the policy outcomes that result. The policy sector approach shifts our attention away from political inputs to categories of issues and outputs of the political system; it suggests that "policy determines politics." (1985, p. 469)

In other words the intrinsic characteristics of the problem or issue "will override whatever tendencies exist toward nationally specific policies" (Freeman 1985, p. 486). To quote Heinelt, "the thesis 'policies determines politics' would imply — given that a policy sector [for example, elite sport] would be seen as the only relevant variable for explaining politics — that institutions, parties, forms of interest mediation, political culture etc. do not matter, only the policy sector does" (2005, p. 7).

One important, and possibly crucial, indicator of convergence in elite sports systems is the extent to which a broad range of countries with different political, socio-economic and cultural profiles adopt similar policy goals and instruments. As has already been suggested, the proportion of, admittedly more wealthy, countries whose governments have accepted elite success as a sport policy goal is high and growing. If it is accepted that there is convergence in policy goals, then the next area for investigation is in relation to the policy instruments that have been selected to achieve that goal and, crucially, whether the choice of policy instruments is constrained by the nature of the policy objective. In other words it can be hypothesized that there is little scope for variation in instrument selection if a country wants to win Olympic gold medals: either that some policy instruments are so much more effective than others that they are selected even though they may conflict with deeper cultural values or that the repertoire of policy instruments is so limited that there is little scope for variation in policy selection. The hypothesis that "policy determines politics" is partially supported by the comparison of elite sport development systems in the volume edited by Houlihan and Green (2008). With the exception of the United States, the other eight countries exhibited considerable similarity in their elite athlete development strategies despite having welfare traditions that ranged from social democratic (Norway) to neo-liberal (New Zealand), and political systems that included authoritarian (China) and liberal-democratic (Australia). However, in order to move beyond observation to analysis, it would be necessary to explore the policy process in much more detail, particularly in relation to policy option evaluation and selection.

Conclusion

The theorizing and empirical research around the issue of the mechanisms by which international and domestic policy systems interact in relation to elite sport is so scant and fragmented that it is tempting to use the academic's "escape clause" of arguing that "we need more empirical evidence." In attempting to avoid such an anodyne conclusion (although we do need more empirical research) the following observations are offered.

First, it is important to bear in mind that the evidence of increasing similarity of elite sport systems across many economically developed countries does not necessarily indicate the activation and impact of some or indeed any of the mechanisms discussed above. It is possible, though I would argue improbable, that the similarity in elite systems is the consequence of individual domestic policy systems responding to an increasingly uniform global environment. According to this argument the extent to which a more homogenized policy agenda faced by countries is the result of globalization is open to debate, as it may simply be that shared problems and common socio-economic developments, such as the spillover of the use of sports drugs into wider society, or declining family size resulting in the need for greater selectivity and precision in talent identification. As Whitty et al. argued in relation to a study of policies designed to tackle inner city under-achievement in education, policy-makers in the UK and United States "were working with similar frames of reference and producing parallel policy initiatives, rather than directly 'borrowing' from one another" (1993, p. 14). While it is important to be cautious in claiming too significant a role in policy change for any of the mechanisms, it also is important to acknowledge the growing body of research which indicates a steady blurring of the interface between the domestic and the international levels of the policy. On the one hand, the evidence of policy learning and transfer among the richer countries is steadily accumulating, particularly in relation to elite athlete development (Green & Oakley, 2001a, 2001b; Houlihan & Green, 2008); on the other hand there is evidence of effective international policy regimes becoming established, most notably in relation to doping in elite sport (Yamamoto, 2009), but also, at the European Union regional level, in relation to players' conditions of employment. It is consequently arguable that there is a dual process in operation—a domestically initiated process of scanning the policy environment for transferable policies (an aspect of which would be compatibility with domestic culture) and an international process of regime development—which, when taken together, contribute to a trend toward homogenization of aspects of sport policy.

However, while regime analysis and policy transfer theory appear to be complementary, there needs to be a degree of caution in combining different types of theoretical explanation. Although theoretical pluralism is not necessarily problematic, there needs to be an awareness of the different types of theory being combined. Regime theory, for example, is generally located within a neo-liberal interpretation of international politics and as such is an example of what Abend refers to as "an overall perspective from which one sees and interprets the world" (2008, p. 179). This type of macro-level theory contrasts with theories of policy learning, policy transfer and isomorphism, which are much more limited in explanatory ambition and are "explanation[s] of a particular social phenomenon" (Abend, 2008, p. 178).

Following on from the first observation, the second is that individual domestic policy systems are likely to be affected by more than one mechanism. It is plausible to hypothesize that at one level there are "ideas in good currency," examples of which might include the nebulous notion of Olympism as well as more practical policies such as establishing specialist training centers for elite athletes. The latter example could be illustrative of the mechanism of mimetic isomorphism, where change results less from external pressure and more from domestic policy uncertainty. It is also likely that many countries will be consciously (or perhaps subconsciously) involved in an accommodation with powerful international policy regimes and countries. The privileging, for funding purposes, of Olympic sports is likely to be a conscious acknowledgement of the dominance of the Olympic Games in the hierarchy of international sporting events. Conscious accommodations with the power distribution in sport is also likely to be evident in the particular sports that are prioritized within individual countries—for example, avoiding those with established dominance by one or a few countries. Overlaying these two processes of interaction will be the more proactive engagement initiated by individual countries (policy learning and transfer) or by international policy regimes (designed to achieve harmonization and compliance).

The third observation is to emphasize the importance of considering the power relations which each mechanism implies. In relation to policy learning and transfer it would appear that the power of initiative lies with the individual country as it is their decision to scan for alternative policy solutions. However, the strength of global policy discourses around issues such as elite success (and the extent to which it is considered a cipher for national vitality) and doping in sport (and the need to be seen to be active on the issue) may result in some countries feeling obliged to engage in policy learning and transfer because the cost (for example, damage to international prestige and risk of losing votes in the selection process to host major events) of being seen to do nothing would be too great.

In relation to international policy regimes it is important to bear in mind that their impact will be uneven: it is generally the weaker states whose domestic policy is more likely to be influenced. This is not only because the more powerful sporting countries are likely to have been instrumental in forming the regime or at least legitimizing its actions, but also because the more powerful countries are more likely to have the resources to manage compliance in such a way as to minimize the disruption to current practice. Moreover, while the formation of global policy discourse can be a powerful constraint on domestic policy-making, its existence does not imply that policy necessarily becomes homogenized. Indeed, there is strong evidence from studies in other policy areas which demonstrates the capacity of individual states to interpret and adapt external policy pressures to their particular national circumstances and history (Lundahl, 2005; Taylor & Henry, 2000; Ozga & Lingard, 2007; Mares, 2003; McEwen & Moreno, 2005; Deacon, 2000; Iversen, 2005; Ellison, 2006; Glatzer & Rueschmeyer, 2005). Consequently, it is important to see the interface between non-domestic and domestic factors and the mechanisms that facilitate interaction as not only being about solving problems but about protecting and furthering interests whether of states or of international non-governmental organizations.

Acknowledgements

The author would like to thank the three anonymous referees for their helpful comments on the earlier draft of this paper.

Note

1. The Bosman case refers to a decision made by the European Court of Justice (ECJ) in 1995. The case, brought by Jean-Marc Bosman, challenged the legality of the system of transfers for football players and the existence of the quota system which limited the number of foreign players allowed to play in a club match. The ECJ found in favor of Bosman and against RFC Liege, the Belgium Football Association, and UEFA. Transfer fees for out-of-contract players were declared illegal where a player was moving between one EU state and another and the quota system was held to be illegal.

References

Abbott, A., Collins, D., Martindale, R., & Sowerby, K. (2002). *Talent identification and development: An academic review*. Edinburgh: Sport Scotland.

Abend, G., 2008. The meaning of "theory." *Sociological Theory, 26*(2), 173–199.

Amis, J., & Cornwell, B. (Eds.). (2005). *Global sport sponsorship*. Oxford: Berg.

Andersen, S. S., & Eliassen, K. A. (Eds.). (1993). *Making policy in Europe: The Europeification of national policy-making*. London: Sage.

Augestad, P., Bergsgard, N. A., & Hansen, A. O. (2006). The institutionalisation of an elite sport organization in Norway: The case of Olympiatoppen. *Sociology of Sport Journal, 23*(3), 293–313.

Bauman, Z., 1999 *Globalization: The human consequences*. Cambridge: Polity Press.

Bennett, C. J., & Howlett, M. (1992). The lessons of learning: Reconciling theories of policy learning and policy change. *Political Sciences, 25*(3), 275–294.

Benson. J. K. (1982). Networks and policy

sectors: A framework for extending inter-organizational analysis. In D. Rogers & D. Whitton (Eds.), *Inter-organizational coordination*. Iowa: Iowa State University.

Birley, D. (1996). *Playing the game: Sport and British society 1914–1945*. Manchester: Manchester University Press.

Blomqvist, P. (2004). The choice revolution: privatization of Swedish welfare services in the 1990s. *Social Policy and Administration*, *38*(2), 139–155.

Carrington, B., & Macdonald, I. (2000). *"Race," sport and British society*. London: Routledge.

Cerny, P. (1995). Globalization and the changing logic of collective action. *International Organization*, *48*(4), 595–625.

Checkel, J. T. (2005). International institutions and socialization in Europe: Introduction and framework. *International Organization*, *59*(4), 801–826.

Coleman, W., & Perl, A. (1999). Internationalized policy environments and policy network analysis. *Political Studies*, *47*(4), 691–709.

Dale, R. (1999). Specifying globalization effects on national policy: A focus on the mechanisms. *Journal of Education Policy*, *14*(1), 1–17.

David, P. (2005). *Human rights in youth sport: A critical review of children's rights in competitive sports*. London: Routledge.

Deacon, B. (2000). Eastern European welfare states: The impact of the politics of globalization. *Journal of European Social Policy*, *10*(2), 121–146.

Deacon, B., with Hulse, M., & Stubbs, P. (1997). *Global social policy: International organizations and the future of welfare*. London: Sage.

Digel, H. (2002a). Organization of high performance athletics in selected countries. Final report for the International Athletic Foundation. Tübingen, Germany: University of Tübingen.

Digel, H. (2002b). A comparison of competitive sports systems. *New Studies in Athletics*, *17*(1), 37–49.

DiMaggio, P., & Powell, W. (1983). The iron cage revisited: Institutional isomorphism and collective rationality in organizational fields. *American Sociological Review*, *48*(April), 147–160.

Dolowitz, D., & Marsh, D. (1996). Who learns what from whom? A review of the policy transfer literature. *Political Studies*, *44*(2), 343–357.

Dolowitz, D., & Marsh, D. (2000). Learning from abroad: the role of policy transfer in contemporary policy making. *Governance*, *13*(1), 5–24.

Easton, D. (1965). *A framework for political analysis*. Englewood Cliffs, NJ: Prentice Hall.

Ellison, N. (2006). *The transformation of welfare states?* London: Routledge.

Esping-Andersen, G. (1990). *The three worlds of welfare capitalism*. Cambridge: Polity Press.

Fischer, F. (2003). *Reframing public policy: Discursive politics and deliberative practices*. New York: Oxford University Press.

Fitch, R. (1996). *The assassination of New York*. London: Verso.

Freeman, G. P. (1985). National styles and policy sectors: Explaining structured variation. *Journal of Public Policy*, *5*(4), 467–496.

Frohock, F. M. (1979). *Public policy: Scope and logic*. Englewood Cliffs, NJ: Prentice Hall.

Glatzer, M., & Rueschmeyer, D. (Eds.). (2005). *Globalization and the future of the welfare state*. Pittsburgh: University of Pittsburgh Press.

Green, M., & Houlihan, B. (2005). *Elite sport development: Policy learning and political priorities*. London: Routledge.

Green, M., & Oakley, B. (2001a). Elite sport development systems and playing to win: Uniformity and diversity in international approaches. *Leisure Studies*, *20*(4), 247–267.

Green, M., & Oakley, B. (2001b). Lesson drawing: International perspectives on elite sport development systems in established nations. Paper presented at the Nation and Sport Conference. Brunel University, London, June.

Greener, I. (2002). Understanding NHS reform: The policy-transfer, social learning, and path dependency perspectives. *Governance: An International Journal of Policy, Administration, and Institutions*, *15*(2), 161–183.

Haas, P. M. (1992). Introduction: Epistemic communities and international policy co-ordination. *International Organization*, *46*, 1–35.

Hall, P. A. (1986). *Governing the economy: The politics of state intervention in Britain and France*. Cambridge: Polity Press.

Hajer, M., & Wagenaar, H. (Eds.). (2003). *Deliberative policy analysis: Understanding governance in the network society*. Cambridge: Cambridge University Press.

Hargreaves, J. (1994). *Sporting females: Critical issues in the history and sociology of women's sport*. London: Routledge

Hechter, M. (1975). Review essay. *Contemporary Sociology, 4*(2), 217–222.

Heclo, H. (1972). Review article: Policy analysis. *British Journal of Political Science, 11*(1), 83–108.

Heinelt, H. (2005). *Do policies determine politics?*. School for Policy Studies Working Paper No. 11. Bristol: University of Bristol.

Henry, I. (2001). *The politics of leisure policy* (2nd ed.). London: Palgrave.

Hirst, P., & Thompson, G. (1999). *Globalization in question* (2nd ed.). Cambridge: Polity Press.

Hogwood, B. (1987). *From crisis to complacency*. Oxford: Oxford University Press.

Houlihan, B. (2007). Sport and globalization. In B. Houlihan (Ed.), *Sport and society* (2nd ed., pp. 553–573). London: Sage.

Houlihan, B., & Green, M. (Eds.). (2008). *Comparative elite sport development: Systems, structures and public policy*. Oxford: Butterworth-Heinemann.

Houlihan, B., & White, A. (2002). *The politics of sport development: Development of sport or development through sport?* London: Routledge.

Howlett, R., & Ramesh, M. (1995). *Studying public policy: Policy cycles and policy sub-systems*. New York: Oxford University Press.

Iversen, T. (2005). *Capitalism, democracy and welfare*. London: Routledge.

Jenkins, W. I. (1978). *Policy analysis: Political and organizational perspectives*. London: Martin Robertson.

Kay, A. (2005). A critique of the use of path dependency in policy studies. *Public administration, 83*(3), 553–571.

Keohane, R. O., Haas, P. M., & Levy, M. A. (1993). The effectiveness of international environmental institutions. In P. M. Haas, R. O. Keohane, & M. A. Levy (Eds.), *Institutions for the earth: Sources of effective international environmental protection*. Cambridge, MA: The MIT Press.

Keohane, R. O., & Nye, J. (1977). *Power and interdependence*. Boston, MA: Little Brown.

Krasner, S. (1983). Structural causes and regime consequences: Regimes as intervening variables. In S. Krasner (Ed.), *International regimes*. Ithaca, NY: Cornell University Press.

Krauss, R. G. (1990). *Recreation and leisure in modern society* (4th ed.). New York: Harper Collins.

Leibfried, S. (1990). *The classification of welfare state regimes in Europe*. Paper presented at Social Policy Association Annual Conference, June, University of Bath.

Lukes, S. (2005). *Power: A radical view*. Basingstoke: Palgrave.

Lundahl, L. (2005). Swedish, European, global: The transformation of the Swedish welfare state. In D. Coulby & E. Zambeta (Eds.), *World yearbook of education 2005: Globalization and nationalism in education*. London: Routledge Falmer.

Macintosh, D. (1991). Sport and the state: The case of Canada. In F. Landry et al. (Eds.), *Sport . . . The third millennium*. Sainte-Foy: Les Presse de Universitairé de Laval.

Macintosh, D., & Whitson, D. (1990). *The game planners: Transforming Canada's sports system*. Montreal: McGill-Queens University Press.

Mares, I. (2003). *The politics of social risk: Business and welfare state development*. Cambridge: Cambridge University Press.

McEwen, N., & Moreno, L. (Eds.). (2005). *The territorial politics of welfare*. London: Routledge.

Nadelmann, E. A. (1990). Global prohibition regimes: The evolution of norms in international society. *International Organization, 44*(4), 479–526.

Oakley, B., & Green, M. (2001). The production of Olympic champions: International perspectives on elite sport development systems. *European Journal of Sport Management, 8* (Special Issue), 83–105.

Oliver, M. J., 1997. *Whatever happened to monetarism?* Aldershot: Ashgate.

Ozga, J., & Lingard, B. (2007). Globalization, education policy and politics. In B. Lingard & J. Ozga (Eds.), *The Routledge Falmer reader in education policy and politics*. London: Routledge.

Pickup, D. (1996). *Not another messiah: An ac-*

count of the Sports Council 1988–1993. Bishop Aukland: Pentland Press.

Pierson, P. (1993). When effect becomes cause: Policy feedback and policy change. World Politics, 45(4), 595–628.

Risse, T., Ropp, S., & Sikkink, K. (Eds.). (1999). The power of human rights: international norms and domestic change. Cambridge: Cambridge University Press.

Roche, M. (1993). Sport and community: Rhetoric and reality in the development of British sport policy. In J. C. Binfield & J. Stevenson (Eds.), Sport, culture and politics. Sheffield: Sheffield Academic Press.

Rose, R. (2005). Learning from comparative public policy: A practical guide. London: Routledge.

Rosenberg, J. (2005). Globalization theory: A post mortem. International Politics, 42(1), 2–74.

Scholte, J. A. (2003). Globalization: A critical introduction (2nd ed.). Basingstoke: Palgrave.

Siaroff, A. (1994). Work, women and gender equality: A new typology. In D. Sainsbury (Ed.), Gendering welfare states. London: Sage.

Silk, M. L., Andrews, D. L., & Cole, C. L. (Eds.). (2005). Sport and corporate nationalism. Oxford: Berg.

Slack, T. (Ed.). (2004). The commercialisation of sport. London: Routledge.

Strange, S. (1983). Cave! hic dragones: A critique of regime analysis. In S. D. Krasner (Ed.),

International regimes. Ithaca, NY: Cornell University Press.

Taylor, S., & Henry, M. (2000). Globalization and educational policymaking: A case study. Educational theory, 50(4), 487–503.

Thelen, K., & Steinmo, S. (1992). Historical institutionalism in comparative politics. In K. Thelen, S. Steinmo, & F. Longstreth (Eds.), Structuring politics: Historical institutionalism in comparative analysis. Cambridge: Cambridge University Press.

Thomas, N. (2007). Sport and disability. In B. Houlihan (Ed.), Sport and society: A student introduction (2nd ed.). London: Sage.

UK Sport. (2006). Sports policy factors leading to international sporting success: An international comparative study. London: UK Sport.

Whitty, G., Edwards, T., & Gerwitz, S.

(1993). Specialisation and choice in urban education. London: Routledge.

Wilson, J. (1994). Playing by the rules: Sport, society and the state. Detroit: Wayne State University Press.

Yamamoto, M.Y. (2008). Japan. In B. Houlihan & M. Green (Eds.), Comparative elite sport development: Systems, structures and public policy. Oxford: Butterworth-Heinemann.

Yamamoto, M.Y. (2009). The influence of international policy regimes on domestic sport policy. Doctoral thesis. Loughborough University.

17

POLICY TRANSFER, LESSON DRAWING, AND PERSPECTIVES ON ELITE SPORT DEVELOPMENT SYSTEMS

Mick Green

In recent years, public policy analyses have focused increasing attention on the concepts of "policy transfer"—and its more overtly "intentional" counterpart, "lesson drawing"—especially in the UK (James & Lodge, 2003). Academic analyses have probed the salience of these concepts within the context of an increasingly interconnected world (cf. Dolowitz & Marsh, 1996, 2000; Dolowitz et al., 1999; Evans & Davies, 1999; Rose, 1991, 1993, 2005). And in the UK, empirical interrogation of these concepts in different policy sectors (e.g., taxation, housing, and prisons) has been promoted by a £3.5 million Economic and Social Research Council Future Governance Programme (Page, 2000). To date, however, these concepts have yet to be applied to the sport policy and sport management sectors.

The central aim of this paper therefore is to explore the salience of the concepts of policy transfer and lesson drawing in an examination of the various components of elite (Olympic) sport development systems in Australia and the UK. In part, this paper is a contribution toward Chalip's (2006, p. 1) recent exhortations for research in the "sport management discipline" to embrace two complementary branches of study:

1. An investigation of "the relevance and application of theories from other disciplines."
2. That this research is "grounded in sport phenomena."

A second, but no less important aim follows from the first. That is, to explore the transferability and thus relevance of (elite sport) policy ideas, goals, content, and practice from one country's jurisdiction to another. In so doing, this paper is also a contribution toward Green's (2005, p. 249) judicious insight that much more work is required in order to bring our current knowledge about the social, political, and psychological parameters of sport participation "to bear on programme planning, implementation, and evaluation." Similar lacunae are evident in the literature on policy transfer and lesson drawing and the claims made on their behalf. In this respect, Page (2000, pp. 8–9) highlights two (of several) issues yet to be resolved:

1. "the question of significance for whom or what [of policy transfer and lesson drawing]" and
2. the requirement to link "outcomes to processes . . . which would be likely to attract a practitioner audience."

The contemporary significance of elite sport development—the "sport phenomenon" under consideration—is underscored by Green and Houlihan (2005) who note, "Over the past 40 years at least there has been an increasing awareness among governments of the value of elite sporting success" (p. 1). Governments across a diverse range of countries—for example, New Zealand (Sam & Jackson, 2004); China (Hong et al., 2005); Singapore (Teo, 2005); Australia (Stewart et al., 2004), and the UK (Green, 2004a)—have shown a considerable willingness to devote significant sums of public or government controlled money (e.g., national lotteries) to the maintenance or improvement of elite sporting success. This is therefore a timely debate. A former senior official at the English Sports Council (now Sport England) argued, "Over the last 10 years, I think if ideas have been borrowed from anywhere, they've been borrowed more from Australia than anywhere else" (Interview, 26 February 2002). Moreover, a senior research officer at the United Kingdom Sports Council (known as UK Sport) stated that UK Sport is a partner in an ongoing cross-national research program that seeks to "learn from other successful European countries about establishing medal winning elites" (personal communication, 21 March 2001; see also Sport Industry Research Center, 2002).

This paper is structured around a number of questions that provide an organizing framework for this first attempt at examining the salience of the concepts of policy transfer and lesson drawing in the sport policy and sport management sectors: in this case, specifically in respect of elite sport development systems. The questions are:

1. What is policy transfer?
2. Why engage in policy transfer? (within this question, the subquestions, what factors constrain policy transfer? and who transfers policy? are also addressed)
3. From where are lessons drawn?
4. What is transferred? (Dolowitz & Marsh, 1996, 2000).

With this evidence in place, we then address the questions raised above with regard to the significance of the evidence: in short, how useful might the evidence be for future sport policymaking and sport management practice? What follows is not purely a theoretical commentary. This paper draws on a study of elite sport policy development in three sports in Australia, Canada, and the UK conducted between 2000 and 2004, which involved an extensive review and analysis of governmental literature, as well as documents from National Sports Organizations (NSOs), including internal reports and reviews, strategy papers, and minutes of meetings. In addition, a series of interviews was conducted with senior officials in government agencies and NSOs and with academics and analysts of the sport sector in each country. The interviewees were selected on the basis that they:

1. were, or had been, in senior positions,
2. were involved at a strategic level of decision making, and
3. had been involved in sport policy/management deliberations over several years (for more detail, see Green, 2003; Green & Houlihan, 2005).

The interview schedules were derived from a similar set of themes to allow for triangulation (of response) between interviewees from the NSOs, government agencies, and sports analysts. The key themes included:

1. evidence of voluntaristic (intentional) lesson drawing,
2. evidence of tangible indicators of transferred policy and/or lessons drawn,
3. sources of potential incompatibility between jurisdictions, and
4. the potential salience of (any) lessons drawn for future decision making and practice.

In short, interviews were used in order to:

1. gain an understanding of public sport policy programs from the perspective of key policy actors,
2. allow distinctions to be made between the "rhetoric" provided in policy documents and the "reality" of an agent's insights into her/his perspective on a particular policy development, and
3. attempt to discern the normative values and belief systems underlying the agent's singular perspective, as well as an assessment of the constraining/facilitating structural context within which she/he operates.

Disaggregating Policy Transfer and Lesson Drawing

What Is Policy Transfer?

At the outset it should be noted that there is much definitional ambiguity in the literature regarding the concepts of policy transfer and lesson drawing (cf. Evans & Davies, 1999; James & Lodge, 2003; Page, 2000). Therefore, in order to provide some conceptual clarity to what follows, we can note that policy transfer is generally conceived of as a broader concept than lesson drawing as it takes account of ideas of diffusion and coercion rather than just the voluntaristic activity of the latter. Following Evans and Davies' (1999, p. 366) analysis, which problematized boundary definitions of both concepts, for the purposes of this paper "policy transfer is defined in Rose's terms as an action-oriented intentional activity." Moreover, for Rose (2005, p. 16), "A *lesson* is the outcome of learning; it specifies a programme drawing on knowledge of programmes in other countries dealing with much the same problem." A further crucial insight is that "Lesson drawing cannot be politically neutral, because politics is about conflicting values and goals" and "that there is rarely complete political consensus, even about scientific and technical matters" (Rose, 1991, p. 22). This argument draws attention to the discussion in Section 2.2, where it is evident that the potential for conflict between elected politicians and sport bureaucrats involved in policy development hindered attempts to implement a strategy for an elite sport institute in the UK during the 1990s. It is also important to state briefly what lesson drawing is not. Lesson drawing is not a theory of *how* policymakers learn. It is about what is learned, the programs that public officials develop in order to deal with immediate substantive problems. The immediate substantive problem in the case of elite sport development in the UK in the early to mid-1990s was the persistently poor performances of elite athletes and consequent low medal results at the Olympic Games, and at the 1996 Atlanta Games in particular (Green, 2004a).

Thus policymakers are driven by the need to dispel such dissatisfaction and instead of new knowledge per se they prefer the assurance of doing what has worked before, or been effective elsewhere. Therefore, searching is instrumentally directed and in part, due to the fact that policymakers have insufficient time or the knowledge to be continuously seeking an ideal policy (cf. Evans & Davies, 1999; Rose, 2005). Indeed, Houlihan (1991) suggests that governments' preference for solutions in respect of sport policy are those that promise an immediate impact, are cheap, and are simple to administer. Moreover, given the comments above on "what has worked before," lesson drawing is clearly not about "innovation" because innovation research is concerned with novel or original programs. By contrast, lesson drawing "presupposes that even though a programme may be new to a government considering it, something very much like it will be in effect elsewhere" (Rose, 1993, p. 24).

Why Engage in Policy Transfer?

Any search for lessons in other jurisdictions is initiated in the hope that a program that is viewed as working well there can be transferred to the borrowing jurisdiction (cf. Rose, 2005). This section therefore interrogates issues surrounding why both state and non-state actors engaged in the intentional lesson drawing form of policy transfer. Here, the related questions of Who transfers policy? and What factors constrain policy transfer? are also considered. In exploring the reasons why these actors engage in this activity, the distinction between voluntary and coercive transfer is highlighted—yet, as revealed in the examples below, at the margins the distinction between the two remains ambiguous.

Over the past 10–15 years, developments within the UK's elite sport system reveal degrees of intentional lesson drawing or voluntary transfer (Green & Houlihan, 2005). However, it is also argued that there is evidence of "indirect coercive transfer" (Dolowitz & Marsh, 1996, pp. 348–349). It should be noted that Dolowitz and Marsh also refer to "direct coercive transfer": when one government forces another to adopt a policy. The direct imposition of policy transfer on another country is rare, however. Examples of this form of transfer may be more commonly found among former Communist bloc countries (cf.

Girginov, 1998). In respect of voluntary transfer, Dolowitz and Marsh (1996, p. 346) suggest that "the primary catalyst . . . is some form of dissatisfaction or problem with the status quo." The ideas promoted for the development of the UK Sports Institute (UKSI) network of facilities in the early to mid-1990s (originally conceived of as the British Academy of Sport) are suggestive of voluntary lesson drawing. Iain Sproat, the Conservative Minister for Sport at the time, argued that the government embarked on this development because there were problems with low participation in sport, poor Olympic medal results, and alarming health reports regarding young people in Britain (Sproat, 1996). With specific regard to elite sport in the UK and lesson drawing from Australia, Theodoraki (1999) reinforces Dolowitz and Marsh's comments above in respect of voluntary transfer:

> Sproat led the Conservative's initiative of the Academy following his visit to the Australian equivalent [Australian Institute of Sport] where he saw a solution to the problems of elite performers in the UK. The Atlanta 1996 Olympics placed added emphasis on the need for the Academy as low medal scores worsened public perception and morale was low" (p. 196).

However, at least one question that remains unanswered here is whether Sproat was seeking a solution to a political problem rather than purely for policy reasons. If this was the case, then, as Dolowitz (2003) reminds us, the lesson drawing is likely "to involve little actual analysis of its possible impact on an existing situation" (p. 105). The "existing situation" at this time was that the Conservative Government was in crisis on a number of fronts, not least because of its handling of the economy but, as noted above, also because the government faced a number of increasingly intractable sport policy problems that were being played out ever more vociferously in the media. Therefore, it is tempting to conclude that Sproat's initial insistence for a centralized elite sports institute, based on the original Australian model, rather than a decentralized network of centers (the recommendation from sports practitioners on the ground) was at least in part due to broader political concerns to (swiftly) assuage public and media discontent through the establishment of a grandiose, "showcase" elite institute. In short, if claims for lesson drawing are made then we need to be clear about the detail of lessons drawn and the reasons why.

If we accept for a moment that this was the voluntaristic rationale for UK government intervention and subsequent lesson drawing, what were the factors that might have led to indirect coercive transfer? Dolowitz and Marsh (1996) highlight two factors indicative of what occurred in the UK. First, these authors argue that "A country can . . . be indirectly pushed toward policy transfer if political actors perceive their country as falling behind its neighbours or competitors" (p. 349). Indeed, reflecting Theodoraki's (1999) comments above regarding public perception and low morale, Bennett (1991) argues that "fears of being left behind on an important public issue can trigger attention. The cumulative effect of action elsewhere may translate into a feeling of insecurity about being the odd-man-out" (p. 43). Clearly, UK policy-makers were concerned with worsening performances at the elite level, particularly at global mega-events such as the Olympic Games.

The second factor highlighted by Dolowitz and Marsh (1996, p. 349) refers to the emergence of an international consensus acting as a push factor with regard to a particular policy area, and

> when a common solution to that problem has been introduced in a number of nations, then nations not adopting this . . . solution will face increasing pressure to join the international "community" by implementing similar programmes or policies.

Houlihan (1997) draws attention to the potential for a common solution to a sport policy problem, which reinforces the notion of an international consensus acting as a push factor. Houlihan argued that the successful Soviet model of elite sport development was evident in Australia, and to a lesser extent Canada, "including the systematic sifting of school-age children as a means of identifying the potential elite . . . the development of specialist training academies . . . and the use of public money to support individual elite athletes" (pp. 6–7). In respect of the point raised earlier regarding how these two types of transfer (voluntary and indirect coercive) merge at the margins, the example of voluntary transfer and the first example cited above regarding indirect coercive transfer, reveal that there is little to choose between the two types. Yet, whichever theoretical nuance is applied, it is evident that UK sport policymakers and bureaucrats engaged in *some degree* of intentional lesson drawing (for whatever political/policy reasons), at least with regard to the development of the UKSI during the 1990s.

The developments surrounding the establishment of the UKSI also allow us to explore, briefly, the two subquestions, Who transfers policy? and What factors constrain policy transfer? In relation to these questions, the earlier point regarding lesson drawing not being politically neutral, given that politics is about conflicting values and goals, is brought into sharp relief. The potential for such conflict is heightened, given Dolowitz and Marsh's (1996) observation that there are "six main categories of actors involved in policy transfer" (p. 345): elected officials; political parties; bureaucrats/civil servants; pressure groups; policy entrepreneurs/experts; and supra-national institutions. Elected officials and bureaucrats/civil servants are of interest here. In the case of the latter group, David Pickup and Derek Casey, respectively Director-General and Director of National Services at the GB Sports Council, visited Australia in 1992. As Pickup (1996) notes:

> The Government's conclusion that the promotion of excellence should be undertaken on a consistent UK-wide basis provided Derek Casey and me with a helpful point of departure for our imminent visit to Australia, the principal purpose of which was to study Australia's approach to grooming their elite athletes through Canberra's Institute of Sport and its satellite academies (p. 97).

As for elected officials, Iain Sproat's (then Minister for Sport) *later* visit to Australia in 1995 is significant. Indeed, as acknowledged in a statement by UK Sport (1998), "The idea to establish an academy of sport was raised by John Major, the former Prime Minister, after the then Minister for Sport, Iain Sproat, visited the Australian Institute of Sport (AIS) in Canberra in 1995" (p. 4). There are at least two discernible strands to the conflict surrounding the lessons drawn by these two sets of actors. The first strand centers on Pickup's (1996) version of what was learned from the visit to Australia *in 1992*:

> Doubts began to arise as we discovered that each of the State Govern-ments had come to resent Canberra's claimed dominance . . . and the States had moved to develop their own centers of excellence . . . [t]his strengthened our conviction that . . . a decentralized provision of training facilities was more sensible than creating a single mega-factory dedicated to churning out potential gold medalists. (p. 98)

The key point here is that there does not appear to have been any acknowl-edgement by Iain Sproat of the lessons drawn during Pickup and Casey's *ear-lier* visit in 1992. Arguably, this may be related to Pickup's (1996) observation that Sproat "was to prove the least communicative politician responsible for the sport portfolio in my experience" (p. 135). The potential for conflict is borne out to some extent in the evidence surrounding the implementation of the lessons drawn regarding the UKSI. As Theodoraki (1999) notes, there were interminable delays throughout the short-listing stages of the bidding process for the development of what was then termed the British Academy of Sport. These delays centered on an in-built conflict over the Academy's func-tion. As Trelford (1997, p. 30) reported in *The Daily Telegraph*, "Iain Sproat, the Sports Minister, wanted . . . a showcase like the Australian Academy. The sports organizations thought [a network of facilities] would best meet the country's real needs." Thus, a somewhat deeper analysis of Sproat's actions further illustrates the requirement for care when exploring the concepts of policy transfer/lesson drawing. For example, as sport policy is a form of social policy and since social policies are designed within frameworks delimited by the institutions, customs, and traditions of the country within which they are established, policymakers (especially politicians) often misunderstand the poli-cies they see in other countries or find themselves promoting the transfer of lit-tle more than the idea that there might be a policy of some kind that is of use (rather than the specific details of policy). As noted earlier, this appears to have been the case with Sproat's endorsement of the concept of a centralized "showcase" elite institute rather than the less (politically) spectacular concept of a network of regional facilities, but one that would best suit the UK context.

The second strand concerning the conflict and delays surrounding the es-tablishment of the UKSI was, in part, due to a general election during the short-listing process for potential locations and a subsequent change of politi-cal administration in 1997 from Conservative to Labour. What then were the ramifications of such change for the nascent Institute? Theodoraki (1999)

found that, despite comments to the contrary before the election by Tom
Pendry, the then shadow Sports Minister, there remained a disparity of views
between politicians from different political parties about decisions on the location and function of the UKSI.

From Where Are Lessons Drawn?

Although the primary concern of this paper is an interrogation of evidence for
policy transfer/lesson drawing between the UK and Australia in respect of
elite sport systems, it has been argued that the antecedents of these Western
systems can be located in the systematic approaches found in the former Eastern bloc states (cf. Green & Houlihan, 2005; Green & Oakley, 2001; Houlihan, 1997). As Houlihan (1997) observes, "Australia, and to a lesser extent
Canada . . . both adopted policies of elite squad development which are very
close to the Soviet model in a number of key respects" (p. 6). On one level,
Houlihan may be correct that the former Eastern bloc model of elite sport development bears several similarities to elite sport systems in Australia, Canada,
and, indeed, now the UK. However, on another level, a deeper analysis reveals
some stark discontinuities. For example, a former senior official at the British
Athletics Federation (now UK Athletics), was adamant that the GDR was not
more advanced than the UK in the areas of sports science and medicine. This
official argued that "if you were to strip away the drug abuse from their programmes, their success would be no greater than anybody else's" (Interview,
28 May 2002). Moreover, Australian talent identification systems bear little resemblance to what many have claimed about the Soviet Union and GDR. Indeed, in the Olympic sports where Australia has enjoyed considerable success
there remains a strong reliance on club-based development and social systems
of recruitment, rather than formal talent identification programs. The examples of two high-profile Olympic sports — swimming and athletics — help to
make the point. Firstly, a senior official at Australian Swimming (the NSO for
the sport) admitted that the organization does not have a systematic program
of talent identification and relies instead on "underpinning programmes
through age squads . . . and competition and training programmes" (Interview, 5 June 2003). Secondly, a senior official at Australian Athletics acknowledged that, in recent years, "most of, if not all, our talent identification . . . has
flowed through the school system . . . and a very large state schools athletics
championship" (Interview, 4 June 2003).

Regardless of the claims for former Eastern bloc antecedents, Dolowitz et
al. (1999) identify a number of factors that provide conducive conditions for
lesson drawing between different jurisdictions in the West: a common language; a shared (neo-liberal) ideology; personal relations; and the role of think-
tanks and policy entrepreneurs. In respect of the UK drawing lessons from
Australia in relation to the development of elite sport systems, the common
language is clearly significant, removing problems of translation and facilitating a much easier exchange of ideas. Indeed, Green and Houlihan's (2005)

comparative study of elite sport development in Australia, Canada, and the UK found that:

> Australia has been an important influence on the emerging policy framework for elite sport development in the UK through the appointment to pivotal coaching posts of Australians including Bill Sweetenham, National Performance Director for British Swimming, Deidre Anderson, UKSI Programme Manager and Wilma Shakespear, National Director of the English Institute of Sport. (p. 188)

As Green and Houlihan go on to note, "These and other international appointments bring ideas, methods, and experiences from Australia and other leading countries and have been very influential in shaping elite sport in the UK" (p. 188). What appears to be emerging here is that, rather than lessons being drawn from Australia regarding specific policy mechanisms, techniques or content, for example, it is experienced Australian coaches, scientists and senior sports administrators and *their ideas* that are having an important impact on elite sport development in the UK. This is an argument borne out by a senior official at the Amateur Swimming Association and British Swimming, the sport's lead organizations in the UK. This official maintained that recent changes in the sport are not due to any notion of "the Australian model . . . it's the Bill Sweetenham model . . . who has said that the acid test of success is Olympic gold medals, nothing else counts, and I agree" (Interview, 18 March 2002). Moreover, a former UK international athlete who is now involved with UK Sport in redesigning programs for elite performers, argued that "This [UK] government has become obsessed with the [idea of] the Australian model," which has not been universally accepted by all (Interview, 23 August 2002).

The notion of ideology is also important in that not only have both Australian and UK governments prioritized elite sport development as a significant focus of political intervention in general but they have also both adopted neoliberal beliefs (e.g., business principles, target setting, audits and inspection, sanctions for poor performance) in the prioritization of sports for funding in particular (cf. Green & Houlihan, 2006). The notion of personal relations does not just refer to Prime Ministerial/Presidential (political) relationships, rather it is also about relationships formed by policy entrepreneurs/experts. One prominent example during the late 1990s is that of Roger Moreland, then Director of the UKSI project, who was part of an International Forum on Elite Sport (attended by experts from 17 countries), convened for the first time in Sydney in 1999. Amongst other issues, this forum discussed "essential factors in a successful elite program" and the "evaluation of the performance of an elite program" (Moreland, 1999, p. 1).

What Is Transferred?

It is important to note that it is rarely possible to quantify the extent of policies transferred or lessons drawn. As Dolowitz et al. (1999) observe, "Governments do not provide convenient lists of what they borrow or from where they borrow. There are also difficulties in establishing whether transfer has occurred" (p. 719). However, following our earlier stated position, in order to better delineate evidence of lesson drawing, this analysis is restricted to interrogating "action-oriented learning — that which takes place consciously and results in policy action" (Evans & Davies, 1999, p. 368). A key aspect of this definition is the element of intentionality, which makes an agent essential to the policy transfer process. In this respect, the intentional activity of a state actor, Iain Sproat (although Sproat's intentions were questioned earlier) and non-state actors (sport bureaucrats), Derek Casey, David Pickup and Roger Moreland have been highlighted. Further examples of such activity are provided below.

As noted, it appears that ideas and attitudes from Australia have been transferred, primarily through key individuals relocating to the UK. Although the evidence in UK national sport policy statements is less clear-cut, the Conservative Government's document, *Sport: Raising the Game* (Department of National Heritage, 1995) placed far greater emphasis on elite sport achievement than had previously been apparent in the UK. This political legitimation of the significance of elite sport development was reinforced in the Labour Party's first major sport policy statement, *A Sporting Future for All* (Department for Culture, Media and Sport [DCMS], 2000) and more recently in *Game Plan* in 2002 (DCMS/Strategy Unit, 2002). It was suggested in Section 2.2 that a key catalyst for this change in political and policy emphasis was the UK's poor performances at the Olympic Games. This mirrors the Australian experience, where the failure to win any gold medals at the 1976 Montreal Olympics caused a public outcry and created the political environment for change (cf. Stewart et al., 2004). This changing emphasis in the UK is also apparent in the transfer of ideas about institutions, for example, in the lessons drawn regarding elite sport institutes. A UK Sport (1997) internal policy statement reinforces this view, wherein the influence of Australian ideas with regard to the UKSI was unequivocally acknowledged. This statement not only maintained that UK Sport must be "astute enough to utilise the lessons from abroad", but also that the "Director of Sport Sciences at the Australian Institute of Sport was one of the outside consultants recruited to assist in the technical evaluation" (p. 2) for the development of the UKSI.

There is also some evidence of the transfer of ideas in respect of specific policy instruments, for example, in the revision of talent identification procedures. As Sport England's Senior Research Manager acknowledged, "Australia, the former Soviet Union, and East Germany have been identified as having (or having had) a more proactive approach to the development of talent. Australia has been hailed as a good example of how talent can be developed" (cited in English Sports Council, 1998, foreword). However, as noted in respect of the actions of a former Minister for Sport (Iain Sproat), statements such as these from policymakers require a far deeper analysis. Indeed, two years before this English Sports Council statement was released, Prescott (1996) questioned a slavish adherence to talent identification procedures that mirror those found in the former Eastern bloc: "The question of whether the identification of talent was of prime importance or whether the harsh training regimes were largely responsible for the extraordinary success of Soviet and other Eastern European athletes remains unanswered" (pp. 12–13).

The final point here centers on whether the UK has drawn lessons regarding the effective targeting of resources. In other words, given that governments have to allocate scarce resources — and sport is just one of many legitimate claims for such resources — actors involved in elite sport development in the UK are under increasing pressure to further prioritize the range of sports deemed "worthy" of funding (cf. National Audit Office [NAO], 2005). The NAO's (2005) review of support provided to elite athletes recommended that UK Sport should be "prepared to make tough decisions based on whether sports merited funding and on what scale" (p. 6). The NAO review is notable in that it commissioned research into the ways in which Australia, Italy, and the Netherlands fund and support different sports and their elite athletes. The prioritization of sports for funding was established in Australia over a decade ago. As a senior official at the Australian Sports Commission (ASC) acknowledged, "In the early 1990s . . . we had specific sports that we were targeting for success" (Interview, 5 June 2003). Moreover, a major federal government review of sport and recreation in Australia confirms that "The ASC chose eight sports in the early 1990s to receive a boost in funding," in large part due to the forthcoming Sydney Olympic Games (Commonwealth of Australia, 1999, p. 33).

Confirmation that lessons had been drawn from Australia in this respect is provided by a former senior official at the English Sports Council: "We looked at what Australia had done with its focus on eight sports, plus the development of the AIS as part of our planning process for elite athlete development in the UK" (Interview, 26 February 2002). Thus there appears to be persuasive evidence that the development of funding/ support programs in the UK over the past 10–15 years (notably the three-tiered National Lottery-funded World Class funding program, UK Sport's prioritization of sports into four funding categories and the NAO recommendations that even fewer sports should be funded), reflects lessons drawn from Australia during the 1990s.

Discussion and Conclusions

This paper had one primary aim: to interrogate the evidence for the intentional lesson drawing form of policy transfer between the UK and Australia in respect of elite sport development systems. In so doing, a secondary aim was to provide a contribution to recent exhortations in the sport management literature (cf. Chalip, 2006; Green, 2005) that argue for a research agenda that should not only synthesise theoretical insights from other disciplines but also that this research should help to illuminate future sport policymaking and sport management practice.

At first sight it is tempting to argue that the development of the elite sport system in the UK is simply an adaptation of the system in Australia. However, a deeper analysis reveals a much more complicated and complex picture[1] because, at least in part, "Sport programmes are social systems with their own internal dynamics . . . They are embedded in a broader system of social relations" (Green, 2005, p. 243). On a theoretical/conceptual level, insights from the literature on policy transfer and lesson drawing certainly have a degree of salience in alerting sport policymakers and bureaucrats to the possibilities of drawing lessons about programs that have achieved success in one jurisdiction (country) for application in their own country. In the case of UK sport policymakers and bureaucrats drawing (elite sport) lessons from Australia, it is at the level of policy ideas or "policy as discourse" (cf. Bacchi, 2000) — primarily transferred through senior sport administrators, coaches, and scientists — rather than concrete programs, techniques, and tools where we find the greatest evidence of lesson drawing.

In this respect, Houlihan's (2005, p. 176) development of a framework for analysis of public sector sport policy is instructive in pointing to the need for interrogation "in terms of the metaphor of levels." This perspective rests on the argument that, in order to better understand policy processes and policy change, it is necessary to interrogate the interaction between surface levels of policy and the deep structure which determines within limits the range of variation of the surface levels (Benson, 1982). Houlihan (2005) identifies three levels of analysis in the sport policy area. At the shallowest (surface) level is the pattern of administrative arrangements that in the UK sport policy area would include the gradual decline in the role of local authorities and the relative rise in importance of national agencies linked to a variety of central government departments. At the next level, is the pattern of interorganizational resource dependencies, which is concerned with questions of the distribution among organizations of resources such as knowledge, finance, facilities, potential elite athletes, authority, and administrative capacity. A recent example of resource dependence in the area of sport policy would be the requirement for (Olympic sport) NSOs to comply with UK Sport's staggered targets in return for funding allocations in the long lead-in to the Beijing and London Olympic Games. Crucially, one of the key targets set by UK Sport is for NSOs to have in place a "robust process . . . for identifying the necessary talent characteristics to reach the podium" (UK Sport, 2006a, p. 2). At the third (and highly resistant to change) level, are the embedded structural values fundamental to the social formation (e.g., patriarchal attitudes to participation in sport, class-based patterns of participation, and voluntarism preferred to state intervention).

It is at the second level of interorganizational resource dependencies that is of interest, where Houlihan (2005) argues that recently in the UK there have been a number of shifts in the "policy paradigm" within which sport organizations operate. Of note is the gradual retreat "from a policy discourse centred on the value of 'sport for all' as an integral part of the process of elite sport development to one which emphasizes the demonstration effect of elite success as a catalyst for increasing participation" (Houlihan, 2005, p. 181). The former discourse assumed a somewhat ad hoc and fragmented approach to elite development according to which mass participation was important in providing the volume of participants from which the elite would emerge. In contrast, prominence is now given to improving the sophistication of early talent identification and concentrating that talent in a small number of elite sport institutes or development clubs (with the hoped-for outcome of increased numbers of Olympic medals), but clearly insulating the elite development process from wider issues relating to participation. As discussed earlier, an elite sport policy discourse has emerged steadily in the UK, with Australia proving to be a fertile breeding ground for this discourse; a discourse, moreover, that has added force to developments in elite sport in the UK from the mid-1990s onwards. This discourse has been promoted by sport policymakers and bureaucrats as "popular wisdom" (Chalip, 2006, p. 10) for the political legitimation of elite success. The gradual emergence of a strong elite sport development system is not in and of itself particularly contentious. However, as Bacchi (2000, p. 50) argues, from a "policy as discourse" perspective, "the battles [are] not simply at the level of wanting or resisting a particular policy initiative but at the level of constituting the shape of the issues to be considered."

This leads on to an examination of the potential consequences for sport management practice of dominant policy ideas/discourse around elite sport development for the design and implementation of sport programs (cf. Chalip, 2006; Green, 2005). As Chalip (2006, p. 10) argues, sport sociologists and psychologists "have become adept at exposing fallacies in popular wisdom about sport but they rarely consider the implications of those fallacies for sport management." The "problem" for sport management practice is clear, given the evidence that an increasing number of countries (including Australia and the UK) have built or are at least building, entire sport systems based on some form of talent identification systems (Chalip, 2006; Green & Houlihan, 2005). But, as Chalip (2006, p. 11) reminds us, "what if talent is neither identifiable nor sufficient to assure competitive success?" Moreover, Chalip goes on to suggest that the "design and management of sport systems seeking to produce excellence should not be based on talent identification but instead requires processes and practices intended to optimize athlete recruitment, retention, and advancement" (p. 11; see also Green, 2005). In this respect, for Green (2005, p. 243), sport programs must incorporate designs that inculcate and maximize social support systems: "Family and community support groups, team social functions, and mentoring need to be structured into programme design."

These observations resonate with MacPhail and Kirk's (2006) interrogation of young people's socialization into sport. These authors draw on recent developments in the UK, in particular the promotion and implementation of what is known as the Long-Term Athlete Development (LTAD) model, which provides a framework for structuring young athletes' development through a number of stages, from the "FUNdamental" through to the "Training to Win" stage. The promotion, and indeed legitimation, of the LTAD model is a pertinent example of the ways in which dominant policy ideas and discourses generated at central government level (cf. DCMS/Strategy Unit, 2002) become embedded as "common sense" ways of working for sport organizations and practitioners. And one of the prominent characteristics of this dominant discourse around models such as the LTAD is the resource dependency of NSOs on government funding agencies (in the UK, primarily UK Sport). In other words, failure to comply with top-down "policy dictates" (cf. Green, 2004b) that "compel" NSOs to implement such models often results in threats of reduced funding for future program design (UK Sport, 2006a).

It is therefore not sufficient for sport policymakers and bureaucrats to borrow dominant policy ideas about elite sport development from abroad and then "impose" these ideas at home without carefully working through the potential consequences of implementation with sport management practitioners and also with those who are the ultimate object of these policy ideas: talented young athletes. In this respect, a former senior official at the British Athletics Federation (now UK Athletics) drew attention to talent identification mechanisms with regard to young athletes and argued that "Nobody cares what happens to them if they aren't successful. Nobody seems to be asking the question at all about how people put together their lives when they have failed to make it through the talent ID [identification and development] process" (Interview, 28 May 2002).

The deleterious consequences of failing to heed such concerns resonate with MacPhail and Kirk's (2006, p. 72) analysis of an athletics club in England, which found that there was a real lack of procedure in following athletes through their involvement in the club and with little concern for those that "drop out from the sport." Moreover, if lifelong participation in sport and physical activity is one of the normative goals of sport policy interventions — as the policy and political rhetoric in the UK and Australia appears to suggest (DCMS/Strategy/Unit, 2002; Department of Industry, Science, and Resources, 2001) — then the views of young athletes must be taken into account in the design and implementation of programs for sport. Indeed, MacPhail et al.'s (2003, p. 69) analysis — which advocates that we listen to the voices of young people in sport and physical recreation — posed a salutary question for practitioners charged with the design and implementation of sport programs in the UK: "What are the incentives for young people to participate in sport if they are merely there to make up the numbers and later to be discarded while their more talented, and often socially privileged peers, progress?"

To conclude, insights from the literature on policy transfer and lesson drawing in the interrogation of the ways in which UK sport policymakers and bureaucrats have drawn lessons from Australia in respect of elite sport development systems point primarily to the transfer of dominant policy ideas and discourses that prioritize elite objectives. However, as Chalip (2006, p. 12) argues, "excellent sport programmes are distinguished from mediocre programmes not by *what* is done, but rather by *how* it is done." The lesson for sport policymakers, analysts, and management practitioners is clear: the design, implementation, and evaluation of sport programs requires more than just the narrow criterion of "success" (e.g., medals and trophies). A concerted research program is therefore long overdue into the ways in which athletes are recruited and move through development systems such as the LTAD pathway models now in favor in the UK. Such research is an *urgent* requirement, not least in the UK with the 2012 London Olympic Games just six years away. The UK government is currently providing the largest ever investment in elite sport as part of UK Sport's "No Compromise Investment Strategy" (UK Sport, 2006b, p. 2) for the realization of its goals of over 60 medals and fourth place in the Olympic medals table in 2012. It remains to be seen whether sport policymakers and practitioners in the UK reveal a similar desire to investigate *how* (Chalip, 2006) these goals will be achieved.

Note

1. I am grateful to an anonymous reviewer for emphasizing this point in an earlier draft of this paper.

References

Bacchi, C. (2000). Policy as discourse: What does it mean? Where does it get us? *Discourse: Studies in the Cultural Politics of Education, 21*(1), 45–57.

Bennett, C.J. (1991). How states utilise foreign evidence. *Journal of Public Policy, 11*(1), 31–54.

Benson, J. K. (1982). A framework for policy analysis. In D. Rogers & D. Whetten (Eds.), *Interorganisational coordination: Theory, research and implementation* I (pp. 137–176). Iowa: Iowa State University.

Chalip, L. (2006). Toward a distinctive sport management discipline. *Journal of Sport Management, 20*(1), 1–21.

Commonwealth of Australia. (1999). *Shaping up: A review of Commonwealth involvement in sport and recreation in Australia* (Sport 2000 Task Force). Canberra: Commonwealth of Australia.

Department for Culture, Media, and Sport. (2000). *A sporting future for all*. London: Department for Culture, Media, and Sport.

Department for Culture, Media and Sport/Strategy Unit. (2002). *Game plan: A strategy for delivering government's sport and physical activity objectives*. London: Department for Culture, Media, and Sport/Strategy Unit.

Department of Industry, Science and Resources. (2001). *Backing Australia's sporting ability: A more active Australia*. Canberra: Department of Industry, Science, and Resources.

Department of National Heritage. (1995).

Sport: Raising the game. London: Department of National Heritage.

Dolowitz, D. P. (2003). A policymaker's guide to policy transfer. *The Political Quarterly, 74*(1), 101–108.

Dolowitz, D. P., Greenwold, S., & Marsh, D. (1999). Policy transfer: Something old, something borrowed, but why red, white, and blue?' *Parliamentary Affairs, 52*(4), 719–730.

Dolowitz, D. P., & Marsh, D. (1996). Who learns what from whom? A review of the policy transfer literature. *Political Studies, 44*, 343–357.

Dolowitz, D. P., & Marsh, D. (2000). Learning from abroad: the role of policy transfer in contemporary policymaking. *Governance: An International Journal of Policy and Administration, 13*(1), 5–24.

English Sports Council. (1998). *The development of sporting talent 1997*. London: English Sports Council.

Evans, M., & Davies, J. (1999). Understanding policy transfer: a multi-level, multi-disciplinary perspective. *Public Administration, 77*(2), 361–385.

Girginov, V. (1998). Capitalist philosophy and communist practice: The transformation of Eastern European sport and the International Olympic Committee. *Culture, Sport, and Society, 1*(1), 118–148.

Green, B. C. (2005). Building sport programmes to optimise athlete recruitment, retention, and transition: Toward a normative theory of sport development. *Journal of Sport Management, 19*(3), 233–253.

Green, M. (2003). An analysis of elite sport policy change in three sports in Canada and the United Kingdom. Unpublished doctoral thesis, Loughborough: Loughborough University.

Green, M. (2004a). Changing policy priorities for sport in England: The emergence of elite sport development as a key policy concern. *Leisure Studies, 23*(4), 365–385.

Green, M. (2004b). Power, policy, and political priorities: Elite sport development in Canada and the United Kingdom. *Sociology of Sport Journal, 21*(4), 376–396.

Green, M., & Houlihan, B. (2005). *Elite Sport Development: Policy Learning and Political Priorities*. London: Routledge.

Green, M., & Houlihan, B. (2006). Governmentality, modernisation and the "disciplining" of national sporting organisations: Athletics in Australia and the UK. *Sociology of Sport Journal, 231*, 47–71.

Green, M., & Oakley, B. (2001). Elite sport development systems and playing to win: uniformity and diversity in international approaches. *Leisure Studies, 20*(4), 247–267.

Hong, F., Wu, P., & Xiong, H. (2005). Beijing ambitions: An analysis of the Chinese elite sports system and its Olympic strategy for the 2008 Olympic Games. *The International Journal of the History of Sport, 22*(4), 510–529.

Houlihan, B. (1991). *The government and politics of sport*. London: Routledge.

Houlihan, B. (1997). *Sport, policy and politics: A comparative analysis*. London: Routledge.

Houlihan, B. (2005). Public sector sport policy: Developing a framework for analysis. *International Review for the Sociology of Sport, 40*(2), 163–185.

James, O., & Lodge, M. (2003). The limitations of "policy transfer" and "lesson drawing" for public policy research. *Political Studies Review, 1*(2), 179–193.

MacPhail, A., & Kirk, D. (2006). Young people's socialisation into sport: Experiencing the specialising phase. *Leisure Studies, 25*(1), 57–74.

MacPhail, A., Kirk, D., & Eley, D. (2003). Listening to young people's voices: Youth sports leaders' advice on facilitating participation in sport. *European Physical Education Review, 9*(1), 57–73.

Moreland, R. (1999). *Report on the International Forum on Elite Sport: Sydney, Australia*. (September), Unpublished paper.

National Audit Office. (2005). *UK sport: Supporting elite athletes*. (HC 182 — SE/2005/9 Session 2004–2005). London: The Stationery Office.

Page, E. C. (2000, January). *Future governance and the literature on policy transfer and lesson drawing*. Paper presented at the ESRC Future Governance Workshop, London.

Pickup, D. (1996). *Not another Messiah: An account of the Sports Council 1988–93*. Edinburgh: The Pentland Press.

Prescott, J. (1996). Talent identification and development in female gymnasts. *Coaching Focus, 31*, 12–13.

Rose, R. (1991). What is lesson drawing? *Journal of Public Policy, 11*(1), 3–30.

Rose, R. (1993). *Lesson drawing in public policy: A guide to learning across time and space*. Chatham, NJ: Chatham House.

Rose, R. (2005). *Learning from comparative public policy: A practical guide*. London: Routledge.

Sam, M. P., & Jackson, S. J. (2004). Sport policy development in New Zealand: Paradoxes of an integrative paradigm. *International Review for the Sociology of Sport. 39*(2), 205–222.

Sport Industry Research Centre. (2002). *European sporting success: A study of the development of medal winning elites in five European countries*. Sheffield: Sport Industry Research Centre.

Sproat, I. (1996). *Sport: Raising the game: The government's strategy for sport*. London: Department of National Heritage.

Stewart, B., Nicholson, M., Smith, A., & Westerbeek, H. (2004). *Australian sport: Better by design? The evolution of Australian sport policy*. London: Routledge.

Teo, L. (2005). An analysis of elite sport policy in Singapore from 1990 to 2005. Unpublished master's thesis, Loughborough University, UK.

Theodoraki, E. (1999). The making of the UK Sports Institute. *Managing Leisure, 4*(4), 187–200.

Trelford, D. (January 28, 1997). Academy process set to run and run. *The Daily Telegraph*, p. 30.

UK Sport. (1997). *The British Academy of Sport—A vision for success* (internal paper). London: UK Sport.

UK Sport. (1998). United Kingdom's serious intentions for sport and coaching. *Coaching Focus*, 37, 4–5.

UK Sport (2006a). *Funding release triggers* (press release). London: UK Sport. 1–2.

UK Sport. (2006b). *Transforming the UK high performance sport system* (press release). London: UK Sport. 1–4.

CHANGE AND GRASSROOTS MOVEMENT: RECONCEPTUALIZING WOMEN'S HOCKEY GOVERNANCE IN CANADA

Carly Adams and Julie Stevens

Introduction

Although evidence suggests the Ontario Women's Hockey Association (OWHA) has been a catalyst for female hockey participation in Canada, it has not been a catalyst for female hockey governance. In its 1995 strategic plan, the OWHA recognized two key critical issues that faced the organization in the 1990s: How to increase the effectiveness of the provincial executive body in terms of administration, communication, and governance processes and how to develop a single voice within the women's hockey community to lobby for separate control over the female game (OWHA, 1995). The second of these goals, separate control, has been difficult to achieve as the OWHA is the only female hockey provincial association in Canada that endorses and endeavors to maintain a separatist philosophy. Female hockey governance structures vary as different regions of the country may better suit integrated or partially-integrated governance approaches based upon their unique local histories and individual dynamics. However, women's hockey governance in Canada as a whole has not progressed in a manner where the authority of female hockey participants and leaders has increased.

Women's sport governance is an under-researched area in sport management. Previous work has addressed governance in specific contexts, such as the global sport forum (Thoma & Chalip, 1996) and college athletics (VanderZwaag, 1998) or in terms of sport industry segments (Hums & MacLean, 2004). Research has also addressed issues related to gender and public policy in sport (Shaw & Slack, 2002; MacKay, 1997; Hall & Richardson, 1982), women's sport participation in the Canadian context (Hall, 2002; Lenskyj, 1986), and, more specifically, women's involvement in specific sports such as ice hockey (Avery & Stevens, 1997; Etue & Williams, 1996; Theberge, 2000). However, collectively, these studies fail to explicitly raise the importance of governance in the advancement of women in sport.

Sport policy and sport governance are intricately linked (Hums & MacLean, 2004). The ability to increase opportunities for women and girls in sport relies largely on one's influence within policy decision-making forums. Newman and White (2006) suggest that for transformations to occur, women must be brought " . . . in from the margins of the policy process" as active contributors to the decision-making process (p. 131). Governance is important because it deals directly with the power and authority of female sport leaders within sport organizations. We draw upon the following definition to demonstrate this point:

> Sport governance is the exercise of power and authority in sport organizations, including policy making, to determine organizational mission, membership, eligibility, and regulatory power within the organization's appropriate local, national, and international scope. (Hums & MacLean, 2004, p. 5)

Members of sport organizations, particularly at the community level, make critical decisions related to women's and girls' sport provision and therefore, governance can play an essential role in advancing the women in sport objectives.

The purpose of this paper is to initiate a dialogue about women's sport governance by utilizing women's hockey in Canada as a context in which to develop a new perspective. The discussion will first focus upon the concepts that are critical for a discussion on women's hockey governance to evolve and second, on the importance of governance to overcome challenges facing women and girls in hockey. This paper will begin with a discussion that integrates critical feminist and grassroots movement perspectives and proceed with a descriptive analysis of the state of women's hockey governance in Canada, with a focus on the situation in the province of Ontario and more specifically the OWHA.

Theoretical Framework

Critical Feminism and Transformation

The current state of women's hockey in Canada is problematic. While governing bodies such as the OWHA are committed to increasing participation, still there are many women and girls who do not have the opportunity to participate. For those who are involved, their opportunities are far from equal or equitable. The inequality in resources, lack of recognition, limited access to leadership positions, and weak voice in the broader hockey community[1] suggests that women are accommodated into the male game and begs the question: should women's hockey focus on a game of their own, with an independent governance structure? The answer to this question can be partially addressed by a critical feminist view, which promotes activism and places the experiences of women and girls at the center of female hockey governance structures.

Women's and girls' hockey at the grassroots level needs to be grounded in the primary goal of freeing ". . . women from the imposition of so-called 'male values', and creating an alternative culture based on 'female values' " (Willis, 1984). The critical feminist perspective that Beasley (2005) labels "Gender

Difference" feminism, offers a theoretical foundation for a movement toward an alternative governance model for female hockey in Canada. This perspective supports the notion that ". . . there is no *singular* universal human nature that can form the basis of 'equality' " (Beasley, 2005, p. 46). Seeking equal opportunity in sport assumes a commonality between males and females; indeed, "what seems impartial or gender neutral is actually male-defined" (Beasley, 2005, p. 46). Women's and girls' hockey should be considered on its own terms not in relation to the male model. "Gender Difference" theorists accept and even celebrate difference—a difference which should not be an assumed inferiority (Showalter, 1985; Squires, 2001). Consequently, a perspective that incorporates a greater degree of separation between female hockey and male hockey streams than currently exists in the Canadian hockey system, would recognize female hockey as a distinct game as well as place greater authority within the hands of its leaders.

If any form of separation is to emerge, then change or emancipation is needed and strategies to achieve this goal rely heavily upon social action. Change can only occur if individuals organize, take action, and demand change (Martin, 1993). Kincheloe and McClaren (2005) identify that a critical emancipation view can be problematic when those taking action focus their efforts on enabling individuals to attain an ideal empowered position. They argue that there is never one ideal condition as issues of power and oppression pervade all socio-political contexts. Given this cautionary stance, our use of the term *emancipation* recognizes that individuals may reach different conclusions in their efforts to battle social forces that shape their social condition and that these conclusions may be imperfect. We are mindful of the problems associated with the term *emancipation*. However, we have carefully included it in this discussion in order to heighten a key point: future governance efforts should reflect a movement toward greater individual freedom and autonomy for female hockey players within the hockey system. Hence, our view of critical theory couples the notion of emancipation with a tangible change.

In order to ensure that our critique of gender, sport, and governance does not fall short, we promote a critical perspective that embraces and endorses action. Critical theory enables scholars to analyze the social experience of individuals and identify a need for change. Always evolving, the critical tradition encompasses many perspectives (Kincheloe & McClaren, 2005). The diversity of views is further compounded by the post-discourses, which contend the issue of democratic egalitarianism should be reassessed. The post-discourses, which have gained prominence within sport studies (Birrell & Cole, 1994; Rail, 1998), enable one to be highly critical of power and social conditions, but it is important to ask: how relevant is this perspective in efforts to actively assault the limiting effect of the hockey system on the advancement of women's and girls' hockey in Canada? Creating alternative female hockey governance structures is a political struggle and understanding issues of power is important; however, our emphasis is that the critical perspective must be grounded in action. A critical feminist perspective works to actively derail the

assumptions of the mainstream in terms of men and male practices and institutions being at the center with women a part of the periphery (Beasley, 2005).

The London Feminist Salon Collective (2004) published a "viewpoint" piece
that raises the question of how to "do" critical practice while recognizing nuances of difference and complexity. In the piece, Becky Francis argues that
"post-structuralist approaches have helped recognize and explore nuances of
power *but* [emphasis added] strong post-modern views withdraw the tools
with which to critically engage/act" (p. 27). When exploring the notion of self
with agency, the Collective made the following comment:

> The notion of feminist communities of practice was revisited . . . we con-
> sidered how movements in theory towards different understandings of
> the self are not necessarily matched within practice and/or social change
> . . . (p. 31)

Hence, we are left with a sense that post-discourses are not easily applied
since these views generate an awareness but not a method of change.

The literature suggests the critical theory-action bridge is difficult to cross.
For example, Kincheloe and McClaren (2005) suggest criticality is ever-evolv-
ing because it seeks "new ways to irritate dominant forms of power" (p. 306),
which unfortunately places it on the academic margins and makes any transfer to practice difficult. Kitschelt (1993) suggests it is important to understand
the catalysts of social collective movements and the factors that influence the
communication of new claims into the political process that impact policy and
governance, but offers little in terms of rational strategies.

The feminist perspective outlined in this section does not call for a rejection
of mainstream (male-dominated) hockey. In reality, women's and girls' hockey
organizations must connect with the larger male hockey network at some level.
The current full-integration governance approach that dominates within the
local, provincial, and national levels of hockey in Canada and the limitations
for the participation of women and girls that results from such an approach,
calls for the recognition of an existing "problem," diagnosis of the problem,
and the experimentation of alternatives (Meyerson & Fletcher, 2000). If the
democratic institutions established within the Canadian hockey network systematically under-privileged women and girls, and if the governance rules of
Hockey Canada are impossible to change, which seems to be the case after 30
years of OWHA efforts, new options must be considered. Grassroots development is a fundamental value of the OWHA. The OWHA is only able to expand and build legitimacy within the larger hockey network through its connection with local women's and girls' hockey associations.

Kitschelt (1993) contends that, in such a situation where a problem is recognized and change is needed, "dissenters can only step outside the established
framework of political governance and engage in protest" (p. 17). Consequently, we prefer to develop a rational approach where agency is carefully
considered and acted on. However, this raises a key question: where and how
will the social mobilization of female hockey enthusiasts occur? In the follow-

ing section, we turn to the literature on grassroots movements in order to address how to initiate change at the grassroots or community level of the hockey system.

Grassroots Movement

Thoma and Chalip (1996) identify three main levels of policy analysis—national, organizational, and individual. National-level analysis examines policy in terms of government goals and objectives. Organization-level analysis addresses the impact of various organizations involved in formulating and implementing policy. Individual-level analysis considers key participants in policy development—who are involved and what are their goals, interests, and influences. Thoma and Chalip (1996) also argue that changes in sport policy can effect changes in sport governance, which implies policy change is driven from the highest or national level, to the lowest or individual level of the sport system.

Thoma and Chalip (1996) suggest that an effective means by which to examine the individual policy level is through stakeholder analysis. They argue that stakeholder analysis enables one to derive strategies to anticipate stakeholder impact on sport governance and as such is proactive. Other policy scholars recognize the need to accommodate community-based views, specifically in terms of how national sport policy is negotiated and enacted at the local level. Green (2004) suggests future research on the nature of active citizenship in public sport provision, particularly in the UK where new planning dictates for elite sport have recently emerged between government agencies and national sport governing bodies.

For this discussion on female hockey governance, a more detailed understanding of grassroots movement is required. Taylor (2003), writing an insightful account of public policy in the community, details the changing fortunes of community by describing three main stages of development. Firstly, in the 1960s, various Western countries created extensive government programs in response to post-war optimism and the rise of the welfare state, which led to greater community empowerment. However, by the 1980s, economic recession advanced a new market mentality of welfare and subordinated state initiatives, including those within communities, to an economic growth agenda. Recently, however, a third stage has resituated the community in a central, albeit different role. Taylor (2003) explains this recent change as follows:

> The marketization of welfare continues, but as the costs of the globalization of the economy become more apparent, and neither government nor the market seem equipped to address the challenges facing society, "community" has been brought back in from the cold. (p. 8)

Taylor (2003) identifies various triggers that contribute to refocusing the community—a rapidly increasing demand for welfare, the breakdown of moral cohesion and responsibility, the breakdown of democracy and political legitimacy, increasing uncertainty and the need for sustainable development.

A similar transition has also occurred within the subsector of Canadian amateur sport. Scholars highlight the creation and proliferation of a public amateur sport system where several government programs in sport and recreation were created in the 1960s and 1970s (Harvey & Proulx, 1988; Macintosh & Whitson, 1990; Macintosh et al., 1987). Research also identifies a shift toward a corporate management model within the amateur sport domain, which coincided with the fiscal crisis of the Canadian welfare state during the late 1980s and early 1990s. Here, dominant ideas such as efficiency and individual enablement were embraced within public sport and recreation policy (Glover & Burton, 1998; Harvey et al., 1995; Stevens, 2000). However, the sport management literature has not addressed the context of Canadian amateur sport in relation to the most recent stage identified by Taylor (2003) — community renewal.

Outside of the Canadian context, recent work by Elling and Claringbould (2005) researched the in/exclusionary mechanisms for sport participation in the Netherlands. They identify the importance of grassroots democracy in efforts to gain greater access of marginalized social groups to sport activities and facilities. The notion of grassroots movement can offer greater insight about overcoming the challenges facing women and girls in hockey. The re-emergence of community relates closely to issues of grassroots democracy and citizen participation. This new approach shifts the focus away from change via federal government and national sport policy to change via municipal government and grassroots sport action.

A community-based approach redefines the citizen as a participant in, rather than a consumer of, social programs. Taylor (2003) suggests the new welfare market "offers communities the opportunity to take more control over the production of their own services" (p. 30). A consumer mentality suggests that if individuals do not like the service they receive, they can exit to another provider. However, as Taylor (2003) points out, the service exit view has been criticized because it oversimplifies the consumer's position, especially when a consumer's ability to exit is constrained by need, buying power, or the absence of an alternative provider. Hence, she argues:

> . . . consumerist policies allow power in the selection and use of a service, but they do not allow the public power as citizens over the range of services that are available to them or in determining the rights that people should have to those services. Any analysis of participation needs to consider whether communities are involved only in implementation, however important this may be, or whether they are involved in agenda setting and policy development." (Taylor, 2003, p. 119)

Female hockey participants have very little choice over a provider and their authority and control are minimal. Power, control, and authority in the Canadian amateur hockey system rests within a national sport governing body, an organization within each province/territory and a minor hockey association in each local jurisdiction. Consequently, the options for female hockey participants and leaders are very limited — do not play at all, play within a governance structure that inhibits your opportunity, or become your own service provider.

Female Hockey Governance Structures in Canada: Past and Present

Women and girls have been playing hockey in Canada since the late 1880s; however, an organized system with leagues and governing bodies was absent until the 1920s. The Ladies Ontario Hockey Association (LOHA), the first provincial governing body for women's hockey in Canada, was formed in 1922 (Kidd, 1996). Despite efforts to pattern the governing body after the Ontario Hockey Association (OHA), the governing body for the men's game, the women's association was not accepted by the male hockey community. Indeed, in 1923, at a meeting in Port Arthur, Ontario, the Canadian Amateur Hockey Association voted unanimously against giving the LOHA official recognition (OHA, 1923). Plagued by a lack of acceptance in the broader hockey community, limited access to resources, and inconsistent membership numbers, the LOHA spent the majority of its 19-year existence challenging traditional notions of appropriate feminine sport practices. Ultimately, the governing body was unsuccessful in securing a place for women in Ontario's hockey community and, as a result, by 1941 ceased to exist.

To organize hockey at the national level, the Dominion Women's Amateur Hockey Association was formed in the early 1930s. Its primary purpose was to establish and coordinate the women's Dominion championship series—the first was contested in 1933 (Avery & Stevens, 1997).[2] However, in 1940, the Dominion Championship was cancelled and the event and the governing body disappeared. Between 1940 and the early 1960s, women continued to play in their communities mostly in exhibition matches and informal games, but there was no formal governance structure as the momentum from the 1920s and 1930s disappeared. The history of women's hockey governance has been tenuous, inconsistent, and often contested.

During the past ten years, women's hockey has experienced rapid national and international expansion (Avery & Stevens, 1997). Yet, despite claims that women's hockey has grown significantly, women and girls who wish to play still face many barriers (Etue & Williams, 1996; Stevens, 2000b, 2006a). An organization that promotes female hockey and works to minimize the participation barriers that women and girls face is the OWHA. Established in the 1970s, the OWHA provides opportunities for women and girls of all abilities to play hockey provincially and leads the way in pushing the boundaries of women's hockey to national and international levels (OWHA, 2006). Promoting itself as "the only organised hockey association in the world of its kind" (OWHA, 2001, p. 2), the OWHA continues to promote a unique and specific brand for the female game.

The OWHA has increased opportunities for women and girls in hockey. The OWHA governance structure is based upon an organizational mission

that states: "Through a provincially unified, collective voice, the OWHA promotes, provides, and develops opportunities for girls and women to play female hockey in Ontario" (OWHA, 2005, p. 8). The OWHA's utmost concern
is increasing members and attracting teams and leagues to participate under
its organizational umbrella. By 2005, it boasted a program with over 2100
teams and over 35,000 players, from age 3 to 84. During the 2004–2005 season alone, the OWHA membership increased by 130 teams and 1794 players
(OWHA, 2005). The OWHA also reaches beyond the support of women's
hockey in its provincial jurisdiction. Over the last three decades, it has effectively lobbied for the inclusion of women's hockey in the Ontario Winter
Games, the Canada Winter Games, the national championships, the world
championships, and most prominently the Winter Olympics.

In the 1960s, there was little support for women's sport initiatives from the
grassroots women's movement that tended to focus on questions of legal, political, and ideological importance. Sport was marginalized as unimportant to the
"real" struggles over sexual equality (Hall, 1996; Hargreaves, 1994). However,
by the 1970s, like most areas of social life, sport found a place on the feminist
agenda (Hall, 2002). Over the past two decades, feminist activism in sport has
been predominantly "liberal" in description with the primary focus on ensuring women and girls equal access to sport and recreation through systematic
structural change. The reasons for this are complex, as Hall (1996) explains:

> The structure of amateur sport in many Western countries is highly state-
> subsidized and not likely to produce individuals with a radical critique
> willing to bite the hand that feeds them. Most sports have an authoritari-
> an power structure that demands discipline and obedience, and works
> against political awareness . . ." (p. 89)

This limitation of action is also noted by Lenskyj (1991) who argues that because of "the tightly structured, hierarchical nature of Canadian sport systems, there are limited points of entry for feminist activists" (p. 131).

The Canadian Association for the Advancement of Women and Sport
(CAAWS), established in 1981 and initially government funded, is a Canadian
advocacy organization that throughout its 25-year existence has negotiated
various feminist visions of sport. In the 1980s, the purported purpose of the
organization was "to advance the position of women by defining, promoting,
and supporting a feminist perspective on sport and to improve the status of
women in sport" (Hall, 1996). Adopting a decidedly feminist perspective, the
organization focused on four primary activities: advocacy, research, leadership
development, and communication both within and external to the organization. Hall (2002) suggests: "The fact that CAAWS was at the same time openly
feminist and government-funded was not at all unusual given the politics of
the state and the Canadian women's movement of the time" (p. 174). During
the 1980s, reacting to various human rights challenges, the women in sport
agenda in Canada shifted from an "equality" to an "equity" focus (Hall, 2002).
The result was a strategy that targeted the system as opposed to women and

the movement began to have less of an impact. By 1990, CAAWS had abandoned its public feminist position and adopted a more socially-accepted liberal feminist orientation that focused on gender equity and increasing opportunities for women in sport with minimal ties to the larger and often negatively perceived, feminist movement.

In 1986, Sport Canada, the federal government department responsible for amateur sport, established a women's sport policy—a policy that has not been formally revisited or updated since its development 20 years ago. *The Sport Canada Policy on Women in Sport* identifies the following goal: "To attain equality for women in sports" with the purpose of creating "an environment in which no one is forced into a pre-determined role or status because of gender" (Fitness and Amateur Sport, 1986, p. 14). Although the policy was a much-needed initiative, there are limitations that impede its effectiveness, particularly in terms of establishing separate women's sport governance bodies. Firstly, its lack of integration with other Sport Canada and provincial/territorial policies resulted in slow execution and relatively little compliance (Strachan & Tomlinson, 1994). Secondly, the document contains very general goals[3] and, as a result, specific action by national and provincial sport organizations is sporadic and inconsistent[4] (Ponic, 2000). Finally, the poor compliance has been compounded by shifts in the political discourse on women's sport since the early 1990s, such as an ongoing debate on whether equality or equity should be the fundamental goal (Hall, 1996, 2002).

Established in 1975 during the initiatives of the "second wave" feminist movement, the OWHA voiced the concerns of a specific female identity—female hockey players—and provided opportunities for the development of, what Newman and White (2006) describe as, "womanspace" within sport. The vision of the organization's leaders during this period was for the OWHA to equal the OHA in strength and membership—an ambitious goal given the historical mythology of hockey in Canada as the rightful place of boys and men. Feminist goals and values are clearly articulated through the objectives of the organization. The defined purpose of the OWHA is:

1. "To promote the participation of girls and women in all aspects of female hockey,"
2. "To foster and encourage leadership programs in all areas related to the development of female hockey in Ontario," and
3. "To promote hockey as a game played primarily for enjoyment but also fostering sportsmanship and life skills" (OWHA, 2000b, p. 2).

Martin (1990) suggests that any one of five criteria can qualify an organization as feminist, although some organizations will demonstrate several of the following: feminist ideology, feminist values, feminist goals, and feminist outcomes and founding circumstances. Feminist values, as outlined by Martin (1990, 1993), of personal growth, development, and empowerment, coupled with an external action agenda aimed at improving women's status and opportunities both as participants and leaders within the hockey community are clearly articulated within all of the policies of the OWHA. In the following statements, the OWHA expresses its support of an alternative female hockey culture:

> It is recognized that female hockey has its own identity. . . . For the game to continue to develop to its maximum value, it is important to allow the differences to continue. There are many lessons to be learned from "male" hockey, but to impose "male" hockey regulations and standards to female hockey is not in the best interests of hockey. (OWHA, 1998, p. 3)

> Female hockey is unique and should be directed by those who work within this side of the game. The OWHA has proven this to be true. (OWHA, 2000a, p. 2)

Offering a women-centered alternative within a male-dominated hockey community, from its beginnings, the OWHA has endorsed a feminist ideology of separatism.

The OWHA organizational ideology recognizes women as oppressed and disadvantaged within the hockey community and endeavors to make change within the existing sport system. The independent separatist position that the OWHA espouses is grounded in a radical feminist women-centered perspective "that recognizes and celebrates differences among women and seriously questions male-dominated and male-defined sport" (Hall, 1996, p. 91). The issue of separatism is not new to women's sport. The separate versus integrated debate that stems back to the 19th century resulted in a model of "feminine-appropriate" and "masculine-appropriate" sports—an ideological foundation that has lingered in the 21st century (Hargreaves, 1994). Traditional male sports such as ice hockey tend to be the sites of the most intense struggles and the most forceful forms of separatism. Hargreaves (1994) suggests that these struggles have resulted in a separatist position that advocates female control over women's sport and supports female participation in sports that are associated with conventional images of masculinity such as boxing, wrestling, or ice hockey. She suggests that "this form of separatism is not necessarily incompatible with the ideology of equal opportunity—it is seen as a way of balancing the advantages that men have had for so long" (Hargreaves, 1994, p. 31).

The legal battle between 12-year-old Justine Blainey and the OHA was perhaps the OWHA's most public endorsement of its commitment to a separatist philosophy. In 1985, Blainey, supported by CAAWS and the Women's Legal and Education Action Fund (LEAF), lobbied the Ontario Human Rights Commission for the right to play on a boys' team in the Metro Toronto Hockey League (MTHL). Opponents to the Blainey case were the OHA, which had jurisdiction over the MTHL and the OWHA, which argued that "allowing Blainey to play on the boys' team would undermine the development of women's hockey in Canada and that numerous opportunities currently existed within the women's program" (Avery & Stevens, 1997). The OWHA executives feared a successful outcome of this case could lead to the end of their league or at the very least drain it of the top female players. In the end, the

Blainey case lead to the dismantling of a discriminatory clause in the Ontario Human Rights Code that specifically exempted athletic organizations and activities from its sex equality policies (Hall, 1996). While many feminists saw this as a victory for human rights, there were some women, including the executive members of the OWHA, who argued vehemently against Blainey's right to play boys' hockey. Hall (1996) suggests that they supported this position for two reasons:

1. "to assure the maintenance of separate-but-equal hockey for girls" and
2. "to ensure the legitimacy and recognition of *women's* sport" (p. 95).

In the end, this action by the OWHA, had an adverse effect on the progress of women's hockey in Ontario because by 1990, the OWHA was still paying its expenses dedicated to the Blainey case which amounted to approximately $100,000 (Etue & Williams, 1996)[5].

The separatist philosophy of the OWHA has been eroded by a lack of authority within the broader provincial and national hockey communities. Hockey Canada, the national governing body for the sport in Canada, is comprised of 13 provincial and territorial branches, of which three come from the province of Ontario due to its large size: The Ontario Hockey Federation (OHF), The Ottawa District Hockey Association (ODHA) and Hockey Northwestern Ontario (HNO).[6] Despite its provincial mandate, the OWHA has no branch representation in Hockey Canada. The following statements from OWHA documents demonstrate the context in which the association operates within the broader Canadian hockey system:

> The OWHA will continue to work very closely with other [male] hockey associations in Ontario and also within the Canadian Amateur Hockey Association. It is very important that our members are given a strong voice and support at the provincial and national levels. (OWHA, 1992a, p. 9)

> We have stabilized the position of the OWHA within the Hockey Canada structure. This was a very long process that was critical to the strength of female hockey in the province of Ontario. The successful resolve was accomplished due to the strength of the OWHA membership. It was completed with the result of the OWHA sharing a respectful and positive relationship with our brother association[s] in Ontario. (OWHA, 2004, p. 2)

The OHF, the ODHA and HNO designate jurisdiction over female hockey in Ontario to the OWHA. Despite its province-wide role, OWHA representation rests within only one Ontario Branch, the OHF, where it is one of seven members. This voice becomes even weaker at the national level where the OWHA is limited to one seat on the Female Council. The Chair of the Council is only one representative on the 43-member Hockey Canada Board of Directors. Thus, the influence of female hockey leaders, be they from the OWHA or other provinces and territories, is severely limited, as its representation is deeply nested within the larger male-dominated hockey structure.

The lack of recognition of the OWHA as a provincial branch coupled with the weak representation of female hockey within the other 12 provinces/territories, restricts national decision-making authority for female hockey since a great deal of power rests with the 13 Branch Presidents on the Hockey Canada board. The Chair of the Female Council is the only voice for female hockey on the 43-member national Hockey Canada board. Most consequential to the female hockey program is that all development program decisions within Hockey Canada, which impact the grassroots level, channel through the 24-member Hockey Development Council. A decision made by the Female Council is not final as Council recommendations are presented, debated, and approved at the board level. As a result, the national Female Council is relegated to an advisory role with little control over the female game.

Future Considerations for Female Hockey Governance in Canada

The first women's world hockey championship, sanctioned by the International Ice Hockey Federation, held in 1990, signaled a new international era in the sport. Since that time, Hockey Canada has moved its programming away from female grassroots hockey development toward female hockey high-performance. Like many other Canadian national sport organizations, Hockey Canada reflects a corporate management model (Stevens, 2006b), which has constrained democratic aims, such as the provision of hockey opportunities for all women and girls. The existence of the OWHA is solidified from its community-based membership as opposed to its role in policy and governance structures within Hockey Canada. Examples of grassroots efforts are evident within OWHA documents that outline community-based strategies and initiatives:

> Locally, our teams, associations and leagues throughout Ontario continue to grow and base their operations on very positive values. (OWHA, 2000a,b, p. 2)

> The [OWHA] Development Committee is once again accepting applications for initiatives from associations and/or OWHA teams. The purpose of this grant is to promote the development of female hockey across Ontario . . . (OWHA, 1996, p. 4)

> We have revised the manual *How to develop your own Girls' Minor Hockey Association*. With this manual, plus initiative meetings, we respond to the many inquiries we receive about how to get girls' hockey started in a community. (OWHA, 1992b, p. 9)

> I suggest profiling some local minor hockey associations, so we can learn from each other. I'd like to read about the traditions of the large successful [local] programs, and I'd be very interested in the progress of the female hockey programs in the last few years. (OWHA, 1991, p. 15)

These statements demonstrate the OWHA's recognition of the importance of community associations to expand its separate structure model. The utilization of a grassroots movement to build the legitimacy of the association and the separate governance structure it purports, can be expanded both within the OWHA's provincial jurisdiction and in other regions of the country.

Given the integration of feminist and grassroots perspectives we proposed earlier in this paper and recognizing how the historical success of the OWHA has in large part been based upon the development of local female hockey associations, we propose an approach that highlights the community sport level as the point to initiate changes to female hockey governance. While the majority of governance bodies within the current hockey system are male-dominated, the greatest proportion of female-dominated structures is at the local level. Some governance structures for female and male hockey are separate at the local level, partially linked at the provincial level, and integrated at the national level. In order to generate change, one must have the power and authority to formulate a policy from the outset, reformulate a policy after its creation or interpret policy goals in ways that enable effective action during implementation (Taylor, 2003). Since the federal women's sport policy has remained unchanged during the past 20 years, we identify the last of these options — implementation — as an important area to initiate change. Our emphasis is not on the organizational structure of such governing bodies, but rather to propose that these structures, whatever their form, initially develop at the community sport level. By coupling grassroots movement ideals with an action-oriented stance, governance structures that meet the needs of female hockey players may take hold and flourish.

There are various factors that support initiating change at the grassroots sport level. Firstly, strategies mentioned by Thoma and Chalip (1996) may be useful for activating change in female hockey governance. For example, Thoma and Chalip (1996) refer to a build strategy where female hockey supporters recruit other stakeholders, namely high profile social sector leaders and create awareness of and interest in their cause. An alliance strategy presents an effective means by which female hockey supporters could align more closely with other stakeholders in a community, particularly those with greater power. In this case, female hockey leaders could coordinate with local parks and recreation leaders, be they staff or community volunteers, by highlighting shared concerns related to gender equity and youth physical activity.

A second area addresses how public policy domains are accountable to a public governance authority (Burbridge, 2005). In Canada, where amateur sport is strongly embedded within the public sector, a grassroots movement may harness public authority, specifically municipal governments and Parks and Recreation departments therein, as a resource to trigger governance change. For example, female hockey leaders could utilize accountability of public municipal institutions to human rights legislation in order to gain equitable access to facilities and allocation of public funds. The OWHA recommends local girls' hockey organizers who wish to establish a new local association in their community refer to a handbook titled, *Level the Playing Field* (Sport Ontario, c.1994). The OWHA encourages groups interested in founding new female hockey associations to draw upon the strategies presented in the document. In particular, the handbook states local level female sport leaders need "to become catalysts for change in the community and resources which level the playing field for women and girls" (p. 1) and need "to assist you in bringing change forward at a pace and in specific areas, appropriate and relevant to your community" (p. 2).

Ontario is not the only province where women's and girls' hockey leaders face challenges. Concerns regarding new governance models were raised in Quebec where the branch formed a committee to examine the poor state of female hockey in the province. The committee made the following recommendation:

> [T]he gap between the number of players in the OWHA and Hockey Quebec is considerable. However, despite the constraints present in Quebec, it would be possible to adapt the [OWHA] model to the Quebec reality and to borrow certain methods in order to attract more young girls to the sport. (Hockey Quebec, 2001, p. 13)

Currently, female hockey governance structures in other regions of the country may or may not resemble the separate structure promoted by the OWHA. For example, a minor hockey association may govern both girls' and boys' programs or a distinct female hockey board within the provincial branch may manage the game and direct female hockey programs for all local minor hockey associations.

A grassroots movement approach to governance is not a perfect solution to the challenges facing female hockey in Canada. Taylor (2005) suggests a participation-governance view as problematic because it has an over-emphasis upon the democratizing role of stakeholder participation. This view places a great deal of faith in a democratic pluralist model of politics and does not consider the wider context in which grassroots political struggles exist. We recognize this is also the case when examining governance change in women's sport, particularly because gender and sport are highly contested political terrains. However, the important message we wish to emphasize is rather than target federal and provincial levels of the amateur sport system as initiation points for change, future female hockey governance efforts must capture the opportunities democratic grassroots movements at the local level offer.

We have presented a new viewpoint on the issues of gender, sport, and governance that integrates critical feminist and grassroots movement views. This new perspective is buoyed by recent research on gendered non-profit organizations. Meinhard and Foster (2003) examine how women's voluntary organizations respond to changing public policy in Canada. They found these organizations represent a distinct subset of the non-profit sector because they are more critical of policy changes and spend more time engaging in political activity compared to gender–neutral organizations. Foster and Meinhard suggest this is due to a long tradition of women's organizations agitating for their own rights. In other words, action and a need for change are values instilled within and enacted by many women's organizations, including women's hockey organizations.

While much of what we propose is based upon the OWHA model, it is important to acknowledge that the diverse strategies that may be used to initiate governance change at the grassroots level can result in a variety of organizational structures. Future research is required to examine the organizational characteristics of the governance structures that exist in areas where community female hockey flourishes. Research within the gender and organization literature (see, e.g., Ferguson, 1984; Martin, 1990; Oerton, 1996) could be used to inform this work, particularly in terms of understanding the ideological and organizational nature of the community-based female hockey entities and how cultural and structural aspects interrelate within these entities. For example, Birrell and Richter (1994) found the women's softball league they researched reflected a feminist sport model with all-female membership, a play-based philosophy, and a non-hierarchical authority structure.

In the social sector, research also indicates women's voluntary organizations include different organizational structures and systems. For example, women's organizations in Canada collaborate more than gender–neutral organizations (Foster & Meinhard, 2005a). These organizations also differ in their response to public policy challenges, such as decreases in public funding, by adopting different revenue generating strategies compared to non-gendered organizations (Foster & Meinhard, 2005b). Given how institutional pressures facing many non-profit organizations have been relatively broad in nature (Hall & Banting, 2000), it is fair to conclude that the differences are due to internal as opposed to external factors.

Our approach proposes change that focuses upon attaining separate female hockey governance that provides control and authority over the female game. In this way, female hockey leaders avoid what Grant and Tancred (1992) refer to as "adjunct control positions" (p. 121) where they participate in the management of hockey but have limited say in the development of hockey policies. Halford (1992) states that despite the problematic state and its bureaucratic apparatus, "many feminist goals can only be met by state institutions" (p. 159). Thus, our approach also addresses the need to utilize public authority, albeit at the municipal as opposed to the federal government level.

Conclusion

In her discussion of women's hockey as a site of struggle, Stevens (2006a) states, "Without a governing association that exclusively serves the development of women's and girls' hockey, resistance or reorientation of the women's hockey model is unlikely" (p. 97). A strategy to rejuvenate the female hockey model debate is to examine the gender-sport-governance relationship. Hums and MacLean (2004) argue that governance structures and policies must evolve in order to improve effectiveness. They identify economic survival as a key pressure influencing sport governance in the future. However, the pressure for change in women's hockey is far more fundamental than economics; it involves a social need to improve the power and authority of women's hockey leaders. While the OWHA has successfully expanded participation in female hockey, it cannot claim a similar record in the area of governance. This can also be said for other female sport organizations throughout Canada.

Consequently, this paper renews efforts to place women's sport governance on the agenda. By shifting the focus from participation to governance, it is possible to identify how shortcomings still exist for women and girls in hockey in Canada. We argue that effective change is not simply a matter of increasing female hockey registration numbers. Rather, it relates directly to issues of power and authority over sport, which is intricately connected to governance structures. The most effective strategy to address this concern will arise from a fresh and creative approach that integrates a critical feminist perspective with a grassroots democratic focus. Over a period of time, women's sport governance research may help inform and may be informed by, governance issues for other marginalized groups in sport and perhaps even for male-dominated hockey associations. We hope future research on the development of women's sport in Canada will take up the challenge of how to initiate change by exploring and debating alternative women's sport governance according to this integrated perspective.

Notes

1. Resources, recognition, and leadership are all areas that must be addressed in women's hockey and female sport more broadly. In terms of resources, we are specifically referring to financial resources, administrative personnel, and access to facilities and equipment. Girls' and women's hockey receives little recognition in the media (with the occasional exception of international events such as the Olympic Games), in the broader hockey community and within institutions of recognition such as the Hockey Hall of Fame in Toronto, Ontario. Since its inception in 1943, there have been no women inducted into the HHOF as players or builders (Adams & Wamsley, 2005). Similarly, the continuing imbalance between men and women in coaching, administration, and officiating in both hockey and sport more broadly suggests that women continue to have limited leadership roles.

2. The Dominion Women's Amateur Hockey Association (DWAHA) was formed in 1933 to establish regulations for a national Championship series among the top women's teams from across the country. The first Dominion Championship was contested in 1933 with the Edmonton Rustlers defeating the Ontario champions the Preston Rivulettes.

3. The *Sport Canada Policy on Women in Sport* is only 27 pages in length. It offers 13 brief policy statements and the proposed implementation activities in the areas of Policy and Program Development, Sport Stratification, Sport Infrastructure, Leadership Development, High Performance Competition, Participation Development, Resource Allocation, Liaison, Research, Education, Promotion, Advocacy and Monitoring, and Evaluation. For example, the Resource Allocation section states: "Greater Efforts will be made to ensure that financial resources are equitable allocated. In cases where inequities are demonstrated, Sport Canada contributions will be conditional on a guarantee from national sport organizations that resources will be more equitably distributed among males and females" (Fitness and Amateur Sport, 1986, p. 23). The implementation activities associated with this statement include analyzing the allocation of human and financial resources on a sport-specific basis and providing support for the generation of new resources and for the reallocation of present resources where inequalities are demonstrated.

4. In 1994, the Ontario Ministry of Culture, Tourism, and Recreation published a policy statement on women and girls in sport, *Full and Fair Access for Women and Girls in Sport and Physical Activity*, in response to the 1986 federal government initiative that urged the provinces/territories to address the issue at the provincial and

community level. Consistent with the national policy from 1986, this brief eight page document focused on Policy and Program Development, Sport and Recreation Organizations, Leadership Development, Sport Participation and High Performance Development, Participation at the Community Level, Welcoming and Harassment-Free Environment, and Education and General Awareness.

5. Megan Williams conducted interviews with scholar's Nancy Theberge and Helen Lenskyj in 1995 and 1993, respectively. Both scholar's contend that the OWHA and it is executive Director Fran Rider does a disservice to female players through the endorsement of a separatist philosophy for female hockey.

6. The Canadian Amateur Hockey Association served as the national governing body for hockey from 1914 until 1994 when it merged with Hockey Canada to form the Canadian Hockey Association. In 2002, the organization changed its name to Hockey Canada but should not be confused with the original Hockey Canada, which was one of the parent organizations for the merger.

References

Adams, C., & Wamsley, K.B. (2005). Moments of silence in shallow halls of greatness: The hockey hall of fame and the politics of representation. In C.D. Howell (Ed.), *Putting it on ice: Women's hockey-gender issues on and off the ice* (pp. 13–17). Halifax, NS: Gorsebrook Research Institute.

Avery, J., & Stevens, J. (1997). *Too many men on the ice: Women's hockey in North America*. Victoria, BC: Polestar Publishers.

Beasley, C. (2005). *Gender and sexuality: Critical theories, critical thinkers*. Thousand Oaks, CA: Sage.

Birrell, S., & Cole, C. (1994). *Women, sport, and culture*. Champaign, IL: Human Kinetics.

Birrell, S., & Richter, D. (1994). Is a diamond forever? Feminist transformations of sport. In S. Birrell & C. Cole (Eds.), *Women, sport and culture* (pp. 221–244). Champaign, IL: Human Kinetics.

Burbridge, S. (2005). The governance deficit: Reflections on the future of public and private policing. *Canadian Journal of Criminology and Criminal Justice, 47*(1), 63–86.

Elling, A., & Claringbould, I. (2005). Mechanisms of inclusion and exclusion in the Dutch sports landscape: Who can and wants to belong? *Sociology of Sport Journal, 22*, 498–515.

Etue, E. ,& Williams, M. (1996). *On the edge: Women making hockey history*. Toronto, ON: Second Story Press.

Ferguson, K. (1984). *The feminist case against bureaucracy*. Philadelphia: Temple Press.

Fitness and Amateur Sport. (1986). *Sport Canada policy on women and sport*. Ottawa, ON.

Foster, M., & Meinhard, A. (2005a). Women's voluntary organizations in Canada: Bridgers, bonders or both? *Voluntas, 16*, 143–159.

Foster, M., & Meinhard, A. (2005b). Diversifying revenue sources in Canada: Are women's voluntary organizations different? *Nonprofit Management and Leadership, 16*, 43–60.

Glover, T., & Burton, T. (1998). A model of alternative forms of public leisure services delivery. In M. F. Collins & I. S. Cooper (Eds.), *Leisure management: Issues and applications* (pp. 139–155). New York: CAB International.

Grant, J., & Tancred, P. (1992). A feminist perspective on state bureaucracy. In J. Mills & P. Tancred (Eds.), *Gendering organizational analysis* (pp. 112–128). Thousand Oaks, CA: Sage.

Green, M. (2004). Power, policy, and political priorities: Elite sport development in Canada and the United Kingdom. *Sociology of Sport Journal, 21*, 376–396.

Halford, S. (1992). Feminist change in a patriarchial organization: The experience of women's initiatives in local government and implications for feminist perspectives on state institutions In M. Savage & A. Witz (Eds.), *Gender and bureaucracy* (pp. 156–185). Oxford: Blackwell.

Hall, M., & Banting, K. G. (2000). The nonprofit sector in Canada. In K. G. Banting (Ed.), *The nonprofit sector in Canada: Roles and relationships* (pp. 1–28). Montreal, McGill: Queens University Press.

Hall, M. A. (1996). *Feminism and sporting bodies*. Champaign, IL: Human Kinetics.

Hall, M. A. (2002). *The Girl and the game*. Peterborough, ON: Broadview Press.

Hall, M. A., & Richardson, D. A. (1982). *Fair ball: Towards sex equality in Canadian sport*. Ottawa, ON: Canadian Advisory Council on the Status of Women.

Hargreaves, J. (1994). *Sporting females*. New York: Routledge.

Harvey, J., & Proulx, R. (1988). Sport and the state in Canada. In J. Harvey & H. Cantelon (Eds.), *Not just a game: Essays in Canadian sport sociology* (pp. 93–119). Ottawa: University of Ottawa Press.

Harvey, J., Thibault, L., & Rail, G. (1995). Neo-corporatism: The political management system in Canadian amateur sport and fitness. *Journal of Sport and Social Issues*, *19*(3), 249–265.

Hockey Canada. (2006). Organizational and program structures. Accessed on 5 July 2006, at http://www.hockeycanada.ca/index.cfm/ci_id/6843/la_id/1.htm.

Hockey Quebec. (2001). *Female hockey development plan: 2001–2008*.

Hums, M., & MacLean, J. (2004). *Governance and policy in sport organizations*. Scottsdale, AZ: Holcomb Hathaway, Publishers, Inc.

Kidd, B. (1996). *The struggle for Canadian sport*. Toronto, ON: University of Toronto Press.

Kincheloe, J., & McClaren, P. (2005). Rethinking critical theory and qualitative research. In N. Denzin & Y. Lincoln (Eds.), *The Sage handbook of qualitative research* (3rd edition, pp. 303–342). Thousand Oaks, CA: Sage Publications.

Kitschelt, H. (1993). Social movements, political parties, and democratic theory. *Annals, AAPSS*, *528*, 13–29.

Lenskyj, H. (1986). *Out of bounds: Women, sport, and sexuality*. Toronto, ON: Women's Press.

Lenskyj, H. (1991). Good sports: Feminists organizing on sport issues in the 1970s and 1980s. *Resources for Feminist Research/Documentation sur la Recherche Féministe*, *20*(3–4), 130–135.

London Feminist Salon Collective. (2004). The problematization of agency in postmodern theory: As feminist researchers where do we go from here? *Gender and Education*, *16*(1), 25–33.

Macintosh, D., & Whitson, D. (1990). *The game planners: Transforming Canada's sport system*. Kingston, ON: McGill-Queen's University Press.

Macintosh, D., Bedecki, T., & Franks, C. E. S. (1987). *Sport and politics in Canada: Federal government involvement since 1961*. Kingston, ON: McGill-Queen's University Press.

MacKay, J. (1997). *Managing gender: affirmative action and organizational power in Australia, Canada, and New Zealand*. Albany, NY: State University of NY Press.

Martin, P.Y. (1990). Rethinking feminist organizations. *Gender and Society*, *4*(2), 182–206.

Martin, P.Y. (1993). Feminist practice in organizations: Implications for management. In E. A. Fegenson (Ed.), *Women in management: Trends, issues and challenges in managerial diversity* (pp. 274–297).Thousand Oaks, CA: Sage.

Meinhard, A., & Foster, M. (2003). Differences in the response of women's voluntary organizations to shifts in Canadian public policy. *Nonprofit and Voluntary Sector Quarterly*, *32*, 366–393.

Meyerson, D. E., & Fletcher, J. K. (2000). A modest manifesto for shattering the glass ceiling. *Harvard Business Review*, *78*(1), 127–136.

Newman, J., & White, L. A. (2006). *Women, politics, and public policy: The political struggles of Canadian women*. Don Mills, ON: Oxford University Press.

Oerton, S. (1996). Sexualizing the organization, lesbianizing the women: Gender, sexuality, and "flat" organizations. *Gender, Work, and Organization*, *3*(1), 26–37.

Ontario Hockey Association. (1923). *Annual meeting minutes 1923*. Ottawa: O.H.A. Papers, National Library of Canada, M2308.

Ontario Women's Hockey Association. (1991). *OWHA Newsletter*. Mississauga, ON.

Ontario Women's Hockey Association. (1992a). *1991–1992 Executive Reports*. Mississauga, ON.

Ontario Women's Hockey Association. (1992b). *OWHA Newsletter*. Mississauga, ON: Lifetime Consulting Services. Ontario Women's Hockey Association. (1995). *Proud past; bright future together toward 2000: OWHA strategic plan final report*. Mississauga, ON.

Ontario Women's Hockey Association. (1996). *OWHA newsletter*. Mississauga, ON.

Ontario Women's Hockey Association. (1998). *1997–1998 executive reports*. Mississauga, ON.

Ontario Women's Hockey Association. (2000a). *1999–2000 executive reports*. Mississauga, ON.

Ontario Women's Hockey Association. (2000b). *2000–2001 constitution, by-laws, regulations and rules*. Mississauga, ON.

Ontario Women's Hockey Association. (2001). *2000–2001 executive reports*. Mississauga, ON.

Ontario Women's Hockey Association. (2004). *2003–2004 executive reports*. Mississauga, ON.

Ontario Women's Hockey Association. (2005). *2004–2005 executive reports*. Mississauga, ON.

Ontario Women's Hockey Association. (2006). *2005–2006 executive reports* Mississauga, ON.

Ponic, P. (2000). A herstory, a legacy: The Canadian amateur sport branch's women's program. *Avante, 6*(2), 51–63.

Rail, G. (1998). *Sport and postmodern times*. Albany, NY: State University of New York Press.

Shaw, S., & Slack, T. (2002). It's been like that for donkey's years': The construction of gender relations and the culture of sport organizations. *Culture, Sport, Society, 5*(1), 86–106.

Showalter, E. (1985). Feminist criticism in the wilderness. In E. Showalter (Ed.), *The new feminist criticism: Essays on women, literature, and theory*. (pp. 243–270). New York, NY: Pantheon.

Sport Ontario. (c.1994). *Level the playing field: A handbook on how to achieve full and fair access for women and girls in sport and physical activity*. Toronto, Ontario: Ministry of Culture, Tourism, and Recreation.

Squires, J. (2001). Representing groups, deconstructing identities. *Feminist Theory, 2*(1), 7–27.

Stevens, J. (2000). The declining sense of community in Canadian women's hockey. *Women in Sport and Physical Activity Journal, 9*, 123–140.

Stevens, J. (2006a) Women's hockey in Canada: "After the gold rush."' In D. Whitson & R. Gruneau (Eds.), *Artificial ice: Hockey, commerce, and Canadian culture* (pp. 85–100). Aurora, ON: Garamond Press.

Stevens, J. (2006b). The Canadian hockey association merger and the emergence of the amateur sport enterprise. *Journal of Sport Management, 20*(1), 74–100.

Strachan, D., & Tomlinson, P. (1994). *Gender equity in coaching*. Coaching Association of Canada.

Taylor, D. (2005), Governing through evidence: Participation and power in policy evaluation. *Journal of Social Policy, 34*, 601–618.

Taylor, M. (2003). *Public policy in the community*. New York, NY: Palgrave Macmillan.

Theberge, N. (2000). *Higher goals: Women's ice hockey and the politics of gender*. Albany, NY: State University of New York.

Thoma, J., & Chalip, L. (1996). *Sport governance in the global community*. Morgantown, WV: Fitness Information Technology, Inc.

VanderZwaag, H. (1998). *Policy development in sport management*. Westport, CT: Praeger Publishers.

Willis, E. (1984). Radical feminism and feminist radicalism. *Social Text, The 60s Without Apology, 9/10*, 91–118.

19

SPORT, HUMAN RIGHTS, AND INDUSTRIAL RELATIONS

Braham Dabscheck

The opening paragraph of the *Universal Declaration of Human Rights* proclaims "recognition of the inherent dignity and . . . the equal and inalienable rights of all members of the human family."[1] The *Universal Declaration*, and other human rights" instruments, see freedom, or freedoms, associated with employment as integral to the attainment or recognition of human rights. For example, Article 4 of the Universal Declaration states that "No one shall be held in slavery or servitude, slavery and the slave trade shall be prohibited in all their forms." A similar statement condemning slavery is contained in Article 8 of the *International Covenant on Civil and Political Rights*. In addition, the International Labor Organization, in 1930 and again in 1957, adopted conventions condemning and seeking the abolition of forced and compulsory labor.[2]

Article 23(1) of the *Universal Declaration of Human Rights* states, "Everyone has the right to work, to free choice of employment." Article 6 of the *International Covenant on Economic, Social and Cultural Rights* declares that "the State Parties to the present Covenant recognize the right to work which includes the right of everyone to the opportunity to gain his living by work which he freely chooses or accepts, and will take appropriate steps to safeguard these rights."

Various human rights instruments recognize or acknowledge freedom of association and the right of workers to join trade unions to protect their employment rights. For example, Article 23(4), of the *Universal Declaration of Human Rights*[2] states, "Everyone has the right to form and join trade unions for the protection of his rights." Similar statements are contained in Article 8 of the *International Covenant on Economic, Social and Cultural Rights*[3] and Article 22 of the *International Covenant on Civil and Political Rights*,[4] respectively. The International Labor Organization has also adopted conventions upholding the independence of trade unions. In 1948 it adopted the *Freedom of Association and Protection of the Right to Organize Convention*[5] and, in 1949, the *Right to Organize and Collective Bargaining Convention*.[6]

Players of professional team sports have been subjected to a series of labor market rules which have substantially curtailed their economic freedom and human rights. The major rules have been the reserve or option system (North

America) and the transfer system[7] (United Kingdom, Western Europe, and Australia) which binds a player to the initial club which employs them for the rest of their playing life.

In response, players have turned to collective action in the form of player associations/trade unions, seeking to remove or overcome abuses associated with such controls. Different leagues, and their respective constituent clubs, have been opposed to the formation and operation of player bodies. Leagues have portrayed player associations and their leaders as a foreign element, hostile to the operation and "good" management of sport.

With the obvious exception of American baseball (see below), the courts, generally speaking, have struck down various labor market controls, which have restricted the employment rights of players. In the United States of America such controls have fallen foul of the *Sherman Antitrust Act 1890*[8] and the *Clayton Act 1914*;[9] in the United Kingdom and Australia the common law doctrine of restraint of trade;[10] and in Western Europe, in the 1995 *Bosman* case,[11] Article 48 of the Treaty of Rome,[12] which ensures the free movement of workers within the European Economic Community.

The courts have found against such controls from the perspective of classic liberal or natural rights interpretations of human rights.[13] Such controls have been anathema to judges imbued with liberal values. They have been perceived as infringing unreasonably on the natural employment rights of players. The major argument of this paper is that the courts, in finding against such rules on the basis of individualistic or natural rights interpretations of human rights, have, paradoxically, enhanced the collective determination of employment conditions and provided a fillip to player associations.[14]

Unfavorable decisions before the courts have "encouraged" leagues to enter into collective bargaining deals with player associations to protect various labor market controls. Such controls, enshrined in collective bargaining agreements negotiated at arms length in "good faith," can be shielded from antitrust or common law actions. The content of such agreements—the extent of freedoms afforded and benefits provided to players—in turn, are a function of the bargaining strength and negotiating skills of the respective parties.

This paper is concerned with providing an examination of human rights dimensions of industrial relations in professional team sports. It is organized into five sections. Section one briefly describes the different labor market rules which operate in professional team sports. Section two examines various cases where courts have considered the "forced labor" or "slavery" aspects of such controls. The next two sections, which constitute the bulk of the paper, focus on how the courts have responded to rules which have restricted the "mobility" and "freedom" of players to obtain employment with alternative clubs, once their contracts with their "original" clubs have expired. Section three surveys decisions in North America and section four the United Kingdom and Australia. The examinations of the case law in these two sections are integrated with analyzes of developments and issues associated with the activities of player associations and the collective determination of employment conditions. Section five provides a conclusion, where the major threads of the discussion are drawn together.

I. Labor Market Controls in Professional Team Sports

League and club officials have consistently argued that sporting labor markets and, therefore, the contracts of players need to be strictly controlled to ensure the survival of their respective sports. It is argued that such controls help to bring about an equal distribution of playing talent among competing teams. It is claimed that without such restrictions rich clubs would secure the most skilled players and, through their continual domination of the competition, reduce the commercial viability of or destroy the sport. Subsidiary arguments justifying controls have been the need to maintain team stability, minimization of wages and costs, and a conviction that clubs should receive compensation for players who change clubs.

Cairns, Jennett, and Sloane, in a survey of the economics of professional team sports, have said "it is relatively uncontroversial that labor market controls have not given equality of performance."[15] The benefits of labor market controls are negligible or illusory and hardly justify the denial of players' human rights. Moreover, there are alternative methods, consistent with employment freedom and/or human rights instruments, in which sporting equality can be achieved—namely revenue sharing or redistributing income between clubs.[16]

Three different types of labor market controls can be distinguished. They are recruitment of players, the movement of players between clubs, and the use of maximum wages. Excluding normal market mechanisms, where players and clubs negotiate (initial) contracts, two major types of recruitment have been used in professional team sports. The first is zoning. Clubs are given exclusive rights to the services of prospective players who reside in their particular allocated geographic area (zone). Players have no choice in the initial club that might employ them. Zones usually operate in tandem with residential requirements of certain periods, to restrict players from being able to take up employment with other clubs by moving to another zone. Zoning schemes have been a feature of Australian sports.

The second method of recruitment is the draft. With drafting, potential new players are placed in a common pool and are chosen (drafted) by clubs in terms of their reverse order in the competition in the previous year; with the process being repeated a number of times. Drafting, like zoning, denies players the ability to choose and/or negotiate with prospective clubs which might be prepared to employ them. Players can only obtain employment with the club which drafts them. The draft was first adopted in American football in 1935, spreading to other North American sports, and Australia in the late 1980s and early 1990s. In Australia this method of selecting new players is known as the "external" draft.

Once a player signs with a club, leagues have developed a variety of rules which enable clubs to maintain control over and/or restrict the ability of players to obtain employment with other clubs. Six such rules can be distinguished—the transfer system, the reserve or option system, the "Rozelle" rule, right of first refusal, assignment, and the external draft.

Under the transfer system, a player who signs with a club is bound to that club for the rest of their playing life. A player, even though their contract with their original club has expired, can only move to a new club with the permission of their original club. The obtaining of such permission invariably involves the payment of a transfer fee to the original club in "compensation" for the loss of the said player. Fees are also paid for players who change clubs or are bought and sold during the life of their contract. Transfer fees were first introduced in English soccer in 1891. They have been a mainstay of soccer worldwide, and were utilized for a large part of the twentieth century in Australian Rules football and rugby league.

The reserve or option system involves a contract whereby a club has a right (or option) to re-sign a player after the expiry of the contract. Given that each new contract contains an option clause, the club, in effect, has a perpetual right to the services of a player. The reserve system was first introduced in American baseball in 1879. It subsequently spread to other North American sports, and to Australian Rules football from the mid 1980s to mid 1990s.

Two variations of the reserve or option system have been developed. Prior to 1963 the rules of American football allowed players to play out their option year. That is, if a player chose to not sign a new contract, he or she could play out the option of his old contract subject to a mandatory 10 percent salary cut and, at the end of the option period, be declared a free agent. Such a player would then be enabled to seek employment with any club in the league. R. C. Owens used this device to change clubs in 1963.

Following this, the National Football League introduced the so-called "Rozelle" rule to block this source of mobility and employment freedom for players. Under the "Rozelle" rule, a club which obtained a "free agent" had to compensate the club which had lost the so-called "free agent." If the two clubs could not agree on compensation, National Football League commissioner Alvin Ray "Pete" Rozelle was empowered to direct the acquiring club to compensate the club which "lost" the player as he saw fit.

Under the right of first refusal, players, following the expiry of their contract with their current club, are able to enter into negotiations and "sign" with a "new" club. However, the player's previous club can match the offer of the "new" club, thereby negating the ability of the player to take up employment with a new club. The right of first refusal has been a feature of North American basketball and football and has also been used in Australian basketball, baseball, and soccer.

Assignment enables clubs or leagues to relocate or (re-)assign players to another club. Assignment has been a feature of North American sports and has been used in Australian rules football and baseball.

The "internal" draft is a uniquely Australian contribution to the player rules of professional team sports. Under the internal draft, current players who have not negotiated a new contract with their club are placed into a common pool and are selected by clubs through the external draft discussed above. The internal draft was introduced into Australian Rules football in 1988. It was also used, for a brief period, in rugby league in the early 1990s.

Two types of wage maxima have operated in professional team sports. Limits have been placed on the income that can be earned either by individual players or the team (league) as a whole, in what has been referred to as a salary cap. Individual wage maxima have operated in English soccer, a number of Australian sports, and unofficially in American baseball. A salary cap was first introduced in American basketball in 1983 following negotiations between the National Basketball League and the National Basketball Players' Association. Salary caps have spread to American football and a number of Australian sports.

II. Forced Labor and Slavery

As already mentioned the international community has adopted conventions condemning forced or compulsory labor and slavery. Article 2(1) of the International Labor Organization's *Convention Concerning Forced or Compulsory Labor 1930* defines such labor to mean "all work or service which is exacted from any person under the menace of any penalty and for which the said person has not offered himself voluntarily." Article 1 of the 1926 *Slavery Convention*, adopted by the League of Nations, and the 1953 *Amended By Protocol* by the United Nations defines slavery as "the status or condition of a person over whom any or all of the powers attaching to the right of ownership are exercised," and states that the "slave trade includes . . . all acts involved in the acquisition of a slave with a view to selling or exchanging him; all acts of disposal by sale or exchange of a slave acquired with a view to being sold or exchanged."

It could be argued that many of the labor market controls which operate in professional team sports breach these conventions. Neither zoning nor drafts enable players to "voluntarily" choose their employers. If players decide not to play with the club that fate has determined for them, they face the "menace" and "penalty" of being denied employment in their chosen profession. The various rules which take from players the ability to negotiate with prospective employers impose a "penalty" of reduction in income and other entitlements.

"Trades" associated with the transfer system, the "Rozelle" rule, right of first refusal, and assignment require a player to play with a club to which he "has not offered himself voluntarily." Transfer fees and other arrangements involving player trades involve "any or all of the powers attaching to the right of ownership . . . [and] acts involved in . . . acquisition . . . with a view to selling or exchanging."

There are three cases where actions have been mounted against such controls on the basis of forced or compulsory labor and slavery.[17] In 1970, Curt Flood claimed that baseball's employment rules, through which he was traded by the St. Louis Cardinals to the Philadelphia Phillies against his will, constituted a form of peonage and involuntary servitude, in contravention of the

Thirteenth Amendment of the Constitution of the United States of America. The Thirteenth Amendment, which was ratified in 1865 after the American Civil War, states, "Neither slavery nor involuntary servitude, except as a punishment for crime whereof the party shall have been duly convicted, shall exist within the United States, or any place subject to their jurisdiction." Mr. Justice Cooper of the United States District Court rejected Flood's application. He said:

> A showing of compulsion is . . . prerequisite to proof of involuntary servitude . . . [Flood] is not compelled by law or statute to play baseball for Philadelphia. We recognise that under the existing rules of baseball, by refusing to report to Philadelphia [Flood] is by his own act foreclosing himself from continuing a professional baseball career, a consequence to be deplored. Nevertheless, he has the right to retire and embark upon a different enterprise outside organized baseball. The financial loss he might thus sustain may affect his choice, but does not leave him with "no way to avoid continued service" . . . [quote omitted]. Accordingly, we find that [Flood] has not satisfied the essential element of this cause of action, a showing of compulsory service.[18]

In the early 1980s a Dutch soccer player, a Mr. Muhren, brought an action before the European Commission of Human Rights. He maintained that his former club had set a prohibitive transfer fee on him, which precluded his ability to obtain employment with a club of his choice. He claimed that such fees were inconsistent with Article 4(2) of the *European Convention on Human Rights*. It states, "No one shall be required to perform forced or compulsory labor."

The reasoning of the European Commission on Human Rights in this case is similar to that of Mr. Justice Cooper in *Flood*. The Commission said Article 4, Clause 2, contained two elements which required consideration. First, the labor or service must be performed against the person's will; and second, the obligation to perform such labor or service "must be either unjust or oppressive or . . . constitute an avoidable hardship."

With respect to the first element, the Commission suggested that "prior consent is a decisive factor whether the work concerned should or should not be considered as being 'forced or compulsory' . . . the applicant freely chose to become a professional football player knowing that he would in entering the profession be affected by the rules governing the relationship between his future employers." On the second element, the Commission concluded that even if the transfer fee system "produce[s] certain inconveniences . . . it cannot be considered as being oppressive or constituting avoidable hardship." It also found that such a system did not directly affect the player's contractual freedom.[19]

In 1995 the Australian Soccer Players' Association[20] claimed, in an action before the Australian Industrial Relations Commission, that the transfer system conflicted with the freedom of choice in employment as specified by Article 23(1) of the *Universal Declaration of Human Rights* (see above). In a decision which is noteworthy for its brevity on this point, the Australian Industrial Relations Commission found that while "Generally speaking restraints on players will, to some degree, impinge on players" freedom of choice in employment . . . it overstates the position to say that the compensation fee system conflicts with freedom of choice in employment."[21]

On other occasions, the courts have seen fit to comment on, or draw attention to, the "servile" nature of employment rules in professional team sports. In 1914, in *American League Baseball Club of Chicago v. Chase*, Mr. Justice Bissell of the Supreme Court, Erie County, New York, strongly criticized baseball's reserve system. The case involved the Chicago club attempting to stop Hal Chase from taking up employment with the Buffalo club of the Federal League.

Mr. Justice Bissell said, due to the reserve system "the baseball player is made a chattel," and "would seem to establish a species of quasi peonage unlawfully controlling and interfering with the personal freedom of players." He asked, "But why should a player enter into a contract when his liberty of conduct and of contract is thus curtailed"? "The answer," he said, "is that he has no recourse. He must either take the contract under the provisions of the National Agreement,[22] whose organization controls practically all of the good ball players of this country or resort to some other occupation." Mr. Justice Bissell also said:

> While the services of . . . baseball players are ostensibly secured by voluntary contract a study of the [reserve] system . . . reveals the involuntary character of the servitude which is imposed upon players by the strength of the combination controlling the labor of practically all of the players in this country . . . The quasi peonage of baseball players . . . is contrary to the spirit of American institutions and is contrary to the spirit of the Constitution of the United States.[23]

In 1949 Daniel Gardella brought an action against baseball after being "blacklisted" for having played in a rival Mexican league. As part of a 2/1 majority which found for Gardella, Mr. Justice Frank of the United States Court of Appeals, Second Circuit, said:

> We have here a monopoly which, in its effect on ball-players like the plaintiff, possess characteristics shockingly repugnant to moral principle that, at least since the War Between the States, has been basic in America, as shown by the Thirteenth Amendment of the Constitution, condemning "involuntary servitude" . . . For the "reserve clause," as has been observed results in something resembling peonage of the baseball player[24] . . . I may add that, if the players be regarded as quasi-peons, it is of no moment that they are well paid; only the totalitarian-minded will believe that high pay excuses virtual slavery. In what I have said about the nature of the contracts made with the players, I am not to be understood as implying that they violate the Thirteenth Amendment or the statutes enacted pursuant thereto. I mean simply to suggest that those contracts are so opposed to the public policy of the United States.[25]

In 1991 Mr. Justice Wilcox of the Federal Court of Australia, in an appeal action concerning the operation of the internal draft in rugby league, said, "The right to choose between perspective employers is a fundamental element of a free society. It is the existence of this right which separates the free person from the serf."[26]

III. Freedom of Choice in Employment: North America

Baseball's reserve or option system rendered players dependent on the tender mercies of their clubs. Denied the ability to seek alternative employment, clubs could not only "persuade" players to "agree" to low salaries, but also devise means to escape contractual obligations. Clubs deducted sums for uniforms, traveling, and medical expenses and imposed fines for profanities expressed on the diamond and other misdemeanors. Players were also threatened with fines if their play or performance didn't improve and, if it did, they were fined anyway because improved play now was an indicator of slacking in the past. Clubs also employed Pinkerton spies to watch over players in the conduct of their private affairs.[27]

Players resented the reserve system and the associated degree of control it afforded clubs/owners over their employment. On three occasions, during the early decades of baseball's operation, they formed player associations in attempting to improve their lot. They were the National Brotherhood of Professional Baseball Players (1885–1890); the League Protective Players' Association (1900–1902) and the Baseball Players Fraternity (1912–1918). The three lacked the leadership and organizational skills required to survive as entities in the baseball industry.[28]

The operation of these respective player associations coincided with periods where Organized Baseball was challenged by rival leagues: the Players League (1890), when players with the aid of financial backers established "a league of their own"; the American League (1900–1902); and the Federal League (1914–1915).[29] Rival leagues provided players with the chance to seek alternative employment and, in turn, generated a series of actions which tested baseball's reserve system.

John Montgomery Ward was the leading figure in the formation of the National Brotherhood—baseball and sports' first union. The New York club sought an injunction restraining Ward from joining the Players' League under the reserve clause in his 1889 contract. Mr. Justice O'Brien of the Supreme Court of New York County declined this application, for two major reasons. The first was based on the common law notion that "a court of equity will not make a contract which the parties themselves have not made, and . . . will not enforce an indefinite one." Mr. Justice O'Brien found that there was nothing in Ward's 1889 contract which provided guidance on what would be the terms and conditions of his employment in 1890. He said, "Not only are there no terms and conditions fixed, but I do not think it is entirely clear that Ward agrees to do anything further than to accord the right to reserve him upon terms thereafter to be fixed."

Secondly, Ward's 1889 contract contained clauses which enabled the New York club to terminate his contract because he had violated it, and on ten days' notice for any reason. Mr. Justice O'Brien concluded that the reserve clause, set against this ten day term, suffered from a "want of fairness and of mutuality."[30]

New York also sought an injunction restraining Ward's teammate, Buck Ewing, from joining the Federal League. Mr. Justice Wallace at the Circuit Court, New York, drawing on the decision in *Ward*, turned down this request.[31]

The players' victories in these cases, however, proved to be pyrrhic. The Players' League was deserted by its financial backers and collapsed, as did the National Brotherhood. To complete this inning of baseball history, in due course Organized Baseball altered player contracts to include clauses which stated that players received specific sums of money for "agreeing" to the reserve clause, and that part of their "high" pay was compensation for the ten-day notice clause.

In 1902 Napolean Lajoie of Organized Baseball's Philadelphia club signed to play with a Philadelphia club in the rival American League. The former club sought an injunction from the Supreme Court of Pennsylvania restraining such a move. It maintained that the reserve clause contained in Lajoie's contract, particularly the two elements identified above, satisfied tests of mutuality and reasonableness as required by a court of equity. Mr. Justice Potter agreed with this line of reasoning and restrained Lajoie from joining the American League's Philadelphia club.[32] The jurisdiction of this decision was, of course, limited to Pennsylvania. Lajoie was traded to Cleveland in the American League. He was provided with the luxury of a short vacation whenever Cleveland played in Philadelphia, for fear of being arrested if he should visit that city.

Reference has already been made to the 1914 decision of Mr. Justice Bissell in *Chase* where he found the reserve system reduced players to "chattels" and "quasi-peons." Organized Baseball's Chicago club was attempting to block Chase from taking up employment with Buffalo in the Federal League. The case is also of importance because it constitutes the first attempt to utilize the *Sherman Antitrust Act 1890* in the legal battles over players' employment rights. The relevant sections hold:

1. Every contract, combination in the form of trust or otherwise, or conspiracy, in restraint of trade or commerce among the several States, or with foreign nations, is declared to be illegal . . .

2. Every person who shall monopolize, or attempt to monopolize, or combine or conspire with any other person or persons, to monopolize any part of the trade or commerce among the several States, or with foreign nations, shall be deemed guilty of a misdemeanour . . ."[33]

Mr. Justice Bissell found that "Organized Baseball is now as complete a monopoly of the baseball business for profit as any monopoly can be made. It is in contravention of the common law, in that it invades the right to labor as a property right, in that it invades the right to contract as a property right, and in that it is a combination to restrain and control the exercise of a profession or calling." Despite this finding, however, he could not accept "the proposition that the business of baseball for profit is interstate trade or commerce, and therefore subject to the provisions of the Sherman Act."

Mr. Justice Bissell defined commerce as the "interchange of goods, merchandise or property of any kind; trade; traffic . . ." Even though he described players as "chattels" and "quasi-peons," in other parts of his decision (see above), he did not accept the proposition that "baseball players are bought and sold and dealt in among the several states, and are thus reduced and commercialized into commodities." He said, "We are not dealing with the bodies of the players as commodities or articles of merchandise; but with their services as retained or transferred by contract." (Compare this with the statement elsewhere in his decision that players have no choice in their employment—see above). "Baseball," he said, "is an amusement, a sport, a game that clearly comes within the civil and criminal law of the state, and it is not commodity or an article of merchandise subject to the regulation of Congress on the theory that it is interstate commerce."[34]

At the end of 1915 the trade war between Organized Baseball and the Federal League came to an end, with the negotiation of a peace deal in Cincinnati. This agreement, however, did not satisfy the principals of the Baltimore club of the Federal League. The Baltimore Federals initiated legal action claiming that Organized Baseball was a monopoly in breach of the *Sherman Antitrust Act 1890*.

The action eventually found its way to the Supreme Court of the United States of America. In 1922 Mr. Justice Holmes, speaking for a unanimous court, ruled against Baltimore, thereby exempting baseball from the reach of the *Sherman Antitrust Act 1890*. He said:

> The business is giving exhibitions of baseball, which are purely state affairs. It is true that, in order to attain for those exhibitions the great popularity that they have achieved, competitions must be arranged between clubs from different cities and States. But the fact that in order to give exhibitions the League must induce free persons to cross state lines and must arrange and pay for their doing is not enough to change the character of the business . . . the transport is a mere incident, not the essential thing. That to which it is incident, the exhibition, although made for money would not be called trade or commerce in the commonly accepted use of those words.[35]

In 1923 in *Hart* the Supreme Court deliberated on the applicability of the *Sherman Antitrust Act 1890* to vaudeville artists. A promoter claimed, relying on *Federal Baseball*, that the provision of vaudeville artists was purely a state affair, and that the transportation of such artists across state borders was "incidental" to the performances supplied. The Supreme Court rejected this line of reasoning. Mr. Justice Holmes, on behalf of the court, said the matter "was brought before the decision in the *Base Ball Club Case*, and it may be that which in general is incidental, in some instances may rise to a magnitude that requires it to be considered independently."[36] By applying the *Sherman Antitrust Act 1890* to vaudeville artists, *Hart* marked the beginning of the extension of the jurisdiction of the *Sherman Antitrust Act* to a range of activities and sports that the courts were prepared to characterize as "interstate commerce." The exemption of baseball from this jurisdiction became an anomaly.

It is not until 1949 that the next major case concerning employment rules in North American sport occurs. The case involves baseball's blacklisting of Daniel Gardella after playing in a Mexican League (see above). Gardella argued that the substantial sums baseball now received from broadcasting and television rights constituted a new factor which negated *Federal Baseball*. A 2/1 majority of the United States Court of Appeals, Second Circuit, accepted such reasoning.[37]

In 1953 the Supreme Court was provided with an opportunity to reconsider *Federal Baseball*. The case involved George Toolson of the New York Yankees, who objected to being assigned to a minor league team. He maintained that baseball's reserve system violated the *Sherman Antitrust Act 1890*. A majority of the court upheld *Federal Baseball* on the basis of *stare decisis*. The majority said:

> In *Federal Baseball* . . . this Court held that the business of providing public baseball games for profit between clubs of professional baseball players was not within the scope of the federal antitrust laws. Congress has had the ruling under consideration but has not seen fit to bring such business under these laws by legislation having prospective effect. The business has thus been left for thirty years to develop, on the understanding that it was not subject to existing antitrust legislation. . . . We think that if there are evils in this field which now warrant application to it of the antitrust laws it should be by legislation.[38]

Promoters of theatrical entertainments and boxing tried to shield themselves from antitrust actions following the Supreme Court's decision in *Toolson*. On both occasions, in almost identical prose, the Supreme Court said that *Toolson* was a narrow application of *stare decisis* in upholding baseball's exemption as granted in *Federal Baseball*.[39] In *International Boxing Club*, a majority of the court said, "Indeed, this Court's decision in the *Hart* case, less than a year after the *Federal Baseball* decision, clearly established that *Federal Baseball* could not be replied upon as a basis of exemption for other segments of the entertainment business, athletic or otherwise."[40]

Two subsequent cases, fourteen years apart, reaffirmed baseball's privileged antitrust position. In 1957, William Radovich initiated proceedings against the National Football League, who blacklisted him because he had previously played with a rival league. A majority of the Supreme Court found that "the volume of interstate business involved in organized professional football places it within the provisions of the [Sherman] Act." To the extent that this ruling "is unrealistic, inconsistent or illogical," given decisions in *Federal Baseball* and *Toolson*, the majority said, "were we considering the question of baseball for the first time upon a clean slate we would have no doubts."[41]

The second case, in 1971, involved basketballer Spencer Haywood. Under basketball's rules players could only join, or be drafted to, clubs after having played four years in college. Haywood signed with Seattle prior to this effluxion of time; and the National Basketball Association barred his playing. Haywood maintained that such an action constituted a violation of the *Sherman Antitrust Act 1890*. The Supreme Court concurred. It simply said "Basketball . . . does not enjoy exemption from the antitrust law."[42]

In the early 1970s Curt Flood, with the backing of the Major League Baseball Players' Association, challenged baseball's reserve system. He objected to being traded by the St. Louis Cardinals, a club for which he had played for twelve years, to the Philadelphia Phillies. He claimed that such a trade violated antitrust and civil rights legislation and the common law and constituted a form of peonage and involuntary servitude in contravention of the Thirteenth Amendment of the United States Constitution. The peonage, involuntary servitude aspect of this claim has already been discussed above.

With respect to the antitrust aspect of Flood's claim the Supreme Court decided to follow *stare decisis* and reaffirmed its previous rulings in *Federal Baseball* and, more especially, *Toolson*. A majority of the court concluded that "professional baseball is a business and it is engaged in interstate commerce." They also found that "its reserve system [in] enjoying exemption from the federal antitrust laws, . . . is, in a very distinct sense, an exception and an anomaly." They added, the court's earlier decisions in *Federal Baseball* and *Toolson* "have become an aberration confined to baseball." Having said this, the majority, nonetheless, concluded that it was Congress's duty to bring about an end to this aberration. They went on to add, if there was any inconsistency or illogic in their stance:

> If we were to act otherwise, we would be withdrawing from the conclusion as to congressional intent made in *Toolson* and from the concerns as to retrospectivity therein expressed. Under these circumstances, there is merit in consistency even though some might claim that beneath that consistency is a layer of inconsistency.[43]

In a dissenting judgment, Mr. Justice Marshall indicated an alternative legal path for resolving employment issues in baseball and sport. He suggested exploration of federal labor law (the *National Labor Relations Act 1935*) as an alternative to antitrust actions.[44] Moreover, the *Clayton Act 1914* provided deals negotiated by labor (and other) organizations with immunity from antitrust actions. Section 6 states:

> The labor of a human being is not a commodity or article of commerce. Nothing contained in the antitrust laws shall be construed to forbid the existence and operation of labor, agricultural or horticultural organizations, instituted for the purposes of mutual help, and not having capital

stock or conducted for profit, or to forbid or restrain individual members of such organizations from lawfully carrying out the legitimate objects thereof; nor shall such organizations, or the members thereof, be held or construed to be illegal combinations or conspiracies in restraint of trade, under the antitrust laws.

In 1946 there was a fourth abortive attempt to establish a players' association in baseball. It was called the American Baseball Guild. Organized Baseball countered this attempt by providing players with some concessions and the introduction of a representative system, where discussions were held with players chosen from each club. In 1954 the Major League Baseball Players' Association was formed. It was a rather inactive, passive body until the appointment of a former Steelworker Union official in the person of Marvin Miller in 1966. In the 1950s player associations were also formed—some of which were short-lived—in football, basketball, and ice-hockey. As with baseball, it was not until the 1960s, and early 1970s, that these respective organizations became more active in protecting and advancing members' rights.[45]

Following *Flood*, cases concerning players' rights hinged on the extent to which leagues/clubs could use labor law to shield themselves from antitrust attacks. This, in turn, was dependent on the "nature," or "state," of collective bargaining within the respective sports. With the exception of baseball, America's legal regime encouraged the growth of collective negotiations in professional team sports.

In 1972 in *Boston Professional Hockey Association* and *Philadelphia World Hockey Club* the courts were asked to adjudicate on ice-hockey's reserve system, following players taking up employment with a rival league.[46] In both instances ice hockey attempted to deflect antitrust attacks on the basis of an alleged labor exemption. The trial judges in both cases rejected such a defense. In *Philadelphia World Hockey Club*, Mr. Justice Higginbotham, of the United States District Court, Pennsylvania, said it was unclear if the National Hockey League Players' Association had been registered under the relevant provisions of the *National Labor Relations Act 1935*, hockey's Board of Governors had not ratified "agreements" negotiated with the players' association, and that the reserve system had "never been the subject of bona-fide, good-faith collective bargaining."[47] Similarly, in *Boston Professional Hockey Association*, Chief Judge Caffrey, of the United States District Court, Massachusetts, could not find any evidence that bargaining had occurred over the reserve clause.[48]

For want of the existence of collective bargaining agreements the courts also found against football and basketball's respective employment rules.[49] In *Smith*, which found against football's draft, Mr. Justice Bryant, of the United States District Court, Columbia, said that courts needed to consider whether issues "have been "thrust upon" a weak players' union by the owners."[50] In *Mackey*, Mr. Justice Larsen, of the United States District Court, Minnesotta, said that the "weakness" of the union was an issue he took into account in finding against football's "Rozelle" rule. Even though two collective bargaining agreements had been entered into, he could find no evidence of "any trade-off or quid pro quo whereby the union had agreed to the Rozelle rule in return for other benefits."[51]

Berry and Gould maintain that the courts' concern in *Smith* and *Mackey* with employment conditions being "thrust upon a weak union" constitutes "a misunderstanding of federal labor law policy and the realities of the collective bargaining process." The notion of "good faith bargaining" in American labor law has not been interpreted to mean that a party must move from its original position when negotiating. "Good faith bargaining" is essentially an endorsement of a preparedness to take part in a process which involves discussions and negotiations. Parties, in agreeing to not pursue certain issues may be enabled to gain concessions on other issues which are of importance to them. Though, what comes out of bargaining will be highly dependent on the strength, strategic position,and negotiating skills of the respective parties. Returning to the situation in American football in the mid 1970s Berry and Gould observed that "If the union had not . . . relinquished bargaining rights [on the "Rozelle" rule], it might not have had a collective bargaining agreement at all."[52]

The National Hockey League and National Hockey League Players' Association negotiated a collective agreement in 1976. A clause in this agreement stated that ice hockey's employment rules were "fair and reasonable." Dale McCourt, of the Detroit Redwings, objected to being assigned to the Los Angeles Kings as part of a compensation package following the Redwing's acquisition of "free agent" Rogation Vachon. In a two to one majority the United States Court of Appeals, Sixth Circuit, found that the collective bargaining agreement protected ice hockey's assignment rule from antitrust attack.[53]

Labor law and/or the relative strength or skills of the parties in collective bargaining would now become the major determinants of players' rights and employment conditions. Player associations could, however, use the actual or real threat of union decertification to negate the owners' use of the labor exemption in antitrust actions as a tactic in collective negotiations.[54]

One North American player association encountered a new problem. Michels has written how labor organizations may become subject to an "iron law of oligarchy." Among other things this involves a situation where leaders abuse their positions of power to further their own interests, at the expense of their members.[55] Such a fate befell the National Hockey League Players' Association under the leadership of Alan Eagleson from the late 1960s to early 1990s. Staudohar reports that in 1994 Eagleson was indicted on numerous counts of racketeering, embezzlement, and fraud following an FBI investigation of his period as the National Hockey League Players' Association director. The charges included misappropriation of union funds and receiving kickbacks from insurance brokers on league and disability coverage.[56]

Flood protected baseball, and its reserve system, from antitrust actions. Despite this, the Major League Baseball Players' Association found a means to bring about the reserve system's demise. Grievance disputes in baseball, in the absence of a viable players' association, were traditionally "resolved" by baseball's commissioner. Following the appointment of Marvin Miller as its leader in 1966, the Major League Baseball Players' Association sought to bring this practice to an end. In 1970 it convinced Organized Baseball that grievance disputes should be heard before a mutually agreed independent arbitrator, per the usual practice of North American collective bargaining agreements.

In 1975 players Andy Messersmith and Dave McNally declined to sign new contracts with their respective clubs and played out their option year. After playing out their options both players claimed they were free agents and could negotiate with the various clubs prepared to employ them. Organized Baseball disputed this line of reasoning. The issue was resolved by baseball's new grievance procedure. Private arbitrator Peter Seitz ruled in favor of Messersmith and McNally.[57] Baseball's reserve system could simply be brought to an end by all players playing out their option year.

Seitz's decision substantially enhanced the strategic position of the players' association in subsequent dealings with Organized Baseball. The choice which confronted the latter was negotiating an agreement acceptable to the players' association which contained "some" restrictions on player mobility or, in the absence of an agreement, free agency for all players. After a series of negotiations the parties agreed on a new system of rules to govern the future employment of baseballers. The most important of these was that after six years of major league service players would become free agents. They would then be able to negotiate with various clubs interested in obtaining their services.

Industrial relations in baseball has been characterized by distrust and rivalry since Seitz"s decision. Organized Baseball has strenuously attempted to reduce the freedoms afforded to players in the mid 1970s. The Major League Baseball Players' Association has, just as strenuously, resisted such attempts. The "best" example of such tensions is the 232-day lockout which disrupted the 1994 season, and, for the first time since 1904, brought about the cancellation of the World Series.[58]

In October 1998 President Clinton signed the *Curt Flood Act 1998*,[59] which ended the exemption baseball's employment rules had enjoyed from antitrust actions.[60] The 1994 lockout helped persuade Congress to respond to the Supreme Court's request in *Toolson*, almost fifty years earlier, to overcome an "inconsistent," "illogical," and "anomalous" decision which the court found itself unable or disinclined to rectify.

IV. Freedom of Choice in Employment: United Kingdom and Australia

The players of English soccer objected to the various employment rules which were developed and imposed on them by the sport's governing authorities. English soccer adopted a transfer system in 1891 and a maximum wage of four pounds per week in 1901. In 1893 and 1898 there were two abortive attempts to establish a players' union. In December 1907 a third attempt proved more successful with the formation of the Association Football Players' Union:[61] the oldest continuous players' body in world sport. Among its objects the union sought to abolish "all restrictions which affect the social and financial position of players" and to provide legal assistance to members "involving claims under the *Workmen"s Compensation Act 1906*,[62] recovery of wages due, and breaches of contract."[63]

Once the union sought to act on these objects—particularly workers' compensation claims—it encountered increasingly bitter opposition from both the Football League and Football Association. In 1909 the latter sought to bring about the destruction of the players' union. Among other things, it required players to sign contracts for the 1909/1910 season renouncing their membership of the union. The determination of players to maintain their allegiance to the union—particularly the members of Manchester United, and, to a lesser extent, Newcastle United, the respective Cup and League champions of 1908/1909—and a likely disruption to the commencement of the 1909/1910 season resulted in an ultimate backdown by the Football Association. It again agreed to recognize and negotiate with the fledging players' body.

In 1912 the players' union backed player Harry Kingaby in an action against soccer's transfer system. Kingaby had played for Aston Villa in 1906. He had been unable to establish himself as a regular member of the team and had joined a Southern League club in 1907. At the time, the Football and Southern leagues did not have an agreement on transfer fees for players moving between the two leagues. This is something they rectified in 1910. Aston Villa placed a £350 transfer fee on Kingaby, which was later reduced to £300 on appeal. For reasons which are unclear, Kingaby and the union did not base their case around the restraint of trade doctrine. Lord McNaughten in *Nordenfelt* in 1894 defined the doctrine as follows:

> The public have an interest in every person's carrying on his trade freely; so has the individual. All interference with individual liberty of action in trading, and all restraints of trade of themselves, if there is nothing more, are contrary to public policy, and, therefore, void. That is the general rule. But there are exceptions. Restraints of trade and interference with individual liberty of action, may be justified by the special circumstances of a particular case. It is a sufficient justification, and indeed, it is the only justification, if the restriction is reasonable—reasonable, that is in reference to the interests of the parties concerned and reasonable in reference to the interests of the public, so framed and so guarded as to afford adequate protection to the party in whose favour it is imposed, while at the same time it is in no way injurious to the public."[64]

Rather, Kingaby's claim for damages was based on his loss of employment and the malicious charging of an excessive transfer fee. Mr. Justice Lawrence dismissed Kingaby's application. He found that the placement of a transfer fee did not constitute a tort; nor was there any evidence that Aston Villa had acted maliciously against Kingaby.[65]

Mr. Justice Lawrence's decision also contains a passing reference to the *Trade Disputes Act 1906*,[66] as a possible defense against actions attacking soccer's transfer system. Section 1 of the Act states, "An act done in pursuance of an agreement or combination by two or more persons shall, if done in contemplation or furtherance of a trade dispute, not be actionable unless the act, if done without any such agreement or combination, would be actionable." Mr. Justice Lawrence said his "judgment was not based on the Trade Disputes Act, though he doubted if it would not apply to the defendant."[67] With these words Mr. Justice Lawrence opened up the prospect of using labor law as a possible defense for leagues and clubs in restraint of trade cases; prior to the analogous use of such a strategy against antitrust actions in North America.

Costs were awarded against Kingaby and the players' union. The union attempted to organize a game among members to raise funds to meet these costs. The Football Association decided not to grant permission for playing such a game. The union secretary, Alfred Owen, wrote a bitter letter to the Football Association over its stance. The Football Association and Football League would not agree to sanction a game until the union's management committee disassociated themselves from Owen's letter and publicly rebuked him. They acceded to this request. Owen resigned from his position as secretary. Harding, the union's official historian, has said, "The Union had thus allowed its secretary to be hounded out of the game, a disgraceful episode and one that could do it no good in the eyes of its members. . . . [It was now] in virtual bankruptcy and impotent."[68]

It was not until the 1950s, under the stewardship of secretary Cliff Lloyd, that the union (from 1958 renamed as the Professional Footballers' Association) was able to reassert itself as a viable force in English soccer. In the mid 1950s it secured a 10 percent share of television rights; income which has placed it in good store to pursue the benevolent, welfare, and transition to post-soccer career needs of members. Threatened strike action in 1961 brought about the abolition of maximum wages, which stood at £20 per week. In 1963 the players' body backed Newcastle United player George Eastham in a challenge to soccer's transfer system.

Following *Kingaby*, and prior to *Eastham*, there had only been one other occasion where the courts had "commented" on the transfer system. In 1955 Ralph Banks fell out with his club Aldershot. Even though his contract with Aldershot had expired, under the transfer system his future employment was subject to the discretion of the club; who had placed a "high" transfer fee on him. The issue before Mr. Justice Rankin of the County Court was Aldershot's attempt to evict Banks from premises provided by the club. The minutes of the union's annual general meeting of November 14, 1955 record that Mr. Justice Rankin said, "It is a penalty imposed on a professional player for his refusal to accept terms he considered unsatisfactory. As he cannot play elsewhere in Britain or the World it is a closed shop." The minutes also state that Mr. Justice Rankin was not prepared to consider whether the transfer system was a restraint of trade because the case before him was primarily concerned with the possession of a house.[69]

The major issue before the court in *Eastham* was the ability of clubs to stop players from taking up employment with alternative clubs, following the expiry of contracts with their original clubs. Mr. Justice Wilberforce described soccer's employment rules as

> an employers' system, set up in an industry where the employers have succeeded in establishing a monolithic front all over the world, and where it is clear that for the purpose of negotiation the employers are vastly more strongly organized than the employees. No doubt the employers all over the world consider the system a good system, but this does not prevent the court from considering whether it goes further than is reasonably necessary to protect their legitimate interests.[70]

He found rules which restricted the ability of players, out of contract, to take up alternative employment operated as a restraint of trade. The Football League mounted a number of defenses in support of the transfer system. They argued that they encouraged clubs to invest in the coaching and training of younger players, aided the attainment of sporting equality, maintained team stability, and prevented the poaching of players. Mr. Justice Wilberforce rejected these defenses. He found little evidence "that clubs in general do spend large sums in training professional players, other than apprentices." Nor could he find any evidence that Newcastle United had expended the profit they had made in fees in the buying and selling of Eastham "in training the plaintiff to his present pitch of excellence." He also concluded that the transfer system had not brought about the attainment of sporting equality. Staggered long-term contracts could be used by clubs to ensure that players are not attracted to play with other, richer clubs. He also said that such contracts would help clubs to maintain team stability and prevent poaching of players by other clubs.[71]

Eastham and the players' body's victory in this case strengthened the latter's hand in subsequent negotiations with the Football League and Football Association over members' employment rights. In the mid 1960s, and again in the latter part of the 1970s, the Professional Footballers' Association negotiated major changes to soccer's employment rules which enhanced the human rights of members.

The mid 1960s changes included players being given a free transfer if clubs did not offer them contracts equal to last year's terms, and the use of an independent tribunal to resolve salary disputes between players and clubs—with players to receive the terms of their previous contract during the dispute period. The changes in the latter part of the 1970s provided free agency for players aged 33, with five years service with a club. They also made players out of contract free to move to a new club, with a fee to be subsequently negotiated between the clubs concerned. If the clubs are unable to agree the fee will be determined by an independent tribunal.[72]

Australian courts have drawn on *Eastham* in their examination of professional team sports' employment rules. In 1971 in *Tutty*, the High Court of Australia, on appeal, adjudicated on the reasonableness of the New South Wales Rugby League's employment rules. The facts of *Tutty* are similar to those of *Eastham*. Balmain used the transfer system to block attempts by Dennis Tutty to obtain employment with other clubs, even though his contract had expired and he sat out of the game for a season. Like Mr. Justice Wilberforce, the High Court found such rules to be an unreasonable restraint of trade.[73]

Since *Tutty*, the general practice of Australian courts has been to find against various employment rules which restrict the ability of players to obtain employment with alternative clubs.[74] Only three cases will be considered here, because of their connections with the activities of player associations in the respective sports.

Throughout the twentieth century different generations of players across a variety of Australian professional team sports have attempted to form player associations. Beginning with players of the Victorian Football League prior to World War I and continuing through to baseball players in 1997 there have been thirty examples of failed attempts to establish such bodies. With small memberships (sometimes widely dispersed) and members with limited incomes, such player bodies have found it difficult to generate enough funds and obtain leaders to sustain themselves as viable organizations.[75] Australia currently has seven player associations; the majority of whom are only of recent vintage. The oldest is the Australian Football League Players' Association which formed in 1973. The Rugby League Players' Union was formed in 1979; The National Basketball League Players' Association in 1989; the Australian Professional Footballers' Association in 1993; both the Rugby Union Players' Association and the Australian Cricketers' Association in 1995; and, finally, the Australian Netball Players' Association in 1997 — the only organization representing female athletes.[76]

In *Foschini* in 1983 Mr. Justice Crockett of the Supreme Court of Victoria found the then Victorian Football League's transfer rules to be an unreasonable restraint of trade. As with *Eastham* and *Tutty*, South Melbourne, or the Sydney Swans as the club became known, blocked Silvio Foschini, an uncontracted player from joining St. Kilda. The case was further complicated by the fact that South Melbourne were relocating to Sydney and required players, such as Foschini, still a teenager, to also relocate. In his decision, Mr. Justice Crockett also passed comment on the league's zoning rules. He said:

> If the desire is, as claimed to assist the less successful sides by a better access to talented players I should have thought that the "draft" system . . . would . . . be a preferable system to zoning in Victoria."[77]

Following *Foschini* the Victorian Football League substantially altered its employment rules. In 1985 it introduced a salary cap, the external draft in 1986 and the internal draft in 1988.[78]

Foschini's action was bankrolled by St. Kilda. The then Victorian Football League Players' Association — it changed its name in 1989 — played no part in the proceedings of this case. *Foschini* appears to have completely passed the Association by. There is no evidence that it attempted to use *Foschini* as a bargaining lever to enhance players' employment rights, as had occurred in North America and the United Kingdom, following similarly favorable court decisions. Moreover, the Victorian Football League Players' Association hardly had any input into the new employment rules developed by the Victorian Football League in the mid to late 1980s—the salary cap and the two drafts.

In 1988, and again in 1990, the Australian Football League Players' Association agreed to the various terms contained in the Australian Football League's standard player contract, with its various restrictions on player mobility and total earnings. In late 1992 the Australian Football League withdrew recognition of the players' association. The threat of strike action and, more significantly, proceedings before the Australian Industrial Relations Commission and the possibility that the matters in dispute would be arbitrated, induced the Australian Football League to review its stance on recognition.

The parties eventually entered into a collective bargaining agreement for the 1994 and 1995 seasons.[79] It established a minimum wage of $7,500, minus deductions for board and lodging. While the 1994/1995 Collective Bargaining Agreement was silent on such issues it, in effect, endorsed the Australian Football League's player rules—salary cap[80] and drafting. Subsequent collective bargaining agreements in Australian rules football have contained clauses whereby the Australian Football League Players' Association agrees that the league's rules

> including and without limitation, restrictions on the freedom of players to transfer from one Club to another, restrictions on the total payment an AFL Club may give or apply for the benefit of a player . . . are necessary and reasonable for the purpose of protecting the legitimate interests of the AFL.[81]

The second case occurred in 1991 when the Full Court of the Federal Court of Australia found the New South Wales Rugby League's internal draft to be an unreasonable restraint of trade.[82] This is the case where Mr. Justice Wilcox likened the draft to serfdom (see above). This action was mounted by the then Association of Rugby League Professionals. It was the first time in the history of Australian sport that a players' association had initiated action against a league's employment rules—and they were successful to boot.

It might be thought that such a victory would have helped to consolidate the association's position. Nothing could be further from the truth. Since the case the rugby league players' body has virtually collapsed. Throughout most of the 1990s it has hardly had more than twenty members. In 1992 it failed in an attempt to negotiate a collective bargaining deal with the New South Wales Rugby League. In an apparent effort to consolidate its organizational effectiveness it merged with the Media, Entertainment, and Arts Alliance. The next two to three years were devoted to disputes over members between the principals of the "new" and "old" unions. Players found themselves more concerned with cashing in on the high salaries that were on offer during the trade war between the Australian Rugby League and Super League after 1995, than worrying about the concerns of a players' organization.[83] In 1997 the Media, Entertainment, and Arts Alliance based organization negotiated a "bare bones" consent award with the Australian Rugby League, under the auspices of the Australian Industrial Relations Commission. The organization that in 1991 had defeated the internal draft found itself agreeing to a grievance procedure where disputes would be resolved by an appeals committee of the Australian Rugby League.[84]

The third case involved the 1995 attempt by the then Australian Soccer Players' Association to abolish the transfer system before the Australian Industrial Relations Commission (see above). The Commission concluded that the "system in its present form should be abolished." However, it should not "be abolished until consideration has been given to whether something else be put in its place," or whether it "could be modified so as to remove its unsatisfactory features." The Commission went on to advocate that negotiations should occur between the parties under its auspices. The Commission also said that negotiations concerning modification of the transfer system should also include "all the terms of an agreement or award to cover the remuneration and conditions of employment of professional soccer players." The Commission added that if the parties are unable to reach agreement "arbitration may be necessary." The decision's final sentence states, "Without pre-empting what the Commission might do at any time in the future, we reiterate our view that, on the evidence and material before us, the present [transfer] fee system should be abolished."[85]

Since that decision two collective bargaining agreements have been negotiated in Australian soccer. In distinction to Australian Rules football, both agreements contain clauses which enhance players' freedom of choice in employment. First, players who do not receive an offer of employment from their current club thirty days prior to the expiration of their contract on "terms and conditions no less favorable" than their previous contract automatically become free agents. Second, players who are 26 years of age, or have played six seasons, automatically become free agents, and remain so for the balance of their careers in Australia.[86] The former clause models the practice that was adopted in English soccer after *Eastham*, and the latter, North American baseball following negotiations after Peter Seitz's private arbitration brought an end to the reserve system.[87]

V. Summary and Conclusion

Fields and Narr have said that "the world is a field of struggle over [human] rights without any guarantee of success."[88] Such an observation is apposite concerning human rights in professional team sports. From their inception, sports in North America, the United Kingdom, Western Europe, and Australia adopted rules which severely limited the human rights and economic freedom of players. Players have resented such controls. They have looked for means, at worst, to mitigate their affects; at best, to bring about their abolition.

Players have employed two methods in their struggles to win back their rights. First, they have turned to collective action, forming player associations or trade unions. The earliest such bodies were formed in North America and the United Kingdom in the latter part of the nineteenth century, and Australia in the early years of the twentieth century. As Scoville has said, "player associations are almost as old as professional team sports."[89]

Player associations have had a checkered history in the annals of professional team sports. It is only in recent decades that they have experienced success in winning back players' rights and obtaining improvements in income and associated entitlements. In the 1960s the Professional Footballers' Association heralded the rise of player associations with its victories in abolishing soccer's maximum wage and Mr. Justice Wilberforce's finding against the transfer system in *Eastham*. North American player associations, led by the Major League Baseball Players' Association, achieved similar victories in the 1970s. It is only in the 1990s that Australian player bodies have come into prominence.

The second method has been to attack such controls in the courts. While judges have occasionally referred to the "chattel," "peonage," "quasi-peonage," or "serfdom" aspects of such controls, they have found it difficult to strike down arrangements which involve the trading, buying, and selling of players as a form of forced labor or slavery. Judges, however, imbued with natural rights and common law principles of freedom and individual liberty, have found it easier to find against such rules on antitrust grounds, as in North America, or as restraints of trade, as in the United Kingdom and Australia.

Leagues have found their employment rules vulnerable to legal attack. A possible means of protecting themselves against such action is to have player associations endorse such, or modified, rules in collective bargaining agreements negotiated at arms length and in "good faith." The courts, in defending the human rights of players on *individualistic* grounds have, paradoxically, enhanced the *collective* governance of sport. The courts have provided leagues with an incentive and, at times, have explicitly encouraged them to recognize and negotiate with player associations. The law, then, has provided a window of opportunity for the players of professional team sports to make use of collective action. This is not something which has traditionally been afforded to workers in other walks of life. It is a window, moreover, which would close if the leagues of various professional team sports adopted employment rules consistent with various human rights instruments developed by the international community.

Notes

1. Extracts from the various human rights instruments referred to here are drawn from Brownlie I (Ed.), *Basic Documents on Human Rights* (2nd ed., Clarendon, Oxford, 1981).
ILO Convention Concerning Forced or Compulsory Labor 1930, ILO Convention Concerning the Abolition of Forced Labor 1957 ibid, at 173–186.

2. *Universal Declaration of Human Rights*, Art. 23(4) ibid, at 24.

3. *International Covenant on Economic Social and Cultural Rights*, Art. 8 ibid, at 120–121.

4. *International Covenant on Civil and Political Rights*, Art. 22 ibid, at 135–136.

5. ILO 87.

6. ILO 98.

7. This is a generic term. Such arrangements have sometimes been referred to as the retain and transfer system, or the transfer and compensation system.

8. *Sherman Antitrust Act 1890* (USA) (Fed.).

9. *Clayton Act 1914* (USA) (Fed.).

10. The Australian *Trade Practices Act 1974* (Cth) does not extend to "the performance of work under a contract of service"; that is employment contracts, per Section 4(1).

11. See Opinion of Advocate General Lenz,

ASBL Union Royale Belge des Societies de Football Association v. Jean-Marc Bosman (1995) Case C-415/93; *and Union Royale des Societies de Football Association ASBL and Royal Club Leigois SA v. Jean-Marc Bosman*, Case C-415/9, Court of Justice of the European Communities, 3, Luxembourg, 15 December 1995. The opinion and decision, and other relevant cases are reproduced in Blainpain, R., and Inston, R., *The Bosman Case: The End of the Transfer System?* (Sweet & Maxwell/Peeters, Leuven, 1996). For a commentary see Dabscheck, B., "Assaults on Soccer"s Compensation System: Europe and Australia Compared" (1996) 13 *Sporting Traditions* 81.

12. *Treaty Establishing the European Economic Community 1957.*

13. For overviews of debates concerning Human Rights see Davidson, S., *Human Rights* (Open University Press, Buckingham, 1993); Donnelly, J., *Universal Human Rights in Theory and Practice* (Cornell University Press, Ithaca, 1989); Fields, A. B., and Narr, W. D., "Human Rights as a Holistic Concept" (1992) 14 *Human Rights Quarterly* 1; Stammers, N., "Human Rights and Power" (1993) XLI *Political Studies* 70; Stammers, N., "A Critique of Social Approaches to Human Rights" (1995) 17 *Human Rights Quarterly* 488; Galenkamp, M., "Collective Rights" (1995) 16 *Netherlands Institute of Human Rights* 53; and Pritchard, S., "The Jurisprudence of Human Rights: Some Critical Thoughts and Developments in Practice" (1995) 2 *Australian Journal of Human Rights* 3.

14. For discussions of the "merging" of individual and collective sports labor law see Berry, R.C., and Gould, W.B., "A Long Deep Drive to Collective Bargaining: Of Players Owners, Brawls and Strikes" (1981) 31 *Case Western Reserve Law Review* 685; Berry, R.C., Gould, W. B., and Staudohar, P. D., *Labor Relations in Professional Sports* (Auburn House, Dover, Massachusetts, 1986); and Opie, H., and Smith, G., "The Withering of Individualism: Professional Team Sports and Employment Law" (1992) 15 *University of New South Wales Law Journal* 313.

15. Cairns, J., Jennett, N., and Sloane, P. J., "The Economics of Professional Team Sports: A Survey of Theory and Evidence" (1986) 13 *Journal of Economic Studies* 3, at 33.

16. For discussions concerning revenue sharing see ibid; Davenport, S., "Collusive Competition in Major League Baseball: Its Theory and Institutional Development" (1969) 13 *American Economist* 6; Noll, R. G. (Ed.), *Government and the Sports Industry* (Brookings Institution, Washington D.C. 1974); Dabscheck, B., "Sporting Equality: Labor Market vs. Product Market Control" (1975) 17 *The Journal of Industrial Relations* 174; Atkinson, S.E., Stanley, L.R., and Tschirhart, J., "Revenue Sharing as an Incentive in an Agency Problem" (1988) 19 *Rand Journal of Economics* 27; Zimbalist, A., *Baseball and Billions: A Probing Look Inside the Big Business of Our National Pastime* (Basic Books, New York 1992); and Fort, R., and Quirk, J., "Cross-subsidization, Incentives, and Outcomes in Professional Team Sports Leagues" (1995) XXXIII *Journal of Economic Literature* 1265.

17. Lowenfish, L., *The Imperfect Diamond: A History of Baseball's Labor Wars* (revised ed., Da Capo, New York, 1992), at 69 refers to a decision by a Mr. Justice Talty of the St. Louis City Circuit Court, who in 1902 denied an injunction against Jack Harper moving to a rival league, on the basis that baseball's reserve system was a form of involuntary servitude. This matter is also referred to in Seymour, H., *Baseball: The Early Years* (Oxford University Press, New York, 1989), at 315; and Burk, R. F., *Never Just a Game: Players, Owners and American Baseball to 1920* (The University of North Carolina Press, Chapel Hill, 1994), at 154.

18. *Flood v. Kuhn* (1970) 316 F. Supp. 271 at 280–281. The matter was finally determined before the Supreme Court on antitrust principles. See *Flood v. Kuhn* (1972) 407 U.S. 258.

19. *X v. The Netherlands*, Application No. 9322/81, 32 EHRR 180 at 183.

20. In 1999 it changed its name to the Australian Professional Footballers' Association.

21. *Media, Entertainment and Arts Alliance v Marconi Fairfield Soccer Club and Australian Soccer Federation*, Australian Industrial Relations Commission, Dec 1285/95 S Print M2565, Sydney, 9 June 1995, at 56. The soccer players merged with the Alliance in 1993, and went their own way in 1998.

22. An agreement between the various clubs/owners in baseball, which enshrined the rules that governed its operation.

23. *American League Baseball Club of Chicago v. Chase*, 149 NYS 6 (1914), at 12, 17, 13 and 19. Though, as will be shown below, when it came to the issue of antitrust, Mr. Justice Bissell was less strident in his criticisms and analysis of baseball's employment rules.

24. A reference to *Chase* ibid.

25. *Gardella v. Chandler*, 172 F. 2d 402 (1949), at 409–410.

26. *Adamson v. New South Wales Rugby League Limited*, (1991) 31 FCR 242, at 267–268. Also see Adamson v. *New South Wales Rugby League Limited*, (1990) 27 FCR 535 for the decision of the trial judge.

27. For details concerning such practices see Burk above, note 9.

28. For details concerning their respective histories see ibid; Lowenfish above, note 9; Seymour above, note 9; Seymour, H., *Baseball: The Golden Age* (Oxford University Press, New York, 1971); Dworkin, J. B., *Owners Versus Players: Baseball and Collective Bargaining* (Auburn House, Boston, 1981); and Voigt, D. Q., "Serfs versus Magnates: A Century of Labor Strife in Major League Baseball" in Staudohar, P. D., and Mangan, J. A. (Eds.), *The Business of Professional Sports* (University of Illinois Press, Urbana and Chicago, 1991), 95–114.

29. For details consult Seymour above, note 9, and Seymour above, note 20.

30. *Metropolitan Exhibition v. Ward*, 9 NYS 779 (1890), at 781, 784, and 783.

31. *Metropolitan Exhibition v. Ewing*, 42 F 198 (1890) Circuit Court S.D. New York.

32. *Philadelphia Ball Club v. Lajoie*, 51 A 973 (1902).

33. Also see Sections 2, 3, and 4 of the *Clayton Act 1914*.

34. *American League Baseball Club of Chicago v. Chase*, 149 NYS 6 (1914), at 16 and 17.

35. *Federal Baseball Club of Baltimore v. National League of Professional Baseball Clubs*, 259 U.S. 200 (1922), at 208 and 209.

36. *Hart v. BF Keith Vaudeville Exchange*, 262 US 271 (1923), at 274.

37. *Gardella v. Chandler*, 172 F. 2d 402 (1949).

38. *Toolson v. New York Yankees*, 346 U.S. 356 (1953), at 356 and 357.

39. *United States v. Shubert*, 348 U.S. 222 (1955); *United States v. International Boxing Club of New York*, 348 U.S. 236 (1955).

40. *International Boxing Club* at 242. See *Shubert*, at 229 for a similar statement.

41. *Radovich v. National Football League*, 352 U.S. 445 (1957), at 452.

42. *Haywood v. National Football League*, 401 U.S. 1204 (1971), at 1205. For the subsequent decision of the lower court see *Denver Rocketts v. All–Pro Management*, 325 F. Supp. 1049 (1971).

43. *Flood v. Kuhn*, 407 U.S. 258 (1972), at 282–284.

44. Ibid, at 294–296. Also see Jacobs, M. S., and Winter, R. K., "Antitrust Principles and Collective Bargaining by Athletes: Of Superstars in Peonage" (1971) 81 *The Yale Law Journal* 1, which is referred to in Mr. Justice Marshall's dissent.

45. For details concerning the development of player associations in this period see Berry, Gould, and Staudohar above, note 6; Dworkin

above, note 20; Voigt above, note 20; Lowenfish above, note 9; Miller, M., *A Whole Different Ball Game: The Sport and Business of Baseball* (Birch Lane, New York, 1991); Korr, C. P., "Marvin Miller and the New Unionism in Baseball" in Staudohar and Mangan above, note 20, 115; and Staudohar, P. D., *Playing for Dollars: Labor Relations and the Sports Business* (ILR Press, Ithaca, 1996).

46. *Boston Professional Hockey Association v. Cheevers*, 348 F. Supp. 261 (1972); *Philadelphia World Hockey Club v. Philadelphia Hockey Club*, 351 F. Supp. 462 (1972).

47. *Philadelphia World Hockey Club*, at 497, 483 and 485.

48. *Boston Professional Hockey Association*, at 267.

49. See *Kapp v. National Football League*, 390 F. Supp. 73 (1974); *Kapp v. National Football League*, 586 F. 2d 644 (1978); *Smith v. Pro-Football*, 420 F. Supp. 738 (1976); *Smith v. Pro-Football*, 593 F. 2d 1173 (1978); *Robertson v. National Basketball Association*, 389 F. Supp. 867 (1975); and *Robertson v. National Basketball Association*, 556 F. 2d 682 (1977).

50. *Smith v. Pro-Football*, 420 F. Supp. 738 (1976), at 743.

51. *Mackey v. National Football League*, 407 F. Supp. 1000 (1975), at 1010 and 1009. Also see *Mackey v. National Football League*, 543 F. 2d 606 (1976), especially at 616; and *Reynolds v. National Football League*, 584 F. 2d 280 (1978).

52. Berry and Gould, above, note 6, at 768 and 769.

53. *McCourt v. California Sports*, 600 F. 2d 1193 (1979).

54. For details concerning the trajectory of collective bargaining in football, basketball, and ice-hockey see Berry, Gould, and Staudohar above, note 6; and Staudohar above, note 37.

55. Michels, R., *Political Parties: A Sociological Study of the Oligarchic Tendencies of Modern Democracy* (Dover Publication, New York, 1959).

56. Staudohar above, note 37, at 149. For other examinations, or rather critiques, of Eagleson see Cruise, D., and Griffiths, A., *Net Worth: Exploding the Myths of Pro Hockey* (Viking, Toronto, 1991); and Conway, R., *Game Misconduct: Alan Eagleson and the Corruption of Hockey* (MacFarlane Walters and Ross, Toronto, 1995).

57. See Seitz, P., "Are Professional Sports or Business? Or How Much Would You Pay for Catfish Hunter?" *Industrial Relations Research Association 29th Annual Proceedings* (Madison, 1976/77), 324–328. Also see *Kansas City Royals Baseball Corporation v. Major League Baseball Player Associations*, 532 F. 2d 615 (1976) where Organized

Baseball unsuccessfully appealed Seitz's decision.

58. For accounts of these various developments in baseball see Dworkin above, note 20; Lowenfish above, note 9; Miller above, note 37; Berry, Gould, and Staudohar above, note 6; Staudohar above, note 37; Jennings KM *Swings and Misses: Moribund Labor Relations in Professional Baseball* (Praeger, Westport, 1997); and Marburger, D. R., (Ed.), *Stee-Rike Four! What's Wrong with the Business of Baseball* (Praeger, Westport, 1997).

59. *Curt Flood Act (1998)* (USA) (Fed).

60. Major League Baseball Player Associations, *Press Release*, 28 October 1998.

61. In 1958 it changed its name to the Professional Footballers' Association.

62. In 1909 the Court of Appeal ruled that footballers were covered by the Act. See *Walker v Crystal Palace Football Club Limited* [1910] 1 KB 87.

63. *Athletic News*, 23 March 1908.

64. *Nordenfelt v. Maxim Nordenfelt Guns and Ammunition*, [1894] AC 535, at 565.

65. *The Times*, 28 March 1912. Also see Grayson, E., *Sport and the Law* (2nd ed.), (Butterrworths, London, 1994), at 10 and 63–65.

66. *Trade Disputes Act (1906)* (UK).

67. *The Times*, 28 March 1912.

68. Harding, J., *For the Good of the Game: The Official History of the Professional Footballers' Association* (Robson, London, 1991) p. 103.

69. Minutes, Association Football Players' and Trainers' Union, Annual General Meeting, 14 November 1955. In 1919 the union changed its name to include trainers. Also see Grayson, above, note 56 at 8 and 9.

70. *Eastham v Newcastle United Football Club* [1964] Ch 413, at 438.

71. *Eastham v. Newcastle United Football Club* [1964] Ch 413, at 430–431, 436 and 433.

72. For examinations of developments concerning English soccer and the associated role of the players' union/association see Harding, above, note 58; Dabscheck, B., "'A Man or a Puppet?': The Football Association's 1909 Attempt to Destroy the Association Football Players' Union" (1991) 8 *The International Journal of History of Sport* 221; Dabscheck, B., "'Defensive Manchester': A History of the Professional Footballers' Association" in Cashman, R., and McKernan, M. (Eds.), *Sport in History: The Making of Modern Sporting History* (University of Queensland Press, St Lucia, 1979), 227; and Dabscheck, B. "Beating the Off-side Trap: The Case of the Professional Footballers' Association" (1986) 17 *Industrial Relations Journal* 350.

73. *Buckley v. Tutty*, 125 CLR 353 (1971). Also see *Tutty v. Buckley* [1970] 3 NSWR 463.

74. Other relevant cases include *Hawick v. Flegg* (1958) 75 The Weekly Notes 255 (rugby league; League management committee didn't follow due process in administration of rules); *Elford v. Buckley* [1969] 2 NSWR 170 (rugby league; dispute over oral contract, rules not a restraint); *Hall v. Victorian Football League* [1982] VR 64 (Australian rules football, decided in 1977; zoning rules an unreasonable restraint); *Hoszowski v. Brown*, Supreme Court of New South Wales, no 1667 of 1978, unreported (soccer; player able to change clubs, transfer system not a restraint); *Adamson v. West Perth Football Club* (1979) 27 ALR 475 (Australian rules football; transfer system barring player from changing leagues an unreasonable restraint); *Walsh v. Victorian Football League* (1983) 74 FLR 207 (Australian rules football; transfer system, difficult issues of law re *Trade Practices Act 1974* and restraint of trade, matter should proceed to trial); *Hughes v. Western Australian Cricket Association* (1986) ATPR 40-676 (cricket; disqualification for playing in rival league void); *Hawthorn Football Club v. Harding* [1988] VR 49 and *Buckenara v. Hawthorn Football Club* [1988] VR 39 (Australian rules football; option clause not an unreasonable restraint of trade); *McCarthy v. Australian Rough Riders Association* (1988) ATPR 40-836 (rodeo; rules barring joining rival association unreasonable restraint of trade); *Carfino v. Australian Basketball Federation* (1988) ATPR 40-895 (basketball; barring movement to another club in league an unreasonable restraint of trade); *Barnard v. Australian Soccer Federation* (1988) ATPR 40-862 (soccer; rules barring playing with a rival league an unreasonable restraint of trade); *Nobes v. Australian Cricket Board*, Supreme Court of Victoria, no 13613 of 1991, unreported (cricket; zoning and residential qualifications an unreasonable restraint of trade); *Canberra Bushrangers Baseball Team v. Byrne*, Supreme Court of the Australian Capital Territory, no SC 707 of 1994, unreported (baseball; option clause, not tested, absence of contract); and *Penrith District Rugby Football League Club v. Fittler and Sing*, Supreme Court of New South Wales, no. 4562/3 of 1995, unreported (rugby league; contracts with club void as club had joined rival "Super" league).

75. For details concerning these various failed attempts see Dabscheck, B., "Playing the Team Game: Unions in Australian Professional Team Sports" (1996) 38 *The Journal of Industrial Relations* 600; and Dabscheck, B., "Australian Baseball's Second Unsuccessful Attempt to Establish

a Players' Association" (1998) 14 *Sporting Traditions* 87.

76. The majority of these organizations have changed their titles. Their current titles are provided here.

77. *Foschini v. Victorian Football League*, Supreme Court of Victoria, no 9868 of 1982 (unreported), at 25.

78. For a critical analysis of these changes see Dabscheck, B., "Abolishing Transfer Fees: The Victorian Football League's New Employment Rules" (1989) 6 *Sporting Traditions* 63.

79. For an account of these developments see Dabscheck, "Playing the Team Game . . ." above, note 64, at 618–621.

80. Buti, A., "Salary Caps in Professional Team Sports: An Unreasonable Restraint of Trade" (1999) 14 *Journal of Contract Law*, 139 argues that the courts would strike down salary caps. See *Johnston v. Cliftonville Football and Athletic Club*, [1984] N1 9. For further discussion concerning salary caps in Australia see Pengilley, W., "Sporting Drafts and Restraint of Trade" (1994) 10 *Queensland University of Technology Law Journal* 89, at 114–116; and in North America see Foraker, S. J., "The National Basketball Association Salary Cap: An Antitrust Violation?" (1985) 59 *Southern California Law Review* 157; and Daspin, D. A., "Of Hoops, Labor Dupes and Antitrust Ally-Oops: Fouling out the Salary Cap" (1986–1987) 62 *Indiana Law Journal* 95.

81. Australian Football League — Australian Football League Players' Association, Collective Bargaining Agreement, 1995/98, Clause 21, Schedule A. Similar language appears in Clause 6 of the Australian Football League — Australian Football League Players' Association, Collective Bargaining Agreement, 1998–2003; and Clause 11 of the National Basketball League — National Basketball League Players' Association, Collective Bargaining Agreement, 1996–98.

82. *Adamson v. New South Wales Rugby League Limited*, (1991) 31 FCR 242.

83. For details concerning these developments see Dabscheck, "Playing the Team Game . . ." above, note 64, at 616–617.

84. *Media, Entertainment and Arts Alliance v. Balmain District Rugby League Football Club*, Australian Rugby League Players Award 1997, Australian Industrial Relations Commission, A2491 AS Print P5383, 25 September 1997.

85. *Media, Entertainment and Arts Alliance v. Marconi Fairfield Soccer Club and Australian Soccer Federation*, Australian Industrial Relations Commission, Dec 1285/95 S Print M2565, Sydney, 9 June 1995, at 69–70, 79–80.

86. Ericsson Cup Collective Agreement, 1996–1999, Schedule B; and Soccer Australia — Australian Professional Footballers' Association, Ericsson Cup Collective Agreement 1999–2001, Schedule B.

87. The Rugby Union Players' Association was formed following a battle between rival "leagues" when Rugby Union turned professional. The players' association agreed to stay with the establishment after the signing of a letter that 95 percent of television rights would be distributed at the "direction" of the players" association. Once the rival "league" disappeared the players' association experienced problems enforcing this direction. It commenced legal proceedings before the Supreme Court of New South Wales, and, after an initial victory on a procedural matter, subsequently negotiated a comprehensive collective bargaining agreement. In 1997 Australian cricketers threatened strike action in gaining recognition and negotiating a collective bargaining deal, which substantially increased the income of Sheffield Shield players. In 1998 netballers also negotiated a collective deal. For details concerning these developments see Dabscheck, B., "Trying Times: Collective Bargaining in Australian Rugby Union" (1998) 15 *Sporting Traditions* 25; Dabscheck, B., "Running to the Same End: The Australian Cricket Pay Dispute" (1999) 71 *A Q Journal of Contemporary Analysis* 52; and Dabscheck, B., "A Safety Net for Netballers," (1998) 8 *Australian and New Zealand Sports Law Association Newsletter* 9.

88. Fields and Narr above, note 5 at 6.

89. Scoville, J. G., "Labor Relations in Sport" in Noll (Ed.) above, note 8 at 206.

PART III

EMERGENT THEMES: DEVELOPMENT, HUMAN RIGHTS, MEDIA CULTURE, AND SPORTS TOURISM

20

SPORT AND THE TRANSNATIONALIZING MEDIA CORPORATION

David L. Andrews

Over the last two decades, the media economy has become ever more global in its organization and influence. This can be attributed to two pivotal developments. First, the widespread dissemination of new distribution technologies (i.e., cable television, direct broadcast satellite, Internet) has provided the logistical wherewithal necessary for the establishment of advanced global communications networks. Second, the influence of an ascendant neo-liberal politics has established a climate of media deregulation and privatization, effectively removing the political and economic barriers that had precluded the growth of truly global media corporations (Barker, 1997; Fairchild, 1999). Although enabled by technological and political initiatives, the shift toward media deregulation was principally propelled by the economically driven compulsion to expand either within existing or into new media markets. Once freed by the combination of technological advancements and political initiatives, the media industry embarked on a growth phase, characterized by a heightened concentration of ownership within, and convergence between, various media properties around the globe(Albarran,2002;Croteau & Hoynes, 2001).The corollary of media industry growth, concentration, and convergence has been the emergence of an imperfect oligarchy, comprised of globally reaching, multilayered, and multiplatformed information and entertainment corporations (Bagdikian, 1997; Barker, 1997; Chan-Olmsted & Albarran, 1998; Herman & McChesney, 1997).

Colossal in scale and scope, corporations such as AOL Time Warner, Disney Corporation, News Corporation, and Viacom have come to dominate today's global media economy. Moreover, they have developed into truly transnational media corporations (henceforth TNMCs) that function simultaneously in numerous countries around the world, in a manner that obscures the location of their corporate headquarters: benefiting from global production and distribution efficiencies, while operating within the cultural practices and sensibilities of numerous locals (Bartlett & Ghoshal, 1992; Dirlik, 1996; Morley & Robins, 1995). Hollifield (2001) outlined what is a growing body of literature pertaining to the structure, operation, and effects of TNMCs. Nevertheless, the author identified a paucity of research specifically focused on the manner in which TNMCs engage, and act on, the contrasting national settings they encounter in realizing their expansionist agendas. Such studies are important, for

> [I]f we are to develop our understanding of the potential effects of the globalization of media, included in our conceptual models must be a fundamental understanding of the structure, strategy, management, and behavior of the corporations themselves as they operate in the different local markets that collectively make up the global market. (Hollifield, 2001, pp. 134–135)

In light of such an observation, this study seeks to make a contribution to the understanding of how TNMCs are strategically managed as they expand into multiple national media markets. In doing so, it illustrates the necessary relationship between macroeconomic and microeconomic realms (Chan-Olmsted & Albarran, 1998), through an analysis that acknowledges broader changes in media and economic policy, while focusing on the attendant corporate strategies operating within recently deregulated and globalizing media environments.

This study focuses on the workings of one noted example of the TNMC phenomenon—namely, News Corporation. As has been well established (cf. Barker, 1997; Demers, 2002; Gershon, 1997; Herman & McChesney, 1997), during five decades of astounding growth, News Corporation was transformed from being a regional Australian newspaper concern into what is arguably the "first vertically integrated entertainment-and-communications company of truly global reach" (Shawcross, 1997, p. 399). In 2002, News Corporation's global multimedia empire—incorporating nine media formats, spanning six contents, and purportedly reaching two thirds of the world's population—controlled assets of US $40.3 billion that generated US$15.2 billion in revenue. Of these 2002 revenues, 28.1% was derived from television, 26.6% from filmed entertainment, 15.9% from newspapers, 12.3% from cable network programming, 7.1% from book publishing, 5.9% from magazine/inserts, and 4.3% from other sources. With regards to the geographical spread of this generated revenue, 77% derived from the United States, 15% from the United Kingdom and Europe, and 8% from Australasia (News Corporation, 2002a).

News Corporation's numerous global television initiatives (those involving both terrestrial and satellite delivery platforms) are of particular relevance to this discussion. They illustrate how TNMCs formulate their entry strategies, modify their organizational structure, and shape their operational behaviors when venturing into new national television markets. News Corporation is doubly interesting because sport—a form of television content all but ignored by TNMC research—has played a pivotal role, and continues to be a core feature of, a strategic plan whose unambiguous aim has been to fashion News Corporation into a global media entertainment empire (Gershon, 2000).

As evidenced by recent global media initiatives, sport content is becoming an increasingly important aspect of TNMC's television programming. Indeed,

AOL-Time Warner, Bertelsmann AG, Disney Corporation, News Corporation, Viacom, and Vivendi-Universal have been collectively dubbed the "global sport mass media oligopoly" (Law, Harvey, & Kemp, 2002, p. 279). However, with regard to what Picard (1996) referred to as today's "communication empires," it is News Corporation—under the leadership of longtime Chairman and CEO, Rupert Murdoch—that has taken the lead in this regard. As Rowe (1999) noted, "There is no one in the media world who has a greater commitment to the commercial exploitation of sport than Murdoch" (p. 191). Sports programming is, in fact, a central component of the growth strategies that have enabled News Corporation to realize its transnational goals.

In specific terms, this study aims to contribute to the body of knowledge within media economics by providing a detailed examination of News Corporation's consistent use of sport as an instrument for successfully penetrating national television markets within the United States, the United Kingdom, and Australia. To realize this objective, the discussion is divided into three sections, focused on (a) the cultural and economic rationales underpinning News Corporation's use of sport as a core aspect of transnational television market entry strategies, (b) examples of News Corporation's use of sport programming to enter and manage local media markets, and (c) the changes wrought in News Corporation's organizational structure and focus resulting from its transnational sporting orientation. From an examination of News Corporation in particular, it is hoped this discussion will generate knowledge that can further the understanding of the structure, operation, and influence of TNMCs in general.

Media Sport and Economies of Scarcity

During the late 1980s and early 1990s, through a combination of purchasing terrestrial television stations and establishing new satellite networks, News Corporation sought to augment its international newspaper, magazine, and publishing holdings. The result was an expansion into television markets within the United States (Fox Television), the United Kingdom (BSkyB), Australia (Foxtel), Japan (JSkyB), India (Zee TV), New Zealand (Sky), Germany (Vox), and Asia (Star TV). Most (apart from Fox Television) of these initiatives revolved around the introduction of pay direct broadcast satellite networks and channels to populations more attuned to free-to-air terrestrial television arrangements. Hence, for its fledgling television operations to succeed, News Corporation was in the unenviable position of having to attract new viewers (subscribers) to unfamiliar television networks, distribution systems, and commercial relations. According to the company's strategic planning, live sport—a form of programming both familiar and important to viewing audiences—was to play a crucial role in establishing the various nodes of News Corporation's aspirant global television network (Barker, 1997; McChesney, 2000).

Reportedly indifferent toward sport *qua* sport (Bruck, 1997; Pierce, 1995), Murdoch's, and thereby News Corporation's, interest lay in sport's unique place within the everyday lives and consciousness of media audiences (Barnett, 1990; Rowe, 1999; Wenner, 1998). As one biographer noted, "Though

Murdoch hated sports as a boy, as an adult he had quickly realized that sport stories sold newspapers" (Chenoweth, 2001, p. 245). Murdoch thus approached sport as a form of media content whose inherent value lay in its ability to appeal to a mass audience. Therefore, sport was mobilized as a core mechanism for leveraging News Corporation's expansion into numerous national television markets.

According to Albarran (2002), studies of the media economy need to address how corporations utilize scarce resources to produce media content designed to satisfy the interests and desires of consumers. Elements of scarcity can be discerned in a number of different guises, playing a number of important roles, in News Corporation's transnational sport media operations. Within what is a never-fragmenting media universe—and largely due to its entrenched popular appeal—live broadcasts of major sporting competitions and contests remain one of the few forms of programming likely to attract the size and quality of audiences attractive to networks and advertisers alike (Donnelly, 1996). Specifically within the U.S. context, television coverage of high-profile sport possesses a rare capacity for attracting high concentrations of the 18–34-year-old male consumers (the demographics traditionally most prized by corporate advertisers; King, 2002; Rofe, 1999).

The capacity for generating mass television audiences through sport programming is, of course, not restricted to the United States. Global viewing figures for televised coverage of Olympic Games and Fédération Internationale de Football Association (FIFA) World Cup tournaments (Bellamy, 1998) indicate sport's status as an universally popular form of media entertainment. Yet, in addition to the broad appeal of global sporting mega-events (Roche, 2000), within most nations the televised live sport coverage of local teams and competitions represents an integral part of mainstream programming: The dominant game forms may vary from country to country; however, the public interest in them would seem to be remarkably consistent (Bairner, 2001; T. Miller, Lawrence, McKay, & Rowe, 2001). Thus, sport programming can be considered a scarce resource, used by media corporations to attract television audiences as a means of generating advertising revenue.

So why does live televised sport coverage generate such popular interest around the globe? Sport, or what Rowe (1995) succinctly described as "the regulated expression of physical culture" (p. 104), can be considered an unique form of mass entertainment due to its explicit and telegenic physicality (conjoined as it is with an implicit hetero/homoeroticism); its innate competitive structure (which encourages empathy-inducing personal narratives); its nurturing of deep-rooted individual identifications and loyalties (about which corporate brand managers must surely fantasize); its relatively straight-forward and inexpensive production demands (especially compared with equivalent programming lasting more than two hours); and, perhaps most significantly, its potential for generating visceral excitement (created by the uncertainty, real or imagined, surrounding the outcomes of live sporting contests; Bellamy, 1998; Giulianotti, 2002; Kellner, 2002; T. Miller et al., 2001).

As demonstrated by the furor that enveloped NBC's manipulation of time through its unannounced mixing of live, live-on-tape, and taped coverage within its primetime Olympic Games broadcasts (Andrews, 1998; Mayberry, Proctor, & Srb, 1996), sport's authentic and uncertain immediacy distinguishes it from other genres of television entertainment in viewer's minds. Television viewers are drawn to live sport by their anticipated involvement in a real-time event, in which they are captivated by "not merely what happens but what might happen" (Fox, 1995, p.35).Or, as Fox Sports Group Chairman and CEO, David Hill, famously quipped, "Sports is the final frontier of reality on TV. . . . Because it's unscripted and the white knight doesn't always get to kiss the girl" (quoted in Brück, 1997, p. 86).

Murdoch unambiguously identified sport's importance in News Corporation's television market entry strategies. His most revealing pronouncement to this effect came within a 1996 speech at News Corporation's annual meeting in Adelaide:

> Sport absolutely overpowers film and everything else in the entertainment genre. . . . Football, of all sports, is number one. . . . Sport will remain very important and we will be investing in and acquiring long-term rights. . . . We have the long-term rights in most countries to major sporting events and we will be doing in Asia what we intend to do elsewhere in the world, that is, use sports as a "battering ram" and a lead offering in all our pay television operations. (quoted in Milliken, 1996, p. 28)

At the heart of News Corporation's expansionist strategizing is the steadfast belief that "sports programming commands unparalleled viewer loyalty in all markets" (Murdoch, 1996) and can therefore be used to enter media markets more effectively, and indeed rapidly, than any other entertainment genre. This point has been corroborated by Peter Chernin, News Corporation President and Chief Operating Officer, when identifying movies and live sport programming as the pivotal elements in their "worldwide TV ventures . . . and sports is the more important" (quoted in Bruck, 1997, p. 82). Sport thus became the vanguard of News Corporation's global television market entry strategy, routinely headlining a menu of popular entertainment programming (blockbuster movies, situation comedies, teen dramas, cartoons, and tabloid telejournalism), targeted at mainstream sensibilities and interests, and aimed at rapidly generating a sustaining market share.

Within any national television market, however, only a relatively small number of sporting events (usually live coverage of global spectacles such as the Olympic Games and the FIFA World Cup, in addition to the televising of sports that generate intense local interest) have the capacity for attracting mass television audiences. The very scarcity of such sporting mega-events (Roche, 2000) means competing television companies are routinely embroiled in inflationary bidding wars for the broadcast rights to such events—effectively a situation in which scarce financial resources are used to try and secure access to scarce cultural resources. To circumvent this cycle of scarcity, Murdoch's much vaunted speculative tendencies prompted News Corporation's adoption of a high-risk growth strategy based on borrowing huge amounts of investment capital to fund acquisitions of television broadcast rights contracts. Access to such fiscal resources realized by this "borrow-and-buy philosophy" (Gershon, 1997, p. 197) allowed News Corporation to routinely make offers that far exceeded the perceived market value for sought-after media properties (e.g., networks, stations, programming, and broadcast rights contracts).

With regard to the sport media economy, Murdoch thrust News Corporation to the forefront of the global sport media oligopoly by adopting this "debt leverage" (Gershon, 1997, p. 197) strategy within the bidding process for television broadcast rights. In doing so, News Corporation has been charged with inflating cost and undercutting the competitive balance between members of the sport media oligopoly (Law et al., 2002; S. Miller, 1999). However, as Doyle (2002) pointed out, this high-finance, high-risk plan was part of a long-term strategy to thrust News Corporation's various television outlets, and thereby the corporation as a whole, into a "virtuous circle of profitability" (pp. 62–63):

> It is only by sustaining its investment in programming that a broadcaster can hope to break in a "virtuous" circle of improving audiences and higher programme budgets. . . . It may take four or five years or even longer before a new channel has built up its revenue base to the point where it begins to break even (Brown, 1999, p. 14). But once a sufficient number of viewers or subscribers have been attracted to cover fixed operating costs, the broadcasters can start to make considerable profits. Because the marginal costs of serving extra viewers are low, a very high proportion of any additional revenues at this stage will flow through into profits. And as it becomes more profitable, the broadcaster may decide to increase its investment in content so as to underpin the strength and popularity of its programme service. (Doyle, 2002, p. 62)

Although providing News Corporation with a definite advantage within the (sport) media marketplace, the financial profligacy associated with simultaneously developing numerous virtuous cycles of profitability was not without considerable risk, as demonstrated by the corporation's fabled near-bankruptcy in the early 1990s (Chenoweth, 2001; Shawcross, 1997) and more recent financial problems (News Corporation, 2002b). On the whole, however, it has proved an effective strategy in establishing profitable television platforms around the globe, examples of which will be examined in detail within the following section.

Transnational Sport Media Strategizing

Incorporated in Adelaide, South Australia, the owner of significant media holdings across the globe, and led by an Australian born, naturalized American citizen, News Corporation operates without a "discernible corporate center" (Gershon, 1997, p. 17). However, this does not mean national boundaries or differences are ignored within its corporate operations and strategizing. In a manner illustrative of transnational corporatism in general, News Corporation both advances efficiencies and scope of global production while recognizing the need to modify products for local tastes and sensibilities (Bartlett & Ghoshal, 1992; Gershon, 1997). Such transnational strategizing signifies the impracticability of treating the global market as a single, homogenous entity— effectively signaling the demise of the multinational ethos of operating "as if the entire world (or major regions of it) were a single, largely identical entity" and subsequently selling the "same things in the same way everywhere" (Levitt, 1983, p. 22). Far from transcending or eradicating differences in the manner of yesterday's mutinationals, today's transnational corporations recognize the enduring importance of the local, and routinely incorporate elements of localized difference and particularity within their global strategizing (Morley & Robins, 1995; Robertson, 1995).

News Corporation's experience within the international media marketplace certainly sensitized it to the perils of ignoring local media market preferences. As Murdoch himself outlined

> You would be very wrong to forget that what people want to watch in their own country is basically local programming, local language, local culture. . . . I learned that many , many years ago in Australia, when I was loading up . . . with good American programs and we'd get beat with second-rate Australian ones. (quoted in Schmidt, 2001, p. 79)

This necessity for localized content explains News Corporation's reliance on sport programming. Nationally inflected sport coverage provides a mechanism for inserting what are often new and unfamiliar television broadcast platforms into the local cultures News Corporation seeks to penetrate as part of its ongoing transnationalization. This inevitably involves a process of sport-oriented "environmental scanning" (Gershon, 2000, p. 83) as a requisite aspect of strategic planning. Strategic decisions, on a country-by-country basis, have to be made regarding the sport programming most suitable to the function of capturing media market attention and share.

Paraphrasing Chyi and Sylvie (2001), although News Corporation's television network is global, its sporting content is deliberately not. This is illustrated through recourse to News Corporation's use of sport programming to enter and manage local television markets within the United Kingdom and the United States. In 1990, News Corporation obtained a 50% stake in the newly formed British Sky Broadcasting (BSkyB) following the merger of Murdoch's Sky Television with its chief rival in the United Kingdom satellite broadcasting market, British Satellite Broadcasting. The financial struggle that led up to the merger resulted in News Corporation incurring massive losses, which threatened the parent company's very existence. As a pay-television service, BSkyB's long-term profitably, indeed its immediate viability, was dependent on the attraction of significant numbers of subscribers (from whom BSkyB would derive significant subscription revenues and whom they could also use as a justification for levying premium advertising rates). This conundrum was solved in 1992 with BSkyB's signing of a £304 million, five-year deal for exclusive broadcast rights to the newly established English Premier League (EPL). BSkyB executives felt the EPL to be "the only sport that was clearly capable of attracting significant numbers of new customers to satellite TV" (Williams, 1994, p. 387), and their assumption proved correct. Within a year of signing the EPL contract, BSkyB subscribers doubled to approximately 3 million, effectively guaranteeing its future and, to all intents and purposes, that of News Corporation as a whole (Lefton & Warner, 2001).

Having identified the EPL as its "jewel in the crown" (Arundel & Roche, 1998, p. 73), BSkyB moved quickly to quash any competitors by agreeing to pay £670 million for a 4 year deal when its original contract ended in 1997. Four years later, the television rights to the EPL became the focal point of a more competitive bidding process, the main protagonists being Murdoch's BSkyB and NTL Inc., the British-based telecommunications company bankrolled by Bill Gates. Not surprisingly, the outcome was a marked increase in the money required for securing broadcasting rights—BSkyB's £1.1 billion proving to be the successful bid in June 2000. Over the past decade, BSkyB's relationship with the EPL has resulted in these two commercial entities becoming synonymous with each other: "Sky without football would be like Unilever without Persil or Mars without chocolate bars" (Anonymous, 2000, p. 28).

Through its experience with the EPL, BSkyB recognized the audience potential of other sporting contests, and subsequently embarked on a relentless pursuit of Britain's most coveted sporting events (including most of the English national soccer team's games, England's cricket test matches played abroad, many major rugby union games, rugby league in its entirety, and the Ryder Cup), the securing of which allowed Murdoch (1996) to boast that "Sky Sports has a lock on many of the commanding heights of British sport." As a consequence, BSkyB's sport-centered strategies played an important role in securing more than 20% of homes in the United Kingdom as subscribers, thereby establishing the satellite broadcaster as a fixture within the British broadcasting landscape (Lefton & Warner, 2001).

In an effort to encourage sport's migration to pay-television platforms on a truly global scale, the BSkyB/EPL scenario has been replicated across numerous national media and sporting contexts (including Australia, New Zealand, and various parts of Asia), with News Corporation's local satellite subsidiary securing the broadcast rights to the sporting entities that most resonate with local audiences. News Corporation also adopted a similar sport-centered approach when building the brand identity and presence of its Fox Television terrestrial network in the United States. At the vanguard of this network building process was the $1.58 billion, 4 year contract signed with the National Football League (NFL) in December 1993 for broadcasting rights to National Football Conference (NFC) games. Justifying what was a vastly in-

flated sum, proffered in an ultimately successful bid to deter his more established and fiscally conservative competitors, Murdoch later conceded

> We put that $380 million a year on the table to help build Fox. We didn't
> do it so some quarterback can make another half million a year. . . . That's
> just a by-product. What we did, we did selfishly, to build the network. It
> was a selfish business decision. (quoted in Pierce, 1995, p. 182)

Selfish it may have been; effective it most definitely was. As Gershon (1997)
noted, Fox's securing of the television broadcast rights to the NFC brought
the fledgling network a much needed "dose of credibility" (p.208). Moreover,
through the regular Sunday NFC schedule, as well as NFC play-off games
and the rotational broadcasting of the Super Bowl spectacle, Fox's investment
provided significant opportunities for magnifying the network's national visibility, elevating direct advertising revenues, and enhancing opportunities for
network promotions. Fox's relationship with the NFC thus proved hugely influential in establishing and defining its network identity within the American
popular consciousness.It also alerted television executives to that which they
had long suspected, the fact that theNFL represents "the most reliable programming on television. . . . Football on television is the closest thing to essential, network-defining programming" (Carter, 1998, p. C1).

The success of its relationship with the NFL prompted Fox to be at the
forefront of negotiations for the renewal of the contract, and, in early 1998,
Fox ($4.4 billion) joined with ABC/ESPN ($9.2 billion) and CBS ($4.0 bil-
lion) in signing an 8 year, $17.6 billion (or $2.2 billion annually) contract for
NFL television rights. By this time, Fox, in conjunction with NBC and ESPN,
was also in the midst of a $1.7 billion, 5 year contract (1996–2000) for the tele-
vision broadcasting rights to Major League Baseball (MLB). This experience
proved successful enough for Fox to subsequently sign a $2.5 billion contract
with MLB to be the sole broadcaster of every All-Star, play-off, and World
Series game for the period 2001–2006. Having secured broadcasting rights to
two of the more established American sport properties, Fox subsequently
turned its attention to the National Association for Stock Car Auto Racing
(NASCAR), the sporting phenomenon of the last decade (Hagstrom, 1998;
Hamilton, 1996). Hoping to benefit from the sport's growing popularity
(NASCAR is presently the second-rated sport on television, behind the NFL),
Fox joined with NBC and TNT in signing a $2.4 billion television rights con-
tract for NASCAR's Winston Cup and Bush Series races for the period
2001–2008 (Schlosser, 2001).

Within both the United Kingdom and United States scenarios, News Corporation's respective branches (BSkyB and Fox Television) illustrate the importance of local sport programming to media market entry and management
strategies. In both cases, the sports or sporting events of most interest to local
populations were appropriated as core aspects of television programming.
Thus, within these and other national contexts, News Corporation exemplifies

the very essence of corporate transnationality, in the capacity to seamlessly operate within the language of the sporting local, simultaneously, in multiple locations (Dirlik, 1996; Silk & Andrews, 2001).

Dimensions of Transnational Expansion and Integration

Doyle (2002) identified three strategies of corporate restructuring associated with the move toward transnationalization in the media industry—namely, diagonal, vertical, and horizontal expansion—each of which can be discerned within News Corporation's transformation into a TNMC. The notion of diagonal, or lateral, expansion refers to corporation's diversification into new media industry sectors, seeking to benefit from what Albarran and Dimmick (1996) referred to as "economies of multiformity" (p. 43). With its movement into terrestrial and satellite television during the 1980s, News Corporation initiated a phase of aggressive diagonal expansion. However, having diversified into the television industry, News Corporation's subsequent growth strategies, particularly those involving sport, have largely sought to capitalize on the perceived benefits derived from vertical expansion and integration. These interrelated processes are prompted by the desire to manage the market uncertainties associated with reliance on external units for core products and services. Hence, vertically integrating and expanding a corporation represents a process of internalization, whereby "The planning unit takes over the source of supply or the outlet; a transaction that is subject to bargaining over prices and amounts is thus replaced with a transfer within the planning unit" (Galbraith, 1985, p. 28).

The market uncertainties implicit within the sport media economy—particularly the imponderables surrounding bidding wars for television broadcasting rights—galvanized News Corporation's vertical integration agenda (Schmidt, 2001). Having invested in the ownership of numerous broadcast platforms and channels, News Corporation subsequently turned to the procurement of the sport entities (leagues, teams, and stadia) from which programming content is derived and the controlled predictability of vertical integration realized. This provided News Corporation a position of ascendancy within the television rights fees scramble, as the purchasing or establishment of sport leagues relinquishes the need to bid for television rights, while the ownership of sport teams puts media corporations in the advantageous position of negotiating with themselves. In addition, the control afforded by sport property ownership also provides networks with the ability to generate significant revenue from the migration of game coverage to lucrative pay-per-view television platforms—something central to News Corporation's long term transnational strategizing (Herman & McChesney, 1997; Murdoch, 1996).

Murdoch's initial steps toward vertically integrating his sport media empire came within the Australian context in the mid-1990s. Murdoch had been stymied by his media mogul rival, Kerry Packer, whose terrestrial Nine Network and cable/satellite Optus Vision outlets dominated televised sport programming, specifically through lucrative broadcast contracts with the highly popular Australian Rugby League (ARL) and the Australian Football League. Acutely aware of the need to generate popular programming content for his new Foxtel pay television network (somewhat like BSkyB's private/public organizational and ownership structure, Foxtel is a partnership between News Corporation and Telstra, the state-owned telecommunications company), News Corporation expanded into the production of its own sporting content. In April 1995, News Corporation embarked on a AUS$500 million undertaking aimed at establishing the Super League, made up of six teams comprised of elite players prized away from the rival ARL. Commencing in March 1997, by December the inevitable ensued with an ARL—Super League merger to form the National Rugby League (NRL), owned in equal partnership between the Murdoch and Packer camps (McGaughey & Liesch, 2002; Rowe, 1997; Rowe & McKay, 1999). Thus, News Corporation used an expansionist strategy to gain a corporate advantage through the ability to control, even if in partnership, a pivotal source of sporting television content.

The Australian Super League initiative was—albeit the keystone—but one element of News Corporation's broader goal of developing a globally integrated Rugby League competition incorporating contests within, and between, clubs in the northern and southern hemispheres (Denham, 2000; Falcous, 1998). To facilitate this, in 1995 News Corporation gained control of the British Rugby Football League with the signing of an £87 million five year contract, the financial details of which bound Rugby League clubs' very survival to Murdoch's corporate strategizing. News Corporation effectively purchased a controlling interest in a 100-year-old sport culture, ingrained in the working class history and experience of northern England, and transformed it from being financially troubled and poorly administered sport into a financially stable media production unit. BSkyB, Rugby league's de facto owners and administrators, soon set about changing the culture of the game through the execution of a divisional restructuring, the implementation of aggressive management and marketing initiatives, and even the institution of pseudo-American team nicknames (i.e., the Bradford Bulls, Wigan Warriors, and Halifax Blue Sox; Arundel & Roche, 1998). Perhaps the most radical change to Rugby League culture came with the switching of the playing season from the winter to the summer, as dictated by the exigencies of both British and Australian media markets. In terms of the former, the British Super League's summer scheduling meant it would not clash with EPL soccer, BSkyB's prize possession within a British broadcasting rights context. With regard to the latter, News Corporation hoped close season contests between Australian and British teams (realized by the alignment of playing seasons) would add an unmatched international dimension, and thereby enhanced brand equity, to Foxtel's Australian Super League coverage. In this way, and as Falcous (1998) noted, "British Rugby League had been used as a tool in a broader global struggle" (p. 8).

Not infrequently, News Corporation has been confronted with sport organizations and cultures wherein league ownership, or new league development, was neither feasible nor even admissible. Within such circumstances,

Murdoch has turned his attention to the ownership of professional teams as a means of exercising control over the sport media economy. However, his ambition of owning a high-profile NFL franchise within a major U.S. television market was stifled by the league's prohibition on corporate ownership of league franchises. With such restrictions in place, Murdoch turned to America's other major professional sports. Most notably, in March 1998, and after protracted negotiations with MLB, Fox purchased the entire Los Angeles Dodgers organization for $311 million. Thus, Murdoch commandeered "one of the great brand names in America in a world where brand names are increasingly important" (Peter Chernin, News Corporation's president, quoted in Heath & Farhi, 1998, p. A1). Also in 1998, Fox Entertainment gained another foothold in the American sports franchise market with the 40% interest in both the New York Knicks and the New York Rangers (and, incidentally, the Madison Square Gardens arena), acquired as part of News Corporations purchase of a 40% share in Rainbow Media Holdings, a Cablevision subsidiary. Of interest, through these dealings News Corporation added ownership and control of sport stadia to its vertically integrated media delivery system.

Although successful in acquiring the Dodgers, Murdoch's even more audacious £623 million bid for Manchester United was ultimately blocked by the British government's Mergers and Monopolies Commission in April 1999 (Walsh & Brown, 1999). The rationale for this denial centered on the deleterious effects on competition in the broadcast sport industry arising from the competitive advantage BSkyB would command—as owners of the most popular and high-profile EPL club—when negotiating for the league's television rights. Murdoch consequently changed tack and has, through stealth as opposed to brute force, sought to garner influence over the future destination of EPL television rights. To this end, BSkyB embarked on a "buying spree" of up to 9.9% (the maximum percentage allowed for ownership in multiple clubs) of shares in individual clubs, with Manchester United, Manchester City, Leeds, Chelsea, and Sunderland all added to its football portfolio (Cassy & Finch, 1999).

Having outlined, in admittedly brief terms, the various levels of its engagement with sport as part of realizing its goal of vertical integration, it becomes evident that News Corporation is simultaneously part of a horizontal web of competing, yet collaborating, companies within the contemporary media industry. As Doyle (2002) noted, "Horizontal expansion is common strategy in many sectors: it allows firms to expand their market share and, usually, to rationalize resources and gain economies of scale" (p. 22). The associated collaborative industrial order, referred to by the Japanese as a *keiretsu*, is based on intricate networks of cross-company alliances and investments, which protect and strengthen the position of the conjoined mega-corporations while restricting the ability of external competitors to challenge their ascendancy: "While the companies continue to do battle with one another, however, they increasingly collaborate, and the result is a horizontal web of joint partnerships" (Auletta, 1997, p. 227).

Illustrating the core precept of horizontal expansion and integration, News Corporation's various collaborative ventures within the sport media economy include associations with a number of its fiercest competitors. These include: the alliance with Kerry Packer over the Foxtel and NRL ventures; collaborations with rival American networks for shares of the broadcasting rights of premium sports properties (i.e., that with NBC with regard to televising NASCAR, and that with ABC and CBS pertaining to televising the NFL); the convoluted web of relations involved in News Corporation's interest in Rainbow Media Holdings—the Cablevision subsidiary owners of the New York Knicks, New York Rangers, and Madison Square Garden—which is also part owned by General Electric; and perhaps the most unlikely collaboration of all, the ESPN Star Sports partnership in Asia, which brings together News Corporation and Disney, in what has proved to be a highly successful venture (Albarran & Chan-Olmsted, 1998; Law et al., 2002).

Evidently, the vertical integration regularly espoused by Murdoch as the defining feature of News Corporation's organization structure (Schmidt, 2001) cannot be viewed in rigid monolithic terms, such as that which the Ford Corporation instituted during its prewar heyday (Castells, 1996; Harvey, 1989). For each unit within News Corporation's vertically integrated structure relies, to varying degrees, on horizontal relations developed with its market competitors. Hence, in Auletta's (1997) terms, News Corporation could be said to exemplify a new order within the media entertainment industry—a sport media *keiretsu*—dependent on horizontal peer networking to share the risks and responsibilities of, yet continue to derive the benefits from, a vertically integrated organizational structure.

Conclusion

The transnationalization of News Corporation's television interests provides rich empirical data with regard to how "media organizations manage themselves, their products, and their business environments in different national settings" (Hollifield, 2001, p. 143). Despite a predilection for sport as a core component of its expansionist aspirations, the logics and practices underpinning News Corporation's transnational expansion and integration are, nonetheless, indicative of TNMCs in general. As such, examinations of News Corporation's global sport strategizing—of which this is merely a preliminary offering—make important contributions to the body of knowledge concerning TNMCs entry into, and operation of, local media markets. More specifically, this article revealed the importance of popular programming (in this case, broadcasts of live sporting events) to local market entry strategies as a means of rapidly generating significant audience interest and a sustainable market share. It also provided more detailed examples of News Corporation's sport-focused operations within local television markets in the United Kingdom and the United States, with regard to the country-specific strategies utilized concerning the appropriate choice of sport programming required for engaging local audiences. Lastly, this discussion highlighted the changes in News Corporation's organizational structure wrought by its sport-led move toward transnationalization, as illustrated by its significant investment in sport leagues, teams, and even stadia. In sum, and in archetypal TNMC fashion, News Corporation's sport strategizing vindicates Dirlik's (1996) description of transnationalization processes as being contingent on the incorporation of "localities into the imperatives of the global" (p. 34).

References

Albarran, A. B. (2002). *Media economics: Understanding markets, industries and concepts* (2nd ed.). Ames: Iowa State University Press.

Albarran, A. B., & Chan-Olmsted, S. M. (1998). Global patterns and issues. In A. B. Albarran & S. M. Chan-Olmsted (Eds.), *Global media economics: Commercialization, concentration and integration of world media markets* (pp. 331–339). Ames: Iowa State University Press.

Albarran, A. B., & Dimmick, J. (1996). Concentration and economies of multiformity in the communication industries. *Journal of media Economics, 9*(4), 41–50.

Andrews, D. L. (1998). Feminizing Olympic reality: Preliminary dispatches from Baudrillard's Atlanta. *International Review for the Sociology of Sport, 33,* 5–18.

Anonymous. (2000, March 9). Held to ransom. *Marketing Week,* p. 28.

Arundel, J., & Roche, M. (1998). Media sport and local identity: British rugby league and Sky TV. In M. Roche (Ed.), *Sport, popular culture and identity* (Vol. 5, pp. 57–91). Aachen, Germany: Meyer & Meyer Verlag.

Auletta, K. (1997, October 20). The next corporate order: American Keiretsu. *The New Yorker,* pp. 225–227.

Bagdikian, B. H. (1997). *The media monopoly* (5th ed.). Boston: Beacon.

Bairner, A. (2001). *Sport, nationalism, and globalization: European and North American perspectives.* Albany: State University of New York Press.

Barker, C. (1997). *Global television.* Oxford, England: Blackwell.

Barnett, S. (1990). *Games and sets: The changing face of sport on television.* London: British Film Institute.

Bartlett, C. A., & Ghoshal, S. (1992). *Transnational management; Texts, cases, and readings in cross-border management.* Homewood, IL: Irwin.

Bellamy, R. V. (1998). The evolving television sports marketplace. In L. A. Wenner (Ed.), *Mediasport* (pp. 73–87). London: Routledge.

Brown, D. (1999). *European cable and satellite economics: Special report.* London: Screen Digest.

Bruck, C. (1997, December 8). The big hitter. *The New Yorker,* pp. 82–93.

Carter, B. (1998, January 14). N.F.L. is must-have TV: NBC is a have-not. *The New York Times,* p. C1.

Cassy, J., & Finch, J. (1999, August 11). BSkyB linked to new Premiership buying spree. *The Guardian.* Retrieved June 12, 2001, from http://football.guardian.co.uk/News_Story/0,1563,72945,00.html

Castells, M. (1996). *The rise of the network society.* Oxford, England: Blackwell.

Chan-Olmsted, S. M., & Albarran, A. B. (1998). A framework for the study of global media economics. In A. B. Albarran & S. M. Chan-Olmsted (Eds.), *Global media economics: Commercialization, concentration and integration of world media markets* (pp. 3–16). Ames: Iowa State University Press.

Chenoweth, N. (2001). *Rupert Murdoch: The untold story of the world's greatest media wizard.* New York: Crown Business.

Chyi, H. I., & Sylvie, G. (2001). The medium is global, the content is not: The role of geography in online newspaper markets. *Journal of Media Economics, 14,* 231–248.

Croteau, D., & Hoynes, W. (2001). *The business of media: Corporate media and public interest.* Thousand Oaks, CA: Pine Forge Press.

Demers, D. (2002). *Global media: Menace or messiah?* (Rev. ed.). Cresskill, NJ: Hampton.

Denham, D. (2000). Modernism and postmodernism in the professional rugby league in England. *Sociology of Sport Journal, 17,* 275–294.

Dirlik, A. (1996). The global in the local. In R. Wilson & W. Dissanayake (Eds.), *Global local: Cultural production and the transnational imaginary* (pp. 21–45). Durham, NC: Duke University Press.

Donnelly, P. (1996). The local and the global: Globalization in the sociology of sport. *Journal of Sport & Social Issues, 20,* 239–257.

Doyle, G. (2002). *Understanding media economics.* London: Sage.

Fairchild, C. (1999). Deterritorializing radio: Deregulation and the continuing triumph of the corporatist in the USA. *Media, Culture & Society, 21,* 549–561.

Falcous, M. (1998). TV made it all a new game: Not again! — Rugby League and the case of Super League in England. *Occasional Papers in Football Studies, 1,* 4–21.

Fox, P. (1995, September 15). Protection for events that matter. *Daily Telegraph,* p. 35.

Galbraith, J. K. (1985). *The new industrial state.* Boston: Houghton Mifflin.

Gershon, R. A. (1997). *The transnational media corporation: Global messages and free market competition.* Mahwah, NJ: Lawrence Erlbaum Associates, Inc.

Gershon, R. A. (2000). The transnational media corporation: Environmental scanning and strategy formulation. *Journal of Media Economics, 13,* 81–101.

Giulianotti, R. (2002). Supporters, followers, fans, and flaneurs: A taxonomy of spectatorship identities in football. *Journal of Sport & Social Issues, 26,* 25–46.

Hagstrom, R. G. (1998). *The NASCAR way: The business that drives the sport.* New York: Wiley.

Hamilton, M. M. (1996, May 26). NASCAR's popularity fuels a powerful marketing engine. *The Washington Post,* p. A01.

Harvey, D. (1989). *The condition of postmodernity: An enquiry into the origins of cultural change.* Oxford, England: Blackwell.

Heath, T., & Farhi, P. (1998, March 20). Murdoch adds Dodgers to media empire. *The Washington Post,* p. A1.

Herman, E., & McChesney, R. W. (1997). *The global media: The new missionaries of corporate capitalism.* London: Cassell.

Hollifield, C. A. (2001). Crossing borders: media management research in a transnational market environment. *Journal of Media Economics, 14,* 133–146.

Kellner, D. (2002). *Media spectacle.* London: Routledge.

King, B. (2002, March 11–17). Passion that can't be counted puts billions of dollars in play. *Street & Smith's Sports Business Journal,* 25–26.

Law, A., Harvey, J., & Kemp, S. (2002). The global sport mass media oligopoly: The three usual suspects and more. *International Review for the Sociology of Sport, 37,* 279–302.

Lefton, T., & Warner, B. (2001, February 19). He's got global game. *The Industry Standard.* Retrieved October 5, 2001, from http://www.thestandard.com/article/0,1902,22093,00.html

Levitt, T. (1983). *The marketing imagination.* London: Collier-Macmillan.

Mayberry, K., Proctor, M., & Srb, R. (1996). The agony of deceit: Ladies' night at the NBC Olympics. *The Humanist, 56*(4), 4–(NL).

McChesney, R. (2000). *Rich media, poor democracy: Communications politics in dubious times.* New York: Free Press.

McGaughey, S. L., & Liesch, P. W. (2002). The global sports-media nexus; Reflections on the "Super League Saga" in Australia. *Journal of Management Studies, 39,* 383–416.

Miller, S. (1999, August 23–29). Taking sports to the next level: Start with teams, add arenas, media and you've got a sports empire. *Street & Smith's Sports Business Journal,* pp. 23, 32.

Miller, T., Lawrence, G., McKay, J., & Rowe, D. (2001). *Globalization and sport: Playing the world.* London: Sage.

Milliken, R. (1996, October 16). Sports is Murdoch's 'battering ram' for pay TV. *The Independent,* p. 28.

Morley, D., & Robins, K. (1995). *Spaces of identity: Global media, electronic landscapes and cultural boundaries.* London: Routledge.

Murdoch, R. (1996). *Annual report: Chief executive's review.* Retrieved June 12, 2001, from http://www.newscorp.com/report1996/index.html News Corporation. (2002a). *Annual report 2002.* Retrieved October 19, 2002, from http://www.newscorp.com/investor/annual_reports.html

News Corporation. (2002b, February 12). Earnings release for the fourth quarter ended December 31, 2001. Retrieved March 17, 2002, from http://www.news-corp.com/investor/2002earnings_releases.html

Picard, R. G. (1996). The rise and fall of media communication empires. *Journal of Media Economics, 9*(4), 23–40.

Pierce, C. P. (1995, April). Master of the universe. *Gentleman's Quarterly,* pp. 180–187.

Robertson, R. (1995). Glocalization: Time—space and homogeneity—heterogeneity. In M. Featherstone, S. Lash, & R. Robertson (Eds.), *Global modernities* (pp. 25–44). London: Sage.

Roche, M. (2000). *Mega-events and modernity: Olympics, expos and the growth of global culture.* London: Routledge.

Rofe, J. (1999, August 23–29). The 800-pound gorilla keeps growing: Fox discovers that buying sports properties is cheaper than renting—and it heads off the competition. *Street & Smith's Sports Business Journal,* p. 24.

Rowe, D. (1995). *Popular cultures: Rock music, sport and the politics of pleasure.* London: Sage.

Rowe, D. (1997). Rugby league in Australia: The super league saga. *Journal of Sport & Social Issues, 21,* 221–226.

Rowe, D. (1999). *Sport, culture and the media: The unruly trinity.* Buckingham, England: Open University Press.

Rowe, D., & McKay, J. (1999). Field of soaps: Rupert v. Kerry as masculine melodrama. In R. Martin & T. Miller (Eds.), *SportCult* (Vol. 16, pp. 191–210). Minneapolis: University of Minnesota Press.

Schlosser, J. (2001, February 12). Revved up for NASCAR. *Broadcasting and Cable,* p. 18.

Schmidt, R. (2001, June). Murdoch reaches for the sky. *Brill's Content,* pp. 74–79, 126–129.

Shawcross, W. (1997). *Murdoch: The making of a media empire.* New York: Touchstone Books.

Silk, M., & Andrews, D. L. (2001). Beyond a boundary? Sport, transnational advertising, and the reimagining of national culture. *Journal of Sport & Social Issues, 25,* 180–201.

Walsh, A., & Brown, A. (1999). *Not for sale: Manchester United, Murdoch and the defeat of BSkyB.* Manchester, England: Mainstream Press.

Wenner, L. A. (Ed.). (1998). *Mediasport.* London: Routledge.

Williams, J. (1994). The local and the global in English soccer and the rise of satellite television. *Sociology of Sport Journal, 11,* 376–397.

21

RECOVERING (FROM) JANET JACKSON'S BREAST: ETHICS AND THE NEXUS OF MEDIA, SPORTS, AND MANAGEMENT

Lawrence A. Wenner

"We are pleased that a star like Janet Jackson will join the roster of entertainers who have made the Super Bowl Halftime so special."

—NFL Commissioner Paul Tagliabue
December 18, 2003 (Janet Jackson set, 2003)

Some pieces of the wardrobe are, in a manner of speaking, designed to malfunction. The breakaway jersey, long a fixture in American football, is a good case in point. In order to curb dirty play and to enhance safety, the football jersey tears apart when tugged at. As a result, the torn jersey has become a common occurrence, usually of little note in the course of gridiron action.

Who would have thought that the most memorable play of the National Football League's 2004 Super Bowl, and perhaps of the recent year in sports, would be a variation on something so common as a jersey breaking away? How was it that, during the "CBS meets MTV" Super Bowl halftime musical show, when Justin Timberlake was playing defense, that Janet Jackson's offense became so offensive? Why did what was called a "wardrobe malfunction" mean so much to so many? What does the construction of an event that led to the uncovering of Janet Jackson's breast and its cultural aftermath say about the state of affairs in the worlds of media and sports? And what reflections might the incident provoke for the role of ethics in sport management, especially when it comes to promotional communication and response to crisis?

Now that the heat over the uncovering of Janet Jackson's breast has cooled down somewhat with the passing of time, it is possible for one to consider some of the implications of this case study for those involved in the management of sport and its communication. My analytical strategy relies on a select thick reading (Geertz, 1973) of the event and its coverage in cultural context. Accordingly, the broader context of the Super Bowl in the market economy is considered before examining: a) the *construction* of the event by its organizational stakeholders, b) the *reconstruction* of understandings about how the fiasco came to be and what really happened and should have happened, and

c) the *deconstruction* of the event by critics and those in the political environment who had reason to consider the incident and the response to it in a broader social context. I close the essay with some observations about the prospects for "ethical health" in sports promotion and entertainment at a time when the sports and media industries are recovering from the uncovering of Janet Jackson's breast.

Context

As has become custom, the broadcast of the 2004 Super Bowl game was an exercise in building corporate synergy. Synergy, in its most pronounced moderncommunication-industry incarnation, is a vertical-integration strategy aimed at maximizing the ways that complementary holdings can strengthen each other through cross-promotion and marketing to make the corporate whole stronger than the sum of the parts. In recent times there has been a move for communication giants to extend effective control over synergy by going beyond alliances or partnerships with sports organizations to owning teams as a way to develop their own sports hook for the most elusive and desirable of viewers, youthful males. Some of these strategies have been successful, such as the Turner–Warner holding of the Atlanta Braves and Hawks and WGN's ownership of the Chicago Cubs. Others have been awkward marriages that have raised questions about the construction of synergy and the truism that the resultant cross-promotional opportunities that come with common ownership will enhance success. Notable recent belly flops in the synergy sweepstakes have been Newscorp/Fox's holding of the Los Angeles Dodgers and Disney's holding of the Anaheim Angels and Mighty Ducks.

In this synergistic opportunity, although ownership of a sports entity was not involved, the communication giant Viacom looked to use their licensing of the rights to broadcast the NFL's Super Bowl not only to build its flagship CBS brand and its lineup of network programming products (including an upcoming broadcast of the Grammy Awards) but also to mesh with its more youthful MTV brands. It is often difficult for older corporate entities, such as CBS and the NFL, to show that they are hip and use that to market advantage. The "edgy" corporation is too easily spotted as an artifice. Still, hipness can bring more desirable demographics to an aging broadcast network and to the NFL juggernaut long heading the table of the sports mainstream. This was a primary CBS strategy in recommending that the production of the Super Bowl halftime show go to its corporate sibling MTV and for the NFL to officially hire MTV for the task (Jenkins, 2004; Miklasz, 2004).

In essential ways, the goal of successfully creating synergy is a key ingredient in the longevity of the Super Bowl as one of television's rating leaders. The Super Bowl and its broadcast, coming in the dead of winter and comfortably in the lull after the Christmas to New Year's holidays, has been marked and promoted as an "unannounced American holiday" (Wenner, 1989). Across the United States the day has fueled Super Bowl parties and is the occasion of many family get-togethers. The chairman of the Federal Communications

Commission, Michael Powell, reinforced this notion when he described his viewing of the 2004 Super Bowl broadcast: "Like millions of Americans, my family and I gathered around the television for a celebration" (Ahrens & de Moraes, 2004, p, A1).

For the NFL, the synergies that come with the Super Bowl event taking on the stature of a celebratory quasi-national holiday are enormous, extending well beyond the monies that come with any broadcasting-rights pact. The Super Bowl event and its broadcast have catapulted the NFL into the elite of two worlds simultaneously: the corporate world, on one hand, and the world of entertainment on the other. Not only is the Super Bowl weekend of activities and parties perhaps the premier wining and dining opportunity used to advance corporate influence, the advertising time for the Super Bowl broadcast represents the most premium and prestigious seconds that sponsors can buy. In 2004, purchasing 30 seconds of advertising time during the game broadcast would cost as much as $2.9 million (Shales, 2004). These landmark costs and derivative events, such as *USA Today*'s Super Bowl Ad Meter, McKee Wallwork's Adbowl, and CBS' own prime-time special "Super Bowl Greatest Commercials," reinforce that the Super Bowl is the commercial king. As such, the strength of the NFL in fueling the corporate engine is seemingly unmatched (Elliott, 2004; Jenkins, 2004).

Moreover, just as corporations wish to grease the wheels by rubbing elbows with the Super Bowl, the NFL looks to rub elbows with the elite of the entertainment world to advance its brand's glow. The primary symbol of the way that the NFL showcases its status in the world of entertainment is through the Super Bowl halftime show. Here the world of entertainment and all of the stars, hoopla, and panache that it can bring have second billing on what is clearly the NFL's show. Here, where the NFL is king, the entertainment becomes court jesters for the crowd that has been welcomed to the court. But these are no mere court jesters. These are entertainment royalty and worthy of sitting at the king's table. And they have been brought forth by wealthy elders in the kingdom of the communication industry who have paid for the right to put on this show.

Although the NFL-as-king analogy might be taken too far, the larger point is that, in this situation, the NFL not only sits higher than the star-laden world of entertainment that it commingles with, but that the show has been brought forth by contracted partners who are looking to do beneficial business with the king in the future. In such a context Viacom's MTV produced the NFL's Super Bowl halftime show for Viacom's CBS broadcast. As icing on the corporate cake, AOL paid the NFL $7.5 million to serve as the named sponsor of the show, a deal that included three other 30-second spots in the broadcast and the rights to stream a replay of the broadcast show online. With this and an adjacent tie-in promotion of an online ad popularity poll, the event was officially called the "AOL TopSpeed Super Bowl XXXVIII Halftime Show," although AOL had no input over production or content (Powers, 2004; Tresniowski, 2004).

The Super Bowl halftime show presents a challenge in hanging onto a large and diverse audience that extends well beyond die-hard football fans. For many viewers this event may be the only football they watch on television all year. Thus, to appeal in advance to these viewers, the halftime show has been used as an added-value hook to keep the ratings numbers up at a moment when the game (and its extended dissection) may not be enough to keep eyeballs glued to the network that has paid dearly for the rights to the broadcast. There is a greater need to curb the itchy exercise of the remote control and surfing for counter-programmed alternatives designed to siphon viewers. Over the years counter-programming efforts have been amped up beyond marathons of favorite shows to wrestling mega-events and to this year's "Lingerie Bowl" on pay-per-view. Accordingly, Super Bowl broadcasters have increased production values and the level of celebrity in what is now pitched as a halftime "entertainment event."

It is an event, however, that is much in the spirit of Daniel Boorstin's (1961) notion of the "pseudo-event"; nothing is really happening in the lull between the halves except this construction, which has become reliant on flash and flesh. This production that is, by necessity, a gap filler has become a significant cultural event in its own right in that it offers the broadest stage for contemporary shared American experience. Although it is common for the Super Bowl to top the year's television ratings, in recent years the "raised bar" for the halftime-show extravaganza has yielded a ratings' bump beyond the game itself. For the 2004 Super Bowl halftime show, about 2 million extra domestic sets of eyeballs showed up in addition to the 99 million across the U.S. (and over 140 million worldwide) that tuned in for the game. In a sense, then, more was at stake during halftime than during the game itself (Ahrens & de Moraes, 2004; Rich, 2004).

Construction

On the surface the 2004 halftime event that MTV produced largely followed the pattern of its earlier effort three years before. That show, as Rich (2004, p. B1) put it, "featured Britney Spears all but falling out of her halter top and numbers in which both Mr. Timberlake (then appearing with 'Nsync) and Nelly grabbed their crotches." In 2004, with this backdrop of knowledge and experience, MTV was again charged by CBS and the NFL with putting together the show. The evidence suggests, however, that although the MTV teenagers had the keys to the car, CBS and the NFL remained in the driver's seat with the ability to determine where the car would go and how fast it would be driven. Not only did CBS and the NFL have what is called "effective organizational control" (see Turow, 1996), but they also had access to planning and to the test drive. Indeed, CBS and NFL executives, in light of their earlier experiences with MTV as producer, were present at rehearsals to approve the acts, hear the material, and watch the choreography, "signing off" on the tone of the show after seeing "every camera angle" (see Attner, 2004; Drudge, 2004;

Rich, 2004; Rybak, 2004). So the means for corporate oversight were in place, but what about the motives that were operant in oversight?

For observers such as Barbara Lippert, advertising critic for *AdWeek*, the motives were clear: "They signed off on it because the kids would like it" (Rybak, 2004, p. 1A). Leading sports-marketing advisors such as Bonham Group chairman Dean Bonham noted that whereas in the past the NFL had lagged behind in using strategies to appeal to young viewers, "now they're trying to be more edgy and encouraging a younger demographic into the fold" (Martzke, 2004, p. 1C). In a more recent strategy, as a *Time* magazine report put it, the NFL "has not exactly been dainty in courting those vaunted 18- to 34-year-old men," citing as evidence the league's parading of "the bodacious Coors Light twins as game trophies" (Poniewozik, 2004, p. 71). There was a lot to motivate the NFL to appeal to young males and also some risks. As advertising scholar James Twitchell observed, sports "is one of the few places adolescent males will slow down long enough to be sold to," but "when you put your primary goal as reaching young men, your advertisers are going to show dogs jumping into the crotches of people" (Martzke, 2004, p. 1C).

Thus, by strengthening the motives to use the halftime show to appeal in advance to the elusive younger male demographic, a larger conflict of interest might have been created for CBS and the NFL. The conflict pitted appropriate family entertainment against that which would hit the center of the target demographic. The opportunity was certainly there to find a golden mean to meld these conflicting considerations. But the lineup for the show provides evidence that this Aristotelian strategy was likely put aside for what some might have thought was the greater corporate good of corralling the target demographic, rather than the utilitarian approach of doing the greatest good for the greatest number and avoiding harm. As well, with such goals emphasized, it became unlikely that a Kantian "categorical imperative" with the universal best interests of humankind would be exercised, nor was the notion of respect for young children and the less edgy in the audience given significant weight. Indeed, it seems unlikely that such ethical undercurrents came to the fore either during the oversight stage or later, at the rehearsals. Perhaps it was because of this that there would come to be a good deal of regret.

On paper, the show that resulted moved CBS and the NFL toward the goal of boosting their "edginess" quotient. The show's lineup featured four performers: three—P. Diddy, Kid Rock, and Nelly—with the known contemporary edginess of rap and hip-hop, and one—Janet Jackson—a pop star with little modesty in using sexiness in her own marketing. In addition, at the time of the show Jackson brought a bizarre second-hand edginess through her relation to her pop-icon brother, Michael Jackson, who was receiving much attention for an eccentric and extravagant lifestyle that included charges of child molestation. Janet's appearance at the Super Bowl would follow on family tradition: brother Michael's 1993 halftime performance was noted as an "all time high" in crotch-grabbing (Lupica, 2004).

The first three artists offered up performances that tracked well with the re-hearsals and earlier experiences. P. Diddy, the updated public personae of Sean Combs, formerly known as Puff Daddy, was an icon in the rap-music business, a founder of Bad Boy Entertainment, and the overseer of many big acts, including Notorious B.I.G. P. Diddy's performance set the tone with raps glorifying violence and graphic expressions of sexual desire, a theme rein-forced through interaction with dancers in simulated sex. Bob Ritchie, better known by the stage name of Kid Rock, brought a different kind of edginess. A metal rapper who blends rock, country, and hip-hop, Kid Rock was riding on the popularity of $4.2 million in sales of his *Cocky* album and a new album in the *Billboard* top ten (Carter, 2004; Powers, 2004). With the nickname "Pimp of the Nation" and "a reputation for potty mouth public performances," Kid Rock's costume, a shredded American flag as a poncho, struck many as "defile-ment" and "disrespectful to the members of our [U.S.] armed forces" (Goudie, 2004, p. 9). His performance featured a salute to "all you bastards at the IRS," to "hookers all tricking out in Hollywood," and lyrics that paid homage to "he-roes in methadone clinics" (Nason, 2004).

Edginess took a different, more predictable form in the performance that followed. Hip-hopping rapper Nelly was both edgy and a superstar, with over 20 million albums sold in the last 4 years, and his last album, *Nellyville*, selling over 6 million copies (Carter, 2004; Powers, 2004). The hot edginess of Nelly was most apparent in his rendition of "Hot in Herre." While performing the song that featured the lyrics, "I was like, good gracious, ass is bodacious/It's getting hot in here/So take off all your clothes"(Nason, 2004), Nelly repeat-edly grabbed his crotch. Although the NFL claimed that the crotch grabbing was not seen in the rehearsals and would not have been approved of, the song itself had been cleared (Carter, 2004). Of course, the NFL, CBS, and MTV had seen Nelly's crotch grabbing in the halftime show three years before. So it wasn't much of a surprise really, just déjà vu all over again.

Janet Jackson had been scheduled to close the Super Bowl halftime show. Jackson, although not as edgy or as currently popular as Nelly and Kid Rock, came with a long and successful pop and music-video career. Her most recent album, *All for You*, had sold over 3 million copies (Carter, 2004). She brought with her the ever-popular Justin Timberlake, now a success on his own, and his current album, *Justified*, had sold 3.5 million copies (Carter, 2004). Jack-son and the hip-hopping Timberlake teamed up on a duet of his song "Rock Your Body" to close the show. The number featured Jackson — dirty dancing in a sexy, black dominatrix outfit — bumping and grinding with Timberlake. Up until this point their performance tracked with those that had come before in the show. Then, as Rybak (2004, p. 1A) put it:

> Right after Timberlake sang the lyric, "I'm gonna have you naked by the end of this song," he reached across Jackson's gladiator-type bustier and pulled off the fabric covering her right breast, which sported a sun-shaped metal nipple stud.

And with this, Janet Jackson's breast spilled out into homes across America and the world. This was a Super Bowl first, and as a result the NFL season finale would also become "the first bowl game to become the subject of both congressional hearings and a federal investigation on indecency" and the first to bring the words *nipple shield* into many a family discussion (Kelly, Clark, & Kulman, 2004, p. 49).

Reconstruction

As it might have in an earlier era, the "outing" of Janet Jackson's breast did not pass as a small blip; it stayed and replayed on many technological radar screens. Users of the digital video recorder TiVo reportedly set an "instant replay record" with what was characterized as "a clinical alacrity heretofore reserved for the Zapruder film" (Rich, 2004, p. B1). Many without TiVo went quickly to the Internet; the Lycos 50, a service that measures search activity on the net, reported that "the breast" had become the all-time most-searched-for topic on the web, replacing the attacks of September 11. This did not surprise a writer at Lycos, Aaron Schatz, who observed, "I don't know if there's a bigger stage than the Super Bowl halftime show. . . . [It is the] immutable law of the Internet that people will search like crazy to see somebody naked that you would not expect to see naked (Steenberg, 2004, p. 2). And the buzz moved many to action. The FCC received an all-time high of 500,000 complaints for one incident, and its chairman, Michael Powell, promised swift reprisal (Lewczak & Lapidus, 2004). Powell stated that the "family celebration" he had looked forward to "was tainted by a classless, crass, and deplorable stunt" and that "our nation's children, parents, and citizens deserve better" (Ahrens & de Moraes, 2004, p. A1).

An event of this magnitude demanded some explanation. In hindsight, how, exactly, did such a thing happen? Was it a mere accident? Was it planned? Or did the truth lie somewhere in between? The reconstruction of the events moved through the less-screened and coached explanations of participants to the more strategic responses of senior executives and corporate spinmeisters aimed at damage control. Everyone apologized, and in distinct ways, all assigned blame and provided context.

First out of the gate was Timberlake, who commented after the incident that this was an accident. He assigned blame by characterizing it as a "wardrobe malfunction," thereby putting a new euphemism into the American lexicon. In these initial comments, Timberlake was contrite and apologetic, using words like "not intentional" and "regrettable" (Nason, 2004). Later on, however, perhaps after being ceaselessly hounded by questions, Timberlake became more playful on the matter. His laughing comment that "we love giving you all something to talk about," was widely circulated. More importantly, the comment undercut the apologies and raised questions about what was really intended (Rosenthal, 2004, p. 12). With reflection came the realization that a "wardrobe malfunction" of this variety could not have happened if the principals had not been complicit in planning a stunt.

The other principal in the incident, Jackson, waited until late in the following day to come out with a statement, one that reinforced that this was an accident. At the same time, she admitted that a last minute "surprise" along these lines had indeed been planned, only to go awry. In her statement, Jackson said:

> The decision to have a costume reveal at the end of my halftime show performance was made after the final rehearsals. MTV was completely unaware of it. It was not my intention that it go as far as it did. I apologize to anyone offended—including the audience, MTV, CBS, and the NFL. (Carter & Sandomir, 2004, p. D1)

With this statement Jackson took the full brunt of the blame, and yet another euphemism, the technical concept of "costume reveal," entered the public discourse. Later explanations provided context for what was supposed to have happened. Here we heard that the reveal was supposed to expose a red lace bra beneath the black bustier. Given the context of the song and choreography, however, many felt "two microns of red lace over Jackson's areola wouldn't have made that any better" (Poniewozik, 2004, p. 73). For them, the performance remained a glorification of a sexual assault that could easily be construed as a prelude to rape. Still, the nipple shield staring people in the face raised doubts about intentionality. Had the nipple not been in full costume—not so "ready for prime time"—the explanations would have been far more plausible. As we will see, plausibility would be further assailed as the press deconstructed the promotion and planning for Jackson's appearance.

The "suits" in this situation were collectively willing to let Jackson and Timberlake take the blame. Often words like "disappointment" were used, much in the same way parents might reprimand a wayward child after being surprised by a shocking behavior such as drug use that, had the parent been looking for more carefully, they would have seen. Here, the more paternal approaches were taken by the more mature organizations, CBS and the NFL, that were simultaneously most out of touch with and most desirous of the edginess they had contracted for.

In this vein, the statements made by CBS succeed in characterizing them as "clueless." Their formal response to the incident:

> CBS deeply regrets the incident that occurred during the Super Bowl halftime show. We attended all rehearsals throughout the week and there was no indication that any such thing would happen. The moment did not conform to CBS broadcast standards, and we would like to apologize to anyone who was offended. (Shales, 2004, p, C1.)

It is telling that this first response, which continued to anchor the CBS message regarding the incident, clears their conscience for everything in the halftime show except for the exposure of Jackson's breast. Apart from that moment, one could read from this that all was well. After all, they had attended rehearsals, and only this particular moment deviated sufficiently for comment.

Although senior CBS executives provided additional comment, the basic message stayed the course. The chairman of CBS, Leslie Moonves, expressed anger and was "embarrassed that this happened during our superb broadcast" and reiterated that there was no knowledge that "such an inappropriate display was contemplated" (Carter & Sandomir, 2004, p. D1). Viacom President Mel Karmazin, while continuing to point the blame at Jackson and Timberlake, expressed a different kind of cluelessness and a bit more candor when he admitted, "I wouldn't have picked these songs. I would've had Andy Williams. I am told that's the way adults are dancing these days" (Meek, 2004, p. 18). Responses like these spurred many a shaking head such as the observation in *Advertising Age*: "What if executives were truly clueless about the halftime peak show? Then they apparently lack control over what goes over the airwaves" ("Credibility malfunction," 2004, p. 14).

The NFL's strategy was different. Though they expressed surprise, they moved beyond being duped by the performers to being burned by MTV. This fingering of MTV would have been more difficult at CBS because it would have been an internecine attack on a sister organization at Viacom. Although the initial comment by NFL Commissioner Paul Tagliabue was tempered, he recast the problem as one that went well beyond Janet Jackson's breast, saying "We were extremely disappointed by the MTV halftime show" (Nevius, 2004, p. A1). Other official statements by the NFL clarified that they were "embarrassed by the entire show" (Rich, 2004, p. B1). Expressed many times over, this broadening of the problem to the entire halftime show contrasted with CBS's attempt to limit the problem to the exposure of the breast. These conflicting storylines about the breadth of the problem complicated questions of blame. More importantly, it opened the door for corporate culpability.

That something was awry in the corporate suites was suggested in another aspect of the NFL attempt to assess blame and punt the story. In blaming MTV, the NFL outlined that there was a "communication problem." Their casting of the tale is telling. This is seen in Tagliabue's concession that the NFL needed to be "more assertive" in expressing their vantage point in the planning and rehearsal phases. Part of the reason for this, as the Commissioner put it, was that "[w]e found MTV difficult to deal with" (Toedtman, 2004, p. A4). There was much amplification of this difficulty. Joe Browne, the NFL executive vice president, decried that "MTV did not live up to their end of the deal. They told us, 'We'll address your concerns' and then things never changed" (Poniewozik, 2004, p. 70). This message was drilled over and over. A crucial addition to the storyline was Tagliabue's claim that the NFL was "on the verge of terminating MTV as halftime producer," and that it was "perfectly obvious CBS couldn't control MTV" (King, Kennedy, & Bechtel, 2004, p. 15). Because the NFL had actually hired MTV, it might have been this last statement that broke the camel's back.

The continued NFL assault led MTV to mount the Viacom defense. Here, chairman of MTV Networks Tom Freston began by explaining that not only was there mutual review of the songs, choreography, and costumes for the halftime show but also that the NFL had overseen MTV in their Super Bowl production three years earlier. As Freston noted, "If you go back and look, you'll see the artists doing similar types of music with similar choreography. You even have guys in 'Nsync doing crotch grabbing. But none of it fell under the microscope" (Poniewozik, 2004, p. 70).

At the very least Freston's comments served to raise real questions about who had the communication problem. Regardless, to many the accident was foreseeable. As Attner (2004, p. 4) put it, "If the NFL is partnering with MTV, what did it expect to get, Snow White? You play with fire long enough, you get Justin and Janet conniving to tweak Big Brother." Perhaps this was the lesson because, in the end, the NFL made public promises never to hire MTV again. In later reports, they put changes in place to create what in the future would be a "family-friendly" halftime show in line with their now-energized corporate ideals. Foremost, according to an NFL spokesperson, "We'll control all facets of their performances, including song selection, choreography, and, yes, wardrobe selection" ("This time," 2004, p. 2C).

MTV's initial response to the incident was in many ways the most complex and interesting. It had nuance, and it worked to turn the events to their advantage. For MTV, the error was in the "moment" that CBS had initially apologized for. They called it "unrehearsed, unplanned, [and] completely unintentional" (Rybak, 2004, p. 1A). Here MTV head Tom Freston not only played the victim but also defended what had been planned:

> We were victims of a lewd stunt. What happened was deplorable. But if not for the last two seconds, that show would have been seen as a great success. . . . These were artists really down the middle of the youth culture. The most dynamic force in pop music for the past two decades is hip-hop. For anyone under 40 these songs have been heard everywhere. (Carter, 2004, p. E1)

Freston's refrain was telling. On one hand, it smacked of a child's whine to a parent that "everyone else is doing it." On the other, it pointed a finger at how clueless and unhip the executives at CBS and the NFL really were. To many, this helped MTV come out of the incident as the main organizational winner (Tresniowski, 2004). Just as presidential candidates "run for the center," MTV made a dash for the cultural center, and in the process insinuated that those that disagreed—implicitly including CBS and the NFL—while posing at the middle, were in fact retrograde and, if not right wing, were certainly passé. This MTV position mirrors the edict in a *Time* magazine report on fallout from the incident: "Let the bogus outrage and culture wars begin!" (Poniewozik, 2004, p. 70).

The final corporate player at the table, AOL, had the most minor role. Although not involved in the halftime programming, they had the good fortune of buying the title sponsorship for the show from the NFL. Thus, their statement made it clear that they weren't responsible for production. And like CBS and MTV, they "were surprised and disappointed with certain elements" (Tresniowski, 2004, p. 58). Even with their take that this was a limited offense, they moved to throw the baby out with the bath water. They made it clear that the material was inappropriate for online streaming of a rebroadcast of the halftime show as had been originally contracted for. So they dropped their rebroadcast plans and appealed to the NFL, demanding money back on their sponsorship deal (monies which had been paid to the NFL). In response, the NFL passed the buck by telling them to speak to CBS about making them whole (Hopkins, 2004).

Collectively, if one steps back from the initial responses to the incident and looks only at reasons that the breast was uncovered, much is offered here to defend the incident as an accident and, even if not, for the corporate overseers to claim that they were duped. Unfortunately for the senior players at the table, CBS and the NFL, the deconstruction that followed did not look at the event in isolation, and the accident, like one caused by drunk driving, was cast as foreseeable. One breast led to many issues, and the public relations disaster spiraled onto broader political and cultural grounds.

Deconstruction

After the initial reconstruction phase, with its varied explanations of what happened, public apologia, and taking and shifting of blame, how did the event and its handling play? How did the principals fair? Would it be possible for the corporate entities to successfully shift blame to the individual level, to Jackson and Timberlake? Would the spin be able to contain the event by suggesting failings on the part of the communication partners, or would the buck ultimately stop with the NFL? Questions such as these were only part of how these few seconds of exposed breast were to play on a broader public stage. The run of the media show would be a comparatively long one, in part because the issue was "titillating," but also because the media was having a great time with an event that was a punster's dream.

The legs of the story were extended as one pun topped another in headlines and reporting. As a report on CNN (Costello & Moos, 2004) summarized, the storyline had moved beyond "Duo Caught in a Booby Trap" to "Tempest in a C Cup" and its effects of "shock and bra." The affront played on U.S. actions in Vietnam, becoming a "tit offensive" and involvement in Iraq, with the search for WMD (weapons of mass destruction) substituting Jackson's breast as a "weapon of mammary destruction." The term "CBS Jugheads" was being extended from Jackson and Timberlake to the executive suite. The NFL was tagged as well, characterizing the Super Bowl as "Super Boob" and "Super Bowl 38D," and NFL Commissioner Paul Tagliabue as "Taglia-Boob." The puns belied, however, that public reaction was not all in good fun.

The breast was quickly seized as an opportune political football. As media critic Robert Thompson pointed out: "All those people looking to make a cause out of what they see as indecency in the media have just hit the mother lode" (Carter, 2004, p. E1). The head of Common Sense Media, Jim Steyer said "this was MTV meets Middle America, and it was ugly," whereas the president of Morality in Media, Robert Peters, called it the "MTV-ization of the NFL," something that had become a "gladiator spectacle, which people are only watching for blood and sex" (Nevius, 2004, p. A1). Desirous of a more reined-in and less offensive media, advocacy groups were not willing to let the breast pass as an isolated incident. To this end, Phil Burress, president of Citizens for Community Values, vowed "this is going to change things, finally" (Poniewozik, 2004, p. 72).

Pressure from social conservatives was very much mirrored in swift reactions from some at the FCC and in Congress. On the face of it, there was a legitimate concern about the event in terms of a technical infraction: indecency on the public airwaves. After all, the FCC is charged with licensing the CBS-owned and operated stations and its affiliated stations in the "public interest, convenience, and necessity," and a blatant breach in the broadcasting of indecent material could ultimately result in a license not being renewed. Although the latter possibility was unlikely, the event enabled much political haymaking toward strategic ends.

The FCC, under the leadership of its chair Michael Powell, had recently been making more of an issue over sexual and crude content. In the rollup to the Super Bowl, the radio monolith Clear Channel Communications had been walloped with a $755,000 fine for sexually explicit broadcasts that had tongues wagging. Public discussion over infractions by Howard Stern, Bubba the Love Sponge, and U2 lead singer Bono's use of the "F" word at the broadcast of an awards show was high. Powell looked to keep this momentum going by weighing in on the whole halftime show as "onstage copulation" (Ahrens & de Moraes, 2004, p. A1). Perhaps wishing to seize similar incendiary opportunities, select members of Congress quickly got up on this soapbox as well. In short order, at House and Senate hearings, the corporate overseers in the Jackson incident were called on the carpet. Even with their apologies, broadcasters were in trouble. Not atypical was New Mexico's Republican Representative Heather Wilson's dress down of Viacom Chairman Mel Karmazin's testimony: "You knew what you were doing! You wanted to be all abuzz. It lines your pockets" (de Moraes, 2004, p. C7). There were calls for a ten-fold increase in the fines for each infraction of broadcast indecency. A $550,000 fine to the CBS stations was advocated. It was clear that the media thought this was more than the usual election year grandstanding. Industry analysts said there was good reason for the media to be afraid. The Jackson incident had offered up the perfect "poster child" for an expansion of the federal campaign against media indecency that had already been gaining traction. As a result, the consensus was that this had become a very chilly environment (Janofsky, 2004; Poniewozik, 2004).

The puns and the one-two punch of media advocacy groups and the promise of federal action combined to enable this story to stick around and continue to be shaped. The overarching public relations spin that was being given to the Janet Jackson incident as an accident was readily recognized by the press as a "blame game," a strategy to deflect and control damage but not provide real answers. To their credit, the press followed the blame game closely. Ultimately, however, as *Advertising Age* moaned, "don't-blame-me's are tiresome" ("Credibility malfunction," 2004) and the media lost patience with this strategy as a dead end and moved on. Collectively, the "don't blame me's" were cast as corporations not willing to take responsibility and come clean. In essence they were charged with not coming clean to what actually happened, but more importantly, with not being more candid about the lapses in strategic thinking that got them into the "zip code" of this kind of jam in the first place (Stanley, 2004). Thus, the net result of spinning too much was that the press dug deeper, thereby preventing the problem from fading away. There were consequences here for all, but especially for CBS and the NFL.

The course of unraveling this story gave way to specific questions about the plausibility of the planning and being clueless to larger ones about hypocrisy in the corporate suite. On the plausibility front, the nipple shield ultimately opened the door. As the press put together the pieces, they saw a number of telltale signs that more than Jackson and Timberlake knew what was being planned, including some in the corporate hierarchy. In the days leading up to the Super Bowl, a story on MTV's website featuring an interview with Janet Jackson's choreographer had promised "some shocking moments" in her performance (Ahrens & de Moraes, 2004 p. A1). Whereas the press saw this as evidence of premeditation, perhaps they were not reading this in the corporate suites at CBS and the NFL. Regardless, these promises were more than hints in plain public view. A second dent in plausibility came with the admission that a Jackson aide had been sent shopping in the days before the Super Bowl. As Tresniowski (2004, p. 58) reported:

> Her stylist Wayne Scot Lucas went shopping for nipple jewelry at a boutique called Taurian Piercing & Metals in the edgy Montrose section of Houston. According to the owner Byriah Dailey, the stylist took a liking to four rings, including a sterling silver sunburst that would become famous during CBS's Super Bowl halftime show.

This, combined with a number of reports saying that "top executives" at CBS had approved the "reveal," broke down the plausibility of "cluelessness" to the stunt (Nevius, 2004, p. A1). These allegations of complicity tended to stick more at this moment because CBS had recently been developing a credibility gap. Recent explanations, particularly those about the cancellation of a mini-series on "The Reagans" and a "softball" interview with Michael Jackson on *60 Minutes* at the same time they were promoting his entertainment special, had created a climate of "implausible deniability" at the network (Stanley, 2004, p. E1).

The breakdown of plausibility, in turn, had many in the press looking at larger issues of "life in the fast lane" for those in big-time mediated sport. Although the core issue remained the Jackson incident, it was now a convenient taking off point. The incident became symbolic of other sordid strategies in the sport marketplace that many felt the NFL and others had recently embraced.

In their reflection, the press looked to other areas where effective managerial control had not been exercised, where poor moral choices had been made, and accountability was dodgy. Ultimately, this became more than an interrogation of the increasing commercialization in the sport marketplace. Because indecency was involved, the focus became a moral indictment of the nature of that commercialization, and one that saw the ethical climate as ripe with hypocrisy.

For many in the press, where the buck stopped in the blame game was clear. The summation by Jenkins (2004, p. D1) characterized where many others landed:

> No doubt most of the fingers will be aimed at Timberlake and Jackson for further eroding our society. It's that dangerous rap music that makes kids behave this way, right? But I'd rather point my own finger directly at the league. If the Super Bowl halftime show was offensive and unsuitable for family viewing, I blame Paul Tagliabue and his fellow marketing executives at the NFL. It was their show, start to finish.

Many reactions indicated the NFL's strategy and response were disingenuous and they were getting their just desserts for being two-faced. Typical was this assessment by Miklasz (2004, p. D1):

> What did the NFL expect? The league hired MTV because it wanted an edgy halftime show. . . . That's why the NFL's hypocrisy is so amusing. The league isn't opposed to raunchy behavior . . . as long as it doesn't go too far, of course. . . . The NFL is enthusiastic about using sex to promote the sport. . . . And yet we are supposed to applaud Tagliabue because he criticized Janet Jackson's dirty dancing? The NFL helps promote the very culture that it now condemns. Jackson exposed something else: the NFL's absurd double standards.

Such commonplace venting by the press allowed the public discussion to spread to other topics, giving wider than usual attention to the tone now being used in the once highly touted Super Bowl commercials. Here, too, the NFL was being held accountable for the increasing coarseness on their watch because the buck stopped with their veto power over CBS about what kinds of ads would be off limits — a power that is exercised, for example, by the Motion Picture Academy in the Oscar Awards broadcast. This group of 2004 Super Bowl commercials were found to be particularly offensive. As Elliott (2004, p. C5) put it, the ads were being "castigated for bombarding viewers with more vulgarity and tastelessness than in any previous Super Bowl" with "punch lines centered on bodily functions, violence, and double entendres." With much crude "frat house humor," the ads ran the gamut from "sleazy" to "squalid," featuring a flatulent horse, a dog biting men's crotches, and even, with a monkey making an amorous pass at young woman, a hint of bestiality (Elliott, 2004, p. C5). That the NFL was "embarrassed" by the halftime show stuck in the craw of others who gagged at ads to treat "erectile dysfunction."

> But if the NFL was really so shocked and appalled, why didn't it flinch at the Cialis advertisement that promised men 36 hours of relief from impotence, then warned that if they should experience an erection for four hours straight, they should seek "immediate medical care." (Stanley, 2004, p. E1)

This spot and one for the release of a new horror movie, "Van Helsing," which "contained extremely disturbing and graphic images of brutality and gore" galled many as inappropriate to family viewing of the Super Bowl (Shales, 2004, p. C1).

The contagion of animosity toward the NFL's hypocrisy in marketing spread even further, to the themes in its video games and highlight shows. As Madden (2004, p. C2) put it:

> Tagliabue is a walking, talking contradiction. He wants to eliminate trash talking, yet NFL-licensed video games include it. He will fine a player for a helmet-to-helmet hit, then allow such hits to be included on a highlights video.

The reporting used the opportunity to target the NFL for an ever-broadening litany of offenses. One report, by Bondy (2004, p. 50), decried the "sad, immoral state of the NFL" by detailing "10 things Tagliabue really ought to be embarrassed about, that have nothing to do with Ms. Jackson's chest." These offenses ranged from glorifying violence to scantily clad cheerleaders to unfair labor practices to poor efforts at hiring minorities in management to the racially offensive nickname of the Washington Redskins. Others, such as Jenkins (2004, p. D1) took aim at the disingenuousness of the NFL using "faux-militarism" and nationalism in its promotional themes. Thus, in the end, the NFL may have been hardest hit by the fallout of Janet Jackson's breast. What had seemed at first an exercise in crisis management had become much more than that. The short of it, as Jenkins (2004, p. D1) put it, was "The NFL tried to use MTV and got used back." The long story and the learning lesson, however, was "what goes around comes around."

In many other ways, the deconstructive contours of this incident are instructive. There is a progression that stems from it being a titillating but biting joke, to it being no joke as political capital, to the loss of patience for the blame game ultimately fueling a breakdown in plausibility and a larger charge of corporate hypocrisy. It is important to note that it is unusual for the press to go beyond blow-by-blow coverage of the blame game as it did in this particular instance. For a variety of reasons, it is difficult for the media to explain the structural pressures and corporate complicity that underlie, encourage, and facilitate wayward individual action. In many ways, the easy way out is to blame individual performers for over-the-edge behaviors used to advance their careers. Such strategies are common in blaming the individual athlete for pushing the envelope by using performance-enhancing drugs in a system that encourages peak performance and pays substantially for its achievement. Often the tendency is to give the boot to the offending individual, but this does little to curb drug use in the larger system, one in which, if it is seen at all, it is seen more as cure than disease. Such is the case in the logic of advanced capitalism. Here, when the logic of the system is seen, it is generally cast as the "genius of the system." In a sound-bite media economy where the media are largely populated by conglomerates willing to reward the creative community for pushing the cultural bounds in order to break though increasing noise and clutter, the public airing and raising of questions about the structural pressures that lead to media and corporate excess become unusual. Unfortunately for the NFL and CBS, the stars aligned in this instance. Consequently, they found themselves, for one small moment at least, on the path toward a promised recovery.

Recovery

The concept of recovery from addiction is in many ways a good fit to describe what could happen in the shadow of the 2004 Super Bowl halftime show for NFL and CBS. They had become addicted to a drug — edginess — that they didn't understand and that was stronger than they were. They had taken too much and embarrassed themselves publicly. Like addicts, their initial instincts were toward denial and a shifting of blame. The NFL, for one, swore off hanging around with unsavory people like those in the MTV crowd and promised to keep themselves firmly in control the next time around. CBS was issued a citation for their vehicle being driven under the influence of the edginess of youth, resulting in a speeding ticket for indecency that disrupted the entire neighborhood. Although they have vowed to fight the fines, it is likely that next time they will not leave the keys out for a drive down that same road. (Levin, 2004).

Nevertheless, when considering the organizational parents in this situation, the NFL and Viacom's CBS, it is clear that a full and lasting recovery will be challenging. For them to recognize that "they have a problem" in a situation where edginess and its manifestations in more graphic sex, violence, and language are both being advanced and applauded in the marketplace requires a leap of faith. Failing to compete with the cultural tidal trends toward explicitness in music, movies, and cable will likely leave them in a niche position rather than one, as at present, of dominance. Pressures such as these make it unlikely that a "one-day-at-a-time" approach to recovery will stay the course. More likely, as has been the case after the many congressional hearings on television violence, there will be a period of retrenchment followed by heightened levels of what was found offensive. In the short run, however, there are still some lessons here about corporate ethics.

First, there is a need for the ethics and standards in the corporation to be clearly stated and to be taken seriously by those in oversight roles. These should not be swept aside when an edgy opportunity comes up. Nor should senior executives delegate important decisions with broad ethical implications and potential consequences to more trendy underlings, especially those who may be unfamiliar or dismissive of ethical signposts. This charge is only magnified when you are talking about overseeing programming that will be seen by the largest audience in the world.

Second, organizations need to put into place programs that will facilitate the "ethical health" of their employees and, particularly, their leadership. In order for this to happen, the first lesson will have to be put into play. The senior management team will need to make decisions about organizational ethics, standards, and values and enmesh them in the reward systems in a consistent way with demonstrable veracity. And senior managers will have to "walk the talk," serving as role models to heighten ethical consideration in decisions, even at the lowest levels. From this basis, programs in ethical training and role-playing can be more successfully implemented.

Third, when the "shit hits the fan," as it most certainly did in the fanning out of embarrassing and negative publicity as a result of the Super Bowl halftime fiasco, a crisis-management and damage-control protocol should guide corporate public response. In this case study, the blame trail led to competing stories that raised questions about plausibility and undermined veracity. As a result, the lively public interplay over stated motives, the quality of oversight, and real vs. denied intentions led this story in many directions and gave it very long legs. The experiences in this case study point to a heightened need to have a negotiated crisis-management plan in place when organizations, particularly those with disparate agendas and corporate philosophies, come together as partners. This need is magnified when the stakes are as high and as visible as they were in this instance, and when the artists and material were chosen, in part, for their ability to be on a sensitive cultural edge.

Fourth, when organizations come together as a team to produce an event, the designated driver should be known, in the driver's seat, and not be asleep at the wheel. Those not in the driver's seat will have to look out for their own ethical best interests as well. Moreover, it always helps if all organizational partners bring similar ethical priorities to the table. With the Super Bowl halftime show, there is no doubt that the buck stopped with the NFL. The NFL sold the rights to the game to CBS who suggested MTV to the NFL to produce their halftime show. The NFL then hired MTV as producer. The NFL sold the sponsorship rights for the halftime show to AOL. Thus, the NFL was clearly in charge, and they knew what they were getting into because they had hired MTV for the task three years before. They had oversight and the opportunity for intervention, but that power was not effectively managed. That the NFL has observed that it had difficulty communicating with MTV is telling. Communication is a two-way process. Often, when the receiver does not get the message, the problem lies with the sender. Communicative competence lies at the heart of ethical health. When managers in a position of power cannot communicate the ethical priorities effectively to subordinates, it is disingenuous to blame the subordinate. In this case study, however, that is exactly what the NFL did.

Earlier in this essay I mentioned a number of ethical strategies that might have been brought to bear in developing and overseeing the 2004 Super Bowl halftime show. These involved familiar time-tested strategies of looking for a golden mean, being loyal to a duty to act to facilitate universal good, acting out of "other-respecting care," and looking for consequences that would serve the greater good for the greater number while minimizing harm. Basic ethical concepts such as these and others are not complex, not difficult to put into play for applied action, and not unyielding to context. Exercising ethics in an organizational setting is not rocket science, but some semblance of "ethical health" needs to be present in order for organizations to successfully navigate problematic waters. Otherwise, managers will not see conflicts of interest when they occur and will not recognize them as ethical dilemmas. Such was the case in the conflict between displaying edginess because it appealed to a desired demographic and programming appropriate family entertainment for television's largest audience. And in this particular instance, where the ethical landmarks may not have been clearly seen nor acted upon, the NFL and CBS will be recovering from Janet Jackson's breast.

References

Ahrens, F., & de Moraes, L. (2004, February 3). FCC is investigating Super Bowl show: Halftime performance faces indecency standard. *Washington Post*, p. A1.

Attner, P. (2004, February 16). To know list 3: The NFL had it coming. *Sporting News*, p. 4.

Bondy, F. (2004, February 4). NFL has more pressing flesh. *New York Daily News*, p. 50.

Boorstin, D. (1961). *The image: A guide to pseudo-events in America*. New York: Atheneum.

Carter, B., & Sandomir, R. (2004, February 3). Pro football: Halftime-show fallout includes F.C.C. inquiry. *New York Times*, p. D1.

Carter, B. (2004, February 5). Bracing for fallout for super indignation. *New York Times*, p. E1.

Costello, C., & Moos, J. (2004, February 10). Puns generated from Super Bowl controversy. *CNN Daybreak*. [Television Broadcast: Transcript #021012CN.V73]. Atlanta, GA: CNN.

Credibility malfunction. (2004, February 9). *Advertising Age*, p. 14.

Dayan, D., & Katz, E. (1992). *Media events: The live broadcasting of history*. Cambridge, MA: Harvard University Press.

De Moraes, L. (2004, February 26). It's congressional chew-out-the-networks time, episode 2. *Washington Post*, p. C7.

Drudge, M. (2004, February 1). Outrage at CBS after Janet bares breast during dinner hour; Super Bowl show pushes limits. Retrieved August 11, 2004, from http://www.drudgereportarchives.com/data/2004/02/03/20040203_003406_mattjj.htm

Elliott, S. (2004, February 3). Class and taste take a beating as the Adbowl dissolves into the "stupidity sweepstakes." *New York Times*, p. C5.

Geertz, C. (1973). Thick description: Toward an interpretive theory of culture. In *The interpretation of cultures* (pp. 3–30). New York: Basic Books.

Goudie, C. (2004, February 9). Oh say can you see . . . the real disgrace at the Super Bowl. *Chicago Daily Herald*, p. 9.

Hopkins, N. (2004, February 6). AOL demands $7.5m refund after Jackson mishap. *The Times* (London), Business, p. 31.

Janet Jackson set to perform at the Super Bowl. (2003, January 18). *The Sports Network*. [Television broadcast]. Hatboro, PA: The Sports Network. Also available online through LexisNexis Academic Universe.

Janofsky, M. (2004, February 12). Review of TV decency law looks beyond bared breast. *New York Times*, p. A32.

Jenkins, S. (2004, February 3). NFL exposed for what it is." *Washington Post*, p. D1.

Kelly, K., Clark, K., & Kulman, L. (2004, February 16). Trash TV. *U.S. News & World Report*, pp. 48–52.

King, P., Kennedy, K., & Bechtel, M. (2004,

February 16). The stoic. *Sports Illustrated*, pp. 14–15.

Levin, G. (2004, July 19). CBS chief says he will fight any fines. *USA Today*, p. 3D.

Lewczak, J. & Lapidus, M. (2004, May). The impact of the Janet Jackson "incident" on advertising: How the costume malfunction is likely to raise the standards and decency on network television. *Metropolitan Corporate Counsel*, p. 6.

Lupika, M. (2004, February 3). Jackson's stunt exposes league: Game was great, but sex is super. *New York Daily News*, p. 53.

Madden, M. (2004, February 4). Halftime show illustrates NFL's contradictions. *Pittsburgh Post-Gazette*, p. C2.

Martzke, R. (2004, February 4). NFL toes line in effort to draw young male viewers. *USA Today*, p. 1C.

Meek, J.G. (2004, February 12). Execs call nipplegate unbareable. *New York Daily News*, p. 18.

Miklasz, B. (2004, February 5). In the halftime fiasco, it's the NFL that is truly exposed. *St. Louis Post-Dispatch*, p. D1.

Nason, P. (2004, February 3). Analysis: Janet's Houston surprise. *United Press International*. Retrieved August 11, 2004, from LexisNexis Academic Universe.

Nevius, C. W. (2004, February 3). FCC inquiry, uproar over Super Bowl halftime peepshow. *San Francisco Chronicle*, p. A1.

Poniewozik, J. (2004, February 16). The hyposcrisy bowl. *Time*, pp. 70–74.

Powers, K. (2004, January 30). Janet Jackson carries torch. *Worchester Telegram & Gazette*, p. 24.

Rich, F. (2004, February 16). My hero, Janet Jackson. *New York Times*, p. B1.

Rosenthal, P. (2004, February 3). Cover story so bad, even FCC sees through it. *Chicago Sun-Times* [special edition], p. 12.

Rybak, D. C. (2004, February 3). Halftime exposure starts a blame game. *Minneapolis Star Tribune*, p. 1A.

Scannell, P. (1995). Media events. *Media, Culture, & Society*, *17*, 151–157. Shales, T. (2004, February 2). Incomplete! *Washington Post*, p, C1.

Stanley, A. (2004, February 3). A flash of flesh: CBS again is in denial. *New York Times*, p. E1.

Steenberg, A. (2004, February 5). Janet tops on Internet; boob hits record number searches. *Toronto Sun*, p. 2.

This time, NFL will have wardrobe approval. (2004, August 11). *Milwaukee Journal Sentinel*, p. 2C.

Toedtman, J. (2004, February 12). NFL, MTV's parent company make cases over halftime flap. *Houston Chronicle*, p. A4.

Tresniowski, A. (2004, February 16). Janet Jackson: The fallout. *People*, pp. 58–62.

Turow, J. (1996). *Media systems in society: Understanding industries, strategies, and power* (2nd ed.). New York: Longman.

Wenner, L. A. (1989). The Super Bowl pregame show: Cultural fantasies and political subtext. In L. A. Wenner (Ed.), *Media, sports, and society* (pp. 157–179). Newbury Park, CA: Sage.

CORPORATE TRAINING: IDENTITY CONSTRUCTION, PREPARATION FOR THE SYDNEY OLYMPIC GAMES, AND RELATIONSHIPS BETWEEN CANADIAN MEDIA, SWIMMERS, AND SPONSORS[1]

Margaret MacNeill, Peter Donnelly, and Graham Knight

Global media mega sports events, like the Olympics and the soccer World Cup, have become orgies of both nationalism and commodification ("commodified nationalism" perhaps).[2]

Sport has long been a popular and profitable aspect of Canadian culture; yet, little scholarly attention has been devoted to national team "duties," athletes' rights, and to the *actual* relationships Olympic athletes have with media, sponsors, media attache's, and sporting organizations. Despite a long history of political-economic investigations into sport[3] and a recent turn in critical sport studies toward issues of identity which have opened a space for the investigation of cornmodified sporting images,[4] there has been little ethnographic research about relationships between those social actors and the (re)production of *corporatized* identities.[5] Athletes and their images have often been employed to compete for a national audience. To understand how and why corporatized Canadian identities are produced around major sporting events, and to explore the consequences of cultural production for the people and institutions involved, this investigation critically examines the relationships and contexts of identity negotiation *in situ*.

Findings from the pre-Olympic stage of a larger project that investigated the contested production of national identities around and at the 2000 Sydney Olympic Games are presented in this article. Contested notions of nationalism and regionalism, and other intersecting discourses produced within the sport-media-promotional complex—such as commercialism, and the struggle to institute team cohesion as an image building exercise—are ethnographically detailed and critically analyzed. We argue that as elite sport has been forced to seek private sector funding at the high performance level during an era of federal fiscal restraint in Canada, a corporatized discourse has become privileged in both the organization of the sport and the negotiation of key identities that

Swim/Natation Canada (SNC) and the national team offer to fans on site and to the Canadian audience through media coverage and advertising. Branding exercises for the "national team product" by sport officials and media skills training for athletes are two strategies that have been instituted to create the shift to corporatized discourse. Thus, nationalism produced in and through commodified elite sport, considering Andrew Wetnick's[6] arguments, has become a form of *promotionalism* that has celebrated a commercial cluster of values infused with particular notions of sporting culture and nationhood that are then recirculated back through corporate communications. Commercial values such as competitive individualism in a team environment, success based on measurable achievement, and efficiency formed an anchor for national team-corporate sponsorships. Maritime Life, a title sponsor of Swimming/Natation Canada for example, upheld the same ideals of reaching for excellence through "teamwork, performance and achievement;" "As a financially strong, national life insurance company, we feel we have a natural tie with sport that Canadians of all ages, cultures and backgrounds can enjoy."[7]

Ethnographic insights about corporatized identities mediating the Maritime Life Olympic Swim Trials held in Montreal in May of 2000 and athlete media skills training seminars held at a national team training camp after the Sears Summer National Championships in August of 2000 are presented in five sections. In Section I we briefly outline critical cultural studies notions of national identity and discourse, and suggest that identities are always in flux as they are primarily reconstituted by promotional relations in and around the National Swimming Team. The team has come to be situated within a corporatized culture of high performance sport management in Canada. The methodological framework is presented in Section II. In Section III we examine the dialectical conflation of national and local identities during media skills training that served to shift team development from a mutually supportive exercise in team building for athletic performance, to a corporatized sense of team cohesiveness. In Section IV we argue that media skills training primarily supported SNC efforts to leverage the sponsorship value of the association by training athletes to interact with the media and promote SNC values, by cultivating relationships with media in a manner that attempted to address the different levels of interest in swimming by Anglophone and Francophone journalists, and by strictly enforcing SNC interview protocol. In Section V we provide a specific example of competitive media interactions in the press room as print journalists attempted to obtain an interview with an athlete caught between corporate reception duties, responsibilities for media relations, and a desire to privately celebrate making the national team. Finally, Section VI offers a number of conclusions regarding athlete-sponsor-sport-media relations and the reproduction of corporatized identities.

I. National Identity and Imagining Corporate Canada

Identities are always in flux. National, regional, class, gender, ethnic, and language-based identities. among others, are also fragmented and reconstituted by associations constructed through the media and the commodified sports industry.[8] For example, the media's obsession with the technological angle on Speedo Fastskin© swimming suits leading up to the 2000 Olympic Games reified the bodies of athletes: Australian Ian Thorpe became an aquadynamic machine and Canadian Morgan Knabe was depicted as an aggressive shark in international waters by the Canadian Broadcast Corporation (CBC).[9] These full-length black suits were banned at the Canadian Olympic swimming Trials in May of 2000 but were permitted during the final Olympic qualifying championship in Winnipeg in August of 2000. In Montreal, and later in Sydney, the Speedo-clad bodies of swimmers served to commodify athletes into billboards for corporate interests, to become biomechanical testing sites for new technologies,[10] and to act as sites where media attempted to reclaim past swimming glory by merging history with current assumptions of the team members being identified as young drug-free "clean" Canadians.

Identities, including corporate and national, are difficult to define because they have multiple significations.[11] We adopt Anderson's definition of the nation as "an imagined political community."[12] Nationhood is imagined in Canada, for example, because members of this sovereign country may have a vision of their "communion" with other citizens; yet, each Canadian will neither see, hear, nor meet most of the other inhabitants of the vast geographic territory. Memories of past sporting glory, beliefs about national or regional character, maple leaf symbols, and relationships that constitute elements of nation building are an amalgam of social practices, promotional strategies, and discursive formations. Communities, Anderson argues, "are to be distinguished, not by their falsity/genuineness, but by the style in which they are imagined."[13] In an ethno-culturally diverse country like Canada—constituted by peoples with a variety of ancestral homelands, political positions, religious affiliations, genders, sexual identities, physical abilities. etc.—there can never be a singular Canadian identity. Rather there are multiple identities. Therefore, as we have argued elsewhere, Canadian sport must also be wrapped up in a range of visions.[14]

However, the polysemic range of imagined "Canadas" can be more narrowly contained in and through national broadcasts of sport, particularly when agreements with the International Olympic Committee permit only a single broadcasting rights holder for each nation, such as the CBC[15] in the case of the 2000 Games, to exclusively produce and circulate what Stuart Hall would call a "preferred"[16] vision of sport and nation. Dominant visions may embody popular practices, feelings, and structures. Yet they are always partially unrepresentative of the various constituents of the nation. Anderson's notion of the imagined community is helpful when theorizing and investigating the ways national identities are produced as a human creation; however, it has a number of limitations. On one level, as Homi Bhabha[17] has observed, the notion of an imagined community ignores the disenfranchised and those marginalized in a national culture, such as the homeless, refugees, and some immigrant groups with diasporic identities in post-colonial Canada. On another level of identification, such as the case of cross border alliances between ath-

letes that are part of indigenous sport circles, the notion of one imagined nation of Canada is problematic. Canada as a nation-state may have specific
geographic borders, laws, and enshrined constitutional rights, but in this case
nationhood has multiple meanings. Assuming for "Canada" a monolithic meaning as an imagined community is problematic for researchers, media, and marketers alike[18] because to distill the diversity of communities and identities in
Canada into an assumed monoculture prevents an understanding of the complexity of identity constitution and its attendant implications. Furthermore,
ethnographic research in local communities has demonstrated that some individuals and groups pursue political activism through sport to conspicuously
place themselves outside of the imagined nation. An example of this can be
found in Catherine Palmer's[19] recent study of Spanish pro-Basque supporters
who attempted to sabotage the Tour de France. Palmer concluded that the
imagined community is fragile and partial; still, Anderson's contention that national identity is "always a product of the human mind"[20] has been upheld in
her research. Indeed, as Hall has argued,

> nationalism has no independent existence outside of the social relations
> through which it is constructed. This also implies that the "being" of
> which nationalism is said to be an expression — national identity — is a so-
> cially constructed phenomenon. Yet the effect of the social construction —
> the nationalist discourse — is conceived of as an impersonal object, con-
> taining the distinct historical subjects of national citizens. But the
> reproduction must still be made in practical social relations. This means
> that the mediation between discourse and practice — processes of social
> organisation — crucially involves a power over the construction and defi-
> nition of these relations, and that nationalism as a socially employed dis-
> cursive practice, which is conceived of as impersonal by subject-forming
> knowledge-power. Hence nationalism may be an "official" or even "ba-
> nal" discourse of power at the same time as this discourse is always pro-
> duced and reproduced relation-ally.[21]

We, therefore, contend that Anderson's notion of the imagined community has
value for critical sport and media studies because it has opened a space to examine privileged identities, such as official visions of "national" teams and corporate identities, as contested human practice and social constructions.

A major focus of this identity project is to study the struggle over and production of multiple layers of discourses about corporatized nationalism. Discourse, according to a critical cultural studies approach, is considered to be
both a social process of making and reproducing meaning, *and* the product of
making sense.[22] In other words, discourse refers to both the *ideological power relation* involved in the act of communication and the product(s) of this relation.
Thus, for example, the power relationship was evident in the employment of
"team cohesiveness" by coaches to pressure athletes to cheer for each other, to
be loyal and committed to performance goals, and to mentor junior athletes in
media savviness as they promoted Swimming/Natation Canada's and sponsors'

values. The product included constructed narratives of "excellence derived from clean performance' conveyed in media coverage and public relations. SNC, as an incorporated sport governing body, has been in competition with other amateur and professional sports for sponsorship funds. "Clean" and "healthy" were the sharpest promotional "hooks" to attract sponsors and fans. SNC attempted to leverage the value of its "brand" by promoting "clean" excellence. With marquee events, such as the men's 100 metre sprint in athletics, hovering in the stale and tainted aura of Ben Johnson's positive doping tests since the 1988 Seoul Olympics, SNC believed it could capitalize on the long history of "clean" drug tests on swimmers. Moreover, the timing to re-position swimming in Canada's high performance sports system was advantageous during the 2000 Summer Olympics, hosted by Sydney. Swimming has long been considered to be the national sport of Australia. To activate "partnerships" with sponsors, clients, and potential consumers in Canada, SNC engaged national team athletes in media skills training, press conferences, and public relations events that we examine in later sections.

The pursuit of private sector partnerships and sponsorships, as Donald Macintosh and Dave Whitson noted a decade ago,[23] has been part of a wider corporatization of high performance sport in Canada. Beginning in the 1980s, they argued, the organizational context of national sport organisations (NSOs) shifted to one that systematically had to attend to financial management and control due to pressure from Sport Canada at the federal level.[24] Since the 1990s, NSOs have been pressed to raise increasingly larger portions of their budgets from fundraising and corporate sponsorships, at the same time that more formal business and administrative credentials have been demanded for staff positions in NSOs.[25] With a three million dollar annual budget, about 40 percent of funding for SNC is now derived from government sources and 60 percent from sponsorship, fund-raising, and membership fees. As a non-profit organization, SNC came under tremendous pressure to create an image that would attract private sector monies to prepare for the 2000 Olympics. As a national sport organization, SNC received over a million dollars a year for organizational support from Sport Canada to fulfill "sport objectives shared with the federal government" related to national team programming, development of elite coaches and officials, and salaries for staff and coaches.[26] Within this context, the Canadian Amateur Swimming Association (created in 1909) changed its name to Swimming/Natation Canada in 1987 to present the official bilingualism of Canada's national swim team and system. The mission of SNC over the past few years has been to "promote excellence in swimming" across the nation.[27] SNC has boasted that for international competition, including Olympic, Commonwealth, and Pan American Games competition, Canadian athletes have won more medals in swimming than in any other sport.[28]

The pressures to "brand" sport with a particular set of values to enhance this NSO's position in both sporting culture and wider business sectors have emerged from the pressures to professionalize and corporatize the operations of amateur sport. The alignment of SNC's high performance goals and excellence assumed in the quality of sponsor's commodities, such as Speedo swimming attire, figured centrally in SNC's branding exercises.[29] In the current economic climate, sponsorship has offered sport the obvious benefits of funding support and publicity to sporting organizations and the people within them. However, as Victor Head,[30] Chris Gratton, and Peter Taylor[31] have commented, there are a number of drawbacks that accompany the return on investment sponsors expect: (1) sporting organizations may have to relinquish a level of control over their image and promotional activities; (2) athletes are compromised by busy promotional schedules; (3) conflicts may arise between NSOs, that benefit financially, and individual athletes who may not directly benefit from sponsorship funds and/or are denied the opportunity to negotiate their own sponsorship deals due to exclusivity contracts; and finally (4) conflicts in objectives can harm the integrity of sport (e.g. by demanding rule changes, forcing athletes to compete wearing untested equipment, or promoting unrelated values). All of these limitations were evident in the relationships between SNC, sponsors, media, and athletes.

II. Methodological Framework

This swimming team case study was part of a larger ethnographic media project examining the political and cultural economies of producing national, regional, gendered, and other identities contested during the production of the Olympic Games as a mediated event. The qualitative methodological platform was informed by critical cultural studies, which was sensitive to the unequal but productive relationships of power constituting (and constitutive of) identity politics between people and the representations of identity found in sport media and marketing communications. This platform employed a crystallization[32] of three techniques to study identity politics and relationships of power. Qualitative studies have often used triangulation to cross check findings using either a variety of data sources, multiple theories, and/or researchers examining the same phenomena, and/or multiple methods of gathering and analyzing data. However, cross checking has often been employed because of quasi-positivist assumptions that findings should be generalizable and have a historical reliability. However, in critical cultural studies, sport and media productions of sport are assumed to be socio-historical phenomena that are produced and reproduced within unequal relationships of power. Thus, data may be *provisionally* generalizable from studies of dominant sports to other hegemonic situations within the same historical juncture, but data is neither assumed to uphold positivist assumptions of replicability to demonstrate law-like validity, nor a constancy and reliability of data in terms of application to other social contexts. This research supports Laurel Richardson's notion of crystallization.[33] Crystallization assumes multiple angles of approach in research design, including the incorporation of inter-disciplinary frameworks of understanding, that can gather and represent data in a non-amorphous way. Three data gathering methods utilized in this study to reflect light on this topic from various angles included:

1. *video-taped ethnographic observation* of (i) the *2000 Speedo Spring National Swimming Championships* held March 8–11, 2000 in Etobicoke. Ontario, Canada, (ii) the *2000 Maritime Life Olympic Swim Trials* held May 28 to June 4, 2000 in Montreal, Quebec, Canada, (iii) the 2000 *Sears, I Can Swim, Summer National Championships* held July 30–August 6, 2000 in Winnipeg, Manitoba, Canada, and (iv) national team meetings and media skills training held in August 7–9, 2000 in Winnipeg, Manitoba, Canada;

2. *interviews* conducted at the Olympic Trials and national championships with athletes, coaches, and sporting personnel, as well as interviews with other key Olympic "partners" such as print media journalists, television executives and commentators, sponsors, media attaches, and Canadian Olympic Association (COA) representatives in Toronto; and

3. *broadcast textual analysis* of Canadian Broadcasting Corporation's (CBC) Olympic Swimming Trials, which aired on 10 and 17 June 2000.

III. Media Skills Training and Corporatized Esprit De Corps

Just as you train hard in the pool, you must train your media and public relations skills.

—Tom Mayenknecht, The Media Institute.[34]

As professional and high performance sport have become mega event industries, part of athletic training has begun to include sessions in media and public relations skills. The majority of Canadian teams that competed in the Sydney Olympics received media skills and public relations training that linked institutional missions to "individual branding" of athletes by the Media Institute (a partnership of print journalist Tom Mayenknecht and former CBC radio sports announcer Fred Walker). Many high performance sporting associations in Canada have enshrined corporate mission statements in their business and strategic plans to help the participation base of their sport grow in terms of athletes competing and attracting corporate sponsors to fund high performance programs. As a result, all athletes and SNC personnel in the public eye have been expected to develop and polish media relations to present a cohesive national team identity as part of business and strategic planning. Athletes on the national team were expected to strive for excellence in an honorable manner and to be exemplar spokesmodels for title sponsors. Swimming/Natation Canada's mission to promote excellence in swimming while maintaining a clean (drug-free) image meshed well with the "pillar" of Maritime Life's business philosophy: "to maintain superior financial strength . . . with a balanced approach between the goal of excellent return and the need to avoid unwarranted risk."[35]

Yet, to become newsworthy personalities, team members needed a "hook." Individual athletes, such as "free spirit" Morgan Knabe attempted to re-articulate the "bad boy" image of the late Victor Davis after receiving advice from CBC swimming commentator Steve Armitage that, "amateur athletes need to separate himself or herself from the pack."[36] Despite the possibilities of a variety of images emerging, the quest to uniquely package themselves was often reconciled with dominant commercialized national images of "the team" promoted by SNC. Knabe, for example, often stuck out his pierced tongue at the end of interviews, yet never went as far as his hero by throwing tantrums on the pool deck in front of dignitaries and corporate guests. The main objectives of media skills and public relations training for the swim team were, "to create optimal conditions for shared learning while placing media relations within the context of the 'job' of being a high performance Canadian swimmer and member of Swimming/Natation Canada's Olympic team."[37] A corporate climate was created by SNC's overall promotional efforts and media skills training to help athletes establish individual mission statements and to become their own "personal brand" *within SNC* and national team culture.

After being schooled in workshops about the value of corporate sponsorships by Maritime Life representatives, and instructed by CBC sportscaster Steve Armitage[38] about CBC's plans for Olympic coverage and how athletes should respond to typical media questions, athletes were advised "to be themselves." But it was hard for athletes to be themselves when their lives on the team were tightly scheduled around training and competition, when media protocol restricted what they could say and to whom, and when rules about their social lives were made public through the media. Midway through the Montreal Olympic Trials, for example, Coach Dave Johnson told *Montreal Gazette* reporter Dave Stubbs about the abstinence rule. Journalistic license was employed by Stubbs to reinforce the coach's power. Stubbs, a former communications manager for Swim Canada, concluded his article in a manner that legitimated athlete subjugation to coaching authority to post winning performances: "expect the distinctive leaf to swim nearer to the front in Sydney. Funny things happen when most of the horses buy into the system, and decide to pull the plow in one direction."[39]

A few days later, the *Globe and Mail* newspaper picked up on the story and published the headline, "Abstinence again golden rule for Canadian Swimmers."[40] Reporter James Christie informed the Canadian public about the head coach's "no sex" rule for all national swim team athletes. Control of athletes' lifestyles was subsumed under the coach's slogan, "buying into the system," and was legitimated by the media. Again, it was hard for athletes to "be themselves" when official protocol limited athlete-media interviews to talk only about their personal background and performance, and when all national team athletes could wear only the official team uniform and live a controlled life at the Trials. SNC's unfulfilled mission to promote excellence in swimming espoused the values of athlete-centeredness, integrity, accountability, fairness, equity, and equality.[41]

"Being oneself" with the media was at odds with the pressure to create team cohesion. The latter was the dominant rhetoric espoused in and around the national swimming team at the Olympic Trials in the spring of 2000. At the level of sport psychology, it was employed by Coach Johnson to provide a "holistic" training environment for a number of reasons. First, team cohesion was employed as an organizational discourse that officially served to re-instill a sense of belonging and loyalty while athletes lived away from home. Second, it reoriented athletes as cheerleaders for their teammates rather than foes, which they had been at regional club levels.[42] Third, it helped athletes focus in the midst of a "media circus" according to the head coach.[43] As swimmers met Federation Internationale de Natation Amateur (FINA) qualifying times for Olympic eligibility standards during the Trials, a team development process formally attempted to reconstruct their identities. Swimmers, with various ethno-cultural, class, gendered, and localized identities (e.g., they were from Salmon Arm, Fort McMurray, Moose Jaw, Oka, Saskatoon, and more than 25 other hometowns) were soon urged to take on a particular image and value set of the commodified elite swimming world to frame the human interest stories they might have to share with the media during interviews and corporate clients during public relations receptions.

Team cohesiveness had the deeper corporatized connotation. Johnson adamantly underscored that his notion of "team" included athletes, the staff coaches, medical staff, scientific support, SNC communications experts, media, *and* supporting sponsors. Athletes were managed by many levels of SNC professionals and were expected to cater to many SNC partners. At the Olympic Trials, corporate sponsors were prioritized. At the pre-Trials press conference, for example, Coach Johnson first thanked sponsors for their financial and technical support (such as the Speedo suits that national team members had been using to train). He then acknowledged the sponsors' contributions to the national team's *esprit de corps*.[44] Maritime Life, for example, had many corporate hospitality receptions arranged for their independent agents and clients over the course of the Trials, which were supposed to be one of the few "fun and social" events for athletes in heavy training.[45] Swimmers were expected to attend receptions, glad-hand, sign autographs, and convey a cohesive image of youthful achievers "to put them on the podium they truly deserve to be on."[46] Athletes unanimously desired greater corporate funding for the team and themselves, but the main podium they wanted to climb upon was "the medal podium not the reception head table."[47]

A united front was demanded by media protocol around all issues except athletes' personal backgrounds or individual performances. A full cast of characters — loyal team players and free spirits, masculine and feminine youth, eastern and western Canadians, small town and big town heroes, Anglophone and Francophone Canadians, rookies and retiring athletes–provided the media with a variety of human interest stories and multiple affiliations with which potential audiences/consumers could identify. In Western Canada, for example, swimming supporters were assumed by the SNC communications team and the CBC to celebrate "the bashful and studious Curtis Myden (from Calgary) who wanted to become a research scientist,"[48] while Eastern Canada celebrated its athletic heroes by naming streets after athletes, like Marianne Limpert, as Fredericton did.[49] This supported the corporatized mandate guiding SNC, media and sponsors' work to reach a wider swimming participation base, audience, and/or range of consumers. Athletes were encouraged to be proud of their old home teams and retain multiple ties to their many communities, but had to do so in national team uniform endorsing SNC values.

The local/national dialectic was evident during the national championships and Olympic Trials as athletes and coaches strived to achieve national standing. For example, Coach Johnson tried to break down former club and zone affiliations by demanding that pre-qualified Olympic national team members stay in uniform at the Trials to foster team cohesion; yet he encouraged them to be proud of their home clubs and communities in order to be ambassadors for SNC's elite program.[50] During a post-race interview at the Trials, for example, swimmer Joanne Malar waved at the camera and said, "Hi everybody at home in Hamilton and Calgary." Malar was born and raised in Hamilton whereas Calgary was her temporary home while she trained at the National Training Centre. In addition to national team photos, all the athletes from a particular region or province were photographed together in national team uniform at the Trials so that local, provincial, and national levels of swimming organizations could tailor their regional promotions yet still retain the anchor of SNC's official parade nationalism. Nationalist discourses were prioritized through the dialectical conflation of identities, as athletes' bodies were simultaneously marked by maple leaf discourses and multinational corporate logos before other, more local, identifications were made available.

IV. Media Protocol, Public Relations, and Producing the Image of "Clean" Athletes

> You can always tell an athlete who has been media-trained: they thank their sponsors first and have a hard time being themselves.
>   — Robin Brown, CBC Radio[51]

Lead-up events to the Sydney Olympic Games, such as national championships and Olympic Trials, served various purposes for different stakeholders during Olympic preparations. They were opportunities for aspiring Olympians to qualify for Team Canada, for SNC and the CBC to bolster audience support, for sponsors to leverage the value of their brand in the Canadian marketplace, and a cultural opportunity for all to claim excellence by reclaiming past Canadian glory in the pool.

To professionalize the corporate communications portfolio and realize some of these opportunities, SNC's staff expanded in recent years to include media relations and sponsor services personnel to protect the image of SNC and the sport of swimming in terms of event signage and other protocol. Penny Joyce, the Director of Corporate Communications and Media Relations for SNC, promoted the image of swimming as being, "clean cut, family-oriented, universal and honest."[52] The image of a clean water-based sport was meant to refer both to the literal level of being well-washed, to connotative levels of the innocence of school kids (most national team members were middle class Euro-Canadians attending university or high school), and to a long history of national swim team members consistently testing negative for the presence of drugs.[53] An official image of Swimming/Natation Canada being "squeaky clean" was frequently pronounced in comparisons to the Chinese team and swimmers from other nations. The results of past drug tests and a sanitized image of "innocent and victimized" Canadians were utilized to mediate the knowledge and expectations conveyed to national team members by SNC personnel. The image of a drug-free team was also heralded by the media personnel at the Trials, who for example, lamented the loss of a gold medal for Marianne Limpert and a bronze medal for Joanne Malar at the 1996 Atlanta Games to Michelle Smith of Ireland. Smith was later charged with contaminating a urine sample with whiskey, presumably to avoid a positive test for a banned substance. Past potential victories could not be fully claimed without official IOC interventions into the record books, but a history of clean performances was still marketed.

SNC's official promotional plan was extensive. It included regular reporting of results, submitting photographs and stories to the Canadian Press through Canadian Sport News, team media training by CBC and print reporters, one-on-one rookie media training at camps before major competitions with Penny Joyce, creating media-specific guides, preparing in-depth profiles on athletes and team officials, hosting pre-competition press conferences, and building a website with live broadcasts.[54] Coaches, sporting organizations, and the Canadian media have recently collaborated to school national athletes in media and public relations skills. With a few exceptions, the media has usually ignored amateur athletes outside of major international competitions. Thus, the reciprocal familiarity does not obtain at the same level as it does in the media's relationship to professional athletes.

Still, Swimming/Natation Canada is now considered to be one of the most media-savvy amateur sport organizations in the nation.[55] Formal media skills training for athletes and strategies for the active cultivation of relationships with reporters are well established. A bilingual staff of media, public relations, and communications people has consciously tried to be as professional as possible in terms of the standards of the media and their sponsors in the corporate sector.[56] This has led to the integration of image construction, sponsor servicing, athlete media training, and the use of a sport psychologist to enhance team cohesiveness and public relations. In turn, media and public relations training has hegemonically reconciled SNC officials, coaches, and athletes to a corporate agenda. The rhetoric of team cohesiveness on site fostered a vision of unified national teamship set firmly in the goals and values of Speedo, Maritime Life, and Sears.

As swimming has grown into a marquee Olympic sport, the CBC and a number of print reporters from major Canadian dailies have begun to cultivate longer term relationships with amateur swimming athletes. Journalists regularly covering swimming include: Suzanne Blake of *CBC Radio*, Steve Buffery of the *Toronto Sun*, James Christie of the *Globe and Mail*, Randy Starkman of the *Toronto Star*, Dave Stubbs of the *Montreal Gazette*, and Wendy Long of the

Vancouver Sun, among others. According to the media personnel who attended the 2000 Olympic Trials for the Canadian team, the reasons for fostering these relationships have included:

1. a genuine commitment on the part of some individual media personnel and the CBC to tell Canadian stories about amateur sport in Canadian culture;
2. the CBC has been mandated by the Canadian Radio-Television and Telecommunications Commission (CRTC) to tell a diversity of Canadian stories about amateur sport in Canadian culture;
3. swimming has long been a high-profile and "sexy" sport for attracting audiences and sponsors to media corporations;
4. the Canadian media predicted attention would be on swimming at the 2000 Games because Australians consider swimming to be the national sport and numerous world records were expected at the Sydney Olympics (due to the "fast pool" and to Speedo's "Fast Skin" suit); and
5. Canada was expected to win medals in the pool, which CBC had anticipated was required to keep audiences riveted to the television to produce high ratings.

However. cultivating long-term relationships with French language media across Canada and in Quebec was a difficult task for SNC, despite having a bilingual head coach and staff. Francophone media has not, according to Penny Joyce, regularly covered swimming unless there was a significant contingent of Francophone athletes on the team. Few Francophone media members attended the swimming trials, despite the location of the trials in Montreal, Quebec. Although two of the thirty-six athletes eventually named to the Olympic team during the trials were Francophone — Karine Chevrier and Karine Legault — the Francophone media left the swimming trials to camp outside the Maurice Richard Arena adjacent to the Olympic swimming pool. During the Olympic Trials, the legendary French-Canadian hockey player Maurice "The Rocket" Richard died and was given a state funeral in Montreal. Rather than watching swimmers, Francophone reporters were more interested in the conversion of The Rocket's statue into a shrine by mourners. Despite claiming to be "just a hockey player," Richard had signified the emergence of Quebec separatist nationalism following the 1955 hockey riot in Montreal.[57] Local CBC reporters covering the trials on 28 May 2000 used the Swim Canada Media Room to coordinate efforts to recruit a full camera crew over the phone to film children laying flowers at the feet of the statue. By lunch, a battle between mourners over which flag would drape the bronze body was settled and recorded by media: Quebec's flag was attached by duct tape and flew prominently from his shoulder, a Canadian flag was tucked into the crook of his arm, and a red home-knit Montreal Canadiens scarf was draped around the statue's neck. Each hour of pilgrimage to the shrine by fans provided the former swimming media from Francophone outlets with a new layer of identity to decipher. The Anglophone reporters from Toronto remained with the

swimming events. Political news journalists from their respective media organizations, not sports reporters, were assigned to The Rocket story for English-
speaking audiences.

Around the pool, Swimming/Natation Canada implemented a strict media
interview protocol. Head coach Dave Johnson in *A Media Guide for Coaches and
Their Athletes* outlined the justifications for such a protocol.[58] Johnson claimed
many reporters had often been confused about who was the most appropriate
person on the national team to answer various types of questions. He claimed
that interviewing the wrong person had resulted in the public being misin-
formed, that the privacy of swimmers was violated in the locker rooms, and
that some staff coaches made biased remarks about their club athletes on the
national team. To "unclutter" the process, yet to still be courteous and respect-
ful of media work, the protocol was instituted and strictly enforced.[59]

Athletes were expected to strictly adhere to the protocol, while Penny Joyce
and her SNC communications assistants endeavored to respond swiftly to all
media requests. Expediency of response was the major rule during the liaison's
labor process.[60] The six steps of the SNC media interview protocol were:

1. The media request is directed to the team media attache;
2. The request is communicated to the team leader or head coach;
3. The team leader or head coach receives approval for the interview from
   the swimmer's staff coach;
4. The time and place for the interview are established so that everything is
   as convenient as possible for the swimmer;
5. The team leader or head coach responds to the media attache; and,
6. The media attache responds to the reporter and sets up the interview.[61]

Many of the journalists who regularly covered swimming respected the protocol to maintain courteous relations with Swimming Canada until the Olympics. However, at the Olympic Games, some journalists planned to do whatever they needed to do to get the story, including yelling down to athletes from
the stands before they were interviewed by Australian or American rights
holders who were contractually in line before Canadian media,[62] and phoning
athletes directly on personal cellular phones to scoop competing media.[63]

The power to control media interactions rested in the hands of the head
coach and the communications director. Joyce could supply or deny media ac-
creditation to SNC events. Johnson enjoyed full control over when and where
athletes could speak to the media, as well as the subject matter. As well, Joyce
and Johnson insulated some athletes from the media: "If an athlete asks, or if
we feel an athlete is unfocused, we put them in the 'bubble' away from media."[64] Basically, the protocol was a mechanism for controlling athletes, branding SNC, and limiting access to athletes by the media. The protocol limited expression rights by stipulating who could speak on various topics to the media.
For example, only the head coach or the SNC chief executive officer could address controversial issues, such as drugs or the naming of an unqualified coach
to Olympic coach level. Also, the team's overall performance could be com-

mented on by the head coach alone, not by swimmers or their staff coaches on the team.

Protocol limitations were still subverted to an athlete's advantage if she or he did not want to speak to a member of the media because he or she was nervous, tired, or ill (as will be demonstrated in the next section), or wanted to avoid particular journalists. Athletes such as Joanne Malar, for example, have used protocol to stall the media. When Malar wanted to support a teammate still swimming at the Olympic Trials, or when she wanted to avoid emotional questions about the death of teammate Tara Sloan in Calgary just before the start of the Spring National Championships, she was unavailable for interview and protected by the SNC communications staff.

Ultimately, the protocol served to produce and maintain a protected image that SNC branded onto the national team in a manner intended to attract and retain sponsors. Johnson claimed:

> We are a high-profile sport, and it is important that when our athletes go into the public forum they are able to present themselves professionally. If they can come across as being very confident and capable, it reflects very positively on the sport and has an impact on the support and sponsorship side of our endeavors.[65]

Public conflicts between the sponsors, agents of individual athletes, and the team sponsors have been avoided by instilling athletes with a sense that it is a "privilege" to be on a national team and to be sponsored by multi/national corporations. During the Winnipeg media training session, for example, a male swimmer asked the media trainers:

> What do I do if the media asks me if the new Speedo *FastSkin* is helping my performance and I think it's a sham? I don't want to hurt the funding of other athletes by cutting up the sponsor, but I'm not going to risk wearing a full suit.[66]

The trainer replied:

> Protocol. You are only allowed to talk about individual performance, not give opinion about a new technology . . . Can't you wait six weeks until the Games are over? See how you do in Sydney and then decide if you have something to say about your performance in the suit.[67]

A few swimmers rolled their eyeballs as they glanced around the room. A veteran later confided that "if we don't do well at the 2000 Olympics, the media will not be interested in asking questions about our suits after the event." After the Olympics, athletes will be assumed to be responsible for their own "failure."[68] Athletes were divided about whether the new technology would shave a few hundredths of a second off their swimming times or whether the shoulder straps and restrictive limb coverings might hamper their mobility. By the end of three days of spin-doctoring sessions, all athletes adopted the standard response to swimsuit questions that had emerged during on-air practice sessions with the media trainers in Winnipeg: *"It's a matter of personal preference. I prefer to wear (full, tank top, jammer or /traditional) style of Speedo Fastskin because _____ ."* Athletes consented to self-censorship due to the pressures from SNC officials, the media trainers, protocol rules, a fear of letting down the team, as noted above, and to the unstated fear of being cut from the team and destroying the dream of competing at the Olympics.[69]

Veteran athletes with personal agents and sponsors also relinquished overall sponsorship rights to the corporate sponsors of SNC. The phenomenon of swimmers hiring agents to promote their personalities, sell their likenesses, and commodify their bodies has been recent. Penny Joyce admitted that the most frequent inquiries she fielded from athletes, parents, and coaches concerned sponsorship issues and the question, "who owns the image of an athlete?":

> When athletes begin to think of themselves as commodities, they ask questions about sponsorship. They are uncertain about sponsorship and logos. When they compete off shore in non-Olympic international events, they are not under the jurisdiction of the COA. The rules change from sport to sport as well, and from national organisation to organisation. We don't own them unless they are on a plane for us — on a trip for Swim Canada."[70]

Some athletes with individual sponsorship, such as Curtis Myden who has been sponsored by General Mills in 2000 and Met Life in 1996, still attended Maritime Life receptions leading up to the 2000 Olympic Games to sign autographs. Maritime Life sponsorship of SNC and the Olympic Trials conferred a contracted team obligation.[71]

Informing athletes and the Canadian media on the American-based globalized corporate values of Speedo and Maritime Life (a Canadian branch of John Hancock, Inc.) began long before the trials. Previous media training sessions for athletes, according to Jane Davies of Maritime Life, included her "PR perspective" [public relations] to help athletes better understand the partnership between SNC and her corporation, Maritime Life. Davies claimed the sponsor-SNC partnership worked because both organizations had the same goals: name awareness, relationship building, and an image of financial success. "Believe. Achieve. Success," the motto splashed across the Maritime Life Olympic Swim Trials posters for sale at the meet and on the program cover, were values that referred to the financial services business she worked in and to athletes' successes in the pool. At the Olympic Trials in May of 2000, SNC worked hard to promote swimming as a family-friendly sport to reinforce Maritime Life's promotion of family-sound financial products, such as insurance. In the year of the Sydney Summer Olympics, Maritime Life paid SNC $100,000 and provided t-shirts for swim meet officials in exchange for signage around the Olympic Trials pool, television coverage, reserved seating, and athlete services. Her goal at this event was to have 80 percent of media coverage report the corporate name "Maritime Life" in conjunction with mention of the Olympic Trials event, to get coverage in every major Canadian daily newspaper, and to increase the total number of media "impressions."[74] They achieved many broadcast mentions of the corporate name during CBC broadcasts, mainly because they were the title sponsor of the television show as well as the athletic event in Montreal. However, almost all print media refused to put a corporate title before "Olympic Swim Trials." The company has since broken away from sponsoring SNC. Maritime Life did not achieve its goals in sponsoring swimming, but believed SNC had benefited from globalized skills of the John Hancock corporation, which addressed event planning, strategic planning, public relations, and awareness of the "importance of constantly acknowledging marketing."[75]

SNC is now attempting to create fundamental shifts in the structure of the national sport organization towards focusing more on member services, supporting athletes and coaches at the elite level, promoting a "performance first" philosophy, and to attend to the needs of the national team within "corporate realities."[76] The key "reality" that emerged from the Sydney Olympics was that high performance sport could not cull excellence as its primary use-value to sell to corporations when few medals were won by Team Canada. The loss of Maritime Life as a title sponsor following the financial company's shift in marketing focus away from sport promotions, and the poor showing by the Canadian Olympic team at the Olympics in terms of medal yield, have led to further "rebranding" exercises by SNC to strengthen the financial support and image of the organization.[77] The continued expectations of medals and concerns for corporate needs are neither likely to shift the official corporatized identity of the national team, nor create an athlete-centered sport training system due to concerns of catering to corporate sponsors as the following section reveals.

V. Dying to Make the Team—Scooping the Guts and Perseverance Story

Perseverance was, and continues to be, a personality trait respected by athletes, coaches, media, and sponsors. Athletes at the Olympic Trials primarily wanted to qualify for the Sydney Olympic Team. Media members wanted to tell the stories of the process of achieving or failing this quest. To pursue the "Olympic Dream" at the Trials, despite earlier failures or significant personal sacrifices was, therefore, an "important and compelling story" to the media.[78] To pursue "The Dream" while suffering from life-threatening conditions became the coveted story for media during the Olympic Trials.

Owen von Richter's pursuit of a spot on the national swim team for the Sydney Olympics was a "guts and perseverance" story that exemplified how media narratives transposed identities. The media focus of the May 29th evening finals at the Olympic Trials demonstrated the naturalization of unhealthy performance expectations, revealed how nervous athletes used medical excuses and media protocol to avoid interviews, and exposed the competitive relationships between print journalists and the CBC to get the story. Before the start of the evening finals, Byron MacDonald (an on-air analyst for CBC) predicted competition that night would be full of "good theatre—with a very sick athlete and about five of his former girlfriends in the stands to cheer him on."[79] A few minutes later in the Media Room, Steve Buffery of the *Toronto Sun*, was asked [by the researcher] if he knew who the sick athlete was. He shrugged his shoulders and flatly said, "In this business you learn that if an athlete says they're not feeling well, it usually means they just aren't swimming well." This night, the CBC's broadcast team stumbled on a story Buffery had been investigating. A CBC interview after the men's 400-meter individual medley race, later broadcast by CBC on the 10th of June 2000, told the following story: Byron MacDonald (CBC poolside commentator):

> He's just about 10 seconds away from possibly making the Olympic team that he's waited seven years to make. The standard that he needs to make is 4:22:82 to be going to the Olympic games. He's under it! He'll be going to the Olympic Games. [*Close-up on von Richter with Maritime Life logo on clock above shoulder*] A long, long journey for Owen von Richter. A very popular winner in the men's 400-meter individual medley.

Steve Armitage (CBC poolside commentator):

> It was certainly one of those feel-good stories at the Olympic pool. [*CBC logo wipes screen, CBC Sports/Maritime Life Olympic Trials placement chart with race times superimposed on a high-angle pool shot*]. The man who beat Myden in '93, but watched the Games on CBC Television in '96, is finally getting a free ticket to his first Olympics. Guts and perseverance paid off big time for von Richter.

Brenda Russell (CBC post race interviewer on deck):

> [*Deckside interview: medium close-up on upper bodies of CBC's Russell and von Richter with a blue Maritime Life towel adorned with Olympic rings draped over his left shoulder*]. Well I guess I don't have to ask how you feel about this Olympic berth. It's been a long tough road.

Owen von Richter (swimmer):

> Ahh, it's been tough, unreal. This morning I swam really bad. And I was pretty much planning retirement all afternoon. And actually, I was going to scratch this morning, but-ta poppa-pee-poo-see-blahhhh [stutters]. Talked to a few people and calmed down. And I knew I didn't have my "A" swim in, so tonight I knew I had to work on my strengths. So I took it out nice and easy and it was there on the way home. Unreal! . . . I've just had so many problems, you know—healthwise. Its tough for your parents to see you in the hospital, pretty much almost dying, and then to have them support you, you know, getting back in the water. It's been tough. [*He looks up at family and friends in audience, puts his head back, thrusts his fists up and roars*] Yahhhhh!

Maritime Life Promotion:

> Be Focused. Be Driven. Believe. Maritime Life, Worldwide sponsor.

[Sponsor trailer at end of swimming segment leads into subsequent commercial break].

Print journalists were not on deck for the recording of the CBC interview. They eagerly waited their turn to interview von Richter in the Media Room on the 29th of May 2000. They waited for CBC television to finish interviews with the swimmer, his doping tests in the medical area, cool down in the pool, and then for Coach Johnson and medics to possibly grant permission for interviews. The journalists furiously typed their stories, checked their facts, and telephoned editors to update them on possible filing times. The race was over by 9 p.m. At 9:30 p.m., the journalists were getting dangerously close to their editors' deadlines at 10 p.m.

James Hood, a communications assistant for SNC at the Olympic Trials, was constantly badgered about when the swimmer would be available. Hood, normally the general manager of Swim Alberta, orchestrated the movement of athletes between media on and off camera at the Olympic Trials. He worked on the pool deck during broadcast taping, urged winning athletes out of the pool, put the title sponsor's logo towel on their shoulders, delivered them to deckside interviews with CBC, and then to interviews with SNC's Chris Wilson for the audience present at the Montreal Olympic pool. Hood then led winning athletes to the scrums in the Media Room and, finally, to sponsor receptions at the end of the night. Media and sponsor obligations often prevented athletes from savoring their moments of victory and the achievement of a lifelong dream to make an Olympic team by catering to the competitive pressures between media and sponsors. Hood finally arrived in the Media Room to announce von Richter would be there soon but was "nervous and upset."

Randy Starkman (*Toronto Star*): That's because he heard Steve Buffery is here.

Steve Buffery (*Toronto Sun*): Tell Owen to get his von Butt in here.

After this humorous bantering, Starkman and Buffery continued to debate who had the real "pipelines" in this sport and to discuss the politics of athlete media training. Buffery noted that he and the other journalists had known each other for about twelve years:

> We razz each other all the time. It's kind of a weird relationship—we're really good friends, but we drive each other nuts at events. Swimming's not too bad, but if you go to a world track and field championship you always keep one eye on the competition because you're paranoid about what they're doing and you're trying to concentrate on your own job. . . . You're trying to find the perfect angle—quietly. If you've got a great angle, the last thing you want to do is bring the guy in here where everyone hears your questions. . . . You either ask him as he's walking in, or walking out, or try to snag him to the side, or get him on the phone in his hotel in the afternoon.

James Christie of the *Globe and Mail* worked quietly with his back to the room.

Buffery worked with his back to the wall in a comer to protect his angles, while Starkman floated to different media desks throughout the evening. During the wait for the promised von Richter interview, Buffery analyzed the competitive pressures between print media, at the same time his ability to complete the journalistic task at hand was being delayed by CBC interviews on the pool deck, as well as team media protocol and pressures from one of the sponsors to have athletes attend a corporate client reception.

While waiting, Buffery continued to complain about the perceived effects of formal media training of athletes:

> Swimmers in particular are, I won't say "bad" because they're really great interviews, but they're controlled. That drives us nuts. I wish they'd be themselves. . . . It's hard, someone will come in here and we'll have, like, ten minutes with them. And there's four or five of us, and radio guys are trying to get sound bites. It's hard to pick up something about their career or even their personal life. It's tough. You'll see what happens — sometimes an athlete will say something interesting about themselves — like eight years ago Marianne Limpert told us she was born in a little Inuit village in Northern Quebec because her father was a helicopter pilot and her mother went into labor. So her father landed in this little Inuit village. And all of us zeroed in on that and of course it was in everyone's story the next day.

After this story, Buffery described how he hated cliches and technical answers from swimmers. He also revealed that the number one rule among sports journalists was not to "piggyback" on another journalist's interview with an athlete outside of press conference and scum situations, but noted that this still occurred in competitive situations at important Olympic, World, and professional events.

Humor was employed to manage the stress of deadlines and SNC's prohibitive protocol. Coach Johnson entered and conducted a telephone interview with the media, as they grew impatient. While on the phone, Starkman chided the coach for his athlete's tardiness when the coach was not listening. Penny Joyce entered the Media Room and was tackled with questions about the athlete's whereabouts. They were told, "He's still in the building;" they were not informed that he was fulfilling a team obligation by attending a Maritime Life reception. The journalists assumed the rights holding broadcaster, CBC, was still interviewing him.

Buffery: Did he drown? Where is he? I want to ask him some questions. I'm not asking him to marry me.

Starkman: Is CBC doing a "Life and Times" piece on him? [*Laughter*]

Joyce: Buff, I want you off my back.

Despite SNC's strict protocol about who, when, and what could be communicated to the media, the hierarchy of official sources was contested terrain. The news media normally imposes its own division of labor on sources: primary sources have official status and authority, and have typically been asked to speak rationally and strategically in ways that concerned the exercise of effective authority, problem solving, or action-taking. Secondary sources for news have been often called upon to speak emotionally about their experiences. But athletes embodied both aspects of types of sources despite protocol attempting to locate political issues, technique expertise, and team performance analysis solely at the level of the head coach. Athletes were experts at a corporeal level and had the sporting experience level that media wanted to know about. Buffery was the only journalist to have finished his story. He just wanted a quote from the athlete at the center of the story to get a combination of primary and secondary sources of insight.

To pass time, Buffery pestered Starkman. Starkman was criticized for his failure to know von Richter was a local boy: von Richter's hometown was Mississauga, a city adjacent to Toronto where both journalists worked. New to the swimming beat, Buffery has brought a guarded and punchy style of interaction into the media room from previous experiences garnered covering boxing and track and field. His colleagues called him a "bulldog" reporter. According to Buffery, at track events, journalists "mentally and physically beat each other up" in tight holding areas reserved for media scrums. Buffery has also covered Winter Olympic sports and has developed tactics to encourage Olympic broadcasting rights holders to relinquish athletes to the print media:

Buffery:

> The CBC monopolized short track speed skaters in Nagano. We had deadlines, so the journalists started shouting "we want a quote, we want a quote" to shut down their feed [by interrupting CBC]. Now I really want Owen so I can just have a beer, but I don't want to interview him in here with these guys around.

Matt Charbonneau, a Swim Canada communications assistant entered and responded to a battery of questions regarding von Richter's whereabouts.

Charbonneau: Owen's M.I.A.[80] now.

Starkman: Isn't it M.I.D.? Missing in Doping?

Charbonneau: No. I wish he was in doping 'cause then I could hunt him.

Buffery: What's that mean though? Is he sick or something?

Charbonneau: No, it means he's far too excited, he's having dinner with his parents and two girls who were crying in the stands.

James Hood finally entered with the "flash quote" he had obtained from von Richter. He set up his tape recorder on Buffery's desk. Hood proclaimed the athlete to be "fine." "He was just a little too excited for his own good. By the time he finished cool-down, he just wanted to have dinner and maybe a hug."

Buffery: I'll give him a hug if it means getting an interview.

Hood: He almost died with a heart problem at altitude.

Buffery: Don't tell everybody that [Buffery quietly pleaded to Hood, who did not hear due to the cross talk with other reporters].

As journalists gathered around Buffery's desk to listen to the audio clip of the athlete who was avoiding them, Starkman teased Hood, "We're trying to do our job and you didn't do your job," he said. Hood repeated the near-death story and elaborated as Buffery looked angry and then defeated. The flash quote dealt with von Richter's poor swim in the morning heats when he was "unshaved and unrested." The athlete said nothing about his health in the flash quote in the recording. The full quote was replayed a few times. Starkman was more interested in gathering further details about the near-death experience from Hood, than he was in listening to the tape about race strategies again. No one asked if von Richter was in any danger swimming at the trials. The perseverance story detailing von Richter's seven-year wait to make the Olympic "cut" suddenly became a sacrificial story of putting one's heart literally on the line to compete for Canada. "Guts" was more poetic than technique when telling stories about graduation from a local Toronto club scene to the national Olympic team.

Buffery quietly fumed. The other journalists had scooped the story he had been working on for weeks about von Richter's "near-death" story. Unfortunately for Buffery, Hood had overheard the earlier taping of the CBC pool deck interview. CBC would not be broadcasting the story for two weeks. Most of the journalists were pleased to scoop CBC due to timing. Buffery, on the other hand, had been the sole journalist who had uncovered and researched the sacrifice and danger angle before the race. He felt he owned the story. Buffery pointed to his laptop screen, as the other journalists rushed back to their desks to rewrite their articles:

There's my story as it was written, I'm so pissed. Oh, well. You do what you gotta do. You win some, you lose some. It's not Hood's fault — with von Richter M.I.A. he had to give us some crumbs.[81]

In the end, the relations that athletes were expected to build with print journalists and broadcast media before the Olympics were traded off in favor of corporate public relations. In this case, an athlete was able to use interview protocol to his advantage to avoid media interviews due to nervousness and exhaustion from the competition; yet he was not able to avoid all team obligations and chose to attend the corporate reception rather than be surrounded in a scrum of reporters in the Media Room. Protocol did, indeed, serve as a gatekeeping device for access to athletes and particular storylines at the trials. Competing for Canada was a dream, a goal, and a sacrifice for which at least one athlete was willing to put his life on the line. Traditionally, the discourse of sacrifice has referred to the long hours of training and narrowed life-choices that delay schooling, work, and relationships for national team athletes. In other words, the sacrifice narrative in media coverage once referred primarily to dedication within sport. However, for athletes like swimmer von Richter, the willingness to die for one's country in an attempt to win a berth on the national team took the risk to a new level.

Corporate nationalist discourse and nationalist corporate discourse are *particular systems of representations* that are historically constructed and struggled over. Discourse was introduced earlier in terms of *meaning making*, following the notion of O'Sullivan et al.,[82] but discourse is also about *claims making*. That is, the politicization of discourse is built into the way it functions as a strategic resource in social interaction as an ongoing struggle over interests, benefits, and successes. Everyone in the chain of relations at the Olympic Trials, national championships, and training had strategic interests at stake, and part of the claims-making process was about taking and being given credit for success. The field of corporatized nationalism discourse has become another second-order competition over the distribution of responsibility. Sacrifice as a storyline. the media claimed, has been able to create lines of instant identification with audiences. Nationalism was a narrative that was taken for granted as something that would sell by SNC and the CBC. However, at the same time, the use of nationalism in this context not only reproduced a general sense of nationalism that reminded readers and viewers who they were and how they possibly should have felt about it. It also articulated nationalism to specific practices (such as overcoming barriers and hardships, or facing one's fears).

Thus, following Andrew Wernick's notion of promotionalism,[83] the celebration of an official team nationalism as the team was chosen at the trials promoted another cluster of corporate values—*"be focused, be driven, believe"* inferring that audiences/ consumers need financial products to protect the financial well-being of the family. Corporations, in turn, promoted nationalism backing the notion of: "believe" in the Olympic dream of success and "be driven" to achieve it for the nation. The lack of medals won by the swim team at the 2000 Olympics (except one bronze medal by Curtis Myden), and the Canadian media coverage of the 2000 Olympic Games as the "disappointment games,"[84] resulted in public calls for greater government funding.[85] This provided SNC with a renewed impetus for a commitment to winning medals to celebrate excellence in high performance sport and to attract corporate funding. The CEO, Harold Cliff, was fired after the Sydney Olympics, and the Board of Directors negotiated a four-year plan based on a philosophy of "performance first" intent on positioning "our athletes on the podium."[86] Hall has argued, "History does not 'make' discourses, discourses make history."[87] Corporatized discourse did indeed make history as it was the dominant discourse that mediated the events and relationships of the Olympic Trials and media training of the national swim team headed to Sydney.

VI. Concluding Comments

This ethnography has examined the politics of corporatized identity that mediated relationships between national team athletes, media, sponsors, media attaches, and other sporting officials. The images of the national team and corporate visions of the nation(s) of Canada were abstract in meaning but experienced in concrete forms such as in the media productions of sport and related promotions for the 2000 Olympics. The examination of contested imagined visions of nationalism during preparations of the National Swim Team for the 2000 Olympics Games revealed multiple layers of "team cohesion" discourses which were employed by the head coach, media trainers, SNC officials, and sponsors during swim and media training to position the official identity. This narrative of daily team interaction mediated public and private team interactions but served, ultimately, to prioritize a corporatized mission for SNC. The formal national team identity of "clean" athletes committed to high performance goals has tended to marginalize the values and identities of athletes during public appearances. Communications about SNC programs, athletes, and their accomplishments in the pool were carefully crafted, branded, and circulated back to the media and Canadian public with values preferred by sponsors.

Moreover, the investigation of the pre-Olympic media training uncovered the lack of athlete-centeredness and abuse of basic human rights. Training that reinforced SNC interview protocol denied athletes the constitutional right to freedom of expression when athletes were told not to speak negatively about sponsors' products, told not to discuss team performances, and warned not to discuss political issues affecting SNC and the team, such as the hiring of an under-qualified female coach. Only the head coach and SNC executives were permitted to comment on such matters to the media. With such a small "window" of peak athletic performance and four years between each set of Summer Olympic Games, athletes were not willing to break protocol for fear of being dropped from the team. Moreover, the hierarchy of official sources created by SNC protocol functioned as filtration devices when problematic events or actions arose. With respect to controversial issues, the institutionalization of the protocol acted as a gate-keeping system to control media access to athletes and to allow SNC to reduce symbolic and financial damage.

Finally, the corporatization of high performance sport through exclusivity agreements for team sponsorship and title sponsorship of events, created tensions between (1) the media and SNC over access to athletes compared to sponsors for their receptions and public relations events; (2) between exclusive media and non-rights holding media created by interview protocol and exclusivity rights; and (3) between media over the issue of CBC's conflict of interest in the network's direct involvement in media skills training because Olympic coverage by the network spanned both entertainment and news formats that meant current and retired CBC announcers were informing the very sporting and political news they were reporting on at the Olympic Trials and Games.

Thus, it is clear that corporatized identity discourses were both descriptive and productive of the social reality of relationships and images forged between sponsors, Swimming/Natation Canada, athletes, media, and media skills trainers. We argue that media skills and public relations training needs to be resituated first and foremost within a human rights perspective to achieve an athlete-centered approach to high performance sport and to democratize the relationships between athletes, national sporting organizations, media, and sponsors that are currently imbalanced in the exclusive rights setting.

Notes

1. A preliminary version of this article was presented at the *Fifth International Symposium for Olympic Research, Bridging Three Centuries: Intellectual Crossroads and the Modern Olympic Movement* (Sydney, Australia, September 2000) and is published in the proceedings edited by Kevin B. Wamsley et al. (London, ON: University of Western Ontario/International Centre for Olympic Studies, 2000), pp. 17–28. The authors would like to thank the two anonymous reviewers for their helpful suggestions, the Social Sciences and Humanities Research Council for funding this research, and all the athletes, media, and sporting officials who allowed us to enter their training and work spaces to observe the culture of high performance sport.

2. David Rowe, *Sport, Culture and the Media* (Buckingham: Open University Press, 1999), p. 23.

3. See, for example, Canadian political-economic studies such as: John Barnes, *Sports and the Law in Canada*, 3rd edition (Toronto: Butterworths, 1996); Rob Beamish, "Socio-Economic and Demographic Characteristics of the National Executives of Selected Amateur Sports in Canada," *Working Papers in the Sociology in the Sociological Study of Sports and Leisure 1* (Kingston: Queen's University, 1978); Eric Broom and Richard Baka, *Canadian Governments and Sport* (Ottawa: CAHPER Sociology of Sport Monograph Series, 1978); Varda Burstyn, *The Rites of Men: Manhood, Politics, and the Culture of Sport* (Toronto: University of Toronto Press, 1999); Hart Cantelon, *Leisure, Sport, and Working Class Cultures* (Toronto: Garamond Press. 1988); Hart Cantelon and Richard Gruneau, *Sport, Culture and the Modern State* (Toronto: University of Toronto Press, 1982); Peter Donnelly and Jean Harvey, "Class and Gender: Intersections in Sport and Physical Activity," Eds., Philip White and Kevin Young, *Sport and Gender in Canada* (Toronto: Oxford University Press, 1999), pp. 40–64; Richard Gruneau, "Commercialism and the Modern Olympic Games," Eds., Alan Tomlinson and Garry Whannel, *Five Ring Circus: Money, Power, and Politics at the Olympic Games*, (London: Pluto Press, 1984), pp. 1–15; Richard Gruneau, *Class, Sports, and Social Development* (Champaign: Human Kinetics Press, 1999); Jean Harvey and Roger Proulx. "Sport and the State in Canada," Eds., Jean Harvey and Hart Cantelon, *Not Just*

a Game: Essays in Canadian Sport Sociology (Ottawa: University of Ottawa Press), pp. 93–119; Bruce Kidd, *The Political Economy of Sport* (Calgary: Canadian Association for Health, Physical Education and Recreation, 1979); Bruce Kidd with Mary Eberts, *Athletes Rights in Canada* (Toronto: Ontario Ministry of Tourism and Recreation, 1982); Bruce Kidd and John MacFarlane, *The Death of Hockey* (Toronto: New Press, 1972); Bruce Kidd, *The Struggle for Canadian Sport* (Toronto: University of Toronto Press, 1996); Donald Macintosh, with Tom Bedecki and C.E.S. Franks, *Sports and Politics in Canada: Federal Government Involvement since 1961* (Montreal/Kingston: McGill-Queen's University Press, 1987); Donald Macintosh and Michael Hawes, *Sport and Canadian Diplomacy* (Montreal/Kingston: McGill-Queen's University Press, 1994); Donald Macintosh and Dave Whitson, *The Game Planners: Transforming Canada's Sport System* (Montreal/Kingston: McGill-Queen's University Press, 1990).

4. Recent developments in research examining commodified images and issues of identity have emerged primarily in postmodern studies of sport. See, for example, David Andrews, "Michael Jordan: A Commodity-Sign of [post] Reaganite Times," in *Working Papers in Popular Cultural Studies 2*, no. 1, (1984) pp. 1–50. Cheryl Cole and Amy Hribar, "Celebrity Feminism: *Nike Style* Post Fordism, Transcendence, and Consumer Power, *Sociology of Sport Journal 12*, no.4, 347–369. Melisse Lafrance, "Colonizing the Feminine: Nike's Intersections of Post-feminism and Hyperconsumption," in Ed., Genevieve Rail, *Sport and Postmodern Times* (New York: SUNY Press, 1998), pp. 117–139.

5. Ethnographic research about the production of commodified sporting images include Richard Gruneau's research about World Cup Skiing, Margaret Mac-Neill's study about Olympic ice hockey, and Michael Silk's study of the Commonwealth Games: Richard Gruneau, "Making Spectacle: A Case Study in Televised Sport Production," Ed., Lawrence Wenner, *Media, Sports and Society* (Newbury Park, CA: Sage, 1989). pp. 134–154; Margaret MacNeill, "Networks: Producing Olympic Ice Hockey for a National Television Audience," *Sociology of Sport Journal 13*, pp. 103–24; Michael Silk, "Together We're One? The 'Place' of the Nation in Media

Representations of the 1998 Kuala Lumpur Commonwealth Games," *Sociology of Sport Journal 18*, pp. 277–301.

6. Andrew Wernick, *Promotional Culture* (Thousand Oaks, CA: Sage, 1991).

7. Maritime Life Website, "Sponsorship: Teamwork, Performance, Achievement," *Maritime Life* (<Maritimelife.ca/mainWWW/MLAC...entLook up/SiteMainContent-SponsorMain?Op>, November 2001).

8. Commodification, to adapt the work of Bero Rigauer, is the process and product of producing someone [e.g., an athlete] or some thing [e.g., gold medal Olympic performances and world records] "not to satisfy the producer's needs but to be exchanged in the marketplace for other values" such as money. See Bero Rigauer, *Sport and Work*, trans., Allen Guttmann (New York: Columbia University Press, 1969/1981), p. 67.

9. The new Speedo suits were banned at the Olympic Trials because the company could not produce enough for all competitors. The CBC coverage of the Olympic Trials still contained a segment in Part I of the broadcast (10 June 2000), in which commentator Byron MacDonald modeled a suit and explained the new technology of the fabric. Part II, broadcast on June 17, 2000 included the Vice-President of Speedo explaining how the protests against the suits were being leveled by athletes or nations who were sponsored by Speedo's competitors. Penny Joyce, the Director of Corporate Communications and Media Officer, noted that the French non-sport media were very intrigued by the technological angle on the suit story (interview by Margaret MacNeill, tape recording, Montreal, 27 May 2000).

10. After the 2000 Olympics, *Swimming World* has become a promotional vehicle to immortalize the "technological advancement" of the new swimsuit. Inside covers of this leading periodical — subscribed to by athletes, coaches, and media — contained full-page advertisements with an image of American Swimmer Jenny Thompson. The ads announced the number of world records, Olympic records, and medals garnered by athletes wearing the *Fastskin* suit. After the Sydney Olympics, Speedo's American-owned parent company, Warnico, filed for bankruptcy. Speedo is one of the few profitable arms of Warnico, which has avoided bankruptcy after acquiring loans according to Byron MacDonald, a CBC swimming commentator (interview by Margaret MacNeill, telephone, 4 October 2001). Speedo continues to support SNC and has reassured this sports organization that it continues

to be financially secure (interview with Penny Joyce by Margaret MacNeill, telephone, 5 October 2001).

11. Benedict Anderson, *Imagined communities: Reflections on the origin and spread of nationalism* (New York: Verso, 1991; revised edition/1983). p. 4.

12. Ibid, p. 6.

13. Ibid.

14. Margaret MacNeill, "Canadian Culture and the Politics of Identity," in *iichiko intercultural*, no. 69, p. 119.

15. CBC negotiated a partnership with The Sports Network, a 24-hour a day Canadaian sports channel, to cover certain team sports (such as basketball) in their entirety. CBC was still contractually considered the "host" broadcaster for the nation and TSN crews were under the executive producership of CBC's Joel Darling.

16. Stuart Hall, "Cultural Studies: Two Paradigms in Cultural Studies," in Tony Bennett, ed., *Culture, Ideology and Social Processes* (London: Bratsford Press, 1989), pp. 19–39.

17. Homi Bhabha, *The Location of Culture* (London: Routledge. 1994).

18. CBC executives, such as Nancy Lee (Head of CBC Sports) and Joel Darling (Executive Producer of CBC's 2000 Olympic Summer Games) assumed that "all" Canadians would watch the Games for at least 15 minutes each based on accumulative audience ratings from the 1996 Atlanta Games. When asked if they would be cultivating particular segments of the audience, they answered "no" because they simply assumed that CBC's Canadian "stories" from the Sydney Games would speak to all citizens (interview by Margaret MacNeill and Peter Donnelly, tape recording, Toronto, 19 July 2000). Maritime Life marketing spokesperson, Jane Davies, imagined the nation to be families (interview by Margaret MacNeill, tape recording, Montreal, 27 May 2000).

19. Catherine Palmer, "Outside the imagined community: Basque terrorism, political activism, and the Tour de France," *Sociology of Sport Journal 18*, pp. 143–161.

20. Ibid, p. 159.

21. P. Hall, *The social construction of nationalism* (Lund, Sweden: Lund University Press, 1998), p. 253.

22. Tim O'Sullivan, et al., *Key concepts in communication and cultural studies, 2nd ed.* (New York: Routledge, 1994), p. 236.

23. Macintosh and Whitson, pp. 67–68.

24. Today, Sport Canada is a branch of the federal Department of Canadian Heritage within the Canadian Identity Sector (until the

mid 1990s Sport Canada was a junior ministry of the former Ministry of Health and Welfare).

25. Macintosh and Whitson, p. 68.

26. Sport Canada, "Sport Canada Funding Programs", Sport Canada (<www.pch.gc.ca/SportcanaddSc_eEscC.html>, 5 October 2001), pp. 1–2.

27. At present, SNC governs 350 clubs, 50,000 competitive swimmers, and 75,000 other people in programs such as the "Sears, I Can Swim" program.

28. Swimming Canada, "Association Profile" (<www.swimming.ca/profile.html>, 3 October 2001).

29. Joyce, interview, 27 May 2000.

30. Victor Head, *Sponsorship: The Newest Marketing Skill* (Cambridge: Woodhead-Faulkner, 1982).

31. Chris Gratton and Peter Taylor, *Economics of Sport and Recreation* (London: E & FP Spon), pp. 175–6.

32. See Laurel Richardson, "Writing a Method of Inquiry," in Norman K. Denzin and Yvonna S. Lincoln, eds., *Handbook of Qualitative Research* (Thousand Oaks, CA: Sage, 1994) pp. 516–529.

33. Ibid.

34. Tom Mayenknecht, media training presentation, video-taped, Winnipeg, 7 August 2000.

35. Maritime Life Website, "Financial Strength," *Maritime Life* <Maritimelife.ca/ mainWWW/MLAC...entLookup/SiteMainContent-strength?Op>), November 2001).

36. Steve Armotage, CBC swim commentator, interview by Margaret MacNeill, tape recording, Montreal, 29 May 2000.

37. Tom Mayenknecht and Fred Walker, *Media Training Workshop Notes* (Winnipeg: The Media Institute, 7 August 2000), p. 1.

38. Moreover, the involvement of the CBC sports personnel in media skills training for the SNC was seen to be a conflict of interest by some print and broadcast news journalists covering the Olympics, such as Randy Starkman of the *Toronto Star* (interview by Margaret MacNeill, in transit to Sydney, 5 September 2000) and Robin Brown of *CBC Radio* (interview by Margaret MacNeill, taping recording, Toronto, 31 August 2000).

39. Dave Stubbs, "Buying into the System," *The Montreal Gazette* (<www.montrealgazette.com/sports/pages/00602/4206585.html>, June 2, 2000).

40. James Christie, "Abstinence again Golden Rule for Canadian Swimmers, *Globe and Mail* (June, 5, 2000), p. A5.

41. Swimming/Natation Canada, *1999 Annual Report* (Ottawa: <www.swimming.ca>, 1999), p. 7.

42. During the Olympic Trials, Swimming Canada distributed a press release that announced Joanne Malar (who earlier rejected a citizenship offer from Australia to swim for their national team) and 1996 Olympic silver medalist Marianne Limpert were no longer bitter enemies. The team psychologist had intervened. Although they competed in the same event, the 200-meter individual medley, the media transposed the reconciliation as a joining of forces for Canada to take on the world at the Olympics.

43. Dave Johnson (head coach), interview by Margaret MacNeill, tape recording, Montreal, 27 May 2000.

44. Dave Johnson, Pre-Olympic Trials press conference, video recording, Montreal, 25 May 2000.

45. Johnson, interview.

46. Davies, interview.

47. Female national team member, interview by Margaret MacNeill, video recording, Montreal, 29 May 2000.

48. Armitage, interview.

49. Davies, interview.

50. Johnson, interview.

51. Brown, interview.

52. Joyce, interview, 27 May 2000.

53. Head coach Johnson claimed that no Canadian on the national team has ever had a positive drug test, although at least one Canadian competing for an American University has tested positive (interview).

54. SNC, pp. 22–24; Joyce, interview, 27 May 2000.

55. Starkman, interview.

56. Joyce interview, 17 May 2000; Johnson interview.

57. See Jean R. Dupereault, "L'Affaire Richard: A Situational Analysis of the Montreal Hockey Riot of 1955." *Canadian Journal of History of Sport*, May 1981, Vol. XII, No. 1. pp. 66–83.

58. Dave Johnson and Sheila Robertson, "Why a Media Interview Request Protocol: Swimming Head Coach Dave Johnson Explains." In Sheila Robertson, ed., *A Media Guide For Athletes and Their Coaches* (Ottawa: Canadian Association for the Advanced of Women in Sport and Canadian Coaching Association), pp. 71–72.

59. Ibid.

60. She was hired by the COA to serve as the media liaison for the swimming and beach volleyball events at the Sydney Olympic Games.

61. Dave Johnson and Sheila Robertson, pp. 71–72. The strict media protocol demonstra-

ted that athlete-centeredness was not being realized as a primary philosophy mediating the rules, practices, and relationships. The formal strategic priorities of Swim/Natation Canada between 1999 and 2004 included: pursue world championship, Olympic, and Paralympic medals; provide a holistic training environment for athletes and coaches through the network of national swimming centers; develop events and properties to increase exposure and sponsorship; capitalize on technological advantages to effectively communicate to SNC members; and revise and implement the swimming development model (SNC, p. 7).

62. Armitage, interview.

63. Steve Buffery, *Toronto Sun* Reporter, tape recording, interview by Margaret Mac-Neill, Montreal, 29 May 2000.

64. Joyce, interview, 28 May 2000.

65. Johnson and Robertson, p. 72.

66. Male national team swimmer, media skills workshop, video recording, Winnipeg, 7 August 2000.

67. Tom Mayenknecht, media skills workshop facilitation, video recording, 7 August 2000.

68. Male national team swimmer, interview by Margaret MacNeill, tape recording, 7 August 2000.

69. Ann Peel, former chair of Athletes' Can, telephone communication with Margaret Mac-Neill, 15 October 1999. This observation by Ann Peel was made after almost a decade of interaction with national team members of Athlete's Can.

70. Penny Joyce, interview by Margaret MacNeill, telephone, 9 May 2000.

71. Davies, interview.

72. Maritime Life was the title sponsor for both the Trials in Montreal and CBC's national television coverage of the event. It is the Canadian subsidiary of the American-based John Hancock company (a TOP sponsor of the Olympics).

73. Jane Davies, the public relations specialist from title sponsor Maritime Life, had two official roles at the Olympic Trials: (1) to support Penny Joyce and the Swim Canada communications and media relations staff to pull together the six months of planning regarding signage for the title sponsor and relations with CBC to "maximize the name awareness component of Maritime Life," and (2) to manage her company's hospitality program. The Olympic Trials was her last "gig" with sports marketing. She was to be moved to a new portfolio in promoting financial services after the trials. Maritime Life was not present at the Olympics because its parent company, John Hancock, was the exclusive TOP partner (Davis, interview). After the 2000 Games, Maritime Life did not renew its sponsorship of Swim Canada. Penny Joyce, the corporate communications director for SNC, claimed the parting was amicable and that Maritime Life had moved out of sports sponsorship completely (Joyce, interview, 5 October 2001). This decision may be a response to John Hancock's temporary break from the IOC in 1999 in the wake of the bribery scandal regarding the 2002 Salt Lake City Games and the low number of medals earned by swimmers at the 2000 Olympic Games.

74. Athletes earned $150 for each broadcast clip that framed them wearing the blue Maritime Life towel on their shoulder during media interviews according to Davies (interview).

75. Maritime Life personnel and signage were not at the 2000 Summer Olympic Games because, as mentioned earlier, John Hancock Insurance, its parent company, focused on its global name in Sydney. At the Montreal Olympic Swimming trials, title sponsorship reigned supreme leading the liaison to proclaim, "This is my Olympics" (Davies, interview).

76. Ken Radford, "Notes from the Acting Executive Director, *Swimming/Natation Canada E-News* (<www.swimming.ca>, July 2001), p. 2.

77. Joyce, interview, 5 October 2001.

78. Armitage, interview.

79. MacDonald, interview, 29 May 2001.

80. M.I.A. is a military acronym for "missing in action."

81. Buffery, interview.

82. Tim O'Sullivan et al., 1994.

83. Andrew Wernick, *Promotional Culture* (Thousand Oaks, CA: Sage, 1991).

84. Graham Knight, "The Disappointment Games," forthcoming.

85. Graham Knight, panel presentation on "Nationalism and Olympic Sport," *Annual Conference for the North American Society for the Sociology of Sport* (Colorado Springs, 6 November 2000).

86. Rob Colburn (Acting President of Swimming/Natation Canada), "Notes from the Acting President", *Swimming/Natation Canada E-News 1* (<www.swimming.ca>. July 2001), p. 1.

87. Hall, *The social construction of nationalism*, p. 6.

THE JUXTAPOSITION OF SPORT AND COMMUNICATION: DEFINING THE FIELD OF SPORT COMMUNICATION

Paul M. Pedersen, Pamela C. Laucella,
Kimberly S. Miloch, and Larry W. Fielding

Introduction

Sport communication has progressed from a field primarily consisting of print sport journalism to a multi-faceted and multi-billion-dollar industry with significant potential for continued growth. The $4.48 billion television agreement that begins in 2007 between the National Association for Stock Car Auto Racing (NASCAR) and four US networks is only one of myriad examples that can be used to illustrate the growing significance of sport communication in the sport industry. The growth in sport communication has been witnessed around the globe. As Grainger and Andrews (2005) commented:

> Given both the broad appeal of global sporting mega-events as well as regional interest in televised coverage of local teams and competitions, it is perhaps hardly surprising that sport has become a central component of the strategies of the global media. (p. 4)

In an examination of mediated sport, Bernstein and Blain (2002) noted that, "sport and the media have become associated to such an extent that it is often difficult to discuss sport in modern society without acknowledging its relationship with media" (p. 3). Although such a statement expresses the significance of sport and the media, the field of sport communication goes beyond this. The discipline of sport communication today is expansive as it encompasses everything from interpersonal relationships, public relations, and electronic media to advertising, theory, research, and emerging technologies. Its activities include a conversation between two front office professionals with Real Madrid and a live chat on the Frankfurt Galaxy's website to a podcast of Olympic highlights or the broadcast of the Super Bowl.

Recognizing the growing and broad nature of sport communication, a need exists for a conceptual examination of the field. To appropriately evaluate and illustrate the facets and interrelated aspects of a discipline, sport scholars have often relied on conceptual frameworks (Pitts et al., 1994; Van Leeuwen et al.,

2002; Westerbeek & Shilbury, 2003). Such examinations allow for the appropriate illustrations and definitions of a specific discipline and provide a foundation for the development of multiple areas of scholarly inquiry. They assist researchers in the identification of the "big picture" while recognizing the concepts and variables that impact the nature and scope of the discipline. A conceptual analysis of the field of sport communication should present the sport communication process and classify its distinct aspects presenting both micro and macro perspectives of the discipline. Therefore, the purpose of this analysis is to examine the nature and scope of sport communication and define its role within the study of sport. Specifically, this research codifies the definitional elements and presents a conceptual perspective of this emerging field.

Defining Sport Communication

Although the intersection of sport and communication has been examined for nearly a half-century, the juxtaposition of these two areas into an academic discipline is a recent phenomenon. Because of this relatively young existence, there is a need to define sport communication and its various components. As Costa (2005) explained in an analysis of sport management, "an exploration of who we are" is one of the "pivotal realms of self-exploration for a young field that seeks to establish itself and its relevance" (p. 118). Studying sport communication is more complicated than analyzing the textual, production, and reception domains of the sport media.

There are many aspects beyond the sport media that constitute sport communication. These aspects—extrapolated from Burton (2002) and applied to the sport context—include such areas as sport communication institutions, production systems, conditions, and sport communication meanings. Sport communication institutions include entities that own and operate sport media or the departments of public and media relations in sport entities. Production systems include those activities that center on developing the content and context of sport messages disseminated to mass and niche audiences. Conditions refer to the setting where sport communication takes place while sport communication meanings refer to the examination of sport audiences. All of these aspects can be found in the definitional examination of sport communication below. The analysis includes an evaluation of the sport communication process, the various communication channels and transfer of messages, the senders and receivers of messages, the language used to create symbolism and meaning of messages, and communication as interaction.

The communication process is quite complex and because of this complexity it is challenging to define (Battenfield, 2004). The same can be said of sport communication. A primal definition of sport communication denotes the discipline as an exchange of sport related and non-sport related information occurring through sport. However, to truly recognize the broad scope of the discipline, a more complex definition is most appropriate. Sport communication is a process by which people in sport, in a sport setting, or through a sport endeavor, share symbols as they create meaning through interaction. Like John

Dewey, Robert Park, and other Chicago School sociologists, who viewed communication as "an active process of community creation and maintenance" (Carey, 1997, p. 26), this definition stems from a cultural approach to examining communication. Although its foundation is in the definition of communication offered by Heath and Bryant (2000), by integrating every aspect of communication through sport and in sport, this definition clearly denotes the broad scope of the discipline. It encompasses interpersonal sport communication, group sport communication, mediated sport communication, and any other type of communicative activity in sport. This analysis proposes the following definition: sport communication is a process by which people in sport, in a sport setting, or through a sport endeavor, share symbols as they create meaning through interaction. This definition contains five unique elements, each of which is detailed below.

"Sport communication is a process . . .

The definition's foundation relies on mass communication theory, which provides insight into the study of sport communication and specifically into its process. A theoretical definition needs to include more than "theory as abstract ideas and theory as predictable findings" (Chaffee, 1996, p. 15) in order to capture the complexity of the term and its fundamental processes. Theory also includes concept explication, which links and connects abstract theory with a more positivist view of knowledge and replicable results. Empirical theory elucidates interrelationships between independent and dependent variables at the conceptual level, exposition of concepts and definitions, and the ensuing findings at the operational level. Therefore, the whole process—from the original idea to the hypotheses, literature review, and research—comprises theorizing and fosters intellectually rigorous and thought-provoking research (Chaffee, 1996).

In sport communication, the theorizing process includes both the academic field of research as well as the practical side of the sport industry, and falls in the "process" section of the definition. Scholars conduct sound research in the quantitative and qualitative traditions using content analysis, surveys, narrative analysis, oral history, and other methods to delve into the many intricacies of sport communication. They study everything from sports journalists' routines and the selection of content; the explicit and implicit meanings of sport texts and the emerging narratives and frames; the ratings of programs like ESPN's *The Sports Reporters* and network game broadcasts; and the financial implications and value of the Wimbledon Championships or the Australian Grand Prix; to human communication in day-to-day activities and interactions at leagues, clubs, teams, sport organizations, university athletic offices, and media outlets.

As evident in the examples above, sport communication is a dynamic process that includes active, interactive, and reactive processes between institutions, texts, and audiences in the public sphere. Sport, according to Wenner (1998), "has always been a conduit or medium through which feelings, values, and priorities are communicated" (p. xiii). Media organizations, networks, leagues, sport organizations, fans, and audiences communicate with each other and through each other. While most entities seek profit first and foremost, communication is a vital element of every single activity and function in sport. Networks seek high ratings and advertising revenue from sponsors and corporations, leagues, teams, and athletes. Teams and leagues seek high exposure through the media, large gate profits through fans and sport enthusiasts, and rely on the successes of their individual workers for sustenance. Organizations use networks, cable outlets, and emerging technologies like the internet and satellite radio to gain recognition, exposure, and value for their products and programs. Correspondingly, fans and the media audience or receivers of sport communication messages can accept or reject the message by watching, listening, viewing, reading, or buying, thereby influencing effects, ratings, and exerting purchasing power in their preferences.

Communication in sport involves interdependent and interactive communication and allows for feedback from all entities. This can be as simple as eye contact, but also includes responses to online fan polls and trivia questions, phone calls or e-mails to commend or criticize sport coverage, or provocative and controversial conversations during sports radio talk shows. Sport communication feedback and effects are apparent not only in television ratings and e-commerce spending, but within sports organizations, leagues, teams, and networks. At the National Football League Players Association (NFLPA), communication informs the public about current players' community service contributions, encourages retired athletes to participate in alumni activities, and can also facilitate the marketing of past, current, and future NFL Pro Bowl selections and MVP candidates. For sport media outlets, sport communication could increase fan support for a team, increase ratings, or increase purchases of advertising and commercials. When a team like the Pittsburgh Steelers has a stellar season, media attention increases locally through network affiliates and nationally through cable channels such as ESPN as well as traditional network coverage of games on ABC or CBS. Networks also use information attained from fans to make programming decisions. For sports fans worldwide, they share unique experiences and can communicate with sport communication professionals through various outlets and through other fans. Fans from a Manchester United soccer match in England, a polo match in Argentina, a game featuring the Carlton Blues of the Australian Rules Football League, or a contest involving the Amsterdam Admirals of NFL Europe can then share experiences. They can discuss what they saw at games or on television, what they read in magazines or newspapers, or what they heard from sports anchors. This gives them many opportunities in various contexts to discuss and communicate the multitudinous sport events and activities (Rowe, 1999). For these reasons, all components share a symbiotic relationship with mutually beneficial results. Whether the result is profit or individual pleasure, the process of communication among sport communication entities is vibrant, interactive, and infinite.

While sport communication is interactive and multi-dimensional with communication flowing multilaterally, simple, linear communication models serve as a foundation for processes and communicative actions. The first recognized type of communication models were transmission models, where communication flowed in a linear direction and were Sender-Message-Channel-Receiver (SMCR) models. Early communication pioneers possessed educational backgrounds in sociology or psychology (Greenberg & Salwen, 1996). One such scholar was Lasswell (1949), who posed the question, "Who says what in which channel to whom with what effect?" In the Lasswell formula, the communicator, message, medium, receiver/audience, and effects are studied. His formula and other early communication models viewed communication as a persuasive process where the sender sought to influence a receiver with no mention of feedback in the process. Although these original models explained mass communication, certain components can be applied to sport communication although today's audiences possess much more power than scholars originally envisioned. When sport sponsors spend billions of dollars for national and international sporting events, companies such as Joyce Julius or SRI International study and measure for message potency. In SRI's study of NBC's coverage of the Athens Olympics, it discovered that brand exposure was highest for Swatch and second for Coca-Cola (Analysis: NBC Olympics coverage, 2004). This example demonstrates the importance of exposure in the persuasive process of communicating products' messages to consumers. This linear flow of information to audiences is also apparent in NBC's broadcasts of the Games and its desire to capture viewers. In Athens, NBC garnered a profit of between $60 and $70 million and averaged a primetime rating of 15.0 (Bernstein, 2004).

In addition to reducing communication to a one-way process of information from senders to receivers, linear models failed to recognize that many messages are not sent smoothly from sender to receiver. When a communicator sends a message to the audience, the channel affects how the message is communicated and conveyed and noise or interference as well as context, or the environment, can also impede or promote communication and feedback (Griffin, 2004). For sport communication, this is especially apropos when considering technical difficulties in sports broadcasts or fan noise in a major post-season game. Although these early models failed to consider context, the effect of the channel that is used, and the relationship between the sender and receiver, they provided the foundation for a more accepted communication model first developed by communication researcher Wilbur Schramm. Schramm developed the Simplified Communications Model and the ensuing Schramm-Osgood Model with Charles Osgood in 1954, which included understanding, feedback, and two-way communication in the process. Schramm sought to bolster communication's legitimacy in the field of academia with his emphasis on behavioral sciences (Greenberg & Salwen, 1996). Schramm's model involved a source who encodes a message or signal that is transmitted through interpersonal communication or through a medium, and a destination where the receiver decodes the message or signal (Pavlik & McIntosh, 2004). Unlike the earlier linear models, this model was circular and accounted for the behavior of various actors in the process. In sport communication, this process is evident in Outdoor Life Network's (OLN) broadcasts of the Tour de France with its analysts and visuals providing detailed coverage for viewers around the globe, who interpret messages and process them either by staying tuned to help increase ratings or switching to another channel, thereby exerting power in the process.

As communication continued its emergence as an academic discipline, the process moved from more empirical approaches to cultural and critical analyses of communication (Pavlik & McIntosh, 2004). "Society not only continues to exist by transmission, by communication, but it may fairly be said to exist in transmission, in communication," according to philosopher Dewey (1916).

> There is more than a verbal tie between the words common, community, and communication. Men live in a community in virtue of the things which they have in common; and communication is the way in which they come to possess things in common. (p. 10)

Dewey and cultural historian James Carey viewed communication as a ritual. The ritual model took a more interactive, meaningful, and interpretive approach to communication (McQual & Windhahl, 1993). According to Carey (1989), "communication is linked to terms such as 'sharing,' 'participation,' 'association,' 'fellowship,' and the 'possession of a common faith' " (p. 18). Carey (1989) added, "A ritual view of communication is directed not toward the extension of messages in space but toward the maintenance of society in time; not the act of imparting information but the representation of shared beliefs" (p. 18). Pauly (1997) noted that such a perspective views communication as "conversation" (p. 10) and a "social practice" (p. 13) rather than a scientific, utilitarian phenomenon.

In addition to a cultural perspective, The Frankfurt School of Critical Theory originated in Germany during the 1920s and 1930s and Marxist analyses in sport originated after 1950 (Rigauer, 2002). In this tradition, sport is viewed as a historical and social phenomenon affording opportunities for studying the working class and sport. The Frankfurt School, and specifically Horkheimer, Adorno, and Habermas, developed a model of base and superstructure and studied sport in capitalist and socialist societies (Rigauer, 2002). Marxists believed that power is in the hands of a select few, thereby minimizing a diversity of voices and ideas and promoting class domination (Shoemaker & Reese, 1996). In this area, hegemony and the consolidation of the sport media industry are relevant areas of inquiry. Messages produced by the elites and dominant ideologies do not always express society's marginalized populations or culturally and ethnically diverse perspectives.

Shoemaker and Reese (1996) recommended analyzing factors inside and outside media organizations. While many scholars have studied the process of communication and the effects, other important variables affecting media content must also be considered. Among these entities, according to Shoemaker and Reese, are the media workers and their perceptions of reality; organizational routines at media organizations; certain social, economic, and cultural forces; and hegemony, or the view that the powerful elites' ideologies influence content. Micro-level studies investigate communication between individuals and macrolevel studies networks, organizations, and entire cultures. Lippmann (1922) realized the importance of routines on the news process when he wrote in the seminal work *Public Opinion*, "without standardization, without stereotypes, without routine judgments, without a fairly ruthless disregard of subtlety, the editor would soon die of excitement" (p. 123). Tuchman (1973) also studied the routinization of work and investigated the problem of how newsroom workers processed and imposed routines on nonspecialized unexpected events.

This is in line with the notion of gatekeepers at each level from corporate executives to sports editors, producers, media managers, and reporters, who all function as message filters. The term "gate keeper" originated in White's (1950, p. 384) seminal study, which defined a gate keeper as a wire editor who selected the national and international news for newspapers, including and excluding stories based upon what he or she deems important. This pioneering study showed the subjective and value-based judgments that affect all media content as well as processes. In sport coverage, certain games are shown, certain events are televised, and certain athletes are highlighted. These are just some of the subjective decisions that are part of the sport communication process. There are processes of selection, creation, dissemination, and reception in all processes (Greenberg & Salwen, 1996). In Greenberg and Salwen's model for communication, the selection of messages and content deals with personal attributes of decision-makers, their agendas and preferences, gatekeeping functions, accessibility issues, and the decoding of messages. Creation includes the actual development of messages and the encoding and channels used as well as the objective of the creators. The dissemination part of the process once again deals with gate keeping and the diffusion of news. And finally, reception deals with the audience, their decoding of messages, their uses and pleasure gained, responses, and selections made as well as individual and aggregate effects.

Sport communication, whether face-to-face or mediated, can be conceptualized as the process of producing and delivering messages to an audience of one individual, a few colleagues at the front office of a professional team, or a massive group of sports television viewers watching World Cup soccer around the world. There are many components, including sport institutions, media, audience members, and the various entities within and outside these arenas. Like most communication, sport communication is intentional/unintentional, complex, circular, irreversible, transactional, unrepeatable, dynamic, multi-dimensional, verbal and non-verbal, constant, and continuous. Sports journalists constantly communicate with their sources, editors, managers, and readers through conversations, gestures, e-mails, letters, and articles. Fans communicate with organizations through e-mails, letters, and ticket sales and with other fans through chat rooms, fantasy leagues, and daily discussions of their teams' progress. A front office employee for a team communicates with the media, other managers, colleagues, and fans through daily job routines and responsibilities. The definition of sport communication provided in this analysis relies on a firm foundation of communication theory and takes into account all communication processes.

. . . by which people . . .

Sport communication includes communicators/senders and recipients who are the audience or receivers. Senders and/or receivers can be individuals, small groups, private discussion participants, public discussants, bystanders, lurkers (i.e., individuals who go to a sports internet site and read posts but never write), and any other sport communication participant. Those involved with sport communication and sport media are both senders and receivers for sport communication. For example, the broadcast professionals associated with a broadcast both communicate (send) messages as well as receive message from other stakeholders (i.e., superiors, producers, engineers) and audience members (i.e., ratings, postings on websites).

In sport entities, senders are often managers, owners, athletes, employees, fellow colleagues, and even sport consumers. For example, a sport entity may communicate to its stakeholders by a newsletter, e-mail, a live chat, or a podcast. The receivers in sport organizations are identical individuals taking on other roles. Similarly, the sport entity may field complaints of sport consumers, thus becoming the receiver. In sport media outlets, senders can be general managers, authors, sports editors, producers, reporters, broadcasters, and any other sport media personnel. The receivers in sport media outlets are the listeners, viewers, customers, advertisers, readers, consumers, and any other individual or group who has to decode a sport-related message.

. . . in sport, in a sport setting, or through sport . . .

Any communication that involves sport can be found in the definition of sport communication. This is because of the three areas in which sport communication exists in the sport industry. First, sport communication is communication in sport. An example of this is the communication that athletes and coaches engage in on the field of play. Second, sport communication is communication in a sport setting. For example, when executives write memos for or hold meetings with the employees of the sport organization, they are engaging in communication in a sport setting. Third, sport communication is communication through sport. This involves such activities as advertising a product in a game program or broadcasting a sporting event.

The channels of sport communication refer to the medium of communication. In sport organizations, channels of communication often relate to interpersonal communicative activities. This often involves mediated and non-mediated communicating through the use of e-mail, phone calls, the intranet, and various verbal and non-verbal messages. For a sport media outlet, mediated communication involves the spoken, visual, auditory, radio signal, satellite, and other channels. Therefore, the means of communication in sport, in a sport setting, or through sport include everything from websites, written documents, and cell phones to technological innovations, oral communications, and publications.

. . . share symbols . . .

Symbolism is language used in sport to create, maintain, and reinforce the values, beliefs, and culture of sport entities and sporting publics. Symbolism assists sport entities in conveying and assigning meanings to messages. It is a key element in sport communication and widely used in the industry when communicating with internal and external publics. Sharing symbols in the discipline of sport communication refers to the manner in which language is used to create symbolism in sport. The language may create or reinforce certain beliefs and values that are held by sport entities as well as sporting publics. Symbolism conveys meaning, and the interpretation of this language is mostly influenced by the context in which it is used. According to Griffin (2004), language is "the system of verbal or gestural symbols a community uses to communicate with one another" (p. 276). Cohen (1976) defined symbols as objects, acts, or relationships that may have many meanings which solicit many emotions in many people. Christian and Dillman (2004) noted that, "symbolic language uses signs that have cultural meaning to convey information" (p. 60). In sport communication, this refers to the transmission of messages. These messages include the verbal, non-verbal, spoken, unspoken, written, sport programs, sport texts, images and sounds of sport, and product advertisements in sport. The shared symbols in sport organizations are those messages, advice, support, and any other communicative act in the sport organization. In the sport media outlet, the shared symbols are also communicative acts, but they add the components of sport reports, game stories, feature stories, investigative reports, and other mediated communicative activities. The sharing of symbols is affected by many variables such as sense, content, size, style, language, trustworthiness, type of argument, intelligence, and clarity.

Individuals assign multiple meanings based on the context and content of the symbols and messages (Vaughn, 1995). These meanings may be contradictory and can link individuals to other worlds which they may not completely understand but know they should not ignore (Van Buskirk & McGrath, 1999). The context and content of messages and symbols are important because they influence interpretation and culture. Relative to sport organizations, symbols assist in creating an organizational identity and in reinforcing the organizational culture and values of its employees. Organizational symbolism refers to the manner in which members of an organization utilize various aspects of the organization to convey the values of the organization (Dandridge et al., 1980). According to Van Buskirk and McGrath (1999), symbols are the "building blocks of culture" and are bundles of meaning (p. 805). These bundles of meaning play a key role in framing the "perceptions, orientations, commitments, and meanings that cultures hold in place" (p. 805).

Symbols have been characterized in numerous ways by scholars. Symbols are thought to illustrate reality, help preserve a calm atmosphere in trying and challenging times, and protect individuals' self-esteem and perceptions of self-worth (Broms & Gahmberg, 1983; Jackson & Carter, 1984). Vaughn (1995) suggested that although scholars differ in their characterizations of symbols, most agree that symbols take the form of "stories, ritualized events, specialized language, and material manifestations" (p. 222). Stories are narratives which are grounded in factual events but often include false aspects or even elements that are fictional and sensationalized. These stories symbolically illustrate norms and values and ultimately assist in defining an organization's character (Vaughn, 1995). Many sport entities create and reinforce their image through the various stories they promote and publicize to the sporting public. For example, the perception and brand image of the Green Bay Packers is firmly rooted in its history and idealized through images of Vince Lombardi. The Packers also create a sense of sporting culture by referring to their venue as "the frozen tundra of Lambeau Field" conjuring up images of fierce competition in an extreme environment of snow and ice. Similarly, storied histories include the Four Horsemen of the University of Notre Dame and Norwegian cross country skiers Vegard Ulvang and Bjørn Dæhlie who each won three gold medals at the 1992 Winter Olympics in Albertville, France. These examples illustrate how stories serve as symbols in creating a certain sport culture.

Ritualized events are those activities that are symbolic, formalized, and repeated. This is exemplified in sport in various forms. For example, one of New Zealand's premier rugby teams, the All Blacks, perform the haka dance prior to each game. This ritualistic activity underscores the culture of rugby in New Zealand and serves to reinforce the values of the All Blacks team. The Olympics also embody ritualistic symbolism in sport through utilization of the Olympic rings as well as the Opening and Closing ceremonies. The Olympics assist in creating a sport culture without boundaries while also reinforcing national identities. At Wimbledon each year, fans and players dine on strawberries and cream and players, before leaving the court, will bow to the royal box. These rituals have become synonymous with Wimbledon and enhance the mystique and values of the tournament. These traditions establish a Wimbledon culture that is different from the other Grand Slam events in professional tennis.

Specialized language is often utilized to create symbolism and reinforce culture in sport. The use of jargon, slang, or specific phrases and slogans reinforce perceptions and values while symbolically communicating a specific identity (Vaughn, 1995). Phrases such as "light the lamp" and "biscuit in the basket" signify the scoring of a goal in the sport of hockey, and these phrases are commonly associated with the sport and are regularly utilized in commentary by members of the sport media. Similar phrases are used in depicting certain aspects in the sport of basketball. The terminology "nothing but net" signifies a clean shot that does not hit the rim or use the backboard, while "behind the arc" is terminology characterizing a shot from the three point line. The phrase "cheap shot" is a term used in most sports to illustrate an unnecessary foul or act against another player that falls outside the realm of the rules and is considered unsportsmanlike. Specialized language also includes slogans. Many sport slogans are used as branding tools for both sport entities and non-sport entities. Nike is synonymous with "Just Do It," while Wheaties is considered the "Breakfast of Champions."

Other means of symbolism in sport include material manifestations. Material manifestations are often the key aspects or elements of an organization and are commonly used in branding and marketing the sport entity. Vaughn (1995) noted that:

> Material elements of an organization include logos, badges, awards, physical settings, and company products. Material symbols are concrete signs that express the central characteristics of an organization and symbolize what an organization has to say about itself, both internally and externally. (p. 222)

The lighting bolt represents and symbolizes Gatorade sports drink, while the Olympic rings are recognized worldwide. Logos not only communicate a brand image and market the sport entity, but they reinforce its values and culture. As Cohen (1996) suggested, "advertisers whose targets are culturally diverse can benefit greatly by identifying symbols which are universal to mankind" (p. 187). The utilization of symbols is just one of the many facets of sport communication and represents an area in need of further scholarly inquiry.

. . . as they create meaning through interaction."

Language is central to communication. Griffin (2004) defined language as, "the system of verbal or gestural symbols a community uses to communicate with one another" (p. 276). Communication at its most basic level is intrapersonal, or the way we process messages and communicate within ourselves (Goss, 1996). After all, communication starts as individuals learn about the world by and through symbols (Steinfatt & Christophel, 1996). In Griffin's (2004) explanation of the semantic triangle of meaning, the symbol at the bottom left is the actual word used by the communicator. In the bottom right, the referent is the object or concept that the symbol depicts and is agreed upon socially. The thought or reference appears at the top of the triangle and represents the past experiences a person has with something. They are personalized interpretations of objects and concepts, and generally a reference evokes emotions. While language is ambiguous and varies from culture to culture, individuals seek meaning through the communication process and their varied experiences. According to Dewey (1916):

> All communication is like art. It may fairly be said, therefore, that any social arrangement that remains vitally social, or vitally shared, is educative to those who participate in it. Only when it becomes cast in a mould and runs in a routine way does it lose its educative power. (p. 13)

Like Dewey's experiential learning and sharing, sport communication creates meaning through action, interaction, and reactions between the communicators, recipients, and all participants from diverse backgrounds and perspectives. The communicators are the individuals, groups, and organizations that send messages and they are considered encoders. According to Griffin (2004, p. 13), encoding is "translating ideas and feelings into words, sounds, and gestures." In sports broadcasting, encoding involves everything from reporting to production and editing. The recipients, or viewers, must then decode or interpret messages, ideologies, and cultural meanings. Decoding is, "translating words, sounds, and gestures into ideas and feelings in an attempt to understand the message" (Griffin, 2004, p. 13). The audience receives messages and also provides verbal or non-verbal responses or feedback, setting the interactive process into motion.

The audience has been a large focus of communication research, especially in terms of media effects. With the modernization, urbanization, and industrialization of US society in the early 20th century, mass society changed relationships creating a more detached social environment (Lowery & DeFleur, 1995). As a result, individuals turned to the media for social cohesion and critical information in their lives. Mass communication research started prior to World War I due to the growing apprehension of wartime propaganda. The "hypodermic needle model," otherwise known as "magic bullet" theory or "model of unlimited effects" portrayed audiences as powerless to the puissant messages of the media (Carey, 1997, p. 15). In mass society, the media injected messages into the audience like a hypodermic needle and they responded uniformly to the pervasive and persuasive messages. From this early theory, social scientists studied the media as a result of the concern on media effects. Some key theories of effects research include uses and gratifications theory, agenda setting theory, adoption of innovation theory, the two-step flow and the diffusion of information, selective influences theory, modeling theory, and cultivation theory.

In 1948, Joseph Klapper disputed the propaganda fears and the "magic bullet" theory, establishing that empirical research found that the media had limited effects. The limited and selective influences theory proposes that individuals' unique characteristics, social categories, and relationships affect how they react to the media. This turned research more toward the study of uses and gratifications. This theory centered more on psychological attributes of the audience and why they sought specific types of content and avoided other types of content. While the "magic bullet" theory viewed the audience as defenseless, this theory presented a view of an audience that sought to use the media for specific uses.

Communication scholars also were interested in the power of the press. McCombs' and Shaw's (1972) pioneering agenda setting study explained the importance of individuals' perceptions of reality based upon news media accounts. The media may not have the power to tell the audience what to think, but have the power to tell the audience what to think about. Managers, editors, and reporters have an influence on perceptions of reality since they select important issues to report and place stories in order of priority. In sports journalism, when stories about female athletes contain sexualized and trivialized portrayals, this potentially shapes readers' perceptions of athletes and women in sport (Pedersen et al., 2003).

The adoption of innovation theory describes the process through which individuals adopt a new innovation whether it is a new ideology, a new trend in fashion, or a new mass medium. Because the media bring individuals information about new inventions, this theory is relevant in all facets of consumption (Lowery & DeFleur, 1995). In sport communication, how quickly do sports fans buy HDTV or satellite subscription packages to increase the quality and content of sport coverage? This is just one example of how this theory is relevant today.

In other effects theories, the two-step flow and diffusion of information relate to the audience's acquisition of media messages indirectly from friends, colleagues, and family members. In a media- and information-rich society, information spreads and diffuses through opinion leaders (in the two-step flow) or through friends and family in the diffusion of information. When there is a monumental catastrophic event such as 11 September 2001, or an uncommon occurrence in sports such as when the Boston Red Sox won the 2004 World Series, these theories are especially apropos. In behavior-related effects theories, modeling theory proposes that the audience models behaviors on actions viewed on television or other media. Children might purchase Nike Lebron III basketball shoes or chew Bubblicious bubble gum if they are fans of the NBA's LeBron James. And finally, cultivation theory was based on George Gerbner's Violence Commission's report on television violence and the effects on children in the 1960s. Gerbner found that individuals who watched a lot of television would view the world as more violent than those who did not due to the amount of violence depicted in television (Lowery & DeFleur, 1995). In sport communication, this could relate to media broadcasts of boxing events and football hooliganism.

Whether the previous theories dealt with short-term or long-term effects, it is important to study how messages shape values, unite people, celebrate events, create a sense of identity, convey information, teach people, and lead them to action or inaction. Just as audiences use the media to gratify needs, throughout history they have used sport to connect with others, to evoke competitiveness, or simply to satiate a sense of belonging. As Rader (2004) notes, in the 1927 boxing rematch between Jack Dempsey and Gene Tunney at Soldier Field in Chicago, more than 104,000 fans attended, contributing to a $2 million gate. An additional 50 million US fans listened to the NBC radio network from living rooms, saloons, and town halls as Graham McNamee offered play-by-play coverage. The event enabled fans to share the moment with others in a meaningful and communicative experience.

Discussion and Conclusion

Despite exponential increases in the economic, social, political, and cultural implications of sport, a dearth of research exists in sport communication. By definition, sport communication is a process by which people in sport, in a sport setting, or through a sport endeavor, share symbols as they create meaning through interaction. The varied processes and components of this definition as discussed above introduce and reinforce the vitality of this evolving field. While there are some who believe singular elements define sport communication, this view is too simplistic as the dynamic and diverse aspects show the complex nature and tremendous breadth of the field. Sport communication possesses tremendous growth potential around the world in its many facets from print journalism and electronic media to public relations, advertising, theory, research, and emerging technologies.

Sport communication involves the sport communication process, its components, and the communication between sport industry practitioners, organizations, and internal and external stakeholders and the interrelationships between them. Included in this umbrella are texts, content, and symbolic representations as well as institutions, or the organizations that own, run, and finance sport media or sport communication departments; production systems, or the activities involved in putting a sports message together; conditions, including the environment in which the communication in sport or the sport media material takes place; sport communication meanings; audiences; and context. Research is vital in all these areas and will help foster understanding and further scholarly inquiry in this emerging academic discipline. By defining the field and analyzing its unique components, another step has been taken in advancing the study of sport and communication and establishing this area as an academic discipline. All sport communication processes, careers, and activities are part of this definition. As a result, the definition provides a framework for critically analyzing the field, developing scholarly inquiries, and empirically testing the expansive influences within the discipline.

References

Analysis: NBC Olympics coverage. (September 6, 2004). Analysis: NBC Olympics coverage *Sports Business Journal*, p. 18.

Battenfield, F. L. (2004). An ethnographic study of the culture of communication in the sports information office in a Division I-A athletic program. *Unpublished doctoral dissertation*, Florida State University.

Bernstein, A. (September 6, 2004). GE's bid for future games looks even brighter in light of Athens profit. *Sports Business Journal*, p. 19.

Bernstein, A., & Blain, N. (2002). Sport and the media: The emergence of a major re-

search field. *Sport, Media, Culture, 5*(3), 1–30.

Broms, H., & Gahmberg, H. (1983). Communication to self in organizations and cultures. *Administrative Science Quarterly, 28*, 482–495.

Burton, G. (2002). *More than meets the eye: An introduction to media studies.* Oxford, New York.

Carey, J. (1997). The Chicago school and the history of mass communication research. In E. S. Munson & C. A. Warren (Eds.), *James Carey: A critical reader* (pp. 14–33). Minneapolis, MN: University of Minnesota Press.

Carey, J. W. (1989). *Communication as culture: Essays on media and society.* New York: Routledge.

Chaffee, S. (1996). Thinking about theory. In M. B. Salwen & D. W. Stacks (Eds.), *An integrated approach to communication theory and research* (pp. 15–32). Mahwah, NJ: Lawrence Erlbaum Associates.

Christian, L., & Dillman, D. (2004). The influence of graphical and symbolic language manipulations on responses to self-administered questions. *Public Opinion Quarterly, 28*(1), 57–80.

Cohen, A. (1976). *Two dimensional man.* Berkeley, CA: University of California Press.

Cohen, J. (1996). The search for universal symbols: The case of right and left. *Journal of International Consumer Marketing, 8*(3–4), 187–210.

Costa, C. A. (2005). The status and future of sport management: a Delphi study. *Journal of Sport Management, 19*(2), 117–142.

Dandridge, T., Mitroff, I. A., & Joyce, W. (1980). Organizational symbolism: A topic to expand organizational analysis. *Academy of Management Review, 5,* 77–82.

Dewey, J. (1916) *Democracy and education,* Retrieved December 24, 2005, from http://www.ilt.columbia.edu/publications/Projects/digitexts/dewey/d_e/chapter01.html

Goss, B. (1996). Intrapersonal communication. In M. B. Salwen & D. W. Stacks (Eds.), *An integrated approach to communication theory and research* (pp. 335–344). Mahwah, NJ: Lawrence Erlbaum Associates.

Grainger, A., & Andrews, D. L. (2005). Resisting Rupert through sporting rituals?: The transnational media corporation and global-local sport cultures. *International Journal of Sport Management and Marketing, 1*(1–2), 3–16.

Greenberg, B. S., & Salwen, M. B. (1996). Mass communication theory and research: Concepts and models. In M. B. Salwen & D. W. Stacks (Eds.), *An integrated approach to communication theory and research* (pp. 63–78). Mahwah, NJ: Lawrence Erlbaum Associates.

Griffin, C. L. (2004). *Invitation to public speaking.* Belmont, CA: Thomson Wadsworth.

Heath, R. L., & Bryant, J. (2000). *Human communication theory and research: Concepts, contexts, and challenges* (2nd ed.). Mahwah, NJ: Lawrence Erlbaum.

Jackson, N., & Carter, P. (1984). The attenuating function of myth in human understanding. *Human Relations, 37*(7), 515–533.

Lasswell, H. D. (1949). The structure and function of communication in society. In W. Schramm (Ed.), *Mass communications* (pp. 102–115). Urbana, IL: University of Illinois Press.

Lippmann, W. (1922). *Public opinion.* New York: Harcourt Brace.

Lowery, S. A., & DeFleur, M. L. (1995). *Milestones in mass communication research* (3rd ed.). White Plains, NY: Longman.

McCombs, M. E., & Shaw, D. L. (1972). The agenda-setting function of mass media. *The Public Opinion Quarterly, 36*(2), 176–187.

McQuail, D., & Windahl, S. (1993). *Communication models for the study of mass communications* (2nd ed.). London: Longman.

Pauly, J. (1997). Introduction on the origins of media studies (and media scholars). In E. S. Munson & C. A. Warren (Eds.), *James Carey: A critical reader* (pp. 3–13). Minneapolis, MN: University of Minnesota Press.

Pavlik, J. V., & McIntosh, S. (2004). *Converging media: An introduction to mass communication.* Boston: Pearson.

Pedersen, P. M., Whisenant, W. A., & Schneider, R. G. (2003). Using a content analysis to examine the gendering of sports newspaper personnel and their coverage. *Journal of Sport Management, 17*(4), 376–383.

Pitts, B. G., Fielding, L. W., & Miller, L. K. (1994). Industry segmentation theory and the sport industry: Developing a sport industry segment model. *Sport Marketing Quarterly, 3*(1), 15–24.

Rader, B. G. (2004). *American sports: From the age of folk games to the age of televised sports* (5th ed).. Upper Saddle River, NJ: Prentice Hall.

Rigauer, B. (2002). Marxist theories. In J. Coakley & E. Dunning (Eds.), *Handbook of sports studies* (pp. 28–47). London: Sage.

Rowe, D. (1999). *Sport, culture, and the media: The unruly trinity.* Philadelphia: Open University Press.

Shoemaker, P. J., & Reese, S. D. (1996). *Mediating the message: Theories of influence on mass media content*. White Plains, NY: Longman.

Steinfatt, T., & Christophel, D. M. (1996). Intercultural communication. In M. B. Salwen & D. W. Stacks (Eds.), *An integrated approach to communication theory and research* (pp. 317–344). Mahwah, NJ: Lawrence Erlbaum Associates.

Tuchman, G. (1973). Making news by doing work: Routinizing the unexpected. *The American Journal of Sociology, 79*(1), 110–131.

Van Buskirk, W., & McGrath, D. (1999). Organizational cultures as holding environments: A psychodynamic look at organizational symbolism. *Human Relations, 52*(6), 805–832.

Van Leeuwen, L., Quick, S., & Daniel, K. (2002). The sport spectator satisfaction model: A conceptual framework for understanding the satisfaction of spectators. *Sport Management Review, 5*(2), 99–128.

Vaughn, M. (1995). Organization symbols: An analysis of their types and functions in a reborn organization. *Management Communication Quarterly, 9*(2), 219–250.

Wenner, L. A. (1998). *Mediasport*. New York, NY: Routledge.

Westerbeek, H. M., & Shilbury, D. (2003). A conceptual model for sport services marketing research: Integrating quality, value and satisfaction. *International Journal of Sports Marketing and Sponsorship, 5*(1), 11–27.

White, D. M. (1950). The "gate keeper": A case study in the selection of news. *Journalism Quarterly, 27*(4), 383–390.

THE INFLUENCE OF POLICY MAKERS' PERCEPTIONS ON SPORT-TOURISM POLICY DEVELOPMENT

Mike Weed

Introduction

Interest in the study of policy activity related to sport has grown in the last 15 years as interest in sport itself has continued to grow on a worldwide scale. Issues such as the bidding process for the Olympic Games and other major international sports events such as Football and Rugby World Cups (Getz, 2003), the impact of European Union legislation on the transfer system in football (McCutcheon, 2002), and drug abuse in a range of sports (Houlihan, 1999) have all attracted the attention of policy analysts. In the UK, sports policy has been given a more prominent place on the political agenda as the apathy towards sports policy of the Thatcher governments in the 1980s gave way to a much more significant interest from the Major government in the 1990s and subsequently to an overt exploitation by the Blair governments of the late 1990s and early 2000s (Oakley & Green, 2001). However, this does not appear to be a phenomenon unique to the UK, as national governments in a range of countries around the globe (Chalip, Johnson, & Stachura, 1996; Sam, 2003) attempt to tap into the economic and national prestige benefits that can accrue from an overt attempt to utilize sport in both national and international policy.

Many of the economic benefits that arise from the development of international sport policies are linked to the attraction of international visitors, particularly for major games and festivals. Furthermore, at a subnational regional level, sport is often used to attract visitors from other regions in order to boost the regional economy. In these respects, the economic benefits of sport are linked to tourism, and consequently, a full exploitation of sport for such economic benefits requires integration with tourism policy. However, despite the range of benefits that have been shown to arise from linking sport and tourism, on a worldwide scale there still remain few genuine examples of explicit and strategic links between agencies responsible for policy for sport and tourism (Higham, 2005; Weed & Bull, 2004).

The Sport–Tourism Link

Mirroring the growth in interest in sport policy since the early 1990s, academic interest in sports tourism[1] has burgeoned over the last 15 years. Work by Glyptis (1991) and the subsequent report commissioned by the Great Britain Sports Council (Jackson & Glyptis, 1992) were some of the early substantive works in the field, while other reviews were carried out by De Knop (1990) and Standeven and Tomlinson (1994). The focus of these early works was on advocacy, attempting to establish sports tourism as a legitimate field of study, and one with a potentially significant range of impacts. The first full text relating to sport and tourism was the 1999 work by Standeven and De Knop, which while largely descriptive, outlined the range of economic, sociocultural, environmental, and health impacts of sports tourism.

In the later 1990s and early 2000s, a range of authors carried out more detailed examinations of the sports tourism field in relation to, inter alia: policy (Weed, 1999, 2003), destination development (Vrondou, 1999), seasonality (Higham & Hinch, 2002), participation patterns (Jackson & Reeves, 1998; Reeves, 2000), economic impacts (Collins & Jackson, 1999), and spectators (Weed, 2002a). Furthermore, in the last few years a number of student texts (e.g., Hudson, 2003; Ritchie & Adair, 2004; Turco, Riley, & Swart, 2002) and more research-oriented books (e.g., Higham, 2005; Hinch & Higham, 2004; Weed & Bull, 2004) have been published, as well as special editions of *European Sport Management Quarterly* (2005; Vol. 5, No.3), *Journal of Sport Management* (2003; Vol. 17, No. 3), *Journal of Vacation Marketing* (1998; Vol. 4, No. 1), and *Tourism Recreation Research* (1997; Vol. 22, No. 2). The existence of these works demonstrates academic interest in the area, while their content clearly establishes sports tourism as a real and significant phenomenon in contemporary society.

Policy Responses to the Sport–Tourism Link

As noted above, the response of policy makers to the increasingly evident links between sport and tourism has been, to say the least, muted. While it may be possible to quote organizing committees formed to coordinate approaches for mega-events such as the Olympic Games as positive examples of liaison, such liaison is obviously the exception rather than the rule given the once in a generation occurrence of such events in any one area. In the late 1990s, Weed and Bull (1997a) showed that regional policy makers for sport and for tourism in England, while often promoting sports tourism-related initiatives, were rarely doing so in collaboration with partner agencies in the other sector. Such lack of policy partnerships has also been commented on by authors from other countries (e.g., Gibson, 2002; Higham, 2005; Swart, 1998), and the international dimension has been discussed in detail by Weed and Bull (2004). The initial Weed and Bull (1997a) review was the starting point for a detailed longitudinal grounded theory (Glaser & Strauss, 1967) study of the response of policy makers in the UK to the sport– tourism link (Weed, 2005). This approach followed the emerging constructivist approach to grounded theory advocated by authors such as Charmaz (2000) and Layder (1993). The interactive collection of data and development of theory took place over an 8year period, beginning with the Weed and Bull (1997a) review mentioned above and concluding with the exposition of a formal grounded theory of the policy process for sport and tourism in Weed and Bull (2004). The full details of the development and implementation of this grounded theory approach are described in detail in Weed (2005). The use of the grounded theory method for this work was reflective of the existence of no detailed theoretical research on sport–tourism policy at the time, and to this day the various publications by Weed and Weed and Bull remain the only nondescriptive works that analyze policy responses to the sport–tourism link. Furthermore, such work is derived from and informed by the broader generic policy studies literature (e.g., Marsh, 1998; Marsh & Rhodes, 1992; Rhodes, 1986; M. Smith, 1993; Wilks & Wright, 1987; Wright, 1988) where there is a much greater body of knowledge than in sport, tourism, or sports tourism. Consequently, the theoretical framework developed through that research is used in this article to provide the context for an examination of the perceptions of UK policy makers of their role in developing the sport–tourism link.

The first part of this article briefly discusses the model of the sport–tourism policy process developed by Weed (2001), and its utility in highlighting the importance of a range of factors related to policy makers' perceptions (Weed, 2003; Weed & Bull, 1998) in the development of collaborations between sport and tourism agencies. These discussions provide the context for the second part of the article, which draws on interviews with policy makers for sport and for tourism at regional and national level in the UK. The evidence from the interviews illustrates policy makers' perceptions of their own and other agencies' roles and potential influence in relation to sports tourism. They also highlight the ways in which policy makers understand the nature and extent of the sport–tourism link. The paper's conclusion relocates the findings from the interviews within the model of the sport–tourism policy process described by Weed (2001, 2005) and assesses the continuing relevance of the model.

Conceptual Framework:
A Model of the Sport–Tourism Policy Process

A number of authors have used the concepts of policy community and policy network to show that policy making takes place within a sectorized arena (Marsh & Rhodes, 1992; Rhodes, 1986; Wilks & Wright, 1987; Wright, 1988). Furthermore, such analysis has been applied to sport (Houlihan, 1991, 1997) and related concepts have been used in relation to tourism (Hall, 1994). Consequently, Weed's (2001) model of the sport–tourism policy process draws on the policy community approach to show that policy making for sport and for tourism takes place within two relatively distinct communities that are historically, culturally, and structurally separate from each other.

In the UK, policy making for sport and for tourism has developed separately, through separate agencies that were until relatively recently (1992) linked to separate government departments. As research published elsewhere has shown (Weed, 2002b), policy organizations in sport tend to have very different organizational structures and cultures to those operating in the tourism sector, and this has an effect on the structures of the policy communities for sport and for tourism. However, as the wide range of research on sports tourism shows, there are a considerable range of issues in relation to which sport and tourism agencies might be expected to collaborate. Consequently, the sport and tourism policy communities can be conceptualized as overlapping, and the area of overlap represents the range of issues in relation to which there is the potential for a sport–tourism policy network to emerge. A policy network is described by Wright (1988) as "a linking process, the outcome of those exchanges within a policy community or between a number of policy communities" (p. 606). Thus, it is a particularly useful concept to use in considering sport– tourism policy, which is clearly derived from an interaction of two policy communities. However, the emergence of a sport–tourism policy network is by no means certain, as noted by Houlihan (1991): "while every policy sector will generate a policy community this is no guarantee that a policy network will emerge to deal with particular issues. Some communities may lack the necessary value consensus or strength of mutual interests to provide the basis for the formation of a network" (p. 161).

Evidence suggests (Weed & Bull, 1998) that this has been the case in relation to sport–tourism policy links, and Weed (2001) highlighted a number of differences in the structures of sport and of tourism policy communities that contribute to this, conceptualizing sport policy communities as "policy circles," and tourism communities as "issue networks." Sport policy communities tend to have a primary core of actors that is relatively closed to other agencies, and a more open secondary community to which access is fairly easy, but whose influence on policy is limited. This contrasts with tourism policy communities, which tend to be altogether more open. Such structures are reinforced by a set of dependencies in sports policy communities in which the secondary actors tend to be dependent on resources controlled by the actors in the primary core. The commercial nature of tourism policy communities means that few such dependencies exist, although governments retain influence in some areas of policy through the distribution of funding and legislation. Although in relation to tourism policy communities, sports policy communities show more of the tightly defined features of a policy circle and are often more able to exclude tourism interests than vice versa, both communities are susceptible to the imposition of policies developed in more politically significant policy areas such as law and order or education.

While the relative structures of policy communities themselves can affect sport–tourism liaison, Weed (2003) used empirical research to revise the conceptual work of Weed and Bull (1998) and identify six further factors that influence relationships between policy communities for sport and for tourism:

- Ideologies
- Definitions

- Regional Contexts
- Government Policy
- Organizational Culture and Structure
- Individuals

It is these six influences, along with the structures of sport and tourism policy communities, that provide the context for a consideration of the influence of policy makers' perceptions on the development of a sport–tourism policy network. For example, definitions of sport, tourism, and sports tourism may affect policy makers' perceptions about the extent of their agency's role, while the structures of the policy communities may affect perceptions about the potential influence of various agencies. Similarly, regional contexts may affect the perception of policy makers of the nature of the sport–tourism link, while government policy may shape perceptions relating to the way in which sports tourism should be developed in particular regions. Of course, there is a two-way relationship between individuals and perceptions, as backgrounds and experiences shape individual perceptions that in turn shape individual behaviors. Following a description of method, the next section of this article utilizes interview data to assess the perceptions of policy makers in relation to a range of issues relating to sport–tourism policy development, and considers the responses of such policy makers against the context provided by the influences discussed here.

Method

The policy-making map for sport and for tourism in the UK is not as straightforward as it was 10 years ago, and some brief comment on the range of agencies involved is perhaps appropriate in providing a context for the method. In England, Sport England is the public sector agency responsible for sport policy, for the distribution of government sport funding, and for funding for sport from the National Lottery. It reports to the Department for Culture, Media and Sport (DCMS) in the UK government and has nine regional offices. In addition, two further national agencies, the Sports Council for Wales and sportsscotland, report to the devolved Welsh Assembly and Scottish Parliament, respectively. In relation to tourism, VisitBritain has both a British and English remit at national level and reports to the DCMS, while Visit Scotland and the Wales Tourist Board report to their respective national executives. Regionally in England, tourism funding is now channeled through nine Regional Development Agencies (RDAs), which may either take on a tourism role themselves or fund Regional Tourist Boards (which were, until 2002, direct recipients of government tourism funding). In most cases Regional Tourist Boards, of which there are 10, have been funded, but in some regions the RDAs have taken on a partial role, with the North East RDA, One North East, being almost wholly responsible for tourism development. This complex picture is further complicated by a range of significant subregional tourism agencies, such as Marketing Manchester and The Mersey Partnership, and one supraregional consortium (England's North Country) with the formation of other such consortia being discussed.

There are two issues that this web of policy-making responsibilities raises. Firstly, it complicates the structure of the policy communities, particularly for tourism, thus reinforcing Weed's (2001) conceptualization of tourism policy as taking place within a loosely constituted issue zone. Secondly, it makes the selection of a sample of agencies for interview less than straightforward. The research tool for this article was a series of "informed source interviews" (see King, 1994; Lowe, 1981; Lowe & Goyder, 1983, for a discussion of this technique), similar to those used by Weed (1999). An advantage of this approach is that it provides insights into "the outlook and attitudes of people in such key positions which are also important facts" (Lowe & Goyder, 1983, p. 4). It is therefore particularly useful in assessing the impact of policy makers' perceptions on policy development. However, the range of agencies involved meant that a comprehensive set of interviews was all but impossible; therefore, a strategic sample of agencies was selected, with nine interviews taking place with regional agencies/offices and three interviews with national agencies. Five of the agencies had responsibility for sport, while seven had tourism remits. In respect to the agencies with tourism responsibilities, informed sources in a mix of national agencies, RDAs, Regional Tourist Boards, and other subregional agencies were interviewed. Across all the interviews, each national area (i.e., England, Scotland, and Wales) and region was covered. The interviews were each held with senior staff who could speak authoritatively on the policies and roles of their agency (e.g., Development Directors in tourist/development agencies and Regional Directors or Senior Planning Officers in sports agencies), and lasted between 30 and 60 minutes. The schedule of questions for the interviews was structured around three themes: structure and communication, strategy and policy development, and organizational philosophy and operations. Each of the interviews was recorded and subsequently transcribed in order that they could be analyzed in detail. An inductive thematic issues analysis was conducted, using a procedure analogous to that used by Marshall (1994) in her discourse analysis of interviews with Health CareWorkers. As noted above, there were 12 informed interviews conducted in total; therefore, the analysis focused on 12 transcripts that ranged from 8 to 15 pages of single-spaced script. Firstly, all the scripts were read through and checked with the tapes for both familiarization and verification. As suggested by Marshall (1994), the scripts were then read through again and recurrent themes were identified. Initially, 11 themes were identified, which were then subsequently grouped into four main themes (see Table 1).

The four main themes were used as the framework for the analysis. As suggested by J. A. Smith (1996), the themes were analyzed idiographically (i.e., they were analyzed independently of each other). In an emergent approach, such an idiographic analysis ensures that themes are allowed to emerge from the interview transcripts, rather than the analysis being influenced by prior

Table 1. Themes Emerging from the Analysis

Main Theme	Subthemes
Roles and remits	Relationships with other agencies Priorities Knowledge of other agencies work
Nature of sport–tourism link	Understanding of sport, tourism and sports tourism Scope of sports tourism
Influence of regional agencies	Advocacy role Coordination role Spheres of influence
Specific regional contexts	Regional tourism product strengths Regional sporting heritage Regional geography

evaluations of other thematic areas (Layder, 1993). A broader interpretation of the collection of themes as a whole can subsequently be made in concluding the analysis.

Results

The themes that emerged from the set of interviews in relation to policy makers perceptions were: (a) roles and remits, (b) the nature of the sport–tourism link, (c) influence of regional agencies, and (d) specific regional contexts. These themes are now discussed in detail, illustrated by "comments" extracted from the interviews. The comments are presented in four thematic panels. The use of these panels serves two purposes: firstly, they allow evidence to be presented without disrupting the narrative flow of the text and, secondly, they allow a greater volume of evidence to be presented than would have been possible if excerpts from the interviews were used solely in the main text. However, notwithstanding the greater volume of evidence presented, by the very nature of qualitative interviewing, such evidence can only be illustrative. Ontologically, such illustrative evidence is representative of "truths" (multiple) rather than "the truth" (singular). That such truths are shared across groups and subgroups of policy actors means that they inevitably affect behavior and policy on more than an individual level. As such, they are of clear interest in an analysis of policy makers' perceptions.

Perceptions of the Roles and Remits of Sport and Tourism Agencies

The failure of the Department for Culture Media and Sport (DCMS) to promote or encourage cross-sectoral liaison was initially outlined by Weed and

Bull (1997b) and reinforced more recently by Weed (2003). The extent of this failure is highlighted by the lack of understanding the sport and tourism agencies generally have of each others roles (Panel 1).

Perhaps the comments in Panel 1 are more extreme than most (particularly 1, 2, and 5)—many of those interviewed did demonstrate a knowledge of the remits of their colleagues in the other sector. However, the comments in Panel 1 do highlight a problem that exists in some areas. Comment 2 from a Regional Director at one of the tourism agencies explicitly confesses a lack of awareness of the role of the English sports agencies, and assumes a reciprocal ignorance of the role of tourist agencies by the sports bodies. Furthermore, just prior to admitting to having no knowledge about their role, judgments are made as to which activities fall within the remit of such sports agencies. Similar assumptions are made in comment 1, which refers to recreational facilities that "are beyond the remit of the various sports bodies." Such ignorance of sports agencies' remits, combined with ill-informed assumptions about what activities they are responsible for, obviously militates against liaison between the sport and tourism bodies. This is particularly the case as such assumptions are largely incorrect because, as comment 3 states, Sport England has always accepted the Council of Europe's European Sports Charter, which gives the following definition of sport: "Sport means all forms of physical activity which, through casual or organisation participation, aims at improving physical fitness and mental well being, forming social relationships, or obtaining results in competition at all levels" (Sports Council, 1994).

A review of the respective strategy statements of regional sport and tourism agencies in the late 1990s (Weed & Bull, 1997a) showed that although many of the regional agencies were involved in or advocated sport–tourism initiatives, in most cases their involvement was unilateral. Few examples of genuine, cross-sectoral liaison were found. This article reinforces this earlier work, with comments 1 and 2 highlighting informal cycling, hiking, and bridleways as issues that are important in sports tourism. However, they are not seen as issues that fall within the remit of the regional sports agencies. Weed and Bull's (1997a) regional strategy review showed that virtually all the regional agencies (both sport and tourism) were active in the area of countryside access and integration, but that not one strategy mentioned any joint activity on these issues. Given the comments here (1 and 2), this finding was not surprising. In addition, comment 4 clearly shows that Sport England still sees a role for itself in countryside activities. This evidence inevitably leads to the conclusion that, in some regions, a lack of awareness of the roles and remits between the sports and tourism agencies may lead to a lack of liaison between the two spheres. Both sport and tourism agencies may be involved in sports tourism-related areas that they perceive do not fall within the policy area of the other sector and, as a result, partnerships in these areas may not be formed and activity continues in a unilateral manner.

Of course, as highlighted above, not all interviewees demonstrated a lack of knowledge about the activities of their regional partners in other sectors, and

---

PANEL 1. Perceptions of Sport and Tourism Agencies' Roles and Remits

(1) Partnerships between sport and tourism depend on product strengths. In this region, although activity holidays are growing, it tends to be the more recreational facilities, like walking, hiking, and bridleways, which are beyond the remit of the various sports bodies, that are most significant.

(2) At regional level, we're talking about more soft areas, where sport and recreation merge— things like cycling; we see that as being one of the real growth areas across the region. Recreational use of the waterways, which is not specifically sport. . . . I don't know what the remit of the English Regional Sports Bodies is, they wouldn't know much about us.

(3) Although our priorities have changed greatly over the last ten years, we do accept (and always have done) the definition of sport as set out in the Council of Europe European Sports Charter.

(4) A lot of time has been spent by Sport England trying to work out what its relationship would be with the Countryside Agency and what could loosely be described as water and countryside sport. (4)

(5) I'm afraid I can't really see where—at the regional level where we have tended to focus on developing sports participation through promotional initiatives—I can't see where we would have any common ground with the tourism bodies.

Comments 1 and 2 are from interviews with informed sources in the regional tourism agencies. Comments 3, 4, and 5 are from informed source interviews with sports agencies.

---

as such it is not possible to generalize that this is a factor across all regions. Nevertheless, the interviews suggest that in between 40% and 60% of regions there are misconceptions about roles and remits that may be affecting liaison. However, a further factor, prevalent across all those interviewed, is a generally narrow view of the extent of the sport– tourism link.

Perceptions of the Nature and Extent of the Sport–Tourism Link

Panel 2 includes comments relating to policy makers' perceptions of the nature and extent of the sport–tourism link. Comments 6 and 8 highlight two levels of attitude of sports agencies to the sport–tourism link. The first level, also vividly stated in comment 5 (Panel 1), is that tourism is not something that sports bodies get involved in; it is outside their remit. Obviously this attitude is prohibitive of the development of any partnership with tourism agencies. However, even the second level of sports agency attitude is not particularly enlightened. Comment 8 talks of the need to "break down the question and look at the specifics in more detail," but such specifics still only reach as far as "the impact of the national stadium, justifying lottery investment, impact of the Commonwealth Games, Olympic bid and other events." The attitude that the links between sport and tourism only stretch as far as major events is also prevalent among the regional tourism agencies, with comment 7 being representative of at least 50 percent of such agencies who see major facilities as a prerequisite for the development of the sports tourism product.

The social aspect of sport is quoted by one of the national agencies (comment 9) as a reason why there is not a great deal of linkage between sport and tourism. The respondent contends that people holiday with their family, but take part in sport with their peer group and friends. However, this view fails to recognize the enabling potential of sport on holiday and its sports development potential. There are a number of aspects to this (Jackson & Glyptis, 1992). Firstly, the family holiday may be the only time during the year that

---

PANEL 2. Perceptions of the Extent of the Sport–Tourism Link

(6) It's not a topical issue, and it's partly due to the word "tourism"— it's not something we are involved in or do. If it's particular issues, like the impact of the national stadium, justifying lottery investment, impact of the Commonwealth Games, Olympic bid and other events, then you trigger off different responses. We don't always think laterally.

(7) Nothing has triggered off in my mind any suspicion that there is something major we should be doing in the sports field. . . . If I was in London and I had a lot of leading facilities, the Earls Courts, the big stadia, I'd be saying something different about sport.

(8) The Sport England view is evident— it's not something we're directly interested in, we can't see the relevance of tourism to sport. However, if you break down the questions, and look in detail at the specifics then some areas become relevant . . . [but] . . . the stock Sports England response, on the face of it, eliminates so many things.

(9) A lot of the work that has been done in sport and recreation is about sports development, and people take part in sport with their peer groups and friends, not with their family—they go on holiday with their family. That's probably one of the reasons there's not a great deal of linkage.

(10) People want to go where these activities could be undertaken, they wouldn't actually . . . take part in these activities, far from it, but they wanted them to be available—the fact that we have this clean and healthy outdoors image is important.

(11) I'm not sure where the sport-tourism links are in this town, apart from leisure centers. Water based activity it tends to be—do Sport England put money into wind-surfing, sailing, etc?

(12) Generally, I think its true that it's seen as more legitimate to link tourism with the arts than with sport.

(13) I think there's certain people in the Sports Council (I suppose you could also say it about the tourist agencies) who are— well, I wouldn't say schizophrenic—but there's sometimes been a lack of clarity about the role of the Sports Council, government hasn't helped. It always surprised me that there were a lot of people . . . who couldn't understand why sport and tourism had anything to do with one another. I've tried to say, "it's all part of the broader leisure picture," but they kept coming back to their key sports activities and didn't want to do any more beyond that, which I found strange. Even the fact that visitors coming into the region might be trying new sporting activities didn't seem necessarily anything to do with them.

Comments 7 and 13 are from informed source interviews with regional tourism agencies. Comments 6, 8, 9, and 10 are from national agency informed source interviews. Comments 11 and 12 are from informed source interviews with sub-regional agencies.

people are free of everyday family responsibilities and so they have time to take part in activities that they would not normally do. Secondly, there are often opportunities to take part in activities on holiday that are not readily available in the tourist's home area. Finally, through access to facilities and tuition in a casual atmosphere, holiday sports participation has the potential to introduce people to new activities and to equip them with the skills to feel confident enough to pursue such activities in their home area. The potential of the sport–tourism link in these areas represents a significant lost opportunity for sports development. However, for this opportunity to be taken, considerably more "lateral thinking" (comment 6) than takes place at present needs to occur in the minds of many sports development professionals.

Comment 10 refers to the potential of sport to aid tourism in promoting a "clean and healthy outdoor image" of an area. Aside from the promotion of major events, this seems to be the main area in which the tourism industry uses sport (see Weed & Bull, 1997a). This comment alludes to the need to promote the image of being a sporting area without necessarily having to actually provide the opportunities. Obviously, if the tourist agencies believe that this is the case, there would not be a need to collaborate with sports bodies as it would be a purely promotional measure.

An ignorance of what the links between sport and tourism are also manifests itself at the subregional level. Comment 11 is from a tourism officer responsible for a prominent coastal town and it highlights a lack of appreciation both of where the links lie and of the roles and remits of the various sports agencies. With significant amounts of funding being available from the Lottery Sports Fund it is particularly surprising that this tourism officer is unaware of whether water sports are funded.

Each of the comments in Panel 2 would appear to be indicative of a view among professionals in both sport and tourism policy communities that, generally, there are few links between sport and tourism. The view that a link between tourism and the arts is seen as more legitimate (comment 12) may be a further indication of this. However, perhaps the most compelling evidence is provided by comment 13, which refers to the lack of clarity from both the sport and the tourism agencies about their respective roles, with the respondent attributing some of the blame for this to central government. Nevertheless, he also identifies a general attitude among sports agency staff that sport and tourism are not linked in any way. In addition, earlier in the comment he suggests that there is a similar attitude among some tourism agency staff—a view that, to some extent, has also been highlighted by earlier evidence which highlights a negative or very narrow view of the sport tourism link. Such attitudes are not unusual in policy communities, with M. Smith (1993) referring to a consensus or ideology in policy communities that limits the range of policy areas that might legitimately be discussed. It would appear that within both sport and tourism policy communities this range does not extend to links across the two sectors.

Perceptions of the Influence of Regional Agencies

Further to the above discussion, there is some evidence to suggest that staffs in both the sport and tourism agencies are unaware of the potential they have to influence others. A lack of resources is often quoted as a reason for not becoming involved in sport–tourism partnerships; however, strategic advocacy involves only a negligible amount of funds and is, potentially, very effective in promoting the sport–tourism link (Panel 3).

Comments 14 and 15 highlight, from both a sport and tourism agency perspective, the importance they attach to their role as strategic advocates seeking to "advise, support and promote" in order to influence others. The sport agency even refers to this as an "imitation" of its role. However, the respondents making comments 16 and 17 are keen to emphasize, from a sport and a tourism perspective, respectively, that there is much liaison that occurs that does not appear in regional strategy statements. Given their self-professed roles as strategic advocates seeking to advise and support others, this is somewhat strange. Certainly the responses from subregional agencies (comments 18 and 19) highlight the need for the regional agencies to "be seen in the arena

---

PANEL 3. Perceptions of the Influence of Regional Agencies

(14) We play the part we can given our resources, which will be one of strategic advocacy mainly. We're not able to deliver much.

(15) We . . . [sports agency] . . . develop a strategy to guide the actions of others in developing sport. . . . Whilst it can forge partnerships at the regional level with other bodies such as those responsible for tourism, such partnerships are limited in so far as they can only seek to advise support and promote.

(16) While there is little reference in the regional strategy, in this region we recognize the potential links that exist. . . . The Sports Council works closely at an operational level with colleagues in the Regional Tourist Board, especially on information.

(17) While our regional strategies are important, it is important to understand that many links take place throughout the year that are not mentioned in the regional strategies.

(18) They should work together on things like encouraging cycling, national cycle routes, regional cycle routes, and marketing those things—we're too small to do it. They need to work on the initiation of things of that nature.

(19) There's a large market for events. EG, motor racing—I don't think people such as Brands Hatch are courted by any of the regional agencies (for sport or for tourism). I think they need to be seen in that arena together . . . to set a joint stall up at various points to court these people and bring them together. . . . Brands Hatch don't even know about the Regional Tourist Board.

(20) We can exert maximum influence and leverage at the margins of tourism mainstream. . . . It's about using our knowledge and selling skills to influence plural and more complex agendas.

Comments 14, 17, and 20 are from informed source interviews with regional tourism agencies. Comments 15 and 16 are from informed source interviews with various sports agencies. Comments 18 and 19 are from informed source interviews with sub-regional agencies.

together" and to work together on the initiation of projects. This suggests that organizations working within regions are looking to the regional agencies to provide a lead and set the agenda on these matters. The final comment (20) in Panel 3 implies that this is a role tourist agencies are well equipped to take on, working "at the margins of tourism mainstream"—which is where, as discussed above, sport–tourism links are seen to fall—to "influence plural and more complex agendas." However, this particular agency, like many others, does not recognize nor refer to sports tourism in its regional strategy, and further believes that it is "a product type that has no particular strength in this region," despite the existence within its boundaries of a major urban conurbation that has staged a great number of international sporting events. It is to the perceptions of particular regional influences that the discussion now turns.

Perceptions of the Influence of Regional Contexts on Sport–Tourism Liaison

Despite the negative influences discussed above, in some areas specific regional contexts have led to a greater development of sport–tourism links, and some examples of this are given in Panel 4.

Comments 21 and 22 provide excellent examples of two very different specific regional situations that have pushed sport and tourism agencies closer together. The situation in relation to comment 21 is particularly unique, as a

---

PANEL 4. Perceptions of the Influence of Regional Contexts on Sport-Tourism Liaison

(21) We can't really look at this in isolation. We are part of this region, we're part of the framework within the region. So this region tends to have more of a tradition of public sector initiatives than . . . [other regions] . . . but it has a weaker private sector. . . . We've evolved as an organization within this region in a way that accords with the policy culture around us.

(22) The importance of sport to tourism depends on what you mean by sport—there's different types of sport. . . . a lot depends on the characteristics of the region as well. Here we've got the natural resources for a wide range of outdoor activities . . . that are a strong market segment in this area.

(23) [Work with tourist agencies] . . . is now more likely to be on a region by region basis on occasional topics that bring the organizations together. For example . . . there is more close contact with tourist agencies in regions with more urban areas because of the importance of sport, and particularly sports events, in the big cities.

(24) Our kind of tourism is linked with the countryside, walking, leisure, and heritage. Obviously that means the links with sport and recreation are closer. When we talk of sport we call it recreation and link it to tourism and the arts. I'm sure in other areas that's very different.

Comments 21 and 22 are from informed source interviews with regional tourism agencies. Comment 23 is from informed source interviews with sports agencies. Comment 24 is from informed source interviews with sub-regional tourism agencies.

range of historical socioeconomic problems and issues in this region have combined to increase the importance of public sector agencies and thus to stimulate interagency liaison, not just between sport and tourism, but between a whole range of regional agencies. Comment 22 relates to an English region with a significant rural landscape where the particular needs of the rural economy have brought the sport and tourism sectors closer together. However, as the comment shows, the respondent appreciates that sport can be defined in a number of different ways, and that this region has taken a view of sport that is appropriate to the regional tourism product. This contrasts with some of the attitudes discussed in Panel 2 and further highlights the importance of individual perceptions in successfully developing sport–tourism liaison. In fact, the individual factor could be quoted as an influence in all the quotes in Panel 4.

The sports agency comment (23) notes the importance of allowing for particular regional products, and the example quoted relating to cities and major events would appear to make sense. However, the situation conflicts with other evidence, which suggests that liaison on major events tends to take place at the city rather than the regional level: "Those special events can be exploited, but that is best done by the operator of the facility working with the local consortium of local authorities — it's not something you can do at regional level" (from the regional tourism agency informed source interviews).

This may be symptomatic of a trend to regard regional specificity as way of abdicating responsibility. Comment 23 states that liaison should be greater in other regions that have major facilities. Other tourism agency comments reflect similar sentiments: "We are a land-locked region, and without a coastline you rule out much of the sport–tourism product — other regions have greater strengths in sports tourism than us." "If I had some of the metropolitan areas with the major facilities I would regard sport as a much more significant player in the tourism market" (both comments from the regional tourism agency informed source interviews).

The first comment above comes from a region that has a range of major facilities within its boundaries, while the second comes from a coastal region. Both agencies are claiming that sports tourism is important, but not in their region, thus avoiding any responsibility for its development while still appearing to acknowledge its importance. Such comments disclaiming a need to be involved as a consequence of the situation in the region are representative of around 50 percent of the regions.

Comment 24, which reflects on the importance of the region's natural resources for sports tourism, is perhaps again an example of regional characteristics combining with an individual who has a broader perspective of the nature of the sport–tourism link resulting in a greater recognition being made of the sports tourism product.

Discussion

In summary, the discussions above indicate that a significant number of policy makers in sport and in tourism have a generally narrow view of the sport–

tourism link, a lack of understanding of the roles and remits of other agencies, and a lack of appreciation of the role they can play in influencing other agencies. However, the discussions also indicate that, in some cases, perceptions of the particular needs of the region can play a role in stimulating liaison, although regional differences can also be used as a way of abdicating responsibility for developing sport–tourism partnerships. In conclusion, it is useful to consider these findings within the context of the model of the sport–tourism policy process developed by Weed (2001, 2003).

Weed's model of the policy process, as described earlier, shows that policy making for sport and for tourism takes place within sectorized arenas called policy communities (Marsh & Rhodes, 1992). The issues on which the interests of sport and tourism policy communities overlap is where a sport–tourism policy network (Wright, 1988) may potentially emerge. However, a number of factors have been shown to influence the emergence of such a policy network. Firstly, the varying structures of sport and of tourism policy communities may influence the extent to which a sport–tourism policy network may emerge. Secondly, a range of factors within and between sport and tourism policy communities may also influence the development of a network, these being: ideology, definitions, regional contexts, government policy, organizational culture and structure, and individuals. While it would seem reasonable to assume that issues related to policy makers' perceptions would largely be influenced by individual factors, the discussions above show the interrelated nature of the range of factors that might influence the emergence of a sport–tourism policy network. The relationship between policy makers' perceptions and factors that influence sport–tourism partnerships appears to be dialectical. Perceptions are clearly influenced by a range of factors; however, in turn these perceptions reinforce and reproduce the influence of such factors. This is perhaps best illustrated by some examples from the issues discussed in this paper.

In Panel 1, comments 1 and 2 (from policy makers in regional tourism agencies) both refer to "recreational" facilities/use that are not seen to be part of the remit of sports agencies. Clearly these responses are derived from a perception that sport is defined as competitive or formal activities, and that more informal recreations such as walking, hiking, and recreational cycling are not part of such a definition. While such definitions are derived from the (mistaken) perceptions of policy makers, they also influence the perceptions of policy makers and, consequently, lack of liaison between sport and tourism agencies based on such misconceptions is perpetuated. A similar reinforcing set of perceptions, illustrated by both individual and institutional definitions of sports tourism, is highlighted by Panel 2. Here, comments 6 and 7 show that policy makers, in both sport and tourism agencies, tend to see sports tourism as being almost entirely about major events. Yet an increasing range of evidence has been presented in the literature showing that the links between sport and tourism are far more extensive than major events (e.g., Hinch & Higham, 2004; Hudson, 2003; Ritchie & Adair, 2004; Weed & Bull, 2004). However, as much sport–tourism liaison is limited by a perceived definition of the area of sports tourism as being about sports events, liaison remains limited to this area and thus such perceptions are reinforced.

This dialectical relationship is also evident when the influence of regional contexts is considered. Panel 4 shows that policy makers perceive the regional situation to be important in the development of any sport–tourism partnerships, but the related discussions also highlight the way in which policy makers tend to perceive that other regions have greater strengths in relation to the sports tourism product. Here, a perception that sport–tourism links are not important in their region is reinforced by an interpretation of the regional context that legitimizes such perceptions. Once again, the relationship between perceptions and other influencing factors is shown to be a two-way, dialectical one that reinforces and reproduces the influence of both.

The importance of dialectical relationships in policy community/network analysis has been recognized in the more recent literature (Marsh, 1998; Marsh & Smith, 2000). The overarching aim of this developing dialectical approach has been to increase the explanatory power of such analyses. Marsh and Smith (2000) see a dialectical approach as being concerned with an interactive relationship between two variables in which each has a bearing on the other in an iterative process. They note that policy makers' decisions reflect past and present policy-making culture and values. Furthermore, reinforcing the discussions above, Marsh and Smith (2000) note that policy makers interpret other influencing factors in the policy process and, through that interpretation, such factors are mediated as affecting but not determining policy makers' perceptions. The central message of a dialectical approach is that there is a range of relationships between factors that influence policy and policy makers' perceptions of such factors, but that such relationships are not straightforward unidimensional or causal relationships.

The implications of this dialectical perspective for the model of the policy process for sport and tourism developed by Weed (2001, 2003) are that it is not only the identified factors (community structure, ideology, definitions, regional contexts, government policy, organizational culture and structure, and individuals) that affect the development of sport–tourism liaison, but also, importantly, policy makers' perceptions of such factors. Furthermore, there is a "continuing iterative process" (Marsh & Smith, 2000) in which such factors are interpreted and reinterpreted, thus further influencing the perceptions of policy makers. While this adds a further dimension to Weed's (2001, 2003) work, it also reinforces the continuing relevance of this model in understanding sport–tourism policy development.

Acknowledgment

I would like to acknowledge the contribution of Dr Chris Bull (Canterbury Christ Church University, UK) to the production of this paper, both in terms of assisting with data collection and with advice about the conduct of the analysis.

Note

1. In this article two different terms are used: "sports tourism" and "sport–tourism link/partnerships/liaison/etc." This is quite deliberate and indicative of a specific difference. The term sports tourism is generally taken to refer to tourism that includes some sports participation, either active or passive. The use of the en dash refers to the broader concept of the "sport–tourism link." There are many issues on which there might be a profitable link between sport and tourism organizations, which would not fall within the generally accepted definition of sports tourism. There is also some debate about whether the term "sports tourism" or the term "sport tourism" should be used. The preference here is for the term "sports tourism," the conceptual rationale for which is explained by Weed and Bull (2004, pp. xiv– xv).

References

Chalip, L., Johnson, A., & Stachura, L. (1996). *National sports policies: An international handbook*. Westport, CT: Greenwood Press.

Charmaz, K. (2000). Grounded theory: Objectivist and constructivist methods. In N. K. Denzin & Y. S. Lincoln (Eds.), *Handbook of qualitative research* (2nd ed.). London: Sage.

Collins, M., & Jackson, G. (1999). The economic impact of sport and tourism. In J. Standeven & P. De Knop (Eds.), *Sport tourism*. London: Human Kinetics.

De Knop, P. (1990, Fall). Sport for all and active tourism. *Journal of the World Leisure and Recreation Association*, 30–36.

Getz, D. (2003). Bidding on events: Identifying event selection criteria and critical success factors. *Journal of Convention and Exhibition Management, 5*(2), 1–24.

Glaser, B., & Strauss, A. (1967). *The discovery of grounded theory*. Chicago: Aldine.

Gibson, H. (2002). Sport tourism at a crossroad? Considerations for the future. In S. Gammon & J. Kurtzman (Eds.), *Sport tourism: Principles and practice*. Eastbourne: Leisure Studies Association.

Glyptis, S. (1991). Sport and tourism. In C. Cooper (Ed.), *Progress in tourism, recreation and hospitality management* (Vol. 3). London: Belhaven Press.

Hall, C. (1994). *Tourism and politics: Policy, power and place*. London: Belhaven Press. Higham, J. (Ed.). (2005). *Sport tourism destinations: Issues, opportunities and analysis*. Oxford: Elsevier.

Higham, J., & Hinch, T. (2002). Sport, tourism and seasons: The challenges and potential of overcoming seasonality in the sport and tourism sectors. *Tourism Management, 23*, 175–185.

Hinch, T., & Higham, J. (2004). *Sport tourism development*. Clevedon: Channel View Publications.

Houlihan, B. (1991). *The government and the politics of sport*. London: Routledge.

Houlihan, B. (1997). *Sport, policy and politics: A comparative analysis*. London: Routledge.

Houlihan, B. (1999). *Dying to win: Doping in sport and the development of anti-doping policy*. Strasbourg: Council of Europe.

Hudson. S. (Ed.). (2003). *Sport and adventure tourism*. New York: Haworth Hospitality Press.

Jackson, G., & Glyptis, S. (1992). *Sport and tourism: A review of the literature* (unpublished report to the Sports Council). Loughborough, UK: Loughborough University, Recreation Management Group.

Jackson, G., & Reeves, M. (1998). Evidencing the sport-tourism interrelationship: A case study of elite British athletes. In M. Collins & I. Cooper (Eds.), *Leisure management: Issues and applications*. London: CAB International.

King, N. (1994). The qualitative research interview. In C. Cassell & G. Symon (Eds.), *Qualitative methods in organisational research: A practical guide*. London: Sage.

Layder, D. (1993). *New strategies in social research*. Cambridge: Polity Press.

Lowe, P. (1981). *A political analysis of British rural conservation issues and policies*. Final report to the Social Science Research Council (Rep. No. HR5010). London: University College London.

Lowe, P., & Goyder, J. (1983). *Environmental groups in politics*. London: Allen & Unwin.

Marsh, D. (1998). The utility and future of policy network analysis. In D. Marsh (Ed.), *Comparing policy networks*. Buckingham: Open University Press.

Marsh, D., & Rhodes, R. (1992). Policy communities and issue networks: Beyond typology. In D. Marsh & R. Rhodes (Eds.), *Policy networks in British government*. Oxford: Oxford University Press.

Marsh, D., & Smith, M. (2000). Understanding policy networks: Towards a dialectical approach. *Political Studies, 48*, 4–21.

Marshall, H. (1994). Discourse analysis in an occupational context. In C. Cassell & G. Symon (Eds.), *Qualitative methods in organisational research: A practical guide*. London: Sage.

McCutcheon, J. (2002). Free movement in European sport. *European Sport Management Quarterly, 2*(4), 308–320.

Oakley, B., & Green, M. (2001). Still playing the game at arm's length? The selective reinvestment in British sport, 1995–2000. *Managing Leisure, 6*(2), 74–94.

Reeves, M. (2000). *Evidencing the sport–tourism interrelationship*. Unpublished doctoral thesis, Loughborough University, UK.

Rhodes, R. (1986). *The national world of local government*. London: Macmillan.

Ritchie, B., & Adair, D. (Eds.). (2004). *Sport tourism: Interrelationships, impacts and issues*. Clevedon: Channel View.

Sam, M. (2003). What's the big idea? Reading the rhetoric of a national sport policy process. *Sociology of Sport Journal, 20*(3), 189–213.

Smith, J. A. (1996). Beyond the divide between cognition and discourse: Using interpretive phenomenological analysis in health psychology. *Psychology and Health, 11*, 261–271.

Smith, M. (1993). *Pressure, power and policy*. Hemel Hempstead: Harvester Wheatsheaf.

Sports Council. (1994). *Sport in the nineties–new horizons*. London: Sports Council.

Standeven, J., & De Knop, P. (1999). *Sport tourism*. IL, USA: Human Kinetics.

Standeven, J., & Tomlinson, A. (1994). *Sport and tourism in South East England: A preliminary assessment*. London: SECSR.

Swart, K. (1998). Visions for South African sport tourism. *Visions in Leisure and Business, 17*(2), 4–12.

Turco, D., Riley, R., & Swart, K. (2002). *Sport tourism*. Morgantown: Fitness Information Technology.

Vrondou, O. (1999). *Sports related tourism and the product repositioning of traditional mass tourism destinations: A case study of Greece*. Unpublished doctoral thesis, Loughborough University, UK.

Weed, M. E. (1999). *Consensual policies for sport and tourism in the UK: An analysis of organisational behaviour and problems*. Unpublished doctoral thesis, Canterbury Christ Church University College/University of Kent at Canterbury, UK.

Weed, M. E. (2001). Towards a model of cross-sectoral policy development in leisure: The case of sport and tourism. *Leisure Studies, 20*, 125–141.

Weed, M. E. (2002a). Football hooligans as undesirable sports tourists: Some meta-analytical speculations. In S. Gammon & J. Kurtzman (Eds.), *Sport tourism: Principles and practice*. Eastbourne: LSA.

Weed, M. E. (2002b). Organisational culture and the leisure policy process in Britain: How structure affects strategy in sport-tourism policy development. *Tourism, Culture & Communication, 3*(3), 147–164.

Weed, M. E. (2003). Why the two won't tango: Explaining the lack of integrated policies for sport and tourism in the UK. *Journal of Sport Management, 17*(3), 258–283.

Weed, M. E. (2005). A grounded theory of the policy process for sport and tourism. *Sport and Society, 8*(2), 356–377.

Weed, M. E., & Bull, C. J. (1997a). Integrating sport and tourism: A review of regional policies in England. *Progress in Tourism and Hospitality Research, 4*, 129–148.

Weed, M. E., & Bull, C. J. (1997b). Influences on sport– tourism relations in the UK: The effects of government policy. *Tourism Recreation Research, 22*(2), 5–12.

Weed, M. E., & Bull, C. J. (1998). The search for a sport–tourism policy network . In M. Collins & I. Cooper (Eds.), *Leisure management: Issues and applications*. Oxford, UK: CABI.

Weed, M. E., & Bull, C. J. (2004). *Sports tourism: Participants, policy and providers*. Oxford, UK: Elsevier.

Wilks, S., & Wright, M. (Eds.). (1987). *Comparative government–industry relations*. Oxford: Clarendon Press.

Wright, M. (1988). Policy community, policy network and comparative industrial policies. *Political Studies, 36*, 593–612.

MODERN SPORT AND OLYMPIC GAMES: THE PROBLEMATIC COMPLEXITIES RAISED BY THE DYNAMICS OF GLOBALIZATION

Deane Neubauer

Introduction

The notion of globalization has become commonplace. We find it in everyday conversation, throughout news reports, within scholarly discourse — seemingly everywhere. On closer inspection, however, we observe that what is meant by globalization often differs. In some usages it seems to be shorthand for the impression that the world is a "closer place." We are linked to each other more immediately by transportation and communication. For others of us, this sense of linkage is tangible: we look at the goods we purchase (and increasingly the services as well) and note their distant place of origin. Yet, in other contexts globalization is seen simultaneously as benefit and cost. For example, Americans (and many others in the world) rely on Walmart as a source of inexpensive consumer items — clearly a marker of globalization since most of Walmart's goods emanate from the cheaper labor pools of China. About this they feel good. At the same time, immigration causes consternation the world over as the apparently "border flattening" nature of contemporary globalization promotes migration, legal and undocumented, about which strong attitudes prevail. Obviously, globalization is a many-factored "thing," some aspects of which may be viewed with approval, whereas others are viewed with anxiety or hostility.

In this essay, I would like to attempt some "brush clearing" with the notion of globalization, bringing some clarification to its nature and the uses to which we put the concept. Having done so, I then turn to the issue of professional sport and the Olympic games and seek to situate them problematically within a globalized context.

Some Relevant Dynamics of Globalization

Is globalization a contemporary phenomenon or an ancient phenomenon? And what difference does it make? For globalization scholars this is an important question because how one responds to it largely determines what one seeks to study within the vast amount of phenomena that make it up and the significance that is attributed to findings about it. Essentially, the scholarly world is divided into those who perceive the social history of mankind as one long journey toward the greater integration of peoples and places and those who see important interruptions in this process. From the long history point of view globalization has advanced in some degree with every new discovery, every new act of trade, every new exchange of symbols and values. This perspective has been beautifully rendered in the recent book by Professor Nayan Chandra whose detailing of this long historical movement toward contemporary integration spans huge amounts of human history.[1]

A quite different view holds that while acknowledging the force and effect of such movements toward integration as a common part of human history, something quite different has occurred in the period of the last forty to fifty years that leads us to label this period as an era of *contemporary globalization*. The point is not to contest the historical globalization perspective, but to emphasize that within this recent frame of four or five decades something quite novel and different is taking place in the world.

These changes, as suggested by the term *contemporary globalization*, obviously and importantly build on the whole of the integrative movements that preceded them, much we have come also to acknowledge other labels for the contemporary period such as the information age, or the knowledge society, or the network society as importantly and necessarily derived from the industrial age that preceded them.[2]

What then *is* so different about contemporary globalization? Out of the many possible responses to that question I want to emphasize six. I will refer to these as some of the important *dynamics* of globalization, by which I mean the structures and processes that have emerged over these past several decades to form and drive contemporary globalization, giving it the special character we attribute to it. The six are: the collapse of time and space; migration and urbanization; wealth creation and distribution; the transformation of global media; the primacy of trade and consumption; and the transformation of values. I have selected these six because in ways that I will develop in part two of this paper, these are the dynamics that in my view are having the most transformative impact on global sport, and by extension, the Olympic Games and movement.

The Collapse of Time and Space

As Chandra's work attests, to some degree the historically large advances in globalization have been marked by advances in technology that allowed people to "move closer" to each other in the sense that the exchange of people and goods (and all this entails, e.g. language, culture, arts, exchanges of knowledge) was enhanced. Certainly many of the inventions of the 18th, 19th and early 20th century revolutionized society as powered ships, airplanes, automobiles, radio and telephony and above all, cheap and reliable electricity, fundamentally changed the way people lived in the world and sought out each other. (For, let it be emphasized, purposes good and ill, as this period also represents successive ages of conquest, domination and imperialism as well as the massive destruction of two world wars.) Within a twenty year period from the mid-1950's to the mid-1970's three technological inventions — satellite communications,[3] the Boeing 747 and the modern container ship had the effect of speeding up the interactions of time and space (while dramatically lowering unit transmission costs) sufficiently that by the early 1990's David Harvey would term this phenomena the collapse of time and space and see it as the harbinger of the contemporary age which he termed the "condition of post modernity."[4]

For Harvey and other commentators of this predisposition, a host of structural and behavioral transformations arise from this technological conjunction. Global instantaneous communications such as those made possible by satellite technology have been the preconditions for such different innovations as the creation of 24/7 equity and currency markets, off-shoring of many services (including the people who answer the phones when you purchase something from your favorite catalogue), simultaneous global transmission of mega events including the World Cup and the Olympics and all the marketing demand that results from that, to the sustaining structures of remittance economies, and the uncountable linkages created and sustained by the Internet.[5] Modern air travel has resulted in the ability of literally hundreds of millions of persons annually to cross national borders any place on the globe within the span of a day. Moreover, an entire global industry has arisen based on the reliable and relatively inexpensive delivery of lower weight packages. But, the backbone of what economic globalization has become relies on the revolution in shipping and the continual innovations that bring declining unit costs to global shipping. If one root meaning of globalization is economic globalization — the trading of goods and services — shipping more than any other single variable has made it possible. Collectively, these three innovations stand at the apex of the complex processes that relocated global manufacturing from the older industrial countries to those of what was then the developing world, and which is now constituted largely as the newly developed countries, primarily those of Asia.

Migration and Urbanization

We now live on an urban planet. For the first time in human history by 2000 more people lived in cities than in the countryside, and the trend will continue. As Mike Davis has remarked, following UN Habitat data, within two decades the global countryside will have reached maximum carrying capacity: from that point on, all net growth will be in the cities.[6] Commonly accepted population projections anticipate that the global population will peak in 2150 with approximately 9.6 billion inhabitants. With roughly 6.7 billion inhabitants, the world has experienced enormous population growth over the past four decades, but we are only 2/3's toward this projected peak, currently adding approximately 76 million new inhabitants a year. Most of the growth is occurring in lesser developed countries; indeed, the older, industrial countries of the world exhibit demographic patterns of aging, declining populations.

As we globally cluster together, cities are becoming larger. The largest are now seen as mega cities—aggregations of 15 and 20+ millions of people. As these largest of cities grow, they become complex urban phenomena: aggregations or conurbations. They and their surrounds come to constitute contiguous populations measuring in the twenties and thirties of millions, so large and growing so rapidly that they challenge our very definition of what constitutes a city (What is its governmental definition? What is the source of its authority [ies]? Who is in charge of what?) The urbanist Michael Douglass looks at some of this massive growth and hypothesizes that the next century may witness the rebirth of the "city-state," for it is in these entities that not only populations are aggregated but increasingly also wealth and power.[7] Recent analyses of China indicate just such a power shift between government at the national and at the local and regional level.[8] Cities in the *globalscape* are centers of growing importance, especially as nodes in the linking of global finance, trade, cultural production, social change and communications.[9]

This combination of rapid and continued population growth and its aggregation in urban conglomerates has done much to give contemporary globalization its distinctive character. These factors combine in an almost infinite number of ways to speed up the processes of social and cultural change, especially with respect to the diffusion of technological innovations. One way to characterize globalization is to gauge its *reach* and *density*. Reach in this sense reflects distribution of effects over time and space; density refers to the number of factors that make up social life than can be directly linked to the various identifiable processes of globalization. Collectively, these are sometimes referred to as the "circuits" of globalization, utilizing this metaphor to suggest the kinds of exchanges and traffic taking place, their relative volume and importantly, the speed at which they take place. Harvey emphasizes that the speed of change itself is one of the factors that makes contemporary globalization distinct from its historical predecessors.[10]

Wealth Creation and Distribution

Globalization over the past five decades has been responsible for the enormous growth of overall wealth. Historians suggest that in relative terms, other historical periods may have been responsible for greater increments in the amount of wealth relative to existing social levels, but the amount of aggregate wealth existing in the world having been produced in a given period is unparalleled. The distribution of wealth and income, however, has become increasingly biased, in part the result of most global population growth having occurred in the poorer regions of the world. Overall, throughout the world the distribution of income within and between countries has become more uneven: there are more rich people in the world and there are more poor people in the world. It is estimated that the richest 1 percent of the world has more wealth than the bottom 57 percent.[11] The richer countries of the world are farther away in income terms from the poorer countries than they were thirty years ago. Within most of the industrial and rapidly industrial countries, the social policies developed by neoliberal political regimes have led to a concentration of wealth in a smaller portion of the population — this is true in Europe, North America, South America, Asia and Australasia. Often, these distributions are geographically oriented, as in the case of China where the beneficiaries of the booming industries of the coastal crescent, marked by its expanding cities that have drawn millions upon millions of migrants, stand in stark contrast to the lands and peoples of the western regions, who are commonly referred to in both government policy and popular texts as "the left behind." However, the trend is world-wide: an analysis of global cities documents this pattern of increasing inequality in virtually every case of a rapidly growing global conurbation.[12]

This relationship between globalization and increasing income inequality is not itself uncontested. In the United States for example, the perception of increasing income inequality has become part of the dispute over the relative status of the middle class and whether it is declining in relation to overall wealth and income distribution. Neoliberal commentators will point out that the amount of wealth possessed by the middle-class has grown consistently. Those disputing this view argue that measured in terms of historical (and widely accepted) measures of income inequality such as the Gini Index, inequality in the United States declined in the post-war years through those of the Carter Administration and then have been progressively on the rise. Data from the Congressional Budget Office are often cited to demonstrate the progressively unequal shares of economic growth in the decades of robust globalization. Data compiled by the World Bank to illustrate the extent of world poverty tend to reflect a similar story of growing world wealth capacity in the face of persistent distribution issues.

As this is being written the world is experiencing the most profound recession of the modern globalization era. The crisis emphasizes the complexities of interdependence on a global scale, illustrating that the dynamics of the American housing market can come to be represented in financial instruments that are traded throughout the world. As they evolved from representing "poor banking judgments" to "toxic assets," they have effected the entire global financial system, which in turn has triggered economic downturns throughout the world. It needs to be emphasized in this regard that as the world quickly "gives up" some of the vast amounts of wealth that it accrued over the past several decades, the human costs of this set of events will be distributed in both relative and absolute ways — those who have already found themselves disadvantaged by the structural inequalities of globalization will experience even greater difficulties in managing the necessities of daily life. Those who were significant beneficiaries of the vast wealth explosion with have suffered enormous and traumatic relative declines in their wealth and income status.

Transformation of Global Media

Changes taking place within the overall structure of global media illustrate a pattern of rapid and extensive distribution of capacity and content and relative consolidation and integration of media industries. The older media companies

Table 1. Top Ten Global Media Companies*

1. Time Warner Inc. (USA)	44,224
2. Walt Disney Company (USA)	34,285
3. The News Corporation Ltd. (UK)	25,327
4. Vivendi (USA)	25,148
5. Comcast Corporation (USA)	24,996
6. Bertelsmann AG (Germany)	24,211
7. Lagardère SCA (France)	18,187
8. The DirecTV Group Inc. (USA)	14,756
9. Dai Nippon Printing Co. (Japan)	13,390
10. Toppan Printing Co. (Japan)	13,308

* Ranking by total 2005 revenues ($ US million)
Source: //www.computerwire.com, 17 March 2008

based in print or electronic forms have shown a dramatic propensity to aggregate into larger firms, in part a response of some of the most powerful national firms becoming transnational firms to dominate the global media space. It is widely accepted that global media are dominated by the largest firms, as illustrated in Table 1. This pattern of domination by the largest firms is reproduced at a national level in most countries with well-developed media. This leads to the notion of two levels of media "domination" that of the "A" list—the top six or eight global firms that operate in most of the countries in the world—and the "B" list—those not in the big eight that dominate national media markets.

Global domination by the survivors of the competition among traditional media has been increasingly challenged by the economic power and reach of media conglomerates whose core businesses lie either in newer technologies, such as the largest of the cable companies and direct provision of content (e.g. DIRECTV), or have risen out of the Internet. Table 2 ranks companies based on gross advertising revenue and market capitalization. As can been easily seen, changing the criteria of relative domination brings a new set of players to the list. I wish to emphasize three things about the media as they have developed globally into these configurations. One is the historical argument made by McChesney and others that links the very size of the largest media forms to their capacity to dominate. Such domination takes many forms from the ability of the most wealthy to aggregate their wealth across media platforms, as has now become the case with the integration of media in such firms linking print, film and digital publication, advertising, and distribution throughout the world. Critics link this capacity to an ability to set agendas, to determine what is being said and seen by whom, and to the ability of the largest firms to assure their access to the highest levels of decision making throughout the world. This is an argument about power—political, economic, social and cultural

Table 2. Ranking of Top Ten Global Media Companies*

By estimated 2005 advertising revenue		By estimated 2005 market capitalization	
1. Time Warner	29.834	General Electric	370.2
2. News Corp	16.726	Google	145.7
3. General Electric	14.689	Time Warner	84.1
4. CBS	13.389	Walt Disney	72.0
5. Walt Disney	13.207	Yahoo	43.1
6. DirecTV	12.958	DirecTV	28.6
7. Bertelsmann	9.622	CBS	24.8
8. Cox Enterprises	9.452	News Corp.	24.6
9. Advance (USA)	7.536	BSkyB (UK)	19.3
10. Gannett (USA)	7.162	Clear Channel	18.0

* ($US billion)
Source: Joe Mandese, "Time Warner Dominates Global Media Dollars, Google in Market Value," *Media Post Publications*, Feb. 22, 2007

power — and its concentration in the hands of the few. The clear implication is that the few rarely employ such power for ends that stray far from their own. It is also an argument about *convention* — the largest media have the ability to establish media conventions throughout the globe by their almost limitless capacity to generate images and to iterate them through any number of texts and contexts. For McChesney and Schiller one of the critical social losses to their capacity is the fact and value of difference — the ability of other points of view to gain attention and to establish themselves as sites of legitimate interest and concern — power seeks conformity with the dominant norms and folkways of that power.[13]

From another perspective, and the second point to make, the specter of global media domination and its constrictive effects are lessened by the explosive rise of "face to face" media, represented by You Tube, My space and their many variants, which give relatively cost-less access to anyone. This capacity has demonstrated in any number of instances to be capable of generating an "immediate coherence" around a topical issue or story, a capacity that is enhanced by the equally burgeoning *blogosphere*.[14] Coupled with the unlimited power of Search, it is argued, these new media generate "new realities" as rapidly as the powerful conventional media constrain them. Indeed, it clearly seems the case that when an issue or story emerges in the new media worthy of attention, the conventional media are quick to cover it and make it their own.

The third point is to emphasize how little we still appear to know about the phenomenon of Search and its linkages through new devices to the Internet and various other components of broadband communication. If, as Google and its companionable competitors claim, it will be the case in the not too distant future that the whole of the world's surviving print experience is available to us (at nominal cost), then surely it is probably the case that the digital information world also promises such availability. Indeed, in his exploration of *the long tail* Chris Anderson suggests that digital storage and distribution of media have already begun to significantly affect the economics of storage and distribution for many products — anything that can be digitized — music being perhaps the most immediately noticeable.[15] The point, as most of us suspect in our exploration of our IPhones, cable boxes, related devices, is that the generational cycles of digital invention and diffusion are tending to briefer and shorter periods with ever-decreasing capability for confident prediction about how we will communicate and make up the world one or two cycles down the road. It does seem clear that what we have over the past several decades confidently termed "media" has changed much and will continue to do so.

Trade and Consumption

Nayan Chandra views trade as the historical measure of globalization.

> Trade would transform societies when a trading class would rise to challenge state power. With the expansion of long-distance exchanges, trading diasporas would emerge to connect communities even more strongly. Driven by traders — people who earned a living by exchange of goods and services, or, in the modern parlance, businesspeople — the commercial network would continually expand, thicken, and accelerate to eventually encompass the globe to an ever-tightening web.[16]

This web of increasing inter-connectiveness and interdependence is clearly at the core of the complex of dynamics, interactions and structures that we conventionally term globalization. These are Sassen's "circuits" — a myriad of exchanges, each with a content and a flow, each with a pattern of origination and distribution. Increasingly, what we trade is what we are, and seemingly we trade everything.

In the context we are developing here, and keeping in mind the arguments we will explore in part two of the paper, I want to underscore three elements of trade and consumption: its extent, its distribution, and its relative fragility.

Extent: No one knows quite how to measure the amount of trade that takes place in the contemporary world economy. The trade in goods has historically been defined by convention: it is the sum total of goods that passes borders. To confound this simple notion we need only observe that Illegal trafficking in goods has always made this notion somewhat quaint. In this era of contemporary globalization the sheer number and amounts of things that are illegally trafficked, whether they be drugs (including counterfeit pharmaceuticals), arms, software and other digital content, or persons, renders them uncountable.[17] What we do know is that the magnitudes are significant and make up a sizeable part of global exchanges.

The volume of *officially* traded goods also staggers the imagination. The World Trade Organization designates trade by the two major categories of

Table 3. Global Trade Volumes in Merchandise and Services

Value ($US trillion)		Annual Change (percent)			
Year	2006	2000–06	2004	2005	2006
Merchandise	11.762	11	22	14	15
Services	2.710	10	10	11	11

Source: World Trade Organization, *World Trade Report 2007*

goods and services. Table Three indicates both the volume of merchandise and services traded in 2006 ($11.762 trillion and $2.710 trillion respectively) and the percentage change over the past six years. (By comparison, global GDP for 2007 is established by the World Bank at $42.799.2 trillion.)[18]

Distribution: Three facts stand out when examining the distribution of world trade. One, most trade in the world is still intra-regional, rather than inter-regional. Despite the enormous advances made in cutting the cost and raising the efficiency of transportation, distance matters. And, second, despite the enormous in-roads that digitalization has made on communication (a critical element of the trade in many services), most global trade is still in merchandise as opposed to services as indicated above. Third, the growth of Asia as a contributor to world trade continues to grow, fueled primarily by the continued spectacular growth of China, particularly as an exporting nation.

Fragility

Despite the enormous volumes of global trade and the extraordinary growth and participation rates demonstrated by new economically developed nations in global trade, as a system it exhibits a fragility that can easily be overlooked. It is useful to remember that inter-dependence has two sides to it. One is made up of the relative synergies that take place within complex systems in the face of growth dynamics — as one component of the system grows, it may do so in ways that produce corresponding growth in other parts of the system as well. This is the "up" side to global trade, the one most emphasized by the WTO when it argues that the growth of global trade acts as a "pull" factor for the overall growth of gross domestic products. The other side of inter-dependence is clearly demonstrated when one part of the system contracts — especially if that is an important component, and the contraction is sudden. This happened with the bursting of the "Japanese economic bubble" in 1988, the effects of which were experienced throughout the world. As I write, a similar dynamic is apparent in the United States where the sub-prime mortgage crisis and the subsequent credit crunch have led to a weakening of consumer demand and an economy probably already in recession. The United States is the largest single nation importer of goods in the world, increasingly those produced in China. A contraction of the US consumer market leads quickly to a slow-down in orders for Chinese goods, which leads to laying off workers and shutting factories, etc.[19]

These familiar dynamics of inter-dependence have been "speeded" up by the existence of a 24/7 financial equity system, and instant communications. A sudden downturn in US equity markets is quickly experienced in others. One part of the system transmits its signals to another in a time frame and with an effect that is unique to contemporary globalization.

Consumption: In ways suggested by the immediate foregoing, contemporary globalization has its core driving force in its economic component, and this has led to an unprecedented world-wide emphasis on consumption. In a prescient volume written in 1982 Mary Douglas and Baron Isherwood characterize the contemporary world as a "world of goods." They mean by this to underscore the degree to which virtually all elements of social life, certainly in the advanced economic societies, are dominated by the search for and the ability to acquire "goods."[20] It is a commonplace in speaking of the US economy to point out that it is driven by consumption, and then to add almost as an afterpoint that the relative health of the economy has become dependent on the willingness of consumers to sustain record amounts of personal debt in pursuit of this now-necessary consumption.

Three aspects of consumption are interest. One is the sense in which consumption in the contemporary global experience has come to constitute a "good" as either a material object or as a service. The second is that most world trade — the primary vehicle by which global interdependence and connectedness has been achieved — is primarily organized around consumption, as opposed to manufacture. The world economy increasingly depends on how much people consume — demand has come to be of relatively greater importance than supply. And, three, because of this aspect and importance of consumption, it lies at the core of global interdependence. *All* of the facts that underlie consumption, but perhaps most specifically the distribution of income and wealth, are critical to the overall health of the global system and what it is motivated and able to trade and consume.

Transformation of Value

In a world of goods, they are what matters. Both the argument in support of further globalization and the critiques lodged against it take this as a primary premise. The proponents of globalization look to a world made continually better by trade, by increases in the amount of global wealth, by the rationalization and liberalization of political and economic systems. In the world of this vision, the private sector comes to be privileged over the public sector; incomes should be taxed as minimally as possible so that money can be in the hands of private investors who through processes of savings, consumption and investment will make the kinds of decisions that drive markets, which in turn contribute to the overall health of economies, and from that societies. This is a familiar story, some version of which is present in every debate in parliament, and in some form or another a part of the evening news. In work that we do at the Globalization Research Center, we call this the "globalization as progress" narrative. This is the "story" of globalization that abounds in the *Wall Street*

Journal, The Economist, and with their relentless message of "you are what you acquire and consume," the tabloids as well.

Those opposed to globalization in one or another way tend to pursue a "globalization as disaster narrative." Here the "story" of globalization is related not as one of continued progress, but as various disasters, real and portending. In some versions of the story local economic viability is overcome by the massive forces of external economic development. In this story usually something precious in the provision of a local good or service is foregone to the less humanly relevant attributes of the global intruder. This, for example, this is a familiar story of loss often related to bemoan the incursion of corporate fast food into local culturally related food patterns. Frequently the "local" is situated directly in the locus of language, custom and culture, which are threatened from the "outside"—a familiar human story of endogeny being challenged by exogeny. (Many of Chandra's tales of ever increasing globalization are set at this interface.) The disaster narrative has many variants and elements, ranging from the loss of local languages[21] to the threats to human planetary viability itself occasioned by global warming, sea level rise, emerging world food shortages as industrial countries convert food stocks into fuel, and the tensions that arise from steadily increasing patterns of inequality. If economic reductionism is the primary value of the progress narrative, other values such as those associated with notions of community and non-economic social values are featured in the disaster narrative.

My point is that globalization has capitalized (literally) on a value shift that reorients other historically relevant values on which society has traditionally been based, values that assign status and place within communities, guide behavior and purport to give meaning to life. The economic imperatives of globalization either act to replace such values with those of the marketplace or to diminish the relative status that non-economic values—the meaning assigned to goods—have within a nation or community's social cosmology.[22] I return to this point below.

Global Professional Sport and the Olympics

Let me draw out these six globalization themes (or dynamics) with direct reference to global professional and Olympic sport. In doing so, I emphasize that globalization in virtually every aspect displays its role as an element in a complex interdependent system whose components are all interlinked. For ease of analysis and discussion it is possible to isolate and separate these elements. In practice the interrelations are omnipresent—one part is always affecting another.

The collapse of time and space creates the immediacy that enables global sport. The instantaneous movement of images across time and space makes possible the sense of team and athlete identification on which sport marketing depends. Its vehicle is global media, which provide the enormous sums that fuel the leagues, teams and athletes and capture the attention of billions throughout the world. The current and rapidly growing linkage of sport to the emergent media of hand-held devices emphasizes this immediacy even further by creating a world in which the dedicated fan is offered significant options in the way events are portrayed across various sporting platforms. Commercially, providers of such media array consumption options across a wide range of "products" to differentiate markets and seek to brand this differentiation itself as a way of interacting with sports.

The immediacy of sport allows for the creation of global circuits involving the exchange (trade) of symbols, images and goods. These exchanges have a local impact, in that they involve real events, happening in real time in front of real people. Simultaneously, however, they produce a value capable of being multiplied hundreds and thousands of times over through the transmission of the event image and all the spin-offs that are produced in both traditional and emergent media. As an overall phenomenon the circulation of such images generate derivative *value-eddies* throughout the globe, collected and concentrated in the vast centers of a now urbanized world.

Over the past three decades, global sport has followed the developmental course of the more inclusive global economy. In this respect there is little that is unique to global sport, but much that is representative of other global structures. It is also useful to note that the progressive collapse of time and space of globalization was previewed in the development of national economies over a century earlier as new technologies — railroads, the telephone, electricity, internal combustion vehicles, airplanes and powered ships brought people closer together in time and space. In this earlier period these innovations in national economies and societies led to increasing integration of both production and consumption, and in time new national identities and behaviors.[23]

Modern industrial society created a middle class and with it the invention of "leisure" — time taken away from work to enjoy the increasing pleasures of a rapidly changing world. Those pleasures included the rapid expansion of arts and letters — and sport. Increased wealth allowed the commodification of sport organized first into local and then regional teams and leagues. The modern Olympics themselves appear on the world scene in 1896 in the midst of what Daniel Boorstin would call the most "inventive" decades of world history, meaning the period from roughly 1875 to the outbreak of the first world war.[24] In the 20th century, sport developed across national scales. With the advent of contemporary globalization and the new accelerations of communication and transport, sport has become increasingly organized as a hierarchy of professionalized and global endeavors.

Sport's Dependence on Urbanization

Rapid and substantial urbanization have historically been important for the growth of professional sport. The concentration of wealth associated with urbanization combines with the human density required to provide acceptable economic return to teams and the complexity of social interactions required to produce and reproduce a viable fan base, especially one capable of sustaining regularly rising prices. Typically, significant and rapid urban growth occurred as people moved from rural to urban employment in manufacturing and service. This is precisely the phenomenon currently taking place in the developing world. For example, the rural to urban migration in China during the 1990s is held to be the largest migration in human history. In the experience of the older industrial nations, urban concentrations became aggregates for capital and finance, knowledge entities such as schools and universities, communication and media. The actions taken by China to produce the sites and arrangements for the 2008 Olympics own virtually everything to the vast collection of wealth and services capable of being aggregated in a contemporary global city, which Beijing has rapidly become.

Transportation and vast service industries such as those for healthcare, recreation, food provision, etc., are essential elements of high urbanization and historically developed quickly and with great energy. In their mature form the highly developed economies of the world are remarkably similar in economic structure: capital is concentrated in a relatively small wealth holding group, with most sectors of the economy dominated by a small number of very large, and powerful corporations, which in turn express their influence throughout society. Governmental and economic power are closely aligned. Historically, in structural terms as these economies moved toward maturity, they were characterized by high differentiation (their economies produce a large variety of products and services) and concentration (virtually all sectors function in a quasi-oligopolistic manner.)

These characteristics apply to contemporary professional sport throughout the world. The franchises of the top leagues are owned by individuals who have become significantly wealthy in industries directly tied to the vast and rapid expansion of global wealth, particularly those having made their fortunes in real estate in the global cities, in media, telecommunications or transportation, and the dot.com boom. High differentiation has come through the varieties of merchandizing of sport, its secondary distribution (e.g. 24/7 television, radio and Ipod dissemination), and the development of tertiary leagues and new, derived sports (e.g. arena football.) Its essential structures are oligopolistic. The number of franchises is strictly limited. New ownership requires the approval of existing owners. Many leagues have contracts that limit the amount that can be paid to players. And in the contemporary era, revenues are frequently shared among owners to "equal out" market gains, ensuring that the overall "product" of the competition remains suitable for its intended markets.

Wealth and Sport have become handmaidens, in large measure because of the critical role played by the media as the primary creator of wealth (a point I will discuss further shortly.) The highly inter-related bundle of "things" that make up modern sport combine to privilege wealth — as in other dimensions of globalized business this is an area in which the rich get richer.

As businesses, professional leagues and franchises behave like other transnational firms, pursing a logic of development firmly embedded in the "manufacture" of a product and a brand that can produce significant returns on investment by vastly expanding the pool of consumers who recognize and identify with the brand and are willing to consume it in some commodified form. The purchase of the New York Yankees in 1978 by George Steinbrenner is a useful case in point. In 1978, he paid $10 million for the team. The team's estimated value in 2006 was $1.026 billion.[25] Much of the value of the Yankee franchise arises out of the combination of location in America's most famous city, a "storied" history, distinctive and established brand graphics, and ownership of dedicated radio and television networks in the nation's most dense media market. This increase in corporate "unit value" compares favorably with the most successful of American Transnational Corporations, such as General Electric that grew in almost identical proportions during the same period under the leadership of Jack Welch. (Gross GE sales in 2007 were $163 billion.)

The oligopoly nature of most professional leagues tends to assure that when the activity is subsidized by long-term media contracts, franchises can prosper even when they are poorly run or are only marginally competitive. Joe Nocera, for example, points to the Los Angeles Clippers as a spectacular case in point. Perennially hapless under owner Donald Sterling, the value of the franchise, which he purchased in 1981 for $13.5 million is now estimated at between $300–400 million, and he refuses to sell, knowing that all he needs to do is not sell for the property and its value will continue to increase along with the NBA as it continues to expand into a global enterprise.[26] Salary caps and revenue assure the financial fortunes of professional sport in an odd reversal of the kinds of dynamics that exist throughout the global economy as a whole. In perspective the inequalities of professional sport are those between individuals who are allowed to enter the enterprise and those who are restricted. Anomalies such as the Green Bay Packers, a community owned team, tend increasingly to be the exceptions that prove the rule.

American college sports, especially football and basketball, can be viewed as quasi-professional sports. Their structure has been much affected in both football and basketball by the structure of season ending events such as the BCS games and March Madness, both of which exist in the bosom of extremely lucrative media contracts.[27] The "take away" from such activities has grown increasingly large for the winning teams and created a growing barrier to other teams that seek to break into the *routine* domination by the top schools. For the so-called non-elite schools, either those in weaker classifications or with less invested programs, the cost of competing with the elite schools is constantly growing, a convenient metric for which is the annual salary of the head coach in both sports, sums that often dwarf that of the ostensible professional leaders of the campus. When universities must move outside their own dedicated resources for financial assistance to better and sustain such programs, they focus on donations from alumni. Many schools have achieved reputations based not only on the storied largess of their athletic department oriented donors, but for the difficulties that arise in seeking to regulate their relationships to the departments in question.

Global Media

The linkage, or alignment, between the broader pattern of global development and that of the Olympic Games, can be similarly told for all of the major global sports. The Olympics, having started as an international event, was well poised for its commodified elevation into authentic globalism than were many national sporting leagues. To repeat points made above: the core of these developments has been the relentless commodification of the current global system, the vast populations gathered in urban centers, their linkage by modern transportation and communication, and above all the package of media and advertising essential for the creation of demand for the goods that produce the revenues. All of these have been coupled to vast reservoirs of disposable income (often subsidized by private corporations) that can support the pricing structures of these events.[28]

The media, having themselves exploded in size and diversity over the same period, experience a rapacious appetite for content — software for the hardware as it were. Sport for this purpose is no more but no less distinctive than reality survival shows or *American Idol*. Each meets the demand for an arranged progression from the many to the few, from contenders to survivors, in an open cycle of repetition that favors the continual re-supply of heroes and stars, who in the current consumption cycle (the analogy to a production cycle) recreate novelty out of the familiar, with each portion of the cycle producing a targeted marketing niche.

This web of consumption and commodification provides a constant tension between the authentic and the artificial, between the familiar and the novel, between the revered and the fresh appeal (often gender based) of the (frequently brash) new. At one end of the television/marketing/commodification nexus of novelty lie the made-for-television (read: filler) "sports" designed to match broadcast minutes with advertising dollars. At the other end lie the "new" sports for which leagues, festivals and games are developed within a professionalized hierarchy of privileged market value. Some of these will "feed" the mega events at the top of the sports food chain, for example joining the Olympics as new events. Others will find a permanent niche in a modestly trafficked area of professionalized repetition (such as the ESPN Extreme Sports Games.) The link between the media and a given sport is irreducibly the "advertising demographic" that it is able to attract and capture. The addition of newer sports to the Olympic Games, particularly the Winter Festival, owes much to this equation.

The mega event becomes an end in itself, having a status not unlike that Daniel Boorstin attributed to being a celebrity — being known for being known.[29] Association with the event, statused in part because of the enormous sums spent on it, (e.g., the $2 million a minute Super Bowl commercial) or by the vast sums paid by official sponsors of the event. Outside this circle of pay-to-play participants is an ever-expanding ring of status distributed by any association with the event, ranging from actual attendance (especially in privileged seating), to corporate sponsorship events, to "seeing" a participating athlete, to eventually having watched the event on television. This hyper-value of the mega event underscores the importance of not "de-valuing" its currency through over-exposure, a lesson well-understood by Olympic and World Cup Organizers.[30]

The great unknown in this relationship is how "big" sport will fare in the rapidly evolving world of digital personalized media. As the recent screen-writer's strike in the United States illustrated, no one is quite certain how the radical diffusion of media will affect overall income—or, more precisely, how the new media may disrupt the existing business model of large-scale sport. We currently have only the music business and the movies as models of how hand-held devices and the diffusion mechanisms of face to face media impact the business model. In both industries unlicensed reproduction has devastated former income flows. Newer models, such as Itunes which "un-bundle" music have yet to prove sustainable or equal the former volumes of the bundling proc-esses of conventional movies, DVD's and CD's. IPOD streaming of sports, e.g. within the ESPN world, would seem to be growing in popularity, but again, the overall business model has yet to be proved. In the long run, profes-sional and Olympic sport at all levels will need to be capable of resisting the deterioration of their branded advertising base to continue to reap the enor-mous income that has come from the model of centralized broadcasting.[31]

Trade and Commodification

The globalization of professional sport has been accomplished primarily by its location in world trade circuits and within the dominant value mix of commodi-fication. As such professional sport provides ample evidence for Thomas Friedman's notion of a flat world of receding borders.[32] This is evident in the cross border flow of athletes, by the cross country ownership of sport fran-chises, by the location of professional games in countries outside their league schedules,[33] and by the explicit ideology in many cases (certainly those of the National Basketball Association, Major League Baseball, the National Football League and the National Hockey League, the English Premiere League, etc.) of making these sports global in their appeal, execution and future location.[34]

Viewing it from the perspective of trade and consumption indicators, the precise size and dollar value of global sport are difficult to determine and thus their value as *trade* is also indeterminate. Some indicators, however, suggest the enormity of its activities. One study examining four major components of sport consumables—footware, equipment, apparel and bikes, estimated in 2006 that these products accounted for $256 billion of activity, with a growth trend of 4 percent. In fractions this amounted to: footware, $49 billion at 3 percent; equipment $67 billion at 4 percent; apparel, $113 billion at 6 percent; and bikes, $27 billion at a stable 1 percent. A significant majority of these "sport outputs" (as it were) are manufactured, of course, in China.[35]

The English Premiere League, formed in 1992 out of the first division by clubs intent on maximizing their financial potential, is arguably the richest and most profitable sport league in the world. Its current television contract through 2010, cost broadcasters £1.7 billion, and an additional £625 million for overseas rights, the largest overseas deal in the history of sport.[36] The Deloitte Football Money League Table, published annually by the accountancy firm Deloitte and Touche, gives the revenue of the top 20 football teams in the 2005–6 season as €3.3 billion, with Real Madrid, followed by Barcelona topping the chart. Real Madrid indicated revenues of €292 million. At the time of the report, prospects were for continued growth, fueled largely by ever-increasing television revenues, underscoring the critical role of media in creating and sustaining global sport.

> Developments in the broadcast market have underpinned many of the changes in the Money League, and these give some pointers to the composition of future Football Money Leagues. Alan Switzer commented: "Revenue from the new French broadcasting deal has seen Olympique Lyonnais move up to their highest Money League position of 11th, while Real Madrid and Barcelona's announcement of new deals should see them challenge at the top of the table in coming years. The Premier League's recently concluded broadcasting deals may see English teams contribute half of the top 20 clubs in 2007/08."[37]

Compare these data with those for the four largest US sport leagues. For the first time in many years major league baseball has revenues approximating those of the National Football League at just over $ 6 billion annually. Baseball has doubled its revenues since the 2000 season, and has a growth rate twice that of football.[38] 2007 revenues for the NBA amounted to $3.6 billion, and for the National Hockey League to $2.4 billion.[39] The major sources of income for professional sports are television, gate receipts, corporate sponsorship, naming rights and branded merchandise, and premium seating. There are over 800 professional teams in the US. Franchise value tends to vary from 2.5–6 times total annual revenues.

Professional sport in Africa demonstrates a similar pattern, albeit on a smaller scale, but extraordinary nevertheless for the size and nature of the economies supporting it. The African National Cup 2008, for example, is expected to draw a global television audience of 2 billion people. Corporate support and television revenues will provide over $100 million dollars of support for the games.

As Table 4 indicates, even Latin America boasts soccer leagues with surprising levels of financial support, compared to the major European professional leagues.

Virtually all professional sports have culmination events at the conclusion of their league seasons. All take a play-off format, the better to highlight drama, extend the length of the season, and promote additional revenues from these "second" seasons. Increasingly, mega events such as the World Cup serve the purpose of focusing global attention on the particular sport.[40]

These dynamics directly parallel those of the Olympic Games, especially since the ascendance of Mr. Samaranch to the head of the IOC in 1980. The

Table 4. International Soccer League Revenues (US $millions)

Premiership	130.00
Series A	90.00
Bundesliga	89.00
La Liga	70.00
Ligue 1	50.00
Mexican Football League	35.00
I-League	28.33
FrediVisie	25.90
Championship	25.50
Brazilian League	24.60

Source: http://www.bigsoccer.com/forum/showthread.php?t=644025, 2008.

story of the commodification and commercialization of the Games is wonderfully told by Barney, Wenn and Martyn, pivoting around the Los Angeles Games of 1984, which established the template for subsequent private sector support of the Games and their enormous increase in commodification.[41] In this sense, the "story" of the Games is a special case of the globalization of sport, which in turn is a special case of global-ist expansion in general.

Transformation of Value and the Narratives of Sport

The transition of professional sport from national to global commodities illustrates a common "problem" with "reading" and interpreting globalization, its scope, dynamics and impacts. Our languages tend to be fashioned out of national examples and texts, and their referents are predominantly located in those national contexts. We can "see" national teams and leagues. It is more difficult to "see" the global system and its circuits of exchange because they operate in a nationally referred context: "the national" is where people live, and where many basic economic and political decisions are made. An analogy may be a federal system in which the constituent units constitute the "place" where events and relationships take place. Over time, however, the federal relationship becomes a repository of power. As this occurs, the national capital comes to be viewed as an equivalent federal power, lodged symbolically in institutions, buildings, rituals and a good deal of actual authority and power that can be marshaled to accomplish federal purposes.

Globalization has some of these attributes without the symbolic "center" of the federal units that gives it identity, responsibility, etc. In the global system transnational corporations and non-governmental organizations are the nearest approximation to these "next level" institutions of global governance. Some of the murkiness of what globalization is (who is responsible for what actions and outcomes, etc.) derives from this lack of a definable and responsible center. In an important way, "no one" runs globalization. Yet, many of the ways in which this system is developing are directly analogous to those of emergent national economies and states in earlier historical periods. This observation is relevant for how one "sees" and "tells" the globalization story.

It is a seemingly universal human trait to compress experienced and imagined worlds into stories. Their many ways of being told are an essential part of the human experience. However, when we refer to the "nature of things" that involve businesses, especially large businesses, we conventionally do not use the language of "a story" to describe and analyze the event. Again, a good example is the examination of increasing commodification of the Olympic Games related by Barney, Wenn and Martyn. As one moves through the volume's chapters, the authors identify a discrete pattern of commodification, told from within the frame of reference of the Olympic movement. It is a story of the Olympics.

One could equally see it, however, as a story made possible in significant part because the developmental course of the Games from Melbourne in 1956 to Athens in 2004 and Beijing in 2008 follows—and is part of—the trajectory of global economic development. The critical shift that took place in the organization and presentation of the Los Angeles games, rendering them largely the creation of private corporate capital, directly parallels the explosion of capital out of the older industrial nations and into the developing world. As detailed above, this shift would result in the enormous expansion of global corporate wealth. The critical decades of the 1980s and 1990s would also witness vast increases in both corporate and individual wealth resulting from neoliberal reforms that dramatically reduced taxes on both corporate and individual incomes.[42] Within this twenty-year period national policies had become wedded to global economic strategies.

In the Olympic context the vast sums of corporate largess available for the succession of TOPS programs and the ever-increasing level of television revenues for both summer and winter festivals would have been unthinkable outside this pattern of global corporate expansion with its ability to reach a global audience of 3.4 billion viewers, the creation of a successful culture of corporate branding, etc. The transformation of the Olympic movement during these four decades was one of an association of national movements, fashioned and held together with the symbolism and nomenclature of *inter-nationalism*, into that of a genuinely global entity where participation at all levels of the process by its various actors takes place within the circuits of globalization.

In the globalization version of the story there is much more to Mr. Samaranch's remark on leaving office that "the IOC I am leaving my successor has nothing to do with the IOC I received in 1980."[43] He arrived at the takeoff stage of corporate globalism and can be given credit either for steering the Olympic ship along a bountiful course in this flood tide, or simply having been fortunate to garner a benefit that came with the massive increase in global wealth during his tenure.

These elements are central to globalization's value transformation: the triumph of economic reductionism and commodification. Athletes in this structure have been significantly instrumentalized. It may, because of the compensation involved, be a willing instrumentalization. Nonetheless, the system reproduces its version of the global disparity in wealth and income through the enormous salaries provided the "athlete as star." Mirroring other global labor distributions, literally hundreds of thousands of prospective athletes are drawn into the "labor climb" toward the very small number of top-paying positions at the top.[44] In the case of most professional sports this produces a ladder of failure for the vast numbers of young aspirants who enter the process, but who will never reach the upper rungs. In the case of the modern highly commodified Olympic Games, a narrow window exists for even the most successful athletes to "cash in" on their achievements, especially in the so-called minor sports. Clearly in all professional sports this structure of fame and remuneration leads to the seeming ubiquity of performance enhancing substances.

A more fundamental confusion of value exists within the supposed "market context" of contemporary sports, as teams seek to find and establish measures, metrics and data for determining the "value" of an athlete to a team. This whole complex of the assignment of values and the symbols that accompany them is commonly held to be articulated through and justified by the fabled "signals of the market." In the midst of this maelstrom of capital and spending, it is believed, lies the core of Adam Smith's irreducible logic of the market that the unfettered exchange of supply and demand creates value. Peter Goodman has recently raised an important question about this presumption that draws our attention to the unexpected behaviors and consequences that arise out of massive complexly interactive systems such as globalization.[45]

> Who among us would have imagined that the same forces of financial ambiguity could at once choke the real estate market, Wall Street, network television and Major League Baseball? Yet somehow a rippling crisis of belief in the traditional ways of valuing so many things, from mortgage-backed bonds to a joke written for Jon Stewart, simultaneously grips many areas of American commerce.[46]

Setting prices in global markets, Goodman maintains, is no longer the clear-cut exercise familiar to most of us from our economics textbooks because the very nature of the product is obscured by the complexity of the markets in which it appears. This is true for the complex bundled securities that flowed from the US real-estate market into the pathways of global commerce with the ability to negatively impact financial institutions throughout the world when they "came down." The generalization similarly holds for the recent US writers' strike in which contending sides were stuck trying to figure out the "value" of the writers' contribution in an internet marketplace that has yet to develop.

A similar situation, Goodman asserts, is true of the dilemma faced by the New York Yankees in seeking to re-sign their star, Alex Rodriguez. Traditionally, baseball contacts were based on the statistics produced by the player in that game where statistics have historically been all important. But, in a world in which the current major league homerun leader, Barry Bonds, has had his stature impugned by drug use allegations, the "clean" Rodriguez, young enough and in sufficient good health to be the all-time challenger to the record, represents a value that is understandable only through the Yankee's proprietary television contract.

> The A-Rod contract talks represent a new mode of calculating value that appears to be slowing down the dance. By most accounts, Rodriguez will command something around $30 million a year when the ink is dry. Though he is among the most prodigious hitters in history, that number still makes little sense when confined to what happens on the field, baseball people say. It begins to make sense only when the game is seen as an industry reshaped by technology and globalization? . . . A-Rod then provides crucial content for the cable television channel owned by the Yankees, and a means of hawking caps and jerseys on interactive Internet services. Factor in how he may break the all-time home run record wearing Yankee pinstripes, which convey a global brand, and perhaps? — but only perhaps? — does the money make sense. "A-Rod could be worth trillions if you get enough eyeballs in China to start watching him," said Mark Zandi, chief economist at Moody's Economy.com.[47]

The point of this tale is that within the complexities of the global marketplace, predictability departs many economic equations. Again, viewed as a narrative, globalization rejects linear treatment, whereas most of the other narratives that define professional sport (and surely the Olympics) construct and depend on linear narratives. In this sense, the narratives of professional sport and the Olympics are fundamentally the kind of progress narratives that we discussed above.

The tension between the overall covering narrative of progress and various sport and Olympic disaster narratives follows the same pattern as globalization narratives — indeed they are subclasses of such arguments. The most dramatic of these centers around the consequences of urban redesign and refurbishment involved in developing all mega events, the Olympic games included.

Problematizing Sport in this Global Era: Enter China

The foregoing suggests the deep alignment between professional sport, the Olympics and the more inclusive structures of globalization.[48] This implies that many less obvious features of globalization may also be present in various ways for these sporting activities. Or, to return to our previous language, sport tends to promote a narrative structure that is closely related to the linkage between the performer and the event. A sport "story" presumes the athletic content as the dominant subject matter of the narrative. When sport is "told" this way, it develops an immediate and attenuated focus: the personalized competition of the athletic event, whether team or individual. Ultimately, there is a winner and a loser. In organized sport, the sequencing of many such contests is performed, told and registered, until there is only one remaining focus to the story: the champion. This highly ritualized story owes much of its social/cultural linkage to other forms of social competition, from business, to politics, to war.[49]

The "sport" narrative tends to overshadow the structural narrative out of which it arises. The business of sport—while understood as increasingly important—tends to be treated as a secondary narrative, one often overlooked in the context of the immediacy of the events themselves. Thus, as Barney et al. make clear in their discussion of the commodification of the Olympic events and movement, when fore-grounded, the commodification narrative accounts in significant measure for the events that take place. It is a more inclusive narrative involving a much broader context of causation and explanation than that encompassed by the events themselves. Similarly, the globalization narrative like the political narrative or the political economic narrative, expands the frame of "the reality" that is encompassed by what we have labeled the event or sport.

The globalization narrative is necessarily complex—at some level it engages virtually every human activity. Selecting professional sport or the Olympics as a subject within the globalization narrative links them directly to globalization's broader structural dynamics, for example the creation and distribution of wealth, or the creation and exchanges of symbols and images. Beyond these, however disguised or unacknowledged, they are linked as well to the broadest aspects of globalization entailments, such as the workings of the global financial system or contributions to environmental stress.

Our customary "event" narratives tend to ignore these other elements unless they intrude so obviously that they cannot be by-passed, such as the terrorist attacks at Munich or the corruption scandal of the Salt Lake Winter Olympics. Even in the face of such disruptions, however, the dominant media tendency is to frame events such as these as individual stories of corruption, tragedy or grief: they have a beginning, a middle and an end. The media are not good "tellers" of structural elements, which after all, are difficult to film. However, when viewed from broader, structural points of view, even such "deviant" events as terror and corruption can be understood as relatively predictable outcomes produced in the interaction of the global system—products of global dynamics. Framed in this way, globalization is in some irreducible way a structural narrative that seeks to identify the many contributing parts of the phenomenon (what is it?), its dynamics (how does it work?), and its impacts (so what?)

Presented in its customary forms, professional and Olympic stories are first and foremost sports narratives. When they are presented as either business or political economy narratives, the predominant predisposition is to frame them as versions of the globalization as progress narrative. As stories of mega events, the Olympics and World Cup narratives, for example, favor a telling of seemingly inevitable progress or of eventual triumphs of the will, often associated with the difficulties of mounting the games in the context of urban transformation. As such, their language often emphasizes the positive transformation of distressed portions of the urban landscape by the development agenda of the mega event. Those promoting the progress narrative advance it through the media and with the legitimating force of supportive government and business sectors. It is a narrative of power and accomplishment.

In contrast, disaster narratives are likely to be told by lower-statused spokespersons, especially when the subject matter is development and its putative costs and benefits. Those negatively affected by such developments are likely to be poor and/or the dispossessed, without means for legitimating their complaints and little access to conventional media. Partially motivated to change this asymmetry of voice within globalization discourses, non-governmental organizations have come to occupy some of the "policy space" between the driving sectors of globalization and various of the most negatively affected sectors, especially in issues involving health, income, poverty, water provision, etc.

By way of illustration, the Centre on Housing Rights and Evictions (COHRE), supported by the Geneva International Academic Network, has recently published *Fair Play for Housing Rights: Mega-Events, Olympic Games and Housing: Opportunities for the Olympic Movement*.[50] The form of the report embraces a disaster narrative to examine mega-event site developments. The report details the story of the displacement of people from their homes and workplaces by the site creation and conduct of mega events. The report holds that over the past 20 years fully two million people, mostly minorities, have suffered this fate. With specific attention to Beijing, it alleges that by the time the games are held, fully 1.5 million people will have been displaced. In a related previous development the 1988 the Seoul games displaced 720,000 persons.

In response to the report, a 2008 Olympic Games spokesperson has rejected the figures as groundless, holding that 6,037 households have been demolished to make room for nine venues, and that compensation for such relocation was generous. In anticipation of the up-coming Games, the COHRE report points to 1,000 people already facing relocation and the loss of 700 low income rental units in Vancouver, despite public commitments on the part of the 2010 Winter Games organizers that such relocations would not be a part of the games. The report details alleged relocations arising from other mega events including the 2010 World Expo in Shanghai in which 18,000 families are to be evicted and 400,000 displaced. Similarly, the 2010 Commonwealth Games scheduled for Delhi are reported to result in the forcible eviction of 35,000 people, with related slum clearance leading to the eviction of 300,000 others. Events as diverse as global beauty conferences and IMF/World Bank meetings have led to similar relocations.[51]

The tension between globalization progress and disaster narratives is perfectly illustrated by the report. Progress narratives exhibit a structure that tightly focuses their causes, structures, and consequences, much in the manner that the classical economics of the firm proceeds by developing a set of assumptions, processes and consequences bound by the structural limitations of the firm itself. To succeed within such a framework, a good manager, leader or investor, seeks to contain analysis, behavior *and accounting* within the organizational boundaries of the firm itself. Additional impacts (good or ill) are viewed as and labeled *externalities*. They are literally external to the frame of analysis and the overall accounting of what the activity *costs*.

Mega events famously displace costs onto the public sector, leaving them to be paid in a disaggregated fashion by public sector mechanisms, often bonds. Ultimately, such costs are paid out of public taxes. Commonly, this is referred to as the *socialization of private* costs. Many studies critical of the current course of globalization focus on the manner in which benefits to global corporations, such as the creation of infrastructure and tax holidays, are viewed as necessary inducements that countries must pay to gain global corporate activity.[52] Other critics focus on negative accretions to the natural environment by the highly generalized externalities of globalization.[53] Yet others point to the outcomes of the structural adjustments promoted by the neoliberal oriented World Bank International Monetary Fund as having the effect of weakening public sectors by the privatization of public goods such as water.[54]

The relocations, evictions and negative impacts on the lives of people — overwhelmingly the poor and minorities — of mega events problematize the kinds of selective disregard for externalities promoted by their organizers. (In contrast note that the publication of other externalities such as the creation of multiplier effects of direct and indirect spending on such events is a highly advanced art.) In kind and style, they are characteristic of the ways in which global capital has invested lavishly to refashion the world's cities, especially those that are the central nodes to the global circuits of capital and finance.[55] One feature of these cities is that in the name of "modernization" and "globalization," their redesign all too frequently results in a significant decline of what Michael Douglass terms "civic space," unregulated and uncommodified spaces available to the citizenry as an authentic public good — a good available through the simple right of citizenship.[56]

Linking professional sport and the Olympics as inter-related structures takes on a new dimension when we raise the question of whether globalization in its contemporary form, having the attributes outlined in this paper, is itself sustainable. This question could also be put as asking whether from a macro perspective the externalities of globalization are becoming so great that they may change the course of globalization itself. Considerable evidence is gathering to suggest that this may be the case.

China is at the center of this case. In a literal sense, although the era of contemporary globalization was initiated with China on the economic sidelines, the core of contemporary globalization *is* China, which has come to hold the current title as the "workshop of the world" (displacing workers not only in the older industrial countries, but within the newer developed countries, and the developing world as well).[57] The U.S. economy is troubled in part because the particular combination of neoliberal economic policies and neoconservative political policies has led to reductions in governmental revenues (and a weak dollar) on the one hand and on the other, enormous debt ($9 trillion) much of which is owned abroad. All of this is attenuated by the unbridgeable trade deficit with China. It is no exaggeration to argue that China is driving critical aspects of globalization. It is entirely fitting in this regard that the 2008 Games should be in Beijing — at an estimated costs of $40 billion no less, that the country be at the point of national hysteria in assuring that they will be "done right," and that in virtually every way the Games deserve the phrase which has been so often recently associated with them as "China's Coming Out Party." It can be argued that China holds the keys to the continued course of globalization and through them will strongly affect the ability of other countries to continue their own patterns of economic growth of which professional sport and their mega events are component parts.

Judged from a globalization perspective, *nothing* about China is *normal*. The rapidity with which it emerged from the structural weaknesses of the Great Leap Forward and the Cultural Revolution is unparalleled. On any globalization index, China stands out as exceptional: in rates of growth, in concentrations of inequality and wealth, in employment, in unemployment, (to illustrate: if every job in the United States were exported to China, it would *still* suffer from unemployment) in the numbers of people in universities, etc. Just a brief trip across some illustrative comparative data makes the point. With a population of 1.4 billion China is 42.2 times more populous than Canada and 4.65 times the size of the United States. The government publication *China Daily* estimates that 13.5 million Chinese enter the middle class every year — that is 5.42 times the population of Toronto. Approximately 26 million Chinese are currently students in higher education. The number of towns in China exceeds 20,000. The total urban population is 540 million. Forty-nine cities have a population over one million.[58]

If it continues along this current economic course, China will be the largest economy in the world by 2050. The list of amazing facts about China can be extended almost without end, in part because no country in the history of the world with a population of this size has ever become "modern" in terms of its economic and social institutions.

The critical globalization question posed by the growth of the Chinese economy over the past two decades is sustainability. At the heart of the globalization as progress narrative is the conviction that it can be sustained and that globalization in its current configuration is sustainable as well. The disaster narrative poses more difficult questions that are only now beginning to be taken with a measure of seriousness.

To pursue this question we might invent a kind of "goldilocks equation" — one for which the answers come with small, medium, and large implications. The small speculation — the baby bear hypothesis if you will, to preserve the metaphor — arises out of historic analyses of economic growth. No modern economy has ever been able to achieve continuous economic growth at the 9–10 percent a year level. Eventually, the various logics of expansion submit to those of consolidation and contraction, much as the US economy did in the early 1990s, in early 2000 and seems to be doing currently. As some economists are wont to put it, globalization has not repealed the business cycle. Unexpected economic events in other parts of the system can lead to unexpected downturns of significant proportion, evidence the Asian economic flu of 1997. If we are poised again on the brink of a world economic slowdown, these "recessionary" blues will quickly ripple across the global system. Professional sport and its periodic manifestations as the Olympics will then again test the hypothesis of whether it is recession proof—as a major distraction from the mundane realities of everyday life—or whether it has, indeed, become a structural captive to discretionary spending linked directly to the global economy.

That globalization should continue as a pattern of linear expanding growth without some form of downturn is most unlikely. Peter Drucker, the guru of business and management wrote before his death in 2005 that the United States in particular seemed embarked on a course that at best might result in a period of global financial instability, built on the combination of its massive trade and budgetary deficits and various structural weaknesses in the economy that could trigger global financial instability.[59] The current contracting state of the US economy seems to fit this prediction, to which need be added the world-wide condition of tight energy supplies and high oil prices, progressively increasing food costs, massive governmental expenditures to sustain wars in Iraq and Afghanistan and the forthcoming structural shock of the country's demographic aging that will vastly escalate health care and pension costs, even as available labor for the economy declines. It is commonly said that the US economy sneezes and the rest of the world catches a cold. If any of this scenario holds, the US interdependence with China will have a reciprocal effect, leading to various forms of economic downturn. In such a situation the dependence of professional sport to gain its largess from those at the top of the economic wealth pyramid may be sorely tested. A global downturn will, arguably, sap much of the energy from the collection of forces that have produced such largess.[60]

The middle speculation—the "momma bear" implication—focuses on the rapid growth of overall consumption in India and China. With millions each year entering the middle class, a status defined in large measure by goods and service consumption, both societies are experiencing rapid increases in energy use. Consequently both societies are rapidly increasing their production of green house gasses (China's contribution is set to double in seven years) and are seeking energy agreements with countries all over the planet in an effort to assure stable energy supplies. Neither shows much interest in social, economic or political policies that would reduce carbon emissions at the expense of either economic growth or social transformation.[61] With considerable justification, both countries now ask the developed world why they should restrict their own development after the more developed countries have already produced the green house gas situation characterized as unsustainable by recent and various scientific reports. The issue is not one of development, they argue, as it is one of justice. Again, the crux of the situation lies within the law of large numbers involved in both countries. We conventionally use a measure of 40 percent (or more) to describe the middle class in a developed society. In the United States with a population of just over 300 million, a middle class of 120 million is assumed. In Canada with its population of approximately 33 million, one can assume a middle class of about 13.2 million. If we take the same fractions for China and India, the corresponding figures are 560, 000,000 and 440,000,000. Add to this equation that India has one of the most rapidly growing populations in the world and the challenges to both world carrying capacity for emissions and supply are clear.

The world faces increased energy competition and growing uncertainty that the global economy can both produce sufficient energy to satisfy its growing needs and hold fuel costs at levels that do not themselves create negative effects. One possible consequence could be uncontrolled inflationary impacts, or, in echoes of the late 1970's another bout of stagflation: recession combined with inflation. Lester Brown's conclusion concerning the world after peak oil is increasingly widely shared.[62]

> National political leaders seem reluctant to face the coming downturn in oil and to plan for it even through it will become one of the great fault lines in world economic history. Trends now taken for granted, such as rapid urbanization and globalization could be slowed almost overnight as oil becomes scare and costly. Economic historians writing about this period may routinely distinguish between before peak oil (BPO) and after peak oil (APO).[63]

This middle level scenario argues that globalization as we have come to know it cannot continue. With oil at $108 a barrel and likely on its way to $150 and higher negative economic consequences are unavoidable. Even at these higher prices a time will come shortly in which insufficient amounts of fossil fuels will be available to support the kinds of growth levels societies regard as normal and necessary. As societies come to deal with these facts, social change will be profound, not ruling out fundamental realignments in world politics and relations between states, including more warfare to control fuel rich nations. The close linkages between social and economic progress and the continued expansion of global sport suggest inescapably that they too will be negatively impacted. If we follow this scenario, we might want to look to the oil rich nations of the middle-east as the forthcoming underwriters of high end professional sport. Perhaps an Olympic Games in Dubai?

The biggest impact scenario—the "papa bear" scenario—is heralded by those who see not only the end of globalization as we know it arising out of fuel issues, but the fundamental transformation of society as we know it through climate change and sea level rise. This is the disaster narrative of globalization writ as large as it gets. We live, it asserts, in perilous times and we ignore them at our peril. Perhaps the leading text in this regard is Jared Diamond's recent examination of societal collapse, the message of which is framed decisively in the book's subtitle: how societies choose to fail or succeed.[64] Some scholars and activists are already beginning to call for planning for "environmental refugees" from climate change and sea level rise, predicting a need to accommodate as many as 50 million. Almost daily one can find in a combination of environmental science and public interest sources additional evidence of climate change elements that threaten some aspect of "our normal way of life," most recently as this involves issues of providing food security for the expanding world population.[65] This premises a world in survival mode, in a future that is increasingly more proximate than almost anyone had imagined.

Conclusion

Under any of these more extreme scenarios, or versions of them, the course of contemporary globalization will change. As Robert Reich observed in an oft-repeated remark in the early 1990's, "globalization is about winners and losers."[66] The struggles of globalization are many and hardly limited to the relentless search of ever more goods for people who already have a good deal. The genius of the post-modern world has been this very capacity to produce goods and services in almost unimaginable amounts and kinds. The failure of the post-modern world has been its ability to develop effective means of equitable distribution. Within the frames of globalization, dominated by economic reductionism, the meaning of progress has itself been reduced from its historical implications of providing a better life for all within a framework of an expanding public good, to the far more limited meaning of the expansion of goods. And with this diminution of the notion of progress has come, as the forgoing section details, an almost wanton disregard for the articulation of global public goods and preservation of the global commons.

As with the other aspects of globalization, the Beijing Olympics have become the prime exemplar of these tensions and contradictions. It is instructive that almost every conversation one has with people who have traveled to Beijing in recent years quickly includes the question of how the authorities can clean up the air in the midst of August in what has become one of the most atmospherically toxic cities on the globe. The answer, given readily by Chinese authorities is "not to worry. We will do it." The reality, almost every outsider believes, is that the authorities will simply stop economic activity and transport within a sufficient radius to allow the air to clear. The irony of needing to repudiate the very economic activity and accomplishments that are being celebrated by the Games, is at the very least lost in public articulations about the games.

China and the Games model other important dimensions of globalization. Income equality data from China dramatically make clear which parts of the population have been included within the progress of globalization and which have been "left behind," a segment of the population often estimated at 400,000,000. It is the classic "glass half full or half empty" metaphor. By any measure, as suggested above, the economic and social achievements of China over the past two decades are unparalleled in the modern world. If 400,000,000 million in China have been left behind, that means a billion have been "brought along" by these radical transformations.

But, the very pragmatism enshrined by Deng Xiaoping's opening to capitalism invites China to occupy a political economic "space" replete with ambiguity, especially in regard to how issues of the public good are framed and debated within both the political and economic systems and the manner in which responsibility is obfuscated and diffused within and between governmental and non-governmental sectors. Armed with this pragmatism China has been a bold adopter of selective neo liberal policies, demonstrating a capacity to pick and choose those aspects of being "global" that meet the particular needs of government, while being far less sensitive to the "entailments" for those affected by the reforms. For a case in point, China has "reformed" its health care system to promote local responsibilities and initiative in health care. In practice, after the manner of neo liberal reforms in other parts of the world, this reform reduces the financial burdens of the central government while displacing costs on lower level governmental units and users. The result is an appalling system of health care in the country with the world's second largest economy and millions who are unable to afford any level of care.[67] And, while superficially trade has had the effect of making parts of China a modern country, it remains an authoritarian if not totalitarian country, firmly committed to and able to suppress dissent, violate individual privacy, and impose governmental will on its people — capacities fully in evidence in the current violent protests in Tibet.[68]

At many policy levels and with respect to governance, China operates not unlike the industrial revolution nations of the 19th century in which politics and economics were dominated by larger-than-life entrepreneurs with little patience for the niceties of governmental regulation, especially as regulation impacted on their ability to organize and coerce labor, protect it from industrial hazard,[69] respect the property (e.g. land) rights of others, or indeed respect the rights to safe products so essential to a modern consumer culture both within and outside China. The reality is that the industrial/manufacturing sectors of China are both poorly regulated and rampant with corruption. This, again, is a circumstance that mirrors the early industrial story of the western industrial nations, evocative of that period in their history that bred governmental intervention to provide safety regulation and led eventually to the rise of progressive and reform movements, often based on labor power, to re-balance the political system. But China is not a democracy and is unlikely to become one. The prospect of allowing dissent and the articulation of interests opposed to any sitting government is entirely off the agenda for China.

Thus, the current conflation of various politics from Dafur to Tibet that seek to "embarrass China before the world" in the focused attention on the Olympic games. It is a politics unlikely to succeed for any number of reasons, not the least of which is that whatever the costs in "global embarrassment" that such events may have, they in no way trump the enormity of the national pride that has been created throughout China. In the wake of the Tibet riots the comparison between Berlin in 1936 and China in 2008 is being freely made. Superficial similarities to the contrary notwithstanding, the critical difference between the two situations lies in the place China has come to occupy within the global economy. Under the impress of the logic of global interdependence the other major countries of the world have made China "one of them," and have done so without imposing on China the "rest of the package," namely the requirement that it abide by supposed standards of international comportment with respect to human rights, "progress toward democracy" and the rest.

The Beijing Games have succeeded. Wildly. More people attended. Venues were often jammed, however "minor" the sport. Records were set. China dominated many events. Much money was made. At every level, I expect that the accounting will be more than satisfactory. But, the aftermath may be difficult to swallow. China by virtue of its very uniqueness, its size, its sense of itself in history, and much more gives rise to excess. As suggested above, the law of large numbers ensures that everything about the Games will in some sense be abnormal. As I have passed several newly developed venues over the past three years, I have been struck that the very structural dynamics that have allowed China to overpower global trade, making itself the producer and much of the rest of the world consumers, is at work here. Cheap labor combined with readily available capital and a fast track within the governmental systems of authorization and support will, no doubt, on many dimensions distinguish the 2008 Olympics as the "best ever." What is likely to be the effect, one wonders, on those who come after Beijing—those who must develop the games in the context of the more deliberately limiting circumstances of societies and cultures such as Canada in 2010 and Britain in 2012? Perhaps a final irony is that we will never know how much China "spent" to mount these games, until we have an opportunity to compare the results with the more transparent efforts of their successors.

Notes

1. Nyan Chandra, *Bound Together: How Traders, Preachers, Adventurers, and Warriors Shaped Globalization* (New Haven and London: Yale University Press, 2007).

2. Manuel Castells, *The Rise of the Network Society*, second edition (Oxford: Blackwells, 2000).

3. Here "satellite communications" is shorthand for the entity of the computing industry and its explosion of products that takes place over these decades into what has now come to be properly known as the "digital age." Increasingly, the realization has come that digitalization lies at the heart of the continuous energies to locate and re-locate global industry and commerce, especially through the phenomenon we have come to call off-shoring. In its initial stages these technologies worked to relocate material processes, especially manufacturing. Increasingly they have come to include services as well, leading to the bromide: if it can be digitized, it can be off-shored. See Thomas Friedman, *The World Is Flat, Release 3.0.* (New York: Picador/Strauss and Giroux, 2007).

4. David Harvey, *The Condition of Postmodernity:*

An Inquiry into the Origins of Cultural Change (Cambridge, Mass. and Oxford, UK: Blackwells, 1990).

5. Friedman, *The World Is Flat*, 185–199.

6. Mike Davis, *Planet of Slums*. (London: Verso, 2006).

7. This argument has developed considerable currency among urban scholars who see the global city as the locus of social, economic and political power in many modern nation states, shifting these elements away from national governments. See for example Neil Brenner and Roger Keil, eds., *The Global Cities Reader* (London: Routledge, Taylor and Francis, 2006).

8. Melina Liu, "Mao to Now," *Newsweek*, Jan. 7, 2008.

9. Brenner and Keil see global cities as: "basing points for the global operations of TNCs; production sites and markets for producer and financial services; articulating nodes within a broader hierarch of cities stratified according to their differential modes of integration into the world economy; and dominant locational centers within large-scale regional economies or urban

fields" (Brenner and Keil, *Global Cities Reader*, 11). See also Saskia Sassan, "Economic Globalization and World Migration as Factors in the Mapping of Today's Advanced Urban Economy," paper commissioned in 2003 for the Globalization Research Network (www.global.grn.org).

10. David Harvey, *The Spaces of Global Capitalism: Toward a Theory of Uneven Geographical Development* (London: Verso, 2006).

11. According to the University of California Income Inequality Atlas (University of California Santa Cruz, 2008, *UC Atlas of Global Inequality*; http: ucatlas.ucs.edu/income.php, accessed 14 April 2008):

> Global income inequality is probably greater than it has ever been in human history. There is some debate about whether it is getting worse or getting better. Currently, the richest 1 percent of people in the world receive as much as the bottom 57 percent. The ratio between the average income of the top 5 percent in the world to the bottom 5 percent increased from 78 to 1 in 1988 to 114 to 1 in 1993.

12. Susan Fainstein, "Inequality in Global Cities," in Brenner and Keil, *The Global Cities Reader*, 111–117.

13. Robert McChesney and Dan Schiller, "The Political Economy of International Communications: Foundations for the Emerging Global Debate About Media Ownership and Regulation, *United National Research Institute for Social Development, Technology, Business and Society Program Paper*, Number 11, October, 2003.

14. The blogosphere has its own daily newspaper, on line of course: see, www.blogherald.com. In 2005 the Bloghearld estimated there to be 60,000,000 blogs worldwide and growing at a rate of 100,000 per day (see, htt://www.blogherald.com/2005/05/25/world-wide-blog-count-for-may-now-over-60-million-blogs).

15. Chris Anderson, *The Long Tail: Why the Future of Business Is Selling Less of More* (New York: Hyperion, 2006).

16. Chandra, *Bound Together*, 28–29.

17. By way of illustration, one organization that seeks to keep abreast of such things estimates that 27 million persons are currently enslaved in the world, a significant number of which have become so by being trafficked over national borders (see, *Human Trafficking*, http://www.NotForSaleCampaign.org, accessed April 14, 2008).

18. *World Bank, World Development Indicators — Global GDP*; http://www.worldbank.org/data/countrydata/countrydata.html.

19. Reuters, "U.S. slowdown may affect China tightening — HSBC," Jan. 16; http://in.reuters.com/article/asiaCompanyAndMarkets/idINSHA1883220080116.

20. Mary Douglas and Baron Isherwood, *A World of Goods: Towards an Anthropology of Consumption* (London and New York: Routledge, 1996).

21. Language is clearly a flashpoint globalization "site." Throughout the world English is being recognized as the language of globalization. The extinction of local languages is taking place at an alarming rate. It has been estimated that of the 6,000 languages extant in the world, one is lost to human exchange every two weeks. See: John Noble Wilford, "World's Languages Dying Off Fast," *New York Times*, September 18, 2007; http://www.nytimes.com/2007/09/19/science/19language.html

22. This usage may unnecessarily complicate the nature of the issues involved. Let me suggest three examples of how these dynamics may work in daily practice. First, many labor economists talk about the "race to the bottom" in which they posit a consequence of the fact that overall global capital is more mobile than labor. (Although globalization has promoted huge labor migrations as well.) One consequence is that global industries move from country to country in search of ever cheaper labor, which at the end of the value chain of production and consumption, means ultimately greater profits for the users of labor. Over a forty-year period, following this logic, manufacturing moved first from the older industrial countries to the newer industrial nations with cheaper labor, primarily countries in Asia and Latin America. This is famously the period of the rise of the four Tiger economies of Asia, and lesser contributors to global labor. With the rise of China as a modern economic power, the labor base of these countries was replaced with cheaper Chinese labor, to the deficit of former producer countries. Some of these like Korea have been able to supply capital and technology to its labor base to remain a significant economic power. Others, such as the economies of South East Asia have been displaced as manufacturers of finished economic goods to contributors of parts to manufacturing chairs in China — a role which provides relatively less value and income to labor. In common language they have been pushed further down the "labor food chain." In line with this theory of labor mobility, China — having developed economically sufficient to unleash its own much higher levels of domestic income and consumption — is now complaining about India as a global

force undercutting Chinese wages. Thomas Mitchell, "China's competitiveness on the decline?" *Financial Times*, March 22, 2006, 18:21

In a second example, unnoticed in most of the developed world, the still developing world is undergoing any number of crises related to water, especially suitable potable water for cooking and drinking. It is not uncommon in many parts of the world for one to two hours of daily labor being devoted to gathering minimally sufficient water supplies, usually by young girls and women. Indeed, UN Habitat estimates that 1.6 billion people in the world lack sufficient access to clean water and 2 billion to adequate sewage. United Nations Habitat, 2003, *The Challenge of Slums-Global Report on Human Settlements 2003*; http: www.unhabitat.org/pmss/getPage.asp?page =downloads.

Throughout countries in Africa, Asia and South America neoliberal influenced policies have promoted the privatization of water, particularly in urban areas, under the presumption that making water a commodity will assist both in regularizing its use and providing capital for further water utility development. Whatever the outcomes of these efforts — and they are intensely debated, cf. Patrick Bond, *Looting Africa: The Economics of Exploitation* (London: Zed Books, 2006). Pursuit of such policies represents a significant value shift from one in which the notion of the public good is embodied in providing a resource for the whole of a community, and linking consumption of the resource to income. Most tellingly, the greatest impact of such policies is among the urban poor, hundreds of millions of whom lack sufficient income even to satisfy their daily caloric intake needs. See: Davis, *A Planet of Slums*, 24–26.

The third example again represents a shift away from a public good set of values to those of privatization. Throughout the developed world, and even in portions of the developing, again, neoliberal economic policies have been adopted that seek to deregulate higher education and promote market entry for private educational entities. The overall effect of these neoliberal "reforms" has been to commodify higher education, especially graduate education, reducing public sector financial support for public higher education and shifting fees onto to students, who in this model — as in the water example — are reconstituted discursively as consumers. The results of such policies are predictable, with the newly affluent taking a disproportionate number of "seats" within higher education, creating in the process a new class of "the left behind." This dynamic has been particularly acute in

China where the enormous numbers of those seeking admission to higher education (which in another value shift is now deemed as an essential ingredient of economic success) leave a population fraction of the "left behind" of staggering numbers. For a fuller treatment of the education dynamics of increased global interdependence, see: Peter D. Hershock, Mark Mason & John N. Hawkins, eds., *Changing Education: Leadership, Innovation and Development in a Globalizing Asia Pacific* (Hong Kong: Springer, 2007).

23. Paul Johnson, *The Birth of the Modern: World Society 1815–1830* (New York: Harper Collins Publishers, 1991).

24. Daniel Boorstin, *The Americans: the Historical Experience, Vol. II* (New York: Vintage Press, 1965).

25. Forbes, New York Yankees, The Green Technology Special Report; http://www.forbes .com/lists/2006/33/334613.html.

26. Joe Nocera, "Big Time Losers: Why do the owners of so many lousy sports teams refuse to let go? Because there are other ways to end up a winner," *New York Times Sports Magazine*, March, 2008, 30–32.

27. The NCAA gains $500 million a year from its 11 year television contract with CBS for March Madness. It distributed in 2006–07 $136.4 million to the participant teams in the tournament. Most of the revenue goes to the top programs. Ohio State overall earns $109 million a year in sports revenue. Luebchow, Lindsey, "March Madness Big Money," The Higher Education Watch Blog, New America Foundation; http://www.newamerica.net/blog/higher-ed-watch/2008/march-madness-big-money-2541.

28. Pricing itself has the capacity to transform a professional sport "game" into an "event." As the combination of seating, parking and concessions have increased in price, the ability of the middle and working class to attend such events is stressed, leaving them either as the preserve of the wealthy or as isolated events that a middle class family enjoys only on an occasional basis. Both sides of this equation have the short-run effect of raising the status of the activity (higher priced "things" have higher presumptive value). One down-side of this transformation includes the subtle alienation of those within a population who do not have direct experience with the event, and thus over their life-time may not become "real fans" (those who will spend to attend games and collect merchandise). Another is the sensitivity to economic downturn of the now significant amounts of discretionary income involved in game attendance. A test of this hypothesis will be the 2008 major league baseball season,

which will take place in a pattern of increasing attendance that will bump into a rapidly declining economy, which has already in the first quarter of 2008 had its effect in other areas of discretionary spending such as consumer electronics.

29. Daniel Boorstin, *The Image: A Guide to Pseudo-events in America* (New York: Antheneum, 1980).

30. This point is very well made by Barney, et al. in their excellent study of Olympic Games commodification; see, Robert K. Barney, Stephen R. Wenn and Scott G. Martyn, *Selling the Five Rings: The International Olympic Committee and the Rise of Olympic Commercialism*, revised edition (Salt Lake: University of Utah Press, 2004).

31. CBS seems to have discovered one fruitful formula with its on-line participation of March Madness. The following, for example, summarizes the early round participation in the tournament when the large number of teams maximizes interest in "bracket play." 2008 NCAA March Madness on Demand traffic figures through Sunday, March 23—3,318,844 total daily unique visitors to the NCAA March Madness on Demand video player (comparable 2007 figure was 1,448,546—129 percent growth)—Total minutes of live streaming video and audio consumed in the first fours days of the tournament (March 20–23): 3,705,092 total hours (222,305,520 minutes). This figure surpasses the entire 2007 total of minutes of live video and audio consumption (2,716,236 hours—162,974,160 minutes) resulting in 36 percent year-over-year growth and counting.—Over 3.6 million fans are currently playing in CBSSports.com bracket games across the web, including the largest bracket application on Facebook. The total number CBSSports.com brackets participants is up 62 percent from 2007. (2.2 million)—2,190,488 clicks of the "Boss Button" (figure not available for 2007)—571,297 VIP registrants (2007 figure was 468,720—22 percent growth) 2008 NCAA March Madness on Demand Consumption tidbits—The First Round Georgia vs. Xavier game on 3/20/08 had a record-setting total of 376,000 hours of consumption. This mark easily eclipsed the previous record high of 133,000 total hours which was set in 2006. (Winthrop vs. Tennessee) Kentucky vs. Marquette on 3/20/08 also broke the 300K barrier with 325,000 hours.—The average stream for Cornell vs. Stanford on 3/20/08 (23.5 minutes per stream) was over four minutes longer than any other game thus far. This is due to the fact that the game tipped off at 4:40 PM ET and was the only game playing at the time (*Smart Brief*; http://www.smartbrief.com/news, accessed April 11, 2008).

32. Friedman, *The World Is Flat*, 51–77.

33. This remains contested terrain. In February 2008 the Premiere League announced its intention to play regularly scheduled matches abroad. Already Manchester United, Chelsea and Liverpool have had the occasional match in the USA, South Africa, Hong Kong, China, Japan and South Korea. This plan to "go global" as regular business starting in the 2010–11 season, however, has been challenged by the Football Association. The primary reason for the opposition, the FA states, is that the league's proposal may affect England's 2018 World cup bid. See: Chris Bevans and Jonathan Stevenson, "Premiere League Going Global," BBC, February 7; http://news.bbc.co.uk/sport2/hi/football/eng_prem/7232378.stm. See also, BBC 2008, "FA concerned over top-flight plan," BBC Sport, February 15; http://news.bbc.co.uk/sport2/hi/football/eng_prem/7246314.stm.

34. Nocera, "Big-time Losers," 30–32.

35. NPD Group, 2006, "Global Sport Market Size Estimate, 2006;" http://www.sportsandplay.com/news/npd_estimates_2006_low.pdf

36. Bevan and Stevenson, "Premiere League Going Global."

37. Sportbusiness.com 2007, "Spanish Clubs Top Football Money League;" http://www.sportbusiness.com/news/161396/spanish-clubs-top-football-money-league.

38. Charles Isidore, "Baseball close to catching NFL as top $ sport," *Sportsbiz., 2007*; http://money.cnn.com/2007/10/25/commentary/sportbiz/index.html.

39. The US sport revenue figures are probably under-reported, as they have tended in the past not to include revenues from such sources as luxury boxes. This becomes a matter of contention in those situations in which players' salaries are tied to revenues.

40. One indicator of the success of this strategy is the data compiled by the Nielsen Corporation on television viewers. Since 1981, of the 40 most watched television shows in the United States, all but four of them have been Super Bowls. Nielsen Corporation 2008, "The Nielsen Company's 2008 Guide to the Super Bowl," January 24; http://www.nielsen.com/media/2008/pr_080124.html.

41. Barney et al., *Selling the Five Rings*, see especially Chapters 6 and 7.

42. Harvey, *Spaces of Global Capitalism*, 11–25.

43. Barney et al., *Selling the Five Rings*, 295

44. One aspect of the global restructuring of labor is the bifurcation of domestic labor markets in advanced industrial countries into fewer "good" jobs at the top, driven in part by the ex-

pansion of knowledge industry jobs, and far more "poor" jobs at the bottom of the labor hierarchy with the middle increasingly squeezed. This pattern can be viewed throughout the economy from finance, to manufacturing, to health care, to universities. Interestingly, even as a country still viewed by itself and many others as a "developing" economy (albeit 2nd wealthiest country in the world ranked by PPP GDP), this pattern has already begun to emerge in China. See, Richard Sennett, *The Culture of the New Capitalism* (New Haven and London: Yale University Press, 2006).

45. I have also pointed to this critique in a recent book review of Paul Close et al. See: Deane Neubauer, Review of Paul Close, David Askey and Xu Xin, *The Beijing Olympiad: The Political Economy of a Sporting Mega-Event*, Routledge, Taylor and Francis—London and New York, 2007, in *Olympika: The International Journal of Olympic Studies XVI* (2007), 99–103.

46. Peter S. Goodman, "When the Price Isn't Right," *New York Times, Week in Review*, December 9, 2007.

47. Ibid. See a companion piece by Goodman, "The Free Market: A False Idol After All?" *New York Times*, December 30, 2007.

48. Close et al. use the language of "extraordinary convergence" and "elective affinity" to refer to the linkage between modern Olympism and modern market capitalism (*The Beijing Olympiad*, cf. Chapter One.

49. Grant Jarvie, *Sport Culture and Society: An Introduction* (London: Routledge, Taylor and Francis, 2006).

50. Centre for Housing Rights and Evictions, *Fair Play for Housing Rights: Mega-Events, Olympic Games and Housing: Opportunities for the Olympic Movement* (Geneva: COHRE, 2007).

51. Ibid., and *International Herald Tribune* 2008, "Rights group: Olympiads displace 2 million people over last 20 years, 1.25 million in Beijing; http://www.iht.com/bin/print.php?id=6000859

Everything global must sooner or later be experienced through the local. Bringing these site location issues closer to home often involves the intrusion of "big box" retailers who are in the end the major distributional outlets for global production. Tense cases most often involve Walmart, which has a history of displacing the local by importing the global. The loss to the local is to tradition and often jobs; the gain to the local— that which is pushed onto planning boards and town and city councils as the compelling rationale to permit the siting of the stores—is lower goods costs for local consumers. The Walmart "story" has become an issue in global studies in and of itself. For a study of Walmart see Charles Fishman, *The Wal-Mart Effect* (New York: Penquin, 2006).

A long-running dispute over store siting with a particular twist on the displace of local values and tradition has been the campaign to locate a Walmart store in Guelph, Ontario adjacent to the site of a Jesuit retreat center and related wetlands. See: Meghan Wood, "Jesuits lose legal battle with Wal-Mart;" http://www.canadianchristianity.com, March 17, 2008.

52. Robert Gilpin, *The Challenge of Global Capitalism: The World Economy in the 21st Century* (Princeton: Princeton University Press, 2000).

53. Lester R. Brown, *Plan B 3.0: Mobilizing to Save Civilization* (New York: W.W. Norton & Company, 2008).

54. Harvey, *Spaces of Global Capitalism*, 48–54.

55. Saskia Sassen, "Locating Cites on Global Circuits," in Brenner and Keil (Eds.), *Global Cities Reader*, 89–95.

56. Mike Douglass, K.C. Ho and Giok-ling Ooi, *Globalization, the Rise of Civil Society and Civic Spaces in Pacific Asia Cities* (London: Routledge, 2007).

57. Gilpin, *The Challenge of Global Capitalism*, 282–287.

58. *China Today*; http://www.chinatoday.com/city/a.htm, accessed 14 April 2008.

59. Peter Drucker, "Will the U.S. Dollar Be the Source of the Next Economic Crisis, *The National Interest*, March 29, 2005; http://the-econoclast.blogspot.com/2005/03/will-us-dollar-be-source-of-next.html.

60. In Part One I discuss the fragility of trade and consumption in contemporary globalization. If we see the global financial sector as a special case of trade in services, note the following: The less known, less understood, credit markets dwarf the stock markets in size. According to Merrill Lynch the global bond markets including government, corporate and securitized debt securities like the infamous CDO's based on subprime mortgages total nearly 50 trillion dollars. Then derivatives based on that debt add up to almost 516 trillion dollars. By contrast the market value of the U.S. stock market, the largest in the world is a mere 19 trillion. See: Telegraph co.uk, "Fed's rescue halted a derivatives Chernobyl," March 24, 08; http://www.telegraph.co.uk/money/main.

61. At its current rate of growth, India is expected to quadruple its energy consumption in the next 25 years. At a global scale this would result in an enormous increase in greenhouse gases. India points out, however, that it currently contributes only 4.6 of the world's greenhouse

gases, even though it has 17 percent of world population. Currently, India's emissions are the fourth largest in the world after the United States, China and Russia. Somini Sengupta, "Thirsting for Energy in India's Boomtowns and Beyond," *New York Times*, March 2, 2008, 4.

62. The following quote from Lester Brown focuses primarily on gross energy production and use, but note that these equations have become almost unimaginably more complex as parts of the world seek to shift from growing crops for food, to growing crops for fuel, as in the current US ethanol programs, which are already having devastating effects on food available and prices throughout the world, especially poorer countries. Brown continues to observe:

> Developing countries will be hit doubly hard as still-expanding populations collide with a shrinking oil supply to steadily reduce oil use per person. Without a rapid restructuring of the energy economy, such a decline could quickly translate into a fall in living standards, with those of the poorest countries falling below survival levels? . . . The peaking of world oil production raises questions more difficult than any since civilization began. Will world population growth survive a continuing decline in world oil production? How will a shrinking oil supply be allocated among countries?" (Brown, Plan B 3.0, 45)

63. Ibid.

64. Jared Diamond, *Collapse: How Societies Choose to Fail or Succeed* (New York: Viking Penguin, 2006).

65. Illustratively, this segment from an Earth-policy press release dated 20 March 20 (http://www.earth-policy.org, accessed 14 April 2008):

> Melting Mountain Glaciers Will Shrink Grain Harvests in China and India. — The world is now facing a climate-driven shrinkage of river-based irrigation water supplies. Mountain glaciers in the Himalayas and on the Tibet-Qinghai Plateau are melting and could soon deprive the major rivers of India and China of the ice melt needed to sustain them during the dry season. In the Ganges, the Yellow, and the Yangtze river basins, where irrigated agriculture depends heavily on rivers, this loss of dry-season flow will shrink harvests.

For a broader review of water issues in general as part of the dynamics of contemporary globalization see Brown, *Plan B 3.0*, 68–84.

66. Robert Reich, *The Work of Nations: Preparing for the 21st Century* (New York: Vintage Books, 1991).

67. David Blumenthal and William Hsiao, "Privatization and Its Discontents: The Evolving Chinese Healthcare System, *New England Journal of Medicine* 353, no. 11 (2005), 1165–1170.

68. One feature of growing media ubiquity is the inability of China as a form of totalitarian government to control all news. Events in late 2005 in which farmers were killed by local police during a protest over a contested land acquisition by local authorities found its way into the world news through Reuters. Soon even the government was forced to concede as many as 87,000 protests and other 'incidents of discontent' had occurred during 2005. Evidence suggests that this level of discontent continues. Most protests focus around land acquisitions by local officials for development, labor disputes, and protests against unsafe working conditions, especially in mines. The instance is from *China View*, cited by Close, et al., *The Beijing Olympiad*, 13.

69. From January to October 2007, China reported 419,000 industrial accidents with an associated death toll of 79,000. The good news is that these figures were declines from the previous year. People's Daily Online, "China reports marked decline in industrial accident deaths," 6 November 2007; http://english.people.com.cn/90001/90776/90882/6297624.html.

ASSESSING THE IMPACT OF SPORTS MEGA-EVENTS IN TRANSITION ECONOMIES: EURO 2012 IN POLAND AND UKRAINE

Brad R. Humphreys and Szymon Prokopowicz

Introduction

The Union of European Football Associations (UEFA), the governing body for football in the European continent, is currently soliciting bids for host regions for EURO 2012, the European football championship. In November 2005 the field was narrowed to three possible host regions: Italy, Croatia/Hungary and Poland/Ukraine. In December 2006 a final decision will be made about the location of EURO 2012.

Sports mega-events like the Olympic Games, the Soccer World Cup and the UEFA Championship, have important impacts on the host regions. These events are very popular, drawing large numbers of spectators and television audiences. For example the 2004 UEFA Football Championship in Portugal was watched by 7.9 billion TV viewers throughout the world, with an average of 150 million viewers per match, which is a 157 percent increase over the 2000 European Championship in Belgium and the Netherlands. An estimated 500 thousand spectators traveled to Portugal to watch the tournament (www.uefa.com).

To date, most mega sporting events have been held in developed countries. However, a number of developing and transitional economies, including regions in central Europe and sub-Saharan Africa, have been lobbying the international sports organizations for the right to host mega sporting events like the World Cup and the Olympic Games (Baade & Matheson, 2004b). We focus on Poland and Ukraine because these two countries represent an interesting contrast to typical regions that host sports mega-events in economic, political and cultural terms. Both are transition economies, and Poland is a member of the European Union (EU). Hungary and Croatia constitute a similar pairing, but Hungary is an EU member and Croatia is an applicant country to the EU and will likely make numerous economic, legal and institutional changes in the coming years as a part of the EU application process. As of this time Ukraine has no such plans. An examination of the costs and benefits of hosting EURO 2012 on Poland and Ukraine can illustrate a number of important lessons from the economic impact literature as they apply to the transitional and developing economies.

UEFA Requirements for Host Countries

Most of the costs of hosting the UEFA 2012 European Football Championship will be driven by the UEFA's requirements for a host region. UEFA has developed an extensive list of requirements that any host country or region must meet (*Phase 1 Bid Requirements*, 2005). These requirements dictate a wide array of economic, legal, cultural and political prerequisite conditions for the host countries. Many of these conditions would clearly be beneficial if they were absent in a prospective host country. For example the political conditions include the existence of a stable political system and effective government agencies and the legal conditions include a legal system, capable of protecting the intellectual property rights associates with the tournament and the existence of a body of employment law that allows for open labor markets with no constraints on foreign workers, protects employees from exploitation and guarantees fringe benefits for employees.

UEFA requires the host regions to provide a significant amount of capital and labor to host EURO 2012, including 8 "state-of-the-art" stadiums with skyboxes and capacities of 30,000 to 50,000 spectators, parking in proximity to the stadiums, hospitality facilities for VIPs, multiple five-star hotels in each host city for the exclusive use of UEFA officials and participating teams, sixteen training facilities for the participating teams, "modern, well-developed, high-quality" transportation infrastructure linking host cities and public transportation networks within each host city, extensive security at venues and other factors. The cost of all infrastructure improvements must be paid for by the host country.

UEFA's "state-of-the-art" stadium requirements include three stadiums seating at least 40,000 spectators and one seating at least 50,000 spectators. All of the stadiums must have luxury suites, and UEFA reserves the control of all of the luxury suites for the entire period of the tournament. UEFA also requires between 5,000 to 8,000 car parking spaces and from 400 to 800 bus parking spaces adjacent and near the venues. These venues must also have extensive facilities for media, teams and UEFA officials.

Table 1 contains information about the current inventory of large football stadiums in Poland and Ukraine, and the population of the cities where these stadiums are located. The existing inventory of stadiums in Poland and Ukraine is old and lacks amenities like covered seats and VIP seating required by UEFA. The region currently does not meet UEFA's stadium requirements and a significant amount of stadium construction and renovation will have to occur to meet UEFA's requirements.

UEFA requires a large number of five-star hotels in the host cities that must be reserved exclusively for the use of UEFA officials and support staff and the participating teams, for the duration of the tournament. UEFA requires one entire five-star hotel with at least 400 bedrooms in the city that will host the cham-

Table 1. Stadiums in Poland and the Ukraine

Host city	Population	Net capacity	Planned matches	Status
Warsaw (Pol)	1,690,000	50,000	4	Planned Construction
Gdansk (Pol)	461,000	44,000	4	Planned Construction
Wroclaw (Pol)	636,000	40,000	3	Planned Renovation
Chorzow (Pol)	116,000	54,000	4	Under Construction
Poznan (Pol)*	572,341	42,000	3	Under Construction
Krakow (Pol)*	757,430	30,000	3	Under Renovation
Kiev (Ukr)	2,611,000	77,000	5 (Final)	Planned Renovation
Lvov (Ukr)	733,000	36,000	3	Planned Renovation
Donetsk (Ukr)	1,017,000	50,000	5	Under Construction
Dnipropetrovsk (Ukr)	1,065,000	31,000	3	Under Construction

*'backup' stadiums, relationship to Championship unclear.
Source: UEFA (2005) Phase I Evaluation Report.

pionship match for the duration of the tournament. UEFA also requires one five-star hotel within a 45 minute drive from the stadium and with at least 40 beds in all cities hosting matches. Sixteen hotels, most five-star, must be provided for each of the 16 participating national teams. UEFA also requires a five-star hotel near the stadiums for the referees and another five-star hotel with at least 20 rooms "in the countryside" for the exclusive use of the doping control doctors. The bid requirements explicitly limit the prices charged for these five-star hotel rooms in 2012 to the average rate charged in 2005 in inflation adjusted terms. Finally, UEFA requires between 1,000 and 5,000 beds in four and five-star hotels in cities hosting matches for UEFA's "commercial partners."

The bid requirements also state that the host cities must have suitable accommodations for the spectators who will attend the matches. UEFA estimated that half a million fans traveled to Portugal for the 2004 tournament and that 75 percent of these fans stayed for at least four days in the country. Presumably, a similar number of fans are to be expected to attend the 2012 tournament, and these fans will require accommodations. According to the bid requirements, the accommodations for spectators should range from "five-star hotels to simple campgrounds," and will have "moderate price levels that will not put potential guests off.? Furthermore, the bid requirements explicitly prohibit hotels from imposing "onerous terms and conditions, such as the enforcement of minimum overnight stays" on spectators (UEFA, 2005, *Phase 1 Bid Requirements*, p. 35).

Table 2 shows the existing hotel inventory, in terms of hotels and total number of rooms, for the Polish and Ukrainian cities containing proposed stadiums for the tournament. According to the Polish Tourism Institute, the number of hotels in Poland increased by 10 percent over the period of 2001–2004, and the five-star hotels increased by 29 percent. It is important to note that most of the existing high quality hotels in both Poland and Ukraine are owned by international companies, and not the local hotel operators. Based on the UEFA requirements, UEFA officials, teams and staff will require 16 five-star hotels located near the host stadiums. From Table 2, there are currently only 19 five-star hotels in the two countries combined in close proximity to the stadiums. Both Poland and Ukraine currently lack sufficient hotel capacity, especially at the high end of the quality spectrum, to host the championship and will have to undertake a significant amount of hotel construction and renovation in order to meet the bid requirements.

Table 2. Hotels in Poland and in Ukraine within 10 kms radius of proposed stadium sites

Host city	5 star	Rooms	4 star	Rooms	3 star	Rooms	2 star	Rooms	1 star	Rooms
Warsaw (Pol)	10	3842	4	1754	22	6953	14	2742	8	2512
Gdansk (Pol)	3	52	2	203	9	1034	2	71	—	—
Wroclaw (Pol)	0	0	8	1188	15	869	9	610	5	169
Chorzow (Pol)	0	0	3	469	7	484	6	501	—	—
Poznan (Pol)	0	0	3	334	21	1645	18	712	37	1000
Krakow (Pol)	3	476	8	764	47	2955	18	877	6	422
Kiev (Ukr)	1	289	5	906	11	2116	8	436	1	17
Lvov (Ukr)	0	0	3	405	3	198	3	288	31	655
Donetsk (Ukr)	1	129	2	79	2	251	2	288	2	41
Dnipropetrovsk (Ukr)	1	71	3	47	4	422	1	140	1	59

Source: UEFA (2005) Phase I Evaluation Report.

Finally, UEFA places requirements on the infrastructure of the prospective host countries. These requirements are not as detailed as the requirements for facilities and accommodations. The transportation infrastructure requirements are both vague and potentially expensive to meet. Each host country must have "a modern, well-developed, high quality transportation infrastructure that links each host city. Travel within the host cities should be convenient and travel times should be reasonable." Furthermore, each host city "must have a modern, well-developed, high-quality public transport network that links each Official Site to the city centre, the airport, railway stations and other transportation links" (UEFA, 2005, *Phase 1 Bid Requirements*, p. 40). The host cities must also have international airports located near the centre, and UEFA officials must be assured priority at these airports during the tournament. Each host city must also have a comprehensive hospital located near each stadium with 24 hours emergency treatment available on a priority basis for UEFA officials and other designated persons.

Table 3 summarizes the existing transportation infrastructure in Poland and Ukraine. Both are large countries in terms of area, and contain relatively large road networks. However, the density of the road networks, in terms of kilometer of highway per 100 square kilometers of area, is much less than the 160 km/sq.km in the EU nations.

Clearly, both the countries will have to upgrade their transportation networks in order to meet the UEFA requirements. Poland has been upgrading its road and motorway network for some time, but it still has relatively few kilometers of motorways. Over the period 2002–2005, Poland spent $8.2 billion for motorways and $19 billion for all roads (www.road.pl). The largest Polish airport, in Warsaw, has connections to 55 world cities. Thanks to the air network, tourists can fly to different European cities in 2 hours and many

Table 3. Transportation infrastructure

	Poland	Ukraine	EU-15
Km of roads	377,000	273,700	53,104,000
Road density	80 km/100 sq.km	45 km/100 sq.km	160 km/100 sq.km
Km of motorways	565	1,777	61,656
Km of railroads	20,665	22,510	153,003
International airports	8	6	68
International sea ports	3	3	—

Source: www.wikipedia.pl, www.paiz.gov.pl

domestic destinations in less time. The density of the Polish railways is one of
the highest in the world, according to the Polish Agency of Foreign Investments (www.paiz.gov.pl), although eastern Poland, on the Ukraine boarder, is
relatively poor in railways and roads. The rail and road network in Ukraine is
much smaller and less well maintained to those in Poland.

Assessing the Costs and Benefits of UEFA 2012

If selected, hosting the UEFA Football Championship in 2012 will clearly
have a significant impact on Poland and Ukraine in many ways. Billions of
people around the world will watch the football matches held in the two countries, and be exposed to these two countries and cultures in some way. Based
on the attendance at the previous UEFA Championships, more than 500 thousand spectators from all over Europe could visit these countries and, in the
course of their visit, purchase hotel rooms, meals, drinks, transportation, tickets to the matches and other goods and services produced in the region. In order to host the tournament, both the countries will have to spent large sums of
money upgrading their sports facilities, transportation infrastructure and hotel, restaurant and bar capacity. Any economic assessment of this event must
begin with a comparison of the total economic costs and total economic benefits generated by the tournament. An *a priori* cost-benefit assessment for a
sports-mega event like UEFA 2012 in a transition economy must be viewed as
a highly speculative undertaking. Transition economies represent difficult
forecasting environments because of the potential for widespread changes in
political and economic institutions and basic societal conditions like the social
welfare system that tend to be more stable in developed economies.

Given these caveats, we searched the print and internet media in Poland,
and to a lesser extent Ukraine, for published estimates of the forecasted total
economic costs and benefits associated with hosting UEFA 2012. All of the following estimates have been converted from local currencies to US dollar values using the Purchasing Power Parity (PPP) exchange rates published by
the International Monetary Fund's World Economic Outlook Database (http:
//www.imf.org/external/pubs/ft/weo/2004/02/data/).

The total economic costs of hosting UEFA 2012 can be categorized into
four broad areas: upgrades in transportation infrastructure like motorways
and rail, construction and renovation of football stadiums, construction and
renovation of hotels and spending for the safety of the participants and spectators. In past months, the Polish national newspaper *Rzeczpospolita* has reported a number of estimates of the expected costs of hosting UEFA 2012 in
Poland in each of these four areas.

Table 4 summarizes the reported cost estimates for Poland, in thousands of
undiscounted US dollars. As was discussed above, the existing transportation
network in both Poland and Ukraine is much less extensive than the corresponding network in the EU. Since the large numbers of spectators will need
to move between the host cities in the region, the existing transportation will
need to be upgraded. Much of this construction will be focused on building

motorways between the host cities. From now till 2012, Poland will reportedly spend over $8 billion dollars on motorways to comply with the UEFA requirements. In particular, all proposed UEFA host cities in Poland are expected to be connected by motorway and one motorway will connect Poland and Ukraine (in the direction of Lvov). Apart from that, two other motorways will connect the countries.

Poland also plans to spend $4.6 billion on upgrading inter-city rail connections and $1.7 billion on public transport in large cities over this period. Some of this construction will come from the EU. Much of it will take place no matter what the outcome of the bidding for UEFA 2012. The amount of transportation infrastructure spending that should be attributed directly to hosting the football championship is unclear.

UEFA estimates that the tournament will require hotel rooms for 200,000 people, including participants, UEFA officials and staff, VIPs and spectators. Poland currently has hotel capacity for about 130,000 visitors, and meeting the UEFA hotel requirements will require just over one billion dollars in hotel construction by 2012. Based on the comparison of the existing hotel stock and the UEFA requirements in the previous section, much of this new hotel construction will be four and five-star hotels.

The UEFA requirements specify a high level of security for participants, officials and spectators. The UEFA Phase I bid requirements specify that the stadiums hosting games must have state-of-the-art security, including internal and external public surveillance television cameras mounted on fixed posi-

Table 4. Estimated costs of hosting UEFA 2012, Poland

Cost category	City	Estimated cost (US$000)
Motorway construction		8,064,000
Hotel construction		1,026,000
Public safety spending		750,000
Stadium spending		
	Warsaw	179,671
	Gdansk	92,603
	Wroclaw	92,166
	Chorzow	55,185
Stadium total cost		384,625
Total estimated cost		10,260,398

tions, a control room for this surveillance system, electronic ticketing access systems and an independent emergency electric power supply. Poland expects to spend $750 million in construction and operations associated with security before and during the tournament.

Both Poland and Ukraine will have to undertake extensive existing stadium renovation projects and new stadium construction projects to meet UEFA's requirements. Poland and Ukraine's bid proposes four stadiums in each country as hosts of UEFA matches. Poland has one relatively large existing stadium, the national stadium in Chorzow. This stadium, built in 1956, is currently being renovated at a cost of $55 million and will seat 54,000–60,000 spectators when completed. There are still no "state-of-the-art" stadiums in Warsaw, Gdansk, or Wroclaw. Warsaw officials plan to either renovate an existing stadium with current capacity of 50,000 seats or build a new one. The construction of a new stadium is expected to cost between $138 million (without a roof) and $276 million (with a roof and air conditioning); one current construction cost estimate for a new stadium in Warsaw is approximately $180 million.

Other stadium renovation cost estimates are somewhat hard to come by. However, according to the Polish Wikipedia (www.wikipedia.pl) the Gdansk stadium construction and the Wroclaw renovation will each cost about $90 million. Ukraine will also undertake significant stadium construction and renovation projects. We were unable to locate much information about stadium construction costs in Ukraine, but according to one estimate the Donetsk stadium construction project is estimated to cost around $200 million. Table 4 shows the estimated construction costs for the four stadiums in Poland, where about $385 million will be spent on stadium renovation and construction before the tournament. Note that some stadium renovation projects in Poland would have taken place no matter what the outcome of the UEFA bidding process, so the stadium spending directly attributable to hosting the tournament is less than this amount.

We estimate that Poland plans to spend over $10 billion over the period of 2006–2012 in their effort to host UEFA 2012. To put this spending in perspective, in 2004 the gross domestic product of Poland was $444 billion. We were unable to obtain any cost estimates for Ukraine, but given the state of the motorway system, stadiums and the current hotel inventory in Ukraine, spending by that country will probably be as large, or larger, than the spending by Poland. In contrast to more developed host regions, much of the costs of hosting the event in Poland will take the form of high-end hotel construction and upgrades to the existing transportation network.

The economic benefits generated by hosting UEFA 2012 can be classified into four broad groups, which are as follows:

1. Direct and indirect benefits generated from spending by foreign tourists who visitPoland and Ukraine to watch or participate in the championship.
2. Direct and indirect benefits generated from spending by foreign tourists who visit Poland and Ukraine after these countries are awarded UEFA

2012 who would not have visited these countries if they did not host the championship.

3. Benefits generated by the upgrades to the transportation, hotel and stadium infrastructure.
4. Psychic benefits accruing to Poles and Ukrainians from hosting a prestigious sporting event.

Estimating the direct and indirect economic impact of the spending by foreign tourists who visit Poland and Ukraine to attend football matches during the 2012 Championships would require estimates of the number of visitors, the average duration of their stays, the average spending per day by these visitors and a regional input-output model of the Polish and Ukrainian economies to convert the direct spending estimates into broader economic impacts on household income (Crompton, Lee, & Shuster, 2001). Performing an economic impact analysis of UEFA 2012 is beyond the scope of this paper. However, the UEFA 2004 Championship in Portugal, and published estimates of the expected economic impact of UEFA 2008 in Switzerland and Austria can provide some evidence of the potential direct economic impact of UEFA 2012. A study commissioned by UEFA, estimated approximately $300 million of current direct and indirect economic impact of UEFA 2004 on Portugal, and between $206 and $411 million in future economic impact from additional tourism after the event was held.[1] Rutter et al. (2004) estimated that UEFA 2008 will generate $298 million in total economic impact in Switzerland, which will host half the matches—the other half will be held in Austria.

Madden (2006) used a Computable General Equilibrium (CGE) model to analyze the total economic impact of the 2000 Summer Olympic Games on the Australian economy. This study concluded that the Summer Games—an event much larger than the UEFA Championship—increased the Gross State Product in New South Wales (the region including Sydney) by 0.25 percent above what it would have been if the Olympic Games had not taken place. This represents an upper bound on the potential economic impact of a mega sporting event. Poland's GDP was $444 billion in 2004, and a 0.25 percent increase in GDP amounts to $1.1 billion. Thus the Polish economy would have to experience this amount of positive economic impact for over nine years, to generate enough additional income to equal the estimated costs of hosting UEFA 2012. Excluding the $8 billion in transportation infrastructure spending, the Polish economy would still have to experience an economic impact of this size for two years to equal the cost of hosting UEFA 2012.

Unless the direct economic impact on the Polish and Ukrainian economies is significantly larger than the direct impact in Switzerland and Portugal—indeed they would need to be approximately the magnitude of the economic impact of hosting the Summer Olympic Games for four consecutive years—the costs of hosting UEFA 2012 will exceed the direct economic benefits. There does not appear to be any reason to expect that the direct economic impact in Poland and Ukraine will be significantly larger than the past direct economic impacts. However, the spending in Poland and Ukraine related to hosting the 2012 Championship may produce additional long-term economic benefits. In particular, infrastructure spending on improving the transportation infra-structure could generate significant long-term economic benefits. Rephann and Isserman (1994) show that the improved highways lead to lower produc-tion costs and increased manufacturing activity in cities. Lowering production costs can lead to lower prices for many goods purchased by households, and this cost reduction would be permanent. Lower prices on food, clothing and other consumer staples would leave more household income for the purchase of entertainment and leisure services, leading to an increase in the quality of living in both the countries.

Finally, even if the direct and indirect economic impact due to increased tourist spending and the effect of improved infrastructure on the economy do not produce enough of the total economic benefit to cover the costs of hosting UEFA 2012, it is possible that the intangible benefits, like an enhanced sense of national pride and the prestige associated with hosting a world famous sporting event might produce sufficient "psychic income" to justify $4.5 billion in spending to host the tournament. Valuing such benefits is a difficult under-taking, but the existing evidence does not support the idea that hosting the UEFA Championship produces significant intangible benefits. In particular, Barros (2002) used the Contingent Valuation Method to estimate the value of the intangible benefits generated in Portugal from the 2004 UEFA Champion-ship. Barros's estimate of the value of the intangible benefits to the residents of Portugal was a tiny fraction, less than one percent of the total cost of hosting that tournament. Unless Poles and Ukrainians derive significantly more intan-gible benefits from hosting UEFA 2012 than the Portuguese, it is unlikely that these benefits can justify the cost of hosting the event. Although residents of a transition economy might derive more psychic benefit from hosting a world fa-mous sporting event than residents of a developed economy, it seems unlikely that the difference would be several orders of magnitude.

The total costs and benefits of a sports mega-event extend well beyond the direct effects of the additional tourists who visit the region and spectators watching on television. Many of these factors were identified by Crompton (1995). In particular, a number of factors can be identified in the literature that overstate the actual benefits or understate the actual costs of sports mega-events. In some cases, these factors may be more important in a host region in a transitional economy than in a developed economy.

Crowding Out

This effect was described by Baade and Matheson (2004a) in the context of the 2000 Sydney Olympics Games, as: "some non-residents, who might have visited the country, decide not to do so because of congestion and high prices during the event's period" and ". . . even the host city's residents who do not at-tend the games may reduce their expenditures in the city if they avoid tem-porarily the neighbourhoods of the stadiums" (p. 346). In other words, because of the widespread speculation about congestion, lack of ticket availability and high prices, some tourists avoid the host region and choose other destinations. Other tourists who might have visited the host region for reasons other than the sports mega-event may be unable to find accommodations or transportation and decide not to visit. Since the sports mega-events are planned six or more years ahead, potential tourists have many opportunities to plan the travel to other destinations. This phenomenon has been identified at other sports mega-events as well. For instance, Lee and Taylor (2005) estimated that $163 million in tourists' expenditures were lost in Los Angeles during the 1984 Olympics because of the crowding out effect.

While a sports mega-event may have a negative effect on tourist visits in the host region, it may also depress the tourism outside the host region. In other words, when one city's tourism revenues grow, other areas may experience declines. For instance, tourists who intended to travel to different places in Australia in Summer 2000, may have chosen Sydney instead of other cities because of the Olympic games. As a consequence, hotel reservations fell by 19 percent in Melbourne in the second half of the September, compared to the first half of the month (Baade & Matheson, 2004a). Teigland (1999) observes that during 1994 Winter Olympic Games in Lillehammer, there was a decline in the domestic tourism in hotel rates in resorts away from the host Olympic city.

There are also some asymmetric effects visible even in host cities. While visitors' spending is higher in event related areas, they decline out of the event area (Chalip & McGuirty, 2004). This trend may last after the sport mega-event as well, if only a part of the city gained new facilities and infrastructure (Teigland, 1999).

According to the Polish Tourism Organization (www.pot.gov.pl), in 2004 Poland was visited by 15.1 million tourists and every year this number grows by at least 5 percent. Most of the visitors come in July and August. The share of Ukrainian tourists visiting Poland is above 300,000 in an average summer month. This may be a problem because Ukrainians may stay at home during the tournament, resulting in significant lost spending due to crowding out. This may also be a problem in Ukraine, as Poles account for a large share of Ukrainian tourism and they probably will stay at home as well during the games. In 2004, 200,000 Polish tourists visited Ukraine.

Hidden Stadium Costs

As discussed above, UEFA requires a host region that have eight "modern state-of-the- art" stadiums to hold the championship. These facilities must be completed two years before the event, by June 2010. Stadium construction and renovation costs are typically one of the largest costs associated with hosting the mega sporting events. As Crompton (1995) pointed out, money spent on construction of sports facilities should be counted as a part of the cost of hosting mega-events, and not as a part of the economic benefit. Many economic impact studies erroneously include stadium construction costs as part of the benefits.

If selected as host region, Poland and Ukraine will have to undertake a significant amount of stadium construction and renovation. While the existence of these new and renovated facilities will generate a large amount of economic impact during the football tournament, it will also generate significant operation and maintenance costs in the end. Also, the size of these new stadiums may be too big for the current and future needs of sports teams in Poland and Ukraine. According to the *Phase I Bid Report* (UEFA, 2005), average attendance at football matches in the top league in Poland was little more than 5,000 spectators in the 2004–2005 season. The corresponding figure was little more than 7,000 in Ukraine. The largest attendance at any match in Poland during that season was 18,000 and the largest attendance at any match in Ukraine was 32,000. If the attendance remains unchanged or even increases by 10 to 20 percent, following the UEFA tournament, the eight new and renovated stadiums will not be utilized fully. Operation and maintenance expenses vary relatively little with the intensity of use. By meeting the UEFA guidelines, the host region runs the risk of building the stadium of large capacity.

Hidden Hotel Costs

Increasing the inventory of high-end hotels will have important economic benefits for the host region. The construction phase will lead to greater demand for jobs in building trades and greater demand for building materials and transportation. After opening, new and relatively high wage jobs will be created as part of the staff of these hotels. However, increasing the inventory of the high-end hotels in developing and transition countries also poses two risks.

1. The new hotels may be built and operated by the foreign companies. In this case, a significant portion of the profits generated by these establishments may flow out of the country and into the pockets of foreign owners.
2. The host region may overbuild high-end hotels, relative to the demand for these accommodations after the sports mega-event is over.

Too much hotel capacity will put downward pressure on room rates and may force some hotels into bankruptcy. If larger foreign owned hotels are better financed than smaller domestically owned hotels, a glut of hotel rooms may have more of a negative impact on the local owners, further magnifying the negative consequences. A similar situation occurred in Lillehammer, Norway, following the 1994 winter Olympic Games. Teigland (1999) reported that several years after these Olympic Games 40 percent of the full-service hotels in Lillehammer had gone bankrupt.

The net long run effect of increased hotel capacity in the host region depends critically on the ability of the tourism sector to convert the increased world attention drawn by a sports mega-event into increased tourist arrivals. Billions of television viewers around the world will watch matches held in the host region. If a small fraction of these viewers can be persuaded to visit the host region after a sports mega- event takes place, then there could be important long-run economic benefits generated. Developing and transitional economies probably stand to gain more from this sort of advertising effect than developed countries like Italy, that are already lodged in the collective consciousness of tourists around the world.

Continuing Infrastructure Operation and Maintenance

The best examples of new or renovated infrastructure construction projects are stadiums, roads and airports. Essex and Chalkley (2004) report that non-event related infrastructure investment for winter Olympic Games over the past 20 years were often as large, or larger, than the direct costs of hosting these mega-events, so this type of spending can be significant. Investment in these projects may improve the quality of life of the local population long after a sports mega-event takes place. It is important to plan new infrastructure construction that can be used after an event by local residents, because the infrastructure costs account for majority of all event-related costs. However, based on the example from Korea, more big stadiums than necessary were built for World Cup 2002. Now even those occupied are too big for local teams and they are located too far from cities to be regularly used (Baade & Matheson, 2004b). Gratton, Shibli and Coleman (2005) provide a similar example from the 1989 Volvo Tennis Tournament in New Haven Connecticut, USA where a tennis arena was built for $15 million but was not used by the locals after the event. A large amount of stadium construction, more than would take place in a developed region, must take place in Poland and Ukraine to host UEFA 2012. This will in turn generate a significant amount of maintenance and upkeep expenditure.

Opportunity Costs

Both the countries, as developing ones, have crucial non-event related needs, like debt repayment, investment in health, education and safety, and even problems concerning negative population growth rate. The $1 billion in stadium renovation and construction and the unknown cost of hotel renovation and construction could be used to promote other economic growth-friendly policies, like improved secondary and higher education, encouraging small business formation, improved health care delivery or technological enhancements, with more efficient effects. Also, new technology development tends to be at very low levels in developing and transitional economies, like Poland and Ukraine.

Conclusions

Hosting a sports mega-event clearly brings a variety of important economic, social and psychic benefits to a host region. Increasingly, developing and transitional economies have argued that sports mega-events like the World Cup, the summer and winter Olympic Games and the UEFA Championship should be awarded to regions outside the developed economies of Europe, North

America and Asia, because developing and transitional countries need economic stimulus more than developed countries. The joint Poland/Ukraine bid to host UEFA 2012 is one example of this trend.

Hosting UEFA 2012 will produce both monetary and non-monetary benefits in developing and transitional economies like Poland and Ukraine. Thousands of UEFA officials, athletes and support staff from participating teams, and media covering the tournament will spend weeks in the host region. Hundreds of thousands of visitors will descend on the host region to attend the matches. Billions of television viewers will watch these matches on television and follow the outcomes of the matches in other media like the World Wide Web. Many new hotels will have to be built to meet the needs of the spectators and participants in the mega-event. The host region will have to significantly upgrade both the current inventory of sports stadiums and the transportation infrastructure. These costs differ significantly from the costs of hosting a sports mega event in developed countries that already have a large inventory of high-end hotels and extensive transportation networks. Improvements to the transportation infrastructure will pay important economic dividends, in terms of lower transportation costs, easier mobility and higher productivity for years to come, especially in developing and transitional economies.

But our simple back of the envelope cost benefit analysis suggests that Poland alone will spend over $10 billion, and if past UEFA Championships are any guide, the direct and indirect benefits generated by the championship will not match these costs. We argue that these benefits must also be qualified, in order to avoid overstating the overall size and scope of the benefits generated by sports mega-events. In the case of Poland and Ukraine, the inter-related nature of the two countries' tourist sectors, and the fact that Poland already draws many visitors from Germany and other European countries that make up a large number of the potential participants in UEFA 2012 suggest that tourists attracted to the tournament may crowd out a significant number of others who would have visited the host region in the absence of the tournament.

These two countries will have to significantly upgrade their current inventory of sports stadiums, perhaps spending over $1 billion on this endeavor. A large number of new hotels, most of them at the high-end of the quality spectrum, will have to be built to meet the requirements of UEFA on host regions. Some portion of these construction projects will be performed by foreign companies, perhaps using foreign workers. After the tournament ends, the host region will have a larger stock of stadiums and hotels that will require a larger amount of operation and maintenance costs. Depending on the long- run effect of UEFA 2012 on tourism, the hotel industry may have excess capacity, and the expended sports stadiums may not be efficiently utilized. Spending on stadium and five-star hotel construction projects in transitional economies has a higher opportunity cost, in terms of alternative projects not funded, than in developed economies. For this reason alone, the organizers of mega sporting events should proceed cautiously before awarding these events to regions in transition and developing economies.

Note

1. This estimate is based on a report by the DTZ consulting firm. The estimate was widely reported in the press, but we have been unable to locate a copy of the report.

References

Baade, R., & Matheson, V. (2004a). The quest for the cup: Assessing the economic impact of the World Cup. *Regional Studies*, 38, 343–354.

Baade, R., & Matheson, V. (2004b). Mega-sporting events in developing nations: Playing the way to prosperity. *South African Journal of Economics*, 72, 1085–1103.

Barros, C. (2002). Evaluating the regulatory procedure of host-country selections for the UEFA European Championship: A case study of Euro 2004. *European Sport Management Quarterly*, 2, 321–349.

Chalip, L., & McGuirty, J. (2004). Bundling sport events with the host destination. *Journal of Sport Tourism*, 9, 267–282.

Crompton, J. (1995). Economic impact analysis of sports facilities and events: Eleven sources of misapplication. *Journal of Sport Management*, 9, 14–35.

Crompton, J., Lee, S., Shuster T. (2001). A guide for undertaking economic impact studies: The Springfest example, *Journal of Travel Research*, 40, 79–87.

Essex, S., & Chalkley, B. (2004). Mega-sporting events in urban and regional policy: A history of the Winter Olympics. *Planning Perspectives*, 19, 201–232.

Gratton, C., Shibli, S., & Coleman, R. (2005). Sport and economic regeneration in cities. *Urban Studies*, 42, 985–999.

Lee, C., & Taylor, T. (2005). Critical reflections on the economic impact assessment of a mega-event: The case of 2002 FIFA world cup. *Tourism Management*, 26, 595–603.

Madden, J. (2006). Economic and fiscal impacts of mega sporting events: A general equilibrium assessment. *Public Finance and Management*, 6, 38–89.

Rephann, T., & Isserman, A. (1994). New highways as economic development tools: An evaluation using quasi-experimental matching methods. *Regional Science and Urban Economics*, 24, 723–751.

Rutter, H., Stettler, J., Amstutz, M., & Grozea-Helmenstein, A. (2004). *Economic Impact of the UEFA EURO2008® in Switzerland*. Institute of Tourism, Lucerne School of Business: Lucerne, Switzerland.

Teigland, J. (1999). Mega-events and impacts of tourism: The predictions and realities of the Lillehammer Olympics. *Impact Assessment and Project Appraisal*, 17, 305–317.

UEFA. (2005). *Phase 1 Bid Requirements*, Available at: http://www.uefa.com/newsfiles/279728.pdf, (Last accessed on 30 January 2006).

UEFA. (2005). *Phase 1 Evaluation Report*, Available at: http://www.uefa.com/newsfiles/362039.pdf, (Last accessed on 30 January 2006).

CAN NEW ORLEANS PLAY ITS WAY PAST KATRINA? THE ROLE OF PROFESSIONAL SPORTS IN THE REDEVELOPMENT OF NEW ORLEANS

Robert A. Baade and Victor A. Matheson

Introduction

Hurricane Katrina devastated New Orleans physically and economically after making landfall on August 29, 2005. Full recovery, which generally follows natural catastrophes in the US given the inflow of funds for reconstruction, seems less certain in the Crescent City. Citizens and businesses that abandoned New Orleans have exhibited a reluctance to return. The city's professional sports teams are included among those enterprises that left New Orleans in the wake of Hurricane Katrina. The National Football League (NFL) Saints played home games in three different cities during 2005; the National Basketball Association (NBA) Hornets have taken up residence in Oklahoma City for their 2005–2006 home games; and the Arena Football League's Voodoo have abandoned their entire 2005–2006 schedule.

Saints owner Tom Benson recently announced that the team would return home for the 2006 season, but their future in the city after the 2006 season is unclear (Duncan, 2005). Benson and the city have had a contentious relationship due largely to the fact that the Superdome could not compete with the new generation of NFL stadiums as a revenue producer, prompting Benson to threaten relocation in the absence of a new playing facility. This relationship has soured further as a consequence of the damage Katrina inflicted on the Superdome making the need for a new or renovated stadium even more pronounced. The purpose of this paper is to analyze the extent to which the city of New Orleans should direct its development dollars toward its sports infrastructure. Has New Orleans benefited economically from its role as host to major professional sports teams and a disproportionate number of mega-sports events given its size and demographics? Do commercial sports enable a rebuilding of New Orleans's storm-ravaged infrastructure or does it force civic trade-offs made even more painful by the storm?

Independent scholarship in general has not supported the thesis that professional sports induce significant increases in economic activity for host cities. New Orleans, however, may be different. The city is smaller and less affluent than other host cities in general, and it may be that the frequency with which large sports events are hosted by New Orleans makes the area an exception to the experience of most cities with regard to sports and economic development. The gravity of the city's economic situation in the wake of Katrina necessitates an individual and more complete appraisal as strategies for economic redevelopment are explored. Answers to the questions raised in this introduction require a review, among other things, of the damage Katrina wrought, the amount of redevelopment money the city must commit, and the evidence with regard to the impact sports has on host city economies.

Measuring Katrina's Devastation

Hurricane Katrina, which swept into New Orleans and the Gulf Coast on August 29, 2005, caused far and away the largest damages in real dollar terms of any hurricane in US history, with uninsured losses topping US$100 billion (Bloomberg News, 2005) and insured losses estimated at US$34.4 billion (Powell, 2005). Its final death toll of over 1,400 also places it among the worst natural disasters ever suffered by the US. New Orleans was particularly hard hit by the storm, as flood waters remained for weeks after Katrina while levies were repaired, and rebuilding the city is an epic undertaking unmatched in scope and expense in recent US history.

The cost of reconstructing New Orleans itself has been placed at more than US$100 billion dollars (Tennessean News Service, 2005). Approximately 80% of New Orleans' 188,000 occupied housing units were severely damaged by the storm. Furthermore, more than half of the city's 100,000 owner-occupied homes were built before 1950, and their repair and replacement will require expensive modifications to meet modern building codes designed to prevent future hurricane damage (Tennessean News Services, 2005).

The damage to middle-class neighborhoods has substantial implications for the redevelopment effort both as it relates to production and consumption. Without a middle class, New Orleans will not have the workers it needs to run the economy that existed prior to Katrina, and the spending necessary to restore the economy to pre-hurricane levels will be deficient. Katrina devastated the housing stock, schools, and other infrastructure vital to normal life for all socio-economic classes.

The extent of the damage to the social infrastructure must also be carefully assessed since the return of middle class workers and consumers is essential to the revitalization of the New Orleans economy. Even before Katrina, by nearly every measure of economic development, New Orleans lagged behind other large cities in USA. Labor force participation rates and employment to population ratios in New Orleans averaged 5–10% below national levels for most demographic groups (Gabe et al., 2005). Hurricane damaged areas in Louisiana had poverty rates above the national average (21.4 vs. 12.4%), and New Orleans residents were less likely (55 vs. 66%) to live in owner-occupied housing than residents of other large cities (Gabe et al., 2005). Finally, the educational attainment of younger adults (age 18–34) for storm-damaged areas is generally below that for the rest of the nation. For example, 22.9% of young adults in hurricane damaged areas had not completed a high school degree compared with 20.6% nationwide, while only 22.5% had completed a college degree compared with 29.3% nationwide (Gabe et al., 2005).

These figures have several implications for the likelihood that people displaced will return. First, Katrina hit the economically disadvantaged hardest. Statistics indicate that other places in the nation to which they have relocated will improve their opportunities for employment. Second, significant portions of the middle class were displaced in the storm-ravaged area; 47.4% of those displaced had education equivalent to some college or above (Gabe et al., 2005). Third, 45% of those displaced did not live in homes that they owned indicating that a significant portion of the people displaced by Hurricane Katrina have weak financial ties to the communities they abandoned. A significant permanent displacement of the population affected by the storm will undermine or may substantially alter the socio-demographic character of neighborhoods mostly adversely affected by the storm. It should also be noted that virtually entire neighborhoods and parishes were wiped out by the storm, and devastation of that magnitude may well negate any pull that community loyalty and ties may exert in bringing people back. It has been estimated, for example, that Orleans Parish and St. Bernard Parish lost 65.9% and 89.8% of their populations over the period from October 2005 to January 2006 (Greater New Orleans Community Data Center, 2006).

The report of the Bring Back New Orleans Commission recommended that all of New Orleans not necessarily be rebuilt. If that recommendation is followed, the post-Katrina New Orleans will be smaller than it was before the storm, and that has implications for the ability (or willingness) of sports to serve as a catalyst for economic redevelopment. Prior to considering what sport potentially can contribute to the redevelopment effort, it is logical to identify a blueprint for redevelopment. That topic will be discussed in the next section of the paper.

A Blueprint for the Redevelopment of New Orleans and the Role of the Leisure Industry

The New Orleans economy serves the nation as a tourist center and transportation hub for water transport in particular, and therefore, any economic redevelopment effort should focus on those traditional industries, an opinion endorsed by members of an *ad hoc* committee of urban experts assembled under the auspices of the Urban Land Institute. Of course, commercial sport is one important aspect of the tourist/leisure industry, and it could play a role in the economic revitalization of New Orleans.

Much of the tourism industry in New Orleans is "high-ground," based in the French Quarter, the Central Business District (CBD), or the Garden District. The Urban Land Institute committee, which met on November 18, 2005 opined:

> New Orleans should concentrate its rebuilding efforts on the sections of
> the city that occupy the high ground, while securing lower-lying areas for

potential long-term rebirth . . . it's not practical to redevelop every acre of New Orleans in the short term, considering that 300,000 residents and 160,000 jobs have been lost. It's also not socially equitable to allow residents back into neighborhoods that do not have adequate levee protection and may be toxic . . . (Carr, 2005)

Prior to the storm New Orleans annually attracted more than 10 million visitors who spent in excess of US $5 billion per year according to the New Orleans Metropolitan and Tourism Bureau. Even though New Orleans is a relatively small city, it ranked fifth in the United States in the number of conventions hosted (Tennessean News Services, 2005). Tourists will not likely return to a city that cannot provide essential services, and in the absence of tourists, the New Orleans economy will flounder. One part of the blueprint for restoration of the New Orleans economy will require restoration of housing and essential services for its middle class who provide the labor and entrepreneurial talent for the tourism industry, followed by a revitalization of those businesses that cater to tourists.

The extent to which professional sports and mega-events contribute to the tourist trade must be assessed in determining the fraction of scarce capital resources that should be devoted to the restoration of the infrastructure necessary to accommodate professional and mega-sports events. The last few years before Hurricane Katrina struck, the city of New Orleans hosted two major league professional sports teams, several minor league teams, and a division one collegiate athletic program at Tulane University. In addition, since opening in 1975, the Superdome has hosted numerous sporting events of national significance including the NFL's Super Bowl in 1978, 1981, 1986, 1990, 1997, and 2002, the National Intercollegiate Athletic Association Men's Basketball Final Four in 1982, 1987, 1993, and 2003. In addition, the Superdome annually hosts the Sugar Bowl, one of college football's top post-season matches and a game which has determined college football's national champion nine times since 1975.

Replacing the infrastructure for professional sports and mega-sports events can be justified if the benefits provided by the facilities exceed the costs incurred in the reconstruction. Both costs and benefits have to be measured over time since the facilities provided a stream of benefits as well as generating costs associated with Operations and Maintenance (O&M). Comprehensive economic analysis would include not only the explicit benefits but also the implicit benefits and costs, which are difficult not only to measure but in many cases to identify.

Data do exist for New Orleans for the number of establishments, annual payroll, and number of employees for a variety of entertainment related industries defined according to the North American Industrial Classification System (NAICS). In Table 1, information is recorded on professional sports' fraction of the three measures of economic activity previously identified.

All data point to the fact that the economic activity accounted for through the "Arts, Entertainment, and Recreation" industry for New Orleans is small.

Table 1. Aggregate measures of the fraction of New Orleans economic activity in total represented by spectator sports for 2003

Ratio/NAICS number	NAICS 71: arts, entertainment, and recreation (%)	NAICS 711: performing arts, spectator sports, and related industries (%)	NAICS 7112: spectator sports (%)
Industry employees/ New Orleans total	4.07	1.16	0.62
Annual industry payroll/ New Orleans total	3.48	1.39	0.34
Industry establishments/ New Orleans total	1.74	0.94	0.20

Source: County Business Patterns (2003).

The contribution of "Spectator Sports" is less than 1% by any of the measures identified in Table 2. Despite the hefty salaries paid professional athletes, the spectator sports industry typically accounts for less than 1% of a city's payroll, and, by that measure, the industry is not economically vital to cities in the US, including New Orleans.

The Cost of Sports Infrastructure and Team Subsidies in New Orleans

The competition to host sports mega-events and/or a professional sports team is often as fierce as the competition among athletes on game day. Sports infrastructure is vital in not only attracting commercial sport but in retaining teams or events. Prior to Hurricane Katrina, New Orleans appeared to be on the verge of losing their NFL franchise, the Saints. Tom Benson, the owner of the Saints, had reportedly rejected the state's final offer to keep the Saints in New Orleans in late April of 2005. The state's offer included not only public financing of over 75% of a proposed $174 million Superdome renovation, but also direct cash payments to the Saints totaling $64 million through 2008 and $9.5 million per year after the completion of the renovations to the Superdome in 2008. (USA Today, 2005). The state's offer to the Saints to include the annual cash subsidy would place the team in the top half of the financial standings in the NFL.

The fact that Benson would reject such an offer speaks volumes about the financial realities of the NFL and the inordinate transfer of business risk from teams to their host cities. While the state struggled to meet its contractual cash payments to the team in the wake of reduced tax revenues following 9/11, the only significant financial risk facing Tom Benson is the $81 million he would be required to pay (representing the subsidies that the Saints have received since 2001), if he breaks his Superdome contract, which he can do following the 2006 season (Konigsmark, 2005). That risk pales in comparison to the US $1 billion written offer Benson claims to have received for the team in 2005, a 1,400% increase over the US $70 million price Benson paid for the Saints in 1985 (Robinson, 2005). The lucrative offer Benson received for the team reflects at least in part the money-making potential of NFL teams, which is explained in large part by the subsidies cities extend to attract a supply of teams that is limited by the NFL and its owners.

Why would Benson consider leaving New Orleans? The answer, of course, is a more lucrative offer or better economic prospects by locating in another city such as Los Angeles, which has been without a team since 1995. The fans in New Orleans have done their part as attendance has been solid, but the overall financial resources of the city are limited. Prior to Katrina, among NFL cities, New Orleans was the fourth lowest in population trailing only Jacksonville, Buffalo, and Green Bay, and the fourth poorest, trailing Buffalo, Tampa Bay, and Phoenix. Even if New Orleans' *per capita* income were to recover to its pre-Katrina levels, if as few as 25% of the population were to fail to return, New Orleans would be smaller than any other American host city except for Green Bay, Wisconsin, in any of the big four professional sports leagues.

Corporations also play a major role in keeping a team financially competitive. It is one thing to provide luxury seating; it is another thing to fill those seats. New Orleans serves as a headquarters for few major corporations, and there is not the market for loges and club seats that can be found in the other NFL cities with which New Orleans competes. One writer somewhat whimsically stated the NFL financial equation in the following way:

> Instead of fans, the NFL seeks corporations. . . . While the NBA and Major League Baseball have guaranteed contracts for their players, the NFL with its exorbitant TV rights deals and corporate backing has practically given their owners guaranteed dollars. . . .

> The way business is done now is the owner convinces his buddies who own the largest businesses in their respective cities to buy majority (sic) of the season tickets and luxury boxes. The result: a term exclusive to the NFL, the guaranteed sellout. Saints owner Tom Benson can't do that in New Orleans because there are no major corporations other than Entergy to back him. (Terrebonne Parrish Courier, 2005)

New Orleans is at a considerable disadvantage in supporting and, therefore, retaining either the Saints or its NBA franchise, the Hornets. The lack of financial capacity creates a relative shortfall in team revenues, which explains the cash subsidies and tax concessions New Orleans has had to provide to retain its professional teams. New Orleans had a total capital budget of US $74,627,540 in 2002 (City of New Orleans, Ordinance #23,957, November 2001). The estimated cost of replacing the Superdome is $600 million. Spreading that cost over 30 years would constitute 27% of the capital budget for 2002 without considering debt service on the bonds to finance replacing or renovating the structure.

Following Katrina any plans for completely replacing the Superdome have been scuttled, but the city will have to provide for a portion of the costs involved in repairing the facility and the adjacent New Orleans Arena. State officials made clear following Katrina that they intended to update the facility with new audio and visual equipment, more luxury seating, concession stands, and wider concourses so that it would be competitive with the newer structures that exist in the NFL. However, Louisiana had only a US $500 million insurance policy on state buildings along with $100 million in flood insurance, and the Superdome was just one of the many public buildings damaged by the storm. The Federal Emergency Management Agency (FEMA) will also contribute to the rebuilding effort, but the funds will have to be efficiently allocated.

Given the very small percentage of economic activity in New Orleans accounted for by the sports industry, it may not be prudent to devote a disproportionate share of scarce redevelopment funds to that sector. An even stronger argument can be made against refurbishing the Superdome to accommodate the financial needs of the NFL Saints since their owner has consistently sought economic concessions from a city and state that were financially stressed even prior to Katrina.

The economic incentive for the Saints owner to keep the team in New Orleans has been severely compromised by Katrina. Lacking the financial wherewithal to support professional sports following Katrina, it is not reasonable to expect that the team will make the financial sacrifices that are necessary as New Orleans attempts to rebuild. Furthermore, unlike the efforts made by large oil companies to repair the capital intensive oil refineries in and around the city, there exists no motivation for the Saints to recoup fixed or sunk costs since their investment in infrastructure has been minimal. This points to a larger problem with the financial structure of the professional sports industry throughout the US: the existence of substantial subsidies for infrastructure undermines the team commitment to their host cities, and absent any meaningful risk to their own capital, what incentive do teams have to stay in a city that experiences a catastrophe on the scale wrought by Hurricane Katrina? There is no question that the financial risk accompanying hosting professional sports in the United States is disproportionately borne by the host community. Katrina provides striking testimony to the reality of how subsidies for sports infrastructure have contributed to that financial vulnerability.

Theory Regarding the Economic Impact of Sport

The argument for subsidies for professional sports has often been based on the economic impact it provides; however, independent scholarship arguing against sports as a catalyst for economic development is abundant (Noll & Zimbalist, 1997). The often-spectacular economic impact estimates advocates for subsidizing sports infrastructure advance fail to accurately estimate the economic impact of sports for at least three reasons. First, often the costs associated with hosting the event, building the structure, or accommodating the team are treated as expansionary expenditures. Such a tactic ignores the budgetary reality that money spent on such endeavors precludes spending that money on something else. The benefit from the use of that money for some other purpose, for example building a levee as opposed to a stadium, represents a cost to the community and should be considered in evaluating the efficacy of any project.

Second, the money spent on attending a sports event by residents of the home team community necessarily precludes them from spending that money on other things. Furthermore, local expenditures on professional sports may actually reduce total spending in the economy as opposed to simply reallocating money among competing ends. Professional sports, which use national resource markets as opposed to locally owned and operated resources for alternative entertainment or recreational activities, may foster a net outflow of money. Most of the money spent on a night at a professional sports event goes to the athletes and owners of the team who may not live in the community in which they play. Value created in the community by the event or team play may not be value that the community recognizes in the way of increased incomes, which are spent again in the community, as might be the case with locally owned and operated entertainment. Professional sports may be a model better described as the circus coming to town for a temporary stay and leaving with a portion of the income spectators created through their economic activity within the community.

Third, to properly gauge the benefit to the public sector, the incremental tax revenues collected should be net of the incremental explicit costs incurred in hosting the event or team. The Super Bowl, for example, places a heavy security burden on the host city and that cost needs to be identified in estimating the net benefit to the city from hosting the event.

Taken together the implication of the three qualifiers noted is that the appropriate measure of the benefit imparted by the subsidy is the measure of *net value added*. The inability or unwillingness to recognize the difference between gross expenditures in conjunction with an event and the net value added it induces explains the substantial disagreements relating to the economic impact of sports teams and mega-events on host community economies. Once the economic impact of sport is properly measured, independent scholarship indicates that most teams and mega-events fail to increase net value added for the host community.

An Empirical Examination of the Impact of Professional Sports on New Orleans

Baade and Dye (1990) examined the impact of NFL teams and Major League Baseball franchises as well as new stadiums on personal incomes in nine host cities, including New Orleans, between 1965 and 1983. In addition, in order to account for regional economic fluctuations, Baade and Dye (1990) also examined the impact of professional sports on the ratio of personal income in host cities to the larger geographic regions in which these cities resided. Their oft-cited results indicate that the construction of new stadiums had a statistically significant negative impact on the personal income ratio for the sample of cities examined. For New Orleans specifically, the construction of the Superdome appeared to have a significant positive impact on the personal income ratio, but that impact was then offset by a significant negative impact induced by the NFL Saints. In their model utilizing personal income rather than the personal income ratio, the presence of the Saints had a positive but not statistically significant impact on the local economy while the construction of the Superdome was positive and just on the border of statistical significance at the 10% level. Baade and Dye's analysis of New Orleans is replicated here updated through 2003 and modified to include the effects of mega-events such as the Super Bowl and NCAA Final Four and the presence of an NBA franchise in the city. In addition, as noted by Baade and Matheson (2001), oil prices have an important effect on economic activities in oil patch cities such as New Orleans, and Baade and Dye's analysis is updated to account for this. Finally, data compatibility necessitates using figures from 1969 through 2003, so that four early years of data in Baade and Dye's original study are not usable. Since the Saints began play in 1967, the economic impact of the Saints cannot be tested with this data set.

Equations (1) and (2) present regression equations that can be used to analyze the economic impact of professional sports on the New Orleans economy:

$$Y_t = b_0 + b_1 Y_{t-1} + b_2 POP_t + b_3 STAD_t + b_4 MEGA_t + b_5 NBA_t$$
$$+ b_6 OIL_t + B_7 TREND_t + e_t \tag{1}$$

where Y_t is the personal income of the New Orleans Metropolitan Statistical Area (MSA) in time period t, POP_t is the population of the New Orleans MSA over time, STAD is a dummy variable for the construction of the Superdome and takes a value of 0 prior to 1975 and 1 from 1975 on, MEGA is a dummy variable of one if the city hosted either the Super Bowl or the NCAA Final Four in a particular year, NBA is a dummy variable accounting for the presence of an NBA team in New Orleans, OIL is real price of a barrel of crude oil, TREND is variable assigned a value of 1 for 1969 and rising to 35 by 2003, and et is the stochastic error.

$$Y_t/YR_t = b_0 + b_1 Y_t/YR_t + b_2 (POP_t/POPR_t) + b_3 STAD_t$$
$$+ b_4 MEGA_t + b_5 NBA_t + b_6 OIL_t + b_7 TREND_t + e_t \tag{2}$$

where Y_t/YR_t is the fraction of personal income in the southeastern region of the US accounted for by the New Orleans economy, and $POP_t / POPR_t$ is the fraction of the southeastern US population living in the New Orleans MSA. Results of OLS regression on Equations (1) and (2) are shown in Table 2.

The results in Table 2 present two stories. In Model 1, no sports variables emerged as statistically significant and the coefficients on both the Superdome and mega-events variable were of the wrong sign. Both of these findings suggest, in accordance with most of the academic literature, that sports have little impact on the economic activity within a city. The results for Model 2, how-

Table 2. OLS regression results for Equations (1) and (2)

Variable	Model 1 (t-stats in parens.)	Model 2 (t-stats in parens.)
Constant	7,431,637 (1.370)	0.03742 (7.536)
Y_{t-1} or Y_{t-1}/YR_{t-1}	0.814 (5.846)	1.135 (14.160)
POP or POP / POPR	−4.240 (−0.752)	−1.613 (−6.353)
STAD	−127,597 (−0.232)	0.0006 (2.657)
MEGA	−130,956 (−0.706)	0.0001 (1.324)
NBA	67,275 (0.270)	− (−0.679)
OIL	25,775 (2.633)	0.00003 (6.913)
TREND	149,056 (1.852)	− (−7.524)
Fit statistics	Adj. R^2 = 0.995; Durbin Watson = 1.891	Adj. R^2 = 0.995; Durbin Watson = 2.217

ever, present a different story. While the coefficients on the NBA and mega-events variables are not significant, the Superdome coefficient is positive and significant at the 5% level confirming the results of Baade and Dye (1990) in the same model. This model presents evidence that the Superdome itself may be an important component of the New Orleans economy, but the teams that play there as well as a handful of the biggest sporting events that take place in the Superdome do not have much impact on the overall economy.

This result is, perhaps, not surprising. The utilization of the Superdome has increased over time, and it has been successful in providing a venue that accommodated events, most of which are not related to sports, that brought visitors and spending to New Orleans from outside the metropolis. Professional football and basketball, on the other hand, induced substitute spending that ultimately deflected resident spending to areas outside New Orleans. The teams, furthermore, drained scarce city resources through subsidies that became income for non-resident players, coaches, and owners. The Saints, as the primary tenant, may have influenced Superdome scheduling and effectively prevented the facility from being utilized for other events that could have expanded the New Orleans economy.

The spectator sports industry, in light of the preponderance of scholarly evidence, is properly viewed as a lagging rather than a leading economic activity. Sports yields hedonic value, in other words, and the quality of life benefit it imparts is a luxury affordable in affluent communities rather than an activity that helps a community achieve affluence. Sport for the most part is properly viewed as a luxury good and not a productive resource although some sports infrastructure, such as the Superdome, is flexible enough to provide use outside the sports sector.

Spectator Sport and the Revitalization of New Orleans

A part of the reconstruction debate will focus on the Superdome and New Orleans Arena, and it is important to assess, therefore, what the public can expect in the way of a return on those investments. The devastation of the middle and lower classes has a profound impact on the professional sports industry in New Orleans. These classes provided workers for the leisure industry as well as other industries, and their abandonment of New Orleans has impaired the ability of the City to adequately meet the needs of service establishments in the French Quarter and CBD that cater to the needs of tourists. The loss of the middle class has also diminished consumption in New Orleans. In other words, Katrina has eliminated both the workers and the customers upon which professional sports relies.

The labor shortage makes it doubtful that the Superdome could host a major event at this juncture. Each large event at the Superdome requires approximately 2,500 part-time workers. Unfortunately, the lack of housing in New Orleans means that no such pool of potential part-time workers is available in the city. Indeed, for a short time longer at least the workers who maintain the hotels and provide restaurant and bar business are housed in the hotels. A Superdome and convention center that is up and running tomorrow would bring in guests who would displace the very workers that provide guest services. Therefore, even if an event could be physically hosted in the Superdome right now, a good fraction of the workers at the facility would very likely have to come from outside the city. The leakage of money from New Orleans through athletes repatriating their incomes to their primary residences would further be enhanced by ordinary workers doing the same thing in some appreciable amount because of a lack of housing in many New Orleans neighborhoods. Post-Katrina, it is even less likely that income generated through commercial sports activities would remain in the City.

Likewise, the devastation in New Orleans has made it less likely that professional athletes would remain in the community to spend their money. The lack of social services and the destruction, which has transformed New Orleans physically, would compel many with the financial wherewithal to live elsewhere. Thus, Katrina likely enhanced the size of the substitution effects noted in the previous section of the paper and enhanced the risk of investment in sports infrastructure substantially.

The money spent on professional sports infrastructure in this environment of acute housing shortages can only slow down the restoration of the housing stock and ultimately frustrate the financial interests of the sports establishment. Money spent on sports infrastructure is money not spent on housing and deflects construction work from where it is needed most.

Restoring the Superdome and New Orleans Arena does send the message that New Orleans is on the road to healing. The message, however, is a tease if those renovated facilities cannot host events for which local residents provide the necessary labor. A better reconstruction strategy would be to repair and replace the damaged housing stock first.

It is also hard to imagine the benefit to the city of New Orleans of repairing sports facilities that the owners will not use due to the compromised economics of events hosted by those structures, especially for commercial sport. If there are few residents, there will be few fans. Few fans translates into little spending, and since tax dollars are derived from the demand for goods and services, tax revenues generated by governments through activities at the facilities will be less, perhaps appreciably less, than before Katrina. Indeed, declining business activity following the terrorist attacks on 9/11 had already resulted in deficit spending by the Louisiana Stadium and Exposition District to meet its cash subsidy obligations to the Saints and Hornets. The shortfall had led to serious discussions about tax increases for car rentals and hotels in addition to sales tax and cigarette tax increases prior to Katrina's arrival. Under present conditions no tax increases are possible, and it is better from the city's point of view to have the teams play elsewhere rather than assume those obligations. If the Saints and Hornets fostered deficit state spending pre-Katrina of approximately US $15 million, surely those deficits would increase substantially following Katrina. The costs of continuing to host professional sports outweigh the benefits and will continue to do so until the economy can be reinvigorated back to pre-Katrina levels.

The professional sports teams in New Orleans would have to be motivated by something other than their financial self interest to help New Orleans move beyond Katrina, but the evidence is overwhelming that the owner of the New Orleans Saints has operated pre- and post-Katrina out of financial self interest. Prior to the storm, the evidence indicates that he was reluctant to accept a refurbished Superdome because Benson apparently believed that even an updated Superdome could not generate sufficient income to allow him to be financially competitive in New Orleans. When evaluating the nature of the negotiations between Benson and the city, the problem for Benson is New Orleans and not the Superdome. Benson has the option to move the team to Los Angeles, but Paul Tagliabue, the Commissioner of the NFL, and the League would have a massive public relations problem if he allowed that move. While the NFL may share revenues, cities that host teams are hardly given a free ride. The *quid pro quo* for having access to revenues generated by NFL teams playing in the New York and Chicago markets is to build state-of-the-art stadiums that allow each team to contribute as much as they can to the pool of stadium-generated revenues. Eventually the NFL will find a way to move the Saints out of New Orleans rather than have the team become a ward of the League.

Conclusions and Policy Implications

Hurricane Katrina induced a massive outflow of residents and businesses from the city of New Orleans. Included among those businesses that fled are the city's two major professional sports teams, the NFL Saints and NBA Hornets. The capital costs necessary to encourage the return of the Saints and the Hornets for the long term are substantial. The images of the NFL and NBA will be damaged if the Saints and Hornets do not at least make cameo appearances, but in the longer term, the teams and their leagues will demand greater revenue streams than can be generated in their current facilities. The fact that New Orleans and the State of Louisiana were directly subsidizing the teams indicates that pre-Katrina the teams were not generating revenues in their venues that allowed them to be financially competitive in their leagues. This paper has concluded that it would be singularly unwise in the post-Katrina world to direct substantial funds at refurbishing the Superdome and New Orleans Arena specifically to make the teams financially competitive.

Capital expenditures on the Superdome supplant capital expenditures on housing, schooling, and other middle class amenities that will bring the middle class back. The evidence from Baade and Dye (1990) and this paper indicates that the Superdome did account for significant net value, but the NFL and NBA franchises did not as a consequence of powerful substitution effects. Therefore, expenditures on the sports facilities that are undertaken should be consistent with attracting those Superdome related activities that have contributed to the New Orleans economy. It should be kept in mind, however, that even though the Superdome has brought net benefits to the city, the reconstruction of the Superdome in the short run should be undertaken only after spending on housing, and that restoration efforts not necessarily be directed toward amenities that provide the highest revenues for sports franchises, but instead providing a multipurpose facility for non-sporting events. Providing physical accommodation for professional sports teams does not advance the economics interests of New Orleans in the short term. Doing so would exacerbate the economic problems that currently exist.

Cities in general should be mindful of the fact that subsidies for professional sports teams eliminate the financial incentives teams would have to remain in the community following a natural or manmade disaster. Businesses that have risked their own capital and built infrastructure have a financial stake in their host community, but the Saints and Hornets, as well as most professional sports teams in the US, have few such ties to their local communities. Paradoxically, cities have contributed in a very substantial way to the incentive for teams to abandon a city in the face of a disaster on the scale of Katrina. The owner of the New Orleans Saints, Tom Benson, was making his way out of New Orleans before Katrina, and the storm has undoubtedly increased his perception of risk and diminished his financial prospects in New Orleans to a point that it is not in his financial interest to stay there.

New Orleans will be rebuilt at the grassroots: home-by-home and business by business. The rebuilding of New Orleans will not occur purely out of economic incentive but because people are attached emotionally to their city. The economic motivation comes from recouping their fixed costs. If businesses cannot cover their variable costs of operation in relatively short order, they will leave. The best way to cover the variable costs is to encourage consumers to return to the community, and therefore, government's role should be to do what they can to encourage the return of the middle class. To this end, the order of capital expenditures in New Orleans should be levees, housing, middle class amenities, infrastructure for non-resident businesses and last those industries that cater to the entertainment needs of the middle class.

The role of sports in the economic recovery of the city is dubious other than serving as a symbol that the city remains vital. The repair of the Superdome and the New Orleans Arena is an expensive tease in that regard, but does little to provide what is needed for the community to recover from the storm. Sports and the hosting of mega-events may actually undermine long-term recovery through deflecting capital spending from where it is needed most and crowding out those workers and residents who are involved in the essential rebuilding process. Sport may provide hedonic value, but at this juncture hedonic value and the economic interests of the sport elites must, out of financial and developmental necessity, take a back seat in the interest of the greater good.

References

Baade, R. A., & Richard, F. D. (1990). The impact of stadiums and professional sports on metropolitan area development. *Growth and Change, 21*, 1–14.

Baade, R. A., & Victor, A. M. (2001). Home run or wild pitch? Assessing the economic impact of major league baseball's all-star game. *Journal of Sports Economics, 2*, 307–327.

Bloomberg News, (October 1, 2005). Katrina cost: $100 billion. *Chicago Tribune*.

Carr, M. (2005). Rebuilding should begin on high ground, group says. *The Times-Picayune*, Retrieved November 19, 2005, from http://www.nola.com/printer/printer.ssf?/base/news-4/113238540235800.xml

County Business Patterns. (2003). NAICS. Retrieved January 31, 2006, from http://censtats.census.gov/cgibin/cbpnaic/cbpdeti.pl

Duncan, J. (December 31, 2005). Saints to play at home next year. *The Times-Picayune*.

Gabe, T., Falk, G., McCarty, M., & Mason, V.W. (2005). Hurricane Katrina: Social-Demographic characteristics of impacted areas. CRS Report for Congress, November 4, 2005.

Greater New Orleans Community Data Center. (2006). Post-disaster population estimates. *Post-Katrina Estimates and Impact Data*. Available at: http://www.gnocdc.org.

Konigsmark, A. R. (December 29, 2005). Superdome major part of New Orleans comeback. *USA Today*.

Noll, R., & Andrew Z. (1997). *Sports, jobs, & taxes*. Washington, DC: Brookings Institution.

Powell, E. A. (October 4, 2005). Survey foresees $34.4 B in Katrina claims. *Associated Press*.

Robinson, C. (May 24, 2005). Saints on the march? *Yahoo! Sports*, Available at: http://sports.yahoo.com/ nfl/news?slug=cr-owners052405&prov=yhoo&type=lgns.

Tennessean News Services. (September 5, 2005). Rebuilding of New Orleans incredibly big, far from easy: Massive job will take billions of dollars and tons of national resolve. *Nashville Tennessean*.

Terrebonne Parrish Courier. (2005). Retrieved May 16, 2005, from http://www.houmatoday.com/apps/pbcs.dll/article?AID=/20050515/SPORTS/505150331/1034/SPORTS02.

USA Today (2005) Available at: http://www.usatoday.com/sports/football/nfl/saints/2005-04 - 29stadium-issues_x.htm?POE=SPOISVA

28

A NEW SOCIAL MOVEMENT:
SPORT FOR DEVELOPMENT AND PEACE

Bruce Kidd

During the last two decades, there has been a concerted effort to remobilize sport as a vehicle for broad, sustainable social development, especially in the most disadvantaged communities in the world. In AIDS-torn east Africa, for example, a coalition of African and first-world agencies called the Kicking Aids Out network uses sport to teach personal health and sexual responsibility to vulnerable youth, no mean challenge when more than half of those newly affected by HIV/AIDS are between the ages of 15 and 24 and they typically die before their 35th birthday. In the former Yugoslavia, UNICEF has created "Open Fun Football Schools" to teach children and youth about the perils of landmines, while the US-based non-governmental organization (NGO) Peace Players International teaches basketball to encourage communication and cooperation between children and youth from different ethnic or religious backgrounds in Israel, Northern Ireland, and South Africa. In the slums of Nairobi, Kenya, the Mathare Youth Sports Association promotes soccer as a vehicle for the inclusion of girls and women, school retention and environmental cleanup.[1] These efforts are not limited to the low- and middle-income countries (LMICs)[2] and regions of conflict, but extend to the slums of First World cities and the impoverished aboriginal reserves of Canada.[3] They are all part of a rapidly mushrooming phenomenon, the use of sport and physical activity to advance sport and broad social development in disadvantaged communities. There are 166 organizations engaged in such work currently listed on the "International Platform on Sport for Development" maintained by the Swiss Academy for Development.[4] Through a series of international conferences and the convening power of the Internet, these often disparate activities are loosely linked together in what is increasingly recognized as the international movement of Sport for Development and Peace (SDP). In many of its ambitions and activities, SDP draws heavily upon the idealism and energy of youth, including a growing number of Olympic and Commonwealth Games athletes, who have formed NGOs, initiated new program, and volunteered as organizers and leaders. A growing number of First World universities, colleges, and high schools provide SDP internships for their students.

To be sure, social development through sport has a long history. Its aspirations can be traced back to the "rational recreation" interventions of the improving middle and working class in the late nineteenth century, the "playground movement" of the early twentieth century, and the confessional and workers' sports movements of the interwar period, among other antecedents.[5] A more recent incarnation has been the "midnight basketball" interventions in the United States and Canada.[6] International social development through sport dates back to nineteenth-century colonizing.[7] But the current manifestation is different in the rapid explosion of the agencies and organizations that are involved, the tremendous appeal it has for youth volunteering, the financial support it enjoys from the powerful international sports federations, and the extent to which it has been championed by the United Nations, its agencies and significant partners.

SDP has brought considerable benefit to many children and youth in the countries where it is conducted. But it is also woefully under-funded, highly uncoordinated, and completely unregulated. Despite a long calendar of high-level international conferences in the last few years, including intergovernmental roundtables at the recent Olympic, Winter Olympic, and Commonwealth Games, with a few important exceptions, SDP operates beyond the radar of most national governments' domestic and foreign policies.

In this essay, I examine the new ambition of "sport for development and peace" in the current, social, economic, and ideological context, identify the growing number of national and international agencies and organizers involved, and discuss problems and prospects. I do so as much as an advocate and organizer within the movement—what Rick Gruneau and David Whitson call a "moral entrepreneur"[8]—as a social scientist. For the last 15 years, I have been active in one of the programs that I discuss—Commonwealth Games Canada's International Development through Sport program—and I serve on the Commonwealth Secretariat's Advisory Body on Sport. I also contribute to a partnership between the University of Toronto and the University of Zambia designed to strengthen teacher education in physical education as a strategy of anti-stigmatization, gender equity, and preventive education about HIV/AIDS.

SDP is part of —but can be distinguished from—the growing efforts to assist sport development in the disadvantaged communities in the world. By "sport development," I mean programs designed to assist those engaged in organized sport—athletes, coaches, officials, administrators—and to strengthen the infrastructure of facilities and institutions within which organized sport takes place. Here, too, there is a long history. Well before the beginning of the twentieth century, missionary "first-world" coaches or teachers, driven by both improving and controlling political, ideological, and commercial motives, took sports to virtually every corner of the non-European world, while sports enthusiasts in many of these countries sought to acquire and develop sports for themselves. In recent decades, international sport development has been led by the International Olympic Committee's Olympic Solidarity Commission, which reinvests the IOC's bonanza from television revenues into a range of programs to assist sports development. During the four years between Athens and Beijing, for example, Olympic Solidarity will invest US$200 million, and assist some 10,000 athletes, coaches, and volunteer administrators. The focus of Olympic Solidarity has been education and training. Olympic Solidarity funds have financed the development of manuals for volunteer and professional leaders on subjects ranging from sports administration and coaching to sports medicine; trained instructors; and given countless athletes, coaches, and officials an immersion in the history and philosophy of the Olympic Movement in National and the International Olympic Academies. Starting in 1989, promising athletes from LMICs have been given access to outstanding coaching, facilities, scientific and medical support and appropriate competition, and scholarships to cover their costs. Not all of this money is spent in LMICs — rich and powerful National Olympic Committees like those in Canada, USA, and Japan receive their share as well — but it does have a redistributive effect. Most of the 934 athletes who received scholarships to train for the 2004 Olympics, for example, came from poor countries. In addition, the International Paralympic Committee and powerful international federations such as FIFA and IAAF have similar programs, and many "First World" national organizations do the same, including some professional leagues. The Norwegian, German, and Italian Olympic Committees have been significant contributors to such programs, as have national government agencies in Canada, Holland, Norway, Switzerland, the UK, and other countries. One of the Canadian-inspired success stories is the Caribbean Coaching Certification Program, which has now been taken over by the Caribbean Association of National Olympic Committees (NOCs). For a small strategic investment — not much more than a US$1 million over eight years — a structure is now in place to generalize "best practice" in community coaching across the Caribbean. There are also programs conducted by multi-national corporations like NIKE, by fundamentalist churches, and by individual entrepreneurs, as sports agents hold recruiting clinics for promising athletes in sports like basketball, soccer, and track and field.

These programs do enrich the sporting experience of many people. But there is a limit to what they can achieve. They do little to engage the majority of people who currently have little opportunity to participate in sports, but devote most of their resources to helping the very best athletes and coaches in LMICs to climb higher up the pyramid. In many cases, they take the most talented and experienced athletes and coaches out of their own countries, so that they are lost as a source of leadership. If sport has the potential to transform entire communities, these programs do little to fulfill that potential.

From "Sport Development" to "Sport for Development"

It was a group of Olympic athletes, led by four-time speed skating champion Johann Koss, who took the most dramatic step toward broader engagement in the mid-1990s. Seeking to "give something back," in conjunction with the Lillehammer Winter Olympic Games Organizing Committee, the Red Cross, Save the Children, the Norwegian Refugee Council, the Norwegian Church Council, and the Norwegian People's Council, they began a program of sports-focused humanitarian assistance called Olympic Aid. At first they just contributed money—for vaccinations and emergency food and clothing to children in war-torn Sarajevo and Afghanistan, donating their own prize money and raising other funds by auctioning off athletes' memorabilia at Olympic Games. In Sydney, Australian swimmer Ian Thorpe's autographed fast-skin racing suit was sold for A$100,000. After the 2006 Winter Olympics in Turin, US and Canadian speed skaters Joey Cheek's and Clara Hughes' personal contributions spurred public donations that now approach C$1 million. Gradually, Olympic Aid began to conduct its own programs for children in refugee camps and now, as Right to Play, sends teams of volunteer coaches and development professionals into 23 African, Asian, and Middle Eastern countries to enhance healthy child and community development, in conjunction with UN agencies such as UNICEF and the UN High Commission for Refugees. Koss has not only been a visionary, but a gifted strategic leader and diplomat, forging links well beyond the comfortable family of international and national sports organizations. While the Olympic Movement has had fraternal relations with the intergovernmental organizations ever since de Coubertin corresponded with the ILO in the 1920s, more than anyone else, Koss has turned correspondence into genuine partnership.[9]

In this milieu, other athletes, physical educators, and sports leaders initiated two further approaches: the use of sport and physical activity to advance reconciliation and intercultural communication in regions of conflict ("sport for peace"); and the use of sport and physical activity to contribute to the realization of the United Nations Millennium Development Goals (MDGs) ("sport for development"). The latter programs focus on strengthening basic education, public health, community safety, and social cohesion and helping girls and women, youth-at-risk, persons with HIV/AIDS (PWA), and persons with disabilities (PWD) in LMICs. Sport for development can be distinguished from "sport development" in that it seeks out those not already involved, and it is unconcerned about whether participants ever become involved in organized training and competition. Whereas "sport development" is largely a project of sporting organizations, SDP is increasingly pursued by NGOs in partnership with government departments of education and health. The best example to make this point is the Aerobics for Pregnant Women Program in Zimbabwe. It was begun by Commonwealth Games Canada in 1994, financed by the Canadian International Development Agency (CIDA), and continued by local women after Canadian foreign policy required CGC to leave Robert Mugabe's Zimbabwe in 2002. The idea is to strengthen maternal health and combat infant mortality through aerobics combined with education about nutrition, effective parenting, and other social services available in the community. Few of the participants have ever competed in organized sports.[10] An example from Namibia is Physically Active Youth (PAY), initiated by University of Namibia faculty member Donovan Zealand to address a disturbingly high school-dropout rate after grade ten, when a country-wide examination determines whether students continue or end their academic careers. In recent years, the failure rate has been as high as 50 percent, throwing many youths on the street to unemployment and a risky lifestyle of drugs, unprotected sexual activity, and crime. PAY was piloted in 2003 with 40 students identified as likely to fail, each of whom received academic counseling and sex education, combined with one hour of organized physical activity, five afternoons per week after school for the entire term. Initial success rates were 75 percent of the students passing the grade ten exams. The program has now expanded to about 100 participants, and discussions are under way to extend it across the country. Again, while sport and physical activity is the vehicle, there is no thought of recruiting these students for organized sport. The short-term "eye on the ball" is to usher students at risk through their grade ten examinations and on their way to further schooling, with a strengthened sense of sexual responsibility, especially among young men. The medium-term goal is productive employment, a reduction in male sexual violence, and a decline in the incidence of HIV/AIDS. The long-term goal is a demonstrated contribution to sustainable economic growth and social development.[11]

The distinctions I have made between sport development, humanitarian sport assistance, and SDP are often blurred in rhetoric and practice. While policy and promise employ the language of development, the bulk of the funds continue to be invested in sports. Most organizations, including my own, are rooted in sports, ideologically and structurally preoccupied with high performance, and face strong expectations from their members and donors to focus on sports development. These pressures intensify when bid committees and candidates for senior office seek votes from the representatives of NOCs, and sport federations in LMICs seek support for their high-performance programs; they are strongly tempted to promise coaching assistance, equipment, and other forms of sports aid in the bargain. In the case of Commonwealth Games Canada, International Development through Sport (CGC IDS), several years ago we were persuaded by our own priorities, the new Canadian foreign policy, and the Canadian International Development Agency (CIDA), to accelerate the timetable to bring the Caribbean programs to sustainability so that we could shift those resources to the fight against HIV/AIDS in southern Africa. Yet the prospect of such withdrawal threatened Caribbean support for the Canadian city of Halifax's bid for the 2014 Commonwealth Games, and the CGC Board demurred. At the time of writing, CGC IDS continues to operate in the Caribbean.

Athletes' Activism

While each intervention has its own unique origins, the remarkable political and economic transformations of the early 1990s provided stimulus, agency, and encouragement. In the Commonwealth, where solidarity with the struggle against apartheid had become the issue on which the entire future of the association hinged, and adherence to the international moratorium against apartheid sport was the moral and practical basis for successful Commonwealth Games, the fall of apartheid quickly highlighted the need for international assistance in sport. With the end of the international moratorium, there was a flurry of international teams and visitors to South Africa, most of whom returned home even more appalled than expected by the tremendous inequality in sporting opportunity and conditions experienced by the non-white majority in the townships and rural areas. The urgent appeals for international assistance and "reparations" for apartheid from the new non-racial South African sports leadership were echoed by the leadership of the front-line states, whose economic and sports infrastructures had also been devastated by the embargoes and military actions of the long struggle. While it had been difficult to win support among sportspersons for the "No," ending all sporting ties with the established South African sport sector as a means of demonstrating one's abhorrence of apartheid, there was a ready understanding of the need for a "Yes," providing those brutalized by apartheid with the opportunity to engage in sports. In the heady, hopeful days after Nelson Mandela's release from prison and the entry of the first non-racial South African team into the 1992 Olympic Games in Barcelona, several initiatives were begun, including the Canadian-based Commonwealth Sport Development Program (now CGC IDS).

SDP was also enabled by the end of Cold War and the breathtaking changes it set in motion. With the collapse of the Soviet Union and the Warsaw Pact countries, the ideological polarization that had previously complicated development quickly evaporated. With state-interventionist models discredited and liberalism triumphant, there was a new focus on entrepreneurship as a strategy of social development, creating new openings for the creation of non-governmental organizations and private foundations. At the same time, the articulation of the "right to protect" in the wake of the frightening genocides in Rwanda and the former Yugoslavia, the tremendous visibility of the worldwide appeals to combat famine and the pandemic of HIV/AIDS in Africa, and the various campaigns to "make poverty history," all contributed to a spirit of popular humanitarian intervention. These efforts resonated with the growing use of sport in the developed world to address "social problems," the increasing inclusion in human rights campaigns of the rights to sport, physical education, and play, especially with the ratification of the International Convention on the Rights of the Child in 1990; the internationalization of feminist efforts to realize full opportunities for girls and women at the Brighton, Windhoek, Montreal, and Kumamoto conferences; and (ironically, in response to the collapse of state-based programs of physical education and grass-roots sports development in many countries), the reassertion of the benefits of sport and physical activity through the World Health Organization, UNESCO, and other international bodies.[12]

Coming of age against this backdrop was a generation of athletes and sports leaders who sought to take more responsibility for the direction and governance of their sports. Many were highly educated and media-savvy, with decision-making experience as elected or co-opted representatives of other athletes on governing bodies and trade unions. They had imbibed the developmental rhetoric of sport throughout their lives and saw themselves as living testimonials. Increasingly, they were called upon to defend their sport against accusations of rampant doping, corruption, extravagance, or excessive commercialization, charges in the Olympic Movement that led to a mounting crisis of legitimacy during the 1990s. When these concerns exploded in the Olympic bribery and doping scandals of 1998, athletes pushed for the resulting reforms, including the election of athletes to the IOC, and sought to broaden the constituency for healthy sport by "giving something back" to disadvantaged communities. It was not only Johann Koss and the speed skaters. At the 1994 Commonwealth Games in Victoria, a group of athletes led by race walker Ann Peel issued a signed appeal to governments to create a program to enable them to serve as sports leaders in disadvantaged communities around the Commonwealth. Since then, many other athletes have volunteered abroad and have created their own organizations to advance social justice. That spirit is now widespread, not only on teams but among students in degree programs in kinesiology, physical education, and sport management. A colleague at another Canadian university told me recently that more students in her sociology of sport class signed up to write an essay on SDP than any other topic. In 2005, the IOC met in Singapore to consider bids for the 2012 Games. It came as no surprise that former Olympic champion Sebastian Coe, as chair of the London bid committee, ended his pitch with an impassioned testimonial about the benefits of sport and the promise that the London Games would strengthen opportunities for youth sport around the world.[13]

The United Nations, the International Working Group, and CABOS

The most comprehensive policies and programs of international assistance are to be found in Norway, Switzerland, and the United Kingdom. While most governments have national policies and many contribute funds to international projects, very few have developed a concerted policy framework to conduct/assist SDP at the international level, with legislation or clear regulatory guidelines, explicit, dedicated programs and, of course, committed budgets. The Canadian Government, for example, funds both Right to Play and CGC IDS through Canadian Heritage International Sport Directorate and the Canadian International Development Agency, and provides a strong voice of support at international conferences. But this is done by committed ministers and civil servants, through existing programs; there is no formal apparatus to guide these decisions and ensure continuity. As a result, in a strategy that others have followed to realize human rights, advocates and activists have turned to the United Nations and other international, intergovernmental bodies as sites for the development of model policies. In 2003, at the instigation of Koss and several developing countries, with the full support of the Secretary General, the UN commissioned and gave approval to a major report, "Sport for Development and Peace: Towards Achieving the Millennium Development Goals," which recommended that:

1. Sport should be better integrated into the development goals.
2. Sport should be incorporated as a useful tool for development and peace.
3. Sport-based initiatives should be included in the country programmes of the UN, where appropriate and according to locally assessed needs.
4. Programs supporting sport for development and peace need greater attention and resources by governments and the UN system.
5. Communications-based activities using sport should focus on well-targeted advocacy and social mobilization.
6. The most effective way to implement programs is through partnerships.[14]

The report led to a General Assembly resolution endorsing this approach, the declaration of 2005 as the International Year for Sport and Physical Education, and the establishment of offices in Geneva and New York. Subsequent reports and resolutions were approved in 2004, 2005, and 2006.[15] But while the UN provides important rhetorical and symbolic legitimation for SDP, and a rich source of information about projects and success stories, it must call upon others, notably national governments, to provide the actual staff and resources. It is not yet apparent that it has influenced many national governments to do so. Advocates and activists have also sought to pressure national governments through the Sport for Development and Peace International Working Group, which grew out of a series of sports ministers' conferences at the Olympics and Paralympics. The SDP IWG is seeking to develop a template for national policies that a large group of governments could endorse at the next full meeting of sports ministers at the Beijing Olympics.[16] Within the Commonwealth, the Commonwealth Advisory Body on Sport (CABOS) has taken a different tack. Rather than advocating new national policies in sport, it has argued that if governments are to be successful in realizing existing national objectives in health (reducing non-communicable diseases such as cardiovascular illnesses, diabetes, and osteoporosis, for example) and education (strengthening school retention) they should mainstream programs of sport and physical activity. Although it meets regularly with sports ministers, CABOS has focused its lobbying efforts upon ministers of health, education, and youth.[17]

SDP advocates at the UN and other international forums stress that opportunities for sport and physical activity are human rights, grounded in such breakthrough agreements as the Universal Declaration of Human Rights (1948), the International Charter on Physical Education and Sport (1978), the International Convention on the Rights of the Child (1990), and most recently, the International Convention on the Rights of Persons with Disabilities (2006).[18] In a world of increasing inequality, where the well-to-do ensure their own enjoyment of sport and physical activity in private clubs and private schools, while the public institutions that seek to provide similar opportunities to everyone else are in decline, they are right to do so. But an increasing number of decision makers, whether ideologically averse to rights-based arguments or sceptical about the movement's often exaggerated claims for the developmental powers of sport, seek more empirical justification for policies and investments. As a result, during the last few years, there has been an increasing effort to improve the monitoring and evaluation of programs, obtain confident outcome as well as activity data, facilitate careful, comprehensive research into long-term impacts, and share the results.[19] The UN agencies, SDP IWG and CABOS, as well as the Swiss Academy for Development and Sport England, help coordinate this collective effort.[20]

Issues for Activists, Scholars, and Teachers

There are heartening success stories in SDP. The evidence is that, when conducted in responsible, culturally appropriate ways, with community support, SDP has enhanced the education, health, and well-being of participants. Yet despite the plethora of programs, international conferences, and endorsements, international SDP is still in its infancy, woefully underfunded, completely unregulated, poorly planned and coordinated, and largely isolated from mainstream development efforts. None of the programs has been able to address the overwhelming need. Whenever a successful program is launched, the organizers are bombarded by requests from others in the region that they are unable to meet. Moreover, while the entrepreneurial spirit can be a plus, it has also led to a multitude of competing NGOs, and a complete disregard (in this writer's view) of the over-arching need to restore and strengthen state programs of health and education. In fact, in the competition for donors, photo ops, and placements for volunteers, NGOs not only compete against each other but against state schools. In 2006, at a conference at the University of Zambia, President Levy Mwanawasa announced that his government had been persuaded to make physical education, with a preventive education focus on HIV/AIDS, mandatory and examinable in the basic or elementary grades. Most of us in attendance rejoiced, because the advantages of a universal program (approximately 90 percent of Zambian children attend state schools) are enormous. But several NGO leaders were crying bitterly, because they feared that the announcement would hurt their own fund-raising, which was premised on the claim that the state schools were inadequate. Moreover, the conference heard that many NGOs send inexperienced volunteers into schools without notice, let alone a mutually prepared plan for their training and deployment, significantly complicating the work of the already over-burdened teachers (with classes that can have as many as 100 students, without proper facilities and equipment). Others reported that few NGOs venture outside the capital of Lusaka, so that while children in some Lusaka communities may receive training from several NGOs, children in rural areas receive none. There have been several efforts to develop a mechanism for an international division of labor. Kicking AIDS Out is one such partnership, involving the Norwegian Olympic Committee and Confederation of Sports (NIF), UK Sport, RTP,

CGC, MYSA, the South African-based SCORE, and several other African NGOs. Giovanni di Cola at the International Labor Organization has developed an extremely useful "Common Framework" planning matrix to help organizations coordinate goals and resources.[21] But sector-wide coordination of planning, programs, monitoring, and evaluation is still the exception. Moreover, what I have called "regulation," the coordinated vetting and certification of teachers, coaches, and other leaders and the establishment of appropriate policies for equity, harassment, risk management, and financial accountability, remains a distant goal. While discouraging, we must remember that it has taken decades for such coordination and certification to be achieved in youth sports in the rich, "First World" countries.

A related issue is "top down" control. Whereas the best community development is "needs-and asset-based," i.e., premised on the expressed needs and available resources of the local population, articulated during a careful, consultative joint planning process, much of SDP is donor-defined, planned and conducted with missionary zeal. Sadly, the single-minded purpose and confidence that sport instills in champions, a commendable attribute when transferred to many other settings, militates against inter-cultural sensitivity and needs-based programming in development. There is a fear that SDP simply imposes the values of the first-world middle class on the disadvantaged of the LMICs in the assimilative manner of "midnight basketball" in North America.[22] To be sure, the global media and commercial penetration of soccer and basketball, the lure of high-performance sport, and the inequality of power and resources, make these challenges difficult to read in many LMICs, especially when many SDP postings are relatively short, as little as six weeks or three months in the case of many university programs. An increasing number of programs begin with needs-based strategic planning, train volunteers in the LMICs, and encourage "South to South" exchanges, i.e. recruit volunteers from LMI countries. Yet at every single international conference I have attended, I have heard LMIC representatives, in both coded and explicit language, publicly complain about First World programs that were highly popular with donors but made little sense to the recipient communities.[23]

The academy can play an important role in the further development of SDP through research and the preparation of students. In particular, because governments and NGOs are understandably preoccupied with program monitoring and evaluation, we need to advance a research agenda that seeks to examine the broader, long-term benefits and challenges of participation in sport and physical activity. Elsewhere, in literature reviews commissioned by the SDP IWG, colleagues and I at the University of Toronto proposed further research to "add to our growing knowledge of the precise circumstances under which sport may result in positive outcomes for gender relations, disability inclusion, youth development, mental health, peace and conflict resolution . . . for different populations and individuals'.[24] Given the overarching importance of the fight against HIV/AIDS, I believe it is particularly urgent to extend our knowledge about

- how sport and physical activity can extend the life and quality of life of those infected by HIV/AIDS, and reduce their stigmatization.
- how sport and physical activity can address the culture of predatory male sexuality rampant in so many parts of the world, empowering girls and women to protect their own boundaries and space, while imbuing boys and men with sexual responsibility.[25]
- the extent to which sport and physical activity can interact with other forms of social development.[EBL]

To the extent that the knowledge and training of leaders have frequently been identified as key to the achievement of positive benefits as a result of sport participation, it is important to better understand the requirements of leadership in LMICs and to ensure that universities and colleges strengthen the preparation of students planning internships and research in LMICs.

Recommendations for Government

At the time of writing, the recommendations of the SDP IWG for the governments' meeting in Beijing have not been released, so I would like to conclude this survey with my own. SDP constitutes a timely, progressive impulse, one of the most encouraging initiatives in sport in the last few years. But it needs to be grown to scale and much more effectively coordinated to ensure need-based interventions, by qualified personnel, in keeping with country and region-wide strategies of development. While there will always be a role for NGOs, governments must take the lead. It is their obligation to do so, given their undertakings to provide opportunities for sport and physical activity as human rights, and the urgency of the education and health challenges that they face. In the first place, funding to international SDP must be dramatically increased. Just as the leading countries of the world have set a target for themselves of 0.7 percent GDP for overseas development assistance (ODA), so should they set themselves a target of 1 percent ODA for SDP. Moreover, governments should use their spending powers to ensure that only qualified personnel are employed, in programs that demonstrate the needs-based participation of recipients in planning and implementation, in keeping with national/regional strategic development plans, and that equity and anti-harassment policies are in force. The dream would be an internationally accountable partnership, involving governments, sports federations, and NGOs, recruiting, training, and deploying volunteers and professional sports leaders on a coordinated basis to programs of demonstrated need and priority.[26] But the SDP IWG is a good place to start.

Acknowledgements

I am grateful to Peter Donnelly, Kathy Hare, and Lorna Reid for their helpful comments. Of course, any errors or omissions are entirely my own.

Notes

1. http://www.kickingaidsout.net; http://www.unicef.org/football/world/index.html; http://www.peaceplayersintl.org; and http://www.mysakenya.org.

2. The way to refer to such countries is extremely contentious among scholars and policy analysts. Among the terms in common use are: developed/developing nations; global North/global South; majority world/minority world; and countries with developing economies. Although "global South" enjoys wide support, it nevertheless glosses over the considerable differences between countries and groups within countries. In a recent set of literature reviews conducted for the International Working Group on Sport for Development and Peace, my colleagues and I at the University of Toronto settled on the term, "Low and Middle Income Countries" (LMICs). Low-income and middle-income countries are sometimes referred to as developing economies. The term is not intended to imply that all economies in the group are experiencing similar development or that other economies have reached a preferred or final stage of development. Classification by income does not necessarily reflect development status. See Kidd and Donnelly, *Benefits of Sport in International Development*.

3. E.g., http://www.youthsporttrust.org and http://www.esteemteam.com

4. http://www.sportanddev.org/en/index.htm. This must be considered a select sample. Not all organizations have made the link to the International Platform; moreover, many organizations in LMICs do not have website capacity.

5. E.g., Cavallo, *Muscles and Morals*; Putney, *Muscular Christianity*; Gems, "Sport, Religion and Americanization"; and Kruger and Riordan, *Story of Worker Sport*.

6. Pitter and Andrews, "Serving America's Underserved Youth."

7. MacAloon, "Muscular Christianity in Colonial and Post-Colonial Worlds"; Mangan, *Games Ethic and Imperialism*; and Gems, *Athletic Crusade*.

8. Gruneau and Whitson, *Hockey Night in Canada*, 46.

9. Right to Play, "History of Right to Play."

10. See http://www.canada2002.org/e/progress/progress/chapter2_10.htm.

11. http://www.sportanddev.org/en/projects/all-projects/pay-program-physically-active-youth.htm

12. E.g., United Nations, "Convention on the Rights of the Child"; International Working Group on Women and Sport, "Brighton Declaration on Women and Sport"; and International Council on Sport Science and Physical Education, "The Berlin Agenda for Action."

13. Other athlete-initiated developmental organizations include Athletes 4 Change, Athletes for Africa, Athletes United for Peace, Concrete Hoops and the Tegla Loroupe Peace Foundation.

14. United Nations, Inter-Agency Task Force on Sport for Development and Peace, *Sport for Development and Peace*.

15. They include: United Nations, "General Assembly Resolution 58/5"; "Final Report"; "Sport for Development and Peace: The Way Forward"; and "Sport in the United Nations Convention." The International Platform on Sport and Development provides a comprehensive listing of these and other relevant documents; see http://www.sportanddev.org/en/browse-by-type-of-document/united-nations-documents/index.htm.

16. See the Sport for Development and Peace International Working Group site at http://iwg.sportanddev. org/en/index.htm

17. CABOS, "Report January 2006."

18. See Kidd and Donnelly, "Human Rights in Sports."

19. E.g., Coalter, *Sport-in-Development*; NCDO, *Lessons Learned*; and UNICEF, *Monitoring and Evaluation of Sports-based Programming*.

20. E.g., For accounts of "best practice," see Kidd and Donnelly, *Benefits of Sport in International Development*; Sport England, "Value of Sport Monitor," CABOS, "Report January 2006"; and International Platform on Sport and Development, http://www.sportanddev.org.

21. International Labor Organization, "Common Framework for Partnership on Sport and Local Development."

22. Pitter, "Midnight basketball."

23. Veii and Howells, "Building Global Partnerships."

24. Kidd and Donnelly, *Benefits of Sport in International Development*, 4–5.

25. For a particularly insightful analysis of the "protection hypothesis," see Fasting et al., "Participation in College Sports."

26. See my proposal for such a corps in "A New Orientation to the Olympic Games."

References

Cavallo, D. (1981). *Muscles and morals: Organized playgrounds and urban reform, 1880–1920*. Philadelphia, PN: University of Pennsylvania Press.

Coalter, F. (2006). *Sport-in-development: A monitoring and evaluation manual*. London: UK Sport. http://www.sportanddev.org/en/home/resources-tools/index.htm

Commonwealth Advisory Body on Sport. Report January 2006. http://www.thecommonwealth.org/Shared_ASP_Files/UploadedFiles/8968898F-E9FD-4616-BA52-95476503C182_CABOSReport forSportsMinistersmeeting-14-3-06.pdf

Dreams and Teams. http://www.youthsporttrust.org (accessed 30 April 2008).

Esteem Team. http://www.esteemteam.com (accessed 30 April 2008).

Fasting, K., Brackenridge, C. H., Miller, K. E., & Sabo, D. Participation in college sports and protection from sexual victimization." *International Journal of Sport and Exercise Psychology*, forthcoming.

Gems, G. (1993). Sport, religion and Americanization: Bishop Sheil and the Catholic Youth Organization. *International Journal of the History of Sport, 10*(2), 233–241.

Gems, G. (2006). The athletic crusade: Sport and American imperialism. Lincoln: University of Nebraska Press.

Gruneau, R., & Whitson, D. *Hockey night in Canada*. Toronto: Garamond.

International Council on Sport Science and Physical Education. (2001). The Berlin Agenda for Action by governments and ministries responsible for education and sport." In G. Doll-Pepper & D. Scoritz (Eds.), *Proceedings of the World Summit on Physical Education* (p.115). Berlin: ICSSPE.

International Labour Organization. (2003). Common framework for partnership on sport and local development. Mozambique, Bouane province. Geneva: ILO, Universitas. http://www. sportanddev.org/en/home/resources-tools/index.htm

International Platform on Sport for Development. http://www.sportanddev.org (accessed 30 April 2008).

International Working Group on Women and Sport. Brighton Declaration on Women and Sport 1993. http://www.iwg-gti.org/e/index.htm

Kicking AIDS Out. http://www.kickingaidsout.net (accessed 30 April 2008).

Kidd, B. (1990). A new orientation to the Olympic Games. *Queen's Quarterly, 98*(2), 363–374.

Kidd, B., & Donnelly, P. (2000). Human rights in sports. *International Review for the Sociology of Sport, 35*(2), 131–48.

Kidd, B., & Donnelly, P. (Eds.). (2007). *The benefits of sport in international development: Five literature reviews*. Geneva: International Working Group for Sport, Development and Peace. http://iwg.sportanddev.org/data/htmleditor/file/SDP%20IWG/literature%20review%20SDP.pdf

Kruger, A.,& Riordan, J. (Eds.) (1996). *The story of worker sport*. Champagne, IL: Human Kinetics.

MacAloon, J. (2006). Muscular Christianity in colonial and post-colonial worlds. *International Journal of the History of Sport, 23*(5), 687–700.

Mangan, J. A. (1998). *The games ethic and imperialism: Aspects of the diffusion of an ideal*. London: Frank Cass.

Mathare Youth Sports Organization. http://www.mysakenya.org (accessed 30 April 2008).

NCDO. (2007). *Lessons learned: Greater effectiveness with knowledge and tips gleaned from sports and development cooperation in practice*. Amsterdam: NCDO.

Open Fun Football Schools. http://www.unicef.org/football/world/index.html (accessed 30 April 2008).

Peace Players International. http://www.peaceplayersintl.org (accessed 30 April 2008).

Physically Active Youth. http://www.sportanddev.org/en/projects/all-projects/pay-program-physicallyactive-youth.htm (accessed 30 April 2008).

Pitter, R. (2004). Midnight basketball and role modeling programs: Avoiding the problems of assimilative reform. In B. Kidd & J. Phillips (Eds.), *From enforcement and prevention to civic engagement: Research on community safety* (pp. 168–180). Toronto: Centre of Criminology, University of Toronto.

Pitter, R., & Andrews, D. (1997). Serving America's underserved youth: Reflections on sport and recreation in an emerging social problems industry." *Quest, 49*(1).

Putney, C. (2001). *Muscular Christianity: Manhood and sports in Protestant America, 1880–1920*. Cambridge, MA: Harvard University Press.

Right to Play. History of right to play. http://www.righttoplay.com/site/PageServer?pagename_ rtp_History

Sport England. The value of sport monitor. http://www.sportengland.org/vosm/vosm.htm

UNICEF. (2006). *Monitoring and evaluation of sports-based programming for development, sports, recreation and play*. New York: UNICEF.

United Nations. (1990). Convention on the Rights of the Child. http://www.unhchr.ch/html/menu3/b/k2crc.htm

United Nations. (2003). Inter-Agency Task Force on Sport for Development and Peace. *Sport for development and peace: Towards achieving the millennium development goals*. http://www.sportanddev.org/en/home/resources-tools/index.htm

United Nations. (2003). *General Assembly Resolution 58/5: Sport as a Means to Promote Health, Education, Development and Peace*. http://www.sportanddev.org/en/browse-by-type-of-document/ united-nations-documents/index.htm

United Nations. (2006). *Final Report: International Year of Sport and Physical Education*. http://www.sportanddev. org/en/browse-by-type-of-document/united-nations-documents/index.htm

United Nations. (2006). *Sport for development and peace: The way forward*. http://www.sportanddev.org/en/ browse-by-type-of-document/united-nations-documents/index.htm

United Nations. (2007). *Sport in the United Nations Convention on the Rights of Persons with Disabilities*. http:// www.sportanddev.org/en/browse-by-type-of-document/united-nations-documents/index.htm

Veii, V.S., & Howells, S. (2007, September 20). *Building global partnerships for sport and development*. Paper presented at the Next Step Conference, Windhoek, Namibia.

29

REACHING THE "HARD TO REACH": ENGAGEMENT, RELATIONSHIP BUILDING, AND SOCIAL CONTROL IN SPORT-BASED SOCIAL INCLUSION WORK

Tim Crabbe

Introduction

In recent times the notion of the "power of sport" to do social good has increasingly come to prominence on both social policy agendas and sports management and marketing strategies. Whether it is the regenerative potential associated with the staging of "mega events" such as the Olympic games or the need to engage young people in purposeful activity in local neighborhoods, belief in the wider benefits of sport has rarely been so strongly advocated.

There remains a widespread tendency within sporting, political, and popular discourses to regard sport as an entirely wholesome activity for young people to be involved in, an activity which is conferred with a whole series of positive attributes to the exclusion of the social ills facing wider "society." There is of course nothing new about this approach. Arguably, organized modern sport owes its very existence to the Victorians' attempts to influence and shape attitudes within British public schools and to service the needs of the Empire through the concept of "Muscular Christianity." More pertinently, during the nineteenth century, "sports were to play a major part . . . in the creation of a healthy, moral, and orderly workforce" and in shaping the values and behavior of working class youth (Holt, 1989, p. 136).

Without necessarily seeking to do so, social considerations of sport have tended to be framed by such "functionalist" perspectives which emphasize what sport does *to* people and *for* "society" (see Blackshaw & Crabbe, 2004). In keeping with this position a number of North American studies have over the years provided some theoretical and empirical support for the notion that participation in sport serves as a deterrence to delinquency and "deviance" (Hastad et al., 1984; Purdy & Richard, 1983; Buhrmann, 1977; Schafer, 1969). Nevertheless, there remains little definitive evidence of a direct causal relationship between involvement in sports, moral outlook, and criminal or deviant behavior (Smith & Waddington, 2004; Morris et al., 2003; Collins, 2002; Long & Sanderson, 2001; Snydor, 1994; Robins, 1990; Coalter, 1989).

Although Long and Sanderson "are persuaded that there is sufficient cause to believe that community benefits can be obtained from sport and leisure initiatives," they recognize that these may be small scale, exclusionary, and isolated (Long & Sanderson, 2001, p. 201). Furthermore, in terms of the specific relationship between sport and crime, although there are reasons why sport and leisure activity might influence levels of criminality, the objectives and rationales have rarely been made clear, leaving the measurement of outcomes an uncertain exercise. Indeed, paradoxically, while it could be argued that formal images of sport may be policed through societal expectations which stress its wholesome and socially cohesive nature, at the level of experience it is precisely sports' legitimation of "deviance" which is often most compelling (Blackshaw & Crabbe, 2004). For sport provides environments in which acts of violence, confrontation, and drug use are licensed in ritualized fashion and given meaning through their association with the hegemonic masculine ideals of toughness, heroism, and sacrifice.

As such, sporting activity itself does not necessarily seem to offer the most appropriate means for challenging "deviant" or socially disruptive behavior. As Lasch argued, "[g]ames quickly lose their charm when forced into the service of education, character development, or social improvement" (Lasch, 1978, p. 100). Nevertheless, such perspectives retain their authority in many sporting, popular, and political arenas and had a key influence on the support given to the UK Positive Futures initiative, which will provide the focus for the remainder of this paper.

Positive Futures is a UK sports-based social inclusion program managed until April 2006 within the Home Office Drug Strategy Directorate, which aims to have "a positive influence on participants' substance misuse, physical activity, and offending behaviour." Launched in 2000, it is now entering its fourth phase of development and is currently delivered through 108 local partnership projects throughout England and Wales. However, the subsequent growth of the program reflects its *distinction* from, as much as its association with, more conventional "diversionary" and morally laden models of sports intervention as revealed by its assertion that:

> The Positive Futures program has been built up around young people's involvement in sporting activity but it is not concerned with the celebration, development, or promotion of sport as an end in itself. Nor does it merely attempt to use sport as a simple "diversion" or alternative to time spent engaging in drug use and crime. Positive Futures is a relationship strategy based on the principle that engagement through sport and the building of mutual respect and trust can provide cultural "gateways" to alternative lifestyles. (Home Office, 2003, p. 8/)

As such, rather than focusing on "outcomes" and "impact" measures, this paper is concerned to explore the attempts of individual Positive Futures projects to *engage* their target groups, build *relationships*, and achieve meaningful social *development*. In doing so it will consider the extent to which projects are able to act as "cultural intermediaries, providing gateways between what are often seen as alien and mutually intimidating worlds" (Home Office, 2003, p. 9). This will involve consideration of how participants are targeted, how local geographic, demographic, and cultural contours are navigated, the style and delivery of project activities, their appeal to particular target groups and the characteristics and approaches of project staff.

Talking Tactics: Issues of Methodology and Method

This paper draws upon research being conducted for the national Positive Futures Case Study Research Project commissioned by the UK Home Office. The two year research program is focused on seven case study projects located across England and Wales which reflect the diversity of organizational and delivery cultures within the wider program. It was commissioned with a view to assessing, at different stages of individual projects' development, the impact, organizational, and process elements associated with their interventions.

One of the points of departure of the research from other investigations of sports based social interventions is the contention that a meaningful evaluation requires a methodological strategy that goes beyond simple quantitative analysis. As such, the fundamental principle, which guides the study, is to ensure that the voices of the young participants, local residents, community groups, and involved professionals are at the heart of the research.

The research then is underpinned by a commitment to a Participatory Action Research (PAR) approach. PAR provides a family of research methods united by a set of principles and a style. It is cyclical, moving between action and critical reflection and seeks to bring together action, theory, and practice, in participation with others, in the pursuit of practical solutions to issues of concern to people and their communities. It aspires to empower participants through this collaboration, by promoting the acquisition of knowledge to achieve social change, while attempting to circumvent traditional hierarchies associated with researcher/researched dichotomies.

A variety of methods of inquiry have been mobilized, located predominantly around the actual lived experiences of project staff and the participants and residents in the selected areas. Extensive participant observation has been conducted on housing estates; at training sessions, matches, and competitive tournaments; on trips and residentials away from the estates; in project offices and the more informal "social" locations inhabited by project staff, participants, and residents; as well as in policy forums and conferences.

In each of the case study locations we have identified a sample of participants, groups, and activities, which we have been tracking through the course of our research. In relation to these a combination of intermittent life history interviews as well as group qualitative interviews and discussions are being conducted. These interviews have themselves been augmented by the use of a range of participative techniques that have sought to engage participants and residents in the research process in more innovative and self determined ways. These have included the use of a range of innovative visually based methods, such as using maps, photo-diaries, disposable cameras, mock TV talk-shows, etc. Through the use of these approaches we have sought to establish how a variety of individuals and social groups talk about the place of sport within their lives and to account for the "taken-for-granted" assumptions about how "facts" and "realities" come to be represented and the different ways in which communicative resources are used (Atkinson, 1990).

With additional surveys of local archive sources these approaches have enabled us to produce detailed "thick" descriptions (Geertz, 1973) of the contexts in which the work is situated, the engagement strategies employed, particular sporting practices, and the social worlds that surround them. This material has been used to locate the place of sports based social interventions within the social ecology of the areas and to explore sport's relationship with particular regional histories and notions of neighborhood. In this way we hope to achieve a certain latitudinal "breadth" and longitudinal "depth" in the study which is only partially reflected in the selected testimony and narrative description offered here.[1]

Looking for Trouble: Identifying Participants and Spaces

Despite its status as a national program, the organization of Positive Futures is essentially a locally negotiated enterprise embodying a variety of management approaches, which have given rise to a diverse and distinct set of project management styles. As such, though there is a clear national strategy which articulates a particular Positive Futures approach (Home Office, 2003), there is less consistency in terms of its application. Indeed in terms of the initial engagement of participants we can identify something of a bifurcation between what might loosely be characterized as "instrumental" and "organic" approaches.

The "instrumental" approach reflects a more conventional "top down" method, which identifies those young people who are perceived as problematic in the eyes of welfare institutions who then direct them towards some form of correctional program. In many ways this is reflective of Lianos and Douglas' identification of deviance as "a side effect of new forms of social regulation" based on dangerization, which has seen society develop "the tendency to perceive and analyze the world through categories of menace" (Lianos & Douglas, 2000, p. 110). This approach invokes the tacit assumption that the world "out there" is unsafe and that as a consequence it becomes essential "to continuously scan and assess public and private spaces in terms of potential threats by other people" (Lianos & Douglas, 2000, p. 111).

However, in many ways this mode of operation, which has been most readily associated with statutory local government and criminal justice agency led projects, conflicts with the approach identified in Positive Futures own strategy document which suggests that:

> In each area the problems and opportunities faced by marginalized groups of young people themselves provide the template for the development of work plans, with non judgmental and culturally appropriate lo-

cal opportunities for personal development emerging organically on the basis of what engages effectively. (Home Office, 2003, p. 10)

The support for this "organic" approach is currently better reflected in the style, which is more typically, though not exclusively, adopted by projects led by community based voluntary sector agencies. When one of our case study projects which fits this categorization begins a new session, they usually start with planned outreach in the area, utilizing an "anywhere that we know young people congregate" approach, doing street work as well as going into schools and shopping centers, as the project co-ordinator, "Kate," explains:

> One of the main things we do is outreach, where we go out on the streets with flyers and use our charm tactics. We speak to the young people on the street and we tell people what we do. We tell them what's on offer for them, we give them a flyer and a phone number and hope that they get along. For more targeted work it's a lot more one to one. We meet with them regularly to build the relationship first.

A crucial distinction is identified here in the sense that there is recognition that identification and targeting cannot be conducted independently of *relationship* building. Rather than personalized calculations of "risk" (Beck, 1992) being made at a distance, which provide the general public with tangible targets of dangerousness, the neighborhood setting is seen to produce potential participants, who in many circumstances then turn out to be the very young people who would otherwise need to be coerced into attendance by referral agents. Rather than providing any mystical revelation, the engagement of young people in this way is ultimately revealed as more straightforward and less stigmatizing since attendance at sessions is voluntary and tied into less formal modes of relationship building as revealed in the following narrative field description:

> Kate seemed disappointed with the attendance at the session. She was worried that the football club coaches who were coming the next day would be disillusioned if they only had a few kids to work with. Rather than sit around and worry about it she decided to get out and see who was about, see if there were any kids hanging around the streets who could be encouraged to come along. Driving around the area it was not the day to be rustling up support for a "sports day." The pouring rain had put paid to street corner society as those who were brave enough to face the elements or had no other options made for what shelter they could find. A couple of hardy souls crunched up under the hoarding of a newsagent were similarly struggling for punters willing to offer reward for their rather poorly improvised effigy of Guy Fawkes. Spotting the opportunity Kate stopped and walked over.
> Rather than a coin she handed them a flyer and asked if they wanted to come down.
> "It's better than sitting out here in the rain."

Spotting that one of the kids was carrying a crutch the offer was re-enforced.

"It's ok if you're injured cos there are x-boxes and other indoor activities that you can get involved with."

"I'm not injured—it's for whacking people with," he smirked as he smashed the stick against the metal shutter boarding up the shop next door for effect.

Kate, utilizing her local knowledge, ignored the bravado and turned to his mate,

"I know you," she said, asking how his mum was. He was soon on board and ran off home to get his mum to sign the form.

Looking to make his excuses the kid with the stick asked,

"Is it where the Pitz is? That's miles away. I'm not goin' there. I'd have to get a bus."

When his mate returned, Kate took the form off him and told the boys that it was on all week so they should just come along. As we got back into the car to rustle up some more would-be participants Kate waved at the lad's mum who was walking down the street.

There were several more at the session the next day.

This account reflects the project's understanding of the dynamic nature of the engagement process and the need to take account of individual circumstances rather than relying on existing referral pathways. Even those projects that are focused on more targeted approaches, while *on paper*, the referrals process can be quite rigid and formulaic, it is more often operationalized by front line staff in a much more flexible manner. As a youth worker explained:

I have had people ask me, "How do you reach the hard to reach young people?" I say, "Well, knock on their door. . . ." Of my core 50, some of them are very hard to reach. Although I might know them and have their date of birth and address, it is not always that easy to engage them because you can get to their door and they tell you to "F off," or they could come. Of the 50, there are at least 15 who I would say are the hardest to reach, that I find difficult . . . I will try and arrange a meeting at their school, so they feel comfortable with their teachers there . . . I'll go to their houses and talk to their parents and try to get the parents on board and we'll all try to talk to them together. If they are involved in the YOT we can arrange a meeting with the YOT and them so they feel comfortable there, and if all that fails then I'll just knock on their door and say, "Can I speak to _____ , please" and then I just make the project sound so fantastic. But there are some who are not engaged and that can be through fear of other young people. They have various reasons as to why they won't come . . . some of my core group have been severely bullied in school and for that reason they find it difficult to be in group settings.

In some ways this perspective transforms the conventional image of the "hard to reach." Instead of this being a label attached to young people, the staff at this project subverted the outlook. They recognize that there are reasons why a young person may be difficult for a worker to make contact with. As such, being designated "hard to reach" is not seen in terms of a broad behavioral category but in relation to an individual's situation. In this context the emphasis is on the need to work harder at combating the reasons why young people might not be able to access the project.

Yet if part of the attraction of Positive Futures is that it offers something "different" to participants, this is also related to its capacity to achieve transcendence and escape from those situations. This can be related to its use of venues or activities, which convey "glamour," in order to attract and retain participants. There is no doubt that football, which is the principle activity delivered by Positive Futures, has a glamorous position in many of the young people's lives which can itself present problems for community sports practitioners who may be seeking to counter the superficiality of an over commercialized sport. However, two of the projects included in the study make strong use of their partnership with English Premiership football clubs and have been able to exploit their glamour effectively in terms of initial engagement. The pictures of players on publicity leaflets and the club strip that the coaches wear along with access to stadium tours and the opportunity to watch matches for free if they assist in the clearance of rubbish before and afterwards are factors in attracting young people to the projects, particularly where young people are supporters of the clubs concerned.

Although the young people are never told that involvement in the projects might lead to them being spotted and finding stardom in the Premiership, it is clear in talking to some of them that they still like to imagine this might happen. In turn, though, there is recognition of the ways in which broader possibilities or progression routes *can* open up from these activities.

> It's, you know, that's what we get, that's what kind of interests them. "Okay, wow, it's free first of all, I can get in the studio, I can lay down my demo if I'm interested in becoming an artist, I can do that, and it's a starting point for me." Also, "if I wanted to become a professional footballer I can start off here, this is a good route and I can get training." "I can become a coach at the same time." And these are the kind of things that keep them interested, and they come in twos, we provide them with as much as we can.

This makes clear that Positive Futures is concerned to be about more than simply offering a "youth club" where there is access to a free pool table and a place to "hang out". Several of the projects utilize a range of unusual, special, "cool" activities including BMXing, snowboarding, dancing, climbing, film special effects, and others which stretch the definition of the program as a sport based social inclusion strategy. These activities stand out and reflect the contemporary appeal of more individualistic "lifestyle" or "extreme" sports (Wheaton, 2004). However, although their "currency" can make them very attractive to young people, in an individualistic society there is also the danger that their appeal may prove to be transient as participants search for "highs" rather than helping to build reciprocal forms of cooperation and collectivity. This is because such activities take place in what Lyotard (1988) calls "open space-time," in which the selves of the individual participants are only ephemerally transformed in the performativity of the activities themselves (Blackshaw & Crabbe, 2004, p. 145). As such, Positive Futures has identified its staff, and front line workers in particular, rather than "sport" as the crucial factor in ensuring the development of sustainable progressive pathways for participants.

"One of Us": Styles of Delivery, Staff Roles and Cultural Capital

Focusing on the approach of staff, rather than on the activities offered, it is clear that projects adopt a flexible approach, which is dynamic and alive to individual personalities and circumstance as the following excerpt reveals:

The minibus journey to the Shenley School is invariably deafening, with Gemma and Judy talking to the young people about what they have been up to since the last session. The group members seem to have a closer relationship with Gemma than with Judy, due to Judy's role as a worker responsible for organizing and delivering transport and administration. This frees Gemma up to knock on doors on the estates if the young people are not waiting when the mini bus arrives and to join in the play and talk to the young people when they break from activities.

Dressed in her usual kit of tracksuit bottoms and hoodie, Gemma who has just turned 21, is keen to show off her "dead cool" new trainers. She bounces around, calling everyone "dude," telling people that they are "gnarly." Much to the group's delight, sharing transport with her means having to listen to Britney and as they get off the bus and wait for the session to begin, they chat with her about their plans for the evening, some give her a hug and urge her to play.

The activities are led by Robbie who has been running the sessions since September. Robbie knows the area well, and knows some of the young people and is himself a former Shenley pupil. He also still works locally, as a gym instructor, after having previously spent time in the Forces. He is physically imposing, and when someone spills a catch or people collide, his laugh booms across the gym, and the laugh is infectious. He explains the rules of the game, splits the group into teams and encourages players while he referees or bowls.

The participants are playing their favorite game, Kwik Krikkit which is sold on the back of the staff's enthusiasm. Gemma whips the group up on the minibus so they are raring to go when they arrive. Robbie delivers bowling to suit each batter and Jeff hurls himself around the pitch fielding. When Paul is caught out by a fielder, he throws down his bat and storms off. Jeff follows him and the two of them sit down, talking about why he is so agitated today. Later, Paul returns to the game.

Jeff is an ex football pro and loves showing off his sporting skills and the young people enjoy watching his tricks. He is very vocal, encouraging players to run, telling the captains to organize their field and get batters in line. When something kicks off, its Gemma who takes each of the two lads outside, in turn, and speaks to them about their behavior, reminding them of the Code of Conduct which they have signed up to. Gemma's natural bubbly nature means that when she is suddenly straight faced and moved to take people outside of the session, participants know that they have transgressed and will be banned from that session, and subsequent ones, if they continue to misbehave.

In this example and others, though misbehavior is sometimes met with sanctions and the withdrawal of privileges, there are no fixed disciplinary regimes. Instead the work is about the use of individual, adaptable approaches, which are "true" to each of the different workers' outlooks and which avoid a "top down" authoritarian approach. One project worker, "Serena" described the necessity of establishing trust with young people before attempting to question particular patterns of behavior:

If a young person doesn't gain your trust then they're not going to take that any further and they're not going to try and go any further with a relationship with you. So I mean before you can even—like if you had to pull up a young person for swearing or anything that's not beneficial to them or anyone else, you have to establish a relationship with them first before you can turn around and say, because they'll turn around and say, "Well, who are you, I don't know who you are, you know, you can't be coming to me and telling me that I shouldn't be doing this, I shouldn't be doing that." So in the first instance when you're signing up with them, even when you're outreaching, introduce yourself, let them know who you are, what you do if you can, and then take it from there basically. See them again. It's down to a simple hi, a simple hand gesture in the road when you see them, that keeps the relationship going. If they feel that you were too hard on them and you had to tell them off or tell them that they were doing something wrong, go back to them, explain yourself, if you have to apologise, apologise, but explain that, you know, "this is the reason why I've done that," so always give reasons why and explain yourself.

Here "Serena" clearly illustrates the essential two-way nature of the relationship between young person and worker, where the power balance may be unequal but is made more equitable through negotiation, explanation, and, if necessary, contrition. This approach is entirely consistent with the nonjudgmental frameworks and ability to read and adapt to the alternative social realities of participants through which the staff operate. "Stu" is in his late thirties and, working in the manual environment of a coastal ranger, swears, jokes, and smokes more freely than might be considered appropriate in conventional youth work contexts. When Positive Futures participants are

around and embrace this culture too openly he chooses to remain true to himself by employing humor as a tactical resource. When "Joseph" states, "He's a
fucking little cunt," the riposte is quick witted rather than condemnatory:
"That's not very nice, don't call him little." This light-hearted approach works
well and the young people appear to respond to this more effectively than being
told directly not to do something. "Joseph" confirming how this enables the
participants to:

> just get on with it and have a laugh while you are doing it . . . It's not like
> school cos school is like you have got to do it, you can't do this, you can't
> do that. Out here you can do what . . . you want as long as you do your
> work.

There is, though, no such thing as an archetype "community sports coach."
Rather projects employ a disparate array of staff with distinct skills and backgrounds who can nevertheless be related to a series of Weberian "ideal types"
embodying certain character types such as the "boss," "buddy," "teacher,"
"joker," "cool dude," "geezer," and "expert" (see Crabbe, 2005). Although workers may play to or utilize different aspects of these characters or even occupy a
number of positions simultaneously depending on the group they are working
with, each of the projects is characterized by their employment of staff from a
variety of working backgrounds. However, what seems to be emerging is a
stronger identification amongst participants with members of staff who are of
their area than those who are not. Although the local rootedness of staff is not
the only factor at work here, those staff who have a deep knowledge of the history of their areas, who have or had a similar social background to participants — that is those who have similar "cultural capital" — seem able to make
stronger connections with the young people and command more respect.

This point relates to the late French sociologist Bourdieu's (1962) argument
that all humans inherit dispositions to act in certain ways. In this sense they
possess an inherited concept of society or *habitus*, which they then modify, according to their own specific local conditions and experiences. For Bourdieu
then, the ability to absorb appropriate actions is the key for individuals to be
at ease with themselves and others. Equally the cultures of individuals and
groups are seen as the tokens by which they make "distinctions" in order to
position themselves and establish group identities (Bourdieu, 1984). The usefulness of these concepts here relates to the point that the ability of Positive
Futures workers to engage with participants is connected to their own biogra-
phies and embodied selves and the degree to which they are acknowledged
and valued in these locales. "Serena" elucidated the point:

> So, you know, streetwise is where I'm from, you know, from . . . which is
> local, you know. I lived in Jamaica for some time. That helps with the
> young people that I come into contact with that are from Jamaica and
> don't have, you know, don't have a clue where to start when they come
> here, so that has helped me to relate to them a lot. And just general kids,

I can relate to them all the time, because, you know, I understand where they're coming from and what's going down and what's not and what's in and what's out and you know. Yeah, we can always chat like normal and they don't feel like they have to be different around me. They can be themselves and I can be myself around them as well. And that's how you gain a lot of respect. I think my background definitely helps. It always does. That is what I always take them back to. I show them where I'm coming from, and they're like "Wow. Well, I can do this too."

It is important to note then that each of the character types we have identified reflects a particular social class and gender *habitus*. A working class male might be perceived to perform the "geezer" role much more proficiently and "easily" than a woman or middle class man could. Indeed it is this "easiness" that defines the role. Equally, the "buddy" is a character that is frequently gendered as feminine. Nevertheless in one of the case study locations where the work has proven to be by far the most challenging, locality, social class identifications, and outlook have come to the fore, enabling gender and racial distinctions to be suspended. Those staff who share some of the life experiences of those they are working with, having been brought up in deprived neighborhoods and not initially flourished in a formal educational setting, have shown the greatest commitment to giving the young people who attend activities a second chance. Embodying the "geezer" persona, they seem to understand the local culture, the values in the community and how young people from the area are perceived.

To a very large extent it is the staff's capacity to achieve this that in itself constitutes success, since it is in the nature of the work — the relations formed, the level of access achieved — where the battle for legitimacy is largely fought. At their most effective Positive Futures projects straddle two increasingly different worlds and act as interpreter for each. In this respect the program's success lies in its position as a "cultural intermediary," providing gateways between what are often seen as alien and mutually intimidating worlds. This concept has elsewhere been most readily applied following Bourdieu (1984) and Featherstone's (1991) use of the term as a way of understanding the emergence of a "new middle class" which has helped to collapse some of the old distinctions between "popular" and "high" culture. However, in the context of this research the term is used in relation to a quite different cultural axis and focus on the potential for projects to help generate a class of professionals who are able to collapse the barriers between the socially "excluded" and the "included."

The predominant focus of the plethora of social interventions associated with the "social inclusion agenda," with its emphasis on social capital and communitarian ideals, has been to encourage "us" (policy makers, university lecturers, community development initiatives) to determine what is appropriate for "them" (the poor), despite the rhetoric of community led initiatives. Our research suggests, however, that successful Positive Futures coaches are often seen in different ways to many of the other agents associated with this agenda such as teachers, police officers, probation officers, and youth workers. Part of the reason for this is that when considering what are often regarded as "alien" social groups such as those engaged with Positive Futures, conventional policy "speak" merely seeks to "translate" their ways of living and thinking into its "own" language. What effective Positive Futures projects are concerned to do is to *understand* people on their own terms through reference to more personal experience rather than policy led language games. The cultural intermediary then becomes more than just a communicator with the wherewithal to open "information channels between formerly sealed off areas of culture" (Featherstone, 1991, p. 10). Rather, they act as both an interpreter and a go-between.

In this sense they are regarded as opening up possibilities, providing guidance, and demystifying mainstream society rather than asserting some kind of repressive or overly directive authority. The credibility of a sports background coupled with empathy among staff for the condition of those they work with has encouraged many young people to engage with projects and in some instances to become qualified as coaches themselves, while others have been influenced to go back to school, on to college, or into jobs. Others may have fallen by the wayside but rarely are they ignored, demeaned, or denied access because of the likelihood that they will be troublesome or lose interest. In this sense, part of the appeal of Positive Futures to *participants* maybe that staff are not usually seen as "teachers" and do not enforce the rules participants would associate with youth clubs or traditional youth work settings.

Youth workers differentiate between their role and that of teachers, or police officers, in that the relationships they have with young people are voluntary and informal and founded on trust and understanding. But in estate based contexts when workers are also peer role models, this can be even more effective. In this respect "Jeff" is viewed by his colleagues as "a good lad," a young but experienced and skillful community worker, comfortable working with females and males across a range of activities. His outreach skills, as well as those he brings to his sessional work, are highly valued by his colleagues. His background as a professional sportsman means he has sporting expertise, but this is not translated in his work into competitive demands for high levels of skill; he stresses fun and enthusiasm when he plays. Described by one female participant as "lush," a group of young women told the project co-ordinator that they would only go on a residential if "Jeff" was coming along. He told the girls he'd love to take part in the residential, but that they would only be able to go if they continued to attend sessions and to demonstrate that staff could trust them by being punctual, behaving well, etc. When the young women responded positively to his guidance and came on the residential, rather than maintaining a hierarchical imbalance he was an enthusiastic participant in a mud fight with some of the participants, unafraid to indulge in "frivolous" behavior in order to achieve an engagement with the activities being offered.

Nevertheless when away from sessions, demonstrating his own understanding of the participants, he has spoken of his frustration at not always being able to transmit to strategic staff the need to work in a flexible, non output driven way with some young people. He feels that there is something of a reality gap between project managers who drive initiatives at the local level, and those who deliver and are the "subjects" of them.

> They want sessions that meet targets. We try to explain to the kids that doing this and that will get them a certificate, but it's impossible to do some of the stuff they ask us to. . . . Some of them have done the minimum amounts of practical work and then they're making policy, setting targets.

Though the national strategy has long advocated the style of work that "Jeff" employs, he has identified the desire of senior agency staff to impose ways of working and a search for outcomes which does not necessarily "speak" to those involved in the projects. He attempts to interpret the strategic messages for the young people he works with, but within a working style which sees him behave in a way which is far removed from the rigid, stentorian way he sees initiatives on paper. However, in his status as a sessional worker, "Jeff" does not take part in Positive Futures team meetings and currently appears to have no channel through which to make his feelings and those that he works with known to strategic staff. In this context then, rather than realizing their potential as cultural intermediaries, the workers are forced back into the position of one-way "translator."

For the political and social theorist Antonio Gramsci the role of the cultural intermediary, or what he referred to as the "new intellectual," is necessarily broader than this if they are to realize the capacity for effecting change:

> The mode of being of the [cultural intermediary] can no longer consist of eloquence, which is an exterior and momentary mover of feelings and passions, but in active participation in practical life as constructor, organizer, "permanent persuader," and not just simple orator." (Gramsci, quoted in Joll, 1977, p. 93)

At the time of writing, while imprisoned by Mussolini's Fascist dictatorship, Gramsci was centrally concerned with the issue of realizing the revolutionary potential of subordinated workers and was in essence talking of trade union "shop stewards" in his discussion of the new intellectuals. In a context where work has now become far less central to the processes of contemporary identity formation, social organization, and progressive politics—programs like Positive Futures offer the potential for an alternative means of organizing and realizing the potential of socially marginalized young people by engaging in a similar orientation towards agitation and action.

"Us and Them": Consumption, Social Control and the Myth of Emancipation

The difficulty with such an emancipatory vision is that in the era of "liquid modernity" (Bauman, 2001), rather than social inequalities being defined through resistance and state repression, they are now navigated through the market place. Consumers are now seen as bound into the social by seduction—driven by the images of "perfect," sexy bodies emerging from commercial gyms, the dreams of football superstardom peddled to youngsters at soccer summer camps and the celebrity sports stars adorning the covers of lifestyle magazines. As such, rather than emancipation from want, disease, squalor, ignorance, and idleness that underpinned the creation of the British Welfare State, the welfare services, and by extension social inclusion programs, now ultimately reveal the horrors of non-participation in the consumerism of the free market.

In this sense sporting interventions are more popularly *believed* to work because they continue to be seen to provide relief from a criminogenic environment. With the "scallies," "chavs," and "hoodies" residing on Britain's housing estates dismissed as "the objective of aesthetic, not moral evaluation; as a matter of taste, not responsibility" (Bauman, 1995, p. 100) a romantic fiction of modernist sporting certainties is reproduced which is associated with the conventional functionalist interpretation of sports as inculcating a sense of self-discipline, routine, and personal responsibility (Crabbe, 2000). Now enhanced by the seductive glamour and performativity of the celebrity version, sport represents a metaphor for the positively imbued social values that the "healthy" *majority* claim as their own and which are wheeled out to the zones of exclusion in an effort to alter the behavior and consciousness of "risky" populations.

In this fashion, community sport is more easily recognized as a product of the mainstream rather than a celebration of the cultural achievements of the disadvantaged. It is seen to provide a means of educating the "flawed" or "illegitimate" consumers in "our way of doing things." It emphasizes the legitimate rules of consumer society, which have often proven beyond the community youth worker, probation officer, and educational welfare officer who lack the cache of social and cultural capital that goes with contemporary sport. What this kind of social intervention represents for the mainstream then is an extension of the seductive appeal of its own consumer society.

In this sense, despite the best efforts of the Positive Futures program and individual projects, part of the attraction of these forms of community sports work to the mainstream is their lack of any ideological critique of the consumerism, which contributes to the young people's ghettoization. Indeed the offer of a "passport" or gateway "out" is premised upon the mediated appeal of one of the most rabidly commercialized industries on the planet.

As such, the funding representatives or agents of those who are "legitimate" members of consumer society, the socially "included," are happy to sponsor the endeavors of community sports agencies because of their presumed capacity to "reach" and "manage" a constituency of the "excluded" who have proven increasingly troublesome for more traditional interventionist agencies.

Note

1. The full research reports emerging from this project can be accessed online at http://www.positivefuturesresearch.org.uk/index.php/Section15.html.

References

Atkinson, M. (1990). *The ethnographic imagination: Textual constructions of reality.* Routledge, London.

Bauman, Z. (1995). *Life in fragments: Essays in postmodern morality.* Blackwell, Oxford.

Bauman, Z. (2001). *Community: Seeking safety in an insecure world.* Polity Press, Cambridge.

Beck, U. (1992). *Risk society: Towards a new modernity.* Sage, London.

Blackshaw, T., & Crabbe, T. (2004). *New perspectives on sport and deviance: Consumption, performativity and social control.* Routledge, London.

Bourdieu, P. (1962). *The Algerians.* Beacon Press, Boston, MA.

Bourdieu, P. (1984). *Distinction: A social critique of judgment and taste.* Routledge, London.

Buhrmann, H. (1977). Athletics and deviance: An examination of the relationship between athletic participation and deviant behavior of high school girls. *Review of Sport and Leisure, 3*(2), 17–35.

Coalter, F. (1989). *Sport and anti-social behavior: A literature review.* Scottish Sports Council, Edinburgh.

Collins, M. (2002). *Sport and social exclusion.* Routledge, London.

Crabbe, T. (2000). A sporting chance?: Using sport to tackle drug use and crime. *Drugs: Education, prevention and policy, 7*(4), 381–391.

Crabbe, T. (2005). Getting to know you: Engagement and relationship building. *First Interim National Positive Futures Case Study Research Report.* Retrieved from http://www.positivefuturesresearch.org.uk/index.php/Section15.html.

Featherstone, M. (1991). *Consumer culture and postmodernism.* TCS.

Geertz, C. (1973). *Deep play: Notes on the Balinese cockfight pt 2.* Retrieved from http://webhome.idirect.com/~boweevil/BaliCockGeertz2.html.

Hastad, D., Segrave, J., Pangrazi, R., & Peterson, G. (1984). Youth sport participation and deviant behavior. *Sociology of Sport Journal, 1*(4), 366–373.

Holt, R. (1989). *Sport and the British.* Oxford University Press, Oxford.

Home Office. (2003). *Cul-de-sacs and gateways: Understanding the Positive Futures approach.* Home Office, London.

Joll, J. (1977). *Gramsci.* Fontana, Glasgow.

Lasch, C. (1978). *The culture of narcissism: American life in an age of diminishing expectations.* Norton, New York.

Lianos, M., & Douglas, M. (2000). Dangerization and the end of deviance: The institutional environment. In D. Garland & R. Sparks (Eds.), *Criminology and social theory.* Oxford University Press, Oxford.

Long, J., & Sanderson, I. (2001). The social benefits of sport: Where's the proof? In C. Gratton, I. Henry (Eds.), *Sport in the city: The role of sport in economic and social regeneration.* Routledge, London.

Lyotard, J-F. (1988). *Peregrinations: Law, form, event.* Columbia University Press, New York.

Morris, L., Sallybanks, J., & Willis, K. (2003) *Sport, physical activity, and antisocial behavior in youth.* Australian Institute of Criminology Research and Public Policy Series No. 49, Australian Institute of Criminology, Canberra.

Purdy, D. A., & Richard, S. F. (1983). Sport and juvenile delinquency: An examination and assessment of four major themes. *Pacific Sociological Review, 14,* 328–338.

Robins, D. (1990). *Sport as prevention, the role of sport in crime prevention programs aimed at young people.* Centre for Criminological Research. Oxford University, Oxford.

Schafer, W. (1969). Some sources and consequences of interscholastic athletics: The case of participation and delinquency. *International Review of Sport Sociology, (4),* 63–79.

Smith, A., & Waddington, I. (2004). Using "sport in the community schemes" to tackle crime and drug use among young people: Some policy issues and problems. *European Physical Education Review, 10*(3), 279–298.

Snydor, E. (1994). Interpretations and explanations of deviance among college athletes: A case study. *Sociology of Sport Journal, 11,* 231–248.

Wheaton, B. (2004). *Understanding lifestyle sports: Consumption, identity and difference.* Routledge, London.

WOMEN AND CHILDREN FIRST?
CHILD ABUSE AND CHILD PROTECTION IN SPORT

Celia Brackenridge

Introduction

Child welfare and women's rights both feature prominently in contemporary debates on equal rights. Efforts to combat trafficking and domestic violence, for example, have included adult women and children since age per se is not a defense against such forms of exploitation. Whereas gender equity has been a policy objective for the past 30 years in sport organizations, child protection has only recently emerged as a sport ethics issue, following several public scandals in swimming and other sports in the early 1990s.[1] The response of the state to concerns about child abuse in sport was initially slow but gathered momentum as the result of grassroots pressure and, arguably, child protection has now leapfrogged over gender equity as a policy priority. In this article, I will outline how child protection initiatives in England have developed since those early scandals and raise some questions about whether the focus on the children's rights agenda in sport has helped or hindered the development of gender equity and women's rights in sport.

The article opens with a discussion of the role of children in sport in relation to opposing ideologies of social control and personal freedom. It then examines the place of women in English sports policy and practice, revisiting some of the well-known feminist critiques of sport. Once child abuse in sport had been recognized, the institutionalization of child protection occurred relatively fast, with a dedicated Child Protection in Sport Unit being established jointly by the National Society for the Prevention of Cruelty to Children (NSPCC) and Sport England in 2001. This development is described and the benefits and limitations of it are assessed and placed in a global context. The shift in theoretical focus from "women" to "gender" has been accompanied by a widening of the general social policy focus away from solely heterosexual interests to include the rights of gay men, lesbians, bisexual and transgender people. It is argued here that this shift has not yet occurred in sport policy or practice because of the inherent conservatism of the institution and its continued political marginalization. Child protection has acted as a kind of Trojan horse, wheeled into the center of sports politics more successfully than women's rights (and gender equity) ever could be and, at the same time, opening up the ethics agenda more widely then ever before. The paradox of child protection, laid out in this article, is that it has simultaneously drawn public attention to issues of abuse and exploitation in sport *and* deflected attention away from the specific issue of women's rights in sport.

Children in Sport

Sport has always been riven with class, gender, race and other social divisions. It is essentially a competitive activity and the striving for supremacy has masked these divisions in a false contest of assumed equals and so-called level playing fields.[2] As a social institution, sport shares many of its basic values with the Christian church. Indeed, in the nineteenth century "muscular Christianity," whereby missionaries carried both bibles and footballs, helped to disseminate the virtues of both religion and sport.[3] Sport was also used at that time in public schools and corrective institutions for children as part of the disciplinary practices that were consonant with the Victorian ideal of "spare the rod and spoil the child."

Parton argues that children were constructed by the Victorian Poor Laws as a delinquent threat since their destitute status rendered them social outcasts.[4] It was not until the 1980s, when, according to Franklin, children's rights "came of age," that legislation in Britain ceased to objectify the child and instead created the "child-as-subject," with the right for children to comment on their own lives.[5] The 1989 United Nations (UN) Children's Charter was an international expression of the rights of the child, albeit it within a monocultural context.[6] While this has been adopted across almost all member nations, barring the United States and Somalia, its impact on practice has been variable.[7] Lyon and Parton, for example, argue that the child is now legally defined in order to allow arms-length social and political control over the family.[8] Since the mid-1980s, children have assumed more visibility in English society as their rights as citizens have come to be acknowledged. The citizenship status of the child, however, is still not fully embedded in all spheres of public life, nor in many private settings, since their capability as decision makers is not universally accepted. In sport, for example, it is still rare to find children consulted or represented in the decision-making process, even in matters of direct concern to them.

The cultural construction of childhood varies between nations and, because there is no universally accepted delineation between "adulthood" and "childhood," there are also anomalies and disparities between the rights and responsibilities accruing to these statuses. Variations in the age threshold for criminality, smoking, marriage, sexual relations, voting and gun use are just some illustrations of the age-related confusion of rights. Even within the sport community, age and rights are further confounded because "junior" and "senior" age definitions vary between sports. Adult athletes are frequently treated like children, with their freedom to socialize, eat, drink and travel curtailed by training regimes and coaches. At the same time, talented child athletes are frequently defined as adults, in relation to the expectations placed upon them to function and perform at a high level. It is therefore unsurprising that there is confusion about both moral and sexual boundaries in sport.

There has been a long association between sport/body and mind, including the adoption of sport within the nineteenth-century public school system as a mechanism of social control (*mens sana in corpore sano*). The discipline of sport was thus an ideological means to discipline the mind and heart. Ironically, as the child/athlete has been fragmented into his/her physiological, biomechanical and psychological self through sport science, so his/her moral status and its integrated personhood have often been lost. Sport science has perhaps been working, unwittingly, in opposition to the general children's rights movement, representing the child as raw material for performance enhancement.[9] Whereas early twentieth-century physical education focused on development *through* the physical, the most recent sport science credo—Long-Term Athlete Development—effectively excludes any concern for individual moral reasoning or political autonomy in the developing athlete as a performance machine.[10] The suppression of individual autonomy through coaching practice maintains the status of the coach-as-controller.

Indeed, in his analysis of child labor in relation to labor laws, Donnelly uncovered exploitative practices in sport that would never be tolerated in educational or employment settings.[11] Because of the laxity with which children's rights have been applied in sport, various other types of exploitation, such as sexual abuse, have been facilitated.

Women in Sport

The history of women's struggles for recognition in sport has been fully and convincingly recorded by feminist sport historians and sociologists.[12] While such authors have now corrected the record of women's invisibility in sport, they have not yet succeeded in helping to transform the institutions that perpetrate exclusionary sporting practices. In England, there was no policy on women and sport until 1993 and even then the policy was the first ever to be rejected by the Sports Council (the UK sport's ruling body) when it was first presented for approval.[13] Once accepted, and despite its relatively liberal tone, the policy became one of the foundation stones for international advances, leading to the Brighton Declaration in 1994.[14] This Declaration is a ten-point set of principles for women's sport which emanated from the 1994 Brighton international conference on women and sport. It addresses:

- equity and equality in society and sport
- facilities
- school and junior sport
- developing participation
- high-performance sport
- leadership in sport
- education, training, and development

- sports information and research
- resources
- domestic and international competition

The Brighton conference was followed by world congresses of women and sport in Namibia and Montreal at which international progress on the endorsement of the original declaration by government and non-government bodies was reported.[15] Notwithstanding the significance of achieving an international template for women's sports development, critics of the Declaration argue that it, along with a number of parallel organizational and pressure-group initiatives for women's sport, merely reflect, defer to, and therefore perpetuate a patriarchal sporting system.[16] In its attempts to move from exclusion (not being allowed to play), to inclusion (being allowed to play but have no power), to equity (playing with parity), to transformation (humanizing the structures and practices of sport) I would argue that British women's sport has become stuck somewhere between inclusion and equity.[17]

Although England and the other "home countries" of the UK each developed sport policies for women and girls they left the patriarchal substructure of sport intact. A couple of Regional Sports Council and Standing Conferences of Sport were brave enough to mention sexuality in their own policy documents but, in essence, policy formulations for women's sport stalled. This is because they were seen, in and of themselves, as radical within the institution of sport yet were hopelessly behind the times when measured against wider political and feminist developments. In short, women in sport were seen as relevant neither to sport (which was and is male) nor to women (whose conservatives eschewed it as unfeminine and whose radicals eschewed it as anti-feminist).

Birrell and Theberge summarized the main aspects of cultural struggle facing women in sport in fairly familiar ways, as social justice issues (adapted below):[18]

- patriarchal privilege (sexism and male violence)
- unrestricted capital accumulation (classism)
- white skin privilege (racism and sectarianism)
- compulsory heterosexuality (homophobia)
- reproduction of privilege (social exclusion)

While women working within the sport community failed to connect with these wider social justice concerns, it is no wonder that their efforts for recognition and status went largely unrewarded. Heterosexuality is still an "organizing principle" in sport with sex segregation embedded in its constitutive systems and in the ideological and cultural domination enjoyed by heterosexual men.[19] In recognition of this, a number of pro-feminists (male supporters of critical feminist analysis of sport) have attempted to reformulate our understanding of the gender order in sport and to draw attention to the cultural constructions of gender and sexuality that afford privilege to males but that can be reconstructed to challenge such privilege.[20] The politicization of the female athlete has also been an ongoing project for radical feminist critics of sport.[21] According to such critiques, only by challenging the depoliticization that appears to be a by-product of the coaching process and by emphasizing the individual agency of the female athlete will women's sport ever succeed in defining its own future. Importantly, it was these feminist researcher advocates who prepared the way for pro-feminist men to receive acclaim for their "gender work" in sport. What might subsequently have been lost in the process of acknowledging "gender" in sport is the value of the pioneering work on "women." It is arguable whether the sudden rise of child abuse and protection up the sport policy agenda has helped or hindered the process of women's recognition and representation in sport. It is to this issue that we now turn.

Child Abuse and Protection in Sport

The sexual exploitation of children has been one of the more successful radicalizing issues in sport. Sexual exploitation and abuse are not, of course, new dangers in Western society but they are relatively new to the sport community which has previously preferred to see sport as something of a moral oasis. Interestingly, the "moral panic" generated by the issue is closely linked to homophobic fears about the breakdown of normative (that is heterosexual) morality and the nuclear family.[22]

The traditional autonomy of the voluntary sport sector has effectively shielded it from external scrutiny and from the regulatory systems that characterize workplace industrial labor relations. Even major human rights legislation on behalf of children has yet to make an impact on certain exploitative sporting practices.[23] The permissive context of child exploitation—whether sexual, physical, or emotional—in sport, arises from the symbolic separation of sport from social and legal regulation. Individual abuses take place within a network of personal and organizational relationships that are historically resistant to outside interference. These networks collectively place athletes, whether children or adults, in an exploitative relation to authority figures and thus increase their susceptibility to exploitation.

David describes 1989 as a

> . . . crucial benchmark in the field of child protection as it marks the year the United Nations General Assembly adopted the Convention on the Rights of the Child. For the first time ever, a legally binding international treaty recognized, to persons under 18 years of age, a full set of human rights . . . [and] moved child protection from the traditional welfare approach to a more modern and dynamic one, the rights-based approach.[24]

Notwithstanding the legislative force of the UN Declaration, David also suggests that "the promotion and protection of the human rights of young athletes in the context of competitive sport has received almost no recognition and has rarely been discussed."[25] While recognizing the undoubted potential benefits of sport for children, in terms of health, well-being and self-determination, David identifies five main situations that have the potential to threaten the physical and mental integrity of child athletes: involvement in early intensive training; sexual abuse and violence; doping; economic exploitation through the transfer market and trafficking; and limitations on access to education.[26]

Prior to the UN Declaration, throughout the 1980s, there was increasing public awareness of the problem of child abuse in UK society resulting from a number of serious disclosures and legal cases. A national telephone help line, the charity-funded ChildLine, was first established in 1986 and subsequently merged with the NSPCC's own helpline service. In sport, some work on codes of ethics and conduct was done in the mid-1980s.[27] But child protection was not named as an issue in UK sport until the late 1980s.[28] Even by the early 1990s, there had been virtually no child protection work in UK sport organizations, and there was widespread denial of the issue. The arrest in 1993 of a former British Olympic swimming coach first brought child protection to the attention of sportspeople in a dramatic way. Paul Hickson was eventually convicted in 1995 for sexual assaults against teenage swimmers in his care over about a 20-year period. His prison sentence — of 17 years — was the longest ever sentence for rape imposed in an English court at that time (subsequently a sentence of 20 years was passed for sexual assaults by a man in the context of equestrian sport). What became known as "the Hickson case" was a defining moment in the history of sexual exploitation in sport.

The moral panic around sexual exploitation in sport served to expose the processes of social control in sport. Many of those at the top of sporting organizations ridiculed allegations, claiming that cases of abuse were "just a one-off" or suggesting that this was a problem of society and not one that sport itself could address.[29] Over a two or three year period during the mid-1990s, however, the fear of pedophile infiltration of sport grew to such an extent in Britain that many local government departments and governing bodies of sport began to develop their own, separate policy initiatives, duplicating both effort and resources.[30] After several years of upward pressure on government sport authorities by those with little power, such as sports development officers, parents and club officials, a National Child Protection in Sport Task Force was convened by Sport England in 1999.[31] (At that time only about half of the governing bodies of sport that received government grants had in place a CP policy.)[32] This represented a major breakthrough in the strategic efforts to deal with sexual and other forms of exploitation in sport. It led to a jointly-funded NSPCC/Sport England Child Protection in Sport Unit (CPSU), which began work in January 2001 on implementing the Task Force Action Plan.[33] The primary functions of the CPSU, which is based at the NSPCC's National Training Centre in Leicester, are to:

- act as one-stop-shop for governing bodies
- develop policy and procedures
- operate a 24-hour helpline
- advise sport organizations on case management
- run a research group
- liaise with Government

- set national child protection standards together with Sport England
- assist funded sports to develop child protection policies and Action Plans
- accredit and quality assure training.

The Unit addressed a number of these strategic priorities within its first year of operation, including: the establishment of policy standards for sport bodies, the establishment of working groups for education and training, research and policy and functional relationships with a wide range of sports clubs, federal bodies and individual national governing bodies of sport.[34]

A crucial stage in the acceptance of child abuse as a legitimate concern for sport was when "pedophiles" — external to the sport system — were defined as the cause of the problem. Illicit (predominantly heterosexual) sexual relationships between under-age athletes and authority figures (mainly male coaches) had gone on for years and had been tacitly condoned but the moment "the pedophile" became labeled as the folk devil, a perfect scapegoat was offered to members of sport organizations who then rallied together to express their growing concern about the external threat of sexual exploitation to children.[35] For some women who had observed at first hand their past discriminations and sexual excesses against female athletes this hypocrisy was hard to bear.

In addition to the false externalization of abuse threats, sometimes described as the "othering" of the abuser, another consequence of the moral panic surrounding abuse in sport has been a preoccupation among some sport leaders with the possibility of so-called false accusations or false allegations against them or their colleagues.[36] The rights of the "professional" thus appear to have been elevated over those of the child, despite very little empirical evidence to substantiate such concerns. One framework for understanding the dynamics of child protection in sport is offered in Figure 1.[37] This framework sets out four dimensions of protection that sport leaders or professionals should attend to in relation to child abuse:

1. *Protecting the athlete from others:* that is, recognizing and referring anyone who has been subjected to abuse or sexual misconduct by someone else, whether inside sport (by another staff member or athlete) or outside sport (by someone in the family or peer group).
2. *Protecting the athlete from oneself:* that is, observing and encouraging good practice when working with athletes in order to avoid perpetrating abuse.
3. *Protecting oneself from the athlete or others:* that is, taking precautions to avoid false allegations against oneself by athletes or their peers or families.
4. *Protecting one's profession:* that is, safeguarding the good name and integrity of sport, coaching, sport science, and management.

This depiction of four dimensions of protection has potential benefits. For example, as empirical evidence is gathered to support or refute the weight of concerns along each dimension, the model could be used to re-balance policies and practices for child protection in sport. In addition, it should assist with clarifying the interests of the key stakeholders in a way that helps to: allay fears (of adults concerned about false allegations): focus the attention of lead-

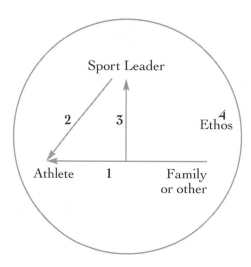

Where:

Sport Leader = the athlete's coach, teacher, physio, or other authority figure.

Athlete = athlete in dependent relationship to sport leader professional.

Family or other = primary carers, siblings, peer coaches, and peer athletes.

Figure 1. Four dimensions of protection in sport

ers in sport on their referral responsibilities (abuses perpetrated outside sport); emphasize good practice (in coaching, teaching, sport science and so on) as a protective measure; and, most importantly, set protection within the broad context of sport ethics. There are examples of interventions in sport relating to all four dimensions, largely promulgated through education and training workshops from Sportscoach UK, the NSPCC and some of the major governing bodies of sport, including The Football Association. Since April 2001, all Exchequer-funded governing bodies of sport in England have been required to have in place a child protection action plan in order to qualify for grant aid.[38] This single change, alone, has had a major positive impact on the uptake of protective interventions. It has forced governing bodies of sport to engage with child protection with an intensity that some have found very challenging indeed. However, it has also helped to take many sport administrators through the "denial barrier" that previously prevented them from accepting the possibility of child abuse in their sports.

Similar initiatives in sport are not easy to find outside the UK, although in Canada, where social welfare objectives in sport have always been comparatively strongly supported by state agencies, there are local and national initiatives to support zero-tolerance towards harassment in sport and where the national equivalent of the UK's Women's Sports Foundation, the Canadian Association for the Advancement of Women in Sport and Recreation (CAAWS), developed its harassment polices as long ago as 1994.[39] Interestingly, the Canadian Red Cross also published one of the first advice and procedures documents on child protection.[40] In Australia, a series of policy documents on harassment-free sport was published in 1998 and has recently been followed by more recent policy directives on child protection.[41]

European attitudes towards gender equity are much more advanced than those elsewhere, with state involvement in gender equity work since the 1980s and a long-standing European Women and Sport Working Group and representing most of the established and some of the emerging European nations.[42] The same cannot be said of child protection in sport. Here, the Council of Europe began to take an interest in 1997 through a national "survey" (in reality, a set of self-report items from member states). Desk studies of sexual harassment of women and children in sport were commissioned by the Council of Europe in 1998 and 1999 and followed by the adoption of a directive at a meeting of European Ministers for Sport in Bratislava.[43] A SPRINT seminar, with 27 member states present, was held in Helsinki in 2001 that attempted to cover issues of welfare and protection for both women and children.[44] The Council of Europe has acted more quickly on this issue than its counterparts in the European Parliament. Some Members of the European Parliament (MEPs) attended a reception in Brussels in May 2002 with staff from the NSPCC and the Child Protection in Sport Task Force, as a result of which child protection was proposed as a theme for the forthcoming "Year of Education Through Sport" in 2004.[45] The International Olympic Committee, while adopting a set of proposals on harassment at its Paris conference on Women and Sport in March 2000, has not addressed child protection per se, perhaps overlooking the fact that some Olympic performers fall within the legal jurisdiction of "child" in some countries.[46]

Concern for the welfare of children and young people in sport is gradually surfacing in some non-European countries, for example through, research work in Japan, but there has not yet been a coordinated effort to collate this work globally.[47]

Gender Equity in Sport

Sport has been described as a prime site for the (re)production of heterosexual masculinity by many eminent feminists and pro-feminists.[48] The segregation of sports on grounds of sex is reinforced by powerful ideological and political mechanisms. The heterosexual imperative privileges particular expressions of masculinity above others and above all types of femininity, thus perpetuating the social domination of particular kinds of men and particular expressions of masculinity. However, in recognition of the pointlessness of a hierarchy of equalities (such as white, male, heterosexual over black, female, disabled) theorization has recently shifted away from biologically determined differences to focus on culturally diverse and relational conceptions of gender and sexualities.

Alongside the shift in theoretical focus from "women" to "gender," social policy is also shifting to account for much more differentiated conceptions of sexual and gender identity (gay, lesbian, bisexual and transgender) than were recognized under hegemonic heterosexuality. It is argued here, however, that this shift has not yet occurred in sport policy or practice because of the inherent conservatism of the institution towards matters of sex and gender and its continued political marginalization.[49] Mainly driven by employment and legal concerns, active consideration is being given to the establishment in the UK of a single equalities body to replace the different commissions (such as the Equal Opportunities Commission, Commission for Racial Equality and so on). In Ireland and Northern Ireland this has already happened with the setting up of the Equality Authority and the Equality Commission for Northern Ireland respectively. The intention of such new bodies is to allow for multiple discriminations to be more effectively addressed and for more prominence to be given to previously marginalized equality "strands." The proposals set out six strands for a new UK body: age, disability, gender, race, religion and sexual orientation.[50] Sport England lists only three strands (or "target groups" as it describes them) in its equity guidelines—"ethnic minority communities, people with disabilities, women" but it does acknowledge that "inequality manifests itself in many ways and that these are not the only sectors of the population that are excluded."[51] Given the non-statutory status of sport and leisure and the private and voluntary settings of most sports clubs, it might seem impossible that sport could be brought within the spirit of these organizational changes. As with their child protection advocacy, however, the Irish have already led the way by stipulating compliance conditions for private sports clubs.[52]

Both sexuality and gender have been differently constructed for women and for men, with sports for men being congruent with masculinity and heterosexuality but sports for women being dissonant with both femininity and heterosexuality.[53] Almost 30 years after Felshin first wrote about the female "apologetic" in sport, women athletes still adopt overtly feminine clothing, jewelry or other trappings of traditional heterosexuality in order to rebut the threat to their (hetero)sexual identity posed by their participation in sport.[54]

The project of maintaining the privileges of heterosexual masculinity in and through sport has been fiercely pursued by those who perceive equity as a zero-sum game, in other words white, middle-class men who fear losing their power if diversity becomes an imperative for sport. Diversity has many faces but, for these privileged males, is most powerfully repelled if it comes in the form of women gaining prominence in sport, the exposure of homosexuality in sport, or by individual men's own failure to live up to the heterosexual masculine standard. The ideological challenges to men's dominance are thus managed through men's homophobic responses. In this way, as Griffin has demonstrated, all women in sport become labeled (and vilified) as lesbian, regardless of their sexual orientations and "out" gay males in sport are deemed the most threatening of all since they embody athleticism yet express homosexuality.[55] They therefore present a direct challenge to the heterosexual imperative.

Individual and collective violence (through discrimination, harassment or abuse) constitutes one response to these perceived threats. The heterosexual imperative ensures that, even when men are absent, women in sport are under constant surveillance, with their adherence to social expectations being monitored. Dress, language, gestures and interpersonal behavior are all targets for subordination and social control. If women choose to resist such control they hazard their access to competitive opportunities, funds or facilities since men control the financial and political infrastructure of sport.

Stereotypical notions of masculine and feminine have been traditionally split along the gender divide. More recently, however, queer theorists have examined the false binaries that characterize sport ideology, the male–female, gay–straight, win–loss relations of sporting practice. In general, however, the material social relations of sport are still far behind queer theorists' analysis and politics. The shift from "sex" into "gender" as a focus for theoretical and political debate, while giving a platform for more socially inclusive sports policy across *all* equity strands, has also masked lack of progress (and some would even argue regression) in *women's* rights. It is ironic, therefore, that the impetus for child protection in sport has gained in strength while that for women's rights has declined. For example, in 2001–02 a grant of £130k, plus a later top-up of £15 k, to the Women's Sports Foundation, the voluntary body that has promoted opportunities for women and girls in sport since 1984 "appear[ed] to be the total amount of Exchequer funding committed by government [directly or through Sport England] to women's sport," less than the turnover of the CPSU in only its first year of operation.[56] Interestingly, in its annual accounts, Sport England lists a total contribution of £1,720 k to "Sports equity and social inclusion," but this is not disaggregated.[57] Further, Bennett reports that the English Federation for Disability Sport applied successfully to the TSB Bank Communities Fund but an application from the WSF failed with the organization being told that women were "too mainstream."[58]

The relative deceleration of women's rights in sport, compared with the acceleration of child protection, may be due to the widely-publicized backlash against feminism and the women's movement.[59] The backlash argument is that equal rights are now perceived as a 1970s and 1980s issue and that equality is no longer a concern for civil society which is characterized by diversity, plurality, choice and contingency in gender relations. Whether an equivalent backlash will occur in child protection is an interesting question. Finkelhor's contribution to this debate suggests that there will be no decline in public interest in child abuse and protection since its moral force is so powerful and enduring.[60]

Conclusions

If sexual exploitation is only deemed to be problematic when perpetrated against children, then there is a hypocritical distortion of rights at work in sport. The phrase "child sexual abuse" has been proven to be an effective motivational device with sport practitioner audiences who have, in contrast, shown limited concern about "sex discrimination" or even "sexual harassment." Equally, the use of the word "child" instead of "athlete" could be said to have detracted from wider concerns about athlete empowerment for *all* ages.

A rights perspective in sport could have a significant beneficial impact on sporting practices. For example, it could lead to the empowerment of individual athletes, better representation, reductions in their hours of training, increases in financial rewards and insurance protection, and better provision for their long-term education and career planning. But a rights perspective that perpetuates a hierarchy of (in)equalities will do little to advance the cause of women in sport.

Child abuse has risen to consciousness within UK sport over relatively short and inglorious few years. No advocate of children's rights could argue against the advances in policy and practice that have accompanied this development, and the transformative effect that it has had on ethical reflection in sport. But it is important to recognize that a false hierarchy of inequalities favors nobody in the end. The relatively narrow focus of the CPSU on children, defined as under 18 years old, draws attention and resources away from those over that age boundary, including many people with disabilities and, especially, adult women in sport. Child abuse is shocking and degrading and child protection, whether in sport or elsewhere, should be the right of every child. It may be too early to tell, however, whether child protection has hijacked sport as a strategic imperative but it certainly seems to have gained a firm footing in the UK, if not global, sport agenda.

Policies for women and sport, both in the UK and in Europe more generally, have not been as effective as they could have been because of apathy towards gender equity. Child sexual abuse, on the other hand, grabbed the media headlines in the UK and has the potential to open up debate on related rights issues across the equality "strands." As the rise and rise of sports ethics continues in response to the many violations apparent in modern sport (doping, fraud, exploitation, violence and others) it will be interesting to observe whether "gender equity" succeeds where "women in sport" failed. Child protection may turn out to be the lever for change that has eluded those groups seeking to promote women's rights in sport. At the same time it might deflect both attention and resources away from women's sport.

Notes

1. C. Brackenridge, *Spoilsports: Understanding and Preventing Sexual Exploitation in Sport* (London: Routledge, 2001).

2. S. Bailey, *Leisure and Class in Victorian England* (London: Routledge & Kegan Paul, 1978).

B. Carrington, & I. McDonald (eds.), *Racism and British Sport* (London: Routledge, 2001).

S. Scraton & A. Flintoff (eds.) *Gender and Sport: A Reader* (London: Routledge, 2002).

3. J. Clarke & C. Critcher, *The Devil Makes Work: Leisure in Capitalist Britain* (London: Macmillan, 1985).

4. N. Parton, *The Politics of Child Abuse* (Basingstoke: Macmillan, 1985).

5. B. Franklin (ed.), *The Handbook of Children's Rights: Comparative Policy and Practice* (London: Routledge, 1995).

6. United Nations, Children's Charter (New York: UN Office of Public Information, 1989).

7. P. David, "The Promotion and Protection of the Human Rights of Child Athletes," paper presented to the Council of Europe Seminar on The Protection of Children, Young People and Women in Sport: How to Guarantee Human Dignity and Equal Rights for These Groups (Hanaholmen, Finland, 14–16 September 2001).

8. C. Lyon & N. Parton, "Children's Rights and the Children Act 1989," in B. Franklin (ed.) *The Handbook of Children's Rights: Comparative Policy and Practice* (London: Routledge, 1995).

9. M. Weiss & D. Gould (eds), *The 1984 Olympic Scientific Congress Proceedings*, Vol. 10, (Champaign, IL: Human Kinetics, 1984). R. Magill, M. Ash & F. Smoll (eds.) *Children in Sport, 3rd Ed.*

(Champaign: Human Kinetics, 1988). V. Grisogono, *Children and Sport: Fitness Injuries and Diet* (London: Murray, 1991).

10. I. Balyi, "Long-Term Athlete Development, the System and Solutions," *Faster, Higher, Stronger, 14* (2002), 6–9.

11. P. Donnelly, "Child Labour, Sport Labour: Applying Child Labour Laws to Sport," *International Review for the Sociology of Sport, 32*(4), (1997), 389–406. A. Tomlinson & I. Yorganci, "Male Coach/Female Athlete Relations: Gender and Power Relations in Competitive Sport," *Journal of Sport and Social Issues, 21*(2), (1997), 134–55.

12. C. Oglesby, *Women and Sport: From Myth to Reality* (Philadelphia, PA: Lea & Febiger, 1978). H. Lenskyj, *Out of Bounds: Women, Sport and Sexuality* (Toronto: The Women's Press, 1986). J. Hargreaves, *Sporting Females: Critical Issues in the History and Sociology of Women's Sports* (London: Routledge, 1994). M. Hall, "Feminist Activism in Sport: A Comparative Study of Women's Sport Advocacy Organizations" in A. Tomlinson (ed.) *Gender, Sport and Leisure: Continuities and Challenges* (Aachen: Meyer & Meyer Verlag, 1997), 217–250.

13. Sports Council, *Women and Sport: Policy and Framework for Action* (London: Sports Council, 1993).

14. Sports Council, *The Brighton Declaration on Women and Sport* (London: Sports Council, 1994).

15. Sport England, *Windhoek Call for Action* (London: Sport England, 1998). www.canada 2002.org. A. White & D. Scoretz, *From Windhoek to Montreal—Women and Sport Progress Report 1998–2000* (Montreal: Sport Canada, 2002).

16. M. Hall (note 12).

17. C. Brackenridge, "Think Global, Act Global": The Future of International Women's Sport, *Journal of the International Council for Health, Physical Education, Recreation, Sport and Dance* 11/4 (Summer 1995), 7–11.

18. S. Birrell & N. Theberge, "Ideological Control of Women in Sport" in D. Costa & S. Guthrie (eds.), *Women and Sport: Interdisciplinary Perspectives* (Champaign, IL: Human Kinetics, 1994), p. 362.

19. L. Kolnes, "Heterosexuality as an Organising Principle in Women's Sports," *International Review for the Sociology of Sport, 30* (1995), 61–80.

20. M. Messner, *Power at Play: Sports and the Problem of Masculinity* (Boston: Beacon Press, 1992). M. Messner & D. Sabo (eds.) *Sport, Men and the Gender Order* (Champaign, IL: Human Kinetics, 1990). M. Messner & D. Sabo, *Sex, Violence and Power in Sports: Rethinking Masculinity* (Freedom, CA: Crossing Press, 1994).

21. M. Hall, *Sport and Gender: A Feminist Perspective on the Sociology of Sport*, CAPHER Sociology of Sport Monograph Series (Ottawa, Ontario: Canadian Association for Health, Physical Education, and Recreation, 1978). M. A. Hall, "How Should We Theorise Sport in a Capitalist Patriarchy?" *International Review for the Sociology of Sport, 1* (1985), 109–13. C. Oglesby (note 12). J. Hargreaves (note 12). H. Lenksyj (note 12).

22. S. Cohen, *Folk Devils and Moral Panics: The Creation of the Mods and Rockers* (London: MacGibbon & Kee, 1972).

23. P. Donnelly (note 11). P. David (note 7).

24. P. David (note 7) p. 1.

25. P. David (note 7) p. 3.

26. P. David (note 7).

27. C. Brackenridge, "Problem? What Problem? Thoughts on a Professional Code of Practice for Coaches," paper presented to the Annual Conference of the British Association of National Coaches, Bristol, England, December 1986. C. H. Brackenridge, "Ethical Concerns in Women's Sports," *Coaching Focus*, National Coaching Foundation Summer (1987). National Coaching Foundation, *Code of Ethics and Conduct for Sports Coaches* (Leeds: NCF Coachwise, 1995).

28. C. Brackenridge, *Child Protection in British Sport: A Position Statement* (Cheltenham: Cheltenham and Gloucester College of HE, 1998).

29. C. Brackenridge, *Spoilsports: Understanding and Preventing Sexual Exploitation in Sport* (London: Routledge, 2001).

30. Sport England, "Child Protection—Task Force Formed", Press release, (London: Sport England, 25 October 1999). Sport England, *Child Protection in Sport Task Force, Draft Action Plan*, unpublished paper (London: Sport England, 5 April 2000).

31. C. White, "Progress Report on Child Protection Policy Development in English National Governing Bodies of Sport", unpublished document presented to a workshop at the NSPCC (14 June 1999).

32. Child Protection in Sport Unit, www .sportprotects.org.uk (2002).

33. Child Protection in Sport Unit, *Child Protection in Sport Unit: Business Plan 2001–2004* (Leicester: NSPCC and Sport England, 2002).

34. C. Brackenridge (note 29). S. Cohen (note 22).

35. C. Brackenridge (note 29).

36. C. Brackenridge, "Ostrich or Eagle? Pro-

tection and Professionalism in Coaching and Sport Science," keynote speech to the annual conference of the British Association of Sport and Exercise Sciences (Newport, September 2001).

37. S. Boocock, The Child Protection in Sport Unit in C. Brackenridge & K. Fasting (eds.), "Sexual Harassment and Abuse in Sport — International Research and Policy Perspectives," special issue of the *Journal of Sexual Aggression*, *8*(2), (2002), 37–48.

38. Canadian Association for the Advancement of Women and Sport, *Harassment in Sport: A Guide to Policies, Procedures and Resources* (Ottawa: CAAWS, 1994). Canadian Association for the Advancement of Women and Sport, What Sport Organisations Need to Know About Sexual Harassment (Ottawa: CAAWS, 1994).

39. Canadian Red Cross, *It's More Than a Game*. The Prevention of Abuse, Harassment and Neglect in Sport (Gloucester, Ontario: Canadian Red Cross, 1997).

40. Australian Sports Commission, *Harassment Free Sport: Guidelines for Sport Administrators* (ACT: ASC, 1998). Australian Sports Commission, *Harassment Free Sport: Guidelines for Sport Organisations* (ACT: ASC, 1998). Australian Sports Commission, *Harassment Free Sport: Guidelines for Athletes* (ACT: ASC, 1998). Australian Sports Commission, *Harassment Free Sport: Guidelines for Coaches* (ACT: ASC, 1998). Australian Sports Commission, *Harassment Free Sport: Protecting Children from Abuse in Sport* (ACT: ASC/Active Australia, 2000).

41. Women and Sport European Working Group.

42. C. Brackenridge & K. Fasting, *An Analysis of Codes of Practice for Preventing Sexual Harassment to Women and Children* (Strasbourg: Council of Europe/Committee for the Development of Sport, 1999). C. Brackenridge & K. Fasting, *The Problems Women and Children Face in Sport with Regard to Sexual Harassment* (Strasbourg: Council of Europe/Committee for the Development of Sport, 1998). Council of Europe, "Sexual Harassment and Abuse in Sport, Especially the Case of Women, Children and Youth," resolution of the ninth conference of European Ministers responsible for sport (Bratislava, 31 May 2000).

43. Council of Europe/Committee for the Development of Sport, *Report on the CDDS Seminar on: The Protection of Children, Young People and Women in Sport: How to Guarantee Human Dignity and Equal Rights for these Groups*, held at Hanasaari, Espoo 14–16 September (Strasbourg: Council of Europe/Committee for the Development of Sport, 2001).

44. Resolution of the Ninth European Sports Forum, Lille, October (www.sportsprotects.org.uk 2002).

45. International Olympic Committee, Resolution of the Second IOC World Conference on Women and Sport, Paris (www.Olympic.org/ioc/news/pressrelease/press_255.e.html 8 March 2000).

46. Personal communication, Takako Iida (email: 11 February 2003).

47. H. Lenskyj, "Sexual Harassment: Female Athletes' Experiences and Coaches' Responsibilities," *Sport Science Periodical on Research and Technology in Sport, Coaching Association of Canada*, *12*(6), (1992), Special Topics B-1. M. A. Hall, *Feminism and Sporting Bodies: Essays on Theory and Practice* (Champaign, IL: Human Kinetics, 1996). S. Thompson, "The Games Begins at Home: Women's Labor in the Service of Sport" in J. Coakley & P. Donnelly (eds.), *Inside Sports* (London: Routledge, 1999), pp. 111–20.

48. M. Messner, *Power at Play: Sports and the Problem of Masculinity* (Boston, MA: Beacon Press, 1992). M. Messner, "Studying up on Sex," *Sociology of Sport Journal*, *13* (1996) 221–37. M. Messner & D. Sabo (eds.) *Sport, Men and the Gender Order* (Champaign, IL: Human Kinetics, 1990). S. Scraton & A. Flintoff (note 2). N. Theberge, Sport and Women's Empowerment, *Women's Studies International Forum*, *10*(4), (1987), 387–393. B. Pronger, *The Arena of Masculinity: Sports, Homosexuality, and the Meaning of Sex* (London: GMP Publishers Ltd, 1990). M. Hall, *Feminism and Sporting Bodies: Essays on Theory and Practice* (Champaign, IL: Human Kinetics, 1996).

49. Department of Trade and Industry, *Equality and Diversity: The Way Ahead* (London: HMSO, 2002).

50. Sport England, *Making English Sport Inclusive: Equity Guidelines for Governing Bodies* www.sportengland.org/resources/pdfs/people/equity/pdf (2000), p. 3.

51. Child Care Northern Ireland, *Our Duty to Care: Principles of Good Practice for the Protection of Children* (Belfast: DHSS, 1995). Irish Sports Council/Sports Council Northern Ireland, *Code of Ethics and Good Practice for Children's Sport* (Dublin: Irish Sports Council/Sports Council Northern Ireland, 2000). B. Merriman, "Single Equality—Speaking from Experience" presentation to a conference "The Future for Equalities: The Implications for Scotland of a Single Equalities Body," Royal Society of Scotland, Edinburgh (25 November 2002).

52. M. Messner, "Studying up on sex" (note 47) pp. 221–37.

53. J. Felshin, *The Dialectic of Woman and Sport*; E. Gerber, J. Felshin, P. Berlin & W. Wyrick (eds.), *The American Women in Sport* (London: Addison-Wesley, 1974) p. 203.

54. P. Griffin, *Strong Women, Deep Closets: Lesbians and Homophobia in Sport* (Champaign, IL: Human Kinetics, 1998). B. Pronger (note 48).

55. R. Acosta & L. Carpenter, *Women in Intercollegiate Sport: A Longitudinal Study — Twenty Five Year Update 1977–2002* (Monograph, Brooklyn College of the City of New York and Project on Women and Social Change of Smith College, 2002).

56. A. Bennett, Personal communication, (email dated 29 November 2002).

57. Sport England, *Annual Report 2000–2001*, www.sportengland.org (2002).

58. A. Bennet (note 56).

59. S. Faludi, Backlash: *The Undeclared War against Women* (New York: Anchor, 1991).

60. D. Finkelhor, "The 'Backlash' and the Future of Child Protection Advocacy"; J. E. B. Myers (ed.), *The Backlash: Child Protection Under Fire* (London: Sage, 1994) pp. 1–16.

ABOUT THE EDITORS

 **John Nauright** is a professor of sport management and the director of the Academy of International Sport at George Mason University in Virginia. He is also a visiting professor of sports studies at Aarhus University in Denmark. He received his Ph.D. from Queen's University in Kingston, Ontario, and his bachelor's and master's degrees from the University of South Carolina. He is author and editor of numerous books in sport management and sport studies including *The Political Economy of Sport*; *Making the Rugby World: Race, Gender, Commerce*; *Sport, Cultures and Identities in South Africa*, and *Global Sport Management* (FIT, 2010). He has taught in Australia, Canada, Denmark, New Zealand, and in the United Kingdom.

 **Steven Pope** is the director of the International Center for Performance Excellence at West Virginia University. He received his Ph.D. from the University of Maine and his B.A. and M.A. at Hope College and the University of Connecticut. He is author of *Patriotic Games: Sporting Traditions in the American Imagination, 1876-1926*; editor of *The New American Sport History: Recent Approaches and Perspectives*; and co-editor (with John Nauright) of *The Routledge Companion to Sports History*. He was a Leverhulme Research Fellow at De Montfort University (United Kingdom) in 2003 and served as program leader of American Studies at the University of Lincoln (United Kingdom) between 2004 and 2008.

ABOUT THE AUTHORS

Carly Adams is an assistant professor in the Department of Kinesiology and Physical Education at the University of Lethbridge, Alberta. Her research interests include twentieth-century Canadian sport, oral, regional, and local histories, gender, women's experiences in sport, and sport governance.

Cara Carmichael Aitchison is dean of the Faculty of Education and Sport and Professor in Leisure and Tourism Studies at the University of Bedfordshire. She was a member of the 2008 UK Research Assessment Exercise Panel for Sports-Related Studies and, until 2008, was professor in human geography and director of the Center for Leisure, Tourism and Society at the University of the West of England, Bristol.

John Amis is an associate professor in the Department of Management in the Fogelman College of Business and Economics at the University of Memphis. He also holds courtesy appointments in the Department of Health & Sports Sciences and the Center for Community Health.

David L. Andrews is a professor of physical cultural studies in the Department of Kinesiology, and an affiliate professor in the Departments of American Studies and Sociology, at the University of Maryland, College Park.

Robert A. Baade is A.B. Dick Professor of Economics and chair of the Economics and Business Department at Lake Forest College. His areas of interest include international trade and financial issues, and a variety of topics relating to the economics of professional and intercollegiate sport.

Angel Barajas is an associate professor of financial management in the Department of Accountancy and Finance at the University of Vigo, Spain, and a researcher for the Spanish Economic Observatory for Sport (FOED). He specializes in the fields of investment valuation and finance of sports, particularly professional football.

Richard Batty is an associate professor in the College of Health and Human Services at California State University, Sacramento. His research interests are in the area of planning and evaluating community recreation programs and events.

Celia Brackenridge is professor of sport sciences (youth sport) and director of the Centre for Youth Sport and Athlete Welfare at Brunel University in West London, UK. She has researched gender relations and sexual exploitation in sport for the past 25 years and has also been an active advocate of gender equity and children's rights in sport.

Nick Burton, at the time of writing, was a doctoral student at Coventry University and researcher for the Center for the International Business of Sport.

Simon Chadwick is a professor of sport business strategy and marketing at Coventry University Business School (UK), where he is also director of the Center for the International Business of Sport. His research interests lie in the areas of sponsorship, endorsements, branding, and fan behavior, as well as other areas of strategy and marketing in sport.

Tim Crabbe is professor of the sociology of sport and popular culture at Sheffield Hallam University and founder member and chair of the Substance Research Cooperative. He has a specialist interest in the social dimensions of sport and popular culture and a long track record of conducting both "pure" academic and applied research in these fields as well as tailored monitoring and evaluation exercises relating to specific programs of activity. His research and writing has focused particularly around young people, race, crime, deviance, and substance misuse and he currently leads the national evaluation of the UK Home Office funded Positive Futures program. Tim is widely regarded as one of the leading authorities in relation to the research, development and analysis of sport and activity based social policy initiatives.

Liz Crolley has published widely on various aspects of the history, politics, business, and sociology of football, including books on nationalism and national identity expressed via football and football writing. She has a particular interest in football in Spain, Italy, and Argentina. She is currently based at the Football Industry Group at the University of Liverpool Management School.

Braham Dabscheck is a senior fellow, Faculty of Law, University of Melbourne. He has published over 80 papers on industrial relations, legal, economic, historical, and comparative aspects of professional team sports. He was the editor of *The Journal of Industrial Relations* from 1991 to 1999 and an active member of the Australian Society for Sports History, serving as president from 1997 to 1999.

Peter Donnelly is a professor and the director of the Center for Sport Policy Studies in the Faculty of Physical Education and Health at the University of Toronto.

Greg Duquette is a doctoral student in the Faculty of Physical Education and Recreation at the University of Alberta. His research focuses on sport, place, and management.

Larry W. Fielding is coordinator of the Sport Marketing/Sport Management Program of Indiana University, Department of Kinesiology, School of Public Health. He is a NASSM Research Fellow.

Michael Friedman, at the time of writing, was a member of the Physical Cultural Studies Research Group in the Sport Commerce and Culture Program, Department of Kinesiology at the University of Maryland. His main focus was on the relationship between sports and the city.

Sam Fullerton is a professor of marketing at Eastern Michigan University and has also served as a visiting professor teaching sports marketing at the University of Michigan and at the University of Waikato in New Zealand.

Mick Green, at the time of writing, was a lecturer in sport and leisure policy and management in the School of Sport and Exercise Sciences (Institute of Sport and Leisure Policy) at Loughborough University. His primary research interest focused on developments in elite sport systems and policy change in different countries.

Richard Giulianotti is a professor and head of the Sociology and Criminology Section in the School of Applied Social Sciences at Durham University. His research interests are in sport, globalization, crime and deviance, popular culture, qualitative research methods and social theory.

Barrie Houlihan is professor of sport policy in the Institute of Sport and Leisure Policy, School of Sport, Health and Exercise Sciences, Loughborough University. He has written widely on many aspects of sport policy including doping, sport development, theorizing the sport policy process, and sport and young people.

Brad Humphreys is associate professor and Chair of Economics of Gaming in the Department of Economics at the University of Alberta. His research areas include economics of sports, sport finance, and economics of higher education.

Bruce Kidd is professor and Dean of the Faculty of Physical Education and Health at the University of Toronto, and the Chair of the Commonwealth Advisory Body on Sport.

Graham Knight, at the time of writing, was a professor in the Department of Sociology at MacMaster University.

Pamela C. Laucella is an assistant professor of sports journalism at Indiana University School of Journalism—Indianapolis. She obtained a Ph.D. in journalism and mass communication from the University of North Carolina—Chapel Hill, and her research investigates socio-cultural-historical aspects of sport communication.

Margaret MacNeill is an associate professor in the Faculty of Physical Education and Health and is cross appointed to the Dalla Lana School of Public Health at the University of Toronto. Her current research interests include sport/fitness media production, postcolonial studies of sport for development and peace, and youth studies of mediated physical literacy.

Barbara Manivet, at the time of writing, had recently earned an MBA in marketing from Université Laval. She collaborated with André Richelieu on several projects related to sports marketing and developed an in marketing research.

Daniel S. Mason is a professor with the Faculty of Physical Education and Recreation and adjunct with the School of Business at the University of Alberta. His research focuses on sport and leisure organizations.

Victor A. Matheson is an associate professor in the Department of Economics at the College of the Holy Cross in Worcester, Massachusetts. He has published extensively regarding the economic impacts of professional sports as well as natural and social disasters on local communities.

G. Russell Merz is a professor of marketing at Eastern Michigan University. His research centers on the use of modeling in the areas of branding and customer satisfaction.

Kimberly S. Miloch is an associate professor in the Kinesiology Department at Texas Woman's University. Her research and teaching interests are sport consumer satisfaction and loyalty, sport public relations and media management, sport brand management, service quality and the sportscape, and online sport communication.

Deane Neubauer is professor emeritus and a senior fellow in the Globalization Research Center in the Department of Political Science, College of Social Sciences, at the University of Hawaii at Manoa. His primary interests lie in policy, especially health policy, and political economy with a particular emphasis on globalization phenomena.

Paul M. Pedersen is the director of the Sport Management Doctoral Program at Indiana University. A NASSM Research Fellow, he has authored or co-authored three books (including *Strategic Sport Communication*) and over 50 peer-reviewed publications in journals. He is the founding editor of the *International Journal of Sport Communication*.

Murray Phillips is a senior lecturer in socio-cultural aspects of sport and physical activity in the School of Human Movement Studies at the University of Queensland. His research interests are in the historical and contemporary dimensions of sport, and he has written on the historical and contemporary aspects of sport and war, sport and gender, sports' coaching, golf, rugby league, rugby union, sport structures as well as the ontological, epistemological and methodological aspects of sport history.

Szymon Prokopowicz, at the time of writing, was a graduate student at the University of Economics in Poznan, Poland. He was a visiting graduate student at the University of Illinois at Urbana-Champaign.

Andre Richelieu specializes in brand management and sports marketing. His research relates to: how professional sports teams can leverage their brand equity by capitalizing on the emotional connection they share with their fans; how professional sports teams can internationalize their brand; and how sports teams can improve fans' experience at the sporting venue and outside the stadium, and increase fans' attachment to the team. He has published extensively in North America and Europe.

J. Andrew Ross teaches courses on sport, business, and economics, and is a postdoctoral fellow in the Historical Data Research Unit at the University of Guelph. He finished his dissertation on the history of the National Hockey League in 2008 and is revising it for publication.

David Rowe is a professor in the School of Humanities and Social Science, Faculty of Education and Arts, at Newcastle University in Australia. His research interests are n culture studies, popular culture, and sports media.

Michael Sam is a senior lecturer with the School of Physical Education at the University of Otago. His research interests broadly encompass areas of policy, politics and governance as they relate to the public administration/management of sport.

Jay Scherer is an assistant professor in the Faculty of Physical Education and Recreation, University of Alberta, Edmonton, Canada. His research focuses on the globalization of sport and popular culture.

Rich Schultz is an adjunct professor in the Department of Liberal Studies at California State University, San Marcos, and in the Department of History at San Diego City College. His current areas of research include US-Mexico border studies.

Michael Silk is a senior lecturer in the Faculty of Humanities and Social Science at the University of Bath. His research and scholarship center on the production and consumption of space, the governance of bodies, and the performative politics of identity within the context of neo-liberalism.

John N. Singer is an assistant professor of sport management in the Department of Health and Kinesiology at Texas A&M University. His research and teaching focus on the broad topic of diversity, with an emphasis on issues pertaining to race.

Julie Stevens is an associate professor in the Department of Sport Management at Brock University. She has published on the governance, development, and structure of hockey in Canada. Her work on female hockey addresses the historical life cycle of the sport in Canada as well as critical commentary on the evolution of the game.

Mike Weed is director of the Center for Sport, Physical Education, and Activity Research, and faculty research director for the Faculty of Social and Applied Sciences at Canterbury Christ Church University. His substantive research interests are in the relationship between sport and tourism, particularly the motivations and behaviors of active sports tourists and traveling sports spectators, and in the implications of hosting the Olympic Games.

Lawrence A. Wenner is the Von der Ahe Professor of Communication and Ethics in the College of Communication and Fine Arts and the School of Film and Television at Loyola Marymount University in Los Angeles, where he directs the *Forum on Media Ethics and Social Responsibility*. Dr. Wenner's research includes seven books and nearly 100 journal articles and book chapters with focus on critical assessments of media content and the values and consumption of mediated sports.

INDEX